Modern Labor Economics
Theory and Public Policy

Ronald G. Ehrenberg / Robert S. Smith

Cornell University

Scott, Foresman and Company

Glenview, Illinois

Dallas, Tex.   Oakland, N.J.   Palo Alto, Cal.   Tucker, Ga.   London, England

For Our Families, With Love

p. 158: Figure 16.1 from Paul A. Samuelson and Robert M. Solow, "Our Menu of
Policy Choices," *The Battle Against Unemployment,* edited by Arthur M. Okun.
Copyright © 1965 by W. W. Norton & Company, Inc.
p. 237: Table 9.1 from Richard B. Freeman, "Overinvestment in College Training?" *The
Journal of Human Resources* 10,3 (Summer 1975), Table 1 (© 1975 by the Board of
Regents of the University of Wisconsin System), p. 288.

Library of Congress Cataloging in Publication Data

Ehrenberg, Ronald G.
 Modern labor economics.

 Includes bibliographical references and index.
  1. Labor economics.   I. Smith, Robert Stewart.
II. Title.
HD4901.E34   331   81-18358
ISBN 0-673-15365-7   AACR2

123456-VHS-868584838281

Preface

Modern Labor Economics: Theory and Public Policy has grown out of our experiences over the last decade in teaching labor-market economics and in conducting research that was meant to influence public policy. Our text develops the modern theory of labor-market behavior, summarizes empirical evidence that supports or contradicts each hypothesis, and illustrates in extensive detail the usefulness of the theory for public-policy analysis. We believe that showing students the social implications of concepts enhances the motivation to learn them and that using the concepts of each chapter in an analytic setting allows students to see the concepts in action. The extensive use of detailed policy applications constitutes a major innovation in this text.

Modern Labor Economics is designed for one-semester or one-quarter courses in labor economics, at either the undergraduate or graduate level, for students who do not necessarily have extensive backgrounds in economics. Since 1974, we have taught such courses at the New York State School of Industrial and Labor Relations at Cornell University. The undergraduate course requires only principles of economics as a prerequisite, and the graduate course (for students in a professional program akin to an MBA program) has no prerequisites. It is our experience that it is not necessary to be highly technical in one's presentation in order to convey important concepts and that students with limited backgrounds in economics *can* comprehend a great deal of material in a single course. Accordingly, while this text is the most comprehensive treatment of modern labor economics available, it is written in a style that makes the important concepts in the field accessible even to those without backgrounds in intermediate-level microeconomics, calculus, or statistics. However, for those students who have had intermediate microeconomics, we have included several appendices that develop a technical concept in much greater detail than the text discussion permits.

Chapter 2 is a review chapter that presents a quick overview of demand and supply in labor markets so that the students will see from the outset the interrelationship of the major forces at work shaping labor-market behavior. This chapter can be skipped or skimmed by students with strong backgrounds in economics or by students in one-quarter courses. Chapters 3 to 5 are concerned primarily with the demand for labor, while Chapters 6 to 11 focus on labor-supply issues. Unionism, public-sector labor markets, and discrimination are treated in Chapters 12, 13, and 14. The final two chapters treat the macroeconomic issues of unemployment and inflation.

As noted above, *Modern Labor Economics* recognizes that many students have only a limited background in economics. All of the necessary analytic tools are carefully developed in the text, and each chapter builds on material that precedes it. We begin the text at a very simple level and explain the derivation of each major concept or tool. We then build up the degree of difficulty in later chapters as the student becomes more familiar with our terminology and methods of analysis.

The text has a number of unique pedagogical features in addition to the use of public-policy examples that reinforce conceptual understanding and the inclusion of technical appendices. First, each chapter contains boxed examples that illustrate an application of that chapter's theory in nontraditional, historical, or cross-cultural settings. Second, each chapter contains a number of discussion or review questions that give students the opportunity to apply what they have learned to specific policy questions. Third, lists of selected readings at the ends of chapters refer students to more advanced sources of study.

Substantively, *Modern Labor Economics* differs from previous textbooks in a number of ways. First and foremost is its extensive emphasis on public-policy applications. The book also attempts to integrate institutional features, such as the existence of internal labor markets, directly into the theoretical models—explaining the institutions within the context of these models rather than discussing them separately. Finally, the coverage of topics in this book is far more comprehensive than in most texts, and the discussion of a number of the more common topics is much more thorough than that found in other texts. We include, for example, discussions of household production and allocation of time, the theory of screening and signaling, labor mobility, hedonic wage theory and compensating wage differentials, the structure of compensation, intertemporal models of employer and employee behavior, the economic foundations and effects of unionism, public-sector labor markets, the relationship of unemployment to underlying labor-markets flows, and the relationship between inflation and unemployment (including the effects of incomes policies). Our chapter on discrimination—in terms of theory and evidence—is much more complete than in other texts and includes a unique section on the conceptual issues of affirmative-action planning.

As the following list of academic acknowledgments indicates, we have had the benefit of substantive and pedagogical comments from numerous friends and colleagues at universities and colleges throughout the country; to these people we are indebted:

George Borjas   *University of California, Santa Barbara*
John F. Burton   *Cornell University*
Glen Cain   *University of Wisconsin*

James Chelius	*Purdue University*
Barry Chiswick	*University of Illinois, Chicago Circle*
Robert Flanagan	*Stanford University*
Donald Frey	*Wake Forest University*
Gilbert Ghez	*Roosevelt University, Chicago*
Daniel Hamermesh	*Michigan State University*
V. Joseph Hotz	*Carnegie-Mellon University*
George Johnson	*University of Michigan*
Lawrence Kahn	*University of Illinois, Urbana*
Randall King	*University of Akron*
H. Gregg Lewis	*Duke University*
Charles Link	*University of Delaware*
J. Peter Mattila	*Iowa State University*
Jacob Mincer	*Columbia University*
George Neumann	*University of Chicago*
Randall Olsen	*Yale University*
Jeffrey Perloff	*University of California, Berkeley*
Jennifer Roback	*Yale University*
Sherwin Rosen	*University of Chicago*
Arthur Schwartz	*University of Michigan*
N.J. Simler	*University of Minnesota*
James P. Smith	*UCLA*
Sharon P. Smith	*Federal Reserve Bank of New York*
Michael Wachter	*University of Pennsylvania*

The length of the above list is only a partial indicator of the extensive developmental editing of *Modern Labor Economics* and the concern of our editor, George Lobell, that we produce a book that accurately reflects the state of the art in labor economics and is comprehensible to students of varying backgrounds. Indeed, to ensure the book's accessibility, drafts of *Modern Labor Economics* have been class tested prior to publication in various labor-economics courses throughout the country. The final draft of our manuscript was ably copyedited by Mary LaMont.

Enormous debts, however, are also owed to three other groups of people. First are those instrumental in teaching us the concepts and social relevance of labor economics when we were students: Frank Brechling, George Delehanty, Dale Mortensen, John Pencavel, Orme Phelps, and Mel Reder. Second are the generations of undergraduate and graduate students we have taught who have forced us to clarify our thinking and who sat through the lectures that preceded *Modern Labor Economics*. Third are the secretaries who typed the many drafts of the manuscript: Jean Brown, Patricia Kauppinen, and Jean Morano.

Contents

12 Unions and Collective Bargaining in the Private Sector   328

13 Public-Sector Labor Markets   366

1

Introduction

Economic theory provides powerful, and often surprising, insights into individual and social behavior. At a purely scientific level these insights are interesting because they help us understand important aspects of our lives. Beyond this, however, government, industry, labor, and other groups have increasingly come to understand the usefulness of the concepts and thought processes of economists in the formulation of social policy. This theory of behavior is simple, yet compelling, and provides a systematic approach to the analysis of problems.

This book presents a comprehensive—and understandable—application of economic analysis to the behavior of, and relationship between, employers and employees. The aggregate compensation received by employees from their employers was $1,350 billion in 1979, while all *other* forms of personal income that year—from investments, self-employment, pensions, and various government welfare programs—amounted to $573 billion. The *employment* relationship, then, is clearly one of the most fundamental relationships in our lives, and as such it is one that attracts a good deal of legislative attention. A mastery of the fundamentals of labor economics is thus essential to an informed understanding of a huge array of social problems and programs.

As economists who have been actively involved in the analysis and evaluation of labor-related programs adopted or considered by the government, we obviously believe labor economics is useful in understanding the effects of these policies. What is perhaps more important for the nature of this text is that we also believe policy analysis can be useful in teaching the fundamentals of labor economics. We have therefore incorporated such analyses into each chapter with two pedagogical reasons in mind. First, we believe that showing students the relevance and social implications of concepts to be studied enhances the motivation to learn. Second, using the concepts of each chapter in an analytical setting serves to reinforce understanding by permitting the student to see them "in action."

THE LABOR MARKET

There is a rumor that one recent Secretary of Labor attempted to abolish the term "labor market" from departmental publications. He believed it demeaned workers to implicitly think of labor as being bought and sold like so much grain, oil, or

1

bonds. True, labor is somewhat unique. Labor services can only be rented; workers themselves cannot be bought and sold. Further, because labor services cannot be separated from workers, the conditions under which such services are rented are often as important as the price. Put differently, *nonpecuniary factors*—such as work environment, risk of injury, personalities of managers and flexibility of work hours—loom larger in employment transactions than they do in markets for commodities. Finally, there are a host of institutions and pieces of legislation influencing the employment relationship that do not exist in other markets.

Nevertheless, the circumstances under which employers and employees rent labor services clearly constitute a "market" for several reasons. First, institutions have developed to facilitate contact between the buyers and sellers of labor services. This contact may come through the want ads, the union hiring hall, employment agencies, placement offices, or at the factory gate. But such contact is necessary and does occur.

Second, once contact is arranged information about price and quality is exchanged. Employment applications, interviews, and even "word-of-mouth" information from friends are illustrative of this kind of exchange in the market for labor.

Third, when agreement is reached some kind of *contract* is executed, covering compensation, conditions of work, job security, and even duration of the job. At times the contract is formal, such as with collective bargaining (union-management) agreements. At times the agreement is unwritten and informal, with only an implied understanding between the parties based on past practices and experience. Nonetheless, it is often useful to think of the employment relationship as governed by a contract.

It is worth noting that labor "contracts" typically call for employers to compensate employees for their *time* and not for the product they produce. Only 14 percent of U.S. workers receive piece-rate wages or commissions, where compensation is computed directly on the basis of output. The vast majority are paid by the hour, week, or month. They are paid, in short, to show up for work and (within limits) to follow orders. This form of compensation requires that employers give careful attention to worker motivation and dependability in the selection and employment process.

The end result of employer-employee transactions in the labor market is, of course, the placement of people in jobs at certain rates of pay. This allocation of labor serves not only the personal needs of individuals but the needs of the larger society as well. Through the labor market our most important national resource—labor—is allocated to firms, industries, occupations, and regions.

LABOR ECONOMICS: SOME BASIC CONCEPTS

Labor economics is the study of the workings and outcomes of the market for labor. More specifically, labor economics is primarily concerned with the behavior of employers and employees in response to the general incentives of wages, prices, profits, and nonpecuniary aspects of the employment relationship (such as working conditions). These incentives serve both to motivate and limit individual choice. The focus in economics is on inducements for behavior that are impersonal and apply to wide groups of people as opposed to incentives that are more personal in nature.

In this book, we will study, for example, the relationship between wages and employment opportunities; the interaction between wages, income, and the decision to work; how general market incentives affect occupational choice; the relationship between wages and undesirable job characteristics; the incentives for, and effects of, educational and training investments; and the effects of unions on wages, productivity, and turnover. In the process, we will analyze the employment and wage effects of such social policies as the minimum wage, overtime legislation, pension reform regulations, the Occupational Safety and Health Act, welfare reform, payroll taxes, unemployment insurance, immigration policies, the rise in the mandatory retirement age, and antidiscrimination laws.

Our study of labor economics will be conducted on two levels. Most of the time we will be using economic theory to analyze "what is"; that is, we will be explaining people's behavior, using a mode of analysis called *positive economics*. Less commonly, we will be using *normative* economic analysis to judge "what should be."

Positive Economics

Positive economics is a theory of behavior in which people are typically assumed to respond favorably to "benefits" and negatively to "costs." In this regard, positive economics closely resembles Skinnerian psychology, which views behavior as shaped by rewards and punishments. The rewards in economic theory are pecuniary and nonpecuniary gains (benefits), while the punishments are forgone opportunities (costs). For example, a person motivated to become a surgeon because of the earnings and status surgeons command must give up the opportunity to be a lawyer and be available for emergency work around the clock. Both the benefits and costs must be considered in making this career choice. Likewise, a firm deciding whether to hire an additional worker must weigh the wage and salary costs against the added revenues or cost savings made possible by expanding its work force.

Scarcity. The most all-pervasive assumption underlying economic theory is that of resource scarcity. According to this assumption, individuals and society alike do not have the resources to meet all their wants. Hence, any resource devoted to satisfying one set of desires could have been used to satisfy other wants, which means that there is always a cost to any decision or action. The real cost of using labor hired by a government contractor to build a road, for example, is the production lost by not devoting this labor to the building of an airport or some other good. Thus, in popular terms, "there is no such thing as a free lunch," and we must always make choices and live with the rewards and costs these choices bring us. Moreover, we are always constrained in our choices by the resources available to us.

Rationality.   The second basic assumption of positive economics is that people are *rational* in the sense that they have an objective and pursue it in a reasonably consistent fashion. When considering *persons,* economists assume that the objective being pursued is *utility maximization;* that is, people are assumed to strive toward the goal of making themselves as happy as they can (given their limited resources). Utility, of course, encompasses both pecuniary and nonpecuniary dimensions. When considering the behavior of *firms,* which are inherently nonpersonal entities, economists assume the goal of behavior to be that of *profit maximization.* Profit maximization is really just a special case of utility maximization—where pecuniary gain is emphasized and nonpecuniary factors are ignored.

The assumption of rationality implies a *consistency* of response to general economic incentives and an *adaptability* of behavior when those incentives change. These two characteristics of behavior underlie predictions about how workers and firms will respond to various incentives. Rationality cannot be directly "proven," however, and it has been suggested that even totally habit-bound or unthinkingly impulsive people would be forced to alter their behavior in predictable ways if the resources at their command change.[1] Thus, while we will maintain the assumption of rationality throughout the textbook, it is clear that this assumption is not absolutely necessary to the derivation of at least *some* of the behavioral predictions contained herein.

The Models and Predictions of Positive Economics

Behavioral predictions in economics flow more or less directly from the two fundamental assumptions of rationality and scarcity. Workers must continually make choices, such as whether to look for other jobs, accept overtime, seek promotions, move to another area, or acquire more education. Employers must also make choices concerning, for example, the level of output and the mix of machines and labor to use in production. Economists usually assume that when making these choices, employees and employers are guided by their desires to maximize utility or profit, as the case may be, and that they weigh the costs and benefits of various decisions in a reasonably careful way.

One may object that these assumptions are unrealistic and that people are not nearly as calculating, as well-informed about alternatives, or as well-endowed with a set of choices as economists assume. Economists are likely to reply that if people are not calculating, are totally uninformed, or do not have any choices, then most predictions suggested by economic theory will not be supported by real-world evidence. They thus argue that the theory underlying positive economics should be judged on the basis of its *predictions* and that there may be *enough* information, calculation, and available options to make the theory useful in explaining or predicting a wide range of behavior.

The reason that we need to make assumptions and create a relatively simple theory of behavior is that the actual workings of the labor market are almost

---

[1]Gary Becker, "Irrational Behavior and Economic Theory," *Journal of Political Economy* 70, 1 (February 1962), pp. 1–13.

impossibly complex. Millions of workers and employers interact daily—all with their own set of motivations, preferences, information, and perceptions of self-interest. A detailed description of the individual outcomes and the processes that determine them would clearly be both of limited feasibility and of limited usefulness. What we need to discover are generalizations or general principles that provide useful insights about the labor market. These principles could not be expected to predict or explain behavior with the same accuracy as the laws of physics predict the movement of an object through space, because we are dealing with human beings capable of making choices. Nevertheless, we hope to show in this book that a few forces are so basic to labor market behavior that they alone can predict or explain much of the outcomes and behaviors we observe in the labor market.

Any time we attempt to explain a complex set of behaviors and outcomes using a few fundamental influences we have created a *model* of such behavior. Models are not intended to capture every complexity of behavior; in fact, they are created for the expressed purpose of stripping away random and idiosyncratic factors so that we can focus on general principles. An analogy from the physical sciences might make the nature of models and their relationship to actual behavior more clear.

Using calculations of velocity and gravitational pull, physicists could predict where a ball would land if it were kicked with a certain force at a given angle to the ground. The actual point of landing might vary from the predicted point due to wind currents and any spin the ball might have—factors that were ignored in the calculations. If 100 balls were kicked none might ever land exactly on the predicted spot, although they would tend to cluster around it. The accuracy of the model, while not perfect, may be good enough for a football coach to make a decision about whether to attempt a field goal or not. The point is that we usually just need to know the *average tendencies* of outcomes for policy purposes. To estimate these tendencies we need to know the important forces at work but must confine ourselves to few enough influences so that calculating estimates remains feasible.

To really grasp the assumptions and predictions of economic models, it is necessary to consider a concrete example. Suppose we begin by asserting that, being subject to resource scarcity, workers will prefer high-wage jobs to low-paying ones *if* all other job characteristics are the same in each job. Thus, in pursuit of their own well-being, they will quit a low-paying job to take a better-paying one for which they qualify if they believe sufficient improvement is likely. This principle does not imply that workers care only about wages or that all are equally likely to quit. Workers obviously care about a number of employment characteristics, and improvement in any of these characteristics makes turnover less likely. Likewise, some workers are more receptive to change than others. Nevertheless, if we hold these other factors constant and increase only wages, we should clearly observe that the probability of quitting will fall.

On the employer side of the market we can consider a similar prediction. Firms need to make a profit to survive. If they have high turnover, their costs will be higher than otherwise because of the need to hire and train replacements. With high turnover they could not, therefore, afford to pay high wages. However, if they could reduce turnover enough by paying higher wages it may well be worth incurring the high wage costs. Thus, both the utility-maximizing behavior of employees and the profit-maximizing behavior of firms lead us to expect low turnover to be associated with high wages and high turnover with low wages, other things equal.[2]

It is important to note several things about the above predictions.

1. The predictions emerge directly from the twin assumptions of rationality and scarcity. Employees and employers, both mindful of their scarce resources, are assumed to be on the lookout for chances to improve their well-being. In addition, the predictions are also based on the assumptions that employees are aware of, or can learn about, alternative jobs and that these alternatives are open to them. If any of these assumptions is invalid or inappropriate, the predictions would not be consistently borne out by observed behavior.

2. The prediction of a negative relationship between wages and voluntary turnover is made holding other things equal. The theory does not deny that job characteristics other than wages matter to employees or that employers can lower turnover by varying policies other than the wage rate. However, holding these other factors constant, we should observe the predicted negative relationship if the basic assumptions are valid.

3. The *assumptions* of the theory concern *individual* behavior of employers and employees, but the *predictions* are about an *aggregate* relationship between wages and turnover. The prediction is *not* that everyone will remain in their jobs if they experience an increase in wages, but that *enough* will for turnover to be cut by raising wages. The test of the prediction thus lies in finding out if the predicted relationship between wages and turnover exists as one looks at aggregate data from firms or industries.

Having waded through this abstract theory of turnover, it may interest the reader to know that there is abundant evidence that its predictions are accurate. Two of the more convincing studies estimate that if an industry increased its wage rate by 10 percent relative to other industries, holding all other job characteristics constant, it would reduce its voluntary turnover from 3–20 percent.[3]

Normative Economics

Any normative statement—a statement about what *ought* to exist—is based on some underlying value. The value premise upon which normative economics rests is that of *mutual benefit*. A mutually beneficial transaction is one in which there

---

[2] In this example the expected relationship between wages and worker/firm behavior is clear-cut. While this is often the case, it is sometimes true that the expected relationship is not all that clear. We will see examples of this later on—especially in Chapter 6.

[3] John Pencavel, *An Analysis of the Quit Rate in Manufacturing Industry* (Princeton: Industrial Relations Section, Princeton University, 1970); Farrell Block, "Labor Turnover in U.S. Manufacturing Industries" *Journal of Human Resources* 14, 2 (Spring 1979), pp. 236–46.

are no losers and, therefore, one that everyone in society could support. A transaction can be unanimously supported when

    a. all parties affected by the transaction gain,

    b. some gain and no one else loses, or

    c. some gain and some lose from the transaction, but the gainers fully compensate the losers.

When the compensation in *c* takes place, case *c* is converted to case *b*. In practice, economists often judge a transaction by whether the gains of the beneficiaries exceed the costs borne by the losers, thus making it *possible* that there would be no losers. If the losers sustain losses that the gainers could not possibly compensate, then the transaction could never be mutually beneficial to all, and the wisdom of the transaction must be questioned.

To illustrate a mutually beneficial transaction, suppose that people who formerly owned and operated small subsistence farms in West Virginia—earning the equivalent of (say) $4000 per year—take jobs in the growing coal mining industry at $15,000 a year. Assuming the switch in jobs is voluntary, these workers are clearly better off. The income gain of $11,000 per year may be offset to some extent by the disagreeableness of working in a mine, but the fact that they voluntarily choose to move into mining tells us that they believe their utility will be enhanced. Mine owners likewise enter into the transaction voluntarily, implying that they obtain at least $15,000 in output from these new workers. The transaction benefits the parties it affects, and as a result it benefits society as a whole. There has been an increase in social output from $4,000 to $15,000 per worker, but, more important, there has been an increase in the overall utility of workers (the miners are better off and no one else is worse off).

To illustrate a transaction that is not mutually beneficial, suppose that society sought to increase the income of these same subsistence farmers by giving them a cash allowance raised by taxing others. This program would simply transfer money from the pockets of some people to the pockets of others, with no increase in output. There is no possibility for the gainers (farmers) to compensate the losers (those taxed), so unanimous consent about the transaction could not be secured. While economists would not say that this transaction is bad or unwarranted, it cannot be justified on the grounds of mutual benefit. Some other ethical principle—not based on unanimous consent—would have to be invoked in order to justify the transaction. (One such principle is that the rich should share their wealth with the poor.)

Normative economics, then, is the analysis of actual and potential transactions to see if they conform to the standard of being mutually beneficial. Transactions may fail to meet this standard—or transactions that meet the standard may not occur—for one of several reasons.

Ignorance. First, people may be ignorant of some important facts and thus led to make decisions that are not in their self-interest. For example, a worker who smokes may take a job in an asbestos-processing plant not knowing that the combination of smoking and inhaling asbestos dust substantially raises the risk of disease. Had the worker known this, he or she would have stopped smoking or changed jobs—but both transactions were "blocked" by ignorance.

Transactions barriers. Second, there may be some barrier to the completion of a transaction that could be mutually beneficial. Often, these barriers are created by government laws. For example, a firm may be willing to offer overtime to production workers at rates no more than 10 percent above their normal wage. Some workers may be willing to accept overtime at the 10 percent premium. However, this transaction—which is desired by both parties—cannot legally be completed in most instances because of a law (the Fair Labor Standards Act) requiring almost all production workers to be paid a 50 percent wage premium for overtime. In this case, overtime will not be worked and both parties will suffer.

Another kind of barrier to mutually beneficial transactions may be the expense of completing the transaction. Unskilled workers facing very limited opportunities in one region may desire to move in order to take better jobs. Alternatively, they may want to enter job training programs. In either case they may lack the funds to finance the desired transaction.

Nonexistence of market. A third reason why transactions that are mutually beneficial may not occur is that it may be impossible or uncustomary for buyers and sellers of certain resources to transact. As an illustration, assume a woman who does not smoke works temporarily next to a man who does. She would be willing to pay as much as 50 cents per hour to keep her working environment smoke-free, and he could be induced to give up smoking for as little as 25 cents per hour. Thus, the potential exists for her to give him, say, 35 cents per hour and for both to benefit. However, custom or the transience of their relationship may prevent her from offering him money in this situation, and the transaction would not occur.

Normative Economics and Government Policy

The solution to problems that impede the completion of mutually beneficial transactions frequently involves government intervention. In cases where a government law is creating the barrier to transaction, the "intervention" might be to repeal the relevant law. Laws prohibiting women from working overtime, for example, have been repealed in recent years as their adverse effects on women have become recognized.

In other cases, however, the government may be able to undertake activities to reduce transactions barriers which the private market would not undertake. We will cite three examples, each of which relates to a barrier discussed above.

Public goods. First let us take the case of information and its dissemination. Suppose that workers in noisy factories are concerned about the effects of noise on their hearing but that to ascertain these effects would require an expensive research program. Suppose, further, that a union representing sawmill workers considers undertaking such research and financing the expensive undertaking by selling its findings to the many other unions or workers involved. The workers would then have the information they desire—albeit at some cost—which they could use to make more intelligent decisions concerning their jobs.

The hitch in the above scheme is that the union doing the research may not have any customers *even though* others find the information it produces valuable. The reason for the lack of customers is that as soon as the union's findings are published to its own members or its first customers, the results can easily become public knowledge—and thus available *for free* from newspapers or by word-of-mouth. Other unions may be understandably reluctant to pay for information they can get for free, and the union doing the research ends up getting very little, if any, reimbursement for its expenses. Anticipating this problem, the union will probably decide not to undertake the research.

The information in the above example is called a *public good*—a good that can be consumed by any number of people at the same time, including those who do not pay for it. Because nonpayers cannot be excluded from consuming the good, no potential customer will have incentives to pay. The result is that the good never gets produced by a private organization. Because the government, however, can *compel* payment through its tax system, it becomes natural to look to the government to produce public goods. If information on occupational health hazards is to be produced on a large scale, it is quite possible that the government will have to be involved.

Capital market imperfections. A second example of a situation in which the government might have to step in to overcome a transaction barrier is the case where loans are not available to finance job training or interregional moves even though such loans could conceivably help workers facing a very poor set of choices to have access to better opportunities. Loans such as these are not typically provided by the private sector, because they are not "backed" (secured) by anything other then the debtor's promise to pay them back. Banks cannot ordinarily afford to take the risks inherent in making such loans, particularly when the loan recipients are poor, because a number of defaults could put them out of business (or at least lower their profitability). This lack of available loans to finance worthwhile transactions represents a "capital market imperfection."

The government, however, might be willing to make loans in the above situation even if it faced the same risk of default, because enabling workers to move to areas of better economic opportunity could improve social welfare and strengthen the economy. In short, because society would reap benefits from encouraging people, in the example given, to enter job training programs or move to areas where their skills could be better utilized, it may be wise for the government to make the loans itself.

Establishing market substitutes. A third type of situation in which government intervention might be necessary to overcome transaction barriers is the case where the market fails to exist for some reason. In the example above, a smoker and nonsmoker were temporarily working next to each other, and their transitory relationship prevented a mutually beneficial transaction from taking place. A solution in this case might be for the government to impose the same result that a market transaction would have generated—and require the employer to designate that area to be a nonsmoking area.

In this case, as in the other examples of government intervention mentioned above, it is important to emphasize that when government does intervene, it must make sure that the transactions it undertakes or imposes on society create more gains for the beneficiaries than they impose in costs on others. Since it is costly to produce information, for example, the government should only do it if the gains are more valuable than the resources used in producing it. Likewise, the government would only want to make loans for job training or interregional moves if these activities enhanced social welfare. Finally, imposing nonsmoking areas would be socially desirable only if the gainers gain more than the losers lose. Thus, while normative economics suggests a role for government in helping accomplish mutually beneficial transactions, the role is not an unlimited one.

PLAN OF THE TEXT

With this brief review of economics in mind, we turn now to the specific subject-matter areas of labor economics. The study of labor economics is mainly a study of the interplay between employers and employees—or between demand and supply. Chapter 2 presents a quick overview of demand and supply in the labor market, allowing the student to see from the outset the interrelationship of the major forces at work shaping labor market behavior. (This chapter contains many concepts that will be familiar to students who have a good background in microeconomics.) Chapters 3–5 are concerned primarily with the demand for labor, while Chapters 6–11 emphasize labor supply issues.

The special topics of unionism and discrimination are treated in Chapters 12–14. The final two chapters deal with the macroeconomic issues of unemployment and inflation.

REVIEW QUESTIONS

1. Using the concepts of normative economics, when would the labor market be judged to be at a point of optimality? What imperfections might prevent the market from achieving this point?

2. Are the following statements "positive" or "normative" in nature? Why?

   a. Society should not prohibit women from working more than 40 hours per week.

   b. If women are prevented from working overtime, they will not be as valuable to employers as their male counterparts of similar skill.

   c. If the military draft is prohibited, military salaries will increase.

   d. The military draft *compels* people to engage in a transaction they would not voluntarily enter into; it should therefore be avoided as a way of recruiting military personnel.

SELECTED READINGS

Ryan C. Amacher, Robert D. Tollison, and Thomas D. Willet, eds., *The Economic Approach to Public Policy* (Ithaca, N.Y.: Cornell University Press, 1976).

Milton Friedman, *Essays in Positive Economics* (Chicago: University of Chicago Press, 1953).

Assar Lindbeck, *The Political Economy of the New Left: An Outsider's View* (New York: Harper and Row, 1971).

2

Overview
of the Labor Market

Every society—regardless of its wealth, form of government, or the organization of its economy—must make certain basic decisions. It must decide what to produce, how to produce it, the quantities to be produced, and how the output shall be distributed. These decisions require finding out what consumers want, what technologies for production are available, and what the skills and preferences of workers are; deciding where to produce; and coordinating all such decisions so that, for example, the millions of people in New York City and the isolated few in an Alaskan fishing village can each buy the milk, bread, meat, vanilla extract, mosquito repellent, and brown shoe polish they desire at the grocery store. The process of coordination involves creating incentives so that the right amount of labor and capital will be employed at the right place at the required time.

These decisions can, of course, be made by administrators employed by a centralized bureaucracy. The amount of information this bureaucracy must obtain and process to make the, literally, millions of needed decisions wisely and the amount of incentives it must give out to ensure that these decisions are coordinated are truly mind boggling. It boggles the mind even more to consider the major alternative to centralized decision making—the decentralized marketplace. Millions of producers striving to make a profit observe prices millions of consumers are willing to pay for products and the wages millions of workers are willing to accept for work. Combining these pieces of information with data on various technologies, they decide where to produce, what to produce, whom to hire, and how much to produce. No one is in charge, and while there are no doubt imperfections that impede progress toward achieving the best allocation of resources, millions of people find jobs that enable them to purchase thousands of items they desire each year. The production, employment, and consumption decisions are all made and coordinated by price signals arising through the marketplace.

The market that has the job of allocating workers to jobs and coordinating employment decisions is *the labor market*. With roughly 100 million workers and 5 million employers in the United States, thousands of decisions about career choice, hiring, quitting, compensation, and technology must be made and coordinated every day. This chapter will present an overview of what the market does and how it works. For those students who may have already mastered microeconomic theory, this chapter can provide a review of basic concepts.

THE LABOR MARKET: DEFINITIONS, FACTS, AND TRENDS

Every market has buyers and sellers, and the labor market is no exception: the "buyers" are employers and the "sellers" are workers. Because there are so many buyers and sellers of labor at any given time, the decisions that are made in any particular case are influenced by the behavior and decisions of others. A firm, for example, may decide to increase compensation in a situation where other employers are doing likewise in order to remain "competitive" in its ability to attract and hold workers. Likewise, an employee may choose to go into personnel work, for example, if he or she discovers that teachers or social workers are having a difficult time finding jobs.

The *labor market* is thus composed of all the buyers and sellers of labor. Some of these participants may not be active at any given moment in the sense that they are not out seeking to find new jobs or new employees. But on any given day, thousands of firms and workers will be "in the market" trying to transact. If, as in the case of doctors or mechanical engineers, buyers and sellers are searching throughout the entire nation for each other, we would describe the market as a *national labor market*. If buyers and sellers only search locally—as in the case of secretaries or automobile mechanics—the labor market is a *local* one.

Some labor markets, particularly those where the sellers of labor are represented by a union, operate under a very formal set of rules that partly govern buyer-seller transactions. In the construction and longshoring trades, for example, employers must hire at the union hiring hall from a list of eligible union members. In other cases, the employer has discretion over who gets hired but is constrained by a union-management agreement in matters like the order in which employees may be laid off, procedures regarding employee complaints, the compensation schedule, the workload or pace of work, and promotions. The markets for government jobs and jobs with large nonunion employers also tend to operate under rules that constrain the authority of management and ensure "fair" treatment of employees. When a formal set of rules and procedures guide and constrain the employment relationship *within* a firm an *internal labor market* is said to exist.[1]

In many cases, of course, labor market transactions are not made within the context of written rules or procedures, as is clearly the case in most transactions where the employee is changing employers or newly entering the market. Written rules or procedures generally do not govern within-firm transactions—such as promotions and layoffs—among smaller, nonunion employers. While jobs in this sector of the labor market can be stable and well paid, many are not. Low-wage, unstable jobs are sometimes considered to be in the *secondary labor market*.[2] We will discuss the concept of secondary labor markets in greater detail in our Chapter 14 on discrimination.

---

[1] P. Doeringer and M. Piore, *Internal Labor Markets and Manpower Analysis* (Lexington, Mass.: D.C. Heath and Company, 1971).

[2] Doeringer and Piore, *Internal Labor Markets and Manpower Analysis*.

When we speak of a particular labor market—for taxi drivers, say—we are using the term *labor market* rather loosely to refer to the companies trying to hire people to drive their cabs and the people seeking employment as cab drivers. The efforts of these buyers and sellers of labor to transact and establish an employment relationship constitute the "market" for cab drivers. However, neither the employers nor the drivers are confined to this market, and in fact both could simultaneously be in other markets as well. An entrepreneur with $100,000 to invest may be thinking of operating either a taxi company or a car wash, depending on the projected revenues and costs of each. A person seeking a cab-driving job may also be trying to find work as an electronics assembler. Thus, all the various "labor markets" that we can define on the basis of industry, occupation, geography, transaction rules, or job character are really interrelated to some degree. We speak of these narrowly defined labor markets for the sake of convenience, and doing so should not suggest that people are necessarily or permanently locked in to a market that is somehow independent of other markets.

The Labor Force and Unemployment

The term *labor force* refers to all the people who are either employed or who would like to be employed for pay at any given time. Those who are not employed for pay but who would like to be are *the unemployed*.[3] People who are not employed and are not looking for work or waiting to be recalled from layoff by their employers are not counted as part of the labor force. The total labor force thus consists of the employed and the unemployed.

In 1979 there were 105 million people in the labor force, representing 64 percent of the entire population over 16 years of age. An overall *labor force participation rate* (labor force divided by population) of 64 percent is substantially higher than the rates around 60 percent that have prevailed throughout the last 30 years, as can be seen by referring to the data in Table 2.1. This table also indicates the single most important fact about labor-force trends in this century; namely, *labor force participation rates for men are falling while those for women are increasing dramatically*. These trends and their causes will be discussed in detail in Chapter 6.

The ratio of those unemployed to those in the labor force is the *unemployment rate*. While this rate is crude and has several imperfections, it is the most widely cited measure of labor market conditions. When the unemployment rate is in the 3–4 percent range in the United States, the labor market is considered *tight*—indicating that jobs in general are plentiful and hard for employers to fill and that most of those who are unemployed will find other work quickly.[4] When the un-

---

[3] The official definition of unemployment for purposes of government statistics includes those who have been laid off by their employers, those who have been fired or have quit and are looking for other work, and those who are just entering or reentering the labor force but have not found a job as yet.

[4] Some people are beginning to argue that labor markets are "tight" when unemployment is around 5 percent or even a bit more. This issue will be discussed in Chapter 15.

**TABLE 2.1 Labor Force Participation Rates by Sex,
1900–1979 (in percent)**

Year	Total		Men		Women	
	Of Those Over 14	*Of Those Over 16*	*Over 14*	*Over 16*	*Over 14*	*Over 16*
1900	54.8 (100)		87.3 (100)		20.4 (100)	
1910	55.7 (102)		86.3 (99)		22.8 (112)	
1920	55.6 (102)		86.5 (99)		23.3 (114)	
1930	54.6 (100)		84.1 (96)		24.3 (119)	
1940	52.2 (95)		79.0 (91)		25.4 (125)	
1950	53.4 (98)	59.9	79.0 (91)	86.8	28.6 (140)	33.9
1960	55.3 (101)	60.2	77.4 (89)	84.0	34.5 (169)	37.8
1970	55.8 (102)	61.3	73.0 (84)	80.6	39.9 (196)	43.4
1979	—	64.2	—	78.4	—	51.1

Note: Index numbers, with 1900 = 100, are shown in parentheses. From 1900–1930, the labor force was defined as those "gainfully employed." Gainful workers were those who, whether they were working at the time or not, reported themselves as having an occupation at which they usually worked. In 1940, the present concept of labor force replaced the concept of gainful worker, with the result that inexperienced people looking for their first job were now counted in the labor force. It is the judgment of Clarence D. Long, *The Labor Force Under Changing Income and Employment*, p. 45, that intercensal comparisons remain meaningful despite this change.

Sources for data on ages 14 and older:

1900–1950: Clarence D. Long, *The Labor Force Under Changing Income and Employment* (Princeton: Princeton University Press, 1958), Table A–2.

1960: U.S. Department of Commerce, Bureau of the Census, *Census of Population, 1960: Employment Status*, Subject Reports, PC(2)–6A, Table 1.

1970: U.S. Department of Commerce, Bureau of the Census, *U.S. Census of Population, 1970: Employment Status and Work Experience*, Subject Reports, PC(2)–6A, Table 1.

Sources for data on ages 16 and older:

U.S. President, *Employment and Training Report of the President* (Washington, D.C.: U.S. Government Printing Office), transmitted to the Congress 1980, Table A–1.

employment rate is higher—say, 7 percent or above—the labor market is described as *loose,* in the sense that workers are abundant and jobs are relatively easy for employers to fill. To say that the labor market as a whole is loose, however, does not imply that no shortages can be found anywhere; to say it is tight, of course, can still mean that in some occupations or places those seeking work exceed the number of jobs available at the prevailing wage.

Table 2.2 displays the overall unemployment rate for the first 80 years of this century. The data clearly show the extraordinarily loose labor market during the Great Depression of the 1930s and the exceptionally tight labor market during World War II. However, when the average unemployment rate of the earliest long stretch of nonwar years (1900–1914) is compared with that of the latest long stretch of nonwar years (1954–1965), we see that unemployment in nonwar, non-depression years is slightly higher now than before (4.4 percent from 1900–1914 vs. 5.3 percent from 1954–65). What is very different is that the *range* within which the unemployment rate fluctuates is much narrower now. In 1900–1914, the unemployment rate varied from 0.8 percent to 8.5 percent, while from 1954–65 the range was 4.2 percent to 6.8 percent. It is evident, then, that the labor market is more stable now than at the turn of the century. Chapter 15 will present a more detailed analysis of the determinants of the unemployment rate.

TABLE 2.2 Unemployment Rates for the Civilian Labor Force over 14 Years Old, 1900–1980

Year	Rate	Year	Rate	Year	Rate
1900	5.0	1916	4.8	1932	23.6
1901	2.4	1917	4.8	1933	24.9
1902	2.7	1918	1.4	1934	21.7
1903	2.6	1919	2.3	1935	20.1
1904	4.8	1920	4.0	1936	17.0
1905	3.1	1921	11.9	1937	14.3
1906	0.8	1922	7.6	1938	19.0
1907	1.8	1923	3.2	1939	17.2
1908	8.5	1924	5.5	1940	14.6
1909	5.2	1925	4.0	1941	9.9
1910	5.9	1926	1.9	1942	4.7
1911	6.2	1927	4.1	1943	1.9
1912	5.2	1928	4.4	1944	1.2
1913	4.4	1929	3.2	1945	1.9
1914	8.0	1930	8.9	1946	3.9
1915	9.7	1931	15.9		

Note: After 1966, unemployment rates for only those 16 and over are published. The differences between the rates for those over 14 and over 16
in the years where both were computed are very small. Therefore, a
parallel series in this table was not considered necessary. The rates
shown from 1967 on relate to those over 16, and the prior data related
to those over 14.

In 1957 the definition of the term *unemployed* was changed to include
those who 1. were waiting to be called back to a job from which they
had been laid off; 2. were waiting to report to a new wage or salary job
scheduled to start within the next 30 days (and were not in school during
the survey week); or 3. would have been looking for work except that
they were temporarily ill or believed no work was available in their line
of work or in the community. Prior to 1957, part of group 1 above—
those whose layoffs were for definite periods of less than 30 days—
were classified as employed, as were all of the persons in group 2
above. This new definition was also applied to unemployment data for
the years 1947–1957.

Industries and Occupations: Adapting to Change

As we pointed out earlier, the labor market is the mechanism through which workers and jobs are matched. Over the years in this century, the number of certain
kinds of jobs has expanded and the number of others has contracted. Both workers
and employers had to adapt to these changes in response to signals provided by
the labor market.

An examination of the industrial distribution of employment from 1900 to
1970 reveals the kinds of changes the labor market has had to facilitate. Table 2.3
discloses a major shift: *agricultural employment has declined drastically while
employment in service industries has expanded.* Manufacturing jobs have increased proportionately to the increase in total employment, so their employment
share has remained more or less constant. The largest employment increases have
been in the service sector. Retail and wholesale trade, which increased from 9.2
percent of employment in 1910 to 20 percent in 1970, showed the largest increases in nongovernment services. However, the largest percentage increase has
been in government employment—which quadrupled its share of total employment over the 70-year period. Some describe this shift in employment from agri-

TABLE 2.2 (continued)

Year	Rate (old series)	Rate (new series)	Year	Rate
1947	3.6	3.9	1958	6.8
1948	3.4	3.9	1959	5.5
1949	5.5	5.9	1960	5.6
1950	5.0	5.3	1961	6.7
1951	3.0	3.3	1962	5.6
1952	2.7	3.1	1963	5.7
1953	2.5	2.9	1964	5.2
1954	5.0	5.6	1965	4.6
1955	4.0	4.4	1966	3.8
1956	3.8	4.2	1967	3.8
1957	4.0	4.3	1968	3.6
			1969	3.5
			1970	4.9
			1971	5.9
			1972	5.6
			1973	4.9
			1974	5.6
			1975	8.5
			1976	7.7
			1977	7.0
			1978	6.0
			1979	5.8
			1980	7.1

SOURCES: 1900–1954 (old series): Stanley Lebergott, "Annual Estimates of Unemployment in the United States, 1900–1950," *The Measurement and Behavior of Unemployment*, NBER Special Committee Conference Series no. 8 (Princeton, 1957), pp. 213–239.

1955–1957 (old series): U.S. Bureau of the Census, *Annual Report on the Labor Force*, Current Population Reports, Series P–50 (1955, 1956, 1957).

1947–1966 (new series): U.S. Bureau of Labor Statistics, *Employment and Earnings*, vol. 13, no. 7 (January 1967), Table A–1.

1967–1980: U.S. President, *Economic Report of the President* (Washington, D.C.: U.S. Government Printing Office, January 1981), p. 267.

culture to services as a shift from the *primary* to the *tertiary* sector (manufacturing being labeled the *secondary* sector). Others describe the shift to services as the arrival of the "post-industrial" state. In any case, the shift in employment has been accompanied by large population movements off the farms and to urban areas. These population movements have also been largely coordinated by the labor market, as Chapter 10 will show.

The combination of shifts in the industrial distribution of jobs and shifts in the production technology within each sector has also necessitated that workers acquire new skills and work in new jobs. Table 2.4 shows that a large increase in *white-collar*, or nonmanual, jobs has taken place concurrently with a large decline in agricultural jobs. Manual workers and personal-service workers have shown relatively modest increases since 1900. The largest single gain has come about in

TABLE 2.3   **Employment Distribution by Major Industrial Sector,
1900–1970 (in percent)**

Year	Agriculture[a]	Goods-Producing Industries[b]	Nongovernment Services[c]	Government Services[d]
1900	38.1	37.8	20.0	4.1
1910	32.1	40.9	22.3	4.7
1920	27.6	44.8	21.6	6.0
1930	22.7	42.1	28.1	7.1
1940	18.5	41.6	31.1	8.8
1950	12.1	41.3	36.4	10.2
1960	6.6	41.4	38.8	13.2
1970	3.8	39.8	40.5	15.9

Note: From 1900 to 1930, employment refers to "gainful workers." From 1940, employment refers to experienced civilian labor force. Where applicable, persons not assigned to an industry were assumed to have the same employment distribution as those were were.
[a]Agriculture includes forestry and fishing.
[b]Included are manufacturing, mining, construction, transportation, communications, and public utilities.
[c]Included are trade; personal, professional, and business services; entertainment; finance; and real estate.
[d]Includes federal, state, and local government workers.
SOURCES: 1900–1940: U.S. Bureau of the Census, *Historical Statistics of the United States, Colonial Times to 1957*, 1960. Table D57–71.
        1950: *U.S. Census of Population 1950*, Subject Reports. Vol. IV, Chapter 1D, 1955. Table 15.
        1960: *U.S. Census of Population 1960*, Subject Reports. PC (2)–7F. 1967, Table 1.
        1970: *U.S. Census of Population 1970*, Subject Reports. PC (2)–7B. 1972, Table 1.

clerical jobs, although professional and technical jobs (teachers, engineers, lawyers, and so forth) have also increased disproportionately fast.

Labor markets must work very effectively if enormous shifts in the industrial and occupational distribution of employment are to be accomplished without long delays or undue hardship. There is disagreement over how effectively and humanely labor markets operate, but there can be no disagreement that the labor market has an incredibly large and important role to perform in society.

The Earnings of Labor

The actions of buyers and sellers in the labor market serve both to allocate and to set prices for various kinds of labor. From a social perspective, these prices act as signals or incentives in the allocation process—a process that relies primarily on individual and voluntary decisions. From the worker's point of view, the price of labor is important in determining income—and hence purchasing power.

The *wage rate* is the price of labor per working hour.[5] The *nominal wage* is what workers get paid per hour in current dollars; nominal wages are most useful

---

[5]In this book, we define the hourly wage in the way most workers would if asked to state their "straight-time" wage. It is the money a worker would lose per hour if he or she has an unauthorized absence. When wages are defined in this way, a paid holiday becomes a "fringe benefit," as we note below, because leisure time is granted while pay continues. Thus, a worker paid $100 for 25 hours—20 of which are working hours and 5 of which are time off—will be said to earn a wage of $4.00 per hour and receive time off worth $20.

An alternative is to define the wage in terms of actual hours worked—or as $5.00 per hour in the above example. We prefer our definition, because if the worker seizes an opportunity to work one less hour in a particular week, his or her earnings would fall by $4.00, not $5.00 (as long as the reduction in hours does not affect the hours of paid holiday or vacation time for which the worker is eligible).

**TABLE 2.4 Occupational Distribution of Experienced Civilian Labor Force,
1900–1979 (in percent)**

	1900	1910	1920	1930	1940	1950	1960	1970	1979
White-collar workers	17.6	21.0	25.0	29.4	31.1	36.6	42.2	47.5	50.9
Professional and technical	4.3	4.6	5.4	6.8	7.5	8.6	11.3	14.6	15.5
Managers	5.9	6.5	6.6	7.4	7.3	8.7	8.5	8.1	10.8
Clerical	3.0	5.2	8.0	8.9	9.6	12.3	14.9	17.8	18.2
Sales	4.5	4.6	4.9	6.3	6.7	7.0	7.5	7.0	6.4
Manual workers	35.8	37.5	40.2	39.6	39.8	41.1	39.7	36.6	33.1
Craft workers	10.6	11.4	13.0	12.8	12.0	14.2	14.3	13.9	13.3
Operatives	12.8	14.4	15.6	15.8	18.4	20.4	19.9	17.9	15.0
Laborers (nonfarm)	12.5	11.8	11.6	11.0	9.4	6.6	5.5	4.7	4.8
Personal-service workers	9.1	9.4	7.9	9.8	11.8	10.5	11.7	12.9	13.2
Domestics	5.4	4.9	3.3	4.1	4.7	2.6	2.8	1.5	1.1
Other[a]	3.6	4.5	4.5	5.7	7.1	7.9	8.9	11.3	12.1
Farm workers	37.5	30.4	27.0	21.2	17.4	11.8	6.3	3.1	2.8
Farmers and farm managers	19.9	16.3	15.3	12.4	10.4	7.4	3.9	1.8	1.5
Farm laborers	17.7	14.2	11.7	8.8	7.0	4.4	2.4	1.3	1.3

Note: From 1900–1930, employment data relate to "gainful workers." From 1940 on, data relate to experienced civilian labor force. 1979 data are not strictly comparable because they relate only to the *employed* labor force 16 and over.

[a]Included are attendants, barbers, cooks, guards, janitors, police, practical nurses, ushers, waiters, etc.

SOURCES: 1900–1950: U.S. Bureau of the Census, *Historical Statistics of the United States, Colonial Times to 1957,* (1960), Table D72–122.
1960: U.S. Bureau of the Census, *Census of Population 1960,* Subject Reports, PC(2)–7A, 1967, Table 1.
1970: U.S. Bureau of the Census, *Census of Population 1970,* Subject Reports, PC(2)–7A, 1972, Table 1.
1979: U.S. President, *Employment and Training Report of the President* (Washington, D.C.: U.S. Government Printing Office, 1980), p. 245.

in comparing the pay of various workers at a given time. To compare the pay of workers over long periods of time we need to account for changes in the purchasing power of a dollar. Nominal wages divided by some index of prices constitutes the definition of *real wages*. Real wages are normally expressed as an *index number*[6] —which provides a rough notion of how the purchasing power of an hour of work compares over time or across cities or countries.

We often apply the term *wages* to the payments received by workers who are paid on a salaried (monthly, for example) basis rather than an hourly basis. The term is used this way merely for convenience and is of no consequence for most purposes. It is important, however, to distinguish among *wages, earnings,* and *income*. The term *wages* refers to the payment for a *unit* of time, while *earnings* refers to wages multiplied by the number of time units (typically hours) worked. Thus, earnings depend on both wages and the length of time the employee works. *Income*—the total spending power of a person or family during some time period (usually a year)—includes both earnings and *unearned income,* which includes

---

[6]An index number is expressed as a fraction of some base, where the base is set equal to 100. To understand how index numbers are constructed, please refer to the last column in Table 2.5, where the index of real hourly wages in 1980 is listed as 403. This means that hourly real wages were four times higher in 1980 than in the base year, which was chosen arbitrarily as 1914.

To arrive at an index of *real* hourly wages requires that we calculate an index of nominal wages *and* an index of prices. An index of nominal wages can be constructed for each year with 1914 as a base by dividing the wage in each year by $0.22—the hourly wage in 1914—and multiplying by 100. This fixes the index at 100 in 1914 and yields an index number of 3305 for 1980 [(7.29 ÷ 0.22) × 100]. The Consumer Price Index, which is based on "pricing out" an unchanging market basket of goods from year to year, is 820 for the year 1980 if 1914 is the base year. Dividing the price index (820) into the index for nominal wages (3305) and multiplying by 100 gives us the figure of 403 noted in the table.

**TABLE 2.5   Average Wages and Earnings of Production Workers in Manufacturing,
1914–1980**

Year	Weekly Earnings (current dollars)	Average Weekly Hours Paid For	Average Hourly Wage (current dollars)	Consumer Price Index (1914 = 100)[a]	Index of Real Weekly Earnings (1914 = 100)	Index of Real Hourly Wages (1914 = 100)
1914	10.92	49.4	0.22	100	100	100
1920	26.02	47.4	0.55	199	120	126
1925	24.11	44.5	0.54	174	127	141
1930	23.00	42.1	0.55	166	127	151
1935	19.91	36.6	0.54	137	133	179
1940	24.96	38.1	0.66	140	163	214
1945	44.20	43.5	1.02	179	226	259
1950	58.32	40.5	1.44	240	223	273
1955	75.70	40.7	1.86	266	261	318
1960	89.72	39.7	2.26	295	278	348
1965	107.53	41.2	2.61	314	314	378
1970	133.73	39.8	3.36	386	317	396
1975	189.51	39.4	4.81	536	324	408
1980	288.62	39.7	7.27	820	322	403

[a]The figures in this column should be interpreted with some caution. They are generated by pricing out a fixed "market basket" of consumer goods each year. Over time, however, new goods have become available and old ones improved in quality, so that comparability of the "baskets" used in making the index diminishes over time.

SOURCES: U.S. Bureau of the Census, *Historical Statistics of the United States, Colonial Times to 1970* (Washington, D.C.: U.S. Government Printing Office), 1975.

U.S. Department of Labor, Bureau of Labor Statistics, *Handbook of Labor Statistics 1977*, Bulletin 1966 (Washington, D.C.: U.S. Government Printing Office), 1977.

U.S. President, *Economic Report of the President* (Washington, D.C.: U.S. Government Printing Office, January 1981).

dividends or interest received on investments and transfer payments received from the government in the form of food stamps, welfare payments, unemployment compensation, and the like.

Table 2.5 shows the long-run trends in earnings and wages for U.S. manufacturing production workers. While real weekly earnings were about three and one quarter times higher in 1980 than in 1914, the fall in paid weekly hours from 49 to about 40 represented an additional gain in the general standard of living for workers. Probably the best index of living standards is how much workers receive *per hour,* and Table 2.5 shows that real hourly wages were four times as high in 1980 as in 1914, which implies that an hour of work paid for four times more goods and services in 1980 than in 1914.

The actual increase in living standards attainable by the ordinary worker is perhaps even greater than indicated in Table 2.5. Both wages and earnings are normally defined and measured in terms of direct monetary payments to employees (before taxes for which the employee is liable). *Total compensation,* on the other hand, consists of earnings plus *fringe benefits*—benefits that are either payments-in-kind or deferred. Examples of *payments-in-kind* are employer-provided health care or health insurance, where the employee receives a service or an insurance policy rather than money. Paid vacation time is also in this category, since employees are given days off instead of cash. Deferred payments can take the form of employer-financed retirement benefits, including Social Security taxes, where employers set aside money now that enables their employees to receive pensions later.

In 1976, earnings as conventionally defined constituted only 75 percent of the total compensation of manufacturing production workers. Vacations, pensions, and health care were the largest categories of fringe benefits. Because fringe benefits were virtually nonexistent before 1940, we can assume that total earnings and total compensation were essentially the same in the early 1900s. If earnings in more recent years are adjusted to reflect fringe benefits, we arrive at the conclusion that real compensation per hour in the mid-'70s was more than five times higher than in 1914 for the typical manufacturing worker.

The next section will shift from the foregoing brief description of labor market *outcomes* over time to an analysis of how the market *operates* to generate these outcomes. This analysis of labor market functioning is the central focus of labor economics.

HOW THE MARKET WORKS

The study of the labor market begins and ends with an analysis of the demand for and supply of labor. On the demand side of the labor market, we will study employer behavior regarding the hiring of labor. On the supply side, the behavior of both workers and potential workers will be explored. The interaction of demand and supply is basically what determines working conditions, employment and compensation levels, and the allocation of labor to various occupations, industries, and employers. One can thus think of any labor market outcome as always affected, to one degree or another, by the forces of both demand and supply. To paraphrase economist Alfred Marshall, it takes both demand and supply to determine economic outcomes just as it takes two blades of a scissors to cut cloth.

In this chapter we present the basic outlines and broadest implications of the simplest economic model of the labor market. In later chapters we will add some complexities to this basic model and explain assumptions and implications more fully. However, the simple model of demand and supply presented here generates some rather profound insights into labor market behavior which can be very useful in the formation of social policy. Every piece of analysis in this text is either an extension or modification of the basic model presented in this chapter.

The Demand for Labor

Firms are in the business of combining various factors of production—mainly capital and labor—to produce goods or services that are sold in a product market. Their total output and the way in which they combine labor and capital depends on 1. product demand, 2. how much labor and capital they can acquire at given prices, and 3. the choice of technologies available to them. When we study the demand for labor, we are interested in finding out how the number of workers employed by a firm or set of firms is affected by changes in one or more of these three forces. To simplify the discussion, we will study one change at a time and hold all other forces constant.

Wage changes. Of primary interest for most purposes is the question of how the number of employees (or total labor hours) demanded varies when wages change. Suppose, for example, that we could vary the wages facing a certain industry over a long period of time but keep the technology available, the conditions under which capital is supplied, and the relationship between product price and product demand all unchanged. What will happen to the demand for labor when, say, the wage rate is *increased?*

First, higher wages imply higher costs and, usually, higher product prices. Because consumers respond to higher prices by buying less, employers would tend to reduce their level of output. Lower output levels, of course, imply lower employment levels (other things equal). This decline in employment is called a *scale effect*—the effect on desired employment of a smaller scale of production.

Second, as wages increase (assuming the price of capital does not change, at least initially), employers have incentives to cut costs by adopting a technology that relies more on capital and less on labor. Thus, if wages were to rise, desired employment would fall because of a shift toward a more "capital-intensive" mode of production. This second effect might be termed a *substitution effect* because as wages rise capital is *substituted* for labor in the production process.

The effects of various wages on employment levels might be summarized in a table showing the labor demanded at each wage level. Table 2.6 is an example of such a *demand schedule*. The relationship between wages and employment tabulated in Table 2.6 could be graphed as a *demand curve*. Figure 2.1 shows the demand curve generated by the data in Table 2.6. Note that the curve has a negative slope—indicating that as wages rise, less labor is demanded.

A demand curve for labor tells us how the desired level of employment— measured in either labor hours or number of employees—varies with changes in the price of labor when other forces affecting demand are held constant. These other forces, to repeat, are the product demand schedule, the conditions under which capital can be obtained, and the set of technologies available. If wages change and these other factors do not, one can determine the change in labor demanded by moving up or down along the demand curve.

Changes in other forces affecting demand. What happens when one of the other forces affecting labor demand changes?

First, suppose that *demand for the product* of a particular industry were to

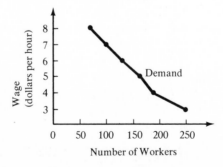

FIGURE 2.1 Labor Demand Curve

**TABLE 2.6 Labor Demand
Schedule for A Hypothetical
Industry**

Wage Rate	Desired Employment Level:
$3.00	250
4.00	190
5.00	160
6.00	130
7.00	100
8.00	70

Note: Employment levels can be measured in number of employees *or* number of labor hours demanded. We have chosen here to use number of employees.

increase, so that at any output price more of the goods or services in question could be sold. Suppose in this case that technology and the conditions under which capital and labor are made available to the industry do not change. Output levels would clearly rise as firms in the industry sought to maximize profits, and this *scale* (or *output*) *effect* would increase the amount of labor demanded. (As long as the relative prices of capital and labor remain unchanged, there is no *substitution effect*.)

How would this change in the demand for labor be illustrated using a demand curve? Since the technology available and the conditions under which capital and labor are supplied have remained constant, this change in product demand would increase the labor desired at any wage level that might prevail. In other words, the entire labor demand curve *shifts* to the right. This rightward shift, shown as a movement from D to D' in Figure 2.2, indicates that at every possible wage rate the number of workers demanded has increased.

Second, consider what would happen if the product demand schedule, technology, and labor-supply conditions were to remain unchanged, but *the supply of capital* changes so that capital prices fall to 50 percent (say) of their prior level. How would this change affect the demand for labor?

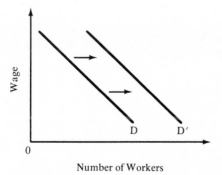

**FIGURE 2.2 Demand for Labor Shifts
Due to an Increase
in Product Demand**

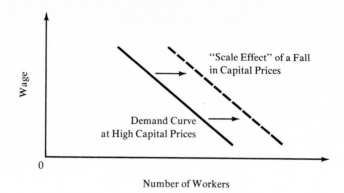

FIGURE 2.3   Demand for Labor Shifts Due to "Scale Effect" Resulting from Fall in Capital Prices

Our analysis of this situation is exactly the same as our analysis of a wage change. First, when capital prices decline the costs of producing tend to decline. Reduced costs stimulate increases in production and these increases will tend to raise the level of desired employment at any given wage. The scale effect of a fall in capital prices thus tends to increase the demand for labor at each wage level—which can be represented in Figure 2.3 by a shift to the right of the labor demand curve.

The second effect of a fall in capital prices would be a substitution effect, whereby firms adopt more capital-intensive technologies in response to cheaper capital. Such firms would substitute capital for labor and would use less labor to produce a given amount of output than before. With less labor being desired at each wage rate, the demand-for-labor curve shifts to the left, as shown in Figure 2.4. In some cases this leftward-shifting tendency of the substitution effect would be stronger than the rightward-shifting tendency of the scale effect; in other cases, the scale effect would be stronger.

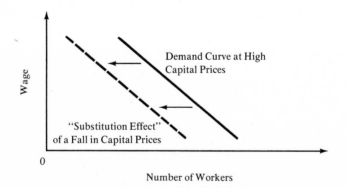

FIGURE 2.4   Demand for Labor Shifts due to "Substitution Effect" Resulting from Fall in Capital Prices

The hypothesized changes in product demand and capital supply just discussed have tended to *shift* the demand curve for labor. It is important to distinguish between a *shift* in a demand curve and *movement along* a curve. A labor demand curve graphically shows the *labor desired* as a function of the *wage rate* (the wage is on one axis and the number employed is on the other axis of the graph). When the *wage* changes and other forces are held unchanged, one *moves along* the curve. However, when one of the *other forces* changes, the labor demand curve will *shift*. Unlike wages, these forces are not directly shown when the demand curve for labor is drawn. Thus, when they change, a different relationship between wages and employment will prevail, and this shows up as a shift of the demand curve. If more labor is desired at any given wage rate, then the curve has shifted to the right. If less labor is demanded at each wage rate that might prevail, then the demand curve has shifted left.

Market, industry, and firm demand. The demand for labor can be analyzed on any one of three different levels.

1. To analyze the demand for labor *by a particular firm,* we would examine how an increase in the wage of machinists (say) would affect their employment by a particular aircraft manufacturer.
2. To analyze the effects of this wage increase on the employment of machinists *in the entire aircraft industry,* we would utilize an industry demand curve.
3. Finally, to see how the wage increase would affect the *entire labor market* for machinists, in all industries in which they are used, we would use a market demand curve.

We will see in Chapters 3 and 4 that firm, industry, and market labor demand curves will vary in *shape* to some extent, because *scale* and *substitution effects* have different strengths at each of the three levels. However, it is important to know at this point that the output and substitution effects work in the same direction at each level, so that firm, industry, and market demand curves *all slope downward*.

Long run vs. short run. One can also distinguish between *long-run* and *short-run* labor demand curves. Over very short periods of time, employers find it difficult to substitute capital for labor (or vice versa), and customers may not change their product demand very much in response to a price increase. It takes *time* to fully adjust consumption and production behavior. Over longer periods of time, of course, responses to changes in wages or the other forces affecting the demand for labor will be larger and more complete.

In Chapters 3 and 4 we will draw some important distinctions between short-run and long-run labor demand curves. At this point, we only need to point out that while these curves will differ, *they both slope downward*. Thus, an increase in the wage rate will reduce the demand for labor—although perhaps by different amounts—in both the short and long run.

The Supply of Labor

Having looked at a simple model of behavior on the buyer (or demand) side of the labor market, we now turn to the seller (or supply) side of the market. For purposes of this chapter we will assume that workers have already decided to work and that the question facing them is what occupation and what employer to choose.

Market supply.   To first consider the supply of labor to the entire market (as opposed to the supply to a particular firm), let us suppose that the market we are considering is the one for stenographers. How will supply respond to changes in the wages stenographers might receive? In other words, what does the supply schedule of stenographers look like?

If the salaries and wages in *other* occupations are *held constant* and the wages of stenographers rise, we would expect to find more people wanting to become stenographers. For example, suppose that each of 100 people in a high school graduating class has the option of becoming an insurance agent or stenographer. Some of these 100 people will prefer to be insurance agents even if stenographers are better paid, because they like the challenge and sociability of selling. Some would want to be stenographers even if the pay were comparatively poor, because they hate the pressures of selling. Many, however, could see themselves doing either job; for these the compensation in each occupation would be a major factor in their decision. If stenographers were higher paid than insurance agents, more would want to become stenographers. If the pay of insurance agents were higher, the number of people choosing the insurance occupation would increase and the supply of stenographers would decrease. Of course, at some ridiculously low wage for stenographers, *no one* would want to become one.

Thus, the supply of labor to a particular market is positively related to the wage rate prevailing in that market, holding other wages constant. That is, if the wages of insurance agents are held constant and the stenographer wage rises, more people will want to become stenographers because of the relative improvement in compensation (as shown graphically in Figure 2.5).

As with demand curves, each supply curve is drawn holding other prices and wages constant. If one or more of these other prices or wages were to change, it

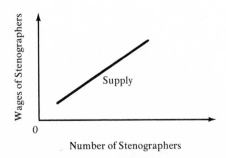

FIGURE 2.5   Supply Curve for Stenographers

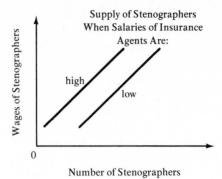

**FIGURE 2.6 Labor Supply Curve
Shifts for Stenographers
as Salaries of
Insurance Agents Rise**

would cause the supply curve to *shift*. As the salaries of insurance agents *rise,* some people will change their minds about becoming stenographers and choose to become insurance agents. Fewer people would want to be stenographers at each level of stenographic wages as salaries of insurance agents rise. In graphical terms (see Figure 2.6), increases in the salaries of insurance agents would cause the supply curve of stenographers to shift to the left.

Supply to firms.   Having decided to become a stenographer, the decision then moves to which offer of employment to accept. If all employers were offering stenographic jobs that were more or less alike, the choice would be based on compensation. Any firm unwise enough to attempt paying a wage below what others pay would find it could not attract any employees (or at least it could not attract any of the caliber it wants). Conversely, no firm would be foolish enough to pay more than the going wage, because it would be paying more than it would have to pay in order to attract a suitable number and quality of employees. The supply curve to a firm, then, would be horizontal, as can be seen in Figure 2.7. The horizontal supply curve to a firm indicates that at the going wage, a firm can get all the stenographers it needs. If it pays less, however, supply shrinks to zero.

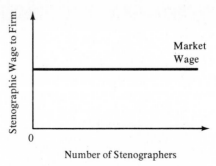

**FIGURE 2.7 Supply of Stenographers
to a Firm**

The difference in slope between the market supply curve and the supply curve to a firm is directly related to the type of choice facing workers. In deciding whether to enter the stenographic labor market or not, workers must weigh both the compensation *and* the job requirements of alternative options (such as being an insurance agent). If wages of stenographers were to fall, fewer people would want to enter the stenographic market. However, not everyone would withdraw from the market, because the jobs of insurance agent and stenographer are not perfect substitutes. Some people would remain stenographers after a wage decline because they dislike the job requirements of insurance agents.

Once having decided to become a stenographer, the choice of which employer to work for is a choice between alternatives where the job requirements are nearly the *same*. Thus, the choice must be made on the grounds of compensation alone. If a firm were to lower its wage offers below those of other firms, it would lose all its applicants. The horizontal supply curve is, therefore, a reflection of supply decisions made among alternatives that are perfect substitutes for each other.

We have argued that firms wishing to hire stenographers must pay the going wage or lose all applicants. While this may seem unrealistic, it is not. If a firm offers jobs *comparable* to those offered by other firms but at a lower level of total compensation, it might be able to attract a few applicants of the quality it desires because a few people will be unaware of compensation elsewhere. Over time, however, knowledge of the firm's poor relative pay would become more wide-spread, and the firm would find it had to rely solely on less qualified people to fill its jobs. It could secure quality employees at below-average pay only if it offered *noncomparable* jobs (more pleasant working conditions, longer paid vacations, and so forth). This factor in labor supply will be discussed in Chapter 8. For now, we will assume that individual firms, like individual workers, are usually *wage takers;* that is, the wages they pay to their workers must be pretty close to the going wage if they face competition in the labor market. Neither individual workers nor firms can set a wage much different from the going wage and still hope to transact. (Exceptions to this general proposition will be noted in later chapters.)

The Determination of the Wage

The wage that prevails in a particular labor market is heavily influenced by the forces of demand and supply, whether or not the market involves a labor union. However, because unions are labor-market institutions designed to alter the market outcome, we will first discuss wage determination in the case of nonunionized labor markets.

The equilibrium wage.   Recall that the market demand curve indicates how many workers employers would want at each wage rate, holding capital prices and consumer incomes constant. The market supply curve indicates how many workers would enter the market at each wage level, holding the wages in other occupations constant. These curves can be overlaid on the same graph to reveal some interesting information, as shown in Figure 2.8.

For example, suppose the market wage were set at W_1. At this low wage, demand is large but supply is small. More importantly, Figure 2.8 indicates that

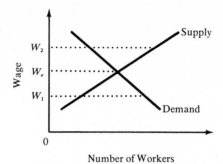

FIGURE 2.8   Market Demand and Supply

at W_1 demand *exceeds* supply. At this point, employers will be competing for the few workers in the market and a "shortage" of workers would exist. Firms' desires to attract more employees would lead them to increase their wage offers, thus driving up the overall level of wage offers in the market.

As wages rise, two things happen. First, more workers would choose to enter the market and look for jobs (a movement along the supply curve); second, at the same time increasing wages would induce employers to seek fewer workers (a movement along the demand curve). If wages were to rise to W_2, supply would exceed demand. Employers would desire fewer workers than the number available, and not all those desiring employment would be able to find jobs—resulting in a "surplus" of workers. Employers would have long lines of eager applicants for any opening. These employers would soon reason that they could still fill their openings with qualified applicants even if they offered lower wages. Further, if they could pay lower wages they would want to hire more employees. Some employees would be more than happy to accept the lower wages if they could just find a job. Others would leave the market and look for work elsewhere as wages fell. Thus, demand and supply would become more equal as wages fell from the level of W_2.

The wage rate at which demand equals supply is the *market-clearing* or *equilibrium* wage. At W_e in Figure 2.8, employers can fill the number of openings they have, and all employees who want jobs in this market can find them. At W_e there is no surplus and no shortage. All parties are satisfied, and no forces exist that would alter the wage. The market is in equilibrium in the sense that the wage will remain at W_e.

The equilibrium wage is the wage that eventually prevails in a market. Wages below W_e, for example, will not prevail because the shortage of workers leads employers to drive up wage offers. Wages above W_e likewise cannot prevail because the surplus leads to downward pressure on wage rates. The market-clearing wage, W_e, thus becomes the *going wage* that individual employers and employees must face. In other words, wage rates are determined by the market and "announced" to individual market participants. Figure 2.9 graphically depicts "market" demand and supply in panel (a) along with the demand and supply curves

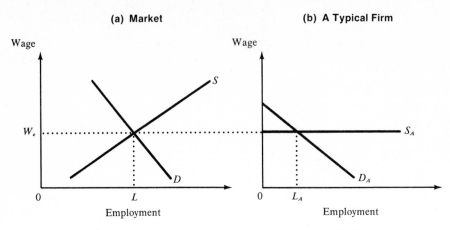

FIGURE 2.9   Demand and Supply at the "Market" and "Firm" Level

for a typical firm in that market in panel (b). All firms in the market pay a wage of W_e, and total employment of L equals the sum of employment in each firm.

Disturbing the equilibrium.   What could happen to change the equilibrium (market) wage once it has been reached? Once equilibrium has been achieved changes could arise from shifts in either the demand or the supply curve. For example, let us consider what might happen to the wages of stenographers (the majority of whom at present are women) if job opportunities for women in management and other prestigious fields were to improve. The greater availability and improved pay for women in these alternative careers would probably cause some women to leave the stenographer market and seek work in these other fields. Fewer women would want to become stenographers at the going wage. As Figure 2.10 shows, the market supply curve for stenographers would shift to the left.

As can be seen from Figure 2.10, after the supply curve has shifted, W_e is no longer the market-clearing wage. There is now a shortage of stenographers (be-

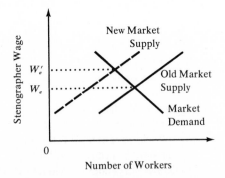

FIGURE 2.10   New Labor Market
Equilibrium after Supply
Shifts Left

Example 2.1
The Black Death and the Wages of Labor

A tragic example of what happens to wages when the supply of labor suddenly shifts occurred when plague—the Black Death—struck England (among other European countries) in 1348–1351. Estimates vary, but it is generally agreed that plague killed between 17 and 40 percent of the English population in the short period of time. This shocking loss of life had the immediate effect of raising the wages of laborers. As supply shifted to the left, a *shortage* of workers was created at the old wage levels, and competition among employers for the surviving workers drove the wage level dramatically upward.

Reliable figures are hard to come by, but many believe wages rose by 50–100 percent over the three-year period. A thresher, for example, earning two and one-half pence per day in 1348 earned four and one-half pence in 1350, while mowers receiving 5 pence per acre in 1348 were receiving 9 pence in 1350. Whether the overall rise in wages was this large or not, there was clearly a labor shortage and an unprecedented increase in wages. A royal proclamation—commanding landlords to share their scarce workers with neighbors and threatening workers with imprisonment if they refused work at the pre-plague wage—was issued to deal with this shortage, but it was ignored. The shortage was too severe and market forces simply too strong for the rise in wages to be thwarted.

The discerning student might wonder at this point about the *demand* curve for labor. Did it not also shift to the left as the population—and the number of consumers—declined? The answer is that it did, but that this leftward shift was not as pronounced as the leftward shift in supply. What happened was that, while there were fewer customers for labor's output, the customers who remained consumed greater amounts of goods and services per capita than before. The money, gold and silver, and durable goods that had existed prior to 1348 were divided among many fewer people by 1350, and this rise in per capita wealth was associated with a widespread and dramatic increase in the level of consumption—especially of luxury goods. Thus the leftward shift in labor demand was dominated by the leftward shift in supply, and the predictable result was a large increase in wages.

SOURCES: Harry A. Miskimin, *The Economy of Early Renaissance Europe 1300–1460* (Englewood Cliffs, N.J.: Prentice-Hall, Inc., 1969); George M. Modlin and Frank T. deVyver, *Development of Economic Society* (Boston: D.C. Heath, 1946); Douglass C. North and Robert Paul Thomas, *The Rise of the Western World* (Cambridge: Cambridge University Press, 1973); Philip Ziegler, *The Black Death* (New York: Harper and Row, 1969).

cause demand exceeds supply) at W_e. As employers scramble to fill stenographic jobs, the wage rate is driven up. The new equilibrium wage is W_e', which of course is higher than W_e. Better opportunities for women in management would thus lead to a smaller supply of stenographers, and to fill stenographic jobs the wage rate paid to stenographers would have to rise. The end result of the improved opportunities elsewhere would be to increase the wages of stenographers.

**FIGURE 2.11   New Labor Market
Equilibrium after Demand
Shifts Right**

Shifts of the demand curve to the right would also cause wages to rise. Suppose, for example, that the increase in paperwork accompanying greater government regulation of industry causes firms to demand more stenographic help than before. Graphically, as in Figure 2.11, this greater demand would be represented as a rightward shift of the demand curve. This rightward shift depicts a situation in which, for any given wage rate, the number of stenographers desired has risen. The old equilibrium wage (W_e) no longer equates demand and supply. If W_e were to persist, there would be a labor shortage in the stenographer market (because demand would exceed supply). This shortage would induce employers to improve their wage offers and eventually drive up the stenographic wage to W_e^*.

Both the leftward shift of supply and the rightward shift in demand initially created shortages—shortages that led to increases in the market wage rate. The supply-caused shift, however, led to a fall in employment (as compared to the old equilibrium level of employment). Conversely, the demand-caused shift induced an increase in the equilibrium level of employment.

Equilibrium wages can also fall, of course. Although *money* wages are rarely cut, in a period of rising prices *real* wages can fall quite readily anyway. Between 1976 and 1977, for example, money wages for nonagricultural production workers

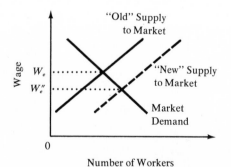

**FIGURE 2.12   New Labor Market
Equilibrium after Supply
Shifts Right**

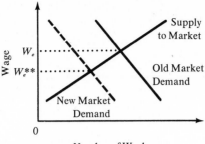

FIGURE 2.13   New Labor Market
Equilibrium after Demand
Shifts Left

rose by 8.0 percent (from $203.70 per week to $219.91), but their real wages fell by 3 percent because prices rose by 11 percent.[7] Money wages in an occupation can also fall relative to wages in other occupations. Thus, when we speak of a declining wage rate it can imply a decline *relative to product prices or to other wages* as well as a fall in the money wage rate.

A fall in the equilibrium wage rate will occur if there is increased supply or reduced demand. An increase in supply would be represented by a rightward shift of the supply curve, as more people enter the market at each wage (see Figure 2.12). This rightward shift causes a surplus to exist at the old equilibrium wage (W_e) and leads to behavior that reduces the wage to W_e'' in Figure 2.12. Note that the equilibrium employment level has increased. What could cause this rightward shift of the supply curve? For stenographers, the causes of increased supply at each wage could be 1. a greater desire among people to become stenographers, or 2. reductions in the wages of competing occupations (such as insurance agents in our example above).

A decrease (leftward shift) in demand would also cause a decrease in the equilibrium wage, although such a shift would be accompanied by a fall in employment, as we can see in Figure 2.13. The leftward demand shift causes a surplus at the original equilibrium wage (W_e). When firms find the ratio of applicants to openings is greater than usual and when workers find that jobs are harder to come by, downward pressure on the wage will exist and the market-clearing wage falls to W_e^{**}. Money wages may go up, but any increases will be smaller than those received in other occupations. Sadly for the authors, the decline in demand for college professors brought on by a number of financial and demographic pressures offers an excellent example of a "surplus" market. The result has been a 17 percent decline in real, after-tax income for college professors over the 1967–78 period.

It is possible, of course, for equilibrium to be disturbed by shifts in both demand and supply at the same time. These simultaneous shifts might either reinforce each other or work against each other. An example of a reinforcing shift is

[7]U.S. President, *Economic Report of the President* (Washington, D.C.: U.S. Government Printing Office, January 1980), Tables B-36 and B-49.

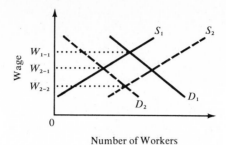

FIGURE 2.14 New Labor Market Equilibrium after Supply Shifts Right and Demand Shifts Left

where a leftward shift in demand is accompanied by a rightward shift in supply, as shown in Figure 2.14. If the demand curve alone shifted, wages would fall from W_{1-1} to W_{2-1}—but when accompanied by a rightward shift in supply wages fall to W_{2-2}.

Shifts may also tend to work against each other. For example, if the invention and spread of tape-recording devices reduced the demand for people with stenographic skills at the same time that opportunities for women outside the clerical occupations were increasing, it would be difficult to predict the effects on stenographers' wages (see Figure 2.15). The leftward shift of demand exerts downward pressure on wages, while the leftward shift of supply has a tendency to cause wages to rise. The ultimate effect depends on which force is greater. In panel (a) of Figure 2.15, the forces generated by the contraction of demand were dominant, and the equilibrium wage is depicted as falling from W_{1-1} to W_{2-2}. In panel (b) of Figure 2.15, however, the contraction of supply was dominant, and wages are shown as rising from W_{1-1} to W_{2-2}.

APPLICATIONS OF THE THEORY

The preceding section presented a simple model of how a labor market functions. Although this model will be refined and elaborated upon in the following chapters, the model is adequate to explain many important phenomena, including those that follow.

The Allocation of Labor to Inhospitable Climates

The labor market, as we emphasized earlier, performs the task of matching employers and employees. In accomplishing this task it fulfills the important social role of allocating a scarce resource—labor—among potential users. Moreover, this allocation takes place voluntarily. Our model of the labor market explains how this allocation happens and with what effects.

Any society wanting to allocate its resouces by taking into account the wishes of both consumer and worker must invent a mechanism that readily reflects both sets of wishes. The market is just such a mechanism. The wishes of consumers are expressed through the labor demand schedules of employers. The more of a

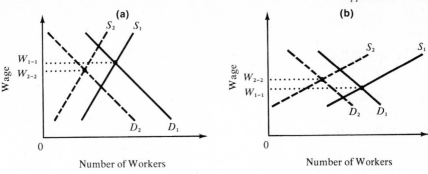

FIGURE 2.15 New Labor Market Equilibria after Supply and Demand Shift Left

particular output consumers want and the more they are willing to pay for it, the more labor (and capital) will be demanded by producers. For example, Figure 2.16 shows that firm A has a stronger demand for workers than does firm B; therefore, at a wage of W_0, it hires more workers.

The labor market also reflects worker preferences. If all jobs were alike, preferences would not be important. However, jobs vary in difficulty, level of tension, location, working conditions, hours, security, and so forth. Workers will understandably be more reluctant to do some kinds of work than other kinds, and the allocation process must take this reluctance into account. The supply curves to various labor markets are a convenient way to represent worker preferences. When the jobs are pleasant, many people will be willing to offer their services at each wage level. When jobs are distasteful, fewer will be willing to do so.

The effect of worker preferences on the allocation of labor can be understood by comparing two labor markets where the job *duties* are the same but where the conditions of work are radically different. Let us suppose, for example, that one market is offering clerical jobs in the continental United States, while the other market is offering such jobs with companies building a pipeline in a harsh, inhospitable, remote location near the Arctic Circle. If wages were equal in both places, the jobs near the Arctic Circle would not be filled, as workers prefer more hospitable climates. To attract workers to the unappealing location requires that compensation be higher there. The high wages cause employers to economize on the

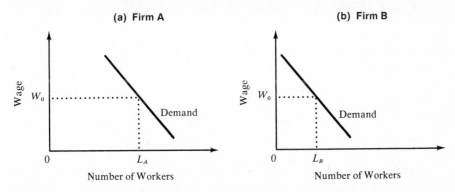

FIGURE 2.16 The Demand for Labor in Two Firms

Example 2.2
Restricted Labor Supply in the Soviet Union

Examples of the effects of a restricted labor supply to areas where the weather is extraordinarily harsh can be found in socialist, as well as capitalist, countries. In the Soviet Union, where production is centrally planned but labor is recruited voluntarily through the use of incentives, workers in the Far North are paid wages and supplements that are 60–180 percent higher than in the populated areas in central, southern, and western Russia. Only part of the differential is to compensate workers for the higher costs of living in Northern Siberia. Even a society that philosophically prefers wage equality must pay its workers in the Far North a *real wage* much higher than elsewhere if it hopes to voluntarily assemble a work force large enough to produce in that region.

SOURCE: Paul R. Gregory and Robert C. Stuart, *Soviet Economic Structure and Performance*, 2nd ed. (New York: Harper & Row, 1981), pp. 190–92.

use of labor in these places—most, in fact, would not even locate there. Some, however, have such strong incentives for locating there that they are willing to pay the high wages. The high wages, of course, serve to compensate workers for the inhospitable location of their jobs.

The building of the trans-Alaska pipeline in the mid-1970s provides an example of how disagreeable working conditions affect wages. The work entailed long hours (84 hours a week), cruel winter weather (frequently 55 degress below zero), and anything but a normal personal life (dormitory living). Under these conditions, it took hourly wages 50 percent higher than those received by similarly skilled workers in the continental United States, with time and one-half for overtime and double time on Sundays, to recruit and hold the required labor force. However, workers who chose to work there could make $60,000 per year—almost four times what they could make in roughly the same job located in the continental United States.

The Accommodation of "Baby Boom" Workers

During the late 1970s, the overall labor market was forced to accommodate a huge influx of new workers searching for jobs. These new entrants were people born in the late 1950s—a period of the so-called "baby boom." The number of 20-year olds in the population in 1977 was 44 percent larger than the number in 1962 and equally large compared to the numbers projected for 1992.[8] Thus, there was a "bulge" in the number of inexperienced workers seeking jobs. What can we predict would happen as this bulge in supply hit the labor market?

[8]Data for this section were obtained from Finis Welch, "Effects of Cohort Size on Earnings: The Baby Boom Babies' Financial Bust," *Journal of Political Economy* 87, 5 (October 1979): S65–98.

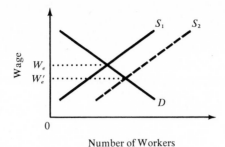

FIGURE 2.17 Labor Market Equilibrium
for Teenagers after
Population Increase

First, new entrants are, by definition, inexperienced workers, and such workers are not very good substitutes for experienced workers. Inexperienced workers tend to be offered *entry-level jobs,* while more complicated or responsible jobs higher up on the career ladder are reserved to some extent for experienced workers. Thus, the experienced and the inexperienced are, to a degree, in different labor markets.

What happens when a big bulge of population enters a labor market? The sheer increase in population will shift the supply curve to the right, because there will be more people offering themselves for work at every wage level. Figure 2.17 illustrates this shift from S_1 to S_2. This shift in supply, if not accompanied by a correspondingly large shift in demand, will have the effect of reducing wages. (Figure 2.17 shows that the equilibrium wage fell from W_e to W_e'.)

Did the "baby boom" bulge in the late 1970s cause wages of inexperienced workers to fall? To answer this question we must pick a standard against which to measure the fall. Money wages rarely fall, especially during periods when prices are rising. We could, therefore, measure whether *real wages* fell over some time period. However, real wages have tended to rise due to improvements in technology—a force we would like to filter out if possible so that we can focus only on changes produced by the shift in supply.

The best way to measure the fall in the wages of inexperienced workers is to compare their wages to those of adults in their peak earnings years. These adults will be the beneficiaries, along with inexperienced workers, of technological advances, but they are far enough removed from the "baby boomers" in experience that the bulge of new labor force entrants will not affect their wages directly. Measured against this group, earnings of new entrants fell dramatically in the late 1970s.

Table 2.7 tells the story. In every educational category, the proportion of inexperienced workers in the labor force increased during the period from 1967 to 1975—a clear indication that the number of young workers was increasing faster than the number of older workers. This abnormally large rise in employment was accompanied by a 12–15 percent decline in the earnings of new workers relative to adults. Thus, as our model of labor-market behavior suggests, the large increase in employment necessary to accomodate the "baby boom" entrants was facilitated

TABLE 2.7   **Economic Position of New Entrants in Labor Force,**
by Level of Schooling

Years of School Completed	Percent of Work Force with Less than 5 Years of Experience in Each Schooling Category		Weekly Wages of New Entrants Relative to Peak Earners	
	1967–69	*1973–75*	*1967–69*	*1973–75*
8–11 years	8.9	15.4	0.53	0.46
12 years	15.0	20.8	0.63	0.55
1–3 years of college	19.0	25.2	0.59	0.52
4 or more years of college	18.7	22.9	0.63	0.54

SOURCE: Finis Welch, "Effects of Cohort Size on Earnings: The Baby Boom Babies' Financial Bust," *Journal of Political Economy* 87, 5 (October 1979): S65–S98.

by a decline in their wage. The influx of inexperienced workers created a "surplus" at the former wage level, and as new workers competed for jobs the wage level was driven down.

Effects of Unions

Although we will discuss the role and effects of unions on the labor market later in this text, it is important here to briefly establish that the model outlined in this chapter can also apply to unions. This analysis will look only generally at the effects of unions on wages. Later chapters will analyze union effects on wages in more detail and will also examine their effects on productivity, turnover, and wage differentials across race and sex groups.

Unions represent workers and, as such, primarily affect the *supply* curves to labor markets. They can affect these supply curves in two ways. First, most unions operate under labor-management agreements—called *contracts* or *collective-bargaining agreements*—that permit employer discretion in the selection of workers. These contracts cover wages, other forms of compensation, working conditions, procedures for employee complaints, and rules governing promotions and layoffs. The provisions of the contracts are the result of a bargain struck between management and all workers collectively. In effect, workers band together, agree to a bargaining position, and negotiate as a group. All are bound by the final provisions of the contract—which means that all must receive the agreed-upon wage.

Many of the most prominent collective-bargaining agreements, in effect, are industrywide. These agreements, which include those in the auto, steel, rubber, coal, and trucking industries, affect the supply curves in the relevant labor markets by making them horizontal. No one can get paid more or less than the wage agreed upon in the contract (see Figure 2.18).

In Figure 2.18, the supply curve without a union is S, and the market-clearing wage is W_e. However, the union raises the wage above W_e to W_u, the wage specified in the contract, by preventing firms and workers from offering or accepting wages below W_u. The result is a wage above equilibrium, employment levels

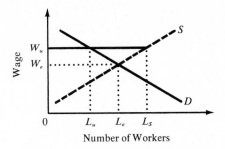

**FIGURE 2.18   Effects on Labor-Market
Equilibrium of
Industrywide Unions**

below those that would prevail if the wage were lower, and a ''surplus'' of labor (at W_u, L_s workers want work in these jobs but only L_u can find work). Because the wage cannot fall, the surplus remains and will manifest itself in long lines of workers applying for job openings with union employers.

The above graphical analysis was based on the assumption that unions raised the wage above market-clearing levels. This is probably a useful assumption, given that unions certainly intend to do this. Not all unions have the power to affect wages much, for reasons we will discuss in Chapter 4. If these unions agree to wages equal to W_e, the market equilibrium wage, then clearly they do not affect wage or employment outcomes in the labor market.

The second way in which some unions affect the supply to markets is by *directly* limiting supply. Some unions operate under agreements in which employers hire all labor from the union and in which the union controls who and how many members it lets in. The dual power of being able to restrict its membership and to require employers to hire only union members permits the union to set the level of labor supply to the market (see Figure 2.19).

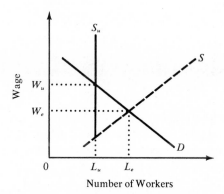

**FIGURE 2.19   How Unions that Control
Supply of Labor to a
Market affect Labor
Market Equilibrium**

In Figure 2.19, S_u represents the level of supply determined by union policy and W_u the resulting wage. S_u is drawn as a vertical line because wage increases or decreases do not affect supply. Supply is set at L_u by union policy.

The wage and employment levels under the union—W_u and L_u—can be compared to the lower wages *(W_e)* and higher employment levels *(L_e)* that would prevail in the absence of a union. The major difference between this case, where unions control supply, and the more common situation, in which employers choose workers but make contracts with all workers collectively, is that there is no surplus of workers standing at the employer's hiring gate. The long line of disappointed people is at the union's office. Examples of labor unions that control supply are those representing skilled construction workers, longshoring workers, and theater lighting technicians.[9]

The model of labor market behavior presented in this chapter has here been used to explain how unions affect wages. If unions are successful in driving such wages above equilibrium, the model can also be used to analyze the consequences of this wage increase. First, as wages rise above the market-clearing level, employment will be reduced. Second, as union wages rise the number of people wanting union jobs will increase. However, the limited job opportunities will make it difficult for many of these people to find work, and a "surplus" of labor will come to exist in the unionized markets. (See Chapters 3 and 12 for an analysis of union effects on wages and employment in nonunion labor markets.)

Who Is Underpaid and Who Is Overpaid?

In casual conversation one often hears a worker say that he or she is "underpaid." Just as often one hears employers claiming workers are "overpaid." Clearly, each is using a different standard for judging wages. People tend to judge the wages paid or received against some notion of what they "need," but there is no universally accepted standard of need. A worker may "need" more income to buy a larger home or finance a recreational vehicle. An employer may "need" greater profits to pay for sending a child to college. In general, almost all of us feel we "need" more income!

Despite the difficulties of assessing needs, there are still important reasons for defining "overpaid" and "underpaid." For example, the public utilities commissions in every state must consider and approve rate increases requested by the telephone, gas, and electric companies. These companies desire increases partly to keep up with production costs, which the companies obviously want to pass on to consumers. Suppose, however, that a public utilities commission observes that the *level* of wages paid by these companies or the *increases* in such wages are "excessive." In the interests of holding down consumer prices, it may want to consider adopting a policy whereby excessive labor costs cannot be passed on to

---

[9]This is not to say that all unions that *can* control supply are equally prone to do it. Some may fear the presence of a large number of qualified workers outside the union, and figure that it is better to take them in, collect their dues, and ration jobs among all members than to face stiff nonunion competition. Restricting entry into the union is *most likely* where employers *must* hire only union workers.

consumers in the form of rate increases. Instead, it may decide that such costs should be borne by the company or its shareholders. Obviously, such a policy would require a definition of what constitutes "overpayment."

We pointed out in Chapter 1 that a fundamental value of normative economics is that, as a society, we should strive to complete all those transactions that are mutually beneficial. Another way of stating this value is to say that we must strive to use our scarce resources as effectively as possible—which implies that output should be produced in the least costly manner so that the most can be obtained from such resources. This goal, combined with the labor market model outlined in this chapter, suggests a useful definition of what it means to be overpaid.

We will define workers as *overpaid* if their wages are higher than the market equilibrium wage for their job. Because a labor "surplus" exists for jobs that are overpaid, a wage above equilibrium has two implications (see Figure 2.20). First, employers are paying more than they have to in order to produce (they pay W_H instead of W_e). They could cut wages and still find enough qualified workers for their job openings. In fact, if they did cut wages they could expand output and make their product cheaper and more accessible to consumers. Second, more workers want jobs than can find them (Y workers want jobs, and only V openings are available). If wages were reduced a bit, more of these disappointed workers could find work. A wage above equilibrium thus causes consumer prices to be higher and output to be smaller than is possible, and it creates a situation where not all workers who want the jobs in question can get them.

With this definition of overpayment, the public utilities commission in question would want to look for evidence that wages were above equilibrium. The commission might be able to compare wages paid by utilities to those of comparable workers in the general labor market. Doing so would require measures of worker quality, of course—data that are hard to quantify in some cases. Alternatively, the commission could look to employee behavior for signs of above-market wages. If wages are above those for comparable jobs current employees will be *very* reluctant to quit, because they know their chances of doing better are small. Likewise, the number of applicants will be unusually large.

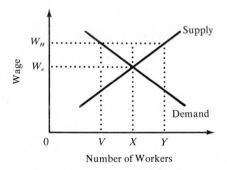

**FIGURE 2.20   Effects of an Above-
Equilibrium Wage**

An interesting—although perhaps extreme—example of above-equilibrium wage rates could be seen in New York City in 1974–75. New York City fire fighters and police officers during this period were receiving salaries roughly 40 percent greater than skilled mechanics and machinists working in the city and some 50 percent greater than area truck drivers. Perhaps the most convincing evidence of "overpayment" and the attendant surplus is that there were enormous numbers of qualified applicants who had passed job-related tests and were waiting for openings. For fire fighters, there were about 12,000 qualified applicants— compared to a total employment of only 10,000—at a time when the city was not even hiring fire fighters. For police officers, there were more than 42,000 quali- fied applicants on the waiting list, 23,000 current employees, and no hiring to speak of.[10]

An even larger surplus existed for sanitation workers, whose $14,770 yearly salary (in 1974 dollars) was 60 percent higher than the area average for laborers/ materials handlers. In that department, there were 36,849 on the waiting list of people who had passed a job-related examination—or 3.4 qualified applicants for each current employee! Again, hiring was almost nil during this period. These numbers clearly point to a labor "surplus"—and thus to "overpayment."

To better understand the social losses attendant to overpayment, let us return to the principles of normative economics. Can it be shown that reducing overpay- ment will create a situation where the gainers gain more than the losers lose? Suppose in the case of sanitation workers that *only* the wages of *newly hired* sanitation workers were lowered—to $10,000, say. Current workers thus do not lose, but many laborers working at $9200 per year (the prevailing wage for them in 1974) will jump at the chance to take a $10,000-a-year job. Taxpayers, know- ing that garbage-collection services can now be expanded at lower cost than before will increase their demand for such services, thus creating jobs for these new workers.[11] Thus, some workers gain while no one loses—and social well-being is clearly enhanced.[12]

Employees can be defined as *underpaid* if their wage is below equilibrium. At below-equilibrium wages employers have difficulty in finding workers to meet the demands by consumers, and a labor "shortage" thus exists (firms want more workers than they can find at the prevailing wage). They also have trouble keeping

---

[10]Sharon P. Smith, *Equal Pay in the Public Sector: Fact or Fantasy* (Princeton, N.J.: Industrial Rela- tions Section, Princeton University, Research Report Series No. 122, 1977), p. 20.

[11]These new workers, of course, have wanted sanitation jobs with New York City all along, but the high wage prevented job opportunities in that field from expanding.

   It should be noted that if the wages of *current* sanitation workers were lowered, city taxpayers could obtain their current level of service for less money. Their gains (in tax savings) equal the income losses of sanitation workers, and if we are to arrange the transaction so that no one loses, the gainers would have to compensate the losers by restoring their lost income. For this reason we have assumed that salaries for current sanitation workers are not cut.

[12]If the workers who switch jobs are getting paid approximately what they are worth to their former employers, these employers lose $9200 in output but save $9200 in costs—and their welfare is thus not affected. The presumption that employees are paid what they are worth to the employer is discussed at length in Chapter 3.

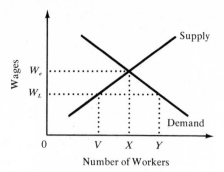

**FIGURE 2.21   Effects of a Below-
Equilibrium Wage**

the workers they do find. If wages were increased, output would rise, and more workers would be attracted to the market. Thus, an increase would benefit the people in society in *both* their consumer and worker roles. Figure 2.21 shows how a wage increase from W_L to W_e would increase employment to V from X (at the same time wages were rising).

A classic example of below-equilibrium wages are those in the U.S. Army. In 1962, for example, when the military draft was in effect, the military paid new entrants room and board and a cash payment that was 54 percent of the average weekly wage of manufacturing production workers. Total compensation was so low for the job that an enormous gap between demand and supply existed. As a result, a large percentage of all new recruits had to be *drafted* in order to deal with the shortage. Fifteen years later, when shortages could no longer be met through conscription, cash wages for Army recruits had risen to 70 percent of the manufacturing wage. Still, there is evidence that Army wages are below equilibrium: there are unfilled openings and the average quality and discipline of recruits is reportedly low.

How do these definitions of underpayment and overpayment accord with notions of fairness or equity? They square very well with the concept of *horizontal equity*—treating equals equally. If the equilibrium wage were paid to each worker in a particular labor market, no one would be underpaid or overpaid. Equal workers would receive equal pay for essentially the same work.

These definitions, however, are ambiguous in relation to the concept of *vertical equity*—treating different groups differently. How can we justify paying a professor more or less than a sanitation worker? The answer suggested by our definitions is that it is less a matter of justice than it is of getting the job done. We have to pay professors and sanitation workers whatever it takes to get them to provide the level of services we desire. If so few people want to collect garbage that it requires a relatively high wage to attract them, so be it. If we are to have this valuable service performed without resorting to involuntary servitude, there is no choice but to pay the wages necessary to attract the required number and quality of workers.

Labor "Shortages": A Policy Application

The government is frequently urged to undertake programs designed to cope with perceived labor shortages. Underlying these proposals is usually an assumption that market forces are not working effectively to generate an adequate supply of workers to the occupations in question, but this assumption is often based on concepts or reasoning that are faulty. We can use the insights developed in this chapter to point out two common errors in this assumption and the dangers of not recognizing them.

Wrong definition of shortage.   Perhaps the most common error is to define a "shortage" in terms that are independent of demand. For example, a recent book on occupational safety and health argued that there was a shortage (in 1973) of 19,700 industrial nurses even though the same book estimated that the number of jobs available for such nurses exceeded their supply by only 700.[13] In what sense does the author perceive a "shortage?"

It is clear that the author's definition of a shortage is inconsistent with the concept as we have defined it. According to our definition a shortage exists if, at the prevailing wage rate for a given occupation, demand exceeds supply. If the figures quoted above for industrial nurses are correct, a minor shortage of 700 may be said to exist. The author, however, ignores what demand *actually* is and bases his definition of a shortage on what he feels demand *should be!* He argues that to do an "adequate" job of protecting workers from the dangers of health hazards on the job, we "need" to have 19,700 more nurses than we currently have. His definition is thus based on a perception of *"need"* as compared to supply—rather than on *demand* as compared to supply.

The distinction between a needs-based definition of a shortage and a demand-based definition is not a trivial matter of semantics. The central problem addressed by economics is that resources are scarce, so that our individual or social *needs* for newer cars, larger houses, cleaner air, better schools, and more mass transit will not necessarily get translated into *demand*. That workers would be healthier if we employed 19,700 more industrial nurses no more indicates that these nurses would be hired than the fact that all families would be happier with five-bedroom houses suggests more such homes could be sold! Given limited resources, firms and homeowners alike may not choose to pay the added costs of meeting the "need."

Acceptance of a needs-based definition of labor shortage by the government poses two related dangers. Declaring that the "shortage" of industrial nurses amounts to 19,700 may imply to new workers that many more jobs are available than in fact actually exist. Many might mistakenly enter the field believing the opportunities are better than they really are. The other danger is that the government might uncritically adopt expensive programs to increase supply in an environment where the added workers would not find jobs available in the field.

In the 1960s, for example, the government initiated a $300 million program to increase the supply of professional nursing graduates by 29 percent in five

---

[13]Nicholas Ashford, *Crisis in the Workplace* (Cambridge, Mass.: MIT Press, 1976), p. 455.

years. The program was adopted after a report by the Surgeon General calculated a huge shortage of nurses based on a needs approach. The report contended that 50 percent of direct patient care should be provided by registered nurses (as opposed to nursing aides), because below this level patient satisfaction is significantly reduced. The problem with trying to increase the supply of nurses to meet this "shortage" was that at the time supply did not seem to be falling short of effective demand!

The hallmark of a shortage (as we have defined it) is a wage rate that rises faster than average. If demand exceeds supply at the prevailing wage, firms with unfilled vacancies will attempt to attract workers by offering higher wages, and thus wages in the shortage occupation rise relative to those in occupations not experiencing a shortage. (Put differently, shortages exist because the wage rate is below market-clearing levels; the market response is for these wages to rise.) There is no evidence that, as of the mid-1960s, nursing salaries were rising faster than average.[14] The relationship of these salaries to all workers, all female workers, and all female professional workers remained essentially constant from 1950 to 1963, showing no tendency to rise. This fact suggests that the effective demand for nurses did not exceed supply at the prevailing wage,[15] and the essential balance between demand and supply probably explains why the supply of nurses rose by 3 percent, and not by 29 percent, as a result of the government program.[16] Future employment and salary prospects simply did not seem attractive enough to lure more students to the field.

What the Surgeon General and the government failed to recognize was that the problem they perceived in providing adequate patient care was one of *demand,* not supply. Nurses were in abundant enough supply to fill available jobs; it was the number of *jobs* that was the "problem." Ironically, a program shifting the *demand* for nurses was initiated later in the 1960s when Medicare and Medicaid were adopted, and the labor market responses to this program indicate a properly functioning market. Nursing salaries rose relative to those in other occupations, and the number of nurses employed rose quickly (mainly because the higher wages attracted many who were *already* trained as nurses back into the field). These responses suggest that the government's efforts to cure a "supply" problem in the nursing market using subsidies were unnecessary as well as unproductive.

Wrong conclusion of market failure. For a prolonged period in the 1950s, firms complained of unfilled vacancies for engineers despite the fact that wages in this market were rising faster than average. The market signals (of a rising wage) seemed to be working, but the shortage did not appear to abate. This situation led

---

[14]Donald Yett, *An Economic Analysis of the Nursing Shortage* (Lexington, Mass.: Lexington Books, 1975), p. 160.

[15]Many economists believe the nursing labor market is dominated by just a few buyers of labor in each city, as we will discuss in Chapter 3. While a lack of competition on the employer side of the market does have a bearing on the perception of shortages (as we will see), it will nevertheless be true that if hospitals were trying to hire beyond current levels, they would behave in a way that would drive nursing salaries up.

[16]Yett, *An Economic Analysis of the Nursing Shortage.*

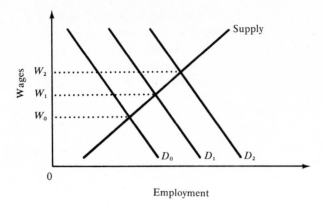

FIGURE 2.22   A Shortage Persists when the Demand Curve Continues to Shift

some to conclude that the market was not functioning effectively and that government "help" was required (in the form of engineering educational subsidies).[17]

The above conclusion was based on the partially *correct* analysis that a rising wage should cure a shortage in two ways. First, as wages rise more workers will be attracted to the occupation in question. Second, the increased wage dampens demand by firms. What the conclusion *missed,* however, is that a shortage can continue despite rising wages if the demand curve *continues to shift* to the right (or the supply curve continues to shift to the left).

To illustrate this point, suppose that the market for engineers begins in equilibrium, but that a shortage occurs when the demand for engineers shifts to the right for some reason. (As Figure 2.22 shows, the demand curve would shift from D_0 to D_1.) Suppose further that it takes a year or two for firms and workers to adjust to the shortage. (A longer adjustment period can cause other problems, which will be discussed in the Chapter 9 section on "cobweb models.") Workers need time to perceive the salary increases and shift occupational plans. Firms need time to discover that their problem of unfilled vacancies is not a random event and to initiate wage increases as a response. However, if no further changes in demand or supply occur, wages would rise to W_1 in a year or two, and the shortage would be over.

Suppose, though, that in the year or two after the *initial* shift in demand, the demand curve shifts *again* (to D_2, say). Figure 2.22 shows how the rise in wages to the level of W_1 would not alleviate the shortage, because after this second shift W_2 is the market-clearing wage. A shortage would continue to exist, and it would persist as long as the demand curve continued to move out and as long as the adjustment to it by firms and workers was not instantaneous!

Something like this pattern appears to have caused the prolonged shortage of engineers in the 1950s. The shortage was felt most acutely among research and

---

[17]See Kenneth Arrow and William Capron, "Dynamic Shortages and Price Rises: The Engineer-Scientist Case," *Quarterly Journal of Economics* 73, 2 (May 1959): 292–308.

development (R & D) engineers and was the apparent result of an increase in R & D expenditures by the federal government. As these expenditures continued to increase, the market never had time to fully adjust before the next increase was felt.[18] The market was not failing; indeed, engineering salaries and employment levels were rising just as theory predicts! The market was simply being asked to facilitate a *series* of changes in demand, and the adjustment to one change was not completed before the next one was felt.

REVIEW QUESTIONS

1. The Central Intelligence Agency (CIA) finds out that compensation for coal miners in the Soviet Union is rising much faster than compensation in general in that country. It knows that the Soviet labor market is free in the sense that it relies on incentives (not compulsion) in the allocation process.

     What can the CIA infer from this sharp rise in mining wages? Can it infer that coal output is increasing? Explain your answers.
2. Analyze the impact of the following changes on wages and employment in a given occupation:
   a. a fall in the danger of the occupation.
   b. an increase in product demand.
   c. increased wages in other occupations.
3. What would happen to the wages and employment levels of engineers if government expenditures on research and development programs were to fall? Show the effect graphically.
4. Suppose a particular labor market is in equilibrium. What could happen to cause the equilibrium wage to fall? If all money wages rise each year, how will this market adjust?

SELECTED READINGS

John T. Dunlop and Walter Galenson, eds., *Labor in the Twentieth Century* (New York: Academic Press, 1978).

Simon Rottenberg, "On Choice in Labor Markets," *Industrial and Labor Relations Review* 9, 2 (January 1956): 183–99; Robert J. Lampman, "On Choice in Labor Markets: Comment," *Industrial and Labor Relations Review* 9, 4 (July 1956): 629–36; and "On Choice in Labor Markets: Reply," *Industrial and Labor Relations Review* 9, 4 (July 1956): 636–41.

Donald Yett, *An Economic Analysis of the Nursing Shortage* (Lexington, Mass.: Lexington Books, 1975).

---

[18]Arrow and Capron, "Dynamic Shortages and Price Rises."

3

The Demand
for
Labor

The demand for labor is a derived demand. In most cases, employers hire labor not for the direct satisfaction that such an action brings them, but rather for the contribution they believe labor can make towards producing some product for sale. Not surprisingly, then, employers' demand for labor is a function of the characteristics of demand in the product market. Employers' demand is also a function of the characteristics of the production process—more specifically the ease with which labor can be substituted for capital and other factors of production. Finally, the demand for labor is a function not only of the price of labor, but also of the prices of other factors of production. This chapter and the next will illustrate how knowledge of the characteristics of the demand for labor can be used in various policy applications.

For purposes of making or evaluating social policy, the demand for labor has two important features. The first is that it can be shown theoretically—and demonstrated empirically—that labor-demand curves slope downward. The second important feature of the demand for labor is the *degree of responsiveness* of this demand to changes in the wage. While it is always true that the quantity of labor demanded declines as the wage increases, in some cases this decline is larger than in other cases. For most policy issues, the degree of responsiveness is of critical importance. Thus, Chapter 4 will discuss the forces that determine this responsiveness and suggest ways in which policy makers can make some guesses about the degree of responsiveness in situations where explicit empirical estimates are not available.

When analyzing the demand for labor, two sets of distinctions are typically made. First, one must specify whether one is concentrating on demand by *firms* or on the demand curves for an entire *market*. As noted in Chapter 2, firm and market labor-demand curves will have different properties, although they will both slope downward. Second, one must specify the *time* period for which the demand curve is drawn: the short run or the long run. The *short run* is defined as a period over which a firm's capital stock is fixed; the only input that is free to be varied is labor. The *long run* is defined as a period over which a firm is free to vary all factors of production, in this case both labor and capital. This distinction between short run and long run is a conceptual one, and the two concepts do not necessarily correspond closely to any actual period of calendar time. For example, an owner of a steel mill may find that it takes several years to construct a new steel plant, in which anything less than two years might be considered the short run. In contrast, the owner of a small firm that hires people to shovel driveways may find that he can vary his capital stock instantaneously (by buying new shovels). In this case, the firm may never face the short run; it will always be involved in making decisions about both labor and capital! However, in spite of the fact that the short run and long run do not correspond neatly to specified calendar periods of time, the distinction does allow us to be more specific about the different forces that influence the demand for labor.

A SIMPLE MODEL OF LABOR DEMAND

Our analysis of the demand for labor will begin with a simple model that yields very basic, but fundamental, behavioral predictions. To simplify the discussion, this model is derived using the four assumptions noted below. Later on in the chapter, two of the assumptions are dropped to see what difference they make. A third assumption is dropped in Chapter 5 and the fourth in Chapter 13.

The Assumptions

In analyzing employers' demand for labor, we will make four assumptions. First, we will assume that employers seek to maximize *profit* (the difference between the revenue they take in from the sales of their product and their costs of production). This is a standard assumption of positive economics, but it is not absolutely necessary to derive the fundamental conclusion of the chapter—namely, that the demand for labor is a downward sloping function of the wage rate.[1] We will relax this assumption in Chapter 13 when we consider the demand for labor in the public sector.

Second, we will initially assume that firms employ two homogeneous factors of production—labor and capital—in their production of goods and services. That is, we assume that there is a two-factor *production function* that indicates how various amounts of labor *(L)* and capital *(K)* can be combined to produce output *(Q)*:

$$Q = f(L,K) \tag{3.1}$$

In equation (3.1) f stands for "a function of" and is used to represent a *general* mathematical relationship between Q and the factors of production. The *specific* relationship between Q and the two factors of production depends on the technology utilized. Later in this chapter we relax this two-factor assumption, noting that

---

[1]Totally impulsive or random demand patterns are consistent with downward-sloping demand curves if people or firms have limited resources—a point made by Gary Becker, "Irrational Behavior and Economic Theory," *Journal of Political Economy* 70, 1 (February 1962).

**TABLE 3.1   The Marginal Product of Labor
in a Hypothetical Car Dealership
(capital held constant)**

Number of Salespersons	Total Cars Sold	Marginal Product of Labor
0	0	
		10
1	10	
		11
2	21	
		5
3	26	

there are many different categories of labor. Firms also use other inputs besides *capital* (defined as machinery, equipment, and structures) in their production process, including materials and energy. Chapter 4 will discuss issues relating to energy usage.

Third, we will assume that the hourly wage cost is the only cost of labor. We will initially ignore the existence of hiring and training costs as well as those fringe benefit costs (like holiday pay, vacation pay, and sick leave as well as many forms of social insurance) that do not vary with weekly hours of work. By ignoring these costs here and by assuming that the length of the work week is fixed, we gloss over the distinction between the number of employees that a firm hires and the total number of person hours[2] of labor that it employs. In Chapter 5 we will drop our simplifying assumption and consider the question of how the firm determines its optimal length of work week—as well as how hiring, training, and nonvariable fringe-benefit costs affect the demand for labor.

Finally, we will initially assume that both a firm's labor market and its product market are competitive. If the firm's labor market is competitive, we can treat the wage rate that it must pay its workers as given; if its product market is competitive, we can treat the product price it faces as given. (Both of these assumptions are relaxed later in the chapter.) The following analyses of labor demand by the firm, in both the long and the short run, are primarily verbal. The derivation of demand curves through graphical analysis is presented in the appendix to this chapter.

Short-Run Demand for Labor by Firms

In the short run, when a firm's capital stock *(K)* and production function are not free to vary, the number of units of output that a firm produces can change only if it changes the number of units of labor that it employs—see equation (3.1). The additional output that can be produced by a firm when it employs one additional unit of labor, with capital held constant, is called the *marginal product of labor (MP$_L$)* For example, if a car dealership can sell 10 cars a month with one salesperson and 21 cars a month with two, the marginal product of hiring one salesperson is 10, and the marginal product of hiring the second is 11 cars per month. If a third equally persuasive salesperson were hired and sales rose to 26

---

[2]Person hours, also called labor hours, are calculated by multiplying the number of employees times the average length of work week per employee.

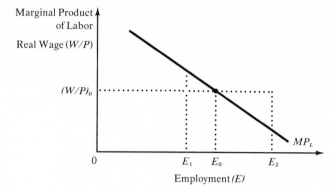

FIGURE 3.1 Demand for Labor in the Short Run

per month, the marginal product of hiring the third salesperson is 5 cars per month. These hypothetical data are summarized in Table 3.1.

Table 3.1 shows that adding an extra salesperson increased output (cars sold) in each case. As long as output *increases* as labor is added, labor's marginal product (the change in output brought about by adding another unit of labor) is *positive*. In our example, however, the marginal product of labor increased at first (from 10 to 11), but then fell (to 5). Why?

The initial rise in marginal product is *not* because the second salesperson is better than the first; we ruled out this possibility by our assumption (stated above) that labor is homogeneous. Rather, the rise could be the result of the two generating promotional ideas or helping each other out in some way. Eventually, however, as more salespeople are hired, the marginal product of labor must fall. A fixed building (remember capital is held constant) can contain only so many customers, and thus each additional increment of labor produces progressively smaller increments of output. This law of *diminishing marginal returns* is an empirical proposition that derives from the fact that as employment expands, each additional worker has a progressively smaller share of the capital stock to work with.

For expository convenience, we will assume that the marginal product of labor is always decreasing.[3] Figure 3.1 shows a marginal product of labor schedule (MP_L) for a representative firm. In this figure, the marginal product of labor is tabulated on the vertical axis and the number of units of labor employed on the horizontal axis. The negative slope of the schedule indicates that each additional unit of labor employed produces a progressively smaller (but still positive) increment in output.

The marginal product of labor is measured as units of added output per unit increase of labor. Suppose we denote the money (nominal) wage rate that the firm pays per unit of labor by W and its product price per unit of output by P. These variables have dimensions of dollars per unit of labor and dollars per unit of

---

[3]We lose nothing by this assumption, because we show later in this section that a firm will never be operated at a point where its marginal product of labor schedule is increasing.

output, respectively. Thus, the *real wage rate* that the firm pays—its money wage divided by its price level *(W/P)*—also has the dimension *units of output per unit of labor*. For example, if a woman is paid $10 per hour and the product she makes sells for $2, she gets paid—from the firm's point of view—five units of output per hour (10 ÷ 2). These five units represent her real wage, and because the real wage and the marginal product of labor are both measured in the same dimension, we can plot both on the vertical axis of Figure 3.1.

In the short run, a firm's demand-for-labor curve coincides with the downward-sloping portion of its marginal-product-of-labor schedule. This result arises from the assumption that firms seek to maximize profit. In order to accomplish this objective, a firm should employ labor up until the point that the marginal revenue (or additional revenue) it receives from hiring the last employee is just equal to its marginal (or additional) cost of employing that worker. Since a firm's profit is simply equal to revenues minus costs, if its marginal revenue exeeds its marginal cost, overall profits can be increased by expanding employment. Analogously, if its marginal revenue is less than its marginal cost, a firm is losing money on the last unit of labor hired, and it could increase its profit by reducing employment. As a result, the only employment level that is consistent with profit maximization is that level at which the marginal revenue of hiring the last unit of labor is just equal to its marginal cost.

Given the assumptions that we have made, the marginal cost of an additional unit of labor is simply the money wage rate *(W)* that must be paid. The marginal revenue of hiring an additional unit of labor, or labors' *marginal revenue product (MRP)*, is equal to the value of the additional output produced. *MRP* equals the marginal product of labor multiplied by the additional revenue that is received per unit of output *(MR)*:

$$MRP = (MP_L) \cdot (MR) \tag{3.2}$$

Because we assumed that the firm sells its output in a competitive market— and hence that that product price does not vary with output—the additional revenue per unit of output is simply the firm's product price *(P)*. As such, the marginal revenue product obtained from an additional unit of labor equals the product price for the firm's output multiplied by its marginal product of labor for firms that operate in competitive output markets:

$$MRP = (MP_L) \cdot P \tag{3.3}$$

The marginal revenue of labor is just equal to its marginal cost—and profits are maximized by the competitive firm—at the point where the marginal revenue product equals the money wage:

$$P \cdot (MP_L) = W. \tag{3.4}$$

Dividing both sides of equation (3.4) by the firm's product price yields an alternative way of stating the profit-maximizing condition, which is that labor should be hired until its marginal product equals the real wage:

$$MP_L = \frac{W}{P}. \tag{3.5}$$

Given any real wage (by the market), the firm should thus employ labor to the point at which the marginal product of labor just equals the real wage. In other words, *the firm's demand for labor in the short run is equivalent to the downward-sloping segment of its marginal-product-of-labor schedule.*[4] To see that this is true, pick any real wage—for example, the real wage denoted by $(W/P)_0$ in Figure 3.1. We have asserted that the firm's demand for labor will be equal to its marginal-product-of-labor schedule and consequently that the firm would employ E_0 employees. Now suppose that a firm initially employed E_2 workers as indicated in Figure 3.1, where E_2 is any employment level greater than E_0. At the employment level E_2, the marginal product of labor is less than the real wage rate; the marginal cost of the last unit of labor hired is therefore greater than its marginal revenue product. As a result, profit could be increased by reducing the level of employment. Similarly, suppose instead that a firm initially employed E_1 employees, where E_1 is *any* employment level less than E_0. Given the specified real wage $(W/P)_0$, the marginal product of labor is greater than the real wage rate at E_1—and consequently the marginal revenue that an additional unit of labor produces is greater than its marginal cost. As a result, a firm could increase its profit level by expanding its level of employment.

Hence, to maximize profit, given any real wage rate, a firm should stop employing labor at the point where any additional labor would cost more than it would produce. This profit-maximization rule implies two things. First, the firm should employ labor up to the point where its real wage equals the marginal product of labor—but not beyond that point. Second, its profit-maximizing level of employment will lie in the range where its marginal product of labor is *declining*. (If $W/P = MP_L$, but MP_L is *increasing*, then adding another unit of labor will create a situation where marginal product *exceeds* W/P. As long as adding labor causes MP_L to exceed W/P, the profit-maximizing firm will continue to hire labor. It will only stop hiring when an extra unit of labor would reduce MP_L below W/P, which will only happen when MP_L is declining. Thus, the only employment levels that could possibly be consistent with profit maximization are those in the range where MP_L is decreasing.)

The demand curve for labor can therefore be thought of in two equivalent ways. It may be thought of as the *downward-sloping section of the firm's marginal-product-of-labor schedule*—in which case it indicates how many units of labor will be hired at each *real wage*. Alternatively, it can be thought of as the *downward-sloping portion of the firm's marginal **revenue** product of labor schedule*—which is simply the *marginal product* schedule multiplied by *marginal revenue* (or product price, for a competitive firm). In this second case, the labor demand curve indicates the profit-maximizing level of employment for any given *money* wage. Which version of the demand curve one employs depends solely on analytical convenience, because they are equivalent alternatives. In Example 3.1, which reviews some of the important aspects of the demand for labor in a concrete

---

[4]One should add here, "provided that the firm's revenue exceeds its labor costs." Above some real wage level this may fail to occur, and the firm will go out of business (employment will drop to zero).

Example 3.1
Store Detectives

The table below shows a hypothetical marginal revenue product *(MRP)* schedule for department-store detectives. Hiring one detective would, in this example, save $50 worth of thefts per hour. Two detectives could save $90 worth of thefts each hour, or $40 more than hiring just one. The *MRP* of hiring a second detective is thus $40. A third detective would add $20 worth more to thefts prevented, and thus adds $20 more to revenues.

Number of Detectives on Duty During Each Hour Store is Open	Total Value of Thefts Prevented per Hour	Marginal Value of Thefts Prevented per Hour (MRP)
0	$ 0	$—
1	50	50
2	90	40
3	110	20
4	115	5
5	117	2

The *MRP* does *not* decline from $40 to $20 because the added detectives are incompetent; in fact, we shall assume that all are equally alert and well trained. *MRP* declines, in part, because surveillance equipment (capital) is fixed; with each added detective, there is less equipment per person. However, the *MRP* also declines because it becomes progressively harder to generate savings. With just a few detectives, the only thieves caught will be the more obvious, less-experienced shoplifters. As more detectives are hired it becomes possible to prevent theft by the more expert shoplifters, but they are harder to detect and fewer in number. Thus, *MRP* falls because theft prevention becomes more difficult once all those who are easy to catch are apprehended.

To draw the demand curve for labor we need to determine how many detectives the store will want to employ at any given wage. For example, at a wage of $50 per hour, how many detectives will the store want? Using the *MRP* = *W* criterion it is easy to see that the answer is "one." At $40 per hour, the store would want to hire two, and at $20 per hour the number demanded would be three. The demand for labor curve that summarizes the store's profit-maximizing employment of detectives is given in the accompanying graph.

The graph illustrates a fundamental point: the demand for labor curve in the short run slopes downward because it *is* the *MRP* curve—and the *MRP* curve slopes downward because of diminishing marginal productivity. The demand curve and the *MRP* curve coincide, as demonstrated by the fact that if one were to graph the *MRP* schedule in the table, one

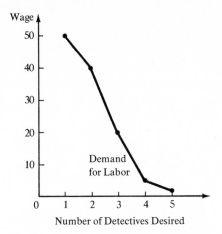

would arrive at exactly the same curve as the one in our graph. When one is hired, *MRP* is $50; when two are hired, *MRP* is $40; and so forth. Since *MRP* always equals *W* for a profit maximizer, the *MRP* and labor demand curves expressed as functions of the money wage must be the same.

---

way, it is more convenient to express the demand curve in terms of marginal revenue product of labor.

It is important to emphasize that the marginal product of any given individual is *not* a function solely of his or her personal characteristics. It should be clear from Figure 3.1 and from Example 3.1 that the marginal product of a worker depends upon the number of employees that the firm has already hired. Similarly, an individual's marginal product depends upon the size of the firm's capital stock; increases in the firm's capital stock shift the entire marginal product of labor schedule up. It is therefore incorrect to speak of an individual's productivity as being an immutable factor that is associated only with his or her characteristics, independent of the characteristics of the other inputs that he or she has to work with.

Marginal productivity and the allocation of baseball players. The fact that one's marginal productivity is not independent of other inputs being used helps explain the allocation of certain professional baseball players across the various teams. Before 1975, professional baseball players were bound to the team for which they played. They could choose not to play baseball, of course, but they could not choose the baseball team for which they would play. Being bound to a team naturally limited their options and held down their salaries. Other teams could not bid them away from the team to which they were bound; the only way a player could change teams was if both owners involved agreed among themselves on a price at which the player would be sold to the new team.

In 1975, a labor-relations ruling was issued (and later followed by a collective-bargaining agreement) that allowed certain players the right to become *free agents,* which meant that these players could sell their services to any team. Owners initially objected to the free-agent system. One argument they advanced was that it would harm competitive balance among the teams by enabling the best and richest teams to grab up all the star players. Our observations about marginal productivity and profit-maximization can be used to evaluate—and refute—the owners' contention about competitive imbalances.

If team owners are profit maximizers, they will hire a star only if the extra revenue he will generate is greater than his salary. That is, the star's *MRP* must not be lower than his wage. If a team is *already* loaded with stars, an additional good player will not bring in very much in terms of added revenues. However, if a team has no star—or very few—the addition of the *same* good player will quite possibly generate a lot in added revenues. Thus, because the *MRP* of a star will probably be lower, *other things equal,* on the best teams, these teams will tend to be the least willing to put up money for the star free agents. Capital stock is one of the "other things" that must be held equal for this prediction to hold, however. For example, if team quality is held constant, one's *MRP* will be higher on teams that have larger stadiums and larger television markets.

The above considerations suggest that the teams that will bid most aggressively for the free agents will be those that tend to have poorer records or are located in areas with large potential markets. Although there are instances to the contrary, it is interesting to note that 20 of the first 29 "star-quality" free agents signed with teams that had poorer records than the team they were on—and of the remaining 9, 6 signed with teams located in larger markets.[5] Thus, free agency has neither had, nor could be expected to have, harmful effects on the competitive balance of professional baseball teams. If anything, it has helped to equalize the distribution of talent across teams.

Objections to the marginal productivity theory of demand. Two kinds of objections are sometimes raised to the theory of labor demand introduced in this section. The first objection is that firms do not know what labor's MP_L is, that almost no employer can ever be heard uttering the words "marginal revenue product of labor," and that the theory assumes a degree of sophistication on the part of employers that just is not there. This objection can be answered as follows: Whether employers can verbalize the profit-maximization conditions or not, they must instinctively *know* them in order to survive in a competitive environment. Competition will "weed out" employers who are not good at generating profits, just as competition will weed out pool players who do not understand the intricacies of how speed, angles, and spin affect the motion of bodies through space. Yet one could canvas the pool halls of America and probably not find one player who could verbalize Newton's laws of motion! The point is that firms can *know* rules without being able to verbalize them. Those who are not good at maximizing profits will not last very long in competitive markets. Conversely, the ones who survive are those who, whether they can verbalize the general rules or not, *do* know how to maximize profits.

---

[5]The authors are indebted to Theo Smith and his enormous collection of baseball cards for these data.

The second objection to the marginal productivity theory of demand is that in many cases it seems that adding labor while holding capital constant would not add to output at all. For example, one secretary and one typewriter can produce output, but it might seem that adding a second secretary (holding the number of typewriters constant) could produce nothing extra, since that secretary would have no machine on which to work. The answer to this objection is that the second secretary could address envelopes by hand—a slower process, but one that would free the secretary at the typewriter to type more letters per day. The two secretaries could trade off using the typewriter, so that neither becomes fatigued to the extent that mistakes increase and typing speeds slow down. The second secretary could also answer the telephone and in other ways expedite work. Thus, even with technologies that seem to require one machine per person, labor will generally have an *MRP* greater than zero (capital held constant).

Long-Run Demand for Labor by Firms

In the long run, employers are free to vary their capital stock as well as the number of workers that they employ. An increase in the wage rate will affect their desired employment levels for two reasons. First, wages affect employment through a *scale* or *output effect.* A profit-maximizing firm will produce up to the point where the marginal revenue from the last unit of output produced is just equal to its marginal cost of production. Now an increase in the wage rate tends to increase the marginal cost of production without affecting the marginal revenue. As a result, at the firm's previous equilibrium level of output, marginal cost *exceeds* marginal revenue. The firm is losing money on the last units of output that it produces, and it can increase its profits after the wage increase by cutting back on its production level. Reducing output will generally cause the firm to reduce its usage both of capital and of labor.

The second reason why an increase in the wage rate affects a firm's desired employment level in the long run is that it induces *factor substitution.* In order to maximize profit, a firm must be minimizing the cost of producing whatever level of output it produces. This cost minimization is achieved when the last dollar the firm spends on employing capital yields the same increment to output as the last dollar that the firm spends employing labor. To illustrate this point, let us assume that a firm has a given level of output, *Q,* and is considering changing its mix of capital and labor to see if it can reduce cost. Suppose it finds that a dollar's worth of labor adds one unit of output to production, but a dollar's worth of capital adds two units to output. If it decreased its employment of labor by the equivalent of a dollar, and increased its employment of capital by the equivalent of 50 cents, it could produce output level *Q* at a lower cost! The *current* mix of capital and labor in this example is clearly not profit-maximizing, and extending this reasoning leads to the conclusion that the firm will reach its optimal mix of inputs only when an added dollar spent on (or taken away from) labor and an added dollar spent on (or taken away from) capital lead to equal changes in output.

To better understand factor substitution, let *C* represent the rental cost per period of a unit of capital equipment. This rental cost depends upon a number of things, including the purchase price of new capital equipment, the interest rate that a firm must pay on borrowed funds, and various provisions that affect the income-tax treatment of firms' investment expenditures (the specific formula for C need not concern us here). Now, if a firm is to minimize the cost of producing any given level of output, it must employ labor and capital up until the point that the marginal cost of producing the last unit of output is the same regardless of whether capital or labor is employed in generating that last unit. A formal way of stating this requirement is that the wage divided by the marginal product of labor (which is the cost of producing an added unit of output using just labor) must equal the cost of capital (C) divided by the marginal product of capital (MP_K):

$$(W/MP_L) = (C/MP_K). \tag{3.6}$$

We can rewrite equation (3.6) as

$$(W/C) = (MP_L/MP_K). \tag{3.7}$$

Equation (3.7) indicates that in order to be minimizing its cost of production, a firm must employ capital and labor up until the point that their relative marginal costs are just equal to their relative marginal productivities.

Consider what happens when wages increase and capital costs do not. The increase in W/C distorts the equality in equation (3.7), and the left-hand side is now greater than the right-hand side. Since the marginal cost of producing a unit of output is now greater when a firm adds new labor than when it adds new capital, the firm has an incentive to substitute capital for labor—to increase its usage of capital and decrease its usage of labor. The increase in usage of capital leads to a decline in the marginal product of capital, while the decrease in usage of labor leads to an increase in the marginal product of labor. Eventually the equality in equation (3.7) is restored, with fewer workers employed.

Market Demand Curves

The demand curve (or schedule) for an individual firm indicates how much labor that firm will want to employ at each real wage level. A *market demand curve* (or schedule) is just the *summation* of the labor demanded by all firms in a particular labor market at each level of the real wage.[6] If there are three firms in a certain labor market, and if at $(W/P)_0$ Firm A wants 12 workers, Firm B wants 6, and Firm C wants 20, then the market demand at $(W/P)_0$ is 38 employees. More importantly, because market demand curves are so closely derived from firm demand curves, they too will *slope downward* as a function of the real wage. When the

---

[6]If firm demand curves are drawn as a function of the money wage, they represent (as we noted) the downward-sloping portion of the firms' marginal revenue product curves. In a competitive industry, the price of the product is "given" to the firm, and thus at the firm level the marginal revenue product of labor has imbedded in it a given product price. When aggregating labor demand to the *market* level, product price can no longer be taken as given, and the aggregation is no longer a simple summation. However, the market demand curves drawn against money wages, like those drawn as a function of real wages, slope downward—which, at this point, is all that is important.

Example 3.2
Coal Mining

That wage increases have both a *scale effect* and a *factor substitution effect,* both of which tend to reduce employment, is widely known—even by many of those pushing for higher wages. John L. Lewis was president of the United Mine Workers during the 1920s, 1930s, and 1940s, when wages for miners were increased considerably with full knowledge that this would induce the substitution of capital for labor. According to Lewis:

> Primarily the United Mine Workers of America insists upon the maintenance of the wage standards guaranteed by the existing contractual relations in the industry, in the interests of its own membership . . . . But in insisting on the maintenance of an American wage standard in the coal fields the United Mine Workers is also doing its part, probably more than its part, to force a reorganization of the basic industry of the country upon scientific and efficient lines. The maintenance of these rates will accelerate the operation of natural economic laws, which will in time eliminate uneconomic mines, obsolete equipment, and incompetent management . . . .
>
> The policy of the United Mine Workers of America will inevitably bring about the utmost employment of machinery of which coal mining is physically capable . . . . Fair wages and American standards of living are inextricably bound up with the progressive substitution of mechanical for human power. It is no accident that fair wages and machinery will walk hand-in-hand.

SOURCE: John L. Lewis, *The Miners' Fight for American Standards* (Indianapolis: The Bell Publishing Company, 1925), pp. 40, 41, 108.

---

real wage falls, the number of workers that existing firms want to employ increases. In addition, the lower real wage may make it profitable for new firms to enter the market. Conversely, when the real wage increases, the number of workers that existing firms want to employ decreases, and some firms may be forced to cease operations completely.

Figure 3.2 shows a hypothetical market demand-for-labor curve *(D_0)* and a labor supply curve *(S_0)*. (Disregard the curve labeled D_1 for the moment.) The supply curve has been drawn as an upward-sloping function of the real wage, since higher real wages induce more individuals to enter this labor market. In this competitive labor market, the equilibrium real wage *(W_0)* and employment *(E_0)* levels are determined by the intersection of the labor demand and supply curves. If the real wage were lower than W_0, the number of workers that employers would want to hire would exceed the number of individuals who want to work. Employers, facing unfilled positions, would be forced to raise their real wage offers to eliminate the job vacancies. In contrast, if the real wage were above W_0, employers would face an excess supply of applicants. The number of individuals willing to work would exceed the number of employees firms want to hire, and employers

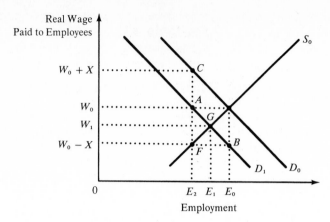

FIGURE 3.2   Who Bears the Burden of an Employer-Financed Payroll Tax?

would eventually realize that they could reduce their real wage offers and still attract the necessary workers.[7]

Policy Application: Who Bears the Burden of the Payroll Tax?

In the United States, several social insurance programs are financed by payroll taxes. Employers, and in some cases employees, make mandatory contributions of a fraction of the employees' salaries, up to a maximum level (or taxable wage base), to the social insurance trust funds. For example, the social security retirement, disability, and medicare programs (OASDHI) are financed by a payroll tax paid by both employers and employees, while in most states the unemployment insurance and workers' compensation insurance programs are financed solely by payroll-tax payments made by employers. It is not clear just why payroll taxes on *employers* are so heavily used in the social insurance area. There seems to be a prevailing notion that such taxes result in employers "footing the bill" for the relevant programs—but this is not necessarily the case.

With our simple labor market model we can show that the party making the social-insurance payment is not necessarily the one that bears the burden of the tax. Suppose for expository convenience that only the employer is required to make payments and that the tax is a fixed dollar amount (X) per employee rather than a percentage of payroll. Now consider the demand curve D_0 in Figure 3.2— which is drawn in such a way that desired employment is plotted against the real wage *employees receive*. Prior to the imposition of the tax, the wage employees receive is the same as the wage employers pay. Thus, if D_0 were the demand curve before the tax was imposed, it would have the conventional interpretation

---

[7]The reduction in real wages need not occur through a reduction in money wages. Rather, all that is required during a period when prices are rising is that money wages remain constant or rise less rapidly than product prices.

of indicating how much labor a firm is willing to hire at any given wage. However, *after* imposition of the tax, employer wage costs are $X above what employees receive. Thus, if employees receive W_0, employers will face costs of $W_0 + X$. They will no longer demand E_0 workers; rather, because their costs are $W_0 + X$, they will demand E_2 workers. Point A becomes a point on a *new* demand curve, formed when demand shifts down because of the tax (remember, the wage on the vertical axis of Figure 3.2 is the wage *employees receive* and not the wage employers pay). Only if employee wages fell to $W_0 - X$ would the firm want to continue hiring E_0 workers—for then *employer* costs would be the same as before the tax. Thus, point B is also on the new, shifted demand curve. Note that with a tax of $X, the new demand curve (D_1) is parallel to the old one and that the vertical distance between the two is X.

Now the tax-related shift in the demand curve to D_1 implies that there is an excess supply of labor at the previous equilibrium real wage of W_0. This surplus of labor creates downward pressure on the real wage, and this downward pressure continues to be exerted until the wage falls to W_1, the point at which the quantity of labor supplied just equals the quantity demanded. At this point, employment has also fallen to E_1. Thus, *employees* bear part of the burden of the payroll tax in the form of *lower wage rates and lower employment levels*. The lesson is clear: the party legally liable to make the contribution (the employer) is not necessarily the one that bears the full burden of the actual cost.

Figure 3.2, however, does suggest that employers will bear at least *some* of the tax, because the wages received by employees do not fall by the full amount of the tax ($W_0 - W_1$ is smaller than X, which is the vertical distance between the two demand curves). The reason for this is that, with an upward-sloping supply curve, employees withdraw labor as their wages fall, and it becomes more difficult for firms to find workers. If wages fell to $W_0 - X$, the withdrawal of workers would create a labor shortage that would serve to drive wages to some point (W_1 in our example) between W_0 and $W_0 - X$. Only if the labor supply curve were *vertical*—meaning that lower wages have no effect on labor supply—would the *entire amount of the tax* be shifted to workers in the form of a decrease in their wages by the amount of X, as shown in panel (a) of Figure 3.3.

In general, the extent to which the labor *supply curve* is *vertical* determines the proportion of the employer payroll tax that gets shifted to employees' wages. The more vertical the supply curve—that is, the less responsive labor supply is to changes in wages—the higher the proportion of the tax that gets shifted to workers in the form of a wage decrease. Panel (a) of Figure 3.3 shows that a payroll tax on the employer will depress employee wages more with supply curve S_0' than with supply curve S_0'' (the wage corresponding to point L is lower than that corresponding to point M). It must also be pointed out, however, that to the degree employee wages do *not* fall, employment levels *will:* employment losses with supply curve S_0'' are larger than with curve S_0'. When employee wages do not fall much in the face of an employer payroll tax increase, employer labor costs are increased—and this increase reduces the quantity of labor they demand.

The other major influence on the extent to which payroll taxes are shifted to

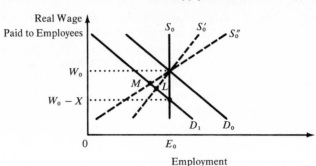

(a) Differences in Slope of Supply Curve

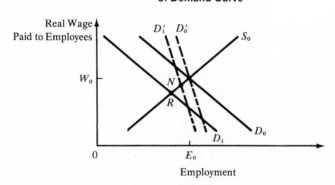

(b) Differences in Slope of Demand Curve

FIGURE 3.3   Conditions that Affect the Shifting of an Employer Payroll Tax

employees is the shape of the demand curve. If the demand curve is relatively horizontal—meaning that employer demand is very sensitive to changes in labor costs—there will be relatively large employment losses and strong downward pressures on employee wages. On the other hand, if employer demand is not very responsive to labor costs—and the demand curve is more vertical—both employment losses and employee wage changes will be small. These two conclusions are illustrated by the two sets of demand curves in panel (b) of Figure 3.3. The wage and employment levels for each initial demand curve (D_0 and D_0') are assumed to be the same (W_0 and E_0). When an employer payroll tax of X is imposed, it shifts *both demand curves down by the vertical distance of* X, so that the new curves are D_1 and D_1'. Point N, which lies on the relatively vertical demand curve D_1', is a lot closer to W_0 and E_0 than is point R—the intersection between the supply curve and the relatively horizontal demand curve D_1.

A number of empirical studies have sought to ascertain what fraction of employers' payroll tax costs are actually passed on to employees in the form of lower wages or lower wage increases. Although the evidence is by no means unambiguous, two recent studies concluded that less than half of employers' payroll tax contributions are actually shifted onto labor in the form of real wage decreases.[8]

MODIFIED MODELS OF LABOR DEMAND
Monopoly in the Product Market

We have assumed so far that firms take product prices as given. If a firm faces a downward-sloping demand curve for its output—so that as it expands employment and output, its product price falls—then the marginal revenue it receives from the last unit of output it produces is not the product price. Rather, the marginal revenue is less than the product price, because the lower price applies to all units it sells, not just the marginal unit. As a result equation (3.4) must be modified in the presence of product market monopoly. In the short run, labor should be employed up until the point at which the wage rate just equals the marginal revenue product of labor *(MRP)*—which, for a firm facing a downward-sloping demand curve in the output market, equals the marginal product of labor multiplied by the marginal revenue *(MR)*:

$$(MR)\ (MP_L) = W \tag{3.8}$$

Now one can express the demand for labor in the short run in terms of the real wage by dividing both sides of equation (3.8) by the firm's product price, *P*, to obtain

$$\frac{MR}{P} \cdot MP_L = \frac{W}{P} \tag{3.9}$$

Since marginal revenue is always less than a monopoly's product price, the ratio *(MR/P)* in equation (3.9) is less than one. As such, the demand-for-labor curve for a firm that has monopoly power in the output market will lie below and to the left of the demand for labor curve for an *otherwise identical* firm that takes product price as given. Put another way, just as output is lower under monopoly than it is under competition, other things equal, so is the level of employment.

The *wage* rates that monopolies pay, however, are not necessarily different from competitive levels even though *employment* levels are. An employer with a product market monopoly may still be a very small part of the market for a particular kind of employee—and thus be a *price taker* in the labor market even though a *price maker* in the product market.[9] For example, a local utility company may have a product market monopoly, but it will have to compete with all other firms to hire secretaries and thus must pay the going wage.

[8]Ronald G. Ehrenberg, Robert Hutchens, and Robert S. Smith, *The Distribution of Unemployment Insurance Benefits and Costs,* Technical Analysis Paper No. 58, ASPER, U.S. Department of Labor, October 1978; Daniel Hamermesh, ''New Estimates of the Incidence of the Payroll Tax,'' *Southern Economic Journal* 45 (February 1979): 1208–19.

[9]A *price taker* is someone who is such a small part of a particular market that he or she cannot influence market price. Thus, to such a person, the market price is a given. A *price maker* is someone with enough monopoly power that he or she can influence prices.

There are circumstances, however, where economists suspect that product market monopolies might pay wages that are *higher* than competitive firms would pay.[10] The monopolies that are legally permitted to exist in the United States are regulated by governmental bodies in an effort to prevent them from exploiting their favored status and earning monopoly profits. This regulation of profits, it can be argued, gives monopolies incentives to pay higher wages than they would otherwise pay for one or two reasons. First, regulatory bodies allow monopolies to pass on the costs of doing business to consumers. Thus, while unable to maximize profits, the managers of a monopoly can enhance their *utility* by paying high wages and passing the cost along to consumers in the form of higher prices. The ability to pay high wages makes a manager's life more pleasant by making it possible to hire people who might be more attractive or more personable or who have other characteristics managers find desirable.

Second, monopolies that are as yet unregulated may not want to attract attention to themselves by earning the very high profits usually associated with monopoly. They, too, may therefore be induced to pay high wages in a partial effort to "hide" their profits. The excess profits of monopolies, in other words, may be partly taken in the form of highly preferred workers—paid a relatively high wage rate—rather than in the usual monetary form.

The evidence on monopoly wages, however, is not very clear as yet. Two studies suggest that monopolies *do* pay higher wages than competitive firms for workers with the same education and experience, while a third finds no such evidence.[11]

Monopsony in the Labor Market

When only one firm is the buyer of labor in a particular labor market, such a firm is called is a *monopsonist*. Because the firm is the only demander of labor in this market, it can influence the wage rate. Rather than being a *price (wage) taker*, and facing the horizontal labor supply curve that competitive firms are confronted with, monopsonists face an upward-sloping supply curve. The supply curve confronting them, in other words, is the *market* supply curve. To expand its work force, a monopsonist must increase its wage rate. (In contrast, a competitive firm can expand its work force while paying the prevailing market wage as long as that wage is not below market-clearing levels.)

The unusual aspect of a *firm's* being confronted with an upward-sloping labor supply curve is that the *marginal cost of hiring labor exceeds the wage*. If a competitive firm wants to hire 10 workers instead of 9, the hourly cost of the additional worker is equal to the wage rate. If a monopsonist hires 10 instead of 9, it must pay a higher wage to all workers *in addition to* paying the bill for the

---

[10]For a full statement of this argument, see Armen Alchian and Reuben Kessel, "Competition, Monopoly, and the Pursuit of Money," H. G. Lewis, ed. *Aspects of Labor Economics* (Princeton, N.J.: Princeton University Press, 1962).

[11]James Dalton and E. J. Ford, "Concentration and Labor Earnings in Manufacturing and Utilities," *Industrial and Labor Relations Review* (October 1977), pp. 45–60; Ronald Ehrenberg, *The Regulatory Process and Labor Earnings* (New York: Academic Press, 1979); Leonard W. Weiss, "Concentration and Labor Earnings," *American Economic Review* 56, 1 (March 1966): 96–117.

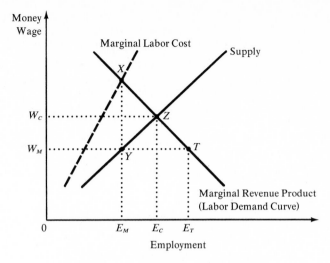

FIGURE 3.4 The Effects of Monopsony

added worker. For example, suppose that a monopsonist could get 9 workers if it paid $7 per hour but that if it wishes to hire 10 workers it would have to pay a wage of $7.50. The labor cost associated with 9 workers is $63 per hour (9 times $7), but the labor cost associated with 10 workers is $75 per hour (10 times $7.50). Hiring the additional worker costs $12 per hour—which is far higher than the $7.50 wage rate![12]

The fact that the marginal cost of hiring labor is above the wage rate affects the labor market behavior of monopsonists. In maximizing profits, any firm should hire labor until the point where marginal revenue product equals marginal cost. Since the marginal cost of hiring labor for a monopsonist is *above* the wage rate, it will stop hiring labor at some point where marginal revenue product is above the wage rate. In terms of Figure 3.4, the monopsonist hires E_M workers because at that point marginal revenue product equals marginal labor costs (point X). However, the wage rate necessary to attract E_M workers to the firm—which can be read off the supply curve—is W_M (see point Y). Thus, wages are below marginal revenue product for a monopsonist.

If the market depicted in Figure 3.4 were competitive, each firm in the market would hire labor until marginal revenue product equals the wage. Thus, if the demand curve in that market were the same as shown, the wage rate would be W_C and the employment level would be E_C—and the conventional result would be obtained. Note that in a market that is monopsonized, wages and employment levels are *below* W_C and E_C.

Examples of pure monopsony in the labor market are difficult to cite: an isolated coal-mining town or a sugar plantation, where the mine or sugar company

---

[12]We assume here that the monopsonist does not know which workers it can hire for $7 per hour and which workers could only be hired at $7.50. All it knows is that if it wants to hire 10 workers it must pay $7.50, while if it wants to hire 9 it can pay only $7.00. Therefore, all workers get paid the same wage.

is literally the only employer, are examples that are increasingly rare. However, some employers may be large relative to the market and may, therefore, find themselves confronted with an upward-sloping supply curve.

Some economists argue that the market for registered nurses—particularly in a small town—is partially monopsonized. Hospitals employ the majority of registered nurses, and in many small towns there is only one hospital. These hospitals, it is argued, behave like monopsonists and pay lower wages than they otherwise would.[13]

If the market for registered nurses is characterized by monopsony, this situation could help explain why the nursing shortage discussed in Chapter 2 was perceived to exist even though nursing salaries were not being bid up. At wage W_M in Figure 3.4, the monopsonized employer (the hospital in this case) will hire only E_M workers because that is where marginal revenue and marginal cost are equal. However, *if* it could do all its additional hiring at W_M, it would *like* to hire E_T. Since at W_M supply falls short of E_T, there might appear to be a shortage! In this case, then, hospitals find themselves in the position of wanting to hire more nurses at wage E_M—and being unable to do so—while at the same time being unwilling to raise wage offers necessary to increase employment beyond E_M! The "shortage" is thus more apparent than real.

Another market that may be monopsonized is the market for public-school teachers outside of metropolitan areas.[14] However, there is not much evidence that private firms in metropolitan areas have monopsony power. Wages that these firms pay appear to be essentially unaffected by the concentration of employment in the hands of a very few employers.[15]

More Than Two Inputs

Thus far we have assumed that there are only two inputs in the production process: capital and labor. In fact, labor can be subdivided into many categories (for example, labor can be categorized by age, race, sex, by educational level, and by occupation). Other inputs besides capital that are used in the production process include materials and energy: If a firm is seeking to maximize profits, in the long run it should employ all inputs up until the point that the additions to output received from spending the last dollar on each input are equal. This generalization of equation (3.6) leads to the somewhat obvious result that the demand for *any* category of labor will be a function not only of its own wage rate, but also of the wage rates of all other categories of labor and of the prices of capital and other inputs.

The demand curve for each category of labor will be a downward-sloping function of the wage rate paid to workers in the category, for the reasons dis-

---

[13]Richard Hurd, "Equilibrium Vacancies in a Labor Market Dominated by Non-Profit Firms: The 'Shortage' of Nurses," *Review of Economics and Statistics* 55, 2 (May 1973): 234–240; C. R. Link and J. H. Landon, "Monopsony and Union Power in the Market for Nurses," *Southern Economic Journal* 41 (April 1975): 649–59.

[14]Ronald Ehrenberg and Gerald Goldstein, "A Model of Public Sector Wage Determination," *Journal of Urban Economics* 2 (April 1975): 223–45.

[15]*See* Robert L. Bunting, *Employer Concentration in Local Labor Markets* (Chapel Hill: University of North Carolina Press, 1962).

(a) Gross Complements   **(b) Gross Substitutes**

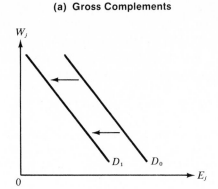 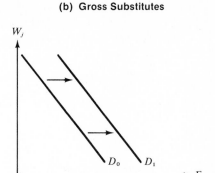

FIGURE 3.5 Effect of an Increase in the Price of One Input *(i)*
on the Demand for Another Input *(j)*

cussed earlier. Changes in the prices of the other categories of labor or in the prices of other inputs may shift the entire demand curve for a given category of labor either to the right or to the left. If an increase in the price of one input shifts the demand for a particular type of labor to the left as in panel (a) of Figure 3.5, the two inputs are *gross complements;* if a price increase shifts the demand for labor to the right, as in panel (b) of Figure 3.5, the two inputs are *gross substitutes.* Whether two inputs are complements or substitutes is a function both of the production process and product demand conditions.

Consider our earlier example of a snow-removal firm. Suppose that snow can be removed using either unskilled workers (with shovels) or skilled workers who drive snowplows, and let us focus on the demand for the skilled workers. Other things equal, an increase in the wage of skilled workers will cause the employer to employ fewer of them; their demand curve is a downward-sloping function of their wage. If the wage rate of unskilled workers increases, the employer would want to employ fewer unskilled workers than before and more of the now relatively cheaper skilled workers to remove any given amount of snow. To the extent that this substitution effect dominates over the scale effect (the higher unskilled wage leading to reduced output and employment of all inputs), the demand for skilled workers would shift to the right. In this case, skilled and unskilled workers are gross substitutes. In contrast, if the price of snowplows went up, the employer would want to cut back on their usage, which would result in a reduced demand, at each wage, for skilled workers who drive the snowplows. Skilled workers and snowplows are gross complements in this example.

To answer many policy questions requires knowledge of the characteristics of demand curves for particular categories of labor. For example, would a subsidy paid to employers who hire teenagers significantly increase teenage employment? The answer depends upon how responsive the demand for teenage labor is to their wage. How would an *investment tax credit,* an implicit subsidy paid to employers for increasing their capital stock, affect the employment of skilled and unskilled workers? The answer here depends upon the extent to which the cost of capital affects the demand curves for skilled and unskilled workers. To take a final example, how does government legislation that prohibits sex discrimination by requiring equal pay for equal work affect the employment levels of males and females? To answer this, one needs to know how the legislation affects male and female wages and then how responsive the demand curve for *each* type of labor is to *both* wage rates.

In each of the above examples, the effect of a policy depends upon the responsiveness of one variable to another. Economists refer to this responsiveness as an *elasticity,* or the percentage change in one variable induced by a given percentage change in another variable. For example, the *own-wage elasticity of demand* for a category of labor is defined as the percentage change in the demand for the category induced by a one percent increase in its wage rate. *Cross-wage elasticity of demand,* or the elasticity of demand for factor *i* with respect to the price of factor *j,* is defined as the percentage change in the demand for category *i* induced by a 1 percent change in the price of factor *j.* Since the magnitude of various elasticities of labor demand are so important for policy discussions, the next chapter will be devoted to a discussion of the determinants of elasticities of demand and will apply this concept to various policy issues. The following discussion of minimum-wage legislation should illustrate the use of the analytical tools developed so far.

POLICY APPLICATION: MINIMUM-WAGE LEGISLATION

History and Description

The *Fair Labor Standards Act of 1938* was the first major piece of protective labor legislation adopted at the national level in the United States. Among its provisions were a minimum-wage rate, or floor, below which hourly wages could not be reduced, an overtime-pay premium for workers who worked long workweeks, and restrictions on the use of child labor. The minimum-wage provisions were designed to guarantee each worker a reasonable wage for his or her work effort and thus to reduce the incidence of poverty.

When initially adopted, the minimum wage was set at $0.25 an hour and covered roughly 43 percent of all nonsupervisory wage and salary workers—primarily those workers employed in larger firms involved in interstate commerce (manufacturing, mining, and construction). As Table 3.2 indicates, both the basic minimum wage and coverage under the minimum wage have expanded over time. Indeed as of January 1, 1981, the minimum wage was set at $3.35 an hour, and about 80 percent of all nonsupervisory workers were covered by its provisions.

It is important to emphasize that the minimum-wage rate is currently specified in *nominal* terms and not in terms *relative* to some other wage or price index. Historically, this definition of minimum wage has led to a pattern of minimum-wage changes that can be represented by Figure 3.6, where time is plotted on the horizontal axis, and the value of the minimum wage relative to average hourly earnings in manufacturing is plotted on the vertical axis. Congress initially specifies the nominal level of the minimum wage (MW_0)—which, given the level of average hourly earnings that prevail in the economy (AHE_0), leads to an initial value of the minimum wage relative to average hourly earnings (MW_0/AHE_0).

Now over time this relative value declines as average hourly earnings increase due to inflation or productivity growth. The reduced relative value of the minimum wage creates pressure on Congress to legislate an increase in the nominal minimum wage, and after the passage of time (point t_1 in Figure 3.6) Congress returns the relative value of the minimum wage approximately to its initial level. Over time, the process is repeated and the saw-toothed time profile of relative minimum-wage values portrayed in Figure 3.6 emerges. Although it varies from peak to peak, the value of the minimum wage relative to average hourly earnings in manufacturing after each legislated change has typically been in the range of 0.45 to 0.50 in recent years (see Table 3.2).

A Model with Uniform Coverage

Unfortunately, as with many social programs, minimum-wage legislation may have unintended side effects that work against the program's goals of reducing poverty. Consider the labor market for unskilled workers and assume, initially, that all are covered by minimum-wage legislation. As Table 3.2 indicates, such uniform coverage certainly would not be a reasonable assumption if we wanted to

TABLE 3.2   Minimum Wage Legislation in the United States, 1938–1980

Effective Date of Minimum Wage Change	*Nominal Minimum Wage*	*Percent of Nonsupervisory Employees Covered*[a]	*Minimum Wage Relative to Average Hourly Wage in Manufacturing*	
			Before	*After*
10/24/38	$0.25	43.4	—	0.403
10/24/39	0.30	47.1	0.398	0.478
10/24/45	0.40	55.4	0.295	0.394
1/25/50	0.75	53.4	0.278	0.521
3/1/56	1.00	53.1	0.385	0.512
9/3/61	1.15	62.1	0.431	0.495
9/3/63	1.25	62.1	0.467	0.508
9/3/64	1.25	62.6		
2/1/67	1.40	75.3	0.441	0.494
2/1/68	1.60	72.6	0.465	0.531
2/1/69	1.60	78.2		
2/1/70	1.60	78.5		
2/1/71	1.60	78.4		
5/1/74	2.00	83.7	0.363	0.454
1/1/75	2.10	83.3	0.423	0.445
1/1/76	2.30		0.410	0.449
1/1/78	2.65		0.430	0.480
1/1/79	2.90		0.402	0.440
1/1/80	3.10		0.417	0.445
1/1/81	3.35			

[a]Excludes executive, administrative, and professional personnel (including teachers in elementary and secondary schools) from the base. Coverage peaked at 87.3 percent of the nonsupervisory work force in September 1977. As of 1978, however, a court decision eliminated most state and local government workers from coverage. As a result, worker coverage fell from 56,100,000 in 1976 to 51,900,000 in 1978.

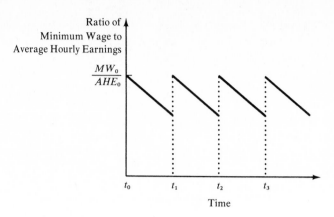

FIGURE 3.6 Time Profile of the Minimum Wage Relative to Average Hourly Earnings

analyze minimum-wage effects during the early years of the legislation. However, a model of full coverage may be more appropriate today than it once was.

Figure 3.7 represents the labor market for unskilled labor, which is in equilibrium prior to the imposition of the minimum wage with an employment level of E_0 and a *real* wage of W_0/P_0. Now suppose Congress legislates a nominal minimum wage of W_1, which is higher than W_0; this legislation will raise the real wage to W_1/P_0 and reduce the number of employees firms want to hire to E_1. Although a larger number of workers (E_2) are willing to offer their services at that wage rate, no downward pressure is exerted on the money wage because by law the wage cannot be reduced below the nominal minimum. As a result, the immediate impact of the increase in the minimum wage is a decrease in employment and an increase in unemployment (which equals $E_2 - E_1$).[16]

Over time, the government may take actions to stimulate the economy in the hope of reducing unemployment. Such actions invariably include pursuing expansionary monetary and fiscal policy (increasing the money supply and government spending, decreasing taxes) and lead to increases in the price level. However, as the price level goes up, the real minimum wage falls, because the nominal minimum wage is being held constant. As the real wage falls, the number of workers employed increases. If Congress takes no other action but continues to pursue expansionary policies, eventually the price level will rise to P_1, where (W_1/P_1)

---

[16]The analysis here is somewhat oversimplified. The supply curve in Figure 3.7 indicates the number of workers who want to work at each real wage, under the assumption that any one who wants to work can find employment. However the imposition of a minimum wage that leads to a real wage (W_1/P_0) above the market-clearing level means that not all workers who want to work at that real wage can actually find employment. This reduced probability of finding employment should reduce the actual number of workers seeking employment below the level indicated by the supply curve (E_2). As a result, the actual increase in unemployment will be less than the depicted excess supply of labor $(E_2 - E_1$ in Figure 3.7). Since this complication does not fundamentally alter any of the conclusions in this chapter, we ignore it in the analysis that follows. Jacob Mincer, in "Unemployment Effects of Minimum Wage Changes," *Journal of Political Economy* 84 (August 1976): S87–S104, has presented evidence that higher minimum-wage rates do lead to reduced labor-force participation rates.

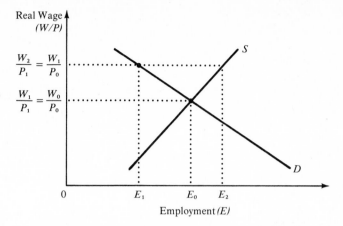

FIGURE 3.7   Minimum Wage Effects: Uniform Coverage

$= (W_0/P_0)$. That is, the real value of the minimum wage will fall back to the market-clearing level, and employment will return to its initial level. While the immediate impact of the minimum-wage increase was to reduce employment, over a longer period of time this employment reduction is eliminated, at the expense of a higher price level.

The story, however, does not end here. As noted above, Congress periodically increases the nominal minimum to restore its value relative to average hourly earnings. An increase, say, to W_2, where $(W_2/P_1) = (W_1/P_0)$, would again reduce employment to E_1 and create further pressure for the government to take action to reduce unemployment. What results then is a cycle of minimum-wage increases inducing short-run employment losses, inflation reducing the real value of the minimum wage and restoring employment, and then Congress increasing the nominal minimum and starting the process all over.

Periodically proposals have been introduced into Congress to tie the minimum wage to either the consumer price level or average hourly earnings; the minimum wage would automatically increase each year to maintain a constant value relative to one of these variables. If tied to the former, the net effect of the legislation would be to fix the real wage of low-skilled labor at a level such as (W_1/P_0) in Figure 3.7. Whether such a policy is desirable for low-skilled workers as a group depends upon whether the higher real wage is sufficiently high to compensate low-skilled workers for their employment losses $(E_0 - E_1)$ and upon the income-support programs, such as unemployment insurance, available to unemployed workers.

What's Wrong with the Model?

Early studies of the employment effects of minimum-wage legislation, conducted in the 1940s and 1950s, often found that employment *increased* after minimum wage increases. They concluded that there are no adverse effects of minimum-wage legislation and that the neoclassical model presented above is all wrong.

These studies, however, do not succeed in disproving the neoclassical model for at least three reasons. First, they ignore the fact that the uniform coverage model is not applicable to the earlier period when coverage was less than com-

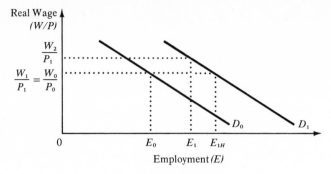

FIGURE 3.8 Minimum Wage Effects: Growing Demand

plete. Second, they ignore the possibility that employers may not fully comply with increases in the minimum wage; noncompliance would reduce the employment effects of the legislated increase (the noncompliance problem will be discussed later in the chapter). Third, and most important, they ignore the fact that all of the predictions from our models are made holding other factors constant. If other factors are not actually constant, changes in one or more of them may obscure the negative relationship between wages and the demand for labor.

To see the effects of such other factors, consider Figure 3.8—where for simplicity we have omitted the labor supply curve and have focused on only the demand side of the market. Suppose that D_0 is the demand curve for low-skilled labor in year 0, in which year the real wage is W_0/P_0 and the employment level is E_0. Further assume that in the absence of any change in the minimum wage the money wage and the price level would both increase by the same percent over the next year, so that the real wage in year 1 (W_1/P_1) would be the same as that in year 0.

Now suppose that in year 1, two things happen. First, the minimum wage rate is raised to W_2, which is greater than W_1, so that the real wage increases to W_2/P_1. Second, because the economy is expanding, the demand for low-skilled labor shifts out to D_1. The result of these two changes is that employment increases from E_0 to E_1 in Figure 3.8.

Comparisons of observed employment levels, such as E_1 and E_0 above, caused the early investigators to conclude that minimum-wage increases had no adverse employment effects. However, this simple before/after comparison is *not* the correct one. Rather, one should ask, "how did the actual employment level in period 1 compare to the level that *would have prevailed in the absence* of the increase in the minimum wage?" Since demand grew between the two periods, this hypothetical employment level would have been E_{1H}. E_{1H} is greater than E_1, the actual level of employment in period 1, so $E_{1H} - E_1$ is the jobs loss caused by the minimum wage.

In sum, in a growing economy with complete coverage the net effect of a one-time increase in the minimum wage is to reduce the rate of growth of employment. By focusing on only the actual employment growth, the early studies

(a) Covered Sector

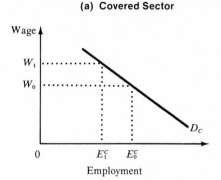

(b) Uncovered Sector

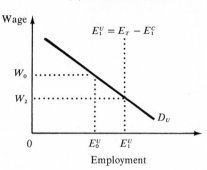

FIGURE 3.9 **Minimum Wage Effects: Incomplete Coverage**

both misunderstood the implications of the neoclassical model and failed to adequately estimate the adverse employment effects of the program.[17]

A Model with Incomplete Coverage

Although minimum wage coverage has grown over time, with somewhere in the range of 87 percent of all nonsupervisory workers in the private sector being covered by the minimum wage, as late as 1965 more than one-third of these private-sector workers were not covered by minimum-wage legislation. The major uncovered sectors then included retail trade, the service industries, and agriculture; today they include primarily employees in these industries who work for small firms. Since coverage is less than complete, it is useful to present a model of minimum-wage effects under incomplete coverage. (A similar model will reappear in Chapter 12 when we discuss the effects of unions on wages.)

To simplify the discussion, we will assume:

a. that prices are constant (so that we can talk interchangeably about real and money wages),
b. that the labor market for unskilled labor is characterized by a vertical supply curve such that total employment of the unskilled is E_T,
c. that this labor market has a covered and an uncovered sector, and
d. that unskilled workers move back and forth between sectors seeking jobs where the wages are highest.

These assumptions suggest that without a minimum wage, the wage in each sector will be the same. Referring to Figure 3.9, let us assume that this "pre-minimum" wage is W_0 and that total employment of E_T is broken down into E_0^C in the "covered" sector plus E_0^U in the other sector.

---

[17]It is important to distinguish between a one-time increase in the minimum wage and recurrent increases that, because of inflation, have tended to keep the ratio of the minimum wage to the price level roughly constant after each increase in the minimum (Figure 3.7). In the case of recurrent increases, the main effect of the minimum-wage legislation is to decrease the average *level* of employment rather than to decrease the average (over time) rate of growth of employment.

If a minimum wage of W_1 is imposed on the covered sector, all unskilled workers will prefer to work there. However, the increase in wages there, from W_0 to W_1, reduces demand—and covered-sector employment will fall from E_0^C to E_1^C. Some workers who previously had, or would have found, jobs in the covered sector must now seek work in the uncovered sector. Thus, to the E_0^U workers formerly working in the uncovered sector are added $E_0^C - E_1^C$ other workers seeking jobs there. Thus, all unskilled workers in the market who are not lucky enough to find "covered jobs" at W_1 now look for work in the uncovered sector,[18] and the supply curve to that sector becomes E_1^U [$= E_0^U + (E_0^C - E_1^C) = E_T - E_1^C$]. The increased supply of workers to that sector drives down the wage there from W_0 to W_2.

As with most government laws, a partial-coverage minimum wage produces both winners and losers. The winners are those covered-sector workers who keep their jobs after the imposition of the minimum and receive the higher minimum wage. The losers are those low-skilled workers who lose their jobs in the covered sector and now are paid lower wages in the uncovered sector. The losers also include those low-skilled workers in the uncovered sector who kept their jobs but now find their real wages depressed, due to the increased supply of labor to that sector. Hence, even in the context of this model, where there are no overall employment effects, it is not obvious that the legislation is desirable on balance. The gains won by some groups must be weighed against the losses suffered by other groups before an unambiguous conclusion can be reached.

Social Losses

Besides predicting that minimum-wage laws produce both gainers and losers among the poor, this chapter also predicts that such laws will create losses for society as a whole. In the case of full coverage, where government-mandated increases in the real wage creates unemployment, the losses of potential output from those who are unemployed is obvious. However, there are also social losses in cases where—as in our Figure 3.9 example of partial coverage above—total employment remains constant. To understand this point requires a quick review of profit-maximization principles.

A firm will hire labor until labor's marginal revenue product equals the money wage rate. In the partial coverage example above (Figure 3.9), unskilled labor—prior to imposition of the minimum wage—would be hired in both sectors to the point where marginal revenue product equalled W_0. Thus, if a worker were transferred from one sector to the other, the value of total output would go down by W_0 in the "sending" sector and up by W_0 in the "receiving" sector. Overall output would remain unchanged by such a transfer.

After the minimum wage has been imposed on the covered sector, however, employment will be reduced there until labor's marginal revenue product equals

---

[18]Under some circumstances it may be rational for these unemployed workers to remain unemployed for a while and to search for jobs in the covered sector. We will discuss this possibility—which is discussed by Jacob Mincer in "Unemployment Effects of Minimum Wage Changes," *Journal of Political Economy* 84 (August 1976): S87–S104—in Chapter 12. At this point we simply note that if it occurs, unemployment will result.

W_1. Wages in the uncovered sector, in contrast, fall to W_2; employment in that sector will thus increase until labor's marginal revenue product equals W_2. The marginal revenue product in the uncovered sector is now *below* that in the covered sector *(W_2 is less than W_1)*, so that if a worker were transferred from the uncovered to the covered sector output could be increased! (The value of output lost in the uncovered sector by this transfer would be W_2, while the value of output gained in the covered sector would be W_1.)

Since W_1 exceeds W_2, *the value of output can be increased* by transferring labor from the uncovered to the covered sector. This transfer would occur naturally if there were no minimum wage, because workers seeking the higher-paying jobs in the covered sector would bid down wages there, and employment in that sector would expand. Transfers of labor would stop when the wages in each sector were equalized—and as we have shown above, when wages are equal in both sectors of the unskilled labor market there are no further gains to be made by transfers of labor between the two sectors of that market.

With a minimum wage, however, labor *cannot* transfer out of the sector with the lower wage (and lower marginal revenue product) to the higher-wage sector. Wages in the latter sector cannot legally fall, and therefore employment cannot expand there. A beneficial transfer of resources is blocked, and social losses occur. Put differently, total output could be increased with no change in our total resources merely by transferring labor from one sector to another, and the effective prevention of this transfer by the minimum-wage law implies social losses.

The Effects of Monopsony

The preceding analysis of the minimum-wage law has assumed that firms are sufficiently small that their hiring decisions do not affect the market wage for low-skilled workers. That is, we have assumed there is no monopsony in the low-skilled labor market. While this assumption is probably appropriate for most employers of low-skilled labor, it is theoretically possible that monopsony exists in some communities. To understand the effects of a minimum wage on monopsonized markets, consider a "full coverage" model (with only one employer and no uncovered sector).

You will recall from our earlier discussion of the demand for labor by monopsonists that their marginal labor costs are above the wage rate. In maximizing profits, they choose an employment level *(E_0 in Figure 3.10)* where marginal labor costs equal marginal revenue product (point A in Figure 3.10). The wage corresponding to employment level E_0 in Figure 3.10 is W_0.

Suppose, now, that a minimum wage of W_m is set in Figure 3.10. This minimum wage prevents the firm from paying a wage less than W_m and effectively creates a horizontal portion in the supply curve facing the firm (which is now *DACS)*. The firm's marginal cost of labor curve is now *DACEM,* because up to employment level E_1 the marginal costs of labor are equal to W_m. The firm, which maximizes profits by equating marginal revenues with marginal costs (which equation now occurs at point A), will still hire E_0 workers—but it will pay them W_m instead of W_0. Moreover, if the minimum were set at a wage rate *between* W_0 and W_m, wages *and* employment would increase.

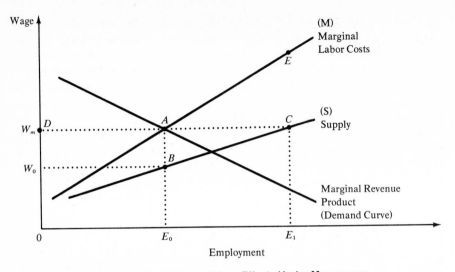

FIGURE 3.10 Minimum Wage Effects Under Monopsony

The apparent conclusion that a minimum wage can increase wages without reducing employment in a monopsonized market is subject to two qualifications. First, in the context of Figure 3.10, the minimum wage cannot be set above W_m if employment is to remain at least as large as E_0. Above W_m there would be employment losses. The second qualification is that the firm must remain in business in order for employment not to fall. While an employer may be the only buyer of labor in a particular market, the employing firm may also have many competitors in its product market. If its product market is competitive, its level of profits will be "normal"—which means that if profits were to fall, the firm would find it could earn more profits in another line of business. If, in our initial example (Figure 3.10), wages rose from W_0 to W_m and employment remained at E_0, firm profits would clearly fall. If the fall were large enough, the firm might go out of business and all E_0 workers would lose their jobs.

Empirical Evidence

Labor economists have devoted much effort to empirically estimating the magnitudes of the effects of minimum-wage legislation on the employment levels of various age/race/sex groups.[19] Although the precise magnitudes of the relationships have yet to be pinned down, it is now widely agreed that increases in minimum wages do reduce employment opportunities, especially among teenagers. The studies use different data and often ask slightly different questions. Virtually all agree, however, that employment opportunities for teenagers have been re-

---

[19]For a very readable, albeit critical, nontechnical survey of economic research on the minimum wage *see* Sar Levitan and Richard Belous, *More Than Subsistence: Minimum Wages for the Working Poor* (Baltimore: John Hopkins Press, 1979). For a more sympathetic view, see Finis Welch, *Minimum Wages: Issues and Evidence* (Washington, D.C.: American Enterprise Institute, 1978).

duced by the minimum wage—although the *size* of the reduction is in doubt. One recent study, for example, estimates that the 1970 minimum wage raised the cost of hiring 18 and 19-year-olds by 11 percent and reduced their employment by 15 percent.[20] Another recent study, using different data, estimated that the minimum wage reduced *full-time* job opportunities for teenagers but increased the availability of *part-time* work. This latter study found that overall teenage *employment* was not much affected by the minimum wage but that *hours of work* among teenagers fell as a result of the law.[21] These discrepancies in estimated effects of the minimum wage are not unusual, given the complexity of the world and the need for researchers to effectively control for *other* factors that influence teenage employment opportunities. There is no consensus on the effects of minimum-wage legislation on adults—perhaps because far fewer adults are directly affected by the minimum wage (most have wages in excess of the minimum).

Somewhat surprisingly, most research on the minimum wage has focused on its unintended adverse outcome: reductions in employment. Very little research, however, has addressed the question of whether minimum-wage legislation is achieving its intended goal of reducing the incidence of poverty. The few studies that have considered this issue have found that minimum-wage legislation actually has only a minor effect on the distribution of income.[22] This finding is not surprising because not all low-wage workers are members of low-income families; many low-wage workers, especially among teenagers, are second earners in middle- or upper-income families. Put another way, minimum-wage legislation directly affects low-wage workers, not necessarily low-income families.

The Fair Labor Standards Act has a certain political sanctity because it was the first piece of protective labor legislation adopted at the federal level; very few people would seriously argue for the repeal of the minimum-wage law today. Instead, given the estimates of the adverse effects of the legislation on youth employment opportunities, many people have recently argued that a youth differential or youth subminimum wage should be instituted. Lower wages for teens, they claim, would help alleviate the teenage unemployment problem. While there appears to be empirical support for this proposition, opponents, including organized labor, point out that reducing the wages of teenagers relative to adults would encourage employers to increase their employment of teenagers at the expense of reduced adult employment. Estimates of the likely magnitude of this substitution are required before intelligent policy decisions can be made with respect to a youth differential (see Chapter 4); in the language of some opponents, one should not substitute parents' unemployment for that of their children.

Two additional reasons may help explain why increases in the minimum wage have not had as dramatic effects on employment or the distribution of income as

[20]Welch, *Minimum Wages.*

[21]Edward Gramlich, "Impact of Minimum Wages on Other Wages, Employment and Family Incomes," *Brookings Papers on Economic Activity* 1976–2, pp. 409–62.

[22]*See* Edward Gramlich, "Impact of Minimum Wages on Other Wages, Employment, and Family Incomes," *Brookings Papers on Economic Activity,* 1976–2, pp. 409–462; Terry Kelly, "Two Policy Questions Regarding the Minimum Wage" (mimeographed, Washington, D.C.: Urban Institute, 1976).

Example 3.3
Minimum Wages in Developing Countries

Does minimum wage legislation reduce employment? The answer depends at least partially on the *level* at which the minimum is set relative to prevailing wages. While in the United States the minimum has stayed at roughly 35 to 50 percent of average hourly earnings, in developing countries the minimum is sometimes set much higher. Not surprisingly the predictions of economic theory are often borne out in situations like the one in Zimbabwe in July 1980. As the *New York Times* reported, a Zimbabwe government decision to set a minimum wage resulted in the dismissal of thousands of workers.

> SALISBURY, Zimbabwe, July 6 (Reuters)—A Government decision to set a minimum wage for workers has backfired for thousands with dismissals reported throughout the country.
>
> Officials of the ruling party of Prime Minister Robert Mugabe said today that in the Salisbury area alone more than 5,000 workers were dismissed before the minimum wage bill went into effect last Tuesday.
>
> Worst hit, according to the officials, were domestic servants and farm workers for whom the minimum had been set at $45 a month. Employees in the commercial and industrial sectors, where the minimum had been fixed at $105 a month, have also been dismissed. The officials said that every party office in the country was dealing with hundreds of workers each day complaining of unfair dismissal.

SOURCE: *New York Times*, July 7, 1980.

one might expect. First, there is no reason to suspect that all employers comply with the legislation; only limited resources are expended on enforcement of the legislation, and the penalties for employers found to be not complying (paying covered workers less than the minimum) are quite small. Indeed, certain evidence suggests that only 50 to 70 percent of covered workers who would have earned less than the minimum in the absence of the law are actually paid the minimum. The remainder are paid a wage that is illegally low.[23]

Second, our discussion has ignored the possibility that employers may respond to increases in the minimum wage by lowering other forms of nonwage compensation that are *not* covered by the minimum wage law. As Chapter 11 will discuss, nonwage forms of compensation (including holiday, vacation, and sick-leave pay, health insurance, and retirement benefits) now comprise a large, and still growing, share of total compensation. To the extent that employers can respond to increases in the minimum wage by lowering the levels (or more likely the rates of growth) of these benefits, increases in the minimum will have smaller effects on total labor costs—and hence smaller employment effects—than one might have otherwise anticipated.

---

[23] Orley Ashenfelter and Robert S. Smith, "Compliance With the Minimum Wage Law," *Journal of Political Economy* 87 (April 1979): 335–50.

REVIEW QUESTIONS

1. "It is generally agreed that the volunteer army is a dismal failure—the quality of volunteers is down and the number is not sufficient to meet desired force levels. The only alternatives are to raise the pay of volunteers or to reinstitute a draft system. Since the cost to society is clearly higher in the former than in the latter case, from an economist's perspective a draft system would be preferable." Evaluate this position.

2. Suppose the government were to subsidize the wages of all women in the population by paying their *employers* 50 cents (say) for every hour they work. What will be the effect on the wage rate women receive? What will be the effect on the unsubsidized wage employers pay? (The unsubsidized wage would be the wage women receive less 50 cents.)

3. The Occupational Safety and Health Administration promulgates safety and health standards. These standards typically apply to machinery—which is required to be equipped with guards, shields, etc. An alternative to these standards is to require the employer to furnish personal protective devices to employees—such as ear plugs, hard hats, safety shoes, etc. *Disregarding* the issue of which alternative approach offers greater protection from injury, what aspects of each alternative must be taken into account when analyzing the possible *employment* effects of the two general approaches to the stimulation of safety?

4. In a certain small city with a large university there appears to be a considerable difference in the hourly wage received by people working part time and those of the same skill working full time.

   a. Using demand and supply curves, and assuming perfect competition, explain the differential in wages.

   b. Suppose university enrollments were to fall. What effect would declining enrollments have on the wage differential?

   c. Suppose full-time and part-time hours were perfect substitutes in production. How would this affect the wage differential?

SELECTED READINGS

Orley Ashenfelter and Robert Smith, "Compliance With the Minimum Wage Law," *Journal of Political Economy,* April 1979.

Edward Gramlich, "Impact of Minimum Wages on Other Wages, Employment and Family Incomes," *Brookings Papers on Economic Activity,* 1976–2.

Sar Levitan and Richard Belous, *More Than Subsistence: Minimum Wages for the Working Poor* (Baltimore: Johns Hopkins University Press, 1979).

Jacob Mincer, "Unemployment Effects of Minimum Wage Changes," *Journal of Political Economy,* August 1976.

Finis Welch, *Minimum Wages: Issues and Evidence* (Washington, D.C.: American Enterprise Institute, 1978).

Graphical Derivation of a Firm's Labor-Demand Curve

Chapter 3 described verbally the derivation of a firm's demand-for-labor curve. This appendix will present the *same* derivation graphically. This graphical representation permits a more rigorous derivation, although our conclusion that demand curves slope downward in both the short and long run remains unchanged.

THE PRODUCTION FUNCTION

Equation (3.1) presented the "production function" as $f(L,K)$. Figure 3A.1 illustrates this production function graphically and depicts several different aspects of the production process.

Consider the convex curve labeled $Q = 100$. Along this line, every combination of labor *(L)* and capital *(K)* produce 100 units of output *(Q)*. That is, the combination of labor and capital at point $A(L_a, K_a)$ generates the same 100 units of output as the combinations at points B and C. Because each point along the $Q = 100$ curve generates the same output, that curve is called an *isoquant* *(iso* = "equal"; *quant* = "quantity").

Two other isoquants are shown in Figure 3A.1 $(Q = 150, Q = 200)$. These isoquants represent higher levels of output than the $Q = 100$ curve. The fact that these isoquants indicate higher output levels can be seen by holding labor constant at L_b (say) and then observing the different levels of capital. If L_b is combined with K_b in capital, 100 units of Q are produced. If L_b is combined with K_b', 150 units are produced $(K_b'$ is greater than $K_b)$. If L_b is combined with even more capital $(K_b''$, say), 200 units of Q could be produced.

Note that the isoquants in Figure 3A.1 have *negative* slopes, reflecting an assumption that labor and capital are substitutes. If, for example, we cut capital from K_a to K_b, we could keep output constant (at 100) by increasing labor from L_a to L_b. Labor, in other words, could be substituted for capital to maintain a given production level.

80

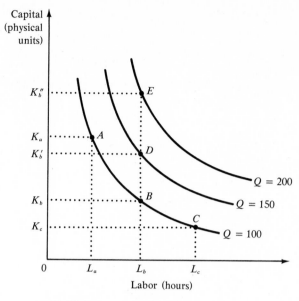

FIGURE 3A.1 A Production Function

Finally, note the *convexity* of the isoquants. At point *A,* the $Q = 100$ iso-quant has a steep slope—suggesting that to keep Q constant at 100, a given decrease in capital could be accompanied by a *modest* increase in labor. At point *C,* however, the slope of the isoquant is relatively flat. This flatter slope means that the same given decrease in capital would require a much *larger* increase in labor for output to be held constant. The decrease in capital permitted by a given increase in labor in order for output to be held constant is called the *marginal rate of technical substitution (MRTS)* between capital and labor. Symbolically, the *MRTS* can be written as

$$MRTS = \frac{\Delta K}{\Delta L} \Big|_{\overline{Q}} \qquad\qquad (3A.1)$$

where Δ means "change in" and $|\overline{Q}$ means "output is held constant." The *MRTS* is *negative,* because if L is increased, K must be reduced to keep Q constant.

Why does the absolute value of the marginal rate of technical substitution diminish as labor increases? When labor is highly used in the production process and capital is not very prevalent (point *C* in Figure 3A.1), there are many jobs that capital can do. Labor is easy to replace; if capital is increased, it will be used as a substitute for labor in parts of the production process where it will have the highest payoff. As capital becomes progressively more utilized and labor less so, the few remaining workers will be doing jobs that are hardest for a machine to do, at which point it will take a lot of capital to substitute for a worker.[1]

---

[1]Only a decade or two ago, most long-distance telephone calls were made through operators. Over time, operators have been increasingly replaced by a very capital-intensive direct-dialing system. Those operators who remain employed, however, perform tasks that are the most difficult for a machine to perform—handling collect calls, dispensing directory assistance, and acting as "trouble shooters" when problems arise.

DEMAND FOR LABOR IN THE SHORT RUN

Chapter 3 argued that firms will maximize profits in the short run *(K* fixed) by hiring labor until labor's marginal product *(MP_L)* is equal to the real wage *(W/P)*. The reason for this decision rule is that the real wage represents the *cost* of an added unit of labor (in terms of output), while the marginal product is the *output* added by the extra unit of labor. As long as the firm, by increasing labor *(K* fixed), gains more in output than it loses in costs, it will continue to hire employees. The firm will stop hiring when the marginal cost of added labor exceeds *MP_L*.

The requirement that $MP_L = W/P$ in order for profits to be maximized means that the firm's labor demand curve in the short run (in terms of the *real* wage) is identical to its marginal-product-of-labor schedule (refer back to Figure 3.1). Remembering that the marginal product of labor is the extra output produced by one-unit increases in the amount of labor employed, holding capital constant, consider the production function displayed in Figure 3A.2. Holding capital constant at K_a, the firm can produce 100 units of Q if it employs labor equal to L_a. If labor is increased to L'_a, the firm can produce 50 more units of *Q;* if labor is increased from L'_a to L''_a the firm can produce an additional 50 units. Notice, however, that the required increase in labor to get the latter 50 units of added output, $L''_a - L'_a$, is larger than the extra labor required to produce the first 50-unit increment $(L'_a - L_a)$. This difference can only mean that as labor is increased when K is held constant, each successive labor-hour hired generates progressively smaller increments in output. Put differently, Figure 3A.2 graphically illustrates the diminishing marginal productivity of labor.

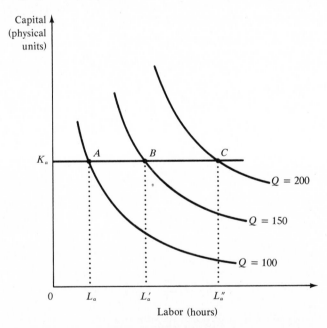

FIGURE 3A.2   The Declining Marginal Productivity of Labor

Why does labor's marginal productivity decline? Chapter 3 explained that labor's marginal productivity declines because, with K fixed, each added worker has less capital (per capita) with which to work. Is this explanation proven in Figure 3A.2? The answer is, regrettably, "No." Figure 3A.2 is drawn *assuming* diminishing marginal productivity. Renumbering the isoquants could produce a different set of marginal productivities. (To see this, change $Q = 150$ to $Q = 200$, and change $Q = 200$ to $Q = 500$. Labor's marginal productivity would then rise.) However, the logic that labor's marginal product must eventually fall as labor is increased, holding buildings, machines, and tools constant, is very compelling. Further, as Chapter 3 pointed out, even if MP_L rises initially, the firm will only stop hiring labor in the range where MP_L is declining—as long as MP_L is above W/P and *rising,* it will pay to continue hiring.

The assumptions that 1. MP_L declines eventually and 2. firms hire until $MP_L = W/P$ are the basis for the assertion that a firm's short-run demand curve for labor slopes downward. The graphical, more rigorous derivation of the demand curve in this appendix serves to confirm and support the verbal analysis in the chapter. However, it also serves to emphasize more clearly than a verbal analysis can that the downward-sloping nature of the short-run labor-demand curve is based on an *assumption*—however reasonable—that MP_L declines as employment is increased.

DEMAND FOR LABOR IN THE LONG RUN

Recall that a firm maximizes its profits by producing at a level of output *(Q*)* where marginal cost equals marginal revenue. That is, the firm will keep increasing output until the addition to its revenues generated by an extra unit of output just equals the marginal cost of producing that extra unit of output. Because marginal revenue—which is equal to output *price* for a competitive firm—is not shown in our graph of the production function, the profit-maximizing level of output cannot be shown either. However, continuing our analysis of the production function can illustrate some important aspects of the demand for labor in the long run.

Conditions for Cost Minimization

In Figure 3A.3, the profit-maximizing level of output is Q^*. How will the firm combine labor and capital to produce Q^*? It can only maximize profits if it produces Q^* in the least expensive way; that is, it must minimize the costs of producing Q^*. To better understand the characteristics of cost minimization, refer to the three *isoexpenditure* lines—*AA', BB', DD'*—in Figure 3A.3. Along any one of these lines the costs of employing labor and capital are equal.

For example, line *AA'* represents total costs of $1000. Given an hourly wage *(W)* of $10 per hour, the firm could hire 100 hours of labor and incur total costs of $1000 if it used no capital (point A'). On the contrary, if the price of a unit of capital *(C)* is $20, the firm could produce at a total cost of $1000 by using 50

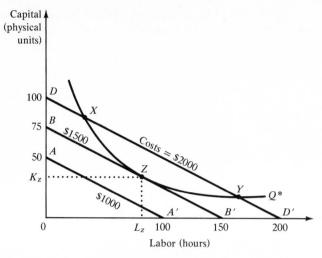

FIGURE 3A.3 **Cost Minimization in the Production of Q***
(Wage = $10 per Hour; Price of a Unit
of Capital = $20)

units of capital (point *A*). All the points between *A* and *A'* represent combinations of *L* and *K* that, at *W* = $10 and *C* = $20, cost $1000 as well.

The problem with the isoexpenditure line of *AA'* is that it does not intersect the isoquant *Q**—implying that *Q** cannot be produced for $1000. At prices of *W* = $10 and *C* = $20, the firm cannot buy enough resources to produce output level *Q** and hold total costs to $1000. The firm can, however, produce *Q** for a total cost of $2000. Isoquant *DD'*, representing expenditures of $2000, intersects the *Q** isoquant at points *X* and *Y*. The problem with these points, however, is that they are not cost-minimizing; *Q** can be produced for less than $2000.

Since isoquant *Q** is convex, the cost-minimizing combination of *L* and *K* in producing *Q** will come at a point where an isoexpenditure line is *tangent* to the isoquant (that is, just barely touches isoquant *Q** at only one place). Point *Z*, where labor equals L_z and capital equals K_z is where *Q** can be produced at minimal cost, *given* that *W* = $10 and C = $20. No lower isoexpenditure curve touches the isoquant—meaning that *Q** cannot be produced for less than $1500.

An important characteristic of point *Z* is that the slope of the isoquant at point *Z* and the slope of the isoexpenditure line are the same (the slope of a curve at a given point is the slope of a line tangent to the curve at that point). The slope of the isoquant at any given point is the *marginal rate of technical substitution* as defined in equation 3A.1. Another way of expressing equation 3A.1 is:

$$MRTS = \frac{-\Delta K / \Delta Q}{\Delta L / \Delta Q} \qquad (3A.2)$$

Equation 3A.2 directly indicates that the *MRTS* is a ratio reflecting the reduction of capital required to *decrease* output by one unit if enough extra labor is hired so that output is tending to *increase* by one unit. (The Δ*Q*s in equation 3A.2 cancel each other and keep output constant.) Pursuing equation 3A.2 one step farther, the numerator and denominator can be rearranged to obtain the following:[2]

$$MRTS = \frac{-\Delta K/\Delta Q}{\Delta L/\Delta Q} = -\frac{\Delta Q/\Delta L}{\Delta Q/\Delta K} = -\frac{MP_L}{MP_K}, \tag{3A.3}$$

where MP_L and MP_K are the marginal productivities of labor and capital, respectively.

The slope of the *isoexpenditure line* is equal to the negative of the ratio W/C (in Figure 3A.3 W/C equals 10/20, or 0.5).[3] Thus at point Z, where Q^* is produced in the minimum-cost fashion, the following equality holds:[4]

$$MRTS = -\frac{MP_L}{MP_K} = -\frac{W}{C} \tag{3A.4}$$

Equation 3A.4 is exactly the same as equation 3.7 in the text.

The economic meaning, or logic, behind the characteristics of cost minimization can most easily be seen by stating the $MRTS$ as $-\dfrac{\Delta K/\Delta Q}{\Delta L/\Delta Q}$ (see equation 3A.3) and equating this version of the $MRTS$ to $-\dfrac{W}{C}$:

$$-\frac{\Delta K/\Delta Q}{\Delta L/\Delta Q} = -\frac{W}{C}, \text{ or} \tag{3A.5}$$

$$\frac{\Delta K}{\Delta Q} \cdot C = \frac{\Delta L}{\Delta Q} \cdot W \tag{3A.6}$$

Equation 3A.6 makes it very plain that to be minimizing costs, the cost of producing an extra unit of output by adding only labor must equal the cost of producing that extra unit by employing only additional capital. If these costs differed, the company could reduce total costs by expanding its use of the factor with which output can be increased more cheaply and cutting back on its use of the other factor. Any point where costs can still be reduced while Q is held constant is obviously not a point of cost minimization.

The Substitution Effect

If the wage rate, which was assumed to be $10 per hour in Figure 3A.3, goes up to $20 per hour (holding C constant), what will happen to the cost-minimizing way of producing output of Q^*? Figure 3A.4 illustrates the answer that common sense would suggest: total costs rise, and more capital and less labor are used to produce Q^*. At $W = \$20$, 150 units of labor can no longer be purchased if total costs are to be held to $1500; in fact, if costs are to equal $1500, only 75 units of

---

[2]This is done by making use of the fact that dividing one number by a second one is equivalent to *multiplying* the first by the *inverse* of the second.

[3]Note that 10/20 = 50/100, or 0A/0A'.

[4]The negative signs on each side of (3A.4) cancel each other and are therefore ignored.

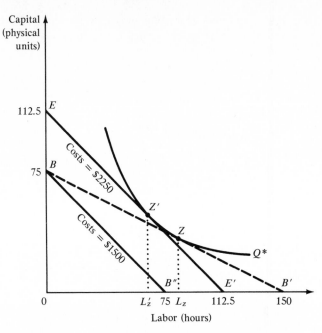

FIGURE 3A.4   Cost Minimization in the Production of Q*
(Wage = $20 per Hour; Price of a Unit
of Capital = $20)

labor can be hired. Thus, the isoexpenditure curve for $1500 in costs shifts from *BB'* to *BB''* and no longer is tangent to isoquant *Q**. *Q** can no longer be produced for $1500, and the minimum-cost way of producing *Q** will rise. In Figure 3A.4 we assume that it rises to $2250 (isoexpenditure line *EE'* is the one tangent to isoquant *Q**).

Moreover, the increase in the cost of labor relative to capital induces the firm to use more capital and less labor. Graphically, the old tangency point of *Z* is replaced by a new one *(Z')*, where the marginal productivity of labor is higher relative to MP_K—as equation 3A.4 explained. Point *Z'* is reached (from *Z*) by adding more capital and reducing employment of labor. The movement from L_Z to L'_Z is the *substitution effect* that is generated by the wage increase.

The Scale Effect

The fact that *Q** can no longer be produced for $1500, but instead involves at least $2250 in costs, will generally mean that it is no longer the profit-maximizing level of production. The new profit-maximizing level of production will be less than *Q** (how much less cannot be determined unless we know something about the product demand curve).

Suppose that the profit-maximizing level of output falls from *Q** to *Q*** in Figure 3A.5. Since all isoexpenditure lines have the new slope of −1 when *W* = $20 and *C* = $20, the cost-minimizing way to produce *Q*** will lie on an isoexpenditure curve parallel to *EE'*. We find this cost-minimizing way to produce *Q*** at point *Z''*, where an isoexpenditure curve *(FF')* is tangent to *Q***.

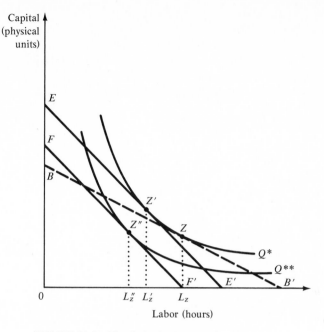

**FIGURE 3A.5   The Substitution and Scale Effects
of a Wage Increase**

The *overall* response in the employment of labor to an increase in the wage rate has been a fall in labor usage from L_Z to L_Z''. The decline from L_Z to L_Z' is called the substitution effect, as we have noted. It results because the *proportions* of K and L used in production change when the ratio of wages to capital prices *(W/C)* changes. The *scale effect* can be seen as the reduction in employment from L_Z' to L_Z''—wherein the usage of both K and L is cut back solely because of the reduced *scale* of production. Both effects are simultaneously present when wages increase and capital prices remain constant, but as Figure 3A.5 emphasizes, the effects are conceptually distinct and occur for different reasons. Together, these effects form the basis for our assertion that the long-run demand for labor curve slopes downward.

4

Elasticities of Demand
for Labor

The previous chapter stressed that the effects of various government policies on employment and wage levels depend crucially on the magnitudes of labor demand elasticities. Given the importance of these elasticities, this chapter will present an extended discussion of the determinants of the elasticities of demand for labor, will summarize the available empirical evidence on the magnitudes of these elasticities, and will then illustrate the importance of this knowledge in a number of policy applications.

ELASTICITY AND CROSS ELASTICITY DEFINED

The Own-Wage Elasticity of Demand

Recall that the _own-wage elasticity of demand_ for a category of labor is defined as the percentage change in its employment (E) induced by a one percent increase in its wage rate (W).

$$\eta_{ii} = \frac{\%\Delta E_i}{\%\Delta W_i} \tag{4.1}$$

In equation (4.1), we have used the subscript i to denote category of labor i, n to represent elasticity, and the notation $\%\Delta$ to represent "percentage change in." Since the last chapter showed that labor demand curves slope downward, an increase (decrease) in the wage rate will lead employment to decrease (increase); the own-wage elasticity of demand is a negative number. What is at issue is its magnitude. The larger its _absolute_ value, the larger will be the percentage decline in employment associated with any given percentage increase in wages.

Labor economists often focus on whether the absolute value of the elasticity of demand for labor is greater than or less than one. If it is greater than one, a one percent increase in wages will lead to an employment decline of greater than one percent; this situation is referred to as an _elastic_ demand curve. In contrast, if the absolute value is less than one, the demand curve is said to be _inelastic;_ a

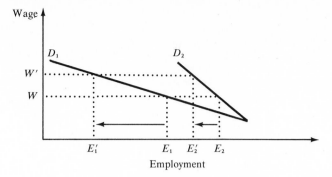

FIGURE 4.1 **Relative Demand Elasticities**

one percent increase in wages will lead to a proportionately smaller decline in employment.[1] If the demand curve is elastic, aggregate earnings (defined here as the wage rate times the employment level) of individuals in the category will decline when the wage rate increases, because employment falls at a faster rate than wages rise. Similarly, if the demand curve is inelastic, aggregate earnings will increase when the wage rate is increased.

To see the importance of the magnitude of elasticity, let us return to our analysis of the minimum wage in a world with *complete coverage*. We saw in Chapter 3 that an increase in the minimum wage would lead to a decrease in employment, if other factors affecting employment are held constant. Does this result imply, from the perspective of low-wage workers as a group, that minimum-wage increases are undesirable? The answer is ambiguous; it depends upon the extent to which the higher minimum wage for those workers who keep their jobs offsets the loss in employment that occurs. There are obvious equity issues involved here that make such comparisons difficult. However, *if* the own-wage elasticity of demand for low-skilled workers is inelastic, an increase in the minimum wage will lead to an increase in aggregate earnings for this group. This increase in aggregate earnings among the low-skilled implies that those who keep their jobs could compensate those who lose them and still be better off.[2] (The fact that *low-skilled* workers, as a *group, might* be made better-off by a minimum-wage law does not imply that the gains to *society* as a whole would exceed the losses. Chapter 3 addressed the social losses.)

Figure 4.1 shows that the flatter of the two demand curves graphed (D_1) has greater elasticity than the steeper (D_2). Beginning with any wage $(W,$ for example), given wage changes (to W', say) will yield greater responses in employment with demand curve D_1 than with D_2 (compare $E_1 - E_1'$ with $E_2 - E_2'$).

To speak of a demand curve as having "an" elasticity, however, is technically incorrect. Given demand curves will generally have elastic and inelastic

---

[1] If the elasticity just equals -1, the demand curve is said to be *unitary elastic*.

[2] Once we include transfer payments, such as unemployment insurance, in the analysis, it becomes possible for the total income of low-skilled workers (including transfer payments) to increase even if the elasticity is greater than one. See Edward Gramlich, "Impact of Minimum Wages on Other Wages, Employment, and Family Incomes," *Brookings Papers on Economic Activity,* 2 (1976).

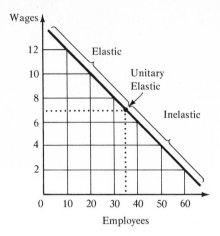

**FIGURE 4.2   Different Elasticities
Along a Demand Curve**

ranges—and while we are usually just interested in the elasticity of demand in the range around the current wage rate in any market, one cannot fully understand elasticity without understanding that it can vary along a given demand curve.

To illustrate, suppose we examine the typical straight-line demand curve that we have used so often in Chapters 2 and 3 (see Figure 4.2). One feature of a straight-line demand curve is that at *each* point along the curve a unit change in wages induces the *same* response in terms of units of employment. For example, at any point along the demand curve shown in Figure 4.2, a $2 decrease in wages will increase employment by 10 workers.

However, the same responses in terms of *unit* changes along the demand curve do *not* imply equal *percentage* changes. To see this point, look first at the upper end of the demand curve in Figure 4.2 (the end where wages are high and employment is low). A $2 decrease in wages when the base is $12 represents a 17 percent reduction in wages—while an addition of 10 workers when the starting point is also 10 represents a 100 percent increase in demand. Demand at this point is clearly *elastic*. However, if one looks at the same unit changes in the lower region of the demand curve (low wages, high employment), demand there is inelastic. A $2 reduction in wages from a $4 base is a 50 percent reduction, while an increase of 10 workers from a base of 50 is only a 20 percent increase. Since the percentage increase in employment is smaller than the percentage increase in wages, demand is seen to be inelastic at this end of the curve.

Thus, the upper end of a straight-line demand curve will exhibit greater elasticity than the lower end. Moreover, a straight-line demand curve will actually be elastic in some ranges and inelastic in others (as shown in Figure 4.2).

The Cross-Wage Elasticity of Demand

Because firms may employ several categories of labor and capital, the demand for any one category can be affected by price changes in the other categories. For example, if the wages of carpenters rose, more people might build brick homes and the demand for *masons* might increase. On the other hand, an increase in carpenters' wages might decrease the overall level of home building in the economy, which would decrease the demand for *plumbers*. Finally, changes in the price of *capital* could increase or decrease the demand for workers in all three trades.

The magnitude of the above effects can be summarized by examining the elasticities of demand for inputs with respect to the prices of other inputs. Recall that in the previous chapter we defined the *elasticity of demand for input* i *with respect to the price of input* j as the percentage change in the demand for input *i* induced by one percent change in the price of input *j*. If the two inputs are both categories of labor, these *cross-wage elasticities of demand* are given by

$$\eta_{ij} = \frac{\%\Delta E_i}{\%\Delta W_j} \tag{4.2}$$

and

$$\eta_{ji} = \frac{\%\Delta E_j}{\%\Delta W_i}$$

If the cross-elasticities are positive (with an increase in the price of one increasing the demand for the other), the two are said to be *gross substitutes*. If these cross-elasticities are negative (and an increase in the price of one reduces the demand for the other), the two are said to be *gross complements*.

Both the sign and magnitude of cross elasticities are important for policy analysis. To return to our minimum-wage example again, would the introduction of a youth subminimum, or youth differential in the minimum wage, be an effective way to increase teenage employment levels? *If* the own-wage elasticity of demand for youth is elastic, a youth differential of, say, 15 percent would lead to a greater than 15 percent increase in teenage employment.[3] However, the story does not end here; one also needs to consider whether *other* groups would face adverse employment effects. If, for example, teens and adult workers are *gross substitutes*, employment of low-skilled *adult* workers would fall if a youth differential were enacted. Estimates of the cross-wage elasticity of demand of adult labor with respect to the teenage wage are thus also required to make intelligent policy decisions. (As later sections will discuss, there *is* evidence that the own-wage elasticity of demand for teenagers is elastic; however, evidence on the size and sign of relevant adult-teenager cross-wage elasticities is generally lacking.[4]

THE HICKS-MARSHALL LAWS OF DERIVED DEMAND

Knowledge of own-wage elasticities of demand is very important for making policy decisions. The factors that influence own-wage elasticity can be summarized by the four "Hicks-Marshall Laws of Derived Demand"—"laws" named after

---

[3] This actually is an overestimate since it assumes all teens earn the minimum wage. In fact, many earn significantly more; their wages would not be directly affected by a youth differential. Hence, the actual reduction in the average teenage wage would be substantially less than 15 percent.

[4] See Daniel Hamermesh and James Grant, "Econometric Studies of Labor-Labor Substitution and Their Implications for Policy," *Journal of Human Resources* 14 (Fall 1979): 518–42.

two distinguished British economists, Alfred Marshall and John Hicks, who are closely associated with their development.[5] These laws assert that, other things equal, the own wage elasticity of demand for a category of labor is high

1. when the price elasticity of demand for the product being produced is high,
2. when other factors of production can be easily substituted for the category of labor,
3. when the supply curves of other factors of production are highly elastic (that is, usage of other factors of production can be increased without substantially increasing their prices), and
4. when the cost of employing the category of labor is a large share of the total costs of production.

Not only are these laws generally valid as an empirical proposition, but the first three can be shown to always hold. There are conditions, however, under which the final law does not hold. (Each of the laws, including the exception just mentioned, is graphically derived in the appendix to this chapter.)

In seeking to explain why these laws hold, it is useful to pretend that we can divide the process by which an increase in the wage rate affects the demand for labor into two steps: First, an increase in the wage rate increases the relative cost of the category of labor in question and induces employers to use less of it and more of other inputs (the *substitution effect*). Second, when the wage increase causes the marginal costs of production to rise, there are pressures to increase product prices and reduce output—causing a fall in employment (the *scale effect*). The four laws of derived demand each deal with substitution or scale effects.

Demand for the Final Product

The greater the price elasticity of demand for the final product, the larger will be the decline in output associated with a given increase in price—and the greater the decrease in output, the greater the loss in employment (other things equal). Thus, *the greater the elasticity of demand for the product, the greater the elasticity of demand for labor will be*. One implication of this result is that, other things equal, the demand for labor at the *firm* level will be more elastic than the demand for labor at the *industry,* or market, level. For example, the product demand curves facing *individual* carpet manufacturing companies are highly elastic, because the carpet of Company X is a very close substitute for the carpet of Company Y. Compared to price increases at the *firm* level, however, price increases at the *industry* level will not have as large an effect on demand because the closest substitutes for carpeting are hardwood, ceramic, or some kind of vinyl floor covering—none of which is a very close substitute for carpeting. The demand for labor is thus much more elastic for an individual carpet manufacturing firm than for the carpet manufacturing industry as a whole. (For the same reasons, the labor demand curve for a monopolist is less elastic than for an individual *firm* in a

---

[5]John R. Hicks, *The Theory of Wages,* 2nd ed. (New York: St. Martins Press, 1966), pp. 241–47; Alfred Marshall, *Principles of Economics,* 8th ed. (London: Macmillan, 1923), pp. 518–38.

competitive industry. Monopolists, after all, face *market* demand curves for their product, because they are the only seller in the particular market.)

Another implication of this first law is that *wage elasticities will be higher in the long run than in the short run*. The reason for this fact is that price elasticities of demand in product markets are higher in the long run. In the short-run there may be no good substitutes for a product, or consumers may be locked into their current stock of consumer durables. However, after a period of time, new products that are substitutes may be introduced, and consumers will begin to replace durables that have worn out.

Substitutability of Other Factors

As the wage rate of a category of labor increases, firms have an incentive to try to substitute other, now relatively cheaper, inputs for the category. Suppose, however, that there were no substitution possibilities; a given number of units of the type of labor *must* be used to produce one unit of output. In this case, the first step in the process described above is not present; there is no reduction in employment due to the substitution effect. In contrast, when substitution possibilities do present themselves, a reduction in employment will occur at this stage. Hence, other things equal, *the easier it is to substitute other factors of production, the higher the wage elasticity of demand will be*.

It is important to note that limitations on substitution possibilities need not be solely technical ones. For example, as we shall see in Chapter 12, unions often try to limit substitution possibilities by including specific work rules in their contracts (e.g., minimum crew size for crews in a railroad locomotive). Alternatively, the government may legislate limitations by specifying minimum employment levels for "safety reasons" (for example, each public swimming pool in New York State must always have a life guard present). Such collectively bargained or legislated restrictions make the demand for labor less elastic. Note, however, that substitution possibilities that are not feasible in the short run may well become feasible over longer periods of time, when employers are free to vary their capital stock. For example, if the wages of railroad workers go up, companies could buy more powerful locomotives and operate with larger trains and fewer locomotives. Likewise, if the wages of lifeguards rose, cities might build larger, but fewer, swimming pools. Both adjustments would occur only in the long run, which is another reason why the demand for labor is more elastic in the long run than in the short run.

The Supply of Other Factors

Suppose that as the wage rate increased and employers attempted to substitute other factors of production for labor, the prices of these inputs were bid up substantially. This situation might occur, for example, if one were trying to substitute capital equipment for labor. If producers of capital equipment were already operating their plants near capacity—so that taking on new orders would cause them substantial increases in costs because they would have to work their employees overtime and pay them a wage premium—they would only accept new orders if they could charge a higher price for their equipment. Such a price increase would

Example 4.1
How to Finance Black Lung Benefits

In 1969, Congress passed the Coal Mine Health and Safety Act, which, among other things, made coal miners and ex-coal miners with black lung disease eligible for monthly benefits ranging from $169 to $340 per month (to be adjusted upward as federal pay scales were adjusted). Black lung disease, which is a lung impairment that occurs when lungs become clogged with coal dust, is disabling and can lead to early death. Any coal miner found eligible in the first five years of the program was to receive benefits financed by the government, but beginning in 1974 the financing of the benefits for new recipients was to fall upon the coal-mine operator for whom the recipient last worked for at least one year.

As 1974 approached, it became clear to the government that many coal-mine operators would buy insurance against their potential liabilities and that the insurance premiums would be charged as a fraction of the operator's *payroll* costs. These premiums, which the government feared would be large, would increase the cost of hiring labor and could have very adverse effects on the employment of coal miners. How large might these effects be?

The first step in estimating employment effects was to obtain an estimate of what the insurance premiums would be. The insurance industry estimated they would average about 11 percent of the payroll in underground mining and 7 percent of the payroll in strip (or surface) mining, where the problem of black lung disease is smaller.

The next step in estimating employment effects was to break these effects down into the *scale* and *substitution* effects. The share of labor in the total costs of underground mining is about 50 percent, so the insurance premiums in that sector would increase costs and prices by about 5.5 percent (in other words, there was an 11 percent increase in half of the total costs). In strip mining, labor costs are only about 25 percent of total costs, so the 7 percent premium there would increase prices in that sector by only 1.7 percent. These calculations clearly made use of data on the *labor share in total cost.*

The price increases in coal that would be caused by the insurance premiums would have two effects. First, the overall price of coal would rise and cause less of it to be used. The overall elasticity of demand for coal was estimated to be − 0.5 (an inelasticity caused by the difficulties and expense of substituting oil or natural gas for coal in electric power generation). Second, because underground and strip-mined coal are good substitutes for each other, the change in their *relative* prices would cause those still using coal to increase their purchases of strip-mined coal at the expense of underground coal.

The total scale effect in the *underground-coal* sector that would take place if the 11 percent and 7 percent rates were charged was estimated to result in a 6 percent reduction in output and employment (a loss of 6,600 jobs). This potential loss was so large because former users of underground-mined coal would tend to substitute away from underground coal toward strip-mined coal *as well as* substituting away from coal altogether. It was estimated that strip mining, by virtue of the shift away from underground coal, would gain 1400 jobs if the 11 percent and 7 percent premiums were charged (a 4 percent increase in employment). These calculations used estimates of the *price elasticity of demand* for both underground and strip-mined coal.

The final step in estimating the employment effects of the Black Lung Benefits Program was to estimate substitution effects. From data on the capital-labor ratios in each sector of the coal mining industry, it appears that a 1 percent increase in the price of labor relative to the price of capital is associated with a 1 percent increase in the capital-labor ratio used in production. (Economists define the percentage change in the ratio of factor inputs associated with a 1% change in the relative prices of these inputs as the "elasticity of substitution.") Using this information on the *substitutability of capital and labor,* it was estimated that about 5200 jobs (4.5 percent of the total) would be lost in the underground sector to capital substitution. The corresponding losses in the strip-mining sector were estimated at 1300 (3.9 percent). (The estimate of the substitution effect was made *assuming that capital prices would remain constant.* Again, this amounts to assuming that the supply curve for capital in the coal-mining industry is horizontal.)

The *overall* estimate of employment losses that would accompany the imposition of financial liability for black-lung payments on coal operators amounted to about 11,700 jobs (virtually all in the underground sector). This estimate implied that even if the coal industry expanded (as it did), there would be around 11,700 fewer jobs in that industry than there would otherwise have been.

The program was not actually implemented as originally planned. There were difficulties in finding the coal-mine operators liable for benefit payments in cases where ex-miners had last worked several years ago. There were also pressures to liberalize the conditions under which ex-miners could be found eligible for the program. As a result of these forces, the program was amended in 1978 in such a way that individual coal-mine operators would only be liable in cases where miners had worked (as miners) since 1970. For those miners who had last worked in coal mining prior to 1970, benefits would be paid out of a trust fund financed by the industry in general from a tax of 50 cents per ton of underground coal and 25 cents per ton of strip-mined coal.

The interesting thing about a *ton tax* is that its employment effects are quite different than those of an insurance premium based on wages. A ton tax would produce scale effects, of course, but because it would not raise the price of labor relative to capital it would produce *no substitution effects.* It was estimated, in fact, that a ton tax large enough to produce the *same* revenues as the 11 percent and 7 percent payroll charges would have caused an overall job loss of only 5200 (which is just the scale effect mentioned above).

Saving jobs, however, is not necessarily the most appropriate criterion by which to choose among alternative means of financing the benefits. One would certainly want to use a financing scheme that provides operators with the incentives to reduce the incidence of disease among their workers. One way to reduce disease is to reduce dust levels, but another is to substitute capital for labor and essentially let *machines* mine coal. An increase in payroll costs, because it does tend to increase the capital-labor ratio, might thus do more to reduce disease, other things equal, than a ton tax (assuming the machines did not create higher dust levels for those workers remaining).

SOURCE: Morris Goldstein and Robert S. Smith, "The Predicted Impact of the Black Lung Benefits Program on the Coal Industry," in Orley Ashenfelter and James Blum, eds., *Evaluating the Labor-Market Effects of Social Programs (Princeton, N.J.: Princeton University, 1976).*

dampen firms' "appetites" for capital and thus limit the substitution of capital for labor.

For another example, suppose an increase in the wages of unskilled workers caused employers to attempt to substitute skilled employees for unskilled employees. If there were only a fixed number of skilled workers in an area, their wages would be bid up by employers. As in the prior example, the incentive to substitute alternative factors would be reduced, and the reduction in employment due to the substitution effect would be smaller. In contrast, if the prices of other inputs did not increase when employers attempted to increase their usage, other things equal, the substitution effect—and thus the wage elasticity of demand—would be larger.

Note again that prices of other inputs are less likely to be bid up in the long run than in the short run. In the long run existing producers of capital equipment can expand their capacity and new producers can enter the market. Similarly, in the long run more skilled workers can be trained. This observation is an additional reason why the demand for labor will be more elastic in the long run.

The Share of Labor in Total Costs

Finally, the share of the category of labor in total costs is crucial to the size of the elasticity of demand. If the category's initial share were 20 percent, a 10 percent increase in the wage rate, other things equal, would raise total costs by 2 percent. In contrast, if its initial share were 80 percent, a 10 percent increase in the wage rate would increase total costs by 8 percent. Since employers would have to increase their product prices by more in the latter case, output—and hence employment—would fall more in that case. *Thus, the greater the category's share in total costs, the higher the wage elasticity of demand will tend to be.*[6]

EMPIRICAL EVIDENCE ON WAGE ELASTICITIES OF DEMAND

Literally hundreds of studies have been published in recent years that present empirical estimates on the magnitudes of wage elasticities of demand. Some of these studies focus on the aggregate demand for labor in the economy as a whole; others focus on the demand by different industries. Some focus on the demand for

---

[6]As we noted earlier, this law does not always hold. More specifically, when it is easy for employers to substitute other factors of production for the category of labor but difficult for consumers to substitute other products for the product being produced (low price elasticity of demand), this law is reversed. A graphical demonstration of this law and its exception is given in the Appendix 4A. For a more formal treatment, see Hicks, *The Theory of Wages.*

different skill classes; still others focus on the demand for different age/race/sex groups. Although our knowledge in a number of these areas is not very precise, it is useful to summarize what we do know.

To be able to draw a particular demand curve with precision requires knowledge of the factors that affect derived demand: the technological possibilities given by the production function (substitutability of capital and labor, labor share in total cost), the supply curve of capital, and the elasticity of product demand. In estimating the elasticity of demand for labor, we do not want to hold these factors constant because they are all crucial in determining the *size* of the elasticity of demand. As a practical matter, however, researchers usually have to estimate demand elasticities holding the *price of capital* constant.[7] This is tantamount to assuming that capital usage can be increased or decreased as wages change with no effect on the price at which capital is supplied; that is, capital supply curves are assumed to be horizontal. All elasticity estimates cited below make this assumption.[8]

The *overall*, own-wage elasticity of demand for labor in the economy as a whole is inelastic and probably in the range of -0.3.[9] This inelasticity is to be expected, because at the level of the economy *as a whole* scale effects are likely to be small. Workers losing jobs due to wage increases will become self-employed in some cases. There are federal policies and programs designed to maintain national output and create full employment. Foreign goods and services are often very hard to substitute for domestic goods and services. For all these reasons, the *overall* wage elasticity of demand is small.

The own-wage elasticities of demand at the *industry* level tend to vary widely across industries and in the main are also inelastic. Table 4.1 presents a representative set of estimates for coal mining, manufacturing, retail trade, and the state and local government sector. That the demand for employees in underground mining (located primarily in the East) is more elastic than the demand for employees in surface or strip mining (located primarily in the West) is not unexpected. Surface mining is much more capital intensive, and labor costs are a smaller share of the total costs of production, in that sector. That the estimated elasticities at the industry level tend to be in the inelastic range is also not surprising because scale effects at that level are likely to be relatively small in many cases. The elasticity of product demand *for a firm* is very high, as mentioned earlier, but *at the industry level* it is not likely to be very large.

A third set of empirical findings suggests that the own-wage elasticity of demand is higher for production workers than for nonproduction workers. This difference appears to be the result of the greater substitutability between capital and *production* labor than between capital and nonproduction workers.[10]

In general, the more substitutable with capital a group of workers is, the

---

[7]*Capital,* even in a given industry, encompasses so many machines, tools, supplies, and buildings that estimating a supply function is really beyond the capability of the data usually available.

[8]Studies in which the level of *output* or the level of capital *usage* is held constant are ignored here since they assume away either scale or substitution effects.

[9]Daniel Hamermesh, "Econometric Studies of Labor Demand and Their Application to Policy Analysis," *Journal of Human Resources* (Fall 1976): 507–25.

[10]Hamermesh and Grant, "Econometric Studies of Labor-Labor Substitution."

TABLE 4.1   Representative Estimates of Long-Run
Wage Elasticities of Demand, by Industry

Industry	Long-Run Wage Elasticity
Coal mining[a]	
Underground	−0.98
Surface	−0.86
Manufacturing[b]	−0.09 to −0.62
Retail trade[c]	−0.34 to −1.20
State and local government[d]	
Employees in education sector	−1.06
Noneducation employees	−0.38

[a]Derived from estimates presented in Morris Goldstein and Robert S. Smith, "The Predicted Impact of the Black Lung Benefits Program on the Coal Industry" in Orley Ashenfelter and James Blum, eds., *Evaluating the Labor-Market Effects of Social Programs* (Princeton, N.J.: Princeton University 1976).

[b]Daniel Hamermesh, "Econometric Studies of Labor Demand and Their Applications to Public Policy," *Journal of Human Resources*" (Fall 1976):507–25.

[c]Philip Cotterill, "The Elasticity of Demand for Low-Wage Labor," *Southern Economic Journal* 41 (January 1975):520–25.

[d]Orley Ashenfelter and Ronald G. Ehrenberg, "The Demand for Labor in the Public Sector," in Daniel Hamermesh, ed., *Labor in the Public and Nonprofit Sectors* (Princeton, N.J.: Princeton University Press, 1975).

greater will be its elasticity of demand, other things equal. Research to date suggests that capital and unskilled labor are more easily substituted than capital and skilled labor,[11] but whether this translates into a greater own-wage elasticity of demand depends upon the "other things" affecting elasticity: product demand elasticities, share of labor in total cost, and the supply curve for capital. *If* these other factors are more or less the same for skilled and unskilled workers, on average, then the own-wage elasticity of demand will tend to be greater for the unskilled. It appears, for example, that the elasticity of demand for teenage labor may be in the range of −7 to −9 and that it is much higher than the elasticity of demand for adults (who tend to be in more skilled jobs).[12]

All of the evidence cited above has concerned *own-wage* elasticities of demand. As indicated earlier, evidence on *cross-wage* elasticities of demand is generally lacking. We *do* have evidence that teenagers and adults, for example, are substitutes in production,[13] but whether they are *gross substitutes* depends on the *scale effect* as well as on the substitution effect. In other words, we know with some certainty that if teenage wages were reduced by a youth differential in the minimum wage, teenagers would be substituted for adults (at least to some degree) in the production process. However, whether adult employment would go up or down depends also on the scale effect a youth subminimum would create. If scale effects are large, teenagers and adults *could* be gross complements (that is, as teenage wages fell, adult employment would rise despite the substitution against

---

[11]Hamermesh and Grant, "Econometric Studies of Labor-Labor Substitution."

[12]Hamermesh and Grant, "Econometric Studies of Labor-Labor Substitution."

[13]Hamermesh and Grant, "Econometric Studies of Labor-Labor Substitution."

them in the production process). Unfortunately, it is not clear at this point whether teenagers and adults are gross complements or gross substitutes.

APPLYING THE LAWS OF DERIVED DEMAND

Because empirical estimates of demand elasticities that may be required for making decisions are lacking in some cases, it is sometimes necessary to try to guess what these elasticities are likely to be. In making these guesses, we can apply the laws of derived demand to predict these magnitudes for various types of labor. Consider first the demand for unionized New York City garment workers. As we shall discuss in Chapter 12, because unions are complex organizations it is not always possible to specify what their goals are. Nevertheless, it is clear that in most cases unions value both their members' wage *and* employment opportunities. This observation leads to the simple prediction that, other things equal, the more elastic the demand for labor, the smaller the wage gain that a union will succeed in winning for its members. The reason for this prediction is that the more elastic the demand curve, the greater the percentage employment decline associated with any given percentage increase in wages. We can expect that

a. unions would win larger wage gains for their members in markets with inelastic demand curves;
b. unions would strive to take actions that reduce the wage elasticity of demand for their members' services; and
c. unions might first seek to organize workers in markets in which demand curves are inelastic (because the potential gains to unionization are higher in these markets).

As we shall see, many of these predictions are born out by empirical evidence (see Chapter 12).

Due to foreign competition, the price elasticity of demand for the clothing produced by New York City garment workers is extremely high. Furthermore, employers can easily find other inputs to substitute for these workers; namely, nonunion garment workers in the South (this substitution would require moving the plant to the South, a strategy that many manufacturers have followed). These facts lead one to predict that the wage elasticity of demand for New York City unionized garment workers should be very elastic—a prediction that seems to be borne out by union policies in the industry. That is, because the garment workers' union faces a highly elastic demand curve, its wage demands historically have been moderate. However, the union has also aggressively sought to reduce the elasticity of product demand by supporting policies that reduce foreign competition—and it has, in addition, pushed for higher federal minimum wages in order to reduce employers' incentives to move their plants to the South.

Next, consider the wage elasticity of demand for unionized airplane pilots on commercial scheduled airlines in the United States. The salaries of pilots are only a small share of the costs of operating large airplanes; they are dwarfed by the fuel and capital costs of airlines. Furthermore, substitution possibilities are limited; there is little room to substitute unskilled labor for skilled labor (although airlines can contemplate substituting capital for labor by reducing the number of flights they offer while increasing the size of airplanes). Although a full analysis would have to consider the factors that influence the elasticity of demand for air travel and the elasticity of supply of capital, the small labor share and the difficulties of substitution suggest that the wage elasticity of demand for commercial airline pilots may be quite inelastic. As one might expect, their wages are quite high, because their union can push for large wage increases without fear that such an increase would substantially reduce their employment levels.

Finally, consider the wage elasticity of demand for *domestic* farm workers. This elasticity will depend heavily on the supply of immigrants, either legal or illegal, who are potentially willing to work as farm workers at wages less than the wages paid to domestic workers. The successful unionization of farm workers, coupled with union or government rules that prevent illegal immigrants from accepting such employment, obviously will make the demand curve for domestic farm workers less elastic. Similarly, government regulations that either limit the quantity of foreign farm products that can be imported into the United States (quotas), place tariffs on such products, or limit foreign producers from *dumping* (selling their farm products in the United States at prices less than they charge in their own countries) will all reduce the price elasticity of demand for U.S. farm products (and hence the wage elasticity of demand for domestic farm workers). This example indicates how government policies can heavily influence wage elasticities in particular labor markets.

POLICY APPLICATIONS

Knowledge of the magnitudes and signs of wage elasticities of demand are important in many policy applications, as the following examples illustrate.

Market Effects of a Government Training Program

Suppose the labor market for a particular type of clerical worker, say typists, is competitive and is initially in equilibrium. This situation is depicted in Figure 4.3; the initial demand curve is D_0, the supply curve is S_0, and E_0 typists are employed and paid the real wage rate W_0. Suppose also that there is unemployment of unskilled workers in the area and that to remedy this situation the government funds a training program to train these unemployed unskilled workers to become typists.[14] If $E_2 - E_0$ unskilled workers are trained, the supply curve of typists in the market will shift to S_1. At the old equilibrium wage (W_0), the number of typists who want to work will exceed the number that firms want to hire (by $E_2 - E_0$). Downward pressure will be placed on the wage rate and eventually equilibrium will be reestablished at the lower real wage rate of W_1 and the higher employment level of E_1.[15]

---

[14]During the late 1970s and early 1980s, the major government training programs for adults were funded under the Comprehensive Employment and Training Act (CETA). See the most recent issue of the *Employment and Training Report of the President* for background data on, and a description of, current training programs.

[15]In a period of rising prices real wages can fall without a cut in money wages. All that is required here is that prices rise more rapidly than money wages.

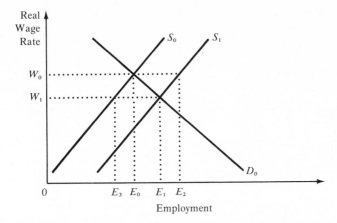

FIGURE 4.3   Market Effects of a Government Training Program

Note that even if all trainees were placed in jobs, the net impact of the program is not to increase employment of typists by the number of trainees. Employment has increased by less than the number of trainees, because the reduction in the real wage rate has induced some previously employed workers to quit their jobs and drop out of the typist labor market. Also, those typists who have kept their jobs are now worse off because their wages are lower than before. Both of these market effects must be taken into account in any evaluation of a training program's effects.

Under what circumstances will both the decline in wages and the loss of jobs by previously employed typists be small? Clearly the answer is, when the wage elasticity of demand for labor is highly elastic. For in this situation, a small decline in wages will lead to a large expansion in the number of employees firms want to hire. Other things equal, trainees should be trained for occupations in which the demand curves are highly elastic.

Of course, this analysis assumes that real wages are flexible in the market for typists, so that initially there is not a shortage of labor in that market. If instead, the real wage could not initially rise above W_1 in Figure 4.3 (which might occur during a period in which wages were directly controlled by federal legislation), then the initial employment level would be E_3. In this situation, employment could increase by the number of trainees and the real wage might not fall. However, if the government attempted to train more than $E_1 - E_3$ new typists, the lesson learned above would apply and employment of typists would not increase by the number trained.

Investment Tax Credit to Reduce Unemployment

An *investment tax credit* allows businesses to subtract a certain percentage of the investments they make in new capital equipment from their tax bills. As such, the credit is an implicit subsidy given to employers for increasing their capital stocks. It has the effect of reducing the price of new capital equipment, which should stimulate such investments. To the extent that this increases the growth rate in the economy, such a tax credit may stimulate employment growth and reduce the unemployment rate. However, working against this scale effect is a substitution effect: the cost of capital is lower because of the tax credit, and this induces the substitution of capital for labor.

Investment tax credits have been part of federal tax legislation since the early 1960s. Indeed, as of 1980 the credit was 10 percent of the purchase price for most capital investments. A policy issue of major interest is whether increasing the level of the tax credit substantially reduces unemployment. Since the cost of the credit to the U.S. Treasury in the form of lost revenue is rather substantial, and because this lost revenue could be used to reduce unemployment in other ways, the effects of the tax credit on employment opportunities is a critical question.

Although the overall effects of an investment tax credit on employment have not been precisely pinned down, we have a fairly good idea which groups would gain or lose from an increase in the credit. As noted above, the data seem to indicate that capital and skilled labor are less substitutable than capital and un- skilled labor. Hence, as increases in the investment tax credit reduce the cost of capital, one would expect greater substitution effects—which adversely affect em- ployment levels—among the unskilled. Whether the *actual* level of employment among the unskilled would fall or not depends, as we have emphasized, on the size of the *scale* effect. However, we would expect a tax credit to cause more displacement of unskilled workers than skilled workers.

Employment Tax Credits or Wage Subsidies

As an alternative to an investment tax credit, one might institute a system of payments to employers for increasing their employment levels. When the payment is made directly to employers (for example, when employers are rebated 50 per- cent of their new employees' wages) the payment is called a *wage subsidy*. If the payment is implicit, in the form of a tax credit, it is called an *employment tax credit*. The analyses, and effects, of both types of payment programs are identical, however. By reducing the price the employer pays for labor, both tend to stimu- late employment.

Employment tax credits, or wage-subsidy schemes, can take many forms.[16] They can apply to all new hires or only to increases in firms' employment levels (in which case they are called *marginal* employment tax credits). Since firms typically hire new employees to replace those employees who have quit, retired, or been involuntarily terminated, they would receive subsidies in the former case even if they maintained a constant employment level.

Employment subsidies can also be either *general* or *selective*. A general sub- sidy is not conditional on the characteristics of the people hired, while a selective, or *targeted,* plan makes payments conditional on hiring people from certain target groups (such as the disadvantaged).

Although European nations have had more experience with employment-tax- credit programs than the United States, both general and selective tax-credit pro-

---

[16]*See* Daniel Hamermesh, "Subsidies for Jobs in the Private Sector," in John Palmer, ed., *Creating Jobs: Public Employment Programs and Wage Subsidies* (Washington, D.C.: Brookings Institu- tion, 1978) for an extended discussion.

Example 4.2
The Slowdown in U.S. Productivity Growth

One measure of productivity that is customarily used is *labor productivity,* or output per hour of labor employed. Between 1948 and 1965 this labor productivity grew at a rate of about 3 percent per year in the manufacturing sector. Between 1973 and 1978, however, it grew at a rate of only about 1.5 percent per year. This slowdown in the rate of growth of productivity is particularly disturbing because, as we shall see in Chapter 16, the rate of growth of labor productivity is directly related to both the rate of growth of real wages and the rate of price inflation that occur in the economy.

Not surprisingly, then, economists have expended considerable effort to try to understand the causes of the slowdown in productivity growth. Although the slowdown is not fully understood, a number of factors are known to contribute to it. These factors include, but are not limited to, changes in the age-sex composition of the labor force, government mandated investments in pollution-abatement equipment (which do not lead to increases in *measured* output since the quality of the environment is not measured in gross national product), and a decline in the capital-labor ratio that has accompanied a slowdown in normal business investment. With less capital to work with, each unit of labor is less productive.

Why has this reduction in capital investment occurred? The answer may hinge on the explosion of energy prices that occurred during the period following the 1974 OPEC oil embargo. Several studies indicate that capital and energy are gross complements and that labor and energy are gross substitutes. Hence, rapid increases in the price of energy should induce employers to reduce their capital stocks and increase employment. Once we realize that energy is an input into the production process and that increases in the price of energy raise the cost of operating capital, it becomes clear why capital/labor ratios have fallen and contributed to the slowdown in measured labor productivity. Government policies to reduce the cost of capital, such as increasing the size of the investment tax credit, could offset energy price increases and stimulate investment, thus increasing labor productivity; however, as already noted, the net effect on *employment,* especially of unskilled workers, will not necessarily be favorable.

SOURCES: J. R. Norsworthy, Michael Harper, and Kent Kunze, "The Slowdown in Productivity Growth: Analysis of Some Contributing Factors," *Brookings Papers on Economic Activity,* 2(1979):387–423; Edward F. Denison, *Accounting for Slower Economic Growth: The United States in the 1970s* (Washington, D.C.: Brookings Institution, 1979).

Ernst Berndt and David Wood, "Technology, Prices and the Derived Demand for Energy," *Review of Economics and Statistics* 57 (August 1975):259–68; Edward A. Hudson and Dale Jorgenson, "Energy Prices and the U.S. Economy, 1972–76," *Data Resources Review* 7 (September 1978): 1.24–1.37. The findings, however, are not unambiguous. James Griffin and Paul Gregory, in "An Intercountry Translog Model of Energy and Substitution Responses," *American Economic Review* 66, (December 1976):845–57, find that capital and energy are gross substitutes.

grams have been tried in the United States in recent years. For example, a New Jobs Tax Credit was part of the 1977 economic stimulus package passed by Congress. This general, marginal employment-tax-credit program was in effect only for 1977 and 1978. Due to limitations on the size of the credit that an employer could receive for each employee (essentially 50 percent of the workers' annual earnings up to a maximum earnings ceiling of $4200), the plan effectively gave employers a proportionately greater subsidy for hiring unskilled and part-time labor than it did for hiring skilled or full-time labor.[17] Because of this, *if* the own-wage elasticities of demand are the same or larger for unskilled or part-time labor *and* if the various skill groups are gross substitutes, one would expect the employment levels of unskilled and part-time workers to be stimulated most by the program.

Preliminary evaluations of the program indicate that it may have had some small positive effect on the overall level of employment; firms that knew of the program's existence seemed to grow more rapidly than firms that did not know.[18] However, one year into the program, less than one-half of all surveyed firms actually knew that the program existed, and one might conjecture that the direction of causation ran from "plans to grow rapidly" to "knowledge of the program," rather than vice versa.[19] That is, firms that were planning to expand their employment, even in the absence of the program, had an incentive to learn about the program so that they could receive the subsidy.

This example again highlights the difficulties social scientists face when they attempt to evaluate the effect of social programs. It also suggests the importance of rapidly disseminating information about the existence of programs; the passage of a law, *per se,* does not guarantee that employers will know about it.

The New Jobs Tax Credit was replaced in 1979 by a Targeted Employment Tax Credit, which was a selective tax credit that subsidized the hiring of unemployed youth (18-24), handicapped individuals, and welfare recipients. Although it is too early to evaluate this program, it is possible to examine some of the evaluation issues.

To the extent that the demand for teenagers is highly elastic, as the empirical estimates indicate, this program does have the potential to substantially increase youth employment. However, it will be important to examine its impact on the employment levels of the nontargeted groups—especially unskilled adults for whom teenagers may be quite close substitutes. Another problem is the lack of data on demand elasticities for the handicapped or welfare recipients. Without these data, *ex post facto* (after the fact) evaluations of the program's effects on the employment levels of the different groups will be required.

[17]For more details of the plan, see Orley Ashenfelter, "Evaluating the Effects of the Employment Tax Credit" in U.S. Department of Labor, *Conference Report on Evaluating the 1977 Economic Stimulus Package* (Washington, D.C., U.S. Government Printing Office, 1979).

[18]*See* Jeffrey Perloff and Michael Wachter, "The New Jobs Tax Credit—an Evaluation of the 1977–78 Wage Subsidy Program," *American Economic Review* 69 (May 1979): 173–79; John Bishop and Robert Haveman, "Selective Employment Subsidies: Can Okun's Law be Repealed?" *American Economic Review* 69 (May 1979): 124–30.

[19]Perloff and Wachter, "The New Jobs Tax Credit"; Bishop and Haveman, "Selective Employment Subsidies."

REVIEW QUESTIONS

1. Suppose Congress has just passed a permanent tax credit applicable to the purchase of machinery. What impact would this tax reduction have on the demand for labor? Under what conditions will the demand for labor be affected *most*?

2. Suppose the government wants to cut expenditures to balance its budget in a way that minimizes the adverse employment effects of such a cutback. Suppose further that it wishes to do this by cutting back expenditures in selected industries (those where employment effects are minimal). Please identify the criteria the government should use in selecting these industries.

3. Union A faces a demand curve where a wage of $4 per hour leads to demand for 20,000 person hours and a wage of $5 per hour leads to demand for 10,000 person hours. What is the elasticity of demand for this union's labor?

    Union B faces a demand curve where a wage of $6 per hour leads to demand for 30,000 person hours while a wage of $5 per hour leads to demand for 33,000 person hours.

    a. Which union faces the *more* elastic demand curve?

    b. Which union will be most successful in increasing the total income (wages times person hours) of its membership?

SELECTED READINGS

Edward F. Denison, *Accounting for Slower Economic Growth: The United States in the 1970s* (Washington, D.C.: Brookings Institution, 1979).

Daniel Hamermesh, "Subsidies for Jobs in the Private Sector" in John Palmer, ed., *Creating Jobs: Public Employment Programs and Wage Subsidies* (Washington, D.C.: Brookings Institution, 1978).

Daniel Hamermesh, "Econometric Studies of Labor Demand and Their Application to Policy Analysis," *Journal of Human Resources,* Fall 1976.

Daniel Hamermesh and James Grant, "Econometric Studies of Labor-Labor Substitution and their Implications for Policy," *Journal of Human Resources,* Fall 1979.

Jeffrey Perloff and Michael Wachter, "The New Jobs Tax Credit—An Evaluation of the 1977–78 Wage Subsidy Program," *American Economic Review,* May 1979.

The "Laws" of Derived Demand

Chapter 4 presented a verbal explanation of the Hicks-Marshall laws of derived demand and briefly mentioned that one of those "laws" does not always hold. This appendix 1. will graphically derive and analyze these laws when the *substitution effect* is zero (that is, it will analyze the determinants of the elasticity of demand when *only* a *scale effect* occurs), and 2. will briefly analyze the above exception when only a *substitution* effect exists.

SCALE EFFECT BUT NO SUBSTITUTION EFFECT

To begin, let us assume that labor and capital must be combined in *fixed proportions* to produce a unit of output.[1] We can assume, for example, that one secretary and one typewriter must be combined if a letter is to be typed. If more labor is added to this one typewriter, no extra output is produced—and if more typewriters are given to one secretary, no extra output is produced.[2] In graphical terms, the isoquants of a fixed-proportions technology are perpendicular lines, as shown in Figure 4A.1. Costs are minimized at the "corner" (point *A* for *Q* = 100), and no matter what the relative prices are of labor and capital, the same amount of each will be used to produce *Q* of 100. (To see that this is the case, observe two isocost curves on which point *A* falls. When the wage *(W)* = $1 and the cost of capital *(C)* = $1, the isocost curve runs between *B* and *D,* while when *W* = $2 and *C* = $0.50 it runs between *E* and *F*. If output of 100 is to be produced, it will be done using *L** and *K** no matter what the relative prices of *L* and *K*. Any other input combination along the isoquant would have a higher total cost.) With this kind of production function, no substitution effect is generated by a change in wages.

---

[1] The analysis in this section leans heavily on Milton Friedman, *Price Theory: A Provisional Text* (Chicago: Aldine Publishing Company, 1962), pp. 148–155.

[2] This assumption is rather extreme and is made for analytical convenience only. We argued in Chapter 3 that adding secretaries to one typewriter *could* increase output, because the extra secretaries would permit them to alternate typing and resting, to address envelopes by hand, or to otherwise expedite work. Likewise, an extra typewriter per secretary could add to output when the inevitable breakdowns occur.

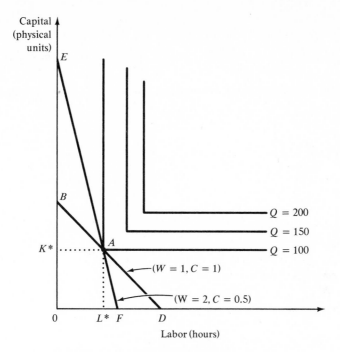

Capital
(physical
units)

$Q = 200$

$Q = 150$

$Q = 100$

$(W = 1, C = 1)$

$(W = 2, C = 0.5)$

Labor (hours)

**FIGURE 4A.1   Isoquants of a Fixed-Proportions
Production Function**

An increase in wages, however, will cause a scale effect. Production costs rise as wages increase, and the profit-maximizing level of output will tend to fall. The extent of the fall, and the forces underlying the degree to which employment also falls, can be easily shown in this fixed-proportions example.

Chapter 4 emphasized that a demand curve for labor is drawn holding three underlying forces constant: the production function, the product demand curve, and the supply curve of capital. These three influences—along with the demand-for-labor curve they imply—are simultaneously illustrated in Figure 4A.2 for a (hypothetical) industry that specializes in typing and mailing letters for customers. The fixed-proportions nature of the technology that we have assumed is shown along the horizontal axis. If 2,000 hours of labor and machine units are combined, 10,000 letters can be produced; if 4,000 hours of labor and capital are combined, 20,000 letters can be produced. The capital/labor combinations shown are the *only* ones that are consistent with cost minimization at any factor price ratio *(W/C)*.

The product demand curve D_P is drawn against the price charged for *bundles of 5 letters*—the hourly output of a unit of labor and a unit of capital—and has the usual negative slope.[3] This demand curve can be interpreted in two mutually consistent ways: it indicates, for given prices, the quantity of output that can be sold; it also indicates, for given levels of output, the price that can be charged.

The third force underlying the demand curve for labor in Figure 4A.2 is the supply curve of capital (S_K). We initially assume that this supply curve is horizon-

---

[3]Output and factor prices must be put on the same hourly basis if they are to be useful in our graphical analysis. It is obvious that one can divide the price per bundle by 5 and get the *unit* price.

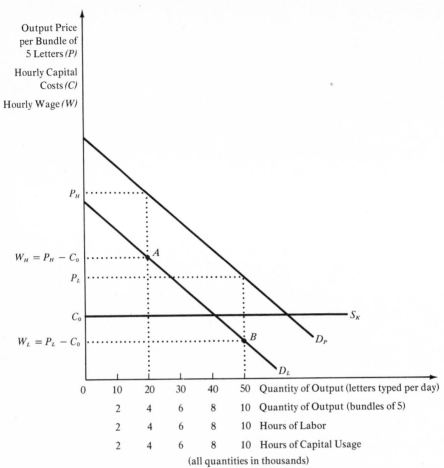

FIGURE 4A.2 **Derivation of the Demand Curve for Labor**
with Fixed-Proportions Technology

tal at C_0, meaning that additional units of capital (in our example, hours of machine usage) can be purchased at the constant price of C_0 per unit.

In deriving the demand-for-labor curve implied by the three forces above, look first at the output level of 20,000 (4,000 bundles of five). If output is 20,000, a price of P_H can be charged for each bundle. The *capital* cost of producing each bundle is C_0, so the maximum wage that could be paid for a labor hour at this level of output is $P_H - C_0$.[4] Point *A* thus becomes one point along the demand curve for labor. If 50,000 units of output are produced, P_L could be charged per bundle, and $P_L - C_0$ is the maximum wage per labor-hour that could be paid. Point *B*, then, is another point on labor's demand curve. D_L becomes the demand-for-labor curve implied by the technology, product demand, and capital supply curve. It shows a. the maximum hourly wage firms would be willing to pay at different levels of employment, or (alternatively) b. the hours of labor firms would desire to employ at any given hourly wage.

---

[4]We assume that C_0 includes a normal profit for the owner.

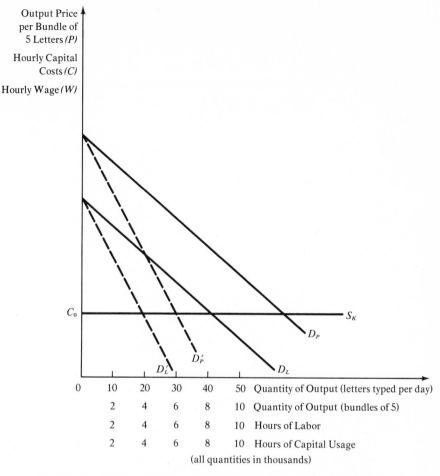

FIGURE 4A.3 The Effect of Product-Demand Elasticity on the Elasticity of Demand for Labor

Once this derivation of the demand-for-labor curve is understood for the fixed-proportions case, three of the "laws" of derived demand can be easily illustrated graphically. First, consider the proposition that *the less elastic is product demand, the less elastic will be the demand for labor*, other things equal. Figure 4A.3, which depicts a relatively elastic product-demand curve represented by the solid curve D_P and a less elastic one represented by the dashed line D_P' illustrates this "law." The labor-demand curve (D_L) derived from the relatively elastic product demand curve has a flatter slope than, and lies above, the dashed labor-demand curve (D_L')—which implies that at any level of labor usage, the dashed curve is less elastic.[5]

---

[5]Students should satisfy themselves that a demand curve with a steeper slope *could* be more elastic (at a given employment level) than a flatter one *if* it lies above its flatter alternative at that point. This possibility relates to the fact that equal changes in the wage rate represent smaller *percentage* changes at higher wage levels.

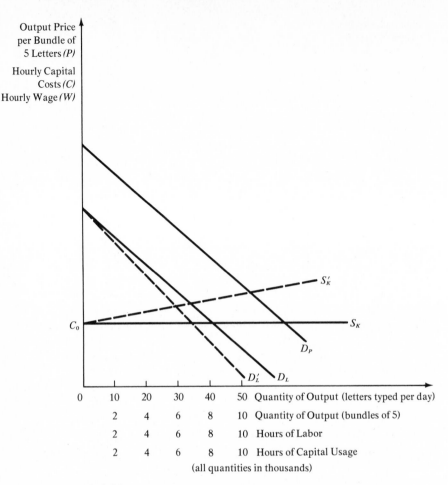

FIGURE 4A.4 The Effect of the Elasticity of Supply of Capital on the Elasticity of Demand for Labor

Next, consider the proposition that *the less elastic is the supply of capital, the less elastic will be the demand for labor* (other things equal). Figure 4A.4 contains two alternative capital supply curves—the perfectly elastic S_K as shown before and a less elastic (dashed) alternative, S_K'. (The product demand curve is held constant.) It is easily seen that D_L, the demand curve consistent with S_K (the perfectly elastic supply-of-capital curve) has a flatter slope than, and lies above, its dashed alternative (D_L'). At each level of employment, then, D_L is more elastic than D_L'.

Finally, consider the law that *when there is no substitution effect, a smaller share of labor in total cost is associated with a less elastic labor demand curve* (other things equal). Figure 4A.5 illustrates this law, showing the product-demand curve (D_P) and two *equally elastic* capital supply curves. When capital is supplied along S_K (at a constant price of C_0), the share of labor in total cost is larger than

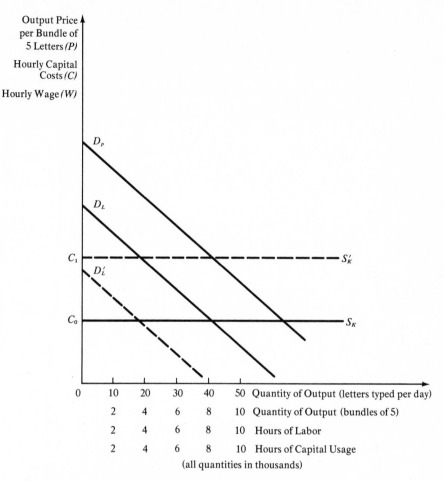

FIGURE 4A.5 The Effects of Labor Share in Total Cost on the Elasticity of Demand for Labor

when a unit of capital costs C_1 (see supply curve S'_K). One can readily see that D_L and D'_L have the same slope (given our assumptions about D_P, S_K and S'_K) but that D'_L lies below D_L at each level of employment. A demand curve with the same slope as one lying above it is the less elastic of the two. Equal changes in wages (at a given employment level) call forth equal absolute and *percentage* changes in employment; however, equal changes in wages represent larger *percentage changes* in wages along the *lower* of the two curves. Since the elasticity of demand for labor is defined as

$$\text{Elasticity of Demand for Labor} = \frac{\% \; \Delta \; \text{Employment}}{\% \; \Delta \; \text{Wages}}, \tag{4A.1}$$

it can easily be seen that the lower of the two demand curves (D'_L in Figure 4A.5) is the less elastic—and is the one associated with the smaller labor share in total costs.[6]

Thus, three of the four laws of derived demand can be geometrically demonstrated if we assume away any substitution effects by assuming a fixed-proportions technology. However, if instead we assume that a substitution effect exists—but now ignore the scale effect—we can better understand why the "law" relating to labor's share does not always hold.

SUBSTITUTION EFFECT BUT NO SCALE EFFECT

In Chapter 4, footnote 6 noted that the "law" relating a smaller labor share with a less elastic demand curve holds only when it is easier for customers to substitute among final products than it is for employers to substitute capital for labor. Since the first half of this appendix assumed that it was *impossible* to substitute capital for labor, this condition was clearly met. To illustrate the reverse condition— where capital/labor substitution can occur but product substitution cannot—we will now work with an example where the product-demand curve is vertical. Consumers will buy the product in the same amounts, no matter what the price; hence, a wage increase will create *no scale effect*. Here we will assume, however, that capital can be substituted for labor.

The version of the labor share "law" that says that a *smaller labor share is associated with a more elastic demand for labor when it is easier to substitute in the production process than among final goods* is true if other things are held constant:

1. the product demand curve, which we assume to be vertical;
2. the supply of capital curve, which we take to be horizontal (perfectly elastic); and
3. the *substitutability* between capital and labor in the production function.

The substitutability of capital and labor can be measured by the *elasticity of substitution*, which is defined as the percentage change in the capital/labor ratio called forth by a one percent change in the ratio of wages to capital costs:

$$\text{Elasticity of Substitution} = \frac{\% \ \Delta \ (K/L)}{\% \ \Delta \ (W/C)} \qquad (4A.2)$$

The elasticity of substitution is clearly a positive number, because as W rises relative to C, capital will be substituted for labor. Expressing substitutability as an elasticity is convenient, because elasticity is measured in units independent of the units in which capital and labor are measured.

Figure 4A.6 displays representative isoquants of two different (industry) production functions. *Both* these production functions have elasticities of substitution

---

[6]Although the share of labor varied in this example because of capital prices, we would obtain the same results if we allowed it to vary for technological reasons (higher ratios of capital to labor that might be required). For example, if *two* units of capital had to be combined with a unit of labor to produce a unit of output, then the required expenditures on capital per unit of output is $2C_0$ (when each capital unit costs C_0).

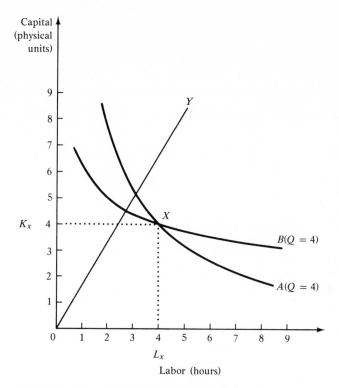

FIGURE 4A.6 Two Production Functions With an Elasticity of Substitution Equal to -1

equal to $+1$. A unitary elasticity of substitution has the property that factor shares remain constant no matter what the relative prices of capital and labor. If wages rise 10 percent relative to capital prices, the use of labor falls 10 percent relative to the use of capital—and labor's share remains constant.[7]

While isoquants *A* and *B* have different shapes, it can be understood (with some work) that their elasticities of substitution are equal. Suppose, for example, that industries A and B were both operating at point *X*, where the capital/labor ratio equals K_X/L_X. Industry A will be at point *X* if wages are relatively high compared to capital costs, while B will be there if wages are relatively low (remember that the marginal rate of technical substitution—as given by the slope of the isoquants—must equal the ratio of *W* to *C*). The equality of the elasticity of substitution for A and B means that if the factor-price ratios in each case change by the same percentage amount, their capital/labor ratios will also change by equal percentages. Since K_X/L_X held for *both* prior to the change in factor price ratios, *K/L after* the change must also be the same. This means that K_A/L_A and K_B/L_B

---

[7]The production functions in Figure 4A.6 are both Cobb-Douglas production functions, meaning they have the form $Q = L^\alpha K^{1-\alpha}$, where $\alpha = $ labor's share and $1-\alpha$ equals capital's share. All Cobb-Douglas production functions have an elasticity of substitution equal to 1. Isoquant *A* is the *Q* $= 4$ isoquant for $Q = L^{0.5} K^{0.5}$. Isoquant *B* is the $Q = 4$ isoquant for $Q = L^{0.25} K^{0.75}$.

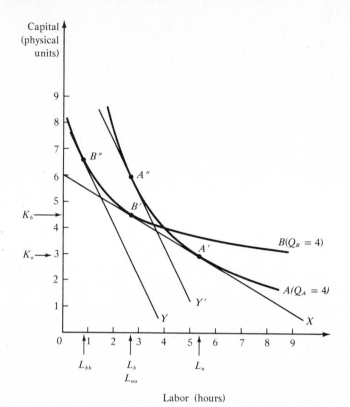

FIGURE 4A.7   **A Smaller Share of Labor in Total Costs Generates a Larger Elasticity of Demand for Labor When the Elasticity of Substitution Between Labor and Capital Exceeds the Elasticity of Product Demand**

after adjustment must lie along the *same ray* passing through the origin of Figure 4A.6. Along a given ray (Y, for example), levels of usage of K and L vary, but the *ratio* of K to L is the same at each point. While the post-adjustment usage of capital and labor will be different in industries A and B, then, the capital/labor *ratios* will be the same if they both start at point X and experience the same *percentage changes* in W/C.

Isoquants A and B are repeated in Figure 4A.7, where it is assumed that the two industries, while having different production functions, face the *same* factor prices. Industry A responds to these factor prices by producing 4 units of output at point A', where the capital/labor ratio is K_a/L_a. Industry B responds by producing its 4 units at point B', where the capital/labor ratio is much higher (at K_b/L_b). Given that factor prices are exactly the same, the share of labor in total cost is much lower in B than A. This can easily be seen using the formula for labor share:

$$\frac{\text{Labor Share in}}{\text{Total Cost}} = \frac{WL}{WL + CK}, \qquad (4A.3)$$

where W and C are the same for each industry, but K/L is much smaller for industry B.

Figure 4A.7 can now be used to analyze the effects of labor share on the elasticity of demand for labor, given a. completely inelastic product demand curves, b. a completely elastic supply of capital, and c. equal elasticities of substitution between K and L. Now suppose that originally W_0 and C_0 were such that isoexpenditure curve X held, but that wages increase to W_1 while C_0 remains constant. This increase in wages tilts the new isoexpenditure curves to Y and Y' — both of which have the same slope of W_1/C_0. Because there is no scale effect, both industries continue producing at $Q = 4$. Industry A moves from a cost-minimizing point of A' to point A'', while B moves from B' to B''. The amount of labor used by A falls from L_a to L_{aa} — a percentage drop of roughly 50 percent as shown in Figure 4A.7. The labor used by B drops by a smaller amount in absolute terms but by a much larger percentage owing to the smaller base; the percentage decrease in B's labor is around 70 percent in the figure. Thus B, with the smaller labor share, has a more elastic demand for labor than does A.

One senses, then, that the exception to the "labor share" law of derived demand is a result of the relatively small initial usage of labor in industries where labor share is also small (other things equal). Given equal elasticities of substitution and no scale effect (or a very small one), a change in the ratio of wages to capital prices will call forth relatively larger percentage changes in employment where labor share is smaller because of the smaller initial level of employment.

5

Extensions of the Theory of Demand

Our analyses of the demand for labor in Chapters 3 and 4, for the most part, ignored the substantial *nonwage* labor costs that exist and the *dynamic* nature of firms' employment decisions. These abstractions allowed us to discuss a number of policy issues in the context of a rather simple model. However, a number of other policy issues can be analyzed only in the context of less restrictive models.

This chapter will begin by discussing the magnitudes and growth of various forms of *nonwage* labor costs, including the costs to firms of hiring and training new employees, the costs of legally required social-insurance programs (such as social security and unemployment compensation), and the costs of privately negotiated fringe benefits (such as health insurance, vacation and sick-leave pay, and private pensions). These costs typically exceed 20 to 30 percent of employers' payroll costs.

This chapter generalizes our model of employers' demand for labor to incorporate decisions about both the numbers of employees to be hired *and* the average length of the work week for these employees. The fact that many of the nonwage labor costs do *not* vary, at the margin, with weekly hours of work explains why employers may decide to regularly work their employees overtime at legally required premium wage rates rather than increasing the level of employment—a phenomenon that has led periodically to the proposal that the legally mandated overtime premium be increased in an effort to discourage employers from authorizing overtime and to encourage them to "spread the work."

Our model of labor demand will also be generalized to explicitly acknowledge the dynamic nature of firms' employment decisions. Employment decisions are often multiperiod in nature. While firms do not always bear the initial costs of employee training, those firms that do must recoup these costs later on. The chapter examines models that incorporate employer-borne hiring and training costs and explores the effects of minimum-wage legislation on teenagers' wage growth, why productivity declines during recessions, and the determinants of voluntary and involuntary labor turnover. The rationales for using hiring standards, such as minimum educational requirements, and for creating internal labor markets are discussed in the context of hiring and training costs.

NONWAGE LABOR COSTS

Although simple textbook models of the labor market often refer to the hourly wage rate paid to workers as the cost of labor, there are in fact substantial *nonwage* labor costs that have important implications for labor market behavior. In general, they fall into two categories: hiring or training costs and fringe benefits.

Hiring and Training Costs

Firms incur substantial costs in hiring and training new employees. *Hiring costs* include all costs involved in advertising positions, screening applicants to evaluate their qualifications, and processing successful applicants who have been offered jobs. One might also include the overhead costs of maintaining employees on the payroll once they have been employed in this category of costs; these costs would include record-keeping costs, the costs of computing and issuing paychecks, and the costs of providing forms to the government (such as W-2 forms to the Internal Revenue Service) about employees' earnings.

New employees typically undergo either formal or informal training and orientation programs. These programs may teach new skills—such as how to use a machine—that directly increase the employees' productive ability. Alternatively, orientation programs may simply provide newcomers with background information on how the firm is structured—such as who to call if a machine breaks down or where the rest room is. Such information, while not changing skill levels, does increase productivity by enabling workers to make more efficient use of time.

Firms incur at least three types of *training costs*:

1. the *explicit* monetary costs of employing individuals to serve as trainers and the costs of materials used up during the training process;
2. the *implicit* or opportunity costs of the trainee's time (while individuals are undergoing training they are not producing as much output as they could if all of their time were devoted to production activities); and
3. the opportunity costs of using capital equipment and experienced employees to do the training in less formal training situations (for example, if training consists solely of an experienced employee demonstrating how he or she does a job to a new recruit, the demonstrator may work at a slower pace than normal).

Because a large share of employers' hiring and training costs are implicit in nature, it is not surprising that detailed estimates of the magnitudes of hiring and training costs in the U.S. economy do not exist. Some estimates for individual firms have been made, however, that suggest that the magnitudes are large. For example, a study conducted by the American Management Association in 1960 concluded that the *hiring* and *orientation* costs of new employees varied from

TABLE 5.1   Compensation of Employees, 1956–1977
(in billions of dollars)

Year	Total	Wages and Salaries (including vacation and holiday pay)	Supplements	Ratio of Supplements to Total (percent)
1956	$ 243.5	$228.3	$ 15.2	6.2
1957	256.5	239.3	17.2	6.7
1958	258.2	240.5	17.7	6.9
1959	279.6	258.9	20.6	7.4
1960	294.9	271.9	23.0	7.8
1961	303.6	279.5	24.1	7.9
1962	325.1	298.0	27.1	8.3
1963	342.9	313.4	29.5	8.6
1964	368.0	336.1	31.8	8.6
1965	396.5	362.0	34.5	8.7
1966	438.3	398.4	40.9	9.3
1967	471.9	427.5	44.4	9.4
1968	519.8	469.5	50.3	9.7
1969	571.4	514.6	56.8	9.9
1970	609.2	546.5	62.7	10.8
1972	715.1	633.8	81.4	11.4
1973	797.7	700.9	96.8	12.1
1974	873.0	763.1	110.0	12.6
1975	931.1	805.9	125.2	13.4
1976	1036.8	890.1	146.7	14.1
1977	1153.4	983.6	169.8	14.7

Notes: "Compensation of Employees" is the income accruing to employees for remuneration for their work.

"Wages & Salaries" consists of the monetary remuneration of employees, including the compensation of corporate officers, commissions, tips, and bonuses, and of payments in kind, which represent income to the recipients.

"Supplements" to wages and salaries consists of employer contributions for social insurance and other labor income. Employer contributions for social insurance comprise employer payments under old-age, survivors, disability, and hospital insurance, state unemployment insurance, railroad retirement and unemployment insurance, government retirement, and a few other minor social insurance programs. Other labor income includes employer contributions to private pension, health and welfare, unemployment, and workers' compensation funds.

SOURCES: U.S. Department of Commerce, Bureau of Economic Analysis, *Business Statistics, 1975*, p. 6; U.S. Department of Commerce, Bureau of Economic Analysis, *Survey of Current Business*, January 1979, p. S–2.

around $200 per unskilled laborer to more than $4500 per engineer.[1] This study did not include estimates of training costs, and the costs that were included are not expressed in terms of today's prices. A 1951 International Harvester Company study did include training costs and estimated that its average *hiring* and *training cost* per employee was about $380;[2] in terms of current prices, this figure would be well over $1000. Each of these estimates must be considered only suggestive, however, because the studies are old, the samples are small, and measuring some of these costs is difficult.

---

[1]See Frederick J. Gaudet, *Labor Turnover: Calculation and Costs* (New York: American Management Association, 1960).

[2]This study is cited in Walter Oi, "Labor As a Quasi-Fixed Factor," *Journal of Political Economy* 70 (December 1962):538–55.

TABLE 5.2   Fringe Benefits as a Percent of Payroll in Manufacturing, 1957–1977

Year	Legally Required Payments (employer's share)	Pensions, Insurance	Paid Rest	Pay for Time Not Worked	Other Items	Total Fringe Benefits
1957	4.1	5.8	2.4	6.5	1.5	20.3
1959	4.5	6.1	2.7	6.7	1.6	21.6
1961	5.5	6.8	2.8	7.2	1.3	23.6
1963	5.9	6.7	2.9	7.3	1.4	24.2
1965	5.3	6.7	2.7	7.2	1.7	23.6
1967	6.4	7.0	3.0	7.3	1.9	25.6
1969	6.8	7.6	3.1	7.8	1.7	27.0
1971	6.9	9.9	3.5	8.6	1.7	30.6
1973	8.3	10.2	3.5	8.5	1.5	32.0
1975	8.8	11.6	3.7	10.1	1.9	36.1
1977	9.3	12.9	3.6	9.2	2.3	37.3

Note: "Payroll" (used as the denominator in calculating the above percentages) includes pay for time not worked, such as vacations and holidays, but does not include pension and insurance costs or payroll taxes. "Other items" includes profit sharing, contributions to thrift plans, bonuses, and employee educational benefits.

SOURCE: U.S. Chamber of Commerce, *Fringe Benefits and Employee Benefits* (various issues).

Fringe Benefits

We have much better data, however, on the other types of *nonwage* labor costs that firms incur. *Fringe benefits* include *legally required* social-insurance contributions and *privately provided* benefits. Examples of legally required benefits are payroll-based payments employers must make to fund programs that compensate workers for unemployment (unemployment insurance), injury (workers' compensation), and retirement (old-age, survivors', disability, and health insurance—or "Social Security"). Examples of privately provided benefits are holiday pay, vacation and sick leave, private pensions, and private health and life insurance.

Tables 5.1 and 5.2 give some idea of the magnitude and growth of these benefits. Department of Commerce data for the nation as a whole, tabulated in Table 5.1, indicate that forms of compensation other than wages and salaries rose from 6.2 percent of total compensation in 1956 to 14.7 percent in 1977. These data understate the importance of nonwage items in total compensation because they include holiday, vacation, and sick pay as wages. A more comprehensive measure, although for a more limited sample, comes from the biennial U.S. Chamber of Commerce survey of large manufacturing establishments. These data, tabulated in Table 5.2, indicate that total fringe benefits as a percent of *payroll* (which does not include pension and insurance costs) rose from 20.3 percent to 37.3 percent during the 1957–77 period.

Both data sets indicate, then, an approximate doubling of the share of fringes in total compensation over the last 25 years or so. This increase has occurred in both legally required employer payments and in privately negotiated benefits. (Chapter 11 will discuss *why* fringe benefits have increased as a fraction of total compensation.)

The Quasi-Fixed Nature of Many Nonwage Costs

The distinction between wage and nonwage costs of employment is important because many nonwage costs are *costs per worker* rather than *costs per hour worked*. That is, many nonwage costs do not vary at the margin with the number of hours an employee works. Economists thus refer to them as *quasi-fixed*—in the sense that once an employee is hired the firm is committed to a cost that does not vary with his or her hours of work.[3]

It should be obvious that hiring and training costs are quasi-fixed; they are associated with each new employee, not with the hours he or she works after the training period. Many fringe costs, however, are also quasi-fixed. For example, in most firms holiday and vacation pay are specified as a fixed number of days per year (which may vary with seniority), and overtime hours do not affect these costs. Or to take another example, an employer's unemployment-insurance payroll-tax liability is specified to be a percentage (the tax rate) of each employee's earnings up until a maximum earnings level (the taxable wage base), which in most states was $6000 in 1980. Since most employees earn more than $6000 per year, having an employee work an additional hour per week will *not* cause any increase in the employer's payroll-tax liability.[4]

The quasi-fixed nature of many nonwage labor costs has important effects on employer hiring and overtime decisions. These effects are discussed below.

THE EMPLOYMENT/HOURS TRADE-OFF

The simple model of the demand for labor presented in the preceding chapters spoke of the quantity of labor demanded and made no distinction between the number of individuals employed by a firm and the average length of its employees' work week. Holding all other inputs constant, however, a firm can produce a given level of output with various combinations of the number of employees hired and the number of hours worked per week. Presumably, increases in the number of employees hired will allow for shorter work weeks, while longer work weeks will allow for fewer employees, other things equal.

In the short run, with capital and all other inputs fixed, the output *(Q)* a firm can produce is related to both its employment level *(M)* and its average work week per employee *(H)* by

$$Q = f(M,H). \tag{5.1}$$

It is reasonable to assume that both inputs in equation (5.1) have positive marginal products $(MP_M > 0; MP_H > 0)$. That is, increasing the number of employees, holding hours constant—or increasing the average work week, holding employment constant—will lead to increases in output. While remaining positive, each of these marginal products must surely decline at some point. In the case where the number of employees is increased this decline may be due to the reduced quantity of capital that each employee will have to work with or the fact that the firm may be forced to employ lower-quality workers. In the case where the hours each employee works per week are increased, the decline in marginal product may

---

[3] *See* Oi, "Labor as a Quasi-Fixed Factor."

[4] This is not true for all fringe benefits. For example, the social security (OASDHI) payroll tax liability of employers is also specified as a percentage of earnings up until a maximum taxable wage base; however, this wage base is considerably higher—$29,000 in 1981. Since this level exceeds the annual earnings of most full-time employees, the employer's payroll tax liability *is* increased when an employer employs a typical employee an additional hour per week.

occur because after some point fatigue sets in.

Given this production function,[5] how does a firm determine its optimal employment/hours combination? Is it ever rational for an employer to work his or her existing employees overtime on a regularly scheduled basis, rather than hiring additional employees?

Determining the Mix of Workers and Hours

The fact that certain labor costs are *not* hour-related and others are makes it important to examine the marginal cost an employer faces when employing an additional *worker* for whatever length work week other employees are working (MC_M). This marginal cost will equal the weekly value of the quasi-fixed labor costs plus the weekly wage and variable (with hours) fringe-benefit costs for the specified length of work week. Similarly, it is important to examine the marginal cost a firm faces when it seeks to increase the *average workweek* of its existing work force by one hour (MC_H). This marginal cost will equal the hourly wage and variable fringe-benefit costs multipled by the number of employees in the work force. Of course, if the employer is in a situation in which an overtime premium (such as time-and-a-half or double time) must be paid for additional hours, that higher rate is the relevant wage rate to use in the latter calculation.

Viewed in this way, a firm's decisions about its optimal employment/hours combination is no different than its decisions about the usage of any two factors of production, which was discussed in Chapter 3. Specifically, to minimize the cost of producing any given level of output, a firm should increase its employment level and its average work week up until the point where spending the last dollar on each yields the same increment to output:

$$\frac{MP_M}{MC_M} = \frac{MP_H}{MC_H} \tag{5.2}$$

Put another way, the marginal cost of hiring an additional employee (MC_M) relative to the marginal cost of working the existing work force an additional hour (MC_H) should be equal to the marginal productivity of an additional employee relative to that of extending the work week by an hour:

$$\frac{MP_M}{MP_H} = \frac{MC_M}{MC_H} \tag{5.3}$$

The Fair Labor Standards Act (FLSA) requires that all employees covered by the legislation receive an overtime pay premium of at least 50 percent of their regular hourly wage (time-and-a-half).[6] Now while a large proportion of overtime

---

[5] For estimates of such a function, *see* Martin Feldstein, "Specification of the Labor Input in the Aggregate Production Function," *Review of Economic Studies* 34 (October 1967):375–86. *See also* Sherwin Rosen, "Short-Run Employment Variation in Class-I Railroads in the U.S., 1947–1967," *Econometrica* 36 (July-October 1968):511–29.

[6] In 1977, approximately 58 percent of all workers were covered by the overtime pay provisions of the FLSA. See U.S. Department of Labor, *Minimum Wage and Maximum Hours Standards under the Fair Labor Standards Act* (Washington, D.C.: U.S. Government Printing Office, October 1978). The major categories of noncovered employees include executive, administrative, and professional personnel, outside salespersons, most state and local government employees, and agricultural workers.

hours are worked because of disequilibrium phenomena—such as rush orders, seasonal demand, mechanical failures, and absenteeism—a substantial amount of overtime appears to be regularly scheduled. Equation (5.3) indicates why this scheduling of overtime may occur. Although overtime hours require premium pay, they also enable an employer to avoid the quasi-fixed employment costs associated with employing an additional worker. This point can be illustrated by considering what would happen if the overtime-wage premium were to be increased.

Policy Analysis: The Overtime-Pay Premium

Periodically, proposals have been introduced in Congress to raise the overtime premium to double time.[7] The argument made to support such an increase is that even though unemployment remains a pressing national problem, the use of overtime hours has not diminished. Moreover, the argument continues, the deterrent effect of the overtime premium on the use of overtime has been weakened since the FLSA was enacted because of the growing share of hiring and training costs, fringe benefits, and government-mandated insurance premiums in total compensation (see Tables 5.1 and 5.2). As already noted, many of these costs are *quasi-fixed*—or employee-related rather than hours-related—and thus do not vary with overtime hours of work. An increase in them increases employers' marginal costs of hiring new employees relative to the costs of working their existing work forces overtime.

In terms of equation (5.3), the increase in quasi-fixed costs that has occurred causes an inequality between the ratio of marginal productivities and marginal costs at the old equilibrium employment/hours combination:

$$\frac{MP_M}{MP_H} < \frac{MC_M}{MC_H} \tag{5.4}$$

To restore the equality (and to thus minimize costs) requires increasing the left-hand side of equation (5.4). Given our assumptions of diminishing marginal productivities, if output were to remain constant, employment would have to be reduced and hours worked per employee would have to increase. It is claimed, therefore, that the growth of these quasi-fixed costs has been at least partially responsible for increased usage of overtime hours and that an increase in the overtime premium is required to better "spread the work."[8] Such an increase, by raising the marginal cost of overtime hours relative to the marginal cost of hiring new workers, should induce employers to substitute new employees for the overtime hours employers might otherwise schedule.

Would an increase in the overtime premium prove to be an effective way of

---

[7] One recent attempt was made by Congressman John Conyers of Michigan in HR 1784, introduced into Congress in February of 1979. To quote a supporter of the proposal, "The AFL-CIO endorses the double-time provision as a means of generating additional jobs. The evidence is persuasive that the overtime pay requirements of the Fair Labor Standards Act have lost their effectiveness as a deterrent to regularly scheduled overtime work." (See the statement by Rudolph Oswald, Director of Research, AFL-CIO, in the minutes of the Hearings before the Subcommittee on Labor Standards on HR 1784, October 23, 1979.)

[8] Average weekly overtime hours of work in manufacturing averaged 2.56 hours per employee between 1956 and 1963. However, over the 1964–1977 period, the average rose to 3.34 hours per employee, an increase of more than 30 percent.

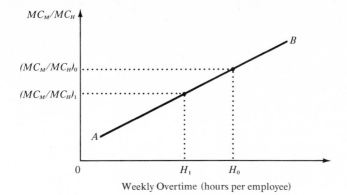

FIGURE 5.1   Simulating the Effect of an Increase in the Overtime Premium to Double Time

increasing employment and reducing unemployment? A number of economists have sought to answer this question. Although the overtime premium is, for the most part, legislatively fixed at a point in time, the ratio MC_M/MC_H varies across establishments because the weekly quasi-fixed costs and the straight-time wage rate vary across establishments. Economists have attempted to estimate the extent to which the usage of overtime hours varies across establishments with the ratio MC_M/MC_H, when all other factors are held constant.[9]

Once this relationship is known, it is possible to simulate what the effect of an increase in the overtime premium would be on overtime hours per employee. For example, suppose that the statistical analyses indicated that the relationship between overtime hours and MC_M/MC_H was given by the line AB in Figure 5.1. Consider a representative firm that faced relative marginal costs $(MC_M/MC_H)_0$ and whose employees worked an average of H_0 overtime hours per week. It is a simple matter to compute the effect on the relative marginal cost of an increase in the overtime premium to double time. If an increased premium caused a decrease to $(MC_M/MC_H)_1$, overtime hours would correspondingly fall to H_1.

Now if one *assumes* that *all* of the reduction in overtime would be converted to new full-time positions, it is possible to estimate what the effect on the employment level would be. The implied results from these studies appear in Table 5.3; these results suggest that employment increases in the range of 0.3 to 4.0 percent would result. At first glance, then, increasing the overtime premium to double time does seem like an effective way of increasing employment and reducing unemployment.

A complete economic analysis, however, suggests that such a conclusion would be an overly optimistic assessment of the effects of a double-time premium.[10] First, these estimates *assume* that the demand for *total* labor hours is completely inelastic with respect to its cost. That is, they ignore the fact that an

---

[9]Since hiring- and training-costs data are not available, these studies utilize data on the other fringe benefits only.

[10]*See* Ronald G. Ehrenberg and Paul L. Schumann, *Longer Hours or More Jobs? An Investigation of Amending Hours Legislation to Create Employment* (Ithaca, N.Y.: New York State School of Industrial and Labor Relations, 1982).

TABLE 5.3 Estimated Changes in Full-Time Employment Resulting From Increasing the Overtime Premium from Time-and-a-Half to Double Time

Study	Group	Absolute Change	Percentage Change
Ehrenberg (1971)	1966 manufacturing production workers	+218,500	+1.6
Nussbaum and Wise (1977)	1968 manufacturing production workers	+491,400	+3.7
	1970 manufacturing production workers	+487,700	+3.7
	1972 manufacturing production workers	+361,900	+2.8
	1974 manufacturing production workers	+549,700	+4.0
	1968–1974 pooled manufacturing interindustry data	+320,000	+2.0
Solnick and Swimmer (1978)	1972 private nonfarm nonsupervisory workers (low estimate)	+159,264	+0.3
	1972 private nonfarm nonsupervisory workers (high estimate)	+1,521,664	+3.1

SOURCES: Ronald G. Ehrenberg, "The Impact of the Overtime Premium on Employment and Hours in U.S. Industry, "*Western Economic Journal* 19 (June 1971): 199–207; Joyce Nussbaum and Donald Wise, "The Employment Impact of the Overtime Provisions of the FLSA" (Final Report submitted to the U.S. Department of Labor, 1977); Loren Solnick and Gene Swimmer, "Overtime and Fringe Benefits—A Simultaneous Equations Approach" (mimeograph, 1978).

increase in the overtime premium raises the average cost of hiring labor (even if overtime is eliminated), and that this may induce a shift to more capital-intensive methods of production. Further, to the extent that the cost increase is passed on to consumers in the form of higher prices, a reduction in the quantity of output will occur. Both these _scale_ and _substitution effects_ should lead to a decline in the number of labor hours purchased by employers; this decline will limit the employment gain associated with any given decline in overtime hours.

Second, these estimates ignore the responses of currently employed workers who would be simultaneously faced with an increase in the overtime premium and a reduction in their hours of work. Although we have yet to discuss the supply side of the labor market in detail, it should be obvious that one possible response to a reduction in overtime hours is for them to _moonlight_—to seek part-time second jobs. Moonlighting would be more likely to occur if the increase in the premium resulted in a decrease in their labor earnings.[11] If increased moonlighting occurred, the creation of new jobs for the unemployed would be further reduced.

Third, these estimates assume that the skill distributions of the unemployed and of those who work overtime are sufficiently similar to permit all of the reduction in overtime to be converted into new full-time employment. However, _if_ those working overtime were primarily skilled workers and the unemployed were primarily unskilled, potential employment gains from raising the overtime premium might be considerably smaller than these estimates.

Finally, these estimates assume that the overtime-pay provisions of the FLSA are fully complied with and that they would continue to be fully complied with after an increase in the premium to double time. However, since an increase in the overtime premium would increase the amount employers save by _not_ comply-

---

[11]Formally, this would occur if employers' demand curves for overtime hours were elastic with respect to the overtime wage.

ing with the legislation, such an increase may well lead to a reduced compliance rate, which would further reduce the positive employment effects of the legislation. A number of studies indicate that noncompliance with the overtime-pay provisions is currently at least in the 10 percent range.[12] That is, at least 10 percent of the individuals working overtime who are covered by the FLSA *fail* to receive a premium of at least time-and-a-half. Hence, the possibility of increased noncompliance cannot be dismissed.

Our analysis of the wisdom of increasing the overtime premium to double time, as a means of stimulating employment growth, unfortunately reminds us that policy analysis is never as easy as one might initially hope it would be. The world is complex and any complete analysis of a policy issue must consider a number of factors. It is in identifying what factors to consider that economic theory is so useful. Indeed, in the present case, even though the *initial* simulations suggested that a double-time premium would lead to an increase in employment, consideration of the *other* factors noted above led to a recommendation against such an overtime premium.[13]

HIRING AND TRAINING COSTS AND THE DEMAND FOR LABOR

The models of the demand for labor given in Chapters 3 and 4 were *static,* in the sense that they considered only *current* marginal productivities and *current* labor costs. If all of a firm's labor costs are variable each year, then clearly it will employ labor in *each period* to the point where labor's marginal product equals the real wage.

However, once we begin to consider hiring and training costs, the analysis changes somewhat.[14] Hiring and training costs are usually heavily concentrated in the initial periods of employment and then do not recur. Later on, however, these early "investments" in hiring and training raise the productivity of employees. Once having made the investment, it is cheaper for the firm to *continue* hiring its previous workers than to hire, at the same wage rate, new ones (who would have to be trained). Likewise, with an investment required for all *new* workers, employers will have to consider not only *current* marginal productivity and labor costs but also *future* marginal productivity and labor costs in deciding whether (and how many) to hire. In short, the presence of investment costs—hiring and training expenses—means that hiring decisions must take into account past, present, and future factors.

To illustrate the hiring decision in the face of labor-investment costs, let us consider a firm that is seeking to determine its employment level over a two-period horizon. Suppose the firm incurs hiring and training costs only in the first

---

[12]See Ehrenberg and Schumann, *Longer Hours or More Jobs?*

[13]Ronald G. Ehrenberg, "The Impact of the Overtime Premium on Employment and Hours in U.S. Industry," *Western Economic Journal* 19 (June 1971): 199–207.

[14]This section draws heavily on Gary Becker's pioneering work, *Human Capital,* 2nd ed. (New York: National Bureau of Economic Research, 1975); and on Oi, "Labor as a Quasi-Fixed Factor."

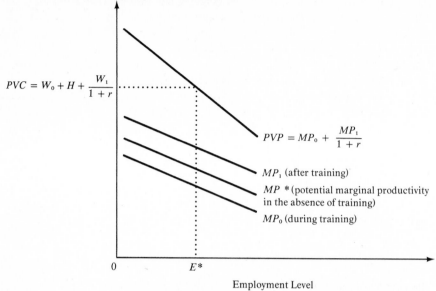

Marginal Product of Labor *(MP)*
Present Value of Marginal Product of Labor *(PVP)*
Present Value of Real Marginal Cost of Labor *(PVC)*

$$PVC = W_0 + H + \frac{W_1}{1 + r}$$

$$PVP = MP_0 + \frac{MP_1}{1 + r}$$

MP_1 (after training)

MP *(potential marginal productivity in the absence of training)*

MP_0 (during training)

0

E^*

Employment Level

FIGURE 5.2   Multiperiod Demand for Labor

period (period 0) and that these *direct outlays* amount to $H per worker. Suppose also that during the initial period, when workers are undergoing training, their actual marginal product schedule is lowered from MP^* to MP_0 (as shown in Figure 5.2)—in other words, $MP^* - MP_0$ represents the *implicit* costs of training. In the period after training (period 1), the marginal productivity of trained employees is higher (MP_1). Finally, suppose that the wage a firm must pay each employee is W_0 and W_1 in periods 0 and 1, respectively; for now, we take these wages as given by the market, although we will shortly examine how they are determined.

The Concept of Present Value

In determining its optimal employment level over the two periods, the firm clearly must consider the costs of employing workers in both periods and their marginal products in both periods. A *naive* approach would be to simply add up the costs $(W_0 + W_1 + H)$, add up the marginal products $(MP_0 + MP_1)$, and then stop hiring when the sum of the marginal products that the last worker produces over the two periods is just equal to the sum of his or her wages and hiring and training costs. This approach is naive because it ignores the fact that benefits accruing in the future are worth less to the firm than an equal level of benefits that accrue now. Similarly, costs that occur in the future are less burdensome to the firm than equal dollar costs that occur in the present.

Why should this be the case? The answer hinges on the role of interest rates. A dollar of revenue earned by a firm today can be invested at some market rate of interest so that by the second period it will be worth more than a dollar. Hence, faced with a choice of employing a worker whose marginal product is 5 in period 0 and 2 in period 1, or a worker whose marginal product is 2 in period 0 and 5 in period 1, the firm would prefer the former (if wages for the two workers were equal in each period). The sooner the product is produced and sold the quicker the firm can gain access to the funds, invest them, and earn interest.[15] Similarly, faced with the option of paying a $100 wage bill today or $100 next period, the firm should prefer the second option. It could earn interest on the $100 in the first period, make the payment in the next period, and have the interest left over. If the firm had made the payment in the initial period, it would not have had the opportunity to earn interest income.

These examples illustrate that firms prefer benefit streams in which the benefits occur as early as possible and prefer cost streams in which the costs occur as late as possible. But how do we compare different benefit and cost streams when benefits and costs occur in more than one period? Economists rely on the concept of *present value,* which we define to be the value *now* of an entire stream of benefits or costs.

Suppose a firm receives the sum of B_0 in the current period and will receive nothing in the next period. How much money could it have in the second period if it invested B_0 at a rate of interest that equals r? It would have its original sum, B_0, plus the interest it earned, rB_0:

$$B_1 = B_0 (1 + r). \tag{5.5}$$

Since assets of B_1 can be automatically acquired by investing B_0 at the market rate of interest, B_0 *now* and B_1 *next period are equivalent values.* That is, a person who is offered B_0 now or B_1 in one year would regard the offers as exactly the same as long as $B_1 = B_0 (1 + r)$.

Following this line of reasoning, suppose that the firm knows it will receive B_1 in the second period. What is the value of that sum to the firm in the first period? The firm would need to have sum X in the first period in order to invest this sum and wind up with principal plus interest equal to B_1 in period 2:

$$X (1 + r) = B_1 \tag{5.6}$$

Dividing both sides by $(1 + r)$,

$$X = \frac{B_1}{1 + r} \tag{5.7}$$

The quantity X in equation (5.7) is called the *discounted value* of B_1 earned one period in the future.

The *present value* of the firm's earnings over two periods is equal to its earnings in the first period plus the discounted value of its earnings in the second period.[16] Returning to our two-period hiring decision example given at the start of this section, the *present value* of marginal productivity *(PVP)* can now be seen as

---

[15]We are assuming here, of course, that the real price the firm receives for its product is constant and that the real rate of interest is positive.

[16]Earnings in the first period are not discounted because they are received *now,* not in the future.

$$PVP = MP_0 + \frac{MP_1}{1 + r}. \tag{5.8}$$

That is, the value of a worker's marginal productivity *now* to the firm is the marginal productivity in the current period (MP_0) plus the marginal productivity in the second period *discounted* by $(1 + r)$. Likewise, the present value of the real marginal *cost* of labor *(PVC)* is equal to

$$PVC = W_0 + H + \frac{W_1}{1 + r}, \tag{5.9}$$

where r is the market rate of interest. W_0 and H are not discounted because they are incurred in the current period. However, W_1 is discounted by $(1 + r)$ because it is incurred one year into the future.

The present value calculation reduces a stream of benefits or costs to a single number that summarizes a firm's entire stream of revenues or liabilities over different time periods. For example, the *PVC* can be thought of as the answer to the question, "Given that a firm incurs costs of $\$(W_0 + H)$ this period and $\$W_1$ next period per worker, how much does it have to set aside today to be able to cover both periods' costs?" The *PVC* is *less* than $W_0 + H + W_1$, because W_1 is not owed until the second period, and any funds set aside to cover W_1 can be invested now. If it sets aside $\$W_1/(1 + r)$ to cover its labor cost in the next period, and invests this amount earning a rate of return r, the interest, $r[W_1/(1 + r)]$, plus principal, $W_1/(1 + r)$, available in the next period will just equal W_1. Similarly, the *PVP* can be thought of as the answer to the question, "Given that a worker's marginal product will be MP_0 in this period and MP_1 next period, what is the value of that output stream to the employer today?" The *PVP* is less than $MP_0 + MP_1$ because if the firm were to attempt to borrow against the employee's future marginal product, it could borrow at most $MP_1/(1 + r)$ today and still afford to repay the principal plus interest, $r[MP_1/(1 + r)]$, out of earnings in the second period.[17]

The Demand for Labor

The concept of present value can help clarify what determines the demand-for-labor function in our two-period model. Rather than focusing on the marginal product of labor in each period, an employee's productivity must be summarized by the *present value* of the marginal-product schedule, which is drawn as the

---

[17]More generally, if the firm expects to receive benefits of $B_0, B_1, B_2, \ldots, B_n$ dollars over the current and next n periods, and if it faces the same interest rate, r, in each period, its present value of benefits *(PVB)* is given by

$$PVB = B_0 + \frac{B_1}{1 + r} + \frac{B_2}{(1 + r)^2} + \frac{B_3}{(1 + r)^3} + \cdots + \frac{B_n}{(1 + r)^n}$$

An analogous expression exists for the present value of costs. The reader should make sure that he or she understands why the denominator of B_2 is $(1 + r)^2$, the denominator of B_3 is $(1 + r)^3$, etc. If one thinks in terms of a series of one-period loans or investments, it should become obvious. For example, X_0 invested for one period yields $X_0(1 + r)$ at the end of the period. Let us call $X_0(1 + r) = X_1$. X_0 invested for two periods is equal to its value after one period (X_1) times $(1 + r)$—or $X_2 = X_1(1 + r)$. But $X_1 = X_0(1 + r)$, so $X_2 = X_0(1 + r)^2$. To find the present value of X_2 we divide by $(1 + r)^2$, so that $X_0 = X_2/(1 + r)^2$.

curve *PVP* in Figure 5.2. Similarly, rather than focusing on the hiring and training costs and the wage rates in each period separately, an employer must consider the *present value* of the marginal cost of labor *(PVC)*. To maximize its present value of profits, a firm should employ labor up until the point that adding an *additional* employee yields as much as it costs (when both yields and costs are stated as present values):

$$PVP = PVC, \text{ or } MP_0 + \frac{MP_1}{1 + r} = W_0 + H + \frac{W_1}{1 + r} \tag{5.10}$$

Given the particular values of W_0, W_1, H, and r that are specified in Figure 5.2, this proves to be the employment level E^*. More generally, the employer's demand-for-labor schedule coincides with the present value of the marginal-product-of-labor schedule.

Now equation (5.10) merely states the familiar profit-maximizing condition— that marginal returns should equal marginal costs—in a multiperiod context. If H were zero, for example, equation (5.10) implies that profits could be maximized when labor is hired so that $MP_0 = W_0$ and $MP_1/(1 + r) = W_1/(1 + r)$—or, since $1 + r$ is the denominator on both sides of the equation, $MP_1 = W_1$. Thus, when H is zero and there are no hiring or training costs, the conditions demonstrated in Chapter 3 are sufficient to guarantee profit maximization in the multiperiod context. However, when H is positive—which means that firms make initial investments in their workers—the conditions for maximizing profits change.

To understand the change in profit-maximizing conditions suggested by equation (5.10), suppose that in the first period the wage the worker receives (W_0) plus the firm's direct outlays (H) exceed the extra worker's output (MP_0). We can call this difference the *net cost* to the firm of hiring an additional worker in the first period (NC_0):

$$NC_0 = W_0 + H - MP_0 > 0 \tag{5.11}$$

In order for the firm to maximize the present value of its profit stream, it must thus get a net *surplus* in the second period—see equation (5.10). If it does not, the firm will not have any incentives to hire the additional worker.

The discounted value of the second period's surplus (G) is defined as:

$$G = \frac{MP_1}{1 + r} - \frac{W_1}{1 + r} = \frac{MP_1 - W_1}{1 + r} \tag{5.12}$$

From equations (5.10), (5.11), and (5.12), we see that the discounted value of the second-period surplus must equal the net cost (NC_0) in the first period if the firm is to maximize profits:

$$W_0 + H - MP_0 = \frac{MP_1 - W_1}{1 + r} \tag{5.13}$$

A second-period surplus can *only* exist if wages in that period (W_1) lie *below* marginal product (MP_1). This surplus makes up for the fact that the employer's labor costs in the first period $(W_0 + H)$ were above the worker's marginal product (MP_0).

–To this point we have established two things. First, equation (5.10) has shown that in a multi-period model of labor demand, the firm's demand curve is the same thing as the curve representing the *present value* of labor's marginal product over the periods of hire. Thus, the firm maximizes profits when the present value of its marginal labor costs equals the present value of labor's marginal product. Second, we demonstrated in equation (5.13), that maximizing profits when the firm's labor costs in the first period exceed the worker's first-period marginal product requires wages in the second period to be below marginal productivity in the second period (so that a surplus is generated). The only situations in which a second-period surplus is not necessary to induce the hiring of an additional employee are a. where investment costs *(H)* are zero in the first period, or b. where investment costs of *H* exist, but the first-period wage is decreased to such an extent that it equals $MP_0 - H$. In this latter case, employees pay for their own training by accepting a wage in the first period that is decreased by the direct costs of training. Understanding how W_0 and W_1 are determined, then, is central to the task of analyzing the demand for labor in the presence of investment costs. To understand the level and time profile of wages, however, we must first examine the nature of job training.

General and Specific Training

Following Gary Becker, it is useful to conceptually distinguish between two types of training: 1. *general training* that increases an individual's productivity *to many employers* equally and 2. *specific training* that increases an individual's productivity *only at the firm* in which he or she is currently employed.[18] Pure general training might include teaching an applicant basic reading skills or teaching a would-be secretary how to type. Pure specific training might include teaching a worker how to use a machine that is unique to a single employer—or showing him or her the organization of the production process in the plant. The distinction is primarily a conceptual one, because most training contains aspects of both types; however, the distinction does yield some interesting insights.

Suppose (continuing our two-period model) that a firm offers *general* training to its employees and incurs a first-period net cost equal to NC_0 of equation (5.11). This training increases employee marginal productivity to MP_1 in the second period, and the firm scales its wages (W_1) in the second period so that there is a surplus in that period whose present value *(G)* equals NC_0. What will happen? The trained employee is worth MP_1 to several other firms, but is getting paid less than MP_1 by the firm doing the training (so that it can obtain the required surplus). The employee can thus get *more* from some other employer—who did not incur training costs and thus will not demand a surplus—than he or she can from the employer offering the training. This situation will induce the employee to quit after training and seek work elsewhere. Assuming all other conditions of employment are the same, the firm would have to pay its employees MP_1 after training to keep them from quitting.

If firms must pay a wage equal to MP_1 after training, they will not be willing to pay for general training of their employees. They either will not offer training or will force the trainees to bear the full cost of their own training by paying

---

[18]Becker, *Human Capital.*

wages that are less than marginal product in the period of training by an amount equal to the direct training costs (that is, NC_0 must equal zero). Exceptions to this conclusion can be found in cases where the employee is bound to the firm in some way. For example, the federal government requires employees it has sent to college (in Master of Business Administration programs, for example) to remain in the federal service for a specified number of years or to repay the costs of the training. Similarly, firms may offer to pay for the general training of long-term employees bound to the firm by pension rights or unique promotion opportunities (see Chapter 11 for further discussion).

In contrast, consider an individual who receives *specific training* that increases marginal productivity with the *current* employer to MP_1 in the second period. Since the training is firm-specific, the trainee's marginal product in *other* firms remains at its pretraining level of MP^*. Now the firm that trains the worker *will* have an incentive to offer (and at least partially pay for) the job training, because it can pay a wage above MP^* but below MP_1 in the second period.

Why will it pay above MP^* in the second period? It will do so because if it makes a first-period investment in the worker it does not want the worker to quit. If it pays MP^*, the worker will not have much of an incentive to stay with the firm, since he or she can get MP^* elsewhere too. The higher W_1 is compared to MP^*, the less likely the worker is to quit. Why will the firm pay less than MP_1? As noted earlier, the firm must obtain a surplus in the second period to recoup its first-period investment costs. Thus, the firm prefers *a second-period* wage that is above MP^* and below MP_1:

$$MP^* < W_1 < MP_1 \tag{5.14}$$

This second-period wage is also preferred by employees. If, for example, they were promised a wage equal to MP_1 in the second period, the lack of employer surplus would mean two things. First, employees would be required to pay the *full* cost of training in the first period, and, second, they would live in fear of being laid-off. Since their second-period wage would be equal to their marginal productivity, a firm would not lose much if it laid them off—and *the workers* would lose all of the investment costs incurred in the first period. However, if the workers generate a surplus for the employer, layoff is less likely in the post-training period.

The wage scheme in equation (5.14) thus suggests that both employer and employee should be willing to share in the costs of specific training. If employees bear *all* of the costs of training, then there will be no second-period surplus to protect them from layoff. If employers bear *all* of the costs, they may not be able to pay their employees enough in the second period to guard against their quitting. It is in their *mutual* interest to foster a long-term employment relationship, which can best be done by sharing the investment costs of the first period.

Implications of the Theory

Layoffs.   One major implication of the presence of specific training is the above-mentioned reluctance of firms to lay off workers in whom they have invested. We have seen that in the post-training period, wages must be less than marginal pro-

Example 5.1
Paternalism in Japan—Is It Rooted in Feudalism or Economics?

In Japan there are many large firms in which employer and employee are mutually committed to a virtual lifetime relationship. These firms almost never lay off workers, and all of their new hires have recently left school. Employees, on the other hand, are given incentives to remain with the firm for their entire career. Wages are strongly linked to seniority, pensions and paid vacations are formulated to encourage a long job tenure, and company loyalty is encouraged through the provision of "paternalistic services," such as company housing, health care, and recreational facilities. James Abegglen describes the consequences of these employment policies:

> At whatever level of organization in the Japanese factory, the worker commits himself on entrance to the company for the remainder of his working career. The company will not discharge him even temporarily except in the most extreme circumstances. He will not quit the company for industrial employment elsewhere. He is a member of the company in a way resembling that in which persons are members of families . . .

While the paternalistic employment relationship described above really pertains to less than half of all Japanese workers—full-time, year-round, predominantly male workers in large firms—the mere existence of such a seemingly permanent employer-employee attachment for so many workers in Japan has drawn much comment. Abegglen views this lifelong relationship as a natural outgrowth of Japan's feudal system prior to industrial development, with its emphasis on the reciprocal loyalty of lord and vassal:

> The loyalty of the worker to the industrial organization, the paternal methods of motivating and rewarding the worker, the close involvement of the company in all manner of what seem to Western eyes to be personal and private affairs of the worker—all have parallels with Japan's preindustrial social organization.

Adherents of this explanation seem to conclude that the Japanese system of industrial relations represents a continuation of an ancient elitist paternalism rather than a system that was consciously chosen for economic reasons by rational industrialists.

An alternative view is that the Japanese system described above finds its roots in profit-maximization calculus. Those who espouse this view argue that Japan's rapid industrialization beginning around 1900 was accompanied by severe shortages of skilled factory workers. Firms competed against each other for skilled labor, and by the end of World War I this fierce competition for workers had led to annual turnover rates of 100 percent for many factories. By 1917 firms were using bribes, cash bonuses, and even physical threats to secure and retain a work force. A government report in 1919 lamented, "The virtue of long and diligent service has been supplanted by a propensity to change jobs."

Faced with such a high degree of employee turnover, firms did not find it profitable to train their own workers; these workers would be gone before they could recoup their investment costs. To reduce the need for constant recruiting, and to induce employees to have long enough job attachments to make training feasible, firms began to offer cash bonuses, company-paid pleasure trips, and shares of company profits to long-term workers. Company housing was provided, and firms took an active interest in improving the quality of worker life both on and off the job. While the "loose" labor markets of the early 1930s provided a setback, industrial growth and attendant labor shortages both during and after World War II fostered the growth of the Japanese system of paternalism throughout the economy. Advocates of this alternative view of Japan's paternalism, such as Koji Taira, argue that the paternalistic system is based more in the need of employers to protect training investments than in feudal tradition.

SOURCES: James C. Abegglen, *The Japanese Factory: Aspects of Its Social Organization* (Glencoe, Ill.: The Free Press, 1958); Clark Kerr, *Industrialization and Industrial Man* (Cambridge, Mass.: Harvard University Press, 1960); Koji Taira, *Economic Development and the Labor Market in Japan* (New York: Columbia University Press, 1970).

---

ductivity if the firm is to have any incentives at all to bear some of the initial training costs. This gap between MP_1 and W_1 provides protection against employee layoffs—even in a recession.

Suppose a recession were to occur and cause product demand to fall. The marginal productivity associated with each employment level would fall (from MP' to MP'' in Figure 5.3). For workers whose wage was equal to marginal productivity before the recession, this fall would reduce their marginal productivity to *below* their wage—and profit-maximizing employers would reduce employment, as shown in panel (a) of Figure 5.3, in order to maximize profits under the changed market conditions. In terms of Figure 5.3(a), employment would fall from E' to E''.

For a worker whose wage was *less* than marginal productivity—owing to past specific training—the decline in marginal productivity might *still* leave such productivity *above* the wage. Firms would not be making enough surplus in the second period to earn back their net labor costs incurred during the training period. However, these costs have already been spent and they cannot get them back. They will not hire and train *new* workers, but neither will they fire the ones they have trained. After all, these trained workers are still generating more than the company is paying them, and to lay them off would only reduce profits further! Thus, as panel (b) of Figure 5.3 shows, workers in whom their employers have invested are shielded to some extent from being laid off in business downturns. Of course, if marginal productivity fell to the point where it was below the wage, even trained workers might be laid off.[19]

Thus, this model suggests that during an economic downswing firms will have

---

[19]If the downturn is expected to be short, and if marginal productivity is not too much below the wage, firms might not lay off workers and chance losing them. Why any adjustment would come in the form of layoffs rather than by workers temporarily reducing their wages is discussed in Chapter 15.

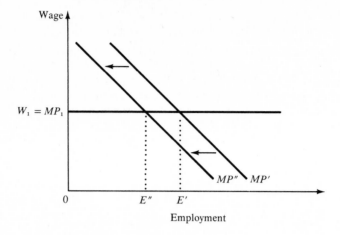

(a) General Training
(a decline in *MP* will reduce employment
for those whose wage = MP_1 initially)

(b) Specific Training
(a decline in *MP* will not necessarily reduce employment
for those whose wage $< MP_1$ initially)

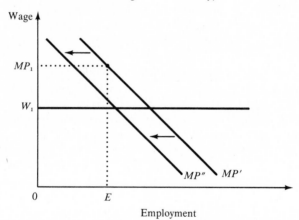

**FIGURE 5.3   The Effect of a Decline in Demand on Employment
with General and Specific Training**

an incentive to lay off workers with either no training or with general training but
that it may prove profitable for firms to retain workers who have specific training.
Although it is difficult to estimate the extent to which workers have specific training "imbedded" in them, there is some evidence that layoffs are lower for workers with higher skill levels, holding all other things including their *wage rates*
constant.[20] Since the divergence between skill (productivity) and wages during the

---

[20] For a summary of the evidence, see Donald O. Parsons, "Models of Labor Market Turnover: A
Theoretical and Empirical Survey" in Ronald G. Ehrenberg, ed., *Research in Labor Economics,*
vol. 1 (Greenwich, Conn.: JAI Press, 1977). Parsons also provides evidence on the existence of
a negative relationship beween quit rates and specific training; as noted earlier, this is another
implication of the theory.

post-training period can be taken as a measure of the extent of specific training, this finding provides some support for the theory.

Labor productivity. A second phenomenon our revised theory of demand can help explain is the fall in average productivity—output per labor hour—that occurs in the early stages of a recession.[21] As demand and output start to fall, firms that have invested in specific training respond by maintaining their specifically trained workers on their payrolls. Such *labor hoarding* causes measured productivity to fall. Of course, the converse of this result is that when demand picks up, firms can increase their output levels without proportionately increasing their employment levels because they, in effect, maintained an *inventory* of skilled labor. Labor hoarding due to specific investments in human capital thus causes average productivity to increase in the early stages of a cyclical expansion and decrease in the early stages of a recession.

Minimum wage effects again. A third implication of our theory has to do with "training" effects of the minimum wage. We have seen that firms will offer *general* training only if the employee fully pays for it. For this to be the case, the employee must receive a first-period wage that is below actual marginal productivity by an amount equal to the direct costs of training. If the minimum wage is set so that receiving such a low wage is precluded, then employers will not offer them training. They may be willing to *hire* workers—if the minimum wage is not above their marginal productivity—but any training would have to take place off the job.

This same analysis would also hold for *specific* training. If the minimum wage prevented the *first* period wage from going low enough, firms offering specific training might *not* be able to offer *second* period wages that are higher than workers' alternative offers. If this is the case, trained workers will always be on the verge of quitting in the second period—which places the firm's first period investment at risk. Under these conditions, firms will have little incentive to offer specific training. Minimum-wage legislation may thus reduce the number of jobs offering training options that are available to low-skilled youths and lower their rates of wage growth. In fact, there is some preliminary evidence that this has occurred.[22]

CREDENTIALS OR SCREENING DEVICES AND THE INTERNAL LABOR MARKET

The addition of hiring and training costs and other quasi-fixed costs of labor into models of labor demand has been shown in this chapter to lead to numerous insights about firms' employment-hours decisions and about the demand for labor in a multiperiod setting. This final section will sketch several additional extensions

---

[21]*See* the 1977 *Employment and Training Report of the President* (Washington, D.C.: U.S. Government Printing Office, 1977), pp. 23–25.

[22]Linda Leighton and Jacob Mincer, "Effects of Minimum Wages on Human Capital Formation," National Bureau of Economic Research, Working Paper No. 441, February 1980.

of these multiperiod models, including the use of credentials or other screening devices and the internal labor market.

Credentials or Screening Devices

Since firms often bear the costs of hiring and training workers, it is in their interests to make these costs as low as possible. Other things equal, firms should prefer to obtain a given quality work force at the least possible cost. Similarly, they should prefer to hire workers who are fast at learning because such workers could be trained at less cost. Unfortunately, it may prove expensive for firms to extensively investigate the backgrounds of every possible individual who applies for a job to ascertain his or her skill level and ability to undertake training.

One way to reduce these costs is to rely on *credentials,* or *signals,* in the hiring process rather than intensively investigating the qualities of individual applicants.[23] For example, if *on average* college graduates are more productive than high-school graduates, an employer might specify that a college degree is a requirement for the job. Rather than interviewing and testing all applicants to try to ascertain the productivity of each, the firm may simply select its new employees from the pool of applicants who meet this educational standard. Similarly, if employers believe that married men are less likely to quit their jobs than single men, or that 25-year-olds are less likely to quit than teenagers, they may give preferential treatment to married men and 25-year-olds over single men and teenagers in their hiring decisions.

Such forms of *statistical discrimination*—judging individuals by *group* characteristics—have obvious costs. On the one hand, for example, there may be some high-school graduates who are fully qualified to work for a firm that insists on college graduates. The exclusion of them from the pool of potential applicants imposes costs on them (they do not get the job); however, it also imposes costs on the employer *if* other qualified applicants cannot be readily found. On the other hand, there may be some "lemons" among the group of college graduates, and if the employer hires them he may well suffer losses while they are employed. However, if the reduction in hiring costs that arises when *signals* (such as educational credentials, marital status, or age) are used is large, it may prove profitable for an employer to use them even if an occasional lemon sneaks through. Put another way, the total costs of hiring, training, and employing workers may well be lower for some firms when hiring standards are used than when such firms rely upon more intensive investigations of applicant characteristics. (Chapter 14 will return to the issue of statistical discrimination.)

Internal Labor Markets

A major problem with the use of credentials, or screening devices, to predict which applicants will become good employees is that these credentials may only be loosely related to actual productivity on the job. Such personal attributes as dependability, motivation, honesty, and flexibility are difficult to observe using

---

[23]See Michael Spence, "Job Market Signaling," *Quarterly Journal of Economics* 87 (August 1973):355–74. See also Appendix 9A, " 'Signaling' in the Labor Market."

Example 5.2
Why Do Employers Discriminate in Hiring?

It is commonly asserted that older workers and women are not given the same preference as *prime-aged* men (men between 25 and 55) in filling many jobs—especially the better-paying ones. While this preference may be rooted in prejudice, there may also be an underlying, nondiscriminatory rationale for it. Chapter 14 will discuss discrimination, but this example will point out that what *appears* to be prejudice may be employer behavior designed to avoid losses on hiring and training investments.

To illustrate how the presence of hiring and training costs bears on the issue of apparent age or sex discrimination, let us assume two people apply for a job where the employer is intending to make a first-period investment of $H in hiring and training costs. It is expected that one applicant will be with the firm for two periods, while the other will remain for three periods. Which will the firm prefer to hire?

If it were possible to find workers and train them without cost, firms would not care about the length of their tenure. If one worker quit, a replacement could easily and costlessly be found. Where hiring a worker involves an initial investment by the firm, however, employers will prefer to hire workers with relatively long expected tenures. The longer an employee is expected to be with the firm, the more likely it is the firm will recoup its initial investment costs. Thus, if the two applicants in our example were alike in every respect except their expected length of tenure with the firm, the one expected to remain with the firm for three periods would be preferred.

This preference can be demonstrated by referring back to equation (5.12). Equation (5.12) calculates the present value of a worker's post-training surplus *(G)* for a case where he or she will be employed for just one period after training. To repeat, the present value of the surplus in cases where there is *one* post-training period—which we will call G_1—is calculated as:

$$G_1 = \frac{MP_1 - W_1}{1 + r} \tag{5.a}$$

If there are *two* post-training periods of employment, the present value of a firm's surplus is found by adding to G_1 the discounted value of the surplus in the second post-training period. The *undiscounted* surplus in this period is the difference between marginal productivity and wages $(MP_2 - W_2)$. However, because this surplus occurs farther into the future than period one's surplus, it must be more heavily discounted when calculating present value. This is done by dividing $(MP_2 - W_2)$ by $(1 + r)^2$—the rationale for which is given in footnote 17. Thus, the present value of a surplus derived over two periods (G_2) is:

$$G_2 = \frac{MP_1 - W_1}{1 + r} + \frac{MP_2 - W_2}{(1 + r)^2} \tag{5.b}$$

It is obvious, by comparing G_2 and G_1, that the post-training surplus a firm can expect to gain from a worker increases as the expected length of the worker's tenure with the firm goes up, if other things are equal. That is, if the differences between marginal productivity and wages are the same for two workers, the one with the longer tenure will generate more post-training "surplus" for the firm.

Applicants who are very close to retirement will not be seriously considered for jobs that require large employer hiring or training investments (*unless* they accept a low post-training wage). That is, if post-training wages are equal, firms will tend to prefer prime-aged applicants to equally productive older ones whenever there are substantial employer hiring or training investments involved because the older applicants may retire before the firm can recoup its investment costs. Older workers could redress this imbalance in hiring preferences only by agreeing to work for a lower wage than younger applicants or by paying at least some of the hiring and training costs themselves—conditions that themselves might raise charges of discrimination!

This same reasoning can help to explain why women may not have had ready access to jobs requiring sizeable initial employer investments. Women—or at least *married* women—have tended to enter and leave the labor force more often then men. Chapter 9 will show, for example, that many married women enter the labor force in their early 20s, drop out to care for children, and then re-enter later on. Chapter 15 will also note that the average white woman worker, aged 25–59, is 15 times more likely to go from having a job to being out of the labor force than a comparable male worker during a one-month period. (For blacks, the probability of going from employment to out of the labor force is 3 times higher for females.) The result of this movement in and out of the labor force among women is that the average length of job tenure for males is about twice what it is for women. That is, the average male worker in 1978 had been on his current job for 4.5 years, while the average woman had been on her job for just 2.6 years.[1]

The shorter average job tenure among women could legitimately induce employers contemplating hiring and training investments to be wary of investing in female workers. This concern has an understandble economic rationale to it, but it also offers a good example of what we earlier called *statistical discrimination* (judging individuals by the characteristics of the group to which they belong). In this case, statistical discrimination could have unfortunate consequences for women who *do* plan continuous careers outside the home. For example, single (never-married) women, aged 25–34, have about the same average job tenure (2.6 years) as men of that age (2.7 years). For single women aged 35–44 the typical length of time on one's current job is 5.7 years, while for men it is only slightly higher (6.9 years). In contrast, the typical married woman worker, aged 35–44, has only been on her job for 3.5 years. Thus, women who never marry are much more likely to have job tenures equivalent to the typical male worker, but a firm using rather general hiring standards (such as age and sex) might not make such distinctions.

In summary, two policy-related points can be drawn from this discussion of hiring and training investments. First, employers may have legitimate economic reasons for preferring to hire employees who are expected to have relatively long job tenures *when* there are significant employer hiring or training investments involved. Thus, it would not necessarily be maliciousness or prejudice that causes older workers and women to have reduced access to jobs that typically require such investments.

The second point, however, is that individuals within groups vary, and using group averages to estimate an individual's expected tenure may do a disservice to atypical members of the group. We have seen, for example, that women who never marry have much longer job tenures than married women. Taking this fact into account when screening applicants would make hiring decisions more "fair" to single women but would probably entail added costs to employers. Firms would have to collect data on their applicants to attempt accurate guesses as to which of their female applicants would remain in the labor force continuously or would never marry.

[1]U.S. Bureau of Labor Statistics, *Job Tenure Declines As Work Force Changes,* Special Labor Force Report No. 235, Washington, D.C.: U.S. Government Printing Office, 1979). As families become smaller, as household duties become more evenly divided among men and women, and as more women seek *careers,* it is very likely that the labor force behavior of women and men will become more similar.

---

credentials, yet for many jobs such attributes may be crucial. This difficulty with screening is one fact that has induced some firms to adopt a policy of hiring workers at low-level jobs, observing their behavior, and filling all upper-level jobs from within the firm—that is, filling all upper-level vacancies with people whose characteristics have been carefully observed in other jobs the firm has given them to do.

This second approach to the problem of minimizing hiring costs while maximizing the productivity of employees creates an *internal labor market,* because most jobs in the firm are filled from within the ranks of current employees.[24] The hiring done from outside the firm tends to be heavily concentrated at certain low-level "ports of entry." These jobs—such as "general laborer," "machine cleaner," and "packer" for blue-collar applicants or "management trainee" for white-collar applicants—are of sufficiently low responsibility levels that a bad employee cannot do too much damage to the firm or its equipment. However, these jobs do give the firm a chance to observe *actual* productive characteristics of the employees hired, and this information is then used to determine who stays with the firm and how fast and how high employees are promoted.

---

[24]For a detailed discussion of internal labor markets, *see* Peter Doeringer and Michael Piore, *Internal Labor Markets and Manpower Analysis* (Lexington, Mass.: D.C. Heath and Company, 1971). The same general concept has been identified by others as "industrial feudalism," "balkanization of labor markets," and "property rights" in a job. *See* Arthur Ross, "Do We Have a New Industrial Feudalism?" *American Economic Review,* 48,5 (December 1958): 914; Clark Kerr, "The Balkanization of Labor Markets," in E. Wight Bakke, et al., *Labor Mobility and Economic Opportunity* (Cambridge Mass.: MIT Press, 1954); and Frederick Meyers, *Ownership of Jobs: A Comparative Study,* Institute of Industrial Relations Monograph Series (Los Angeles: University of California Press, 1964). Other reasons for the existence of internal labor markets are found more recently in Oliver Williamson, et al., "Understanding the Employment Relation: The Analysis of Idiosyncratic Exchange," *Bell Journal of Economics* 16 (Spring 1975): 250–80.

The *benefits* of using an internal labor market to fill vacancies is that the firm knows a lot about the people working for it. Hiring decisions for upper-level jobs in either the blue-collar or white-collar work forces will thus offer few surprises to the firm. The *costs* of using the internal labor market are associated with the restriction of competition for the upper-level jobs to those in the firm. Those in the firm may not be the best employees available, but they are the only ones the firm considers for these jobs. Firms most likely to decide that the benefits of using an internal labor market outweigh the costs are those whose upper-level workers must have a lot of firm-specific knowledge and training that can best be attained by on-the-job learning over the years. For those firms, the number of qualified *outside* applicants for upper-level jobs is relatively small. Firms in the steel, petroleum, and chemical industries tend to rely on internal labor markets to fill vacancies, while those in the garment and shoe industries do not.[25] The former group of industries has highly automated, complicated, and interdependent production technologies that can only be mastered through years on the job. The garment- and shoe-manufacturing industries employ workers who perform certain discrete crafts—skills that are not specific to one firm.

As noted earlier, firms engaged in *specific training* will want to ensure that they obtain a stable, long-term work force—which can learn quickly and perform well later on. For these firms, the internal labor market offers two attractions. First, it allows the firm to observe workers on the job, where it can see firsthand who learns quickly, who is easily motivated, who is dependable, and so forth, and thus make better decisions about which workers will be the recipients of later, perhaps very expensive, training. Second, the internal labor market tends to foster an attachment to the firm by its employees. They know that outsiders will not be considered for upper-level vacancies and that they, therefore, have an inside track on job vacancies. If they quit the firm, they would lose this privileged position. They are thus motivated to become long-term employees of the firm. The full implications of internal labor markets for wage policies within the firm will be discussed in the chapter on compensation (Chapter 11).

REVIEW QUESTIONS

1. Both low-skilled workers and high-paid professors have high rates of voluntary quits. What do they have in common that leads to a high quit rate?
2. Wages in the U.S. Postal Service have been attacked for being higher than wages elsewhere for people of the same age and education. The Postal Service answers that they *must* pay higher wages than workers could get elsewhere in order to keep their quit rate below the quit rate in other jobs. Are there circumstances under which this argument has any merit?
3. Suppose the government wants to reduce recidivism of ex-convicts by improving their employment prospects and job stability. Suppose further that the government is consid-

---

[25]Doeringer and Piore, *Internal Labor Markets and Manpower Analysis,* p. 43.

ering subsidizing half of employer costs incurred in training ex-cons for jobs in their plants. How will this subsidy affect the job prospects and stability of ex-cons, assuming ex-cons are the only group subsidized?

4. Unemployment insurance is financed through a payroll tax levied on the employer. Assume that taxes paid = tax rate × firm's payroll. Generally speaking, the tax rate increases when a firm lays off workers. Assuming the firm is unable to shift the tax, what effect will abolition of this tax have on the firm's decision to:
   a. lay off workers?
   b. hire workers?
   c. schedule overtime work?

5. In its presentation to the Democratic and Republican national platform committees, the AFL-CIO proposed the following changes to the Fair Labor Standards Act in 1976:
   1. Raise the federal minimum wage to $3.00 per hour (the minimum was then less than $3.00);
   2. Increase overtime pay to double the standard wage (it was then 1½ times the standard);
   3. Reduce the standard work week to 35 hours (down from 40), so that overtime pay would be owed to a worker after 35 hours per week.

   Analyze the employment effects of these proposals.

SELECTED READINGS

Gary Becker, *Human Capital,* 2nd. ed. (New York: National Bureau of Economic Research, 1975).

Peter Doeringer and Michael Piore, *Internal Labor Markets and Manpower Analysis* (Lexington, Mass.: D. C. Heath, 1971).

Ronald G. Ehrenberg and Paul L. Schumann, *Longer Hours or More Jobs? An Investigation of Amending Hours Legislation to Create Employment* (Ithaca: New York State School of Industrial and Labor Relations, Cornell University, 1982).

Walter Oi, "Labor As A Quasi-Fixed Factor," *Journal of Political Economy* 70 (December 1962):538–55.

Michael Spence, "Job Market Signalling," *Quarterly Journal of Economics* 87 (August 1973):355–74.

Oliver Williamson et al. "Understanding the Employment Relation: The Analysis of Idiosyncratic Exchange," *Bell Journal of Economics* 16 (Spring 1975):250–80.

6

Supply
of Labor to the Economy:
The Decision to Work

This and the next five chapters will focus on issues of *worker* behavior. That is, Chapters 6–11 will discuss and analyze various aspects of *labor-supply* behavior. Labor-supply decisions can be roughly divided into two categories. The first category, which is addressed in Chapters 6–7, includes decisions about whether to work at all, and if so, how long to work. Questions that must be answered include whether to participate in the labor force, whether to seek part-time or full-time work, the length of one's working life, and how many years a parent will stay home to raise children. The second category of decisions, which is addressed in Chapters 8–11, deals with the questions that must be faced by a person who has decided to seek work: the occupation or general class of occupations in which to seek offers (Chapters 8–9), the geographical area in which the offers will be sought (Chapter 10), and the specific employer for whom to work (Chapter 11).

This chapter begins with some basic facts concerning labor-force participation rates and hours of work and then moves on to an analysis of the decision to work for pay. This analytical framework is useful in the context of formulating income-maintenance programs.

TRENDS IN LABOR-FORCE PARTICIPATION
AND HOURS OF WORK

When a person actively seeks work, he or she is, by definition, in the *labor force*. As pointed out in Chapter 2, the *labor-force participation rate* is the percentage of a given population that either has a job or is looking for one. Thus, one clear-cut statistic important in measuring people's willingness to work outside the home is the labor-force participation rate.

Perhaps the most revolutionary change taking place in the labor market today is the tremendous increase in the proportion of women—particularly married women—working outside the home. Table 6.1 shows the extraordinary dimensions of this change. As late as 1950, only 21.6 percent of married women were

TABLE 6.1   Labor Force Participation Rates of Females over 16 Years of Age, by Marital Status, 1900–1979 (percent)

Year	All Females	Single	Widowed, Divorced	Married
1900	20.6 (100)	45.9 (100)	32.5 (100)	5.6 (100)
1910	25.5 (124)	54.0 (118)	34.1 (105)	10.7 (191)
1920	24.0 (117)			9.0 (161)
1930	25.3 (123)	55.2 (120)	34.4 (106)	11.7 (209)
1940	26.7 (130)	53.1 (116)	33.7 (104)	13.8 (246)
1950	29.7 (144)	53.6 (117)	35.5 (109)	21.6 (386)
1960	35.7 (173)	42.9 (94)	38.7 (119)	30.6 (546)
1970	41.6 (202)	50.9 (111)	39.5 (122)	39.5 (705)
1979	51.1 (248)	62.7 (137)	43.1 (133)	49.4 (882)

Note: Index numbers, with 1900 = 100, are shown in parentheses.

SOURCES: 1900–1950: Clarence D. Long, *The Labor Force Under Changing Income and Employment* (Princeton: Princeton University Press), 1958, Table A–6.

1960: U.S. Department of Commerce, Bureau of the Census, *Census of Population, 1960: Employment Status* (Subject Reports PC(2)–6A), Table 4.

1970: U.S. Department of Commerce, Bureau of the Census, *Census of Population, 1970: Employment Status and Work Experience* (Subject Reports PC(2)–6A), Table 3.

1979: U.S. President, *Employment and Training Report of the President, 1980* (Washington, D.C.: U.S. Government Printing Office, 1980), Tables A2, B1. (The data for 1979 are not strictly comparable because they are derived from a monthly survey, not the decennial census.

in the labor force. By 1960 this percentage had risen to 30.6 percent, and by 1979 it had increased to 49.4 percent—almost two and a half times what it had been in 1950.

We need not dwell here on the social changes that have been associated with this increasing tendency for women to seek work outside the home. Changes in family income, child-rearing practices, and the family relationship itself are obvious. Less obvious are the effects on the demand for education by females and on the unemployment rate which will be discussed in Chapters 9, 15, and 16. The longer life span of females is another factor that will affect labor supply and will become an important issue, for example, in funding pension plans (see Chapter 11). Of paramount concern in this chapter are the factors that have influenced this fundamental change in the propensity of women to seek work outside the home.

A second major trend in labor-force participation is the decrease in the length of careers for males—as can be seen in Table 6.2. The overall labor-force participation rate of men has been falling, as was noted in Chapter 2, but the really substantial decreases have been among the very young and the very old. The labor-force participation rate of teenagers fell from 61.1 percent in 1900 to 35.8 percent in 1970—a 41 percent decline—although the growth of the student labor force since World War II has slowed the decrease somewhat. The decrease for men over 65 has been even more dramatic—from 68.3 percent in 1900 to 25 percent in 1970 and down to 20 percent by 1979. Participation rates for men of "prime age" have declined only slightly. Clearly, men are starting their careers later and ending them earlier than they were at the beginning of this century.

TABLE 6.2   Labor Force Participation Rates For Males,
by Age, 1900–1979 (percent)

	Age Groups				
Year	*14–19*	*20–24*	*25–44*	*45–64*	*Over 65*
1900	61.1 (100)	91.7 (100)	96.3 (100)	93.3 (100)	68.3 (100)
1910	56.2 (92)	91.1 (99)	96.6 (100)	93.6 (100)	58.1 (85)
1920	52.6 (86)	90.9 (99)	97.1 (101)	93.8 (101)	60.1 (88)
1930	41.1 (67)	89.9 (98)	97.5 (101)	94.1 (101)	58.3 (85)
1940	34.4 (56)	88.0 (96)	95.0 (99)	88.7 (95)	41.5 (61)
1950	39.9 (65)	82.8 (90)	92.8 (96)	87.9 (94)	41.6 (61)
1960	38.1 (62)	86.1 (94)	95.2 (99)	89.0 (95)	30.6 (45)
1970	35.8 (59)	80.9 (88)	94.4 (98)	87.3 (94)	25.0 (37)
1979			95.7 (99)	82.8 (89)	20.0 (29)

Note: Index numbers, with 1900 = 100, are shown in parentheses.

SOURCES: 1900–1950: Clarence D. Long, *The Labor Force Under Changing Income and Employment* (Princeton: Princeton University Press), 1958, Table A–2.

1960: U.S. Department of Commerce, Bureau of the Census, *Census of Population, 1960: Employment Status,* Subject Reports PC(2)–6A, Table 1.

1970: U.S. Department of Commerce, Bureau of the Census, *Census of Population, 1970: Employment Status and Work Experience,* Subject Reports PC(2)–6A, Table 1.

1979: U.S. President, *Employment and Training Report of the President, 1980* (Washington, D.C.: U.S. Government Printing Office, 1980), Table A2. (The data for 1979 are not strictly comparable because they are derived from a monthly survey, not the decennial census. Reliable data for males under 25 are unavailable).

Other measures reflecting the decisions people make about work are the weekly hours of work, the fraction of people who work *part-time*, and the proportion of people who hold more than one job ("moonlighting"). It is not common for people to think of the *hours* of work as being a *supply* variable that is subject to *employee* choice. After all, don't employers—in responding to the factors discussed in Chapter 5—establish the hours of work? They do, of course, but this does not mean that employees have no choice of, or influence on, their working hours. The *weekly* hours of work offered by employers vary to some extent, so that in choosing employers the worker can also choose hours of work. The range of choice may be limited—70 percent of all full-time plant workers normally worked a 40-hour week in 1973, for example, and most of the rest were within 5 hours of that—but choice does exist. Among full-time, nonsupervisory office workers in 1973, only 59 percent worked 40 hours a week, while 17 percent worked 37¹/₂ hours, and 13 percent worked 35-hour weeks.[1] Moreover, firms with the same 40-hour standard work week will offer different *yearly* hours of work because of different vacation and holiday policies. Finally, *occupational* choice has a working-hours dimension. The weekly or yearly hours of work are different if one chooses to become a teacher rather than an accountant, a retail clerk rather than a traveling sales representative, or a Wall Street rather than a small-town lawyer.

Thus employees can, in effect, exercise some choice over their hours of work

---

[1]U.S. Department of Labor Employment Standards Administration, *1973 Survey of Establishment Characteristics and Practices* (Washington, D.C.: U.S. Government Printing Office, 1979), Table 15.

**TABLE 6.3 Average Weekly Hours Actually Worked by
Manufacturing Production Workers during the Peak
Employment Years in Each Business Cycle, 1900–1973
(excluding 1940–45)**

	Average Hours Worked	*Average per Decade Decline in Hours Worked*
1901	54.3 ⎫	
1906	55.0 ⎮	
1913	50.9 ⎮	
1919	46.1 ⎬	2.2
1923	48.9 ⎮	
1926	47.8 ⎮	
1929	48.0 ⎭ ⎫	4.6
1948	38.8 ⎬	
1953	38.6 ⎫	
1956	38.2 ⎬	0.3
1969	38.3 ⎮	
1973	38.0 ⎭	

SOURCE: The data for 1900–1957 were taken from Ethel Jones, ''New Estimates of Hours
of Work Per Week and Hourly Earnings, 1900–1957,'' *Review of Economics and
Statistics*, November 1963, pp. 374–385. Data for 1969 and 1973 were calculated
from the *Annual Survey of Manufactures*, which contain worker hours worked (exclusive of vacations, sick leave, and holidays).

in the short run by choosing their employment. In the long run, a similar mechanism gives employees some influence on working hours. If employees receiving
an hourly wage of $X for 40 hours per week really wanted to work only 30 hours
at $X per hour, some enterprising employer would seize on their dissatisfaction
and offer jobs with 30-hour weeks—ending up with a more satisfied work force
in the process. As noted below, large declines in the average hours worked per
week took place in this century well before the advent of unions and of federal
legislation concerning hours of work.

Table 6.3 displays the historical change in *actual* weekly hours of work in
this century after correcting for the fact that these hours tend to rise in prosperity
and fall in recessions.[2] What the table shows is that weekly hours fell steadily
until the 1940s but since then have more or less stabilized. Overall, the typical
manufacturing worker has 16 more hours of leisure each week than he or she had
in 1901—virtually an entire waking day! Yet perhaps equally worth emphasizing
is that almost all of this change came in the first 45 years of this century—much
of it in the first 30 years when unions and federal legislation could not have
exerted much influence. An explanation for this must include an analysis of factors influencing both the demand for, and supply of, weekly hours per worker.
The supply factors are considered in this chapter, while the demand-side influences were treated in Chapter 5.

---

[2]Chapter 2 noted, when defining wages and fringe benefits, that hours of *actual* work and the hours
for which an employee is *paid* are two different things. Since World War II, the *paid* hours of
work are greater than the *actual* hours of work because of the growing prevalence of paid holidays
and paid vacations.

Table 6.4 contains data indicating that the fraction of employed workers who voluntarily work part-time (less than 35 hours per week) has risen from 10.7 percent in 1963 to 14.4 percent in 1977. Partly this rise has occurred because the fastest growing groups in the labor force are teenagers and women—groups for which part-time employment is relatively common. However, it is obvious from Table 6.4 that all major labor-force groups have experienced an increase in the proportion of their members who work part-time.

In contrast to trends in part-time employment, there appears to be no trend in the percentage of workers holding two or more jobs. Since 1956, the proportion of employed workers holding two or more jobs has fluctuated around 5 percent—achieving lows of 4.5 percent in 1959 and 1974 and a high of 5.7 percent in 1963. In 1977 exactly 5 percent of employed workers were ''moonlighters.''

Because labor is the most abundant factor of production, it is fair to say that this country's well-being is heavily dependent on the willingness of its people to work. As we will demonstrate, leisure and other ways of spending time that do not involve work for pay are also important in generating well-being; however, our economy relies heavily on goods and services produced for market transactions. Therefore, it is important to understand the *work-incentive* effects of higher wages and incomes, different kinds of taxes, and various forms of income maintenance programs.

The question of work incentives, for example, will become of critical importance as our population—through longer life spans and a declining birth rate—gradually becomes older. When this happens, there will be a period when relatively few people of working age will have to support a large number of retirees. Their ability to do this and still maintain current standards of living obviously depends on the age at which older people retire and the fraction of the working-age population in the labor force.

A THEORY OF THE DECISION TO WORK

The decision to work is ultimately a decision about how to spend time. One way to use one's available time is to spend it in pleasurable leisure activities. The other major way in which people use time is to work.[3] One can work around the home, performing such *household production* as raising children, sewing, building, or even growing food. Alternatively, one can work for pay and use one's earnings to purchase food, shelter, clothing, and child care.

Because working for pay and engaging in household production are two ways of getting the same jobs done, we will initially ignore the distinction between them and treat work activities as working for pay. We will therefore be characterizing the decision to work as a choice between leisure and working for pay. Most of the crucial factors affecting work incentives can be understood in this context (household-production activities will be examined separately in Chapter 7).

If we regard the time spent eating, sleeping, and otherwise maintaining ourselves as more or less fixed by natural laws, then the discretionary time we have

---

[3]Another category of activity is to spend time acquiring skills or doing other things that enhance one's future earnings capacity. These activities will be discussed in Chapters 9–10.

**TABLE 6.4 Percentage of Employed
Persons Working Part-Time Voluntarily
1963 and 1977 (in percent)**

Group	1963	1977
All workers	10.7	14.4
Males, 20 years and over	3.5	5.0
Females, 20 years and over	19.5	21.3
Both sexes, 16–19	37.8	45.5

Note: A part-time worker is one who works between 1 and 34
hours a week.
SOURCE: U.S. Department of Labor, Bureau of Labor Statistics,
Handbook of Labor Statistics 1978 (Washington D.C.:
U.S. Government Printing Office), Table 21.

(16 hours a day, say) can be allocated to either work or leisure. Since the amount of discretionary time spent on leisure is time not spent on working, and vice versa, the *demand for leisure* can be considered the reverse side of the coin labeled *supply of labor*. It is actually more convenient to analyze work incentives in the context of the demand for leisure—because one can apply the standard analysis of the demand for any good to the demand for leisure—and then simply subtract leisure hours from total discretionary hours available to obtain the *labor-supply* effects.

A Verbal Analysis of the Labor/Leisure Choice

Since we have chosen to analyze work incentives in the context of the demand for leisure, it is instructive to briefly consider the factors that affect the demand for any good. Basically, the demand for a good is a function of three factors:

1. the *opportunity cost* of the good (which is often but not always equal to *market price*),
2. one's level of *wealth,* and
3. one's set of *preferences.*

For example, heating oil consumption will vary with the *cost* of such oil; as that cost rises, consumption will tend to fall unless one of the other two factors intervene. As *wealth* rises people generally want larger and warmer houses that obviously require more oil to heat.[4] Even if the price of energy and the level of personal wealth were to remain constant, the demand for energy could rise if a falling birth rate and lengthened life span resulted in a higher proportion of the population being aged and therefore wanting warmer houses. This change in the composition of the population amounts to a shift in the overall *preferences* for warmer houses and thus leads to a change in the demand for heating oil.

To summarize, the demand *(D)* for any good can be characterized as a function of opportunity costs *(C)* and wealth *(V)*:

$$D = f(\bar{C}, \overset{+}{V}), \tag{6.1}$$

---

[4]When the demand for a good rises with wealth, economists say the good is a *normal good*. If demand falls as wealth rises, the good is said to be an *inferior good* (traveling or commuting by bus is sometimes cited as an example of an inferior good).

where *f*—the particular relationship between demand and the variables *C* and *V* for an individual—depends on preferences. The notation above *C* and *V* indicates the direction in which the demand for a good is expected to go when the variable in question *increases—holding the other one constant*. The demand would move in the opposite direction if *C* or *V* were to decrease.

Note: Economists usually assume that preferences are given and not subject to immediate change. For policy purposes, the changes in *C* and *V*—not changes in the function of *f*—are of paramount interest to us in explaining changes in demand because *C* and *V* are most susceptible to change by government policy. For the most part, we will assume preferences are *given* and *fixed* at any point in time.[5]

To apply this general analysis of demand to the demand for leisure, we must first ask, "What is the opportunity cost of leisure?" The cost of spending an hour watching television is basically what one could earn if one had spent that hour working. Thus, the opportunity cost of an hour of leisure is very closely related to one's *wage rate*—so closely related, in fact, that to simplify the analysis we will say that leisure's opportunity cost *is* the wage rate.[6]

Next, we must understand and be able to measure wealth. Naturally, wealth includes a family's holdings of bank accounts, financial investments, and physical property. Workers' skills can also be considered assets, since these skills can be, in effect, rented out to employers for a price. The more one can get in wages, the larger is the value of one's human assets. Unfortunately, it is not usually possible to directly measure people's wealth. It is much easier to measure the *returns* from that wealth, because data on total *income* are readily available from government surveys. Economists thus often use total income as an indicator of total wealth, since the two are conceptually so closely related.[7]

If we replace the general demand function in equation (6.1) with the *demand for leisure function,* it would become equation (6.2):

$$D_L = f(\overset{-}{W}, \overset{+}{Y}), \tag{6.2}$$

where D_L is the demand for leisure hours, *W* is the wage rate, *Y* is total income, and *f* (as before) depends on preferences people have for leisure independent of *W* and *Y*. The signs over *W* and *Y* indicate what happens to the demand for leisure if the variable in question increases, holding the other variable constant.

If income increases, holding wages (and *f*) constant, equation (6.2) asserts

---

[5]On occasion the government attempts to influence consumption patterns of people by changing preferences rather than prices. For example, rather than raising cigarette taxes to discourage cigarette consumption, the federal government in the 1970s prohibited cigarette manufacturers from advertising on television, and it even sponsored radio and television campaigns against smoking. The effectiveness of these attempts to change preferences is difficult to assess.

[6]This assumes that individuals can work as many hours as they want at a fixed wage rate. While this assumption may seem overly simplistic, it will not lead to wrong conclusions with respect to the issues analyzed in this chapter. More rigorously, it should be said that leisure's *marginal* opportunity cost is the *marginal* wage rate (the wage one could receive for an extra hour of work).

[7]The best indicator of wealth is one's *permanent,* or long-run potential *income*. One's current income may differ from one's permanent income for a variety of reasons (unemployment, illness, or being a student, etc.). For our purposes here, however, the distinction between current and permanent income is not too important, but it is briefly mentioned in Chapter 7.

that the demand for leisure goes up. Put differently, *if income increases (decreases), holding wages constant, hours of work will go down (up).* Economists call this predicted response the *income effect.* The income effect is based on the simple notion that as incomes rise, holding leisure's opportunity cost constant, people will want to consume more leisure (which means working less).

Using algebraic notation, the income effect is defined as the change in the hours of work (ΔH) produced by a change in income (ΔY), holding wages constant ($\overline{W}$):

$$\text{Income Effect} = \frac{\Delta H}{\Delta Y} \Big|\, \overline{W} < 0. \tag{6.3}$$

We say the income effect is *negative* because the *sign* of the *fraction* in equation (6.3) is *negative.* If income goes up (wages held constant), hours of work fall. If income goes down, hours of work increase. The numerator (ΔH) and denominator (ΔY) in equation (6.3) move in opposite directions, giving a negative sign to the income effect.

Equation (6.2) also suggests that *if income is held constant, an increase (decrease) in the wage rate will reduce (increase) the demand for leisure—thereby increasing (decreasing) work incentives.* This *substitution effect* occurs because as the opportunity costs of leisure rise (income held constant), working hours are substituted for leisure hours.

In contrast to the income effect, the substitution effect is *positive.* Because this effect is the change in hours of work (ΔH) induced by a change in the wage (ΔW), holding income constant ($\overline{Y}$), the substitution effect can be written as:

$$\text{Substitution Effect} = \frac{\Delta H}{\Delta W} \Big|\, \overline{Y} > 0. \tag{6.4}$$

Because numerator (ΔH) and denominator (ΔW) always move in the same direction—at least in theory—the substitution effect has a positive sign.

At times, it is possible to observe situations or programs that create "pure" income or substitution effects. Usually, however, both effects are simultaneously present—often working against each other.

A "pure" income effect. Winning a state lottery is an example of the income effect by itself. The winnings enhance one's wealth (income) *independent* of the hours of work. Thus, income is increased *without* a change in the compensation received from an hour of work. In this case, the income effect induces the person to consume more leisure, thereby reducing the willingness to work. (If the change in nonlabor income were *negative,* on the other hand, the income effect suggests that people would work *more.*)

A "pure" substitution effect. In the 1980 Presidential campaign, one of the candidates—John Anderson—proposed a program aimed at conserving gasoline. His plan consisted of raising the gasoline tax but offsetting this increase by a reduced Social Security tax payable by individuals on their earnings. The idea was to raise the price of gasoline without reducing people's overall spendable income.

For our purposes, this plan is interesting because it creates a pure substitution effect on labor supply. Social Security revenues are collected by a tax on earnings, so reductions in the tax are, in effect, an increase in the wage rate.[8] However, for the average person, the increased wealth associated with this wage increase is exactly offset by increases in the gasoline tax.[9] Hence, wages are increased while income is held more or less constant. This program would thus create a substitution effect that induces people to work more hours.

Both effects occur when wages rise.   While the above examples illustrate situations in which the income or substitution effects are present by themselves, normally both effects are present—often working in opposite directions. The presence of both effects creates ambiguity in predicting the overall labor supply response in many cases. Consider the case of a person who receives a wage increase.

The labor-supply response to a simple wage change will involve *both* an income and a substitution effect. The *income effect* is the result of the worker's enhanced wealth (or potential income) after the increase. For a given level of work effort, he or she now has a greater command over resources than before (because more income is received for any given number of hours of work). The *substitution effect* results from the fact that the wage increase raises the opportunity costs of leisure. Because the actual labor supply response is the *sum* of the income and substitution effects, we cannot predict the response in advance; theory simply does not tell us which effect is stronger.

If the *income* effect is dominant, the person will respond to a wage increase by decreasing his or her labor supply. This decrease will be *smaller* than if the same change in wealth were due to an increase in *nonlabor* wealth, because the substitution effect is present and acts as a moderating influence. However, in the case where the *income* effect dominates, the substitution effect is not large enough to prevent labor supply from *declining*. It is entirely plausible, of course, that the *substitution* effect will dominate. If so, the actual response to wage increases will be to *increase* labor supply.

Should the substitution effect dominate, the person's labor-supply curve— relating, say, desired hours of work to wages—will be *positively sloped*. That is, labor supply will increase with the wage rate. If on the other hand, the income effect dominates, the labor-supply curve will be *negatively sloped*. Economic theory cannot say which effect will dominate, and in fact individual labor supply curves could be positively sloped in some ranges of the wage and negatively

---

[8]Social Security taxes are levied on yearly earnings up to some maximum—$29,000 in 1981. Once that maximum level is reached within a year, no more Social Security taxes are paid. People whose yearly earnings exceed the base experience no change in the marginal opportunity cost of leisure, because an additional hour of work per year is not subject to Social Security taxes anyway. However, the marginal opportunity cost of leisure would be increased for many—if not most—workers.

[9]An increase in the price of gasoline will reduce the income people have left for expenditures on nongasoline consumption only if the demand for gasoline is inelastic. In this case, the percentage reduction in gasoline consumption is smaller than the percentage increase in price; total expenditures on gasoline would thus rise. Our analysis assumes this to be the case.

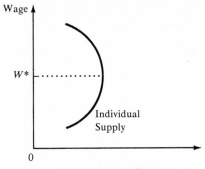

**FIGURE 6.1 An Individual
Supply-of-Labor Curve
Can Bend Backwards**

sloped in others. In Figure 6.1, for example, the person's desired hours of work increase (substitution effect dominates) as wages go up as long as wages are low (below W^*). However, at higher wages, further increases result in reduced hours of work (the income effect dominates): economists refer to such a curve as "backward-bending."

While economic theory is unable to predict whether the income or substitution effect will dominate in an individual's labor-supply curve, it can bring some useful insights to bear on important policy issues. The work-incentive effect of the personal income tax is an important case in point.

Tax-rate cuts and "supply-side" economics. The election of Ronald Reagan as President in 1980 brought to power an administration persuaded that high rates of inflation (that is, rising prices) and lagging labor productivity could be at least partially overcome by cutting taxes in such a way that investment and work effort would be stimulated.[10] The notion that tax-rate cuts and tax-related investment incentives could be used to stimulate output is central to what came to be called "supply-side" economics. An important element of the supply-side strategy proposed by President Reagan was the Kemp-Roth plan to cut personal income-tax rates across the board by 30 percent over a three-year period.[11] It was believed that cuts in personal income-tax rates would, among other things, increase the incentives of people to work:

> According to supply-siders, large tax-rate cuts would cause an increase in investment and work effort that would reduce fundamental inflationary pressures."[12]

---

[10]We are indebted to Sharon Smith of the New York Federal Reserve Bank for suggesting this policy application to us.

[11]The plan is named for its Congressional sponsors, Representative Jack Kemp and Senator William Roth. In the summer of 1981, Congress voted to cut taxes 25 percent over 3 years and to adjust tax brackets for inflation thereafter.

[12]"Reagan's Top Problem: Braking Inflationary Expectations," *Business Week,* December 1, 1980, p. 110.

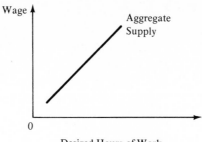

Wage

Aggregate
Supply

0

Desired Hours of Work

**FIGURE 6.2   The Aggregate
Supply-of-Labor Curve
Must Be Upward-Sloping
at Any Point in Time**

Is the belief by supply-siders that income tax-rate cuts will increase work effort theoretically sound? Suppose, first, that Congress were to lower the income tax rates of (say) lower income workers but not cut the level of government services provided for this group. A decrease in their income-tax rates is equivalent to an increase in wages, because the workers would take home more income for each hour of work. This wage increase would generate an income and substitution effect, and theoretical reasoning alone cannot predict which effect will dominate. If the substitution effect dominated, labor supply would increase; if the income effect were dominant, the tax cuts would be accompanied by a *fall* in labor supply! The issue is ultimately an empirical question.[13]

The supply-siders who claim that reducing income-tax rates would increase work incentives have a valid point, however, when one considers *general* income-tax-rate reductions. While at any point in time *individuals* or *small* groups of people can experience income effects if their wages change, workers as a *whole* cannot. The potential wealth of a society is more or less fixed at any point in time by the resources and technology it has available to it, and changing the wage rates of workers does not change this potential wealth. (If it did, we could make ourselves, as a society, arbitrarily wealthy by granting ourselves large wage increases!) Thus, income-tax-rate reductions for everyone would be accompanied by a *substitution* effect but *not* by an *income* effect. The cut in income-tax rates would increase workers' real wage rates—if the government at the same time reduces expenditures so that inflationary pressures do not occur—but it would not immediately affect society's real wealth. There would be a substitution effect with no overall income effect, and labor supply would increase. The *aggregate* supply-of-labor curve, then, must be upward-sloping, as shown in Figure 6.2. *How much* labor supply will increase if tax rates were cut by 30 percent is another question—and the answer is largely unknown at the moment. However, the estimates summarized later in the chapter suggest that the increase will probably be larger for women than men.

To better understand the upward-sloping nature of the aggregate supply-of-

---

[13]Later this chapter will show that the income effect may dominate for men but not for married women.

labor curve, let us examine in more concrete terms how a general 10 percent reduction in income-tax rates might be handled. While a cut in tax rates would, of course, increase workers' wage rates, it would have the *initial* effect of reducing by 10 percent the revenues available to government. The government might respond to reduced revenues by cutting back on various services it formerly provided: mail delivery on Saturday, educational subsidies, and road-construction funds, for example. Thus, while *wages* would be increased, real income would be held more or less constant by the cut in government services.[14] Workers would have more take-home income but fewer government-provided services.[15] There would be a substitution effect but no overall income effect.

The increase in labor supply caused by the tax cut would serve to increase people's money incomes and reduce their consumption of leisure. Some of the increased earnings would be spent on goods or services, and some would go to the government in the form of taxes.[16] However, whether the increased goods or services are provided privately or by the government, the happiness they generate is offset by the reduced consumption of leisure time. In the short run, to repeat, increased goods and services are offset by reduced consumption of leisure, leaving society equally well off.

In the *long run,* however, real national wealth could be increased *if* the increase in goods and services is channelled into *investment* activities and not immediately consumed. Wage increases that accompany the growth of national wealth *do* generate income effects. However, real national welfare could *only* be increased in the long run and only if current investments were to increase.

The following section introduces indifference curves and budget constraints— material that may already be familiar to students with a background in these fundamentals.

A Graphical Analysis of the Labor/Leisure Choice:
The Fundamentals

Graphical analysis requires a level of rigor that is more convincing than verbal analysis and incorporates visual aids that make the analysis easier to understand. The graphical analysis, however, is simply a more rigorous, visible repetition of our verbal analysis; hence, none of the conclusions or definitions reached above will be changed in any way.

Preferences.   Let us assume that there are two major categories of goods that make people happy—leisure and money income (which can, of course, be used

---

[14]Some people would be more affected by the governmental spending cuts than others, but the *overall* change in real wealth would be zero.

[15]The alternative to cutting services, at least initially, is to borrow money. However, borrowing increases the money supply if it is done, as is most often the case, from banks—and this would tend to be inflationary. A rise in *prices* would lower the real wage and mitigate any substitution effects (if before-tax money wages remained constant).

[16]Because earnings are taxed and leisure is not, a 10 percent tax cut that called forth increased labor supply would mean that government revenues would *not* fall by 10 percent in the long run.

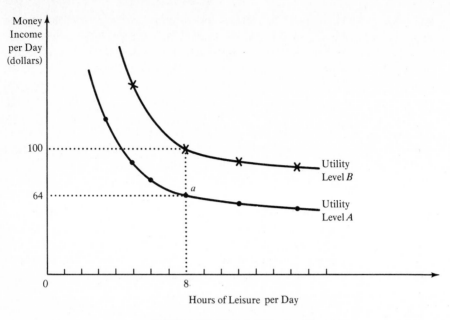

**FIGURE 6.3   Two Indifference Curves
for the Same Person**

to buy other goods). Collapsing all goods into two allows our graphs to be drawn in two-dimensional space.

Since both leisure and money can be used to generate satisfaction (or *utility*), these two goods are to some extent substitutes for each other. If one were forced to give up some money income—by cutting back one's hours of work, for example—there would be some increase in leisure time that could be substituted for this lost income to keep the person as happy as before. A very thoughtful consumer/worker, in fact, could reveal a whole *variety* of combinations of money and leisure hours that would yield him or her this same level of satisfaction.

To understand how preferences can be graphed, suppose a thoughtful consumer/worker is asked to decide how happy he or she would be with a daily income of $64 combined with 8 hours of leisure (point *a* in Figure 6.3). This level of happiness could be called "utility level *A*." Our consumer/worker could name *other combinations* of money income and leisure hours that would *also* yield utility level *A*. Assume that our respondent names five other such combinations. All six combinations of money and leisure that yield utility level *A* are represented by heavy dots in Figure 6.3. The curve connecting these dots is called an *indifference curve*—a curve connecting the various combinations of money and leisure that yield equal utility. (The term *indifference curve* got its name from the fact that, since each point on the curve yields equal utility, a person is truly indifferent about where on the curve he or she will be.)

Our worker/consumer could no doubt achieve a higher level of happiness if he or she could combine the 8 hours of leisure with an income of $100 per day instead of just $64 a day. This higher satisfaction level could be called "utility level *B*." The consumer could name other combinations of money income and leisure that would also yield *this* higher level of utility. These combinations are denoted by the *X*s in Figure 6.3 that are connected by a new indifference curve.

Indifference curves have certain specific characteristics that are reflected by the way they are drawn:

1. Utility level *B* represents more happiness than level *A*. Every level of leisure consumption is combined with a higher income on *B* than on curve *A*. Hence our respondent prefers all points on indifference curve *B* to any point on curve *A*. A whole *set* of indifference curves could be drawn for this one person, each representing a different utility level. Any such curve that lies to the northeast of another one is preferred to any curve to the southwest, because the northeastern curve represents a higher level of utility.

2. Indifference curves *do not intersect*. If they did, the point of intersection would represent *one* combination of money and leisure that yields *two* different levels of satisfaction. We assume our worker/consumer is *not* so inconsistent in stating his or her preferences that this could happen

3. Indifference curves are *negatively sloped,* because if either money or leisure hours is increased, the other is reduced in order to preserve the same level of utility. If the slope is steep—as at segment *LK* in Figure 6.4—a given loss of income need not be accompanied by a large increase in leisure hours in order to keep utility constant.[17] When the curve is relatively flat—as at segment *MN* in Figure 6.4—a given decrease in income must be accompanied by a large increase in the consumption of leisure to hold utility constant. Thus, where indifference curves are relatively steep, people do not value money income as highly as when such curves are relatively flat—for when they are flat, a loss of income can only be compensated by a large increase in leisure if utility is to be kept constant.

4. Indifference curves are *convex*—steeper at the left than at the right. This shape reflects the assumption that when money income is relatively high and leisure hours are relatively few, leisure is more highly valued than when leisure is abundant and money relatively scarce. At segment *LK* in Figure 6.4, a great loss of income (from Y_4 to Y_3, for example) can be compensated for by just a little increase in leisure, whereas a little loss of leisure time (from H_3 to H_4, for example) would require a relatively large increase in income to maintain equal utility. What is relatively scarce is highly valued.

   Conversely, when income is low and leisure is abundant (segment *MN* in Figure 6.4), income is more highly valued. Losing income (by moving from Y_2 to Y_1, for example) requires a huge increase in leisure in order for utility to remain constant. To repeat, what is scarce is assumed to be highly valued.

---

[17]Economists call the change in money income needed to hold utility constant when leisure hours are changed by one unit the *marginal rate of substitution* between leisure and money income. This marginal rate of substitution can be graphically understood as the slope of the indifference curve at any point. At point *L*, for example, the slope is relatively steep so economists would say that the marginal rate of substitution at point *L* is relatively high.

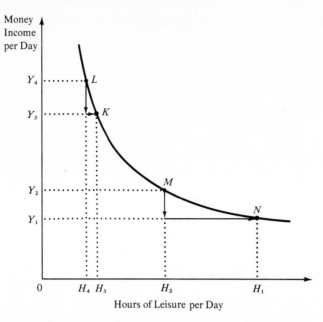

FIGURE 6.4   An Indifference Curve

5. Finally, different people will have different sets of indifference curves. The curves drawn in Figures 6.3 and 6.4 were for *one person only*. Another person would have a completely different set of curves. People who value leisure more highly, for example, would have had indifference curves that were generally steeper (see Figure 6.5). People who do not value leisure highly will have relatively flat curves.[18] Thus, individual preferences can be portrayed graphically.

Income and wage constraints.   Now everyone would like to maximize his or her utility, which could be most nicely done by consuming every available hour of leisure combined with the highest conceivable income. Unfortunately, the resources anyone can command are limited. Thus, all that is possible is to do the best one can, given limited resources. To see these resource limitations graphically requires superimposing constraints over one's set of indifference curves to see which combinations of income and leisure are available and which are not.

Suppose the person whose indifference curves are graphed in Figure 6.3 has no source of income other than labor earnings. Suppose, further, that he or she can earn $8 per hour. Figure 6.6 contains the two indifference curves drawn in Figure 6.3 but also contains a straight line *(DE)* connecting combinations of leisure and income that are possible for a person with an $8 wage and no outside

---

[18]The two curves shown in Figure 6.5 should be compared in *slope* only. Levels of utility for two different people cannot be compared because happiness is not objectively measurable. Figure 6.5 simply shows that people with different preferences will have indifference curves with different *shapes*. The fact that the two curves in Figure 6.5 intersect is thus not important, since the curves are for different people.

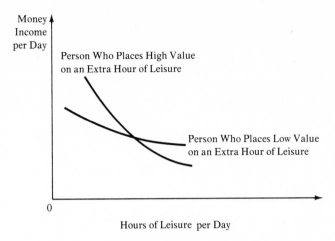

FIGURE 6.5   Indifference Curves for Two Different People

income. If 16 hours per day are available for work and leisure, and if this person consumes all 16 in leisure, then money income will be zero (point *D* in Figure 6.6). If 8 hours a day are devoted to work, income will be $64 per day (point *M*), and if 16 hours a day are worked income would be $128 per day (point *E*). Other points on this line—the point of 15 hours of leisure (1 hour of work) and $8 of income—are also possible. This line, which reflects the combinations of leisure and income that are possible for the individual, is called the *budget constraint.* Any combination to the right of the budget constraint is not achievable; the person's command over resources simply is not sufficient to attain these combinations of leisure and money income.

The *slope* of the budget constraint is a graphical representation of the wage rate. One's wage rate is properly defined as the increment in income *(ΔY)* derived from an increment in the hours of work *(ΔH):*

$$\text{Wage Rate} = \frac{\Delta Y}{\Delta H} \tag{6.5}$$

Now $\frac{\Delta Y}{\Delta H}$ is exactly the slope of the budget constraint (in absolute value).[19] Figure 6.6 shows how the constraint rises $8 for every one-hour increase in work: if the person works zero hours, income per day is zero; if the person works one hour, $8 in income is possible; if he or she works 8 hours, $64 in income can be achieved. The reason the constraint rises $8 for every unit increase in hours of work is because the wage rate the person commands is $8 per hour. If the person could earn $16 per hour, the constraint would rise twice as fast and be twice as steep.

It is clear from Figure 6.6 that our consumer/worker cannot achieve utility level *B*. He or she can achieve *some* points on the indifference curve representing

---

[19]The vertical change for a one-unit change in horizontal distance is the definition for *slope*. *Absolute value* refers to the size of the slope, disregarding whether it is positive or negative.

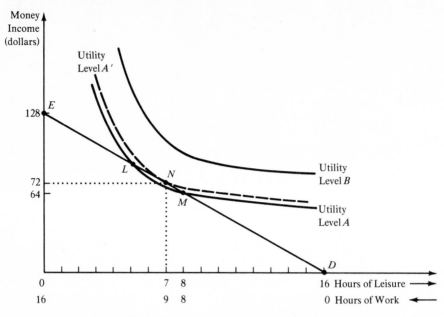

FIGURE 6.6 Indifference Curves and Budget Constraint

utility level A; specifically, those points between L and M in Figure 6.6. However, if our consumer/worker is a utility maximizer, he or she will realize that a utility level *above* A is possible. Remembering that there are an infinite number of indifference curves that can be drawn between curves A and B in Figure 6.6—one representing each possible level of satisfaction between A and B—we can draw a curve (A') that is northeast of curve A and is just *tangent* to the budget constraint. Any movement along the budget constraint *away* from the tangency point places the person on an indifference curve lying *below* A'.

An indifference curve that is just tangent to the constraint represents the highest level of utility that the person can obtain given his or her constraint. It is the most northeast curve with an achievable point on it, and no curve superior to it can be reached. If this highest possible curve is denoted as utility level A' in Figure 6.6, then point N represents the utility-maximizing combination of leisure and income. Thus, our consumer/worker is best off—given his or her preferences and constraints—working 9 hours a day, consuming 7 hours of leisure, and having a daily income of $72. All other possible combinations, such as 8 hours of work and $64 of income, yield lower utility.

The decision not to work. In the example discussed above—and illustrated in Figure 6.6—a point of tangency (N) existed between the individual's indifference curve and the budget constraint. That point of tangency indicated the utility-maximizing labor/leisure combination. What happens if there is no point of tangency? What happens, for example, if the person's indifference curves are at every point more steeply sloped than the budget constraint (see Figure 6.7)?

If indifference curves that represent an individual's preferences are very steeply sloped it indicates that the person places a very high value on extra hours

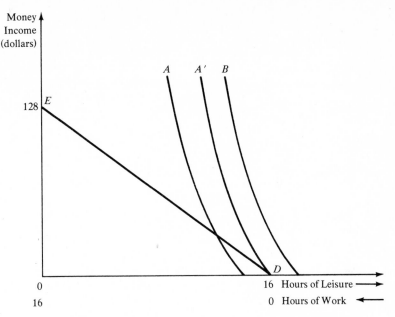

FIGURE 6.7   The Decision Not To Work Is a "Corner Solution"

of leisure (see Figure 6.5). A very high hourly wage would be required to compensate the person for an hour of lost leisure (that is, an hour of work). If the increase in money income required to compensate the worker for an hour of work (to keep utility constant) is greater than the wage rate at every feasible number of leisure hours, then the person simply will choose not to work. Figure 6.7 indicates that utility is maximized at point *D*—a point of zero hours of work. Point *D* is *not* a tangency point; there can be no tangency if the indifference curve has no points at which the slope equals the slope of the budget constraint. Thus, utility in Figure 6.7 is maximized at a *corner*—a point at the extreme end of the budget constraint—and at this point *(D)* the person does not choose to be in the labor force.

The income effect.   Suppose now that the person depicted in Figure 6.6 is lucky and falls into a source of income independent of work. Suppose, further, that this *nonlabor* income amounts to about $36 per day. Thus, even if this person worked zero hours per day, his or her daily income would be $36. Naturally, if the person worked more than zero hours, his or her daily income would be equal to $36 plus earnings (the wage multiplied by the hours of work).

The source of nonlabor income has clearly increased our person's command over resources, as can be shown by drawing a new budget constraint to reflect the nonlabor income. As shown by the broken line in Figure 6.8, the end points of the new constraint are:

1. point *d*—zero hours of work and $36 of money income, and
2. point *e*—16 hours of work and $164 of income ($36 in nonlabor income plus $128 in earnings).

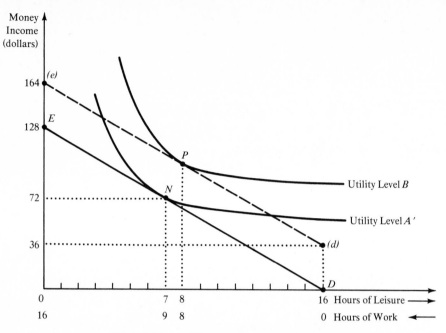

**FIGURE 6.8   Indifference Curves and Budget Constraint
(with an increase in nonlabor income)**

Note that the new constraint is *parallel* to the old one. Parallel lines have the same slope; since the slope of each constraint reflects the wage rate, we can infer that the increase in nonlabor income has not changed the person's wage rate.

We have just described a situation in which a pure *income effect* should be observed. Income (wealth) has been increased, but the wage rate has remained unchanged. The previous section noted that if wealth increased and the opportunity cost of leisure remained constant, the person would consume more leisure and work less. We thus concluded that the income effect was *negative;* as income goes up (down), holding wages constant, hours of work go down (up). This negative relationship is illustrated graphically in Figure 6.8.

When the old (solid) budget constraint was in effect, the person's highest level of utility was reached at point *N,* where he or she worked 9 hours a day. With the new (dashed) constraint, the optimium hours of work are 8 per day. The new source of income, by not altering the wage, has caused an income effect that results in one less hour of work per day.

Income and substitution effects with a wage increase.   Suppose that, instead of increasing one's command over resources by receiving a source of nonlabor income, the wage rate for another person were to be increased from $8.00 to $12.00 per hour. This increase, as noted earlier, will cause *both* an income and a substitution effect; the person is both wealthier *and* faces a higher opportunity cost of leisure. Both effects can be illustrated graphically (see Figures 6.9 and 6.10).

Figures 6.9 and 6.10 illustrate the *observed effects* of the wage change as well as the two (hidden) *components* of the observed change: the income and

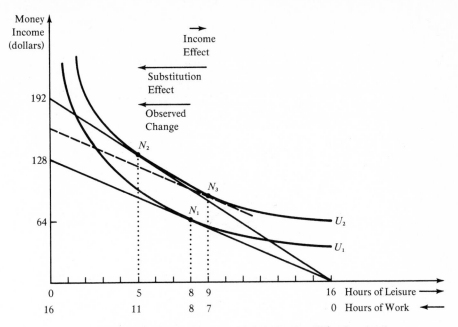

FIGURE 6.9 Wage Change with Substitution Effect Dominating

substitution effects. Figure 6.9 illustrates the case where the observed response is to increase the hours of work; in this case, the substitution effect is stronger than the income effect. Figure 6.10 illustrates the case where the income effect is stronger, and the response to a wage increase is to reduce the hours of work. Both cases are plausible. Theory tells us in what direction the income and substitution effects should go, but theory does not tell us which effect will be stronger. The difference between the two cases lies *solely* in the shape of the indifference curves (preferences); the budget constraints, which reflect wealth and the wage rate, are exactly the same.

Figures 6.9 and 6.10 show a new budget constraint. We are assuming that no source of nonlabor income exists for the person depicted, so that both the old and new constraints in each diagram are anchored at the same place—zero income for zero hours worked. However, the new constraint rises 50 percent faster than the old constraint, reflecting the 50 percent increase in the wage rate (from $8 to $12 per hour). The left endpoint of the new constraint is now at $192 (16 hours of work times $12 per hour) rather than at $128 (16 hours times $8).

In Figure 6.9, the new constraint implies that utility level U_2 is the highest that can be reached, and the tangency at point N_2 suggests that 11 hours of work per day is the optimum. When the old constraint was in effect, the utility-maximizing hours of work were 8 per day. Thus, the wage increase has caused the person's hours of work to increase by three per day.

This observed effect, however, masks the underlying forces at work. These underlying forces are, of course, the income and substitution effects. These forces are not directly observable, but they are there (and working against each other) nonetheless. A physical analogy can be used to explain how these forces work.

Suppose a riderless boat is set adrift in the Mississippi River on a day in

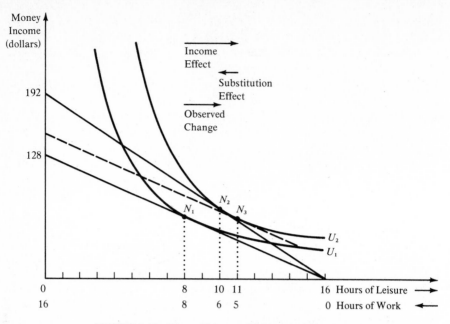

Money Income (dollars)

Income Effect

Substitution Effect

Observed Change

192

128

N_2

N_1 N_3

U_2

U_1

| 0 | 8 | 10 | 11 | 16 | Hours of Leisure $\longrightarrow$ |
| 16 | 8 | 6 | 5 | 0 | Hours of Work $\longleftarrow$ |

FIGURE 6.10 Wage Change with Income Effect Dominating

which the wind is blowing *across* the river. The river's current carries the boat downstream, but the crosswind also exerts a force that blows the boat east (say). We observe where the boat is when it passes under a certain bridge. While we *observe* where the boat crosses under the bridge, we cannot directly see the two independent forces that together dictate where the boat ends up. There is the influence of the current and of the wind, and for some purposes it may be useful to measure these effects separately. How would we do it?

We would measure the influence of the current by asking ourselves, "Where would the boat have passed under the same bridge if there had been no wind?" This hypothetical question holds two elements constant: the wind (zero velocity) and the bridge under which the boat passes. The answer to the question is thus designed to identify the "pure" effect of the current. The influence of the wind could be measured by comparing where the boat actually crossed under the bridge with where it *would have crossed* had there been no wind.

Turning now to Figure 6.9, we will identify the income effect (as we did the "current effect") by asking, "What would have been the change in the hours worked if the person had reached indifference curve U_2 (the bridge) by a change in *nonlabor* income with *no* change in the wage rate (no wind)?"

We answer this question by moving the old constraint to the northeast, maintaining its original slope (reflecting the old wage of $8.00), which holds the wage constant. By definition, we must hold the wage constant when dealing with the income effect. However, moving the old constaint hypothetically "allows" nonlabor income to increase so that the person arrives at the new level of utility. The dashed constraint in Figure 6.9 depicts this hypothetical constraint, which is tangent to indifference curve U_2 at N_3. This tangency suggests that had the person received nonlabor income, with no change in the wage, sufficient to reach the new level of utility, he or she would have *reduced* work hours from 8 (N_1), to 7 (N_3) per day. This shift is a graphical "proof" that the income effect is negative, assuming that leisure is a normal good.

The substitution effect can be measured once the pure effect of the wage change is known. We measure the substitution effect as the difference between where the person ends up and where he or she *would* have ended up without a wage change. *With* the wage change, the person represented in Figure 6.9 ended up at point N_2, working 11 hours a day. *Without* the wage change, the person would have arrived at point N_3, working 7 hours a day. The wage change *by itself* (holding utility, or real wealth, constant) caused work hours to increase by 4 per day. This increase demonstrates that the substitution effect is positive.

To summarize, the observed effect of raising wages from $8 to $12 per hour increased the hours of work in Figure 6.9 from 8 to 11 per day. This observed effect, however, is the *sum* of two component effects. The income effect—which operates because an increased wage increases one's real wealth—tended to *reduce* the hours of work from 8 to 7 per day. The substitution effect—which captures the pure effect of the change in leisure's opportunity cost—tended to push the person toward 4 more hours of work per day. The end result was an increase of 3 in the hours worked each day.

Figure 6.10 can be analyzed in the same way. Here, the *observed* effect of the increased wage is a *reduction* in hours of work from 8 to 6 per day (points N_1 to N_2). This change is the result of an income effect, which by itself tended to *decrease* by 3 hours the hours of work per day, and a substitution effect, which tended to *increase* working hours by one per day. The net result of these forces is, of course, a reduction in hours of work by 2 per day.

The differences in the observed effects of a wage increase between Figures 6.9 and 6.10 are due to differences in the shape of the indifference curves—or, in other words, to different preferences. The substitution and income effects worked in their predicted direction in both cases, but their relative strengths are a function of preferences (which are reflected in the shape and placement of indifference curves).

Although theory cannot predict whether the income or substitution effect will dominate, it can be readily understood that the income effect of any given wage change is *larger* for individuals who are *working many hours* for pay than for those who are working few hours. Changes in income represent changes in one's command over resources, and it is clear that a wage increase (say) fosters greater increases in wealth the more hours one works. (In terms of our graphical analysis, it can be seen from Figures 6.9 and 6.10 that the budget constraint representing a wage of $12 per hour lies further to the northeast of the one representing an $8 wage in its upper portion—where more hours are worked.)

Empirical Findings on the Labor/Leisure Choice

This chapter has argued, both verbally and graphically, that the income effect on labor supply is negative and that the substitution effect is positive. While these predictions are often useful for policy purposes—as we saw in the discussions of the work-incentive effect of the income tax—it is also important to know *how large* the two effects are. It is the *relative size* of each effect that determines the ultimate *observed* effect.

Evidence on the absolute and relative sizes of income and substitution effects can be obtained in two different ways:

1. the *time-series study* can be used to look at *trends* in labor-force participation rates and hours of work over time.
2. the *cross-section study* can be used to analyze the patterns of labor supply across individuals at a given point in time.

Time-series studies.   Chapter 2 pointed out that real hourly wages rose fourfold from 1914 to 1975. Associated with that rise was a rather sharp decline in the labor-force participation rate of older males, clearly reflecting a trend toward earlier retirement. One can also observe substantial declines in the hours of work. One is therefore tempted to conclude from these trends that the income effect dominates the substitution effect—meaning that when wages rise, the propensity to work will fall.

There are three potential objections to, or problems with, the conclusion that the income effect is larger than the substitution effect. First, the earlier retirement of males can be seen as a function of greater availability of pensions. Pensions pay older people for not working, thereby creating incentives not to work at an elderly age. Interestingly, however, a large part of the decline in labor-force participation rates for elderly males came *before* 1940, during an era when pensions were virtually nonexistent.

A second disturbing fact that raises questions about the relative strength of the income and substitution effects is the much smaller decline in hours of work after World War II. Has the income effect grown weaker relative to the substitution effect? Not necessarily. Hours of work are *jointly* determined by employers and employees, and while rising real wages may be inducing employees to want to work less, a number of developments have led employers to offer incentives for workers to work longer hours (these forces were discussed in Chapter 5). It is important to remember that countervailing forces may well be coming from the *demand* side of the market in determining hours of work.

Third, while we cannot rule out the possibility that the income effect dominates the substitution effect for males, how do we interpret the dramatic rise in participation rates among females? One possible explanation is that preferences among women have changed—particularly since their heavy involvement in the labor market during World War II. For example, the stigma against working wives or mothers has weakened. This change in preferences may explain some of the rising propensity of women to work, but it does not explain the *cause* of the changing preferences. Since women's attitudes may be most strongly influenced by the sheer increase in the number of working women, understanding what started the increase originally is fundamental.

Another theory for the growing proportion of working women is based on the observation that women really have a tripartite choice of how to spend time: leisure, market work, and nonmarket (household) work (see Chapter 7 for further discussion of this tripartite choice). The inventions of automatic washers and dryers, frost-free refrigerators, and prepared foods—to name a few—have reduced the time required to perform given household tasks. Being able to perform these tasks faster reduces the savings from staying home instead of working for pay. Thus, yet another force is at work affecting the incentives of women to work for pay.

Finally, it may well be that because wives have tended to work in the home more–and for pay less–than men and unmarried women, the income effect for them will be smaller and the substitution effect will be larger. The plausibility of a smaller income effect rests on the observation that at any point in time, many married women are out of the labor force and many others are working less than full time. Thus, as noted before, a given wage increase will generate a smaller income effect than it would if virtually all were working (for pay) full time. A larger substitution effect is plausible for married women because household and market work are such close substitutes, whereas market work and leisure are not as close substitutes.

Suppose that women and men have roughly the same preferences regarding leisure and work. These two alternative ways to spend time are substitutes, but they are not close substitutes. Thus, a change in the opportunity cost of leisure may not elicit a large change in the supply of working hours for either sex; leisure and work are simply too different for a large responsiveness to changes in opportunity costs to be observed. However, there are two different types of *work* activity—market work (for pay) and household work—and there is a high degree of substitutability between *these* alternatives. If market work is performed, household chores are hired out to specialists (baby-sitters, cleaning services) or done by machines (frost-free refrigerators). If household work is substituted for market work, these costs of hiring out tasks are saved. Thus, doing household work oneself or working for pay and hiring out these chores represent two ways of getting the same job done. They are very close substitutes, so that when the incentives to pursue one alternative change, a large response in time spent doing the other can be expected. Because married women have traditionally performed household work to a greater extent than have men and unmarried women, we would expect this second influence on the overall substitution effect (the substitution between work activities) to be more important for married women. The substitution effect observed in the above studies is thus plausibly larger for married women. (Chapter 7 will return to the issue of household and market work in more detail.)

It is easy to see that looking at *trends* in the propensity of people to work for evidence on the relative strength of income or substitution effects is not completely satisfactory. So many other factors are involved over time that affect these propensities that isolating income and substitution effects is impossible. Indeed, the growth of pensions, changes in employer desires concerning hours of work, time-saving household inventions, and changed attitudes toward working women all cloud our analysis of trends.

Cross-section studies.   Numerous studies of labor-supply behavior have relied on cross-sectional data.[20] These studies basically analyze labor-force participation or annual hours of work as they are affected by wage rates (the slope of the budget constraint) and unearned income (how far out the constraint lies). The most reliable and informative studies are those done on large samples of males, primarily because the labor supply behavior of women is complicated by child-rearing and household-work arrangements for which data are sketchy at best. The findings discussed here are of *nonexperimental studies*—studies in which variations in wages and incomes are *observed*, rather than *generated by*, the researchers (findings from experimental studies are summarized later in this chapter in the discussion of income-maintenance programs).

Just about all studies of male labor-supply behavior indicate that the income effect dominates the substitution effect—and thus that males have (individual) negatively sloped supply curves. There is as yet no universal consensus about the *size* of the labor-supply response. However, one careful review study[21] claims that once various statistical and definitional problems are accounted for the effect of raising a man's wage by 10 percent would be a 1–2 percent reduction in his labor supply. This observed effect is the result of something like a 2.5 percent reduction resulting from the income effect and roughly a 1 percent increase associated with the substitution effect.

The estimates for women are less well defined, perhaps for the reasons cited above. Nevertheless, the results of cross-sectional studies usually indicate that the *substitution* effect dominates, yielding a positively sloped labor supply curve for females.[22] Studies comparable to those for males (noted above) have generally found similar income effects among females, but the substitution effects for women are much larger than those for men, the likely reasons for which were mentioned earlier.[23]

It is interesting—and somewhat heartening—that the results of nonexperimental, statistically sophisticated cross-section studies generally support the observations based on trends over time. Namely, the income effect appears to dominate for males, and the substitution effect appears dominant for females. As noted earlier, the relatively larger substitution effect among women probably reflects the traditional household role of married women rather than sex-related differences in work/leisure preferences.

[20]The studies and conclusions reported here are for *individual* wage changes and *individual* supply-of-labor curves. They do *not* pertain to *aggregate* labor supply responses in response to a general wage change (where, as noted earlier, there can be no overall income effect).

[21]George Borjas and James Heckman, "Labor Supply Estimates for Public Policy Evaluation," *Proceedings of the Industrial Relations Research Association* (1978), pp. 320–31.

[22]See Jacob Mincer, "Labor Force Participation of Married Women," in *Aspects of Labor Economics* (Princeton, N.J.: Princeton University Press, 1962); Glen G. Cain, *Married Women in the Labor Force* (Chicago: University of Chicago Press, 1966); William G. Bowen and T. Aldrich Finegan, *The Economics of Labor Force Participation* (Princeton, N.J.: Princeton University Press, 1969).

[23]See Glen G. Cain and Harold W. Watts, "Toward a Summary and Synthesis of the Evidence," *Income Maintenance and Labor Supply: Econometric Studies,* (Chicago: Markham, 1973).

POLICY APPLICATIONS

Virtually all government income-maintenance programs—from welfare payments to unemployment compensation—have work-incentive effects, and the direction and size of these effects are often critical issues in constructing and enacting such programs. As a society, we have decided to help those among us who are economically disadvantaged for one reason or another. However, it is important to understand how income-maintenance programs can affect the willingness to work. This final section will discuss the labor-supply implications of the unemployment-insurance, workers'-compensation, and welfare programs and their alternatives.

Income-Replacement Programs

Unemployment insurance and workers' compensation are what might be called *income-replacement programs*. Unemployment insurance benefits are paid to workers who have been laid off, permanently or temporarily, by their employers. Workers' compensation is paid to employees who have been injured on the job. Both programs are intended to compensate workers for earnings lost while out of work.[24]

Complete replacement? Given that both the unemployment-insurance and workers'-compensation programs are intended to replace lost earnings, it may seem a bit odd—if not callous—that both programs typically replace roughly just *half* of before-tax lost earnings.[25] It is true that most benefits paid out under these programs are not taxed, so that the fraction of *after-tax* earnings replaced is usually somewhat higher than 50 percent. However, it is also true that lost fringe benefits are not replaced, so that lost compensation is far from completely replaced. Why?

The reason for incomplete earnings replacement has to do with work incentives. Both injured and unemployed workers have some discretion over how long they will remain out of work. A man with a lacerated arm might be able to carry out his normal duties with some discomfort after a few days of recuperation, or he might choose to wait until his wound is completely healed before returning to work. An unemployed woman might accept the first offer of work she obtains, or she may prefer to wait a while and see if she can generate a better offer. In both cases the worker has the legal latitude to decide (within some limits) when to return to work. These decisions will obviously be affected by work incentives inherent in the income-replacement programs affecting them.

Replacing *all* of lost income could result in *overcompensation*—by generating a higher level of utility than before the loss of income[26]—and would motivate

---

[24]For a complete description of these programs, see George E. Rejda, *Social Insurance and Economic Security* (Englewood Cliffs, N.J.: Prentice-Hall, 1976). We will return to the unemployment insurance and workers' compensation programs in the chapters on unemployment (Chapter 15) and compensating differentials (Chapter 8).

[25]Both programs are run at the state level and thus vary in their characteristics across states. Benefits in both programs are bounded by minimums and maximums.

[26]We are assuming here that the psychic costs of injury or layoff are small. It could be argued that complete income replacement is justified on the grounds that it compensates for large psychic losses, but our analysis of work-incentive effects would be unchanged.

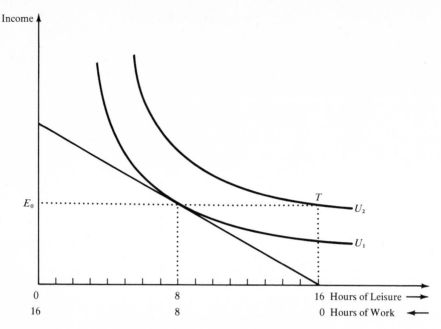

**FIGURE 6.11 Full-Earnings Replacement
Overcompensates Workers**

the recipients of benefits to remain out of work as long as possible. Figure 6.11 shows that before employment ceased, the person earned E_0 and had a level of utility equal to U_1. If, when employment ceases, the worker receives benefits equal to E_0, he or she will be at point T on a higher indifference curve. Before work ceased, the worker earned E_0 and had 8 hours of leisure, whereas at T he or she has E_0 in income and 16 hours of leisure per day. In this case, the recipient would be better off not working than working! Thus, full earnings replacement could clearly inhibit program beneficiaries from returning to work at the earliest possible time (see Example 6.1 for a case where full earnings replacement would *not* completely destroy work incentives).

Actual income loss vs. "scheduled" benefits. A second issue in income replacement programs is how to structure workers' compensation for permanent disabilities. Should workers who are either totally or partially disabled receive benefits that replace their *actual* lost earnings, or should they receive benefits according to some impersonal schedule appropriate for people with their disability? One might initially think that replacing actual losses is more fair, but such a program would create an enormous disincentive to work.

Suppose a worker has become partially disabled because of an injury on the job. Suppose this worker lost three fingers on one hand and, being a manual worker, must now seek work in jobs that pay less than he earned before. His new "market" budget constraint might be the line AD in Figure 6.12. If our injured worker earned E_0 before injury, and workers' compensation replaces all earnings loss up to E_0, the workers' compensation budget constraint facing this worker is like the solid-line constraint *(ABCD)* drawn in Figure 6.12. This income-replace-

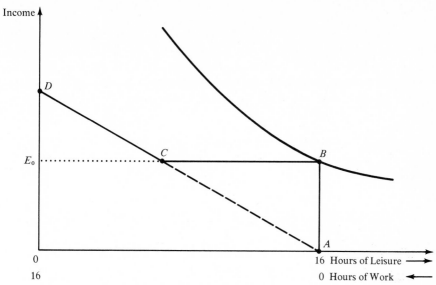

Income

D

E_0

C

B

A

0

16

16 Hours of Leisure ⟶

0 Hours of Work ⟵

FIGURE 6.12 **Budget Constraint with Actual
Income Replacement**

ment constraint has a vertical segment *(AB),* which indicates that if the person
does not work at all he receives a benefit equal to E_0. If he does earn money by
taking a job, the difference between E_0 and his actual earnings becomes his disability benefit. Thus, as long as his actual earnings are below E_0, his benefit is
such that his total income remains at E_0, which is why the segment *BC* is horizontal at E_0. The segment *CD* corresponds to his "market" (unsubsidized) constraint when earnings are above E_0.

Now the interesting thing about Figure 6.12 is that for many people *B*—a
point of no work at all—is the point of maximum utility. Throughout the horizontal segment, *BC,* the individual's net wage is zero, as reflected by the horizontal line. If our worker were to earn an extra $10, the government would reduce
his benefits by $10. In a very real sense, any earnings would be "taxed" away
completely in the form of a dollar-for-dollar reduction in benefits. When people
cannot increase their income by working, there is usually no incentive to work.
There are exceptions, however, where a zero wage *would* be associated with a
positive level of work hours—as illustrated in Example 6.1.

One way to avoid the disincentives inherent in replacing *actual* lost earnings
for disabled workers is to grant benefits according to some schedule drawn up
with reference to the disability but without regard to the individual's actual earnings loss. For example, in the state of New York, a worker losing the first three
fingers of one hand receives two thirds of his before-injury weekly wage for a
period of 101 weeks irrespective of his actual earnings during or after this 101-
week period.[27] After that, he receives no further workers' compensation for that
injury. Other states compensate permanent, partial disabilities in a similar manner.

---

[27]New York State, *Workmen's Compensation Law* (Hempstead, N.Y.: Workmen's Compensation
Board, 1970), p. 65.

Example 6.1
The Economics of the "Workaholic"

The text discussion of work incentives inherent in income-replacement programs has assumed that more leisure time always increases one's utility. This assumption leads to the conclusion that government income subsidies that are reduced one dollar for every dollar earned will induce people not to work. It was argued that such subsidies essentially reduce wages to zero, and that people will not work if they cannot increase their income by working.

Although the above assumption that an hour of leisure yields more in utility than an uncompensated hour at work may be true for most people, we can all think of people we know who love their work and become bored and restless when away from work. For them, work may be a "hobby," a "calling", or a means of socializing. It seems inconceivable that these people would choose *not* to work even if their money income would be the same whether they did or did not work. Can economic theory deal with these "workaholics" who derive more pleasure from work than from leisure, holding money income constant? The answer is yes.

Let us suppose that a "workaholic" places a positive value on leisure when her working hours are high, but after L' hours of daily leisure are consumed any further increases in leisure cause her to be bored and restless. She places *negative* value on leisure at that point and would prefer to be at work even if she were not paid for it! A graphical representation of this woman's indifference curve is given by the curve $ABCD$ in the accompanying figure. Along the arc ABC, the indifference curve is negatively sloped, which means that she would be willing to give up some income to obtain more leisure (that is, she places a positive value on leisure). Increases in leisure hours beyond L', however, place her in a range

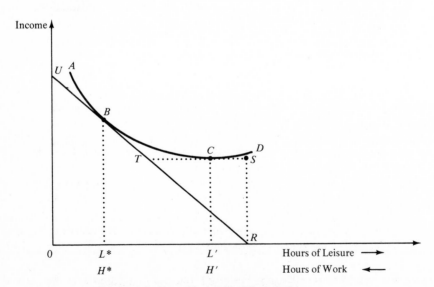

The Work/Leisure Choice of a Workaholic

where her indifference curve is positively sloped (segment *CD*). In this range she places a negative value on leisure and would *give up* income if it meant she could avoid the boredom or social isolation of not working.

If our workaholic faced a budget constraint like *RU* in this figure, she would maximize utility at point *B* and work *H** hours per day. However, even if her budget constraint had a horizontal (zero-wage) segment in it (see, for example, the constraint *RSTU* in the figure) she would work! In this latter case, she would maximize utility at point *C* and work *H'* hours. *H'* represents fewer hours than did *H** but is clearly not equal to zero. Economic theory, then, *can* represent and successfully analyze the behavior of "workaholics."

Using an impersonal schedule of disability benefits preserves at least some incentive to work, because benefits are not reduced if earnings increase. The benefits received become a grant of nonwage income, and they do not alter the recipient's wage rate (price of leisure).

Figure 6.13 contains the "market" constraint *(AD)* and the "actual earnings loss" constraint *(ABCD)* previously depicted in Figure 6.12. Now assume that instead of actual earnings loss, disability benefits for our disabled worker equal E_s no matter how much or how little he earns after the injury. His new constraint is thus *ABE*. This new constraint is parallel to *AD*, his "market" constraint (*ABE* is everywhere E_s higher than constraint *AD*)—reflecting the fact that this form of compensation for injury does not alter his wage rate.

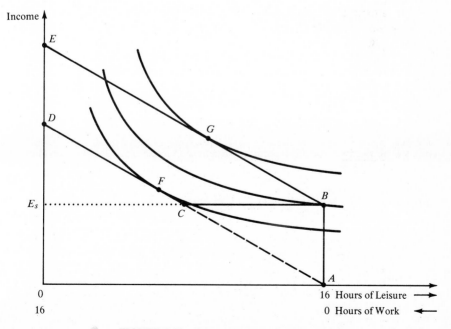

**FIGURE 6.13 Comparing Budget Constraints
of Two Disability Programs**

Figure 6.13 provides a graphical demonstration that with ''scheduled'' benefits there are greater incentives to work than when benefits are based on earnings loss. Our injured worker maximizes utility at point G rather than at point B, even though both disability benefit programs depicted pay equal benefits for those who cannot or do not choose to work.

The conclusion that scheduled payments offer stronger work incentives than benefits based on actual losses clearly becomes even stronger if the scheduled benefits are reduced below E_S. As benefits are reduced, the constraint ABE moves closer to AD, and the point of utility maximization moves farther from G and closer to F (the utility-maximizing point in a world without disability benefits). Maximum work incentives are retained when there is no income-transfer program—a situation in obvious conflict with the overall *goal* of helping workers who find themselves economically disadvantaged.[28]

While the basic aim is to restore income to disadvantaged workers, it is important to preserve work incentives as much as possible. If we take AD as the budget constraint when no benefit program exists and point F as the corresponding optimum work effort, it is easy to see from Figure 6.13 that ''scheduled'' benefits cause only an income effect. The constraint moves out to ABE, but it does not change slope. Work effort declines, since point G is to the right of point F, but it does not cease.[29]

On the contrary, when actual earnings loss becomes the basis for benefits calculation, there is an income *and* a substitution effect—and *both* work in the *same* direction. The benefits simultaneously increase income while *reducing* the wage rate to zero (in the segment BC of constraint $ABCD$). The presence of a zero wage rate reduces the price of leisure to zero and is a powerful disincentive to work. It is not surprising that payments for partial disabilities are generally ''scheduled'' in nature.[30]

Income-Maintenance Programs

Income-maintenance programs—more popularly known as ''welfare'' or ''relief'' programs—have the goal of *raising* the income of the poor to some minimum acceptable level. They thus differ from income-replacement programs, which were aimed at *restoring* lost income. Because poverty is generally an income-related concept, the benefits paid out under income-maintenance programs generally are affected by the level of the beneficiary's actual income. As we shall see, income-conditioned benefits inevitably reduce work incentives below what such incentives would be with no income-support system for the poor. They simultaneously increase income while reducing the price of leisure (the wage rate)—both of which

---

[28]Chapter 8 will show that workers who are injured may be compensated *in advance* of injury by having higher wages (due to the risk inherent in their job) than they would otherwise have. The *compensating wage differentials* must also be taken into account when establishing programs on post-injury compensation.

[29]An exception to this statement would be a situation in which a person's indifference curves are such that a ''corner solution''—as in Figure 6.7—is obtained.

[30]For more details on the Workers' Compensation program, *see* Rejda, *Social Insurance and Economic Security.*

Example 6.2
Worker Adjustment

The discussion of work incentives inherent in income-replacement and income-maintenance programs assumed that workers are well informed about program characteristics—that is, that they have some intuitive understanding of the budget constraint facing them. It also assumes that workers face a sufficiently large array of choices that they are able to find a set of working hours close to their utility-maximizing set. Students often have a healthy skepticism about the degree to which these assumptions approximate reality. The following example suggests that workers *do* have sufficient knowledge and choice to accomodate their behavior to a given set of work incentives.

The State of Wisconsin, like other states, has an unemployment compensation program that pays unemployed workers a weekly benefit. These benefits are different for different recipients, depending primarily on their pre-unemployment earnings. There is a minimum and a maximum weekly benefit, but for most workers the unemployment benefit is about one half of prior earnings. Also like most other states, Wisconsin has a method of allowing for partial benefits to be paid to unemployed workers who obtain part-time or low-wage work during their period of eligibility for unemployment benefits. Unlike most other states, however, Wisconsin's partial benefit scheme is such that recipients can only receive one of three unemployment benefits: their full weekly benefit, a benefit equal to half their full weekly benefit, or zero. This partial benefit program contains some rather interesting work incentives.

The typical recipient of unemployment compensation in Wisconsin can earn up to one fourth of his or her pre-unemployment earnings with

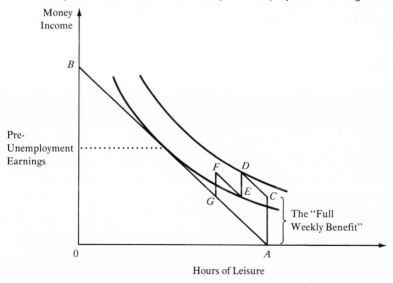

Partial Unemployment Benefits in Wisconsin

no loss of benefits. Being able, in effect, to keep all their earnings up to that point, the wage rate of recipients equals their market wage. This element of the program is graphed in the first figure as segment *CD*, which is parallel to the market constraint (*AB*).

However, once current earnings rise above the critical level of one fourth of prior earnings, benefits are reduced to one-half the weekly benefit. This abrupt drop in benefits causes an equally abrupt drop in total income. Since working an extra hour past point *D* causes income to drop, the wage, in effect, becomes *negative,* as segment *DE* in the first figure illustrates.

Benefits equalling one half the full entitlement are paid, then, to recipients who earn between one fourth and one half of their prior earnings. When earnings rise just beyond the one-half point, all unemployment benefits cease, and the constraint becomes the "market constraint"—as segments *EF, FG,* and *GB* illustrate. The first figure shows a saw-toothed constraint where the market wage alternates with extremely negative wage rates.

A quick look at the first figure indicates that, for many people, point *D* is the utility-maximizing combination of leisure hours and income. People who are not fortunate enough to obtain a job offer where they can earn exactly one fourth of their earnings will try to choose the next best posi-

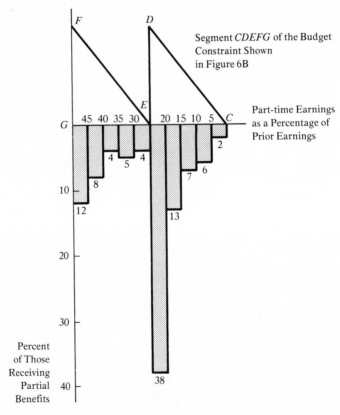

Distribution of Partial Benefits in Wisconsin (1967), by Earnings Level

tion—which is likely to be at points along the upper portions of *CD* or near point *F*. Points along most of *EF* and the lower portions of *CD* are clearly inferior—in terms of utility—to other points along the constraint running from *C* to *G*.

While it is true that most of those receiving unemployment benefits are completely unemployed, it is interesting to observe whether those who *are* able to find part-time work adjust their behavior as indicated above. In other words, *do* people tend to cluster most at point *D*—where earnings are just equal to one fourth of their prior wages? Are there more people at point *F* and the upper portions of *CD* than along the rest of the constraint running from *C* to *G*?

The answer to both these questions—at least for the year 1967 when a study of the questions was undertaken—is yes. In the second figure, segment *CDEFG* of the first figures budget constraint is superimposed on the distribution of those actually receiving partial unemployment benefits, demonstrating that by far the biggest cluster of people is at point *D*, earning 20–25 percent of their prior earnings. Further, the concentrations of people increase as one moves to the upper ends of each segment (*CD* and *EF*)—with two-thirds of all partial-benefits recipients either at *F* or the upper half of *CD*. Thus, it appears that workers who do find partial employment while receiving unemployment benefits do have the knowledge and inclination to adjust their behavior to the constraints (and the related incentives) facing them.

SOURCE: Raymond Munts, "Partial Benefit Schedules in Unemployment Insurance: Their Effect on Work Incentive," *Journal of Human Resources* 5 (Spring 1970); 160–76.

---

should cause the demand for leisure to increase and the supply of labor to fall. This fact is the root of much of the controversy welfare programs have generated over the years. Welfare payments have taken two forms in this country, as described below.

The old welfare system.   Prior to 1967, welfare took the form of a guaranteed annual income. A welfare worker would determine the "needed" income of the eligible person or family, based on family size, area living costs, and local welfare regulations. Actual earnings would be subtracted from this needed level, and a check would be received each month for the difference. If earnings went up, welfare benefits would go down, dollar-for-dollar. This created a budget constraint like *ABCD* shown in Figure 6.14, where total income is Y_n (the "needed" income) as long as the person is subsidized. There is no incentive to work for many people, because there is a zero wage (segment *BC*) over most normal hours of work.

Thus, the old welfare system served to increase income by moving the budget constraint out from *AC* to *ABC*; this shift created an *income effect* tending to reduce labor supply from points *E* to *F* in Figure 6.14. However, it *also* caused the wage to effectively drop to zero: every dollar earned was matched by a dollar reduction of welfare benefits. This dollar-for-dollar reduction in benefits induced a huge *substitution effect*—causing many to reduce their hours of work to zero

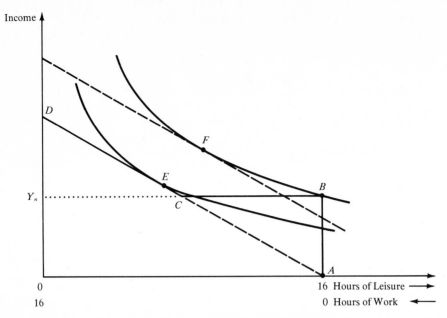

FIGURE 6.14   Income and Substitution Effects for "Old" Welfare System

(point *B*). The old system clearly had strong disincentives for welfare recipients to find work.

The current welfare system.   Recognizing the nonexistent work incentives in the old system, the government restructured welfare benefits in 1967 to eliminate the zero wage rate. Welfare recipients were allowed to keep the first $30 of any earnings per month and one third of the rest. Thus, ignoring the first $30, a welfare recipient who earned an extra $100 by working would have his or her benefits reduced by $67. The take-home wage rate thus became, in effect, one third of the market wage.

While a take-home wage of one third the market wage clearly reduces the wage rate compared to what it would be without welfare, it represents a significant improvement in work incentives over the zero wage rate implicit in the old system (see Figure 6.15).

Let us assume that the government has determined that the minimum needed income, Y_n, for the recipient family is $16 per day. It thus guarantees that the family will have a welfare benefit of $16 if no one works. Suppose, however, that the family head could earn $3 per hour if she worked, or a total of $48 per day if she works 16 hours a day. If we ignore the first $30 of monthly earnings that can be kept completely[31] and remember that for every $3 she earns the government reduces her welfare benefit by $2, we can easily see that if she works 8 hours a

---

[31]To take into account this small sum would complicate our diagram without changing the analysis or its conclusions in any essential way.

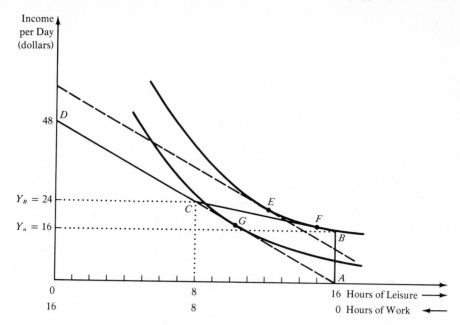

**FIGURE 6.15   Income and Substitution Effects
of the Current Welfare Program**

day—and thus earns $24—she will be taken off welfare and receive no benefit
(two thirds of $24 is $16). An income of $24 thus becomes the *break-even level*
of income (Y_B)—the point at which the family is no longer subsidized.

For incomes higher than $24 per day, the family's budget constraint is *CD*,
the unsubsidized or market constraint of which the slope's absolute value is 3
(reflecting the $3 wage). If the family earnings are zero, the welfare benefit is $16
(point *B* in Figure 6.15). If earnings are between $0–24, the family is subsidized
and has a total income (earnings plus subsidy) that falls along segment *BC* in
Figure 6.15. Segment *BC* rises from $16 (point *B*) to $24 (point *C*) for 8 hours of
work—which suggests this segment has a slope of which the absolute value is
one. This slope is one third the slope of *AD*, which reflects the market wage of
$3. Therefore, as long as the family is subsidized, the take-home wage rate is one
third of the market wage under the current welfare system.

If one looks at the segment *ABC* of Figure 6.15—the welfare system constraint—one can see that the program increases income and reduces the take-home
wage rate (because it "taxes away," in the form of reducing welfare benefits, two
thirds of earnings). The increased income alone—with no change in wage—
would create an *income effect* that decreases labor supply from points *G* to *E*.
However, the fact that the take-home wage is reduced to one-third of its market
level creates a *substitution effect* that further reduces labor supply to point *F*.[32]

---

[32]Note that because of the decrease in the take-home wage, the *income effect* of the income-maintenance program described becomes smaller the *more* one works (as long as income is sufficiently
low to qualify for the subsidy). Graphically, segment *ABC* of the constraint in Figure 6.15 is
further to the northeast of the market constraint *AD* in the region where working hours are few-
est—and closest near 8 hours of work (the point where the subsidy ends).

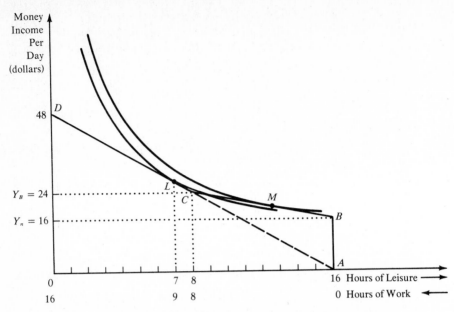

FIGURE 6.16 Some May Reduce Hours of Work and Money Income Under an Income-Maintenance Program

Again, *both* the income and the substitution effect work in the direction of less work *compared to a world with no income subsidies.* However, comparing Figures 6.15 and 6.14, one can see that the current welfare system has stronger work incentives than the old one, because welfare benefits are not reduced dollar-for-dollar with earnings.

Lest the student receive the impression that the obvious solution to this work-incentive problem is to reduce the implicit tax from two thirds to some lower fraction, let us explore what happens if this implicit tax were reduced to one-fourth. Under this plan, the welfare recipient would be allowed to keep three of every four dollars earned. If $16 is still the daily benefit when there are no earnings, the break-even level of income becomes $64 (instead of $24). In other words, no matter what their wage rate, people who earn less than $64 per day would receive welfare benefits. Clearly, a low implicit tax rate and a reasonably generous guarantee level are inconsistent with confining welfare benefits to only the needy! This dilemma pervades just about all disputes over welfare policy. That is, reducing implicit tax rates to increase the work incentive leads to an increase in the number of people eligible for benefits.

It is also worth noting here that because the welfare subsidy is conditioned on income, and because income is to some extent under the control of an individual, it is possible that some people previously above the break-even level of income will reduce their labor supply enough to qualify for the subsidy. This possibility is illustrated in Figure 6.16. Prior to the subsidy, the person depicted maximized utility at point *L*, working 9 hours per day. After the subsidy is instituted and the constraint moves to *ABCD*, this person finds that utility is maximized at point *M*, where hours of work are much fewer. Point *M* is a point of lower money income than point *L,* but the increased leisure time more than makes up for the lost income.

Although making welfare benefits available to people who were not previously eligible for them will clearly decrease their work incentives, the relevant policy question is: By how much will their work incentives be decreased? Some studies used estimates of income and substitution effects obtained from nonexperimental data in the late 1960s to answer this question. These studies imply that, for males, a guaranteed (zero-earnings) benefit of about 75 percent of the poverty level (which was $3300 per year in 1967) and a 50 percent implicit tax rate would cause male labor supply to decrease by 8–15 percent.[33]

Experimental data, however, can also be used to estimate the size of income and substitution effects. Four large social experiments were conducted in New Jersey, Seattle-Denver, Gary (Indiana), and rural North Carolina in the late 1960s and early 1970s for the purpose of measuring labor-supply responses to various alternative income-maintenance policies. They were conceived and funded because researchers and policy makers did not want to rely solely on estimates derived from the nonexperimental studies cited above.

While the details in each experiment varied, the welfare programs offered to the people in the experiments had benefit-guarantee levels (benefits with zero earnings) ranging from 50–125 percent of the poverty level.[34] The implicit tax rates in each experiment ranged from 30–80 percent. The typical response for males in these experiments was to reduce labor supply by 3–8 percent.[35] The somewhat smaller response than the cross-sectional prediction above is perhaps due to the known and limited duration of each experiment; responses might have been larger if recipients knew the program would be available to them indefinitely.

In examining the labor-supply response of females in these experiments, it is useful to recall two facts from the nonexperimental studies. First, the estimates of income and substitution effects for women are much less precise than for men; second, the substitution effect for market work appears to be larger. Remembering that the substitution effect of income-maintenance programs induces a withdrawal of labor supply, it is not surprising to find that the labor-supply responses of women in the experiments tended to be larger than for men and were also more varied. For wives, the responses ranged from zero decline in Gary to a 55 percent

[33]Borjas and Heckman, "Labor Supply Estimates for Public Policy Evaluation," p. 331.

[34]Poverty level incomes are those below which the federal government considers a family to be living in poverty. These income thresholds are defined for farm and nonfarm families separately and are also calculated by family size and the age/sex of the household head. The threshold in each case is based on the 1963 cost of an inexpensive, but nutritionally sound, food plan designed by the Department of Agriculture. This cost was multiplied by 3, reflecting an assumption that families of three or more persons spend one-third of their income on food, and has been adjusted upward each year since 1963 by changes in the Consumer Price Index. For a nonfarm family of four, the 1976 poverty threshold was $5815, up from $3128 in 1963; by 1980 changes in the Consumer Price Index implied a poverty level of around $8600 per year. (See U.S. Bureau of the Census, Current Population Reports, *Consumer Income,* Series P-60, No. 115, issued July 1978 for a more detailed explanation of poverty thresholds.)

[35]Minorities in the New Jersey experiment were an exception to this finding. They did not decrease their labor supply at all.

decline among Spanish-speaking wives in New Jersey, with most other estimates in the 15–30 percent range.[36] For female heads of families, the declines ranged from 11 percent in Seattle-Denver to 30 percent in Gary.

Thus the labor supply effects of expanded welfare coverage are not likely to be innocuous. At some point, society will have to decide whether the improvements in social equity that result from more generous welfare programs are counterbalanced by the social losses attendant to reduced labor supply.[37] In making this decision, of course, society may feel quite different about reductions in market work by some groups (say, mothers of small children) than it feels about the labor-supply reductions of other groups.

REVIEW QUESTIONS

1. Is the following statement true, false, or uncertain:
    "Leisure must be an inferior good for an individual's labor supply curve to be backward-bending." Explain your answer.
2. The way the Workers' Compensation system works now is that employees permanently injured on the job receive a payment of $X each year whether they work or not. Suppose the government were to implement a new program where those who do not work at all get $0.5X but where those who do work get $0.5X plus Workers' Compensation of 50 cents *for every hour worked*. What would be the change in work incentives associated with this change in the way Workers' Compensation payments are calculated?
3. Suppose our welfare system were structured *initially* as follows: all people earning below income $X would be given a cash grant to bring their income up to $X. *Draw a graph showing the budget constraint for this program.*
    Next, suppose we change the welfare system to incorporate a *work test*. This means that persons who work *fewer* than Y hours get no welfare payment at all. Above Y hours of work, the people receive a welfare payment sufficient to bring up their income to $X. *Draw in the relevant budget constraint on your graph.*
    Now answer the question: *Which system has stronger work incentives? Why?*
4. A secret memo from the President has been found in the trash basket in front of an aide's house. It says, in part, "Although I am in favor of eliminating the capital-gains advantages in the income tax system, I am concerned that we maintain the labor supply of the expert managers who run the industry of this country. By forcing them to pay higher taxes on investment income, we may be affecting their labor market behavior. Please have a labor economist figure out the labor supply effects of this proposed tax

---

[36]For a summary of all the experiments, see Robert Moffitt and Kenneth Kehrer, "The Effect of Tax and Transfer Programs on Labor Supply: The Evidence from the Income Maintenance Experiments" *Research in Labor Economics*, ed. R. Ehrenberg (Greenwich, Conn.: JAI Press, 1981). Also see Michael C. Keeley *et al.*, "The Estimation of Labor Supply Models Using Experimental Data," *American Economic Review* (December 1978): pp. 873–87; Robert A. Moffitt, "The Labor Supply Response in the Gary Experiment," *The Journal of Human Resources* 14 (Fall 1979): 477–87; Albert Rees, "An Overview of the Labor-Supply Results," *The Journal of Human Resources* 9 (Spring 1974): 158–80.

[37]The general issue of equity vs. output considerations is treated in a readable manner by Arthur Okun, *Equality and Efficiency: The Big Trade-Off* (Washington, D.C.: The Brookings Institution, 1975).

reform on the wealthy and report back to me as soon as possible. The analysis should be clear as to what might happen and why. Please have your economist write so that an ordinary human can understand.''

Write an analysis for the President. (Note: The capital-gains ''loophole'' applies to the sale of stocks, bonds, and other assets. If the asset has been held for more than six months, only 40 percent of the gain on the sale—the difference between selling price and cost—is taxable. The President would make the whole gain taxable.)

5. The Secretary of Labor has received the following memo from a member of the President's staff:

''The growth of interest in worker-owned enterprises raises some important questions relating to profit sharing. If workers with no previous investment income begin to receive a portion of profits, the effects on labor supply could be large. Would you please have your staff prepare an analysis of the labor-supply implications of widespread worker participation in profits? The paper should cover the direction of the labor-supply effects as indicated by theory and the likely ways in which these labor-supply effects could be manifested. In particular, however, I am interested in a comparison of the labor-supply effects of alternative bases upon which profits can be shared among workers. Which basis or bases have the smallest labor-supply effects?''

Write the paper avoiding the use of undefined jargon words. In other words, explain the concepts and hypotheses fully.

SELECTED READINGS

George Borjas and James Heckman, ''Labor Supply Estimates for Public Policy Evaluation,'' *Proceedings of the Industrial Relations Research Association* (1978), pp. 320–331.

William G. Bowen and T. Aldrich Finegan, *The Economics of Labor Force Participation* (Princeton, N.J.: Princeton University Press, 1969).

Glen G. Cain, *Married Women in the Labor Force* (Chicago: University of Chicago Press, 1966).

Glen G. Cain and Harold W. Watts, eds., *Income Maintenance and Labor Supply* (Chicago: Rand McNally, 1973).

H. G. Lewis, ''Hours of Work and Hours of Leisure,'' *Proceedings of the Industrial Relations Research Association* (1957), pp. 196–206.

J. A. Pechman and P. M. Timpane, eds. *Work Incentives and Income Guarantees: The New Jersey Income Tax Experiment* (Washington, D.C.: The Brookings Institution, 1975).

7

Labor Supply: Household Production and the Family

In Chapter 6 the theory of labor supply focused on *individuals* who were choosing between *labor* and *leisure*. This chapter will recast labor-supply theory to take into account the interdependency of family members' decisions and the fact that much of the time spent at home is on *production,* not consumption, activities. This theory of labor supply in the context of "household production" can yield many useful insights into labor-supply behavior and related policy issues.[1]

THE THEORY OF HOUSEHOLD PRODUCTION

Although many adults are unmarried at some points in their lives, most do marry and form family units. The family thus becomes a very basic decision-making entity in society, and many important decisions concerning both consumption patterns and labor supply are made in a *family* context. Our task in this chapter is to find out in what ways (if any) the implications of the individual labor-supply theory in Chapter 6 are modified or expanded by consideration of the *family*.

Throughout this chapter we will assume that it is the *family unit* that consumes and enjoys goods; that is, we will assume that husband and wife *jointly* derive utility from consumption. We will also assume that many of the goods the family consumes are produced—or can be produced—at home. Thus, food and energy are combined with preparation time to produce the meals from which family enjoyment is derived. A vacuum cleaner and time are combined to contribute to an orderly home. Food, clothing, and supervision time all contribute to the growth of children whom the parents hope to enjoy. Thus, a marriage partner who stays at home may be engaged more in the production of goods from which the family derives utility than in the direct consumption of leisure.

---

[1]Models of household production are based on the pioneering work of Gary Becker, "A Theory of the Allocation of Time," *Economic Journal* 75 (September 1965): 493–517. Another early study in this area is by Reuben Gronau, "The Measurement of Output of the Nonmarket Sector: The Evaluation of Housewives' Time," in Milton Moss, ed., *The Measurement of Economic and Social Performance* (New York: National Bureau of Economic Research, 1973), pp. 163–89.

A Model of Household Production

Household-production models explicitly recognize that both consumption and pro-duction take place in the home. The family unit, then, must make two kinds of decisions: 1. *what* to consume and 2. *how to produce* what it consumes. Consider the second decision first by analyzing a family that does not have to worry about what to consume because it consumes only one good: meals. This family derives its utility from the quantity and quality of food it eats as well as from the general environment surrounding its meal consumption.[2]

Meals that yield equal utility can be produced in several ways. A family can eat out in a restaurant, in which case there is minimum time spent in preparation and a maximum of market commodities (food plus service) consumed. The meal could be prepared at home with food bought from a market—or it could be pre-pared at home with food grown or made at home, which obviously represents a lot of preparation time. Since any of these combinations of commodities and household time can produce meals that are equally valuable (in terms of producing utility) to the family, we can draw a curve that represents all the time-commodity combinations that can produce meals of equal utility. Such a curve can be called a utility *isoquant*—where *iso* means ''equal,'' and *quant* means ''quantity''— and two such isoquants are depicted in Figure 7.1 as M_0 and M_1.

Several things should be noted about the isoquants in Figure 7.1. First, along M_0, the utility provided by family meals is constant. The utility produced by the time-commodity combinations along M_1 is also constant, but it is greater than the

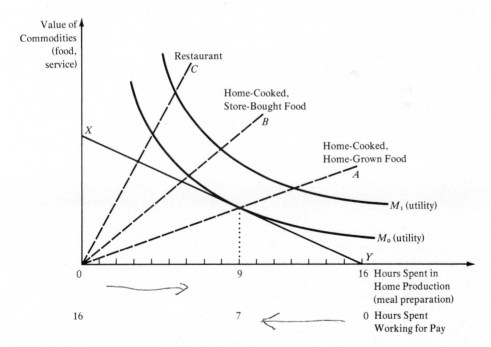

FIGURE 7.1   The Production of Family Meals

---

[2]We will drop the assumption about consuming just one good later, but the assumption permits us to make several basic points in an easily understood fashion.

utility represented by M_0 because meals produced by such combinations generally involve more commodities, more time, or both.

Second, the isoquants M_0 and M_1 are both *negative* in slope and *convex* (as viewed from below) in shape. The *negative* slope reflects an assumption that time and commodities are substitutes in the production of meals. If household time is reduced, meal production can be held constant by increasing the purchase of commodities. Thus, if a family decides not to grow its own food, it can buy food instead—or if it decides to spend less time cooking food it could still maintain the same utility from meals by using a microwave oven or going out to eat.

The *convexity* of the isoquants reflects an assumption that as household meal-preparation time continues to fall, it becomes more difficult to make up for it with commodities. If the family spends a lot of time in meal preparation, it will be easy to replace some of that time with just a few commodities (store-bought food easily replaces home-grown food, for example). However, when preparation time is very short to begin with, a further cut in such time may be very difficult to absorb and still keep utility constant. Thus, it will take many commodities—a large increase in food quality, for example—to substitute for reduced cooking time.

Finally, along any one ray (*A, B,* or *C*) emanating from the origin of Figure 7.1 the ratio of commodities to household preparation time in the production of meals is constant. When time and commodities are combined in the ratio along ray *A,* time-intensive meals are produced using home-grown food. Meals produced with the time-commodity ratio along *B* are home-cooked, using store-bought food—and the time-commodity ratio along ray *C* represents the "production" of restaurant meals.

The utility-maximizing mode of producing meals depends on the wage rate and the nonwage income and utility preferences of the producer of those meals. In Figure 7.1 the budget constraint of a woman whose husband is disabled and cannot work, who has no nonwage income, and who has a relatively low wage is depicted by *XY*. The figure suggests that the utility-maximizing mode of meal preparation is to use home-grown food, for the simple reason that when one has a low wage, time-intensive activities are relatively inexpensive. Time spent weeding, tilling, canning, and freezing does not cost a lot, in terms of forgone earnings (commodities), in this case. Thus, in the example shown, nine hours a day would be spent at home, seven hours performing work for pay, and meal production on isoquant M_0 represents the highest level of utility that can be attained.

Figure 7.2 shows what will happen if the budget constraint in Figure 7.1 shifts because of an increase in *nonwage* income. What happens to the wife's propensity to work outside the home if the family were to receive governmental payments for the husband's disability? This income grant does not change the wife's wage rate, so that the new budget constraint facing the family has the same slope as constraint *XY* in Figure 7.1. However, the new constraint (*X'Y'* in Figure 7.2) lies above the old one and reflects a pure *income effect*. Because it is wealthier, the family will want to enjoy higher-quality meals. It will have more money with which to buy commodities, but it will also decide to have the wife spend more time at home to prepare the meals (remember, both commodities and time

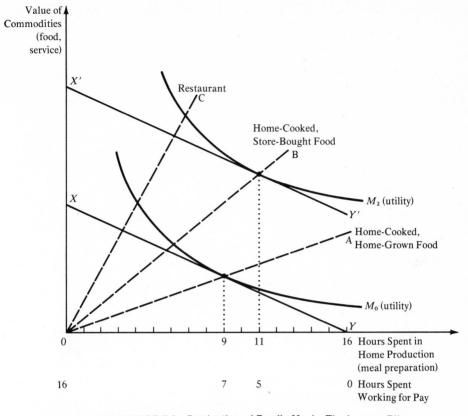

FIGURE 7.2   **Production of Family Meals: The Income Effect**

are valuable in producing meals). She may change the time-commodity ratio, as shown in Figure 7.2 by a movement from Ray A to Ray B—depending on the shape of the isoquants.

Before moving on to discuss the changes that occur as a result of a change in the wife's wage, let us pause to make two points. First, the income effect in this household-production model has exactly the same sign as the effect in the labor/leisure model discussed in the Chapter 6. Second, the amount of work for pay and the mode of household production are jointly determined; that is, they are affected by the same constraint and are made as part of the same decision. Emphasizing household production rather than leisure, therefore, does not change our conclusion about the effects of income on labor supply in this case. Emphasizing production rather than leisure, however, does highlight the interrelated nature of decisions concerning family "production" and decisions about labor supply.

Let us continue for a moment with our example in Figure 7.2 of a wife whose husband was initially disabled and unemployed. If he remains disabled, but she obtained a wage increase, what would happen to her labor supply? Quite simply, there would be two opposing effects (as we found in the "leisure" model previously). The *income effect,* as above, would tend to drive her away from market

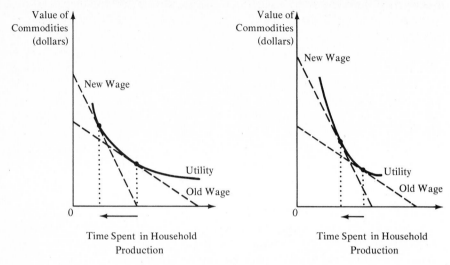

FIGURE 7.3   Large vs. Small Substitution Effects

work and toward more time at home, where she could spend more time in activities (meal preparation) which enhance family utility. However, the *substitution effect* would tend to push her out of the home and toward more work for pay. When her wages are increased, time spent at home preparing meals becomes more expensive than it was before. Thus, she will tend to move away from time-intensive modes of production to modes which rely more on commodities—thus freeing her for more "market" work. The overall, observed effect of her wage increase on her labor supply cannot be predicted based on theory alone.

Household Production and Consumption

We have just seen that when a family member is engaged in household production, an increase in the wage rate will have two effects. There will be an income effect that induces the family to consume more household "output"—and tends to push the household producer out of market work and into the home. However, there is also a substitution effect that induces the family to produce its household output in a less time-intensive fashion—which tends to drive the household producer into working more for pay outside the home. Thus, *substitution in the (household) production process* occurs.

However, *another* substitution effect is also present. If we drop our assumption that the family consumes just one good, it is easy to see that when the market wage rate of the household producer changes the family may change the *mix* of goods that it consumes. If the wife's wage, say, goes up and commodity prices do not, the cost of very time-intensive goods will rise more than goods that are produced using less time. The family will tend to consume more goods, because it is wealthier, but it will alter the *mix* of goods it consumes by reducing the proportion of time-intensive goods in its consumption "basket." Thus, a change in the market wage rate of the household producer causes substitution in household *consumption* as well as in household *production*.

Recall from Chapter 6 that the substitution effect is graphically depicted by changing the slope of the budget constraint, keeping it tangent to a given indifference curve. If the relevant indifference curve is relatively flat, as in panel (a) of Figure 7.3, the substitution effect will be larger than when the indifference curve is steep, as in panel (b). What will cause it to be comparatively flat? In terms of our model, the curve will be flat when it is *easy to substitute commodities for time* without loss of utility. (To prove this to yourself, ask "If an hour of time at home is given up, what amount of commodities will have to be added to keep utility constant?" When it is easy to substitute commodities for time, it will take relatively few commodities to keep utility constant.)

Married women have traditionally been engaged in household production, as well as household consumption. Married men have tended to be less involved in household production, and a higher proportion of their time at home has been spent in consumption, or leisure, activities. As male wages rise, they will experience a substitution effect in *consumption* that tends to push them towards less time-intensive forms of consumption and towards more commodities-intensive consumption. When women's wages rise, however, there will be substitution effects in both *production and consumption*. Women will tend to consume less time-intensive goods, but as household producers they will *also* adopt less time-intensive modes of production. They will substitute frozen foods, day care for children, and automatic washing machines for household-production time; this substitution effect in production is more or less added to the one in consumption to yield a stronger overall substitution effect than is observed for males.

JOINT HUSBAND-WIFE LABOR-SUPPLY DECISIONS

In the preceding example, we assumed that the husband was disabled and thus not very productive in either market or household production in order to analyze the labor-supply decisions for the wife only. When both spouses are capable of work inside and outside of the home, the family must make decisions about who will work where. In other words, because husbands and wives are productive in two places—in market work and in the household—their labor supply decisions will be jointly made.

Who Stays at Home?

Consider a utility-maximizing family trying to decide which spouse will stay at home and engage in "household production" full-time. This family will need to answer two questions: Who is relatively more productive at home? Who is relatively more productive in market work? The answer to the first question depends upon who can produce more goods (more utility) for a given amount of commodities and home-production time. The answer to the second question depends upon who can generate the greater command over commodities by working for pay. Simply put, if a utility-maximizing family decides it must have one spouse at home, it will prefer to have that spouse be the one who is relatively more productive there than in the marketplace.

For example, a family deciding who should stay home and perform most of the child rearing would—if it is going to maximize utility—consider the gains

Example 7.1
Household Productivity and Labor Supply In Japan

One of the fundamental insights of household-production theory is that one's labor supply behavior is, in part, a function of productivity at home relative to that in the marketplace (as reflected in one's wage rate). While formal exposition of the theory is a recent development in economics, the behavior it seeks to explain is not. Many developing countries employ people in their industrial cities who have recently migrated from family farms and whose labor is valuable there at harvest time. In terms of household-production theory, the harvest-related increase in their productivity back on the farm temporarily reduces the relative advantage of market (paid) work; the result is they quit or absent themselves from their factory jobs at this time of year and go back home to help out.

An example of the above behavior can be found in Japan early in this century. Many cotton-spinning mills lost 30 percent of their work force in August, stimulating factory owners to adopt countermeasures. Koji Taira describes the situation as follows:

> It was widely recognized that the seasonal fluctuations were closely related to labor requirements on farms, since the factory operatives were predominantly from farm households. From the point of view of the farm households, the value of work on the farm during busy periods was much higher than the regular wages at the factory. The essence of countermeasures on the part of the factory, therefore, was to offer such inducements as might make staying on the job more attractive than return to the farm during such periods. A variety of inducements developed that were based on this premise. One was to grant bonuses to those who stayed on their jobs during the months of peak activity on the farm. Another was a profit-sharing plan of one kind or another that was related to length of period of consecutive work. The third was a variety of devices such as company-paid pleasure trips, participation in company-sponsored lotteries, and recreational opportunities granted only to workers remaining on the job during busy seasons on the farm.

SOURCE: Koji Taira, *Economic Development and the Labor Market in Japan* (New York: The Columbia University Press, 1970), p. 122.

and losses attendant to either the husband or wife performing this task. The losses from staying home are related to the market wage of each, while the gains depend on their enjoyment of, and skill at, child rearing. (Since enjoyment of the parenting process increases family utility, we can designate both higher levels of enjoyment *and* higher levels of skill as indicative of greater "productivity" in child rearing.) The wage rate for women—perhaps because of discrimination—is usually below that for men. (Discrimination will be treated in Chapter 14; other reasons for male-female wage differences are dealt with in Chapters 8 and 9.) It is also likely that, due to the socialization process, women are more productive than men in child rearing. If in an individual family, the woman's wage rate is lower than the man's and the woman is more productive in child rearing, it is clearly

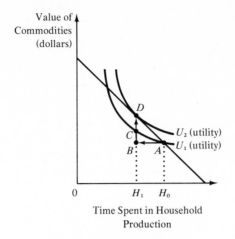

**FIGURE 7.4   Home vs. Market
Productivities**

best for the woman to raise the children. The family gives up less in commodities
and gains more in child rearing.

Modeling the choice of who stays home to raise children as a function of
relative productivities, and not just custom, emphasizes the point that child-rearing
arrangements will probably change as wages and home productivities change. If
discrimination against women is eliminated, or if sex roles in childhood become
less distinct for boys and girls, we could well observe more men rearing children
in the future.

Do Both Spouses Work for Pay?

It is clearly not the case, of course, that either husband or wife must stay at home
full time. Many household chores—from cooking and cleaning to child care—
can be hired out or otherwise performed in a commodity-intensive manner. The
considerations underlying the decision about whether both should work can be
best understood by looking at Figure 7.4. The utility isoquants there (U_1 and U_2)
represent the various combinations of household time and commodities that can
be used to generate family utility of two given levels (level 1 and level 2).

As long as an extra hour of market work by both husband and wife creates
the ability to buy more commodities than are required to make up for the hour of
lost home production time, both spouses will work for pay that extra hour. In
terms of Figure 7.4, if a person spending H_0 hours at home decides to work an
extra hour for pay—so that H_1 hours are now spent at home—he or she will gain
BD in commodities.[3] Since an increase of only BC in commodities is required to
compensate for the lost hour of home production to keep utility constant, the
person is clearly better off working for pay. In other words, at point A the person
is relatively more productive in the market place than at home; therefore, the

---

[3]We are talking here of *after*-tax spending power. The value of what one produces at home is not
taxed, but earnings in the market place are—a difference that forces us to focus here on wages
and earnings *net* of taxes.

decision to perform more market work would be in the family's best interests. Thus, decisions about family labor supply must be made in full consideration of market and household productivities of both marriage partners.

Health and Labor Supply

An analysis of the market and household productivities of a husband and wife must also consider the effects of *health* on labor supply. While a man who tires quickly because of a respiratory problem may be capable of performing market work at reduced hours or wages, his affliction renders his *market* time less productive than that of a healthy person. However, his productivity at home—where resting in between tasks is possible—may not be affected much at all. His changed relative productivity between home and the marketplace may induce his *wife* to replace him as the family's primary breadwinner. He may be almost as productive at home as she is, but her market productivity may now exceed his. Thus she goes to work and he stays home.

Here again, labor-supply decisions are viewed by a utility-maximizing family as matters of choice, not custom or necessity. While custom or necessity are obviously important in some cases, viewing labor-supply decisions as matters of choice provides insight into how government policies or general economic trends will change such decisions. For example, if there is discrimination against women and if this discrimination decreases so that their market wages improve relative to those for males, the labor-supply withdrawal of unhealthly men will probably become more pronounced, for the reasons noted above. For the same reasons, it will become more common for women to be the primary breadwinners in two-adult families.

The "Discouraged" vs. the "Additional" Worker

Changes in one spouse's productivity, either at home or in market work, can alter the family's basic labor-supply decision. Consider, for example, a family in which market work is performed by the husband and in which the wife is employed full-time in the home. What will happen if a recession causes the husband to become unemployed?

The husband's market productivity declines, at least temporarily. He may be a highly specialized worker and unable to find similar work at the moment. The drop in his market productivity relative to his household productivity (which is unaffected by the recession) makes it more likely that the family will find it beneficial for him to engage in household production. If the wage his wife can earn in paid work is not affected, the family *may* decide that, to try to maintain the family's prior level of utility (which might be affected by both consumption and *savings* levels), *she* should seek market work and that *he* should stay home for as long as the recession lasts. He may remain a member of the labor force as an unemployed worker awaiting recall, and as she begins to look for work she becomes an "added" member of the labor force. Thus, in the face of falling family income, the number of family members seeking market work may increase—a phenomenon akin to the *income effect*.

At the same time, however, we must look at the *wage rate* someone without a job can *expect* to receive if he or she looks for work. This expected wage, denoted by *E(W)*, can actually be written as a precise statistical concept:

$$E(W) = \pi W, \tag{7.1}$$

where *W* is the wage rate of people who have the job and π is the probability of obtaining the job. For someone without a job, the price of an hour at home—the opportunity cost of staying home—is *E(W)*. The reduced availability of jobs that occurs when the unemployment rate rises causes the expected wage of those without jobs to fall sharply, for two reasons. First, an excess of labor supply over demand tends to push down real wages (for those with jobs) during recessionary periods. Second, the chances of getting a job fall in a recession. Thus, both *W* and π fall in a recession, causing *E(W)* to decline. Noting the *substitution effect* that accompanies a falling expected wage, some have argued that people who would otherwise have entered the labor force become "discouraged" in a recession and tend to remain out of the labor market. Looking for work has such a low expected payoff for them that such people decide that spending time at home is more productive than spending time in job search. The reduction of the labor force associated with discouraged workers in a recession is a force working opposite to the "added-worker" effect—just as the substitution effect works against the income effect.

It is possible, of course, for both the "added-worker" and "discouraged-worker" effects to coexist, because "added" and "discouraged" workers will be different groups of people. Which group predominates, however, is the important question. If the labor force is swelled by "added workers" during a recession, the published unemployment rate will likewise become swollen (the added workers will increase the number of people looking for work). If workers become "discouraged" and drop out of the labor market when they are unemployed, the decline in people seeking jobs will depress the unemployment rate. Knowledge of which effect predominates is needed in order to make accurate inferences about the actual state of the labor market from the published unemployment rate.

We do know that the added-worker effect does exist. Jacob Mincer, in a clever landmark study, found that the labor-market behavior of wives was very sensitive to temporary changes in their husbands' income. In fact, he found that the labor supply of married women was more responsive to temporary than permanent changes in their husbands' income![4] However, this added-worker effect is confined to the relatively few families whose normal breadwinner loses a job (the overall unemployment rate rarely goes above 10 percent).[5] The fall in expected real wages occurs in nearly *every* household, and remembering that the substitution effect is strong for married women, it is not surprising to find that the discouraged-worker effect is large and predominant. Other things equal, *the labor force tends to shrink during recessions and grow during periods of economic recovery.*

[4]Jacob Mincer, "Labor Force Participation of Married Women," in *Aspects of Labor Economics:* A Conference of the Universities—National Bureau Committee on Economic Research (Princeton, N.J.: Princeton University Press, 1962).

[5]As more and more women become *regularly* employed for pay, the "added" worker effect will tend to decline (and will increasingly be confined to teenagers).

The dominance of the discouraged-worker effect creates what some call the "hidden unemployed"—people who would like to work but who believe that jobs are so scarce that looking for work is of no use. Because they are not looking for work, they are not counted as "unemployed" in government statistics. Focusing on the period 1973–1978, when the overall official unemployment rate went from 4.9 percent to 6.0 percent, can give some indication of the size of hidden unemployment.

In 1973, an average of 4.3 million people were counted as unemployed at any given time—representing 4.9 percent of the labor force. In addition, there were 679,000 people who indicated that they wanted work but were not seeking it because they felt jobs were unavailable to them. This group constituted 1.2 percent of those adults not in the labor force. In 1978, the number of people officially counted as unemployed was 6 million, but there were 850,000 people among the "hidden" unemployed. These 850,000 people represented 1.5 percent of those adults not in the labor force. The rise in the percentage of those out of the labor market for job-related reasons is evidence of the discouraged-worker effect. Incidentally, if "discouraged workers" were counted as unemployed members of the labor force, the unemployment rate would have been 5.6 percent in 1973 and 6.8 percent in 1978.[6] To count these workers, however, would overlook the possibility that many of them desire only an intermittent labor-force attachment and time their periods out of the labor force to coincide with periods when expected wages are low.

How Will an Income-Maintenance Program Affect Work Incentives?

Family labor-supply models can also be applied to the analysis of the effects of income-maintenance programs. Our model in Chapter 6 implied that income-maintenance programs clearly reduce work incentives because they simultaneously increase income and reduce the take-home wage rate. While this effect may be true for the family unit as a whole, it does *not* follow that *both* husband and wife will supply fewer hours to the labor market.[7]

Consider the *wife's* response to a family income-maintenance subsidy and assume she is initially the primary "household producer." The *increase* in family *income* will encourage the family to consume more of all normal goods, including "pure" leisure and other household-produced goods. Both of these "income effects" suggest that total family hours at home will tend to rise. The *decline* in her take-home *wage* induces the family to adopt more time-intensive modes of household production—indicative of a substitution effect that also works in the direction of reduced family labor supply. Both effects depend, of course, on her *remaining* the primary household producer.

---

[6]To say that including "discouraged workers" in unemployment statistics would change the published unemployment rate does not imply that it *should* be done. For a summary of the arguments for and against counting discouraged workers as unemployed, see the final report of the National Commission on Employment and Unemployment Statistics," *Counting the Labor Force* (Washington, D.C., 1979), pp. 44–49.

[7]For a more rigorous and complete analysis of this issue, see Mark R. Killingsworth, "Must A Negative Income Tax Reduce Labor Supply? A Study of the Family's Allocation of Time," *Journal of Human Resources* 11 (Summer 1976): 354–65.

The income-maintenance program, however, also reduces the take-home wage of her *husband*, and this change could result in the family deciding that the *husband* should become the primary household producer. Suppose, for example, that both husband and wife have the same market wage but that the wife is relatively more productive at home when just a few total hours of family time are spent there. Initially, then, the family decides that *she* should do the household production. Suppose, however, that the husband has household skills—such as carpentry and plumbing skills—that can be put to best use when time at home is substantial. When the family decides to allocate more total hours of family time to household production, his household skills become relatively more valuable, and the family may decide *he* should become the primary household producer. (The likelihood of this decision is increased if the family, for example, is renovating a very old house.) He might thus reduce his market labor supply, but she might increase hers.

Thus, it is theoretically possible that the availability of an income-maintenance program could cause *overall* family labor supply to fall, while at the same time inducing one family member to *increase* his or her labor supply. To say that it is a *possibility* should not imply, of course, that it is a theoretical prediction *or* that it actually occurs. The empirical results on this issue are still rather inconclusive.[8]

LIFE-CYCLE ASPECTS OF LABOR SUPPLY

People vary the hours they supply to the labor market over their life cycle. In the early adult years relatively fewer hours are devoted to work than in later years, and more time is devoted to schooling. In the very late years people fully or partially retire—though at varying ages. In the middle years most males are working full time, but many women have careers that are interrupted by years at home raising small children. While the issue of schooling is dealt with in Chapter 9, the model of household production discussed in this chapter can help us understand both the labor-force behavior of married women and decisions about retirement.

The Interrupted Careers of Married Women

The basic premise of the household-production model is that people are productive in two places: in the home and in a "market" job. Their decisions about whether to seek market work and for how many hours are a function of their *relative* productivities in both places. As long as an hour of market work allows the person to buy more commodities than are required to make up for the hour of lost production time at home, the person will work for pay.

The marginal home productivity of married women greatly increases when young children are present. In effect, the presence of young children tilts the

---

[8]See Chapter 6 for citations of numerous labor supply studies based on income-maintenance experiments. See also the following studies: T. J. Wales and A. D. Woodland, "Estimation of Household Utility Functions and Labor Supply Response," *International Economic Review* 17 (June 1976): 397–410; Thomas J. Kniesner, "An Indirect Test of Complementarity in a Family Labor Supply Model," *Econometrica* 44 (July 1976): 651–69; and Wendy Lee Gramm, "The Demand for the Wife's Non-Market Time," *Southern Economic Journal* 41 (July 1974): 124–33.

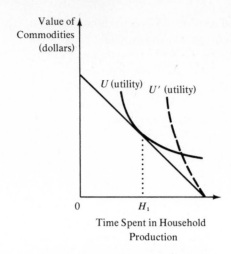

FIGURE 7.5 Household Productivity Can Change over the Life Cycle

utility isoquants of married women from U (say) in Figure 7.5 to something like U'. The important feature of U' is that an hour of home production given up is so valuable that it requires a large compensation of commodities in order for family utility to remain constant. Since market earnings in Figure 7.5 cannot possibly provide the wherewithal to purchase those commodities, the woman decides not to work. As children grow older, her indifference curves tilt back toward U, and she begins to seek more work for pay (see Example 7.2 for a discussion of how household productivity can be measured).

Retirement and Work Effort Over a Lifetime

Just as deciding *who* will work at home at various stages in a family's life involves comparing market and home productivities of husband and wife, deciding *when* to work over the course of one's life involves comparing market and home productivities *over time*. The basic idea here is that a person will tend to perform the most market work when his or her earning capacity is high relative to home productivity. Conversely, people will engage in household production when their earning capacity is relatively low.

Suppose a sales representative working on a commission basis knows that his potential income is around $30,000 in a certain year but that July's income potential will be twice that of November's. Would it be rational for him to schedule his vacation (a time-intensive activity) in November? The answer depends on his market productivity relative to his "household productivity" for the two months. Obviously, his market productivity—his wage rate—is higher in July than November, which means that the opportunity costs of a vacation are greater in July. However, if he has children who are only free to vacation in July, he may decide that his household productivity (in terms of utility) is so much greater in July than November that the benefits of vacationing in July outweigh the costs. If he does not have children of school age, the utility generated by a November vacation

Example 7.2
The Value of a Homemaker's Time

The services performed by homemakers are not sold in the market-place and thus are not counted in estimates of gross national product (GNP). The fact that they are not sold, however, does not imply they are not valuable—and for many purposes it becomes interesting to attempt to estimate the value of these services. There are three different approaches one might take in evaluating these services, and household-production theory can be used to evaluate each.

Market Prices. One method of valuing the services of homemakers is to measure how much these services would cost if they were to be purchased in the marketplace. Thus, the "market" costs of child care, cleaning, cooking, and other services are aggregated to form an overall estimate. In one careful study using this approach, Hawrylyshyn estimated that the value in 1967 of the services performed by a full-time homemaker (in a two-adult family) was $5220. Accounting for inflation, the 1980 value of these services would be roughly $13,000.

The problem with this method is that in cases where market services are available and not purchased, it must be the case that the household believes such services are *not worth their cost.* Either the price is too high or the quality is viewed as too low. Thus, households that do not purchase these services clearly place a value on them that is *less* than the value assigned by the market-prices approach.

Opportunity Costs. A second method of evaluating the value of homemakers' services is to estimate what the homemakers would have been able to earn—net of taxes, employment, and commuting costs—if they had worked for pay. The problem here, of course, is that many married women do not work for pay at all—which implies they value the services they provide at home at *more* than their potential market earnings. Using the forgone wage to estimate the value of services performed by these women thus results in an underestimate. A recent estimate by Gronau of the value of a homemaker's services using this approach comes to about $6800 per year in 1980 (after taxes).

Self-Employment Approach. A third method of valuing household services is to treat homemakers as self-employed individuals. If a self-employed person, for example, increases his or her hours of self-employment by one—and decreases by one hour his or her time spent working for someone else—that person *gains* the value at which the product from that hour can be sold (the "marginal product") and *loses* the wage that could have been earned by working for someone else. If one's marginal product in self-employment exceeds one's wage, one will expand one's hours of self-employment until (a) the marginal product and wage are equal, or (b) the person works totally for oneself (a corner solution reached if one's marginal product always exceeds one's wage). If the marginal product is less than the wage, the person cuts back on the hours of self-employment until condition (a) is reached or until the person works totally for others. Note that if the person is self-employed part of the time and also works for someone else part of the time, theory tells us that the marginal product and wage rate must be equal.

A homemaker who performs household services will either be fully employed in the home—that is, fully self-employed—or will divide the work time between self-employment and working for others. If the homemaker is fully self-employed the value of the marginal product from self-employment clearly exceeds the wage, but since this product is never priced in the market it is difficult to estimate its value. (This value may exceed the cost of employing others to do this work if the family believes that the homemaker will do a better job of cooking and raising children, say, than someone else.)

However, for those homemakers who perform household services *and* who also work for pay, we can infer from theory that the value of their *marginal* productivity at home is equal to their net market wage. Using the wage as an estimate of their marginal productivity at home, it is possible to estimate a production function for the value of household services. Applying this production function to full-time homemakers, Gronau estimated that the typical homemaker working exclusively in the home produces services worth (in 1980 terms) $15,700 to the family. This latter figure is actually a weighted average of those with small children and those without. Full-time married homemakers with *children under age six* were estimated to produce services worth $20,900 per year—an amount very close to what the average males earned.

SOURCES: Oli Hawrylyshyn, "The Value of Household Services: A Survey of Empirical Estimates," *The Review of Income and Wealth* 22, 2 (June 1976): 101–31.

Reuben Gronau, "Home Production—A Forgotten Industry," *Review of Economics and Statistics* 62 (August 1980): 408–15.

The self-employment approach is advocated by Carmel Ullman Chiswick, "The Value of a Housewife's Time," *Journal of Human Resources* (forthcoming).

---

may be sufficiently close to that of a July vacation that the smaller opportunity costs make a November vacation preferable.

Similar decisions are probably made over longer periods of time—perhaps one's entire life. As Chapter 9 will show, market productivity (which is reflected in one's wage) starts low in the young adult years, rises rapidly with age, then tails off and even falls in the later years, as shown in panel (a) of Figure 7.6. *If* home productivity is more or less constant over the years, then we should find people working (for pay) hardest in their middle years and least in the early and late years, as illustrated in panel (b) of Figure 7.6. Likewise, the consumption of very time-intensive goods will occur in one's early and late years—a prediction more or less confirmed when one observes the ages of Americans traveling in Europe. That such travelers are primarily young adults and the elderly is clearly related to the fact that, for these groups, opportunity costs are lower. They make the time to go because, at these stages in their lives, time is relatively inexpensive.

The decision about *when* to work for pay over the life cycle focuses on the productivity and cost of time—in other words, the *substitution effect*. Without explicitly saying so, we have been looking at persons or families of given wealth and analyzing how they arrange their market and "household" production over their lives in response to changing productivities in each place. In this context, the income effect is of little relevance.

For example, once one's educational level, general occupation, and probable

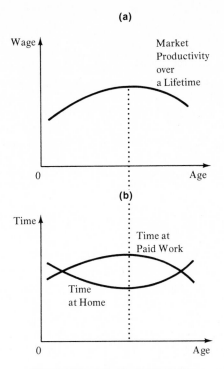

FIGURE 7.6 Life-Cycle Allocation of Time

inherited wealth are known, one's overall lifetime wealth can be foretold with reasonable accuracy. If a woman of wealth level *X* knows she wants to take a trip to Kenya at least once in her life, the question is not *whether* to take it—but *when*. The "when" partly depends on the factors discussed above, which emphasize substitution effects.[9]

Policy Application: The Social Security "Retirement Test"

Nearly everyone who has worked for 7½ years and has reached 62 years of age qualifies for a Social Security pension. The size of the pension depends, within upper and lower limits, on the person's average monthly earnings while working and on the age of retirement—with those retiring at age 62, for example, receiving less per month than those retiring at 65.[10]

One interesting feature of the Social Security system in the United States is that there is a "retirement test" that determines the benefits one can receive. To receive full benefits, one must qualify as being "retired," which in 1980 meant earning less than $5000 per year. (This limit is increased slightly each year and does not apply to people over age 72.) For those earning more than $5000 per year in 1980, Social Security retirement benefits are reduced by 50 cents for every

---

[9]Another factor, of course, is the extent to which the trip will permanently increase her utility (through pleasant memories, for example).

[10]For more details, see George Rejda, *Social Insurance and Economic Security* (Englewood Cliffs, N.J.: Prentice-Hall, 1976).

dollar earned *above* $5000. Thus if a person's "full" Social Security benefit is $4800, and if he or she earns $6000 per year at age 67 (say), the Social Security benefit received would be reduced by $500 (0.5 × $1,000) to $4300.

The existence of the retirement test has long been a subject of controversy. Its supporters maintain that Social Security is a program to help older people without jobs meet their financial needs and that the costs of giving benefits to those older people who have a decent labor income would be burdensome to those of working age who finance the program through a payroll tax. Opponents argue that retirees have earned their benefits through years of paying a payroll tax and that they are entitled to them in old age regardless of their circumstances. Opponents further assert that *removing* the retirement test would *increase* work incentives among the elderly.[11]

As illustrated in Figure 7.7, the retirement test separates the budget constraint facing the elderly into three segments. When earnings are under $5000 (for 1980), the presence of Social Security creates a pure income effect—shifting the constraint up by the amount of the retirement benefit *(AC)* but keeping it parallel to the market constraint (see segment *CD* in Figure 7.7). After $5000 in earnings, however, the slope of the constraint is cut in half, because for every dollar earned, fifty cents in benefits are removed. Thus, in segment *DE* there is an income *and* a substitution effect—*both* of which serve to reduce work incentives. At the point (*E* in the figure), where earnings are great enough that retirement benefits are reduced to zero, the market constraint becomes relevant (segment *EB*).

For people who have indifference curves like X_1 and X_2 in panel (a) of Figure 7.7, the existence of Social Security (with the retirement test) reduces the incentives to work because of the "pure" income effect. For people with indifference curves like Y_1 and Y_2 in panel (b), work incentives are also diminished; the wage reduction creates a substitution effect in addition to the income effect. People with preferences like Z_1 in panel (c) may be unaffected (or they may reduce market work even if it means reduced income—the tangency point, not shown, occurs along *DE*).

Would *keeping* Social Security but *eliminating* the retirement test increase work incentives? What effects would the elimination of the test have on the labor-supply decisions of 1. people who are at or near retirement and 2. people who have not yet reached retirement age?

Immediate effects on older workers.   For those who are near retirement age when the test is eliminated, any increase in benefits resulting from the change will increase wealth. These people receive added benefits but do not have to face years of increased payroll taxes to finance them (their future working years are limited).

Figure 7.7 shows that removing the retirement test will change the budget constraint facing these older people from *ACDEB* to *ACF*. This change preserves the market wage rate—essentially granting elderly people an income supplement independent of their work effort. People with preferences like *X*—people who earned less than $5000 before the retirement test was removed—will be unaf-

---

[11]See, for example, Marshall R. Colberg, *The Social Security Retirement Test: Right or Wrong?* (Washington, D.C.: The American Enterprise Institute for Public Policy Research, 1978), for a review of this and other arguments concerning the retirement test.

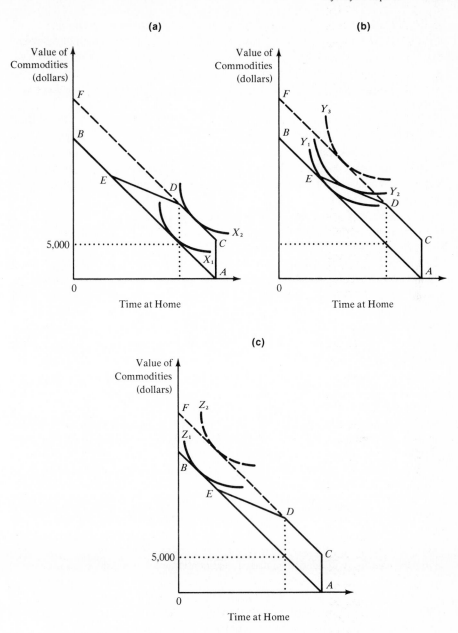

(a)

(b)

(c)

FIGURE 7.7 **Budget Constraint Relevant
to Social Security Retirement Test**

fected. Their work incentives are the same as before the change. People with preferences like Z have *reduced* work incentives. They face a pure income effect (their wage rate does not change), which will induce them to work less. However, for people affected by the portion of the old constraint labeled DE in panel (b) of Figure 7.7 constraint ACF represents a wage increase—and there is *both* an income and substitution effect. Which effect dominates cannot be foretold by theory. If the income effect dominates, then people with preferences like *Y* will have *reduced* work incentives—and the overall effect of eliminating the retirement test may be to reduce hours of work by the elderly! If the substitution effect dominates, labor supply by people like *Y* will increase, while the labor supply of those like *Z* might decrease. The overall effect would be unknown in advance.

Life-cycle effects.   The life-cycle effects of removing the retirement test are a bit more complicated—but still relatively straightforward. The change would clearly increase the total benefits paid out to the elderly, but the increased benefits younger workers can expect to receive in old age will be paid for by higher current payroll taxes. The effect on workers of paying this higher payroll tax depends on which segment of constraint *ACDEB* would have been relevant after age 65 had the retirement test not been removed.

Consider workers of average earning power.[12] For workers constrained by segment *CD* in their old age, neither benefits nor wages (in old age) change. However, the added payroll tax they must pay in their younger years reduces their wage rate—causing an income and a substitution effect. Depending on which effect is dominant, labor supply in one's younger years may be increased or decreased. Given the empirical results noted earlier, the decreased wage is likely to cause an *increase* in labor supply among prime-age males (for whom the income effect appears to be dominant) and a *decrease* in labor supply among similarly aged married women (for whom the substitution effect dominates).

Older workers who were affected by segments *DE* and *EB* of the constraint will receive increased benefits in old age, but these benefits will tend to be offset by larger taxes in their younger years. Their *lifetime wealth* will thus be largely unaffected by this change—or, to put it differently, removing the retirement test will tend to have essentially *no income effect* on the labor supply of these workers *over their lifetime*. Where these workers will be affected is in their allocations of labor supply over their lifetimes.

The increased payroll taxes lowers their wages during their prime years, while increasing the wages in old age for those on segment *DE* (those on *EB* experience no wage change in old age). In both cases, wage rates in one's prime years fall relative to those in old age. This change in relative wages, *in the presence of constant wealth,* will tend to cause a reallocation of household (time-intensive) activities from old age to prime age. Thus, instead of waiting until old age to take one's European tour, some people may seize on the reduced disparity between wage rates in prime age and old age as sufficient reason to take this tour earlier in life. For the people affected by *DE* and *EB*, then, labor supply will tend to *decrease in one's prime years and increase in old age*.

The overall life-cycle effects of removing the retirement test from the Social

---

[12]For workers with average wage rates, Social Security benefits are roughly equivalent to Social Security payroll taxes. Low-wage workers obtain proportionally higher benefits—and high-wage workers proportionally lower benefits—relative to their taxes paid out. Focusing the analysis on the average wage-earner is sufficient for our purpose, which is to illustrate the usefulness of the theory in policy analysis.

Security program cannot be predicted from theory. For some workers (such as X) the effects in *old age* are nil, but removing the test would create income and substitution effects in their prime years that have opposite tendencies on labor supply. For other workers, there may be some reallocation of labor from one's prime years to one's older years, but theory cannot tell us whether this shift will be one-for-one. What we *can* say is that people who argue that removing the retirement test will increase labor supply are being simplistic—unless, of course, they have some empirical evidence that resolves the theoretical ambiguities.

REVIEW QUESTIONS

1. Suppose that 4 percent unemployment is defined as "full employment" and that currently unemployment is equal to 6 percent. Suppose further that we have the following information:

Unemployment Rate	Labor Force	Unemployment	Employment
4 percent	6000	240	5760
6 percent	5600	336	5264

   a. What is the amount of "hidden unemployment" when the unemployment rate is 6 percent?

   b. If the population is 10,000, what is the change in the participation rate that occurs as a result of the marginal change in the unemployment rate?

   c. What are your views on the economic significance of hidden unemployment? Should measured and hidden unemployment be added together directly to obtain a "total unemployment" figure?

2. Several studies have indicated that for prime-age males, the income effect of a wage increase tends to dominate the substitution effect. Other recent studies point out that hourly wages tend to rise over the early stages of the life cycle (the young receive lower wages than the middle-aged) *and* that young males tend to work fewer hours than middle-aged males, *ceteris paribus*. Employing a theory of life-cycle allocation of time, explain the apparent discrepancy.

3. In his first debate against President Ford, Jimmy Carter argued, "While it is true that much of the recent rise in unemployment is due to the entrance of married women and teenagers into the labor force, this influx of people into the labor force is itself a sign of economic decay. The reason these people are now seeking work is because the primary breadwinner in the family is out of work and extra workers are needed to maintain the family income." Comment.

4. Some American observers have worried about a supposed decline in the "work ethic" among U.S. workers. The thesis (which is as yet unproven) of these observers is that U.S. workers are less interested in working than they used to be and that in the long run our national output per capita might fail to grow if gains in productivity are offset by reductions in working hours or labor-force participation rates. These observers conclude: that "A constant per capita output of goods and services is a sure sign of economic decay. It implies that economic progress is halted—that improvements in human

welfare stop. It is unthinkable that our society would tolerate such stagnation in human progress.''

Suppose the *factual* premise of these observers is true. That is, suppose improvements in the marginal productivity of workers over time are offset by declining work hours and participation rates so that gross national product per capita remains constant. Use economic theory to evaluate the *conclusion* drawn by these observers that this represents a stoppage of improvements in human welfare.

5. Is the following statement true, false, or uncertain? Why? ''If a married woman's husband gets a raise, she tends to work less, but if *she* gets a raise she tends to work more.''

SELECTED READINGS

Gary Becker, ''A Theory of the Allocation of Time,'' *Economic Journal* 75 (September 1965): 493–517.

G. R. Ghez and G. S. Becker, *The Allocation of Time and Goods Over the Life Cycle* (New York: Columbia University Press, 1975), Chapter 3.

Reuben Gronau, ''The Measurement of Output of the Nonmarket Sector: The Evaluation of Housewives' Time,'' *The Measurement of Economic and Social Performance,* ed. Milton Moss (New York: National Bureau of Economic Research, 1973), pp. 163–89.

Clarence D. Long, *The Labor Force Under Changing Income and Employment* (Princeton, N.J.: Princeton University Press, 1958).

Jacob Mincer, ''Labor Force Participation and Unemployment: A Review of Recent Evidence,'' in *Prosperity and Unemployment,* eds. Robert A. Gordon and Margaret S. Gordon (New York: John Wiley and Sons, 1966).

Jacob Mincer, ''Labor Force Participation of Married Women,'' in *Aspects of Labor Economics:* A Conference of the Universities—National Bureau Committee on Economic Research (Princeton, N.J.: Princeton University Press, 1962).

8

Compensating
Wage Differentials and
Labor Markets

Chapters 6 and 7 analyzed workers' decisions about *whether to seek employment* and *how long to work*. Chapters 8 and 9 will analyze workers' decisions about the industry, occupation, or firm in which they will work. This chapter will emphasize the influence on job choice of such daily, *recurring* job characteristics as working environment, length of commute from home to work, and risk of injury. The following chapter will analyze the effects of required educational *investments* on occupational choice.

This chapter will present a verbal as well as a graphical analysis of occupational choice that emphasizes the importance of both wages and nonpecuniary job characteristics in the allocation of labor to meet social needs. The empirical research on wage patterns will also be examined to see if job choices and the allocation of labor really are made along the lines suggested by these analyses. The final section applies the concepts of this chapter to two very important and controversial government programs: occupational safety and health regulation and affirmative-action plans for hiring women and minorities.

A VERBAL ANALYSIS OF OCCUPATIONAL CHOICE

If all jobs were exactly alike and located in the same place, an individual's decision about where to seek work would be relatively simple. He or she would attempt to obtain a job where the expected compensation was highest. Any differences in compensation would cause workers to seek work with the highest-paying employers and avoid applying for work with the low-paying ones. The high-paying employers, having an abundance of applicants, might decide they are paying more than they have to in order to staff their vacancies. The low-paying employers would have to raise wage offers in order to compete for workers. Ultimately, if the market works without hindrance, wages of all employers would equalize.

All jobs are not the same, however. Some jobs require much more education or training than others. Some jobs are in clean, modern offices, and others are in noisy, dusty, or dangerous factories. Some permit the employee some discretion over the pace of work at various points throughout the day, while some involve highly rigid assembly-line work. Some are challenging and call for decision making by the employee; others are monotonous. While the influence of educational and training requirements will be discussed at length in the next chapter, we will discuss here how the variations in job characteristics influence individual choice and the observable market outcomes of that choice.

Individual Choice and Its Outcomes

Suppose several unskilled workers have received offers from two employers. Employer X pays $5.00 per hour and offers clean, safe working conditions. Employer Y also pays $5.00 per hour, but offers employment in a dirty, noisy factory. Which employer would the workers choose? Most would undoubtedly choose Employer X, because the pay is the same while the job is performed under less disagreeable conditions.

Clearly, however, $5.00 is not an equilibrium wage in both firms.[1] Because Firm X finds it very easy to attract applicants at $5.00, it will "hold the line" on any future wage increases. Firm Y, however, must either clean up the plant, pay higher wages, or do both if it wants to fill its vacancies. Assuming it decides not to alter working conditions, it must clearly pay a wage *above* $5.00 to be competitive in the labor market. The extra wage it must pay to attract workers is called a *compensating wage differential,* because the higher wage is paid to compensate workers for the undesirable working conditions. If such a differential did not exist, Firm Y could not attract the unskilled workers that Firm X can obtain.

Suppose that Firm Y raises its wage offer to $5.50 while the offer from X remains at $5.00. Will this 50-cent-per-hour differential—an extra $1,000 per year—serve to attract *all* the workers in our group to Firm Y? If it did attract them all, Firm X would have an incentive to raise its wage and Firm Y might want to lower its offers a bit; the 50-cent differential in this case would *not* be an equilibrium differential.

More than likely, however, the 10 percent higher wage in Firm Y would attract only *some* of the group to Firm Y. Some people are not bothered by dirt and noise as much as others are, and these people may decide to take the extra pay and put up with the poorer working conditions.[2] Others, however, may be very sensitive to noise or allergic to dust, and they will decide that they would rather get paid less than expose themselves to working conditions that are very unpleasant. If both firms can obtain the quantity and quality of workers they want, the 50-cent differential *would* be an equilibrium differential—in the sense that there would be no forces causing the differential to change.

The desire of workers to avoid unpleasantness or risk, then, should force

---

[1]There may be a few people who really do not care about noise and dirt in the workplace. We assume here that these people are so rare—or Firm Y's demand for workers so large—that Y cannot fill all its vacancies with just those who are totally insensitive to dirt and noise.

[2]The assertion that people are affected differently by noise is documented in *Community Reaction to Airport Noise,* vol. I (report to the National Aeronautics and Space Administration prepared by Tracor, Inc. of Austin, Texas), July 1971. This study showed, for example, that around 10 percent of people are "highly susceptible" to noise annoyance, while around half are "highly adaptable" to airport noises.

employers offering unpleasant or risky jobs to pay higher wages than they would otherwise have to pay. Put another way, in order to attract a work force, these employers will have to pay higher wages to their workers than firms that offer pleasant, safe jobs to comparable workers. This wage differential serves two related, socially desirable ends. First, it serves a *social* need by giving people an incentive to do—voluntarily—dirty, dangerous, or unpleasant work. Likewise the existence of a compensating wage differential also imposes a financial penalty on employers who have unfavorable working conditions. Second, at an *individual* level, it serves as a reward to workers who accept unpleasant jobs by paying them more than comparable workers in more pleasant jobs.

The allocation of labor.   Society has a number of jobs that are either unavoidably nasty or would be very costly to make safe and pleasant (coal mining, deep-sea diving, and coke-oven cleaning are examples). There are essentially two ways to recruit the necessary labor for such jobs. One is to compel people to do these jobs—the military draft being the most obvious American example of forced labor. The second way is to induce people to do the jobs voluntarily.

Most modern societies rely mainly on incentives—compensating wage differentials—to recruit labor to unpleasant jobs voluntarily. Workers will mine coal, collect garbage, and bolt steel beams together 50 stories off the ground, because, compared to alternative jobs for which they could qualify, these jobs pay well. The 1500 commercial deep-sea divers in the United States, for example, who are exposed to the dangers of drowning, the rigors of construction work with cumbersome gear, a lonely and hostile work environment, and several physiological disorders as a result of compression and decompression, earn $20,000 to $45,000 per year, or about 20 percent to 130 percent more than the average high-school graduate.

As another example, the *failure* to pay sufficiently high wages to U.S. military personnel has created enormous difficulties in recruiting and retaining such

---

Example 8.1
Coal Mining in the Soviet Union

Coal mining is a dangerous, but socially necessary, task the world over. Because it is difficult to recruit people to voluntarily do this unpleasant work, compensating wage differentials exist even in economies where "market" incentives are not *philosophically* recognized. In the Soviet Union, for example, the difficulties of recruiting personnel to work in the coal-mining industry have caused the average earnings of miners to be *double* that of the average factory worker. Further, miners in the most unhealthy and arduous jobs work 30 hours a week, compared to 36 hours in the other mining jobs; in addition, they receive a one-time bonus equivalent to over 25 percent of the yearly pay for manufacturing workers.

SOURCE: Radio Liberty Research, June 11, 1979 (RL 179/79).

people. While military pay rose relative to civilian compensation after the draft was eliminated (see Chapter 2), it has not risen enough to overcome a 74,000-person shortage (as of 1980)—a shortage especially concentrated in the skilled jobs where the alternative of civilian employment is especially attractive. If the government wants to maintain armed services without resorting to the draft, it is clear that military pay must rise to a level sufficient to overcome the hazards and inconveniences of military life.[3]

Compensation for workers.   Compensating wage differentials also serve as *individual* rewards by paying those who accept bad or arduous working conditions more than they would otherwise receive. In a parallel fashion, those who opt for more pleasant conditions have to "buy" them by accepting lower pay. For example, if a person takes the $5.00 per hour job with Firm X, he or she is giving up a $5.50 per hour job with less pleasant conditions. The better conditions are being bought, in a very real sense, for 50 cents per hour.

Thus compensating wage differentials become the price at which good working conditions can be purchased by—or bad ones sold to—workers. Contrary to what is commonly asserted, a monetary value *can* often be attached to events or conditions in which the effects are primarily psychological in nature. Compensating wage differentials provide the key to the valuation of these nonpecuniary aspects of employment.

In the area of occupational-health-and-safety policy, there is continuous debate about whether to make machines safer or whether to protect the worker from machine hazards with personal protective devices.[4] For example, high noise levels can eventually damage the hearing of workers. The Department of Labor has favored reducing noise levels through engineering changes, such as putting mufflers on—or baffles around—noisy machines. Employer representatives have consistently claimed that such engineering changes are inordinately expensive and that compelling workers to wear earplugs would preserve workers' hearing at much less cost. Because resources are scarce, our society would like to achieve hearing protection at minimum cost, but we must be sure to count *all* the costs. One of the costs of wearing earplugs is the *psychic* cost: they are very uncomfortable for most people to wear. The cost of this discomfort *must* be counted along with the purchase price of earplugs in arriving at the total cost of wearing earplugs.

How could we put a dollar value on earplug discomfort? A straightforward way to determine this dollar value would be to find a set of employers who *require* the use of earplugs as a condition of employment and to compare the wages they pay to those of *comparable* firms that allow, but *do not require,* the wearing of earplugs. If workers do in fact find earplugs more uncomfortable than the noise,

---

[3]"The Retention Problem," *The Wall Street Journal* (March 19, 1980), p. 24. What is pleasant or unpleasant is determined in the market at the *margin.* For example, even if most people dislike night work, there might be enough who do not to fill night-shift jobs without a compensating wage differential.

[4]The debate about whether or not the government should be involved at all in the occupational safety and health area is discussed later in this chapter.

wages in the firm that requires their use should be higher—and this wage differential is the estimate of what value workers place on this discomfort.

Suppose, for example, that the research showed that companies requiring earplugs pay 10 cents an hour—or $200 per year—more than *otherwise similar* firms pay for *comparable* labor.[5] Workers accepting work there are indicating by their behavior that they are willing to take $200 per year as compensation for the discomfort they must bear; that is, the cost of the discomfort to them is equal to, or less than, $200 per year. Those refusing to work at the plant place a value higher than that on their discomfort costs, because $200 is insufficient to compensate them. Thus, the cost of discomfort at the margin is $200 per year (that is, to induce one more worker to wear earplugs would require added compensation of about $200 per year).

Before concluding that the psychic costs of wearing earplugs are $200 per year, we must remember that our hypothetical findings above are for the marginal worker. People differ in the amount of discomfort they feel and in the value they place on what they feel. Those most likely to take the extra pay in return for having to wear earplugs are those who are least sensitive to discomfort or most willing to trade discomfort for money. If we were to compel *all* workers in noisy factories to wear earplugs, we would be forcing earplugs on some for whom the costs of discomfort are in excess of $200.

As this example illustrates, compensating wage differentials are the price at which various *qualitative* job characteristics are bought and sold. As such, they offer a way of placing a value on things that most people think of as "noneconomic." This illustration, of course, does not prove that compensating wage differentials exist or that they are equilibrium prices—issues that will be discussed later in the chapter.

Assumptions and Predictions

We have seen how a simple theory of job choice by individuals leads to the *prediction* that compensating wage differentials will be associated with various job characteristics. Positive differentials (higher wages) will accompany "bad" characteristics, while negative differentials (lower wages) will be associated with "good" ones. However, it is very important to understand that this prediction can *only* be made *holding other things equal*.

Our prediction about the existence of compensating wage differentials grows out of the reasonable assumption that if a worker has a choice between a job with "good" working conditions and a job of equal pay with a "bad" set of working conditions, he or she will choose the "good" job. If the employee is an unskilled laborer he or she may be choosing between an unpleasant job spreading hot asphalt or a more comfortable job in an air-conditioned warehouse. In either case, he or she is going to receive something close to the wage rate unskilled workers typically receive. However, our theory would predict that this worker would receive *more* from the asphalt-spreading job than from the warehouse job.

Thus the predicted outcome of our theory of job choice is *not* that employees

---

[5]Firms may be willing to do this if they believe requiring earplugs will reduce workers' compensation claims for hearing loss in the future.

working under "bad" conditions receive more than those working in "good" conditions. The prediction is that, *holding worker characteristics constant,* employees in bad jobs receive higher wages than those working under more pleasant conditions. The characteristics that must be held constant include all the other things that influence wages: skill level, age, race, sex, union status, region of the country, and so forth. Because there are many influences on wages *other* than working conditions, our theory leads us to expect employers offering "bad" jobs to pay higher wages than employers offering "good" jobs to *comparable* workers. This theory is based on the following three assumptions:

Assumption 1: utility maximization.   Our first assumption is that workers seek to maximize their *utility,* not their income. If workers sought to maximize income, they would always choose the highest-paying job available to them. This behavior would eventually cause wages to be equalized across the jobs open to any set of workers, as stated earlier.

In contrast, compensating wage differentials will only arise if some people do *not* choose the highest-paying job offered—preferring instead a lower-paying, but more pleasant, job. This behavior allows the employers offering the lower-paying, pleasant jobs to be competitive for labor. Wages do not equalize in this case. Rather, the *net advantages*—the overall utility from the pay and the psychic aspects of the job—tend to equalize for the marginal worker.

Assumption 2: worker information.   The second assumption implicit in our analysis is that workers are aware of the job characteristics of potential importance to them. Whether they know about them before they take the job or find out soon after taking it is not too important. In either case, a company offering a "bad" job with no compensating wage differentials would have trouble recruiting or retaining workers—trouble that would eventually force it to raise its wage.

It is quite likely, of course, that workers will quickly learn of dust, dirt, noise, rigid work discipline, and other obvious bad working conditions. It is equally likely that they will *not* know the *precise* probability of being laid off, say, or injured on the job. However, even with respect to these probabilities, their own direct observation or word-of-mouth reports from other employees can give them enough information to evaluate the situation with some accuracy. For example, the proportion of employees considering their work "dangerous" has been shown to be rather closely related to the actual injury rates published by the government for the industry in which they work.[6] This finding illustrates that, while workers are probably not able to state the precise probability of being injured, they do form accurate subjective judgments about the relative risk among several jobs.

Where our predictions may disappoint us, however, is with respect to *very* obscure characteristics. For example, while we now know that asbestos dust is highly damaging to worker health, this fact was not widely known 40 years ago. One reason information on asbestos dangers in plants was so long in being gen-

---

[6]W. Kip Viscusi, "Labor Market Valuations of Life and Limb: Empirical Evidence and Policy Implications," *Public Policy* 26 (Summer 1978): 359–86.

erated is that it takes more than 20 years for asbestos-related disease to develop. Cause and effect were thus obscured from workers and researchers alike—creating a situation where worker job choices were made in ignorance of this risk. Compensating wage differentials for this danger thus could not possibly arise at that time. Our predictions about compensating wage differentials, then, hold only for job characteristics that workers know about.

Assumption 3: worker mobility. The final assumption implicit in our theory is that workers have a range of job offers from which to choose. Without a range of offers, workers would not be able to select the combination of job characteristics they desire or avoid the ones to which they do not wish exposure. A compensating wage differential for risk of injury, for example, simply could not arise if workers were able to obtain only dangerous jobs. It is the act of choosing safe jobs over dangerous ones that forces employers offering dangerous work to raise wages.

One manner in which this choice can occur is for each job applicant to receive several job offers from which to choose. However, another way in which choice could be exercised is for workers to be (at least potentially) highly mobile. In other words, workers with few concurrent offers could take a job and continue their search for work if they thought an improvement could be made. Thus, even with few offers at any *one* time, workers could conceivably have relatively wide choice over a *period* of time—which would eventually allow them to select the job that maximizes their utility.

While there are no general data on the number of concurrent offers a typical job applicant receives, it does seem to be true that job mobility among American workers is relatively high. The reported quit rate in manufacturing is normally between 1–2 percent per month—or about 12–24 percent per year. With job openings from quits and from general business expansion, manufacturing businesses newly hire 3 percent of their employees each month. Turnover is so great, in fact, that the median length of job tenure is 3.6 years—meaning that half of all workers have been on their current job less than three and one-half years.[7]

Another way to understand the amount of choice workers have in the job market is to look at job mobility over time. Consider male, blue-collar operatives (semiskilled workers)—a group most people feel faces the greatest restrictions on job choice. Among those operatives who were over age 25 in 1965:18 percent were working in *completely different* occupations by 1970, almost 9 percent had moved to skilled jobs, 3.5 percent had entered managerial or professional/technical occupations, and 3 percent were in unskilled jobs. The main point is that almost one worker in five had had a major occupational change in that five-year period.[8] Many more, of course, changed their jobs or their place of employment while still retaining semiskilled work. It is thus difficult to conclude that workers are typically lacking in job choice.

---

[7]Robert E. Hall, "The Importance of Lifetime Jobs in the U.S. Economy," Working Paper No. 560, National Bureau of Economic Research, Stanford, California, 1981.

[8]U.S. Bureau of the Census, *Characteristics of the Population, 1970: U.S. Summary,* Vol. I, Sec. 2 (Washington, D.C.: U.S. Government Printing Office, 1973), Table 230. These data do not indicate what fraction of those who changed occupation also changed employers.

The next section will present a graphical exposition of the theory of compensating wage differentials that has just been described verbally. This graphical analysis incorporates employer behavior, which has not yet been explicitly considered, and will visually illustrate some important conclusions. Economists have labeled the following analysis a *hedonic theory of wages*—that is, a wage theory based on the assumption of philosophical *hedonism* that workers strive to maximize utility (happiness).[9]

A HEDONIC THEORY OF WAGES

Business firms offer, and employees accept, jobs that may differ greatly in their level of responsibility, pace of work, security from layoff, work environment, and so forth.[10] Those job characteristics that are considered undesirable by workers should have a positive compensating wage differential associated with them, while those that are desired should be purchased by employees in the form of lower wages. To simplify our discussion, we will analyze just one dimension—risk of injury on the job—and *assume* that the compensating wage differentials for every *other* dimension have already been established. This assumption allows us to clearly see the outcomes of the job selection process with respect to *one* undesirable dimension (injury risk); since the same analysis could be repeated for every other dimension, our conclusions are not obscured by it. To obtain a complete understanding of the job-selection process and the outcomes of that process it is necessary, as always, to consider both the employer and employee sides of the market.

Employee Considerations

Employees, it may safely be assumed, dislike the risk of being injured on the job. A worker who is offered a job for $8.00 per hour, in a firm in which 3 percent of the work force is injured each year, would achieve a certain level of utility from that job. If the risk of injury were increased to 4 percent (holding other job characteristics constant) the job would have to pay a higher wage to produce this same level of utility, since risk is considered undesirable. The added wage would compensate the worker for the increase in risk—in the sense that the level of utility would be held constant.[11]

Other combinations of wage rates and risk levels could be devised that would

---

[9]The philosophy of hedonism is usually associated with Jeremy Bentham, a philosopher of the late 18th Century who believed people always behaved in ways that they believed would maximize their happiness.

[10]The analysis in this section is adapted primarily from Sherwin Rosen, "Hedonic Prices and Implicit Markets," *Journal of Political Economy* 82 (January/February 1974): 34–55.

[11]Compensating wage differentials provide for *ex ante*—"before the fact"—compensation related to injury risk. Workers could also be compensated (to keep utility constant) by *ex post*—or after injury—payments for damages. Workers' Compensation insurance provides for such *ex post* payments, but these payments are typically incomplete. There is no way to compensate a worker for his or her own death, and Workers' Compensation does not cover the psychic costs of disfigurement due to permanent impairment. Moreover, the lost income associated with temporary impairments is not *completely* replaced by Workers' Compensation. Because not all injury-related losses are completely compensated *ex post*, compensating wage differentials must exist *ex ante* in order for worker utility to be held constant in the face of increased risk.

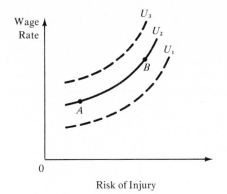

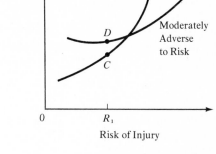

FIGURE 8.1 A Family of Indifference Curves Between Wages and Risk of Injury

FIGURE 8.2 Representative Indifference Curves for Two Workers Who Differ in Their Aversion to Risk of Injury

also yield the same utility as the $8.00/3 percent-risk offer. These combinations can be connected on a graph to form an indifference curve (see the solid curve— U_2—in Figure 8.1). Unlike the indifference curves drawn in Chapters 6 and 7, those in Figure 8.1 slope upward, because risk of injury is a "bad" job characteristic, not a "good" one (such as leisure, for example). In other words, if risk increases, wages must rise if utility is to be held constant.

As in the previous chapters, there is one indifference curve for each possible level of utility. Because a higher wage at a given risk level will generate more utility, indifference curves lying to the northwest represent higher utility.[12] Thus, all points on curve U_3 in Figure 8.1 are preferred to those on U_2, and those on U_2 are preferred to U_1. The fact that each indifference curve is convex (when viewed from below) reflects the normal assumption of diminishing marginal rates of substitution. At point B of curve U_2, the person receives a relatively high wage and faces a high level of risk. He or she will be willing to give up a lot in wages to achieve a given reduction in risk because 1. risk levels are high enough to place one in imminent danger, and 2. the consumption level of the goods that are bought with wages is already high. However, as risk levels and wage rates fall, the person becomes less willing to give up wages in return for the given reduction in risk; the danger is no longer imminent, and consumption of other goods is not as high.

People differ, of course, in their aversion to the risk of being injured. Those who are very sensitive to this risk will require large wage increases for any given increase in risk, while those who are less sensitive will require smaller wage increases to hold utility constant. The sensitive workers will have indifference curves that are steeper at any level of risk than those who are less sensitive, as illustrated in Figure 8.2. At risk level R_1, the slope at point C is steeper than at point D. Point C lies on the indifference curve of a worker who is highly sensitive to risk, while point D lies on an indifference curve of one who is less sensitive.

---

[12]When two "goods" were on the axes of our graphs, as in Chapters 6 and 7, indifference curves lying to the "northeast" represented higher levels of utility (people wanted more of each). When a "bad" is on the horizontal axis (as in Figure 8.1) and a "good" on the vertical axis, people with more of the "good" and less of the "bad" are unambiguously better off—and this combination is achieved by moving in a northwest direction on the graph.

Each person has a whole family of indifference curves that are not shown in Figure 8.2—and each will attempt to achieve the highest level of utility possible.

Employer Considerations

Employers are faced with a wage/risk trade-off of their own that derives from three assumptions. First, we assume it is costly to reduce the risk of injury facing employees. Safety equipment must be placed on machines, production time must be sacrificed for safety training sessions, protective clothing must be furnished to workers, and so forth. Second, we assume that competitive pressures will force many firms to operate at *zero profits* (that is, at a point where all costs are covered and the rate of return on capital is about what it is for similar investments).[13] Third, we have assumed that all *other* job characteristics are given or already determined. The consequence of these three assumptions is that if a firm undertakes a program to reduce the risk of injury, it must reduce wages in order to remain competitive.

Thus, forces on the employer side of the market tend to cause low risk to be associated with low wages—and high risk to be associated with high wages— *holding other things constant*. These "other things" may be fringe benefits or other job characteristics; assuming they are given will not affect the validity of our analysis (even though it may seem at first unrealistic). The major point is that if a firm spends *more on safety* it must spend *less on other things* if it is to remain competitive.[14] The term *wages* can thus be thought of as shorthand for "terms of employment" in our theoretical analyses.

The employer trade-offs between wages and levels of injury risk can be graphed through the use of *isoprofit curves*—curves that show the various combinations of risk and wage levels that yield a given level of profits (*iso* means "equal"). Thus, all the points along a given curve—such as those depicted in Figure 8.3—are wage/risk combinations that yield the *same* level of profits. Curves to the southeast represent higher profit levels, because with all other items in the employment contract given, each risk level is associated with a *lower* wage level. Curves to the northwest represent, conversely, lower profit levels.

Note that the isoprofit curves in Figure 8.3 are concave (from below). This concavity is a graphical representation of our assumption that there are diminishing marginal returns to safety expenditures. Suppose, for example, the firm was operating at point M in Figure 8.3—a point where the risk of injury is high. The first expenditures by the firm to reduce risk will have a relatively high return, because the firm will obviously choose to attack the safety problem by eliminating the most obvious and cheaply eliminated hazards. Because the risk—and accompanying cost—reductions are relatively large, the firm need not reduce wages by very much in order to keep profits constant. Thus, the isoprofit curve at point M

---

[13]If returns are permanently below normal, it would benefit the owners to close down the plant and invest their funds elsewhere. If returns are above normal, investors will be attracted to the industry and profits would eventually be driven down to increase competition.

[14]We *could* focus on the trade-off between safety and fringe benefits or safety and other working conditions, because certainly our theory would predict that such trade-offs exist. However, we choose to focus on the *wage* trade-off because wages are easy to measure and form the largest component of compensation.

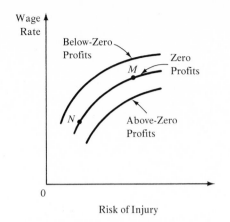

FIGURE 8.3   A Family of Isoprofit Curves
for an Employer

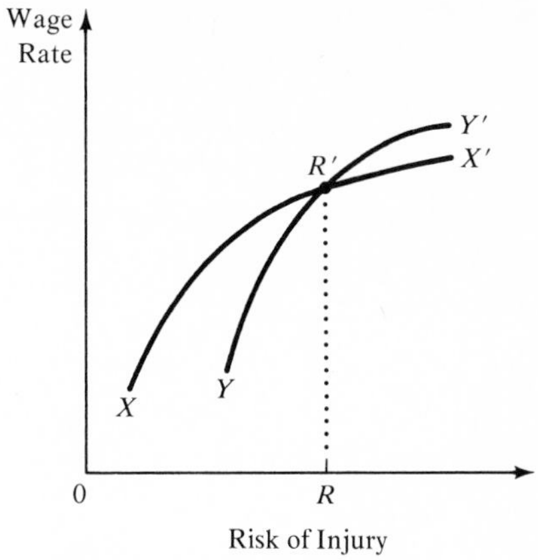

FIGURE 8.4   The Zero-Profit Curves
of Two Firms

is relatively flat. At point *N,* however, the curve is steeply sloped, indicating that wages would have to be reduced by quite a bit if the firm is to maintain its profits in the presence of a program to reduce risk. This large wage reduction is required because, at this point, further increases in safety are very costly; all the easy-to-solve safety problems have been dealt with.

As with employees, we also assume that employers differ in the ease (cost) with which they can eliminate hazards. We have just indicated that the cost of reducing risk levels is reflected in the *slope* of the isoprofit curve. In firms where injuries are costly to reduce, large wage reductions will be required to keep profits constant in the face of a safety program; the isoprofit curve in this case will be steeply sloped. The isoprofit curve of one such firm is shown as *YY'* in Figure 8.4. The isoprofit curves of firms where injuries are easier to eliminate are flatter. Note that curve *XX'* in Figure 8.4 is flatter at each level of risk than *YY'*; this indicates that Firm X can reduce risk more cheaply than Firm Y.

The Matching of Employers and Employees

The aim of employees is to achieve the highest possible utility from their choice of a job. If they receive two offers at the same wage rate, they will choose the lower-risk job. If they receive two offers in which the risk levels are equal, they will accept the offer with the higher wage rate. More generally, they will choose the offer that falls on the highest—or most northwest—indifference curve.

In obtaining jobs, employees are constrained by the offers they receive from employers. Employers, for their part, are constrained by two forces. On the one hand, they cannot make outrageously lucrative offers because they would be driven out of business by firms whose costs were lower. On the other hand, if their offered terms of employment are very low, they will be unable to attract employees (who will work for other firms). These two forces will compel firms in competitive markets to operate on their zero-profit isoprofit curves.

To better understand the offers firms make, refer back to Figure 8.4 where two different firms are depicted. Firm X—the firm that can cheaply reduce injuries—can make higher wage offers at low levels of risk (left of point *R*) than can

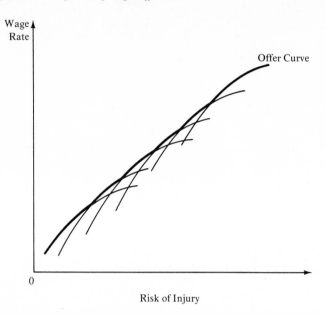

Wage
Rate

Offer Curve

0

Risk of Injury

FIGURE 8.5   An Offer Curve

Firm Y. Because it can produce safety (reduce risk) more cheaply, it can pay higher wages at low levels of risk and still remain competitive. Any point along segment *XR'* will be preferred by employees to any point along *YR'*, because for given levels of risk higher wages are paid.

At higher levels of risk, however, Firm Y can outbid Firm X for employees. Firm X does not save much money if it permits the risk level to rise above *R,* because risk reduction is so cheap. Because Firm Y *does* save itself a lot by operating at levels of risk beyond *R* (it may be a sawmill where risk reduction is prohibitively costly), it is willing to pay relatively high wages at high-risk levels. Since offers along *R'Y'* will be preferable to those along *R'X'*—again, because higher wages at any level of risk are paid by Firm Y—employees working at high-risk jobs will work for Y.

The upshot of the above considerations is that the only offers of jobs to workers with a chance of being accepted will lie along *XR'Y'* in Figure 8.4. The curve *XR'Y'*—combining the relevant portions of each isoprofit curve—is called an "offer curve." The offer curve that emerges from *several* isoprofit curves is drawn in Figure 8.5 as a heavy line. It will be along this curve that offers to employees will be *made and accepted.* One can immediately note that this curve has a positive slope—which means that *wages rise with risk, other things equal.* This curve is a graphical proof that, given our assumptions, we expect compensating wage differentials for risky jobs to exist.

Graphing worker indifference curves and employer isoprofit curves together can show which workers choose which offers. Consider Figure 8.6, which contains the zero-profit curves of two different employers (X and Y) and the indifference curves of two employees (A and B). Employee A maximizes utility by working for Employer X at wage W_{AX} and risk level R_{AX}, while Person B maximizes utility by working for Employer Y at wage W_{BY} and risk level R_{BY}.

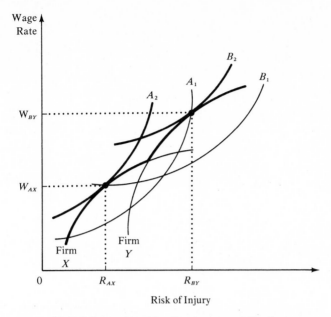

FIGURE 8.6   Matching Employers and Employees

Looking at A's choice more closely, we see that if he or she took the offer B accepted—W_{BY} and R_{BY}—the level of utility achieved would be A_1, which is less than A_2. Person A values safety very highly, and wage W_{BY} is just not high enough to compensate for the high level of risk. Person B, whose indifference curves are flatter—signifying he or she is less averse to risk—finds the offer of W_{BY} and R_{BY} superior to the offer A accepts. Person B is simply not willing to take a cut in pay to W_{AX} in order to reduce risk from R_{BY} to R_{AX}.

The matching of A with Firm X and B with Firm Y is thus not accidental or random. Firm X can generate safety relatively cheaply and does not reduce cost much by operating at high-risk levels. Since X can "produce" safety more cheaply than Y, it is logical that X will be a low-risk producer who attracts employees, like A, who value safety highly. Likewise, Employer Y generates a lot of cost savings by operating at high-risk levels and can thus afford to pay high wages and still be competitive. Y attracts people like B, who have a relatively strong preference for money wages and a relatively weak preference for safety. Firm Y, then, has a comparative advantage (over X) in offering high-risk, high-paying jobs.[15]

Our hedonic model thus generates two major insights. First, wages rise with risk, other things equal. According to this prediction, there will be compensating wage differentials for job characteristics that are viewed as undesirable by workers whom employers must attract. Second, workers with strong preferences for safety will tend to take jobs in firms where safety can be generated most cheaply. They thus tend to seek out and accept safer, lower-paying jobs. Workers who are not

---

[15]The issue of whether society should allow Firm Y to operate at high risk levels is examined later in this chapter.

as averse to accepting risk will seek out and accept the higher-paying, higher-risk jobs offered by firms that find safety costly to "produce." The second insight, then, is that the job-matching process—if it takes place under the conditions of knowledge and choice—is one in which firms and workers offer and accept jobs in a fashion that makes the most of their strengths and preferences.

Before employing the above hedonic model to analyze labor-market problems, it is useful to establish the empirical credibility of the theory of compensating differentials. The major empirically testable prediction of this theory is that, other things equal, wages are higher in jobs with disagreeable characteristics.

EMPIRICAL TESTS OF THE THEORY OF COMPENSATING WAGE DIFFERENTIALS

The prediction that there will be compensating wage differentials for undesirable job characteristics is at least 200 years old. Adam Smith, in his *Wealth of Nations* published in 1776, proposed five "principal circumstances which . . . make up for a small pecuniary gain in some employments, and counterbalance a great one in others."[16] Three of these will be discussed in other chapters: the difficulty of learning the job (Chapter 9), the probability of success (Chapter 11), and the constancy of employment (Chapter 15). However, most relevant to our discussion in this chapter is his assertion that "the wages of labour vary with the ease or hardship, the cleanliness or dirtiness, the honourableness or dishonourableness of the employment."

One would think that 200 years is a sufficient period of time over which to have accumulated substantial evidence concerning an important prediction! Unfortunately, the prediction has only been seriously tested in the last ten years–and even then in only a limited way. The reasons for this lack of evidence are twofold. First, the prediction is that, *other things equal,* wages will be higher in unpleasant or dangerous jobs. The prediction can only be tested validly if the researcher is able to control for the effects of age, education, sex, region, race, union status, and all the other factors that typically influence wages. Only when the effects of these factors on wages are known can the researcher filter out the *separate* influence on wages of (say) injury risk.[17] Statistical procedures can control for these other factors, but these procedures require large data samples and the use of computers—and only in the last ten years or so have the necessary data and computers been widely available to researchers.

The second problem that has hindered the empirical testing for compensating wage differentials is the problem of specifying, in advance of these tests, job

---

[16]*See* Adam Smith, *Wealth of Nations* (New York: Modern Library, 1937), Book I, Chapter 10.

[17]It is especially important to control for these other influences because safety is probably a normal good (meaning that higher income workers desire more of it). A *simple* correlation of risk levels and earnings is thus negative—not positive as predicted by theory. However, the simple correlation fails to account for all the *other* factors that influence earnings. Only if the influence of these factors can be accounted for would we expect to obtain the predicted positive relationship between earnings and risk.

characteristics that are generally regarded as "disagreeable." For example, while some people dislike outdoor work and would have to be paid a premium in order to accept it, others prefer such work and dislike desk jobs. Similar observations can be made about such job characteristics as repetitiveness, chances to make decisions, level of responsibility, and amount of physical exertion. Tests of the theory require selecting job characteristics where there is widespread agreement about what is "good" or "bad" at the margin. For this reason, the most credible and convincing tests of the theory have dealt with the level of *danger* on the job. While people may respond with different intensities to danger, it is difficult to believe that anyone prefers injury to safety; danger is an unambiguous "bad." The risk of injury is also objectively measured from injury rates published by occupation or, more commonly, by industry.

The most striking evidence of compensating wage differentials to date relates to the risk of *fatal* injury on the job. Nine separate studies, all using different data sets—seven from the United States and two from Great Britain—have found that wages are positively associated with the risk of being killed on the job, other things equal.[18] The results suggest that workers receive between $20 and $300 more per year for every one-in-ten-thousand increase in the risk of being killed on the job. (One death for every 10,000 workers is roughly the yearly average for steel mills, while a rate of 10 deaths per 10,000 workers is the average for logging camps.) While these estimates seem small, they do imply that a plant with 1,000 employees could save between $20,000 and $300,000 in wage costs *per year* if it undertook a safety program that would save one life every ten years.

The results for nonfatal injuries are not as supportive of the theory of compensating differentials. Most of these injuries are relatively minor and at least partially compensated for by workers' compensation insurance—which means that the losses incurred by workers are relatively small. Small losses probably do not generate much incentive to obtain large compensating wage differentials, so that any differentials that do exist may simply be too small to distinguish from other forces that influence wages.[19] It is not too surprising, then, that it has been easier to observe compensating wage differentials for fatal than nonfatal work accidents. The victims of a fatal accident cannot possibly be fully compensated after the fact, so that the sheer magnitude of the losses caused by these accidents motivates those at risk to seek compensating differentials that are large enough to observe (see footnote 11).

---

[18]Eight studies are reviewed in Robert S. Smith, "Compensating Wage Differentials and Public Policy: A Review," *Industrial and Labor Relations Review* 32 (April 1979): 339–52. The ninth is by Alan Marin and George Psacharopoulos, "The Reward for Risk in the Labor Market: Evidence from the U.K. and a Reconciliation with Other Studies" (Discussion Paper No. 75, Centre for Labour Economics, London School of Economics), January 1981.

[19]The statistical problem is one of distinguishing the influence of injuries from all the other influences, including random ones, on wages. It is a little bit like trying to locate the position of Pluto in the sky from one's backyard. When Pluto is close to earth, the moon is merely a crescent, there is no haze, and the city is dark, it can be done. If a full moon, great distance from the earth, haze, and ground light are present, Pluto's weak light signal cannot be seen or "filtered" out from all the other stars or planets.

POLICY APPLICATIONS

The insights of hedonic wage theory can be applied to some very critical social issues: the federal occupational safety and health program and affirmative-action plans for hiring minorities.

Occupational Safety and Health

Are workers benefited by the reduction of risk? In 1970, Congress passed the Occupational Safety and Health Act, which directed the U.S. Department of Labor to issue and enforce safety and health standards for all private employers. The stated goal of the act was to ensure the "highest degree of health and safety protection for the employee."[20]

Despite the *ideal* that employees should face the minimum possible risk in the workplace, implementing this ideal as social *policy* is not necessarily in the best interests of workers. Our hedonic model can show that reducing risk in some circumstances will lower the utility of workers! Consider Figure 8.7.

Suppose a labor market is functioning about like our textbook models, in that workers are well informed about dangers inherent in any job and are mobile enough to avoid risks they do not wish to take. In these circumstances, wages will be positively related to risk (other things equal), and workers will sort themselves into jobs according to their preferences. This market can be modeled graphically in Figure 8.7 where, for simplicity's sake, we have assumed there are two kinds

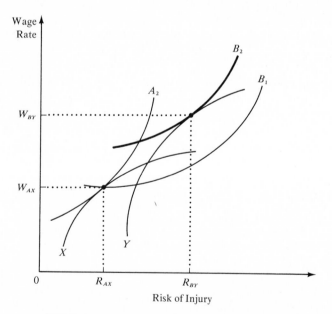

FIGURE 8.7 **The Effects of Government Regulation on a Perfectly Functioning Labor Market**

---

[20]Section 6(b)(5) of the Occupational Safety and Health Act.

Example 8.2
Mandatory Risk Reduction in Coal Mining

The caution with which government should proceed with *mandatory* risk-reduction programs is underscored by events in coal mining. The Federal Coal Mine Health and Safety Act of 1969 directs that miners be offered chest X rays in order to detect black lung disease. (This disease is technically known as *coal workers' pneumoconiosis*—a condition in which the inhalation of coal dust eventually reduces the functional capacity of the lungs. It is progressive, disabling, and sometimes fatal.) When it appears miners have the disease, their employers must, under the law, offer them jobs in less dusty areas of the mine. These jobs are lower-paid and less prestigious than the dusty jobs at the "face" of the mine. Consequently, only 10 percent of the miners offered such jobs in the 1970s accepted them. The behavior of most miners thus tells us that they were willing to undertake a known risk because the compensation (monetary and psychic) of the dangerous jobs was great enough to offset this risk. A law *compelling* them to leave the dusty jobs would clearly reduce their welfare, at least as they see it.

---

of workers and two kinds of firms. Person A, who is very averse to the risk of injury, works at wage W_{AX} and risk R_{AX} for Employer X. Person B works for Employer Y at wage W_{BY} and risk R_{BY}.

Now suppose the Occupational Safety and Health Administration (OSHA)—the Department of Labor agency that is responsible for implementing the federal safety and health program—promulgates a standard that, in effect, says that risk levels above R_{AX} are illegal. The effects, although unintended and perhaps not immediately obvious, would be detrimental to employees like B. Reducing risk is costly, and the best wage offer a worker can obtain at risk R_{AX} is W_{AX}. For Person B, however, wage W_{AX} and risk R_{AX} generate *less utility* than did Y's offer of W_{BY} and R_{BY}. Figure 8.7 shows that X's offer of W_{AX} and R_{AX} lies on indifference curve B_1, whereas Y's old (now illegal) offer was on the higher curve B_2.

When the government mandates the reduction of risk in a market where workers are compensated for the risks they take, it penalizes workers like B, who are not terribly sensitive to risk and appreciate the higher wages associated with higher risk. The critical issue, of course, is whether workers have the knowledge and choice necessary to generate compensating wage differentials. Many people believe that because workers are ignorant, unable to comprehend different risk levels, or immobile, most do not choose risky jobs voluntarily. If this belief were true, government regulation *could* make workers better off—and, indeed, such conditions almost undoubtedly prevail in some markets. However, the arguments already presented concerning information and mobility and the evidence of the positive relationship between wages and risk of death should challenge the assumption that, in general, the labor market fails to generate compensating differentials.

To say that worker utility *can* be reduced by such programs does not, of course, imply that it *will* be reduced. The outcome depends on how well the unregulated market functions and how careful the government is in setting its standards for risk reduction. The following section will analyze a governmental program implemented in a market that has *not* generated enough information about risk for employees to make informed job choices.

How strict should OSHA standards be?

Consider a labor market, like that mentioned previously for asbestos workers, where ignorance or worker immobility hinders labor-market operation. Let us suppose also that the government becomes aware of the health hazard involved and wishes to set a standard regulating worker exposure to this hazard. How stringent should this standard be?

The crux of the problem in standard setting is that reducing hazards is costly; the greater the reduction, the more it costs. While businesses bear these costs initially, they will ultimately respond to them by a. cutting costs elsewhere and b. raising prices (to the extent that cutting costs is not possible). Since labor costs constitute the largest cost category for most businesses, it is natural for firms facing large government-mandated hazard-reduction costs to hold the line on wage increases or to adopt policies that are the equivalent of reducing wages: speeding up production, being less lenient with absenteeism, reducing fringe benefits, and so forth. It is also likely—particularly in view of any price increases (which, of course, tend to reduce product demand)—that employment will be cut back. Some of the job loss will be in the form of permanent layoffs that force workers to find other jobs—jobs they presumably could have had before the layoff but chose not to accept. Some of the loss will be in the form of cutting down on hiring new employees who would have regarded the jobs as their best employment option.

Thus, whether it is in the form of smaller wage increases, more difficult working conditions, or being unable to obtain or retain one's first choice in a job, the costs of compliance with health standards will fall on employees. Employees will bear these costs in ways that reduce their earnings below what they *would have been in the absence of OSHA.* These losses may not be immediate or very obvious, since it is hard to know what wages would have been without the OSHA standard. However, the obscurity of this outcome of government regulation does not justify ignoring it. A graphical example can be used to make an educated guess about whether worker utility will be enhanced or not as a result of the increased protection from risk mandated by an OSHA health standard.

Figure 8.8 depicts a worker who believes she has taken a low-risk job, when in fact she is exposing herself to a hazard that has a relatively large probability of damaging her health in 20 years. She receives, let us suppose, a wage of W_1 and *believes* she is at point A, where the risk level is R_1 and the utility level is U_1. Instead, she is in fact at point B, receiving W_1 for accepting (unknowingly) risk level R_2; she would thus experience lower utility (indifference curve U_0) if she knew the extent of the risk she was taking.

Suppose now that the government discovers that her job is highly hazardous. The government could simply inform the affected workers and let them move to other work. However, if it has little confidence in the ability of workers to under-

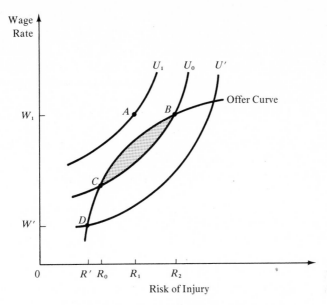

FIGURE 8.8   A Worker Accepting Unknown Risk

stand the information or to find other work, the government could pass a standard that limits employee exposure to this hazard. But what level of protection should this standard offer?

If the government forces the risk level down to R', the best wage offer the woman in our example could obtain is W' (at point D on the offer curve). Given the market, no employer would or could pay her more at risk level R', other things equal. Point D, however, lies on indifference curve U', which represents a lower level of utility than she is in fact getting now (U_0). She would be worse off under the government-imposed standard. On the other hand, if the government forced risk levels down to a level between R_0 and R_2 she would be better off, because she would be able to reach an indifference above U_0 (see shaded area of Figure 8.8).

How can one estimate, in a practical way, how much wage loss workers are willing to bear in exchange for a reduction in risk and still feel at least as well off as they are currently? The answer lies in estimating compensating wage differentials in markets that appear to work. Suppose, in a properly functioning market, that workers facing risk level R_1—the one our hypothetical worker *thought* she was facing in Figure 8.8—accept wage cuts (increases) of $80 per year for reductions (increases) in the yearly death rate of 1 in 10,000. These workers appear to feel that, other things equal, $80 is a price they are willing to pay for this reduction in risk. Thus, as noted earlier in the case of earplug use, compensating wage differentials can be used to estimate the value workers place on seemingly intangible aspects of their jobs. The use of such differentials should not be oversold, because the difficulties of establishing which markets are properly functioning are considerable. However, estimating compensating wage differentials is probably the best way of finding out what value workers attach to various job characteristics.[21]

Since one cannot rule out the possibility—indeed, the likelihood—that one way or another workers will ultimately pay for the costs of their reduced workplace risks, economists argue strongly that the government should conduct studies to estimate whether the value workers place on risk reduction is commensurate with the costs of the program. These studies are called *benefit-cost* studies, and they weigh the costs of a program against the value workers (or other beneficiaries) attach to the benefits of (say) reduced risk. Estimates of compensating wage differentials can be very useful in estimating these benefits.

Consider the OSHA standard that reduced the exposure of 90,000 asbestos workers to two fibers of asbestos per cubic centimeter of air. Inhaling airborne asbestos fibers is strongly and persuasively associated with several types of cancer; it is expected that the two-fiber standard will reduce yearly asbestos-related deaths by 4 per 1000 workers. Extrapolating from the estimates of compensating differentials associated with the risk of death, mentioned earlier, asbestos workers would probably be willing to pay *at least* $800 per year for this four-in-one-thousand reduction in risk.[22] Because the yearly cost of the asbestos standard comes to roughly $800 per worker, it seems reasonably certain that the workers benefited by the standard would be willing to bear any of the program's costs that are shifted to them.[23] Thus, the asbestos standard almost certainly improves the welfare (utility) of asbestos workers.

As another example of benefit-cost analysis, consider two alternative standards limiting the exposure of chemical workers to *acrylonitrile*—a substance used in making acrylic fibers and a certain type of resin. Exposure to acrylonitrile is believed to increase one's chances of contracting cancer; reducing worker exposure from 20 parts per million (ppm) of air to 2 ppm would reduce the yearly risk of cancer-related deaths by 8.4 per 10,000 exposed workers. We know from our estimates of compensating differentials that the *most* we can assume workers would be willing to give up to obtain this reduction in risk is about $2500 per year.[24] Since obtaining this new level of risk would cost $2800 per worker (per year), it is conceivable that the standard would improve worker utility if workers bore the costs, but the costs would come very close to outweighing the benefits.

On the other hand, reducing acrylonitrile exposure to 1 ppm would reduce the death rate by 9 per 10,000 exposed workers at a yearly cost of $25,000 per worker. Given that the most workers seem to be willing to pay for a 9 in 10,000 reduction in risk is $2700 per year, there is no chance that a 1 ppm standard could

---

[21]See E. J. Mishan, "Evaluation of Life and Limb: A Theoretical Approach," *Journal of Political Economy* 79, 4 (July/August 1971): 687–705.

[22]The figure of $800 arises from multiplying the lower estimate of $20 for a one-in-ten-thousand reduction in death risk by a factor of 40 (to bring it up to a four-in-one-thousand reduction).

[23]Russell Settle, "Benefits and Costs of the Federal Asbestos Standard," paper delivered at a Department of Labor Conference on Evaluating the Effects of the Occupational Safety and Health Program, March 18–19, 1975.

[24]This figure is obtained by multiplying the upper estimate of $300 for a one-in-ten-thousand reduction by 8.4.

improve their utility if they bore the costs. Thus, while a 2 ppm standard may be worth promulgating, a 1 ppm standard would not be.[25] Perhaps because of the high costs and small benefits, OSHA chose to set the acrylonitrile standard at 2 ppm.

Judging OSHA under alternative norms. In our analysis of OSHA above, we argued that a safety or health standard is socially desirable only if the value workers place on risk reduction is commensurate with the costs of the standard. The implicit assumptions of this analysis were that a. the only beneficiaries of the standard are the workers whose risk is reduced, and b. the benefits can best be measured by the current willingness of employees to pay for risk reduction. Neither assumption is universally accepted.

It is frequently argued that members of society who are not directly affected by the risk-reduction program might be willing to pay *something* for the benefits that accrue to those workers who *are* directly affected. Presumably, this "willingness to pay" is strongest for family members, relatives, and close friends and weakest for strangers. However, even strangers would have some interest in reducing injury and disease if they were taxed to subsidize the medical treatment of those who are injured or become ill. Thus, it is argued, the benefits of OSHA standards extend beyond the direct beneficiaries to other "external" parties whose "willingness to pay" should also be counted.

The major issue for policy making is not whether these external benefits exist but how large they are and whether they are already included in the "willingness to pay" of those directly benefited by an OSHA standard. For example, one could plausibly argue that a worker's *family* might be heavily involved in his or her choice of jobs, so that compensating wage differentials *already* reflect family preferences. Put differently, the opinions and preferences of family members and close relatives *could* affect the indifference curves of the workers directly at risk and thus play a role in determining what jobs such workers choose at what wages. To date, no research has addressed this issue.

Also unclear at present is the degree to which medical care for job-related injuries and illnesses is subsidized by parties who are not direct beneficiaries of an OSHA standard. Workers' compensation insurance premiums, for example, are established at the *industry* level and are subject to some modification based on the experience of the individual firm in that industry; it seems unlikely that one industry's workers subsidize the medical treatment of injured workers in other industries. Since OSHA standards apply to *entire industries,* it does not appear too probable that subsidies by "external" parties through workers' compensation are very large. However, because most occupational *illnesses* are not effectively covered by workers' compensation, treatment of those who contract a disease from their work is paid for by them, their insurance, or public subsidies (Medicare,

---

[25]This analysis is based on data reported in James Miller, "Occupational Exposure to Acrylonitrile," statement before the Occupational Safety and Health Administration on behalf of Vistron Corporation, Washington, D.C., 1978.

Medicaid).[26] The likelihood that "external" parties subsidize the treatment of those directly at risk of occupational disease is thus very high; what is unknown at present is the magnitude of the subsidy.[27]

Another argument against using only the apparent willingness of workers to pay for risk reduction as a measure of its benefit is that workers really do not know what is best for themselves in the long run. Society frequently prohibits (or at least tries to prohibit) people from indulging in activities that are dangerous to their welfare; laws against the use of narcotics and gambling are two such examples. Some argue that OSHA standards limiting exposure to dangerous substances or situations fall into the category of preventing workers from doing harm to themselves by being lured into dangerous work; therefore, it is argued that to ask how much they value risk reduction is irrelevant. The conflict between those who claim that workers know what is best for themselves and those who claim they do not can only be resolved on philosophical grounds.

However, one offshoot of the argument that workers do not know best for themselves deserves special mention. Some argue that worker preferences are molded by the environment in which they were raised and that there is no reason to take that environment as "given" or unchangeable. Once all workers at risk are required to wear protective clothing and equipment, and once they are prevented from taking certain risks on the job (in return for higher pay perhaps), their attitudes and preferences will accommodate. A few years ago, for example, wearing hard hats was considered "sissified"; today it is not. Thus, OSHA standards are regarded as an engine for changing worker—as well as employer—attitudes and behavior.

How far one wants to go in imposing present costs on workers to induce a change of attitude is a philosophical issue. We should add, however, that the value judgment underlying normative economics—that of mutual benefit, or making some better off and no one else worse off—is usually interpreted as applying to *current* (observed) preferences. Thus, the policy analyses of this text, by taking indifference curves and the current set of prices (compensating wage differentials, for example) as given, have implicitly assumed that workers know what is best for themselves. This section points out that *alternative* assumptions *do* exist.

Affirmative-Action Planning

In an effort to end discriminatory hiring practices, all large firms doing business with the federal government are required to prepare an *affirmative-action plan* listing their goals for the hiring of women and minorities for the coming years. If

---

[26]When a worker contracts lung cancer, it is usually very difficult to tell whether the cause was job-related, due to personal habits, related to residential location, or a combination of all three. Because it cannot usually be proven to be job-related, workers' compensation does not apply.

[27]This ignorance need not prevent us from making benefit estimates, however. We could, for example, calculate benefits in two different ways: We could first assume no subsidy and use compensating wage differentials as discussed in the text. Alternatively, we could assume a 100 percent subsidy of medical costs and add to the willingness to pay implied by the compensating differentials the medical-cost savings associated with the OSHA standard. These calculations would at least indicate the range into which benefits are likely to fall.

these goals are set too low or if approved goals are not met, the firm could conceivably lose its government contracts. Thus, setting realistic goals is important.

In order to construct and evaluate a realistic affirmative-action plan for hiring new employees, firms must know the *availability* of women and minorites. The concept of availability used by the government has been defined in basically two ways as:[28]

1. the percentage of minorities or women among those who have the skills required by a specific job group or who are capable of acquiring them;
2. the percentage of minorities and women who can be expected to become available during the period [in which] the ultimate goal is to be achieved.

A construction contractor seeking to hire 20 carpenters for a big job may be required to establish a goal of having six blacks among them if 30 percent of *all* carpenters in the city are black. Alternatively, an automobile manufacturer that will be hiring 20 beginning mechanical engineers may be required to set a goal of having five women among them if 25 percent of *new graduates* in mechanical engineering are female. The particular definition of availability to be used is the one that makes the most sense in the particular situation.

While this flexibility in defining availability undoubtedly helps achieve the goal of setting realistic targets for firms, the government has usually ignored another aspect of availability: the *interest of workers* in a particular employer. In the case of locally recruited minority workers, for example, the government has typically used the percentage of qualified minorities in the entire city or metropolitan area as the measure of availability, regardless of how far away they may live from the place of employment. This measure of availability disregards the fact that people prefer to work near home, other things equal, and that their interest in applying for jobs diminishes as the commuting distance rises. Commuting costs, in terms of both time and money, are seen by workers as negative aspects of employment—aspects to be avoided unless adequate compensation for them is received. Failure to take them into account when trying to measure availability works against the intention of setting realistic hiring goals.

The Timken Company. An illustration of the severity of the commuting issue arose in 1976, when the government declared The Timken Company ineligible to receive government contracts.[29] The reason for debarment was that Timken's plant in Bucyrus, Ohio, set its minority hiring goals based on a 16-mile recruiting radius—an area with a 0.6 percent minority population—and refused to include the town of Mansfield, which is 25 miles from its plant and contains 15 percent minorities. The government concluded that 25 miles—35-45 minutes by car—was a reasonable commuting distance and that Mansfield should thus be included for goal-setting purposes. Characteristically, the government's hiring goal for Timken assumed that workers in Mansfield were equally likely to be interested in

---

[28]U.S. Department of Labor, Office of Federal Contract Compliance Programs, *Compliance Manual* (October 18, 1978).

[29]*Timken Company* v. *Vaughn* 413 F. Supp. 1183 (N.D., Ohio 1976).

a job at Timken as those in Bucyrus. The government thus calculated its measure of availability by drawing a 25-mile radius around the plant and calculating the percentage (3.5 percent) of minorities living in that entire area.

Timken took the case to court and won a reversal. The court, looking at the jobs available in Mansfield and the commuting pattern of its residents, decided that workers living in Mansfield were unlikely to want to commute to Bucyrus. In this decision, the court relied on a survey of 12 major employers in Bucyrus, none of whom restricted the geographical range of their hiring, which showed only four Mansfield residents out of 2300 workers were working in the Bucyrus firms.

While it is clear that the government was wrong in weighting Mansfield and Bucyrus residents equally in computing Timken's availability, it is not clear that the court was correct in rejecting Mansfield as part of Timken's natural recruiting area.

A hedonic model of commuting.   We asserted earlier that the cost of commuting to work is viewed by workers as a disadvantage; the higher the cost, the greater the disadvantages of the job. In this respect, commuting costs are like the risk of injury—to be avoided unless compensation is received. Thus, we would expect that workers, in order to keep their utility constant, would require higher wages to commute longer distances to otherwise identical jobs.

Figure 8.9 shows worker commuting preferences graphically—by drawing indifference curves that are upward-sloping and convex (similar to indifference curves in the analysis of risk of injury). Workers with the greatest aversion to commuting (like Employee A) have the steepest curves, because they require the greatest wage increases to commute longer distances. Workers with the weakest aversion to commuting (like Employee B) have the flattest indifference curves.

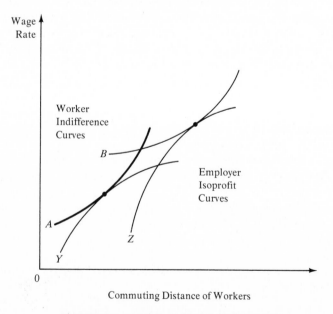

FIGURE 8.9   A Hedonic Model of Commuting

On the employer side of the market, there is also a positive relationship between wages and the commuting distances of their workers. Consider a firm that is dissatisfied with its pool of job applicants and wants to enlarge this pool so it can be more selective in hiring. One solution is to raise its wage offers in order to attract more applicants. This higher wage offer will, among other things, attract applicants who live farther away from the plant. The higher wage offer serves to overcome the commuting costs for these workers.

How high the firm is willing to raise its wage offer depends on how much more productive its work force will be. A large, sophisticated, assembly-line plant may be willing to raise its wages a lot to increase the size of its labor market, because it can select the most skilled *and* the most dependable workers. Unsteady workers, or those prone to absenteeism, can impose high costs on an assembly-line producer. These large, sophisticated firms have the steepest isoprofit curves (like Z in Figure 8.9). A smaller firm looking for workers of the same general skill, but not having a highly interdependent production process, may not obtain a very big increase in productivity if it hires only the most dependable workers. Thus, it may not find that increasing the size of its labor market is as beneficial; this type of small firm (like Y) has a flatter isoprofit curve.

Figure 8.9 suggests two conclusions of interest in the context of antidiscrimination programs. First, there is a *positive* relationship between wages and commuting distances, other things equal. High-wage firms will have geographically larger recruiting areas than low-wage employers. What this means for affirmative-action planning is that the firm's wage policy—whether its pay rate is high, average, or low for the skills it hires—should play a role in determining the size of its labor market and the availability of minorities or women.

In the Timken case, for example, Mansfield may well have been in Timken's legitimate recruiting area (even if it was not for the other twelve employers) *if* Timken's wage rates were higher than average for the jobs involved. Mansfield workers would not, under any circumstances, be considered as equally "available" as Bucyrus workers, but an important consideration—the wage rate—was ignored by the court in defining the availability of minorities to Timken. This consideration, however, was taken into account in a 1979 court decision, wherein it was held that residents of the District of Columbia were not effectively in the labor pool of a suburban employer because, in part, the employer's wages were lower than those paid in the District.[30]

The second major conclusion suggested by Figure 8.9 is that workers select wage offers and commuting distances based on their preferences. People who place a high value on working close to home will accept lower wage offers. These lower offers serve as a compensating wage differential for the desirable characteristic of being able to commute to work quickly and cheaply.

This second conclusion is significant for antidiscrimination policy because women typically work closer to home than do men. Usually having the primary family responsibilities for meal preparation and child rearing, women appear to place a premium on being able to work close to home. Figure 8.9 illustrates that their wages will be somewhat lower as a result of this preference. Thus, *some* of

---

[30]*U.S.* v. *County of Fairfax* 19 FEP Cases 753 (E.O., Va. 1979).

the gross wage differentials between men and women may well be explained by the generally shorter commutes among women.

Chapter 14 will return to a closer examination of male-female wage differences. The point here is that the role women traditionally have had as primary homemaker affects their earnings adversely. While assigning women this role may in itself be considered "discriminatory" by some, this form of discrimination is not the direct object of antidiscrimination programs conducted by the government. These programs by themselves cannot completely eradicate male-female earnings differences.

REVIEW QUESTIONS

1. Is the following true, false, or uncertain: "Certain occupations, such as coal mining, are inherently dangerous to workers' health and safety. Therefore, unambiguously, the most appropriate government policy is the establishment and enforcement of rigid safety and health standards." Explain your answer.
2. Statement 1: "Business executives are greedy profit maximizers, caring only for themselves." Statement 2: "It has been established that workers doing filthy, dangerous work receive higher wages, other things equal." Can both of these statements be generally true? Why?
3. It has often been claimed that an all-volunteer army would be entirely made up of soldiers from minority groups or disadvantaged backgrounds. Using what you have learned in this chapter, analyze the reasoning and assumptions underlying this claim.
4. "The concept of compensating wage premiums for dangerous work does not apply to industries like the coal industry, where the union has forced all wages and other compensation items to be the same. Since all mines must pay the same wage, owners of dangerous mines will have to pay the same wage as owners of safe mines. Therefore, compensating differentials cannot exist." Is this statement correct? (Assume wages and other forms of pay must be equal for dangerous and nondangerous work and consider the implications for individual labor-supply behavior.)

SELECTED READINGS

Milton Friedman, *Price Theory: A Provisional Text* (Chicago: Aldine Publishing Company, 1962). See the chapter entitled, "The Supply of Factors of Production."

Sherwin Rosen, "Hedonic Prices and Implicit Markets," *Journal of Political Economy* 82 (January-February 1974): 34–55.

Adam Smith, *Wealth of Nations* (New York: Modern Library, 1937), Book I, Chapter 10.

Robert S. Smith, "Compensating Wage Differentials and Public Policy: A Review," *Industrial and Labor Relations Review* 32 (April 1979): 339–52.

Robert S. Smith, *The Occupational Safety and Health Act: Its Goals and Its Achievements* (Washington, D.C.: The American Enterprise Institute for Public Policy Research, 1976).

W. Kip Viscusi, *Employment Hazards: An Investigation of Market Performance* (Cambridge, Mass.: Harvard University Press, 1979).

9

Investments in Human Capital: Education and Training

Chapters 6, 7, and 8—on the decision to work and on job choice—have emphasized the effects of *current* wages and psychic income on worker decisions. However, many labor-supply choices require a substantial initial *investment* on the part of the worker. Recall that investments, by definition, entail an initial cost that is then recouped (hopefully) over some period of time. Thus, for many labor-supply decisions, *current* wages and working conditions are not the only deciding factors. To model these decisions, one needs to develop a framework that incorporates investment behavior.

Workers undertake three major kinds of investments: 1. education and training, 2. migration, and 3. search for new jobs. All three investments involve an initial cost, and all three are made in the hope and expectation that the investment will pay off well into the future. To emphasize the essential similarity of these investments to other kinds of investments, economists refer to them as investments in *human capital*—a term that conceptualizes workers as embodying a set of skills that can be "rented" out to employers. The knowledge and skills a worker has—which come from education and training, including the training that experience yields—generate a certain *stock* of productive capital. However, the *value* of this amount of productive capital is derived from how much these skills can earn in the labor market. Job search and migration are activities that increase the value of one's human capital by increasing the price (wage) received for a given stock of skills.

Society's total wealth should therefore be thought of as a combination of both human and nonhuman capital. Human capital includes accumulated investments in such activities as education, job training, and migration, whereas nonhuman wealth includes society's stock of land, buildings, and machinery. Total wealth in the United States was estimated at $15.6 trillion in 1973, or about $75,000 for every man, woman and child. Of this, 52 percent—or $39,000 per capita—took the form of *human* wealth.[1] Thus, investments in human capital are enormously important in our society.

The expected *returns* on human capital investments are, as noted, a higher level of earnings, greater job satisfaction over one's lifetime, and a greater appreciation of nonmarket activities and interests. Generally speaking, the investment *expenditures* can be divided into three categories:

1. *Out-of-pocket* or *direct* expenses include: tuition and books (education), moving expenses (migration), and gasoline (job search).
2. *Forgone earnings* are another source of cost because during the investment period it is usually impossible to work, at least full time.
3. *Psychic losses* are a third kind cost incurred because education is difficult and often boring, because job search is tedious and nerve-wracking, and because migration means saying goodbye to old friends.

This chapter will analyze educational investments and their labor-market implications. Because most such investments are closely related to the supply of labor to a particular occupation or set of occupations, this aspect of human-capital theory adds more depth to the analysis of occupational choice begun in the last chapter. Chapter 10 deals with turnover and migration; other aspects of job search are treated in Chapter 15.

DEMAND FOR EDUCATION BY WORKERS

There are many ways in which workers—or potential workers—can enhance their earning capacity through education. They can attend high school, junior college, or a university. They can go to a trade school or technical institute. They can enter an apprenticeship program, or they can acquire skills on the job. The analysis of the demand for any of these types of education or training is essentially the same. Therefore, this section will analyze the demand for a college education as an illustration and application of human-capital theory.

People will want to attend college when they believe they will be better off by so doing. For some, the benefits may be short-term: they like the courses or the lifestyle of a student. Students attending for these reasons regard college as a *consumption good*—that is, they are going to college primarily for the satisfaction it provides during the period of attendance. Others, however, are attending college because of the *long-term* benefits it provides. These benefits are partly in the form of higher earnings, partly in the form of gaining access to more interesting, challenging, or pleasant jobs, and partly in the form of prestige or enhanced enjoyment of nonmarket activities. Attendance for the long-term benefits—or *investment behavior*—is the behavior this chapter seeks to analyze.

---

[1]U.S. Congress, Joint Economic Committee, *Economic Growth and Total Capital Formation* (Washington, D.C.: U.S. Government Printing Office, February 18, 1976).

An Overview of the Benefits and Costs
of an Educational Investment

Calculating the benefits of an investment over time requires the progressive discounting of benefits lying farther into the future (see Chapter 5). Benefits that are received in the future are worth less to us now than an equal amount of benefits to be received today, for two reasons. First, if people plan to consume their benefits, they will prefer to consume earlier than later. (One is relatively sure of being able to enjoy such consumption now, but the uncertainties of life make future enjoyment problematic.) Second, if people plan to invest the monetary benefits rather than use them for consumption, they can earn interest on the investment and enlarge their funds in the future. Thus, no matter how people intend to use their benefits, they will discount future receipts to some extent.

As Chapter 5 explained, the present value of a stream of yearly benefits (B) over time (T) can be calculated as follows:

$$\text{Present Value} = \frac{B_1}{1+r} + \frac{B_2}{(1+r)^2} + \frac{B_3}{(1+r)^3} + \ldots + \frac{B_T}{(1+r)^T} \tag{9.1}$$

where the interest rate (or discount rate) is r. As long as r is positive, benefits into the future will be progressively discounted. For example, if $r = 0.06$ benefits payable in 30 years would receive a weight that is only 17 percent of the weight placed on benefits payable immediately $(1.06^{30} = 5.73; 1/5.73 = 0.17)$.

The costs of going to college are normally incurred over a relatively short period of time. These costs include 1. the direct costs of tuition, fees, and books; 2. the forgone earnings attendant to being a full-time student; and 3. the psychic costs of studying and being examined. The total costs of going to college are thus very high, with the monetary costs alone (direct costs plus forgone earnings) in the range of $10,000–15,000 per year in 1980.

A person considering college has, in some broad sense, a choice between two streams of income over his or her lifetime. Stream A begins immediately but does not rise very high; it is the earnings stream of a high-school graduate. Stream B (the college graduate) has a negative income for the first four years (owing to college tuition costs), followed by a period when the salary is less than what the high-school graduate makes, but then it takes off and rises above stream A. Both streams are illustrated in Figure 9.1. (Why these streams are *curved* will be discussed later in this chapter.) The streams shown in the figure are stylized so that we can emphasize some basic points. Actual earnings streams are shown later in Figures 9.11 and 9.13.

Obviously, the earnings of the college graduate would have to rise above those of the high-school graduate in order to induce someone to invest in a college education (unless, of course, the psychic or consumption-related returns are large). The gross benefits—the difference in earnings between the two streams—must total much more than the costs because such returns are in the future and are therefore discounted. For example, if it costs $12,000 per year to obtain a four-year college education, and if the interest rate is 6 percent, the after-tax returns (if they are the same each year) must be $3200 for 40 years in order to

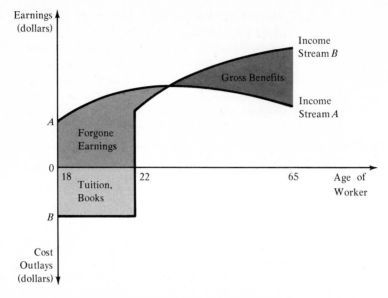

FIGURE 9.1   Alternative Income Streams

justify the investment on purely monetary grounds. These returns must be so high because $48,000 invested at a 6 percent interest rate can provide a payment (of interest and principal) totaling $3200 a year for 40 years.[2]

A Formal Model of Choice and Its Implications

The preceding discussion emphasized that investing in a college education is worthwhile if the present value of the benefits (monetary and psychic) are at least as large as the costs. In mathematical terms this criterion can be expressed as:

$$\frac{B_1}{1+r} + \frac{B_2}{(1+r)^2} + \ldots + \frac{B_T}{(1+r)_T} \geq C, \tag{9.2}$$

where C equals the total costs of a college education and B equals the yearly differences in earnings between college and high-school graduates.

There are two ways one can measure whether the criterion in equation (9.2) is met. Using the *present-value method,* one can specify a value for the discount rate, r, and determine if the present value of benefits is greater than or equal to costs. Alternatively, one can adopt the *internal-rate-of-return-method,* which asks, "How large could the discount rate be and still render college profitable?" Clearly, if the benefits are so large that even a very high discount rate would

---

[2]This calculation is made using the *annuity formula:*

$$Y = X \frac{1 - [1/(1 + r)^n]}{r},$$

where Y equals the total investment ($48,000 in our example), X = the yearly payment ($3200), r = the rate of interest (0.06), and n = the number of years (40). In this example, we treat the costs of a college education as being incurred all in one year rather than being spread out over four—a simplification that does not alter the magnitude of required returns much at all.

render college profitable, then the project is worthwhile. In practice, one calculates this internal rate of return by setting the present value of benefits equal to costs and solving for r. The internal rate of return is then compared to the rate of return on other investments. If the internal rate of return exceeds the alternative rates of return, the investment project is considered profitable.[3]

In deciding whether to attend college, no doubt few students make the very precise calculations suggested in equation (9.2). Nevertheless, if they make less formal estimates that take into account the same factors, four predictions concerning the demand for college education can be made:

1. Present-oriented people are less likely to go to college than forward-looking people (other things equal).
2. Most college students will be young.
3. College attendance will increase if the costs of college fall (other things equal).
4. College attendance will increase if the gap between the earnings of college graduates and high-school graduates widens (again, other things equal).

Present-orientedness.   Psychologists use the term *present-oriented* to refer to people who do not weight future events or outcomes very heavily. While all people discount the future with respect to the present, those who discount it more than average—or, at the extreme, ignore the future altogether—could be considered present-oriented. In terms of equations (9.1) and (9.2), a present-oriented person is one with a very high discount rate *(r)*.

Suppose one were to calculate investment returns using the *present-value method*. If r is large, the present value of benefits associated with college will be lower than if the discount rate being used is smaller. Thus, a present-oriented person would impute smaller benefits to college attendance than one who is less present-oriented, and those who are present-oriented would be less likely to attend college. Using the *internal-rate-of-return method* for evaluating the soundness of a college education, one would arrive at the same result. If a college education earns an 8 percent rate or return, but the individuals in question are so present-oriented that they would insist on a 25 percent rate of return before investing, they would likewise decide not to attend.

The prediction that present-oriented people are less likely to attend college than forward-looking ones is difficult to substantiate or disprove. The rates of discount that people use in making investment decisions are rarely available, because the decisions are not made as formally as equation (9.2) implies. However, the model does suggest that people who have a high propensity to invest in education will also engage in other forward-looking behavior. Certain medical statistics tend to support this prediction.

---

[3]For our purposes here, the present-value and internal-rate-of-return methods may be considered interchangeable in evaluating investment alternatives. In *some* circumstances, however, the two methods would not provide identical rankings of investment opportunities. *See* J. Hirshleifer, "On the Theory of Optimal Investment Decision," *Journal of Political Economy* 66 (August 1958): 329–52.

In the United States there is a strong statistical correlation between education and health status.[4] People with more years of schooling have lower mortality rates, fewer symptoms of disease (such as high blood pressure, high cholesterol levels, abnormal X-rays), and a greater tendency to report themselves to be in good health. This effect of education on health is independent of income, which appears to have no effect of its own on health status except at the lowest poverty levels. Is this correlation between education and health a result of better use of medical resources by the well educated? It appears not. Better-educated people undergoing surgery choose the same doctors, enter the hospital at the same stage of disease, and have the same length of stay as less-educated people of equal income.

What *may* cause this correlation is a more forward-looking attitude among those who have obtained more education. People with lower discount rates will be more likely to attend college, and they will *also* be more likely to adopt forward-looking habits of health. They may choose healthier diets, be more careful of health risks, and make more use of preventative medicine. This explanation for the correlation between education and health is not the only plausible one, but it receives some direct support from British data on cigarette smoking.[5] From 1958–1975, the proportion of men in the most highly educated groups who smoked fell by 50 percent. During the same time period, the proportion of smokers in the more poorly educated class remained unchanged. It is unlikely that the less-educated group was uninformed of the smoking dangers revealed during that period. It is more likely that they were less willing to give up a present source of pleasure for a distant benefit. Thus, we have at least some evidence that people who invest in education also engage in *other* forward-looking behavior.

Age.   Given similar *yearly* benefits of going to college, young people have a larger present value of *total* benefits than older workers simply because they have a longer remaining work life ahead of them. In terms of equation (9.2), T for younger people is greater than for older ones. We would therefore expect younger people to have a greater propensity than older people to obtain a college education or engage in other forms of training activity. This prediction is parallel to the predictions in Chapter 5 about which workers employers will decide to invest in when they make decisions about hiring or specific training.

Costs.   A third prediction of our model is that human-capital investments are more likely when costs are lower. The major monetary costs of college attendance are forgone earnings and the direct costs of tuition, books, and fees. (Food and lodging are not always opportunity costs of going to college, because much of these costs would have to be incurred in any event.) Thus, if forgone earnings or tuition costs fall, other things equal, we would expect an increase in college enrollments.

---

[4]The analysis of the correlation between education and health status is taken from Victor Fuchs, "The Economics of Health in a Post-Industrial Society," *The Public Interest,* Summer 1979, pp. 3–20.

[5]It could be, for example, that healthy people, with longer life spans, are more likely to invest in human capital because they expect to experience a longer payback period. Alternatively, one could argue that the higher incomes of college graduates later in life mean they have more to lose from illness than do non-college graduates.

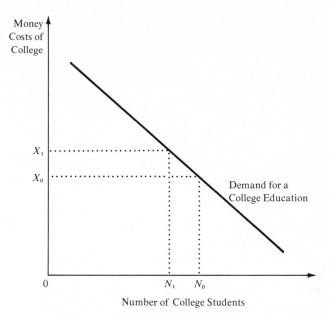

FIGURE 9.2   The Demand for a College Education

The costs of college attendance offer an additional reason why we observe older people attending less often than younger people. As workers age, they acquire levels of experience and maturity that employers are willing to reward with higher wages. Because older workers thus command higher wages (on average), their opportunity costs of college attendance are higher than those for younger students.[6] Older people are thus doubly discouraged from attending college: their forgone earnings are relatively high and the period over which they can capture benefits is comparatively short.

The psychic costs of going to college cannot be ignored. While these costs cannot be easily observed, they are likely to be related to ability. People who learn easily and who do well in school settings have an easier and more pleasant time in college than people who do not.

In any set of market transactions, some people are *at the margin*—which means that they are close to the point of not transacting. For example, consider a downward-sloping demand curve for education, where the number of people attending college is drawn as a function of its money costs (see Figure 9.2). If the money costs were X_0, we would observe that N_0 people would go to college. If the costs were raised to X_1, only N_1 would decide to attend. The people deciding to drop out when costs rise to X_1 are those who were closest to not going when they were X_0. They are the ones who had the hardest time making up their minds at X_0—in other words, those who came closest to deciding not to go when costs were X_0.

Who are the people closest to the margin regarding the decision to go to college? In part, they are people for whom the psychic costs of studying and being

---

[6]This discussion is related to our discussion of the life-cycle supply of labor in Chapter 7. When wages are low, people will engage in time-intensive activities.

examined are relatively high—people who do not especially like school. This group—who, we have argued, might consist to a large extent of less able students—is thus likely to be the most responsive to changes in the money costs of education. (See the Appendix to this chapter for a fuller discussion of the signaling issue.) Indeed, studies that have analyzed the effects of college location on college attendance show that males of moderate ability are much more responsive to college location than those of high ability. That is, whether a college is available in one's hometown seems to matter a lot more to moderate-ability students than it does to high-ability students.[7]

Earnings differentials.   The fourth prediction of human-capital theory is that the demand for education is positively related to the *returns*—that is, to the increases in lifetime earnings or psychic benefits that a college education allows. In practice, this prediction can be tested only with reference to money returns, since psychic returns are unobservable.[8] This prediction has been used to explain the sharp fall in college enrollments that occured in the early 1970s.[9]

Beginning around 1970, the labor market for college graduates began to exhibit signs of a surplus. Jobs in the professional fields where college graduates have typically found employment began to dwindle relative to the supply, and more and more college graduates had to take jobs as sales, clerical, or blue-collar workers. For example, in 1958 only 10.5 percent of recent female college graduates and 13.8 percent of recent male college graduates were employed in non-professional, nonmanagerial jobs—such as sales, clerical, or blue-collar work. For 1970–71 college graduates, these percentages had more than doubled to 24.4 percent for women and 30.5 percent for men. The deterioration in employment prospects for college graduates was also manifest in the starting salaries for graduates with bachelor's degrees. Table 9.1 tells the story for men, for whom comparative data over time are more available and reliable than are the data for women. From 1961-69, starting salaries for male college graduates increased faster than wages and prices in general—indicative of a pre-existing *shortage* of college graduates (see Chapter 2 for a review of the concepts of *shortage* and *surplus*). From 1969–74, starting salaries for male bachelor's graduates increased more slowly than both average wages and the price level, which is what one would expect in sectors where labor surpluses exist.

In analyzing the potential effects of this surplus of college graduates on college enrollments, however, one must not ignore the fact that our model stresses the discounted stream of benefits *over a lifetime,* while the data just presented

---

[7]C. A. Anderson, M. J. Bowman, V. Tinto, *Where Colleges Are and Who Attends* (New York: McGraw-Hill, 1972). Given that loans to attend college often are not readily available, the financial resources of the investor are an important factor in the decision to invest. Thus, people in families with modest wealth are closer to the margin regarding the educational decision.

[8]There is evidence, although it is somewhat weak, that better-educated workers are more likely to describe themselves as "satisfied" with their jobs. (See Daniel Hamermesh, "Economic Aspects of Job Satisfaction," in *Essays in Labor Market Analysis,* eds. Orley Ashenfelter and Wallace Oates (New York: John Wiley and Sons, 1977), pp. 53–72. *Quantifying* job or nonjob psychic benefits however, is still not possible.

[9]The analysis in the succeeding paragraphs relies heavily on Richard Freeman, "Overinvestment in College Training?" *Journal of Human Resources* 10, 3 (Summer 1975): 287–311.

TABLE 9.1.   Compound Annual Changes in the Starting Salaries of Male Bachelor Graduates, 1961–69 and 1969–74

	1961–69 Period of Relative Market Boom		1969–74 Period of Relative Market Bust	
	Annual Percent Change in Salaries	Annual Percent Change Minus Change in CPI[a]	Annual Percent Change in Salaries	Annual Percent Change Minus Change in CPI
Accountant	6.0	3.4	4.0	−2.2
Business-general	5.7	3.1	2.4	−3.8
Humanities and social science	5.3	2.7	1.1	−5.1
Aeronautic engineering	4.8	2.2	3.1	−3.1
Chemical engineering	5.8	3.2	3.8	−2.4
Civil engineering	5.7	3.1	3.9	−2.5
Electrical engineering	5.1	2.5	3.2	−3.0
Mechanical engineering	5.3	2.7	3.5	−2.7
Industrial engineering	4.7	2.1	3.3	−2.9
Physical sciences, mathematics	4.8	2.2	2.1	−4.1
Changes in annual earnings of year-round full-time workers	4.7	2.1	6.6[b]	+0.4

[a]CPI = Consumer Price Index

[b]1974 estimated by percentage change in average hourly earnings of all private industry production workers from March 1973 to March 1974.

SOURCE: Reprinted from Richard Freeman, "Overinvestment in College Training?" *Journal of Human Resources* 10, 3 (Summer 1975): 288.

refer mainly to employment prospects *immediately after graduation.* Nevertheless, there are two reasons to believe that immediate post-college prospects are of crucial importance in the decision to go to college. First, being closer to the present, earnings immediately after graduation are less heavily discounted than earnings later on. Second, in the absence of any better information, people may use current employment trends for college graduates as estimates of what prospects in the more distant future will be like. If there is a surplus now, people may assume it will last long enough to render college a poor investment.

Associated with the surplus of college graduates was a decline in the proportion of young males going to college. Among males—for whom labor-market conditions appeared to change most in the early 1970s—the percentage of high-school graduates going to college fell from 58 percent (1969) to 50 percent (1973). Further, the proportion of 18- to 24-year-old males going to college, after rising almost steadily since 1950, fell from 35 percent (1969) to 27 percent (1973).

Among females, the enrollment response was an abrupt cessation of growth in the proportion of young women enrolled in college rather than a decline. Nevertheless, this response did represent a significant departure from the trend in growing college attendance during the 1960s. (The failure of enrollments to fall can possibly be explained—at least in part—by the tremendous increase in the propensity of women to seek work outside the home that has occurred in recent years. The longer one expects to work outside the home, the greater are the benefits of college attendance.) One might also argue that the differential response of men and women in terms of college attendance was due to changes during the early 1970s in the draft laws—which effectively removed the incentives for men to attend college in order to avoid the draft. While the draft-law changes did have an effect, the timing of the decline in enrollments makes it clear that such changes

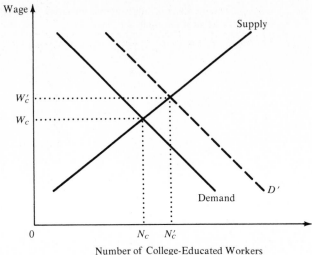

Wage

Supply

W_c'

W_c

Demand

D'

0

N_c N_c'

Number of College-Educated Workers

**FIGURE 9.3   The Market for College Graduates
with a Shift in Demand**

can only explain part of the decline in demand for college education among males. Declining returns to a college education were clearly a major stimulus for the changed patterns of college-attendance in the early 1970s.

Earnings Differences and the Demand for Education

As we have just seen, the demand for education is influenced by the differences in earnings made possible by an educational investment. However, the returns to education are themselves affected by the number of people who attend school. To obtain an overall picture of how enrollments and returns are interrelated, it is necessary to return briefly to our simple model of the labor market.

Figure 9.3 shows the labor market demand for, and supply of, college graduates. We know why the demand curve for labor slopes downward, but why does the supply curve for college graduates in Figure 9.3 slope upward? The reason, discussed earlier in this chapter, is that college is costly. If college graduates typically earn relatively low wages, few people will want to attend college. If the earnings of college graduates were to rise, more would want to attend college. If they were to rise still more, even greater numbers would enroll.

What would happen if the demand for college graduates were to shift outward, so that more such graduates were demanded at any given wage? Figure 9.3 illustrates that if the demand curve shifts to D', the wages of college graduates would rise from W_c to W_c'. This increase in the wages of college graduates would serve as an incentive for more people to attend college, and the number of college graduates would rise.

What would happen if, on the other hand, the supply of college graduates were to shift to the right—indicating that more people want to attend college for any given wage level that can be attained by graduates. Such a shift might occur, for example, if the government were to subsidize students in college or to exempt

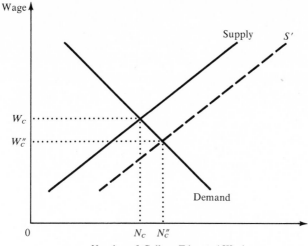

Wage

Supply

S'

W_C

W_C''

Demand

0

N_C N_C''

Number of College-Educated Workers

**FIGURE 9.4   The Market for College Graduates
with a Shift in Supply**

students from the military draft. Figure 9.4 shows that the outward shift in the supply of college graduates drives wages down to W_C'', a reduction that serves to moderate the increase in enrollments (as W_C falls to W_C'', the movement along S' suggests that fewer people decide to attend).

Unfortunately, the adjustment of college enrollments to changes in the returns to education is not always smooth or rapid—particularly in special fields, like engineering and law, that are highly technical. The problem is that if engineering wages (say) were to go up suddenly in 1980, the supply of graduate engineers would not be affected for three or four years (owing to the time it takes to learn the field). Likewise, if engineering wages were to fall, those students enrolled in an engineering curriculum would understandably be reluctant to immediately leave the field. They have already invested a lot of time and effort and may prefer to take their chances in engineering rather than devote more time and money to learning a new field.

The inability to respond immediately to changed market conditions can cause *boom-and-bust cycles* in the market for highly technical workers. If educational planners in government or the private sector were unaware of these cycles, they might seek to stimulate (or reduce) enrollments at a time when they should be doing exactly the opposite, as illustrated below.

Suppose the market for engineers is in equilibrium, where the wage is W_0 and the number of engineers is N_0 (see Figure 9.5). Let us now assume that the demand curve for engineers shifts from D_0 to D_1. Initially, this increase in the demand for engineers does *not* induce the supply of engineers to increase beyond N_0, because it takes a long time to become an engineer once one has decided to do so. Thus, while the increased demand for engineers causes more people to decide to enter the field, the number available for employment at the moment is N_0. These N_0 engineers, therefore, can *currently* obtain a wage of W_1 (in effect,

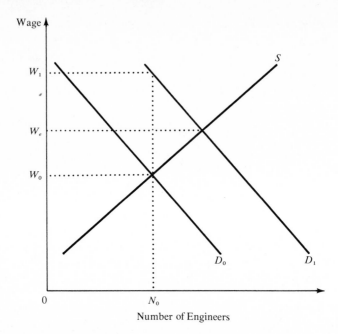

FIGURE 9.5   The Labor Market for Engineers

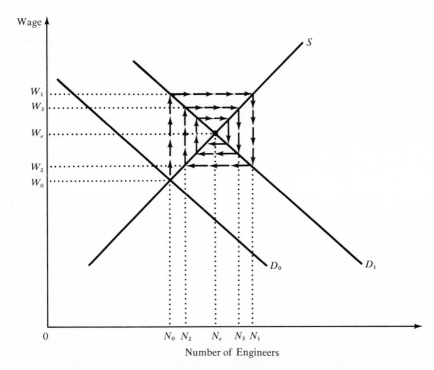

FIGURE 9.6   The Labor Market for Engineers: a Cobweb Model

there is a vertical supply curve, at N_0, for a few years until the supply of engineering graduates is increased).

Now W_1, the *current* engineering wage, is above W_e—the new *long-run* equilibrium wage caused by the intersection of D_1 and S. The market, however, is unaware of W_e—observing only W_1. If people are myopic and assume W_1 is the new engineering wage, N_1 people will enter the engineering field (see Figure 9.6). When these N_1 all graduate, there will be a *surplus* of engineers (remember W_1 is *above* long-run equilibrium).

With the supply of engineers now temporarily fixed at N_1, the wage will fall to W_2. This fall will cause students and workers to shift *out* of engineering, but that effect will not be fully felt for a few years. In the meantime, note that W_2 is below long-run equilibrium (still at W_e). Thus, when supply *does* adjust, it will adjust too much—all the way to N_2. Now there is another shortage of engineers, because at W_2, there is greater demand than supply. This causes wages to rise to W_3, and the cycle repeats itself. Over time, the swings become smaller, and eventually equilibrium is reached. Because the adjustment path in Figure 9.6 looks like a cobweb, the adjustment process described above is sometimes called a *cobweb model*.[10]

Any market characterized by a cobweb adjustment process will experience alternating shortages and surpluses—and any educational institution training students for these fields will also experience booms and busts. Engineering appears to be one such field.[11] In the early 1950s people were talking of a surplus of engineers. In the late 1950s and early 1960s the discussion was of shortages. In the late 1960s there was again a surplus, followed in the 1970s by another shortage. Engineering enrollments fluctuated likewise, clearly reacting to the changed state of the market for engineers.

The lesson to be learned from the cobweb model should not be lost on government policymakers. If the government chooses to take an active role in dealing with labor shortages and surpluses, it must be aware that, because supply adjustments are slow in highly technical markets, wages in those markets tend to *over-adjust*. For example, at the initial stages of a shortage when wages are rising toward W_1 (in our example), the government should be pointing out that W_1 is likely to be *above* the long-run equilibrium. If instead it attempts to meet the current shortage by *subsidizing* study in that field, it will be encouraging an even greater *surplus* later on. The moral of the story is that a rather complete knowledge of how markets adjust to changes in demand or supply is necessary before one can be sure that government intervention will do more good than harm.

---

[10]Critical to cobweb models is the assumption that suppliers—in this case, workers—have static or myopic expectations about prices. In our example, they first assume that W_1 will be the prevailing wage, ignoring the possibility that the behavior of others will in 4 years drive the wage below W_1. One might expect that they would learn of their errors over time; however, as long as they assume the future prevalence of wages that oscillate above and below W_e, cobweb-type behavior will result.

[11]Richard B. Freeman, "A Cobweb Model of the Supply and Starting Salary of New Engineers," *Industrial and Labor Relations Review* 29 (January 1976): 236–46.

THE EDUCATION/WAGE RELATIONSHIP

The preceding section used human-capital theory to explore the demand for education—particularly college education. This section will investigate in more detail the effects of education on earnings and will explore several policy issues to which human-capital theory can be applied.

A Hedonic Model of Education and Wages

The preceding section argued that the prospect of improved lifetime earnings served as a major inducement for people to invest in an education or training program. Indeed, unless education is acquired purely for purposes of consumption, people will not undertake an investment in education or training without the expectation that, by so doing, they can improve their stream of lifetime earnings or psychic rewards. However, in order to obtain these higher benefits, *employers* must be willing to pay for them. Therefore, it is necessary to examine both sides of the market to fully understand the relationship between education and earnings.

Supply (worker) side.   Consider a group of people who have chosen a particular class of job—selling, say—as a desired career. These salespersons-to-be have a choice of how much education or training to invest in, given their career objectives. In making this choice they will have to weigh the returns against the costs, as pointed out in the previous section. Crucial to this decision is how the *actual* returns compare to the returns each would *require* in order to induce them to invest.

Figure 9.7 shows the indifference curves between yearly earnings and education for two workers, A and B. To induce A or B to acquire X years of education would require the assurance of earning W_X after they begin work. However, to induce A to increase his or her education beyond X years (holding utility constant) would require a larger salary increase than B would require. A's greater aversion

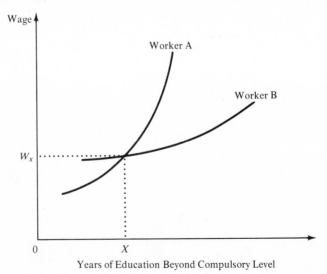

FIGURE 9.7   Indifference Curves for Two Different Workers

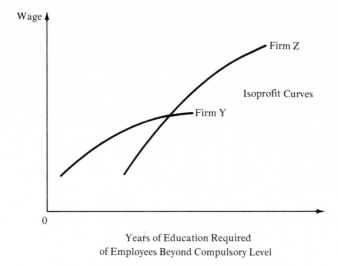

FIGURE 9.8   Isoprofit Curves for Two Different Firms

to making educational investments could be explained in several ways. Person A could be older than B, thus having higher forgone earnings and fewer years over which to recoup investment costs. Person A could be more present-oriented and thus more inclined to discount future benefits heavily—or could have less ability in classroom learning or have a greater dislike of schooling. Finally, A may find it more difficult to finance additional schooling. Whatever the reason, this analysis points up the important fact that people are different in their propensity to invest in schooling.

Demand (employer) side.   On the demand side of the market, employers must consider whether they are willing to pay higher wages for better-educated workers. If they are, they must also decide how much to pay for each additional year. Figure 9.8 illustrates employers' choices about the wage/education relationship. Employers Y and Z are *both* willing to pay more for better-educated sales personnel (to continue our example), because they have found that better-educated workers are more productive.[12] Thus, they can achieve the same profit level by either paying lower wages for less educated workers or higher wages for more educated workers. Their isoprofit curves are thus upward sloping (see Chapter 8 for a description of isoprofit curves).

The isoprofit curves in Figure 9.8 have three important characteristics:

1. For each firm the curves are concave—that is, they get flatter as education increases. This concavity results from the assumption that, at some point, the added benefits to the employer of an additional year of employee schooling begin to decline. In other words, we assume that schooling is subject to diminishing marginal productivity.

---

[12]Whether schooling causes workers to be more productive or whether schooling simply reflects—or "signals"—higher productivity is not important at this point, but we do address this issue later on.

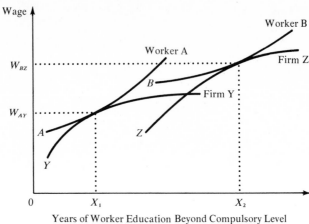

FIGURE 9.9   The Wage/Education Relationship

2. The isoprofit curves are the *zero-profit curves*. Neither firm can pay higher wages for each level of education than those indicated on the curves; if they did so their profits would be negative and they would cease operations.

3. The added benefits from an extra year of schooling are smaller in Firm Y than in Firm Z—causing Y to have a flatter isoprofit curve. Firm Y, for example, may be a discount department store where "selling" is largely a matter of waiting on a counter. While better-educated people may be more productive, they are not *too* much more valuable then less-educated people; hence Firm Y is not willing to pay them much more. Firm Z, on the other hand, may sell technical instruments where knowledge of physics and customer engineering problems are needed. In Firm Z, additional education adds a relatively large increment to one's productivity.

Market Determination of the Wage/Education Relationship.

Putting both sides of the market for educated workers together, it is clear that the wage/education relationship will be positive, as indicated in Figure 9.9. Worker A will work for Y, receiving a wage equal to W_{AY} and obtaining X_1 years of education. The reason for this matching is simple. Firm Z cannot pay higher wages (for each level of education) than those shown on the isoprofit curve in Figure 9.9, for reasons noted above. Clearly, then, Worker A could never derive as much utility from Z as he or she could from Y; working for Firm Z would involve a loss of utility to Worker A. For similar reasons, Worker B will accept work with Firm Z, obtain X_2 years of schooling, and receive higher pay (W_{BZ}).

When examined from an overall social perspective, the positive wage/education relationship is the result of a very sensible sorting of workers and employers performed by the labor market. Workers with the greatest aversion to investing in education *(A)* will work for firms where education adds least to employee productivity *(Y)*. People with the least aversion to educational investment *(B)* are hired by those firms most willing to pay for an educated work force *(Z)*.

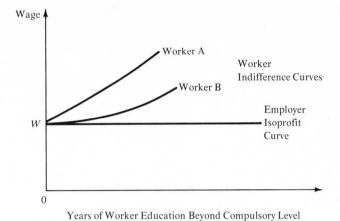

FIGURE 9.10 Unwillingness of Firm to Pay for More Education by Employees

Note: If employers were unwilling to pay higher wages for more educated workers, no education-related differentials would exist, and employer isoprofit curves would be horizontal. Without a positive education/wage relationship, employees would have no incentive to invest in an education (see Figure 9.10).

The relationship between education and earnings is well documented and can be observed graphically in Figure 9.11. This figure presents (for males) *age/earnings profiles*—or lifetime earnings patterns—for five different levels of schooling. Two conclusions are immediately obvious:

1. Better-educated males have higher earnings than less-educated males at each post-schooling age level—as predicted by our theory. Note, however, from the (dashed) earnings profile of men with education beyond the bachelor's degree, that earnings while in school are lower than they would otherwise be (a graphical representation of the concept of forgone earnings).

2. The age/earnings profiles for workers with more education are steeper than the profiles of workers with less education. That is, the differences in earnings associated with education tend to widen as workers grow older. In the early years the earnings gap is small. Workers who have gone to college have not had a chance to acquire the work experience of their colleagues who have been working rather than attending college. Later, after they have had a chance to gain experience, their earnings rise much more sharply. (A more detailed discussion of *why* age/earnings profiles are steeper for more educated workers will be presented later in this chapter.)

IS EDUCATION A GOOD INVESTMENT?

It is well established that workers with more education tend to earn higher wages. However, an individual deciding whether to go to college would naturally ask, "Will I increase my monetary and psychic income enough to justify the costs of

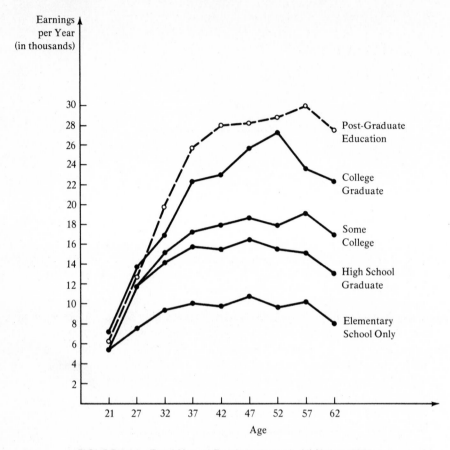

FIGURE 9.11   Total Money Earnings (mean), All Males, 1977

SOURCE: U.S. Bureau of the Census, *Money Income in 1977 of Families and Persons in the United States,* Current Population Reports, Series P-60, No. 118 (March 1979), Table 48.

going to college?'' Further, government policymakers trying to decide whether to expand educational facilities or subsidize increased enrollments must ask, ''Will the benefits of improved productivity outweigh the costs?''

Is Education a Good Investment for Individuals?

Individuals about to make an investment in a college education are committing themselves to costs of at least $10,000 per year. Is there evidence that this investment pays off for the typical student? Several studies have tried to answer this question by calculating the internal rates of return to educational investments. While the methods and data used vary, these studies normally estimate benefits by calculating earnings differentials at each age from age/earnings profiles such as those in Figure 9.11. (*Earnings* are usually used to measure benefits because higher wages and more stable jobs are payoffs to more education.) The *rate of return* is that discount rate which equates the present value of benefits to the cost of acquiring the level of education in question. It should be stressed that all such studies have analyzed only the monetary—and not the psychic—costs and returns to educational investments.

Example 9.1
Schooling, Earnings, and Compensation for Wrongful Death

How does a court determine the size of an award in a wrongful death case? Many states allow the family of a person killed through the negligence of another to collect from the responsible party the present value of the deceased's lost lifetime earnings. The procedure employed in calculating the size of the award often relies heavily on the victim's level of education in predicting earnings had he or she lived. This procedure is illustrated by summarizing an actual case in which one of the authors was involved.

John Doe was a 20-year-old high-school graduate not yet firmly established in a career. While a passenger in a car one night, he was killed when the car's drunk driver hit a truck while drag racing. Doe's family sued the driver of the car, seeking to collect the discounted value of his lost lifetime earnings. In evaluating his loss, the court had to decide (a) which would be the appropriate age/earnings profile to use in estimating lost earnings, and (b) which would be the appropriate interest rate to use in discounting these losses to the present.

It is obvious that John Doe's lifetime earnings losses are impossible to calculate precisely but must instead be estimated. What is the most reasonable estimate? We know that peoples' earnings differ because of differences in both luck and unmeasurable personal characteristics, such as perseverance and the drive to succeed. Since there is no reason to believe Doe would have been exceptionally lucky or unlucky—and since unmeasurable characteristics are by definition difficult to deal with—the court was forced to assume he would have been average in these respects.

We also know that earnings vary because of education, age, race, sex, health status, union membership, region, occupation, and the industry in which employment is found. Had Doe, who was white, been reasonably settled in an occupation—carpentry, say—one could have used age/earnings profiles for the average white male carpenter. Unfortunately, Doe was not in a training program and had worked only briefly in a variety of jobs. (Indeed, occupational mobility in the United States is so high that few people remain in one occupation or industry for an entire career. (Chapter 10 will return to this point.)

If evidence of a career-long job attachment is absent, the best estimate of lifetime earnings is derived from age/earnings profiles specific to the race, sex, and educational level of the individual. In the case of John Doe, earnings that would have prevailed at each age in his working life were estimated by plotting the typical age earnings/profile for white, male high-school graduates in the United States for 1977. The profile applicable to Doe is summarized in the accompanying table. Assuming Doe would have retired at age 65, the simple summation of these yearly earnings totals $624,666. This figure is undiscounted and thus inappropriate for a court settlement which pays a lump-sum payment now. However, it does give the reader an idea of the magnitude of the losses involved.

**Average Earnings of White,
Male High-School Graduates, 1977**

Age	Earnings
18–24	$ 6,708
25–29	11,506
30–34	13,290
35–39	15,667
40–44	15,584
45–49	16,529
50–54	15,843
55–59	15,002
60–64	13,341
65	7,316

Note: Earnings shown are *median* earnings, meaning that half of all high-school graduates earned more than the amount shown and half earned less.

SOURCE: U.S. Bureau of the Census, "Money Income in 1977 of Families and Persons in the United States," *Current Population Reports,* Series P-60, no. 118, March 1979, Table 48.

The age/earnings profile shown in the table would be appropriate to use in calculating Doe's undiscounted losses only if Doe would have earned at each age what workers currently that age were earning in 1977. There are at least three reasons why this is unlikely. First, Doe may not have been average in terms of luck, union membership, health status, or unmeasurable personal characteristics. We have already mentioned this problem and suggested that assuming he would have been average is the best one could do.

Second, inflation alone will increase money wages substantially over one's career. However, the court can downplay inflation because the award to Doe's family is a *lump-sum* settlement payable in the current year. Doe's family could spend all the money in the current year, at *current* prices, or they could invest it. Because interest rates and other forms of investment returns *tend* to reflect inflation, investing the funds would provide a natural adjustment for inflation. (Economists often distinguish between the "real" and "nominal" rate of interest. The *nominal* rate is the one that is quoted by banks or bond dealers. The *real* rate is the nominal rate minus the rate of inflation.)

Third, real wages have grown in the past and will grow in the future because of increased productivity. The court needed to take real wage growth into account in order to arrive at real earnings losses, so it was assumed that real earnings would grow 1.27 percent each year—the average real wage growth during the 1953-77 period. Thus, the 1977 age/earnings profile was adjusted to reflect estimated changes in real wages that would have occurred over Doe's career. The undiscounted total of lifetime earnings adjusted to reflect real wage growth amounts to $855,324.

In making its award, the court must calculate the present value of Doe's lost earnings. The reason is probably obvious: Doe's family will receive *now* all the income Doe would have received over his entire lifetime. If this sum were not discounted, the returns that would be possible if the money were invested would have the effect of increasing the award beyond the level of Doe's actual lost earnings.

Choice of a discount rate is critical to the size of the award. For example, if Doe's age/earnings profile for real earnings were discounted at 7 percent, its present value would have been around $200,000. If it were discounted at 2 percent, however, its present value would be roughly twice as large. In Doe's case, earnings were discounted at 2.14 percent because this was the 1953-77 average *real rate of interest* on the safest corporate bonds. Put differently, 2.14 percent was the rate at which invested funds would grow, in real terms, if invested safely. Discounted at 2.14 percent, the present value of Doe's losses amounted to $389,000. (The case was actually settled out of court for less than discounted earnings losses.)

The rates of return typically estimated in the above studies generally fall in the range of 5–15 percent (after adjusting for inflation). These findings are interesting, because most other investments generate returns in the same range. Thus, it appears—at least at first glance—that an investment in education is about as good as an investment in stocks, bonds, or real estate. This conclusion must be qualified, however, by recognizing that there are systematic biases in the estimated rates of return to education. These biases—which are of unknown size—work in opposite directions.

The upward bias.   The typical estimates of the rate of return to further schooling overstate the gain an individual student could obtain by investing in education because they are unable to separate the contribution *ability* makes to higher earnings from the contribution made by *schooling*. The problem is that (a) people who are smarter, harder-working, and more dynamic are more likely to obtain more schooling, and (b) such people may be more productive, and hence earn higher-than-average wages, even if they did not complete more years of schooling than others. When measures of ability are not observed or accounted for, the studies attribute *all* of the earnings differentials associated with college to college itself and none to ability—even though *some* of the added earnings college graduates typically receive would probably be received by an equally able high-school graduate who did not attend college.

Most studies attempting to identify the separate effects of ability and schooling have concluded that the effects of ability are relatively small—accounting for, at most, one-fifth of observed earnings differentials.[13] However, these studies have used aptitude-test scores—such as IQ or mathematical reasoning—as measures

---

[13]See, for example, Gary Becker, *Human Capital* (New York: National Bureau of Economic Research, 1975); Zvi Griliches and William M. Mason, "Education, Income, and Ability" and John C. Hause, "Earnings Profile: Ability and Schooling," both in *Journal of Political Economy* 80, 3 (May/June 1972).

of ability, and these measures are primarily designed to predict success in school, not in the workplace. Success in the world of work is also affected by interpersonal skills, work habits, motivation, and resourcefulness—attributes that are not easily measured by a test.

One interesting attempt to control for all the unmeasured aspects of ability used data on twins.[14] When the researcher first calculated rates of return to an added year of education ignoring any controls for ability, the estimated return was 8 percent. When he looked only at earnings differences between identical twins— people with a common *genetic and environmental* background—with different levels of schooling, he found that the rate of return to schooling dropped to 3 percent. While no one study is conclusive, the results do suggest that part—and perhaps a large part—of earnings differentials associated with higher levels of schooling are due to inherently abler persons obtaining more schooling.

The downward bias. By focusing only on the earnings differentials associated with an educational investment, the studies of returns to educational investments ignore other aspects of the returns to schooling. First, some benefits of college attendance are not necessarily reflected in higher productivity, but rather in an increased ability to understand and appreciate the behavioral, historic, and philosophical foundations of human existence. While these benefits may be difficult to measure, they exist nonetheless.

Second, most rate-of-return studies fail to include fringe benefits; they measure money earnings, not total compensation. Because fringe benefits as a fraction of total compensation tend to rise as money earnings rise, ignoring fringe benefits tends to create a downward bias in the estimation of rates of return to education. The size of this bias is largely unknown at present.[15]

Third, some of the job-related rewards of college are captured in the form of psychic or nonmonetary benefits. Jobs in executive or professional occupations are probably more interesting and pleasant than the more routine jobs typically available to people with less education. While executive and professional jobs do pay more than others, the total benefits of these jobs are probably understated when just earnings differences are analyzed.

An interesting example of the role nonmonetary costs and benefits play in schooling decisions can be seen in the fact that there is near-universal agreement that conventionally calculated rates of return fall as educational level rises. That is, the rate of return to a high-school education is higher than for a college education, and higher yet than the average returns from going to graduate school. This fact can be understood when psychic benefits and costs are accounted for. Referring back to Figure 9.9, one is reminded that students who acquire the most education are, on average, the ones who dislike school the least. They may also be the ones who, because of their higher learning abilities, derive the most psychic

---

[14]Paul Taubman, "Earnings, Education, Genetics, and Environment," *Journal of Human Resources* 11, 4 (Fall 1976): 447–61.

[15]Greg J. Duncan, "Earnings Functions and Nonpecuniary Benefits," *Journal of Human Resources* 11, 4 (Fall 1976): 462–83.

benefits from college. They thus require a smaller monetary incentive to attend college than do their less able colleagues.[16]

It is difficult to summarize the findings on the question of whether education is a sensible investment for an individual. Considering only monetary costs and benefits, rates of return to educational investments are modest (once ability is accounted for)—but not out of line with the ''real'' returns on many other types of investments. Moreover, if benefits other than money earnings were measured, the estimated returns to education would probably be higher.

Is Education a Good Social Investment?

The United States spends 7 percent of its gross national product—or $166 billion in 1980—on formal education (primary, secondary, and college). If forgone earnings of high-school and college students were included, this figure would rise to 10 percent.[17] In part these expenditures are justified by our need for a literate citizenry, speaking a common language and sharing a common culture. In part, however, education—especially at the secondary and college levels—is justified on the grounds that it enhances worker productivity. Interestingly, an early Soviet economist—S. G. Strumilin—wrote in 1929 that:

> a long time ago we had already arrived at the conclusion, that the expenditure of the state budget to raise the cultural level of the country ought to be considered along with the expenditures on technical reconstruction of production as capital expenditures and as equal in terms of their importance to our economy.[18]

There are some fields, such as mechanics and engineering, where education clearly has a social pay-off in the form of increased productivity. Recently, however, some critics have suggested that, to a large degree, education acts merely as a ''sorting device.'' They argue that rather than making workers more productive, the educational process is merely a screening device that reveals to employers the productive characteristics *already inherent* in prospective workers (we touched on this issue earlier in the discussion of the relationship between education and ability).

Employers—as noted in Chapter 5—are faced with the problem of ascertaining the quality of their job applicants. If they hire people for a trial period to see how they work out, they may face the costs of terminating low-quality employees and of the losses associated with their mistakes. An alternative procedure is to screen applicants through interviews, evaluations from previous employers, or work-related tests. These procedures themselves are costly, of course. They take time and money—and may still give imprecise readings of applicant quality.

---

[16]It may also be true that students from poor families, who lack the financial resources to obtain much education, require a higher rate of return to their educational investments than do students from families where wealth is more abundant.

[17]The forgone earnings of high-school and college students have been estimated to equal 60 percent of the *direct* cost outlays at those schooling levels. See Theodore Schultz, *The Economic Value of Education* (New York: Columbia University Press, 1963).

[18]Arcadius Kahan, ''Russian Scholars and Statesmen on Education as an Investment,'' in *Educational and Economic Development,* eds. C. A. Anderson and M. J. Bowman (Chicago: Aldine Publishing Co., 1965), p. 10.

Employers may also use data on applicant education as a screening tool. To do well in school requires both a capacity to learn and a willingness to work. The intellectual abilities required to succeed in school are obviously more closely correlated with the requirements for success in some jobs than others; however, it is probably true that workers better able to learn in school are easier to train and more flexible in the workplace than others. The discipline required in school—promptness, willingness to follow directions, adherence to deadlines—is very similar to the discipline required to perform well in most jobs. In a real sense, schooling is the "work" of youth and may well be a good test of ability to succeed later on.

The argument of those who regard education *only* as a sorting device goes beyond the argument that employers use educational attainment to screen applicants. Such critics of education assert that schooling does *nothing* to alter productive characteristics, that it does not increase knowledge of the kind useful to employees, and that it does not impart useful attitudes or work habits. In short, they say, nothing happens to students while in school that affects productivity later on. The educational system is seen as simply a filter that has the effect of *signaling* which people are likely to be most productive.[19] (For a discussion of signaling, see the appendix to this chapter.)

It should be recognized that even if schooling is only a screening device, it could have social, as well as private, value. Employers need a reliable method through which to select employees. Obviously, sorting millions of workers into various categories of ability is an enormous job for any society to accomplish, and schooling may be a very efficient means of doing this. The people most likely to acquire more schooling are the ones for whom schooling entails the least psychic cost—and, as we have argued, this group will tend to be heavily populated by the most able people. Investment in schooling, then, sends a *signal* to the labor market that one has a certain level of ability. The costs of investing in schooling purely for its signaling value generate net *private* benefits if the increased wage a graduate can obtain outweighs the costs. Schools in this case would have net *social* value if the decision to attend and the success one attains in school send accurate signals about productive characteristics to employers in the least costly way.

Whether schooling is purely a sorting device or whether it adds to productivity is not a particularly important question for individuals. Whatever role schools play, additional schooling does enhance one's lifetime income. Where the issue of screening is important is at the social level. If the only purpose of schools is to screen, why encourage the expansion of schooling? If 40 years ago being a high-school graduate signaled above-average intelligence and work discipline, why incur the enormous costs of expanding college attendance only to find out that now a bachelor's degree signals above average intelligence and work habits? The issue is of even more importance in less developed countries—where mistakes in allocating extremely scarce capital resources could be disastrous (see Example 9.2).

---

[19]If this was all schools did, it must be noted that they would not do much to alter the influences of family background—and thus would not be terribly useful in breaking down existing class distinctions or providing a vehicle for social mobility.

Example 9.2
The Socially Optimal Level of
Educational Investment

In addition to asking whether schooling is a good social investment, we could also ask, What is the socially optimal *level* of schooling? The general principle guiding our answer to this question is that society should increase or reduce its educational investments until the marginal rate of return (to society) equals the marginal rate of return on other forms of capital investment (investment in physical capital, for example).

The rationale for the above principle is that if society has some funds it wants to invest, it will desire to invest them in projects yielding the highest rates of return. If an investment in physical capital yields a 20 percent rate of return, and the same funds invested in schooling yield (all things considered) only a 10 percent return, society will clearly prefer to invest in physical capital. As long as the two rates of return differ, society could be made better off by reducing its investment in low-yield projects and increasing them in those with higher rates of return.

The text has discussed many of the difficulties and biases inherent in estimating rates of return to schooling. However, the general principle of equating the rates of social return on all forms of investments is still a useful one to consider. It suggests, for example, that capital-poor countries should only invest in additional schooling if the returns are very high—higher, in all probability, than the rates of return required for optimality in more capital-rich countries. Indeed, it is generally true that the rates of return to both secondary schooling and higher education appear to be higher in less developed countries than in developed countries. One study estimated that the rate of return on secondary schooling investments was 9.5 percent to a developed country (on average), while to a less-developed country it was 15.2 percent. Comparable rates of return to investments in higher education were 9.4 percent and 12.3 percent, respectively.

SOURCE: George Psacharopoulos, *Returns to Education* (San Francisco: Jossey-Bass, 1973), p. 67.

Unfortunately, direct evidence on the role schooling plays in society is almost impossible to obtain. Advocates of the screening viewpoint, for example, assert that the fact that rates of return to college *graduates* are higher than for college *dropouts* is evidence that schooling is a screening device.[20] They argue that what is learned in school is proportional to the time spent there and that an added bonus (rate of return) just for a diploma is proof of the screening hypothesis. Advocates of the view that schooling enhances human capital counter that one who graduates after four years probably has learned more than four times what the freshman dropout has learned. They argue that dropouts are more likely to be poorer stu-

---

[20]Dropouts naturally have lower incomes than graduates, but because they have also invested less it is not clear that their *rates of return* should be lower.

dents—the ones who overestimated their returns to schooling and quit when they discovered their mistake. Thus, their relatively low rate of return is not *because* they dropped out but is associated with the *reason* for dropping out.[21]

To take another example, proponents of the human-capital view of education sometimes argue that the fact that earnings differentials between (say) college and high-school graduates continue to grow is evidence supporting their view. They argue that if schooling is just a screening device employers would rely on it *initially* but that as they accumulate direct information from experience with their employees schooling would play a smaller role in determining earnings. Screening advocates could counter that continued growth in earnings differentials and the continued association of schooling and earnings only illustrates that educational levels are a *successful* sorting device; in other words, workers with higher levels of attainment in school do in fact make more productive workers.

Finally, it has been argued that the 1940–1965 change in skill requirements for a large number of jobs was very small, yet the educational requirements for obtaining those jobs rose dramatically.[22] Thus, while shoe salespeople in 1965 performed the same job as in 1940, they were required to have more education because of the general inflation in levels of educational attainment. While this seems like persuasive evidence in favor of the screening hypothesis, it ignores the fact that the real earnings of sales personnel have risen. While the job requirements are the same—fitting and selling shoes—the salesperson of the 1960s must have a higher marginal product than his or her counterpart of the 1940s. This higher marginal productivity could be achieved by harder work and improved store layout or it could be the result of more knowledgeable sales personnel. Exactly how the increase has been obtained is unknown, but one cannot rule out improvements in human capital as a partial cause.

Thus, just about any evidence offered to support one side of the argument can be accomodated by the other side. Perhaps the best resolution of this issue is one that relies on economic reasoning. We know that college, for example, is very expensive and that to induce students to attend requires a reasonable return on their investment. Thus, to obtain college graduates, employers must pay them wages high enough to compensate them for their investment. If their investment costs are $40,000, employers must pay them wages whose present value is at least $40,000 higher than if they did not attend. In short, to get a college graduate costs an employer at least $40,000 more than a high-school graduate in present-value terms.

Now the college graduate may in fact be worth $40,000 more because of his or her productive characteristics. However, if these characteristics existed prior to college—and were unaffected by college—it would pay the firm to find its own method of sorting high-school graduates in order to find the best potential workers. As long as the methods it used were as reliable and cost less than a college education ($40,000 per worker), it would be profitable to adopt them. The firm

---

[21]See Barry Chiswick, "Schooling, Screening, and Income," in *Does College Matter?* ed. Lewis Solomon and Paul Taubman (New York: Academic Press, 1973).

[22]See Ivar Berg, *Education and Jobs: The Great Training Robbery* (New York: Praeger Publishers, 1970).

could pay lower wages to their workers, because these workers would be spared the expense of college.

The fact that firms have not generally substituted their own screening devices for the educational requirements widely used suggests one of two things. Either education *does* enhance worker productivity, or it is a *cheaper* screening tool than any other firms could use. In either case, the fact that employers are willing to pay a high price for an educated work force *seems* to suggest that education produces social benefits.

Government Training Programs

Questions about the social benefits and costs of educational investments can be extended from general schooling to *particular* job-training programs—where the questions are generally easier to answer.

Since the early 1960s, the federal government has been rather heavily involved in programs designed to increase worker skills. In 1978, for example, 856,000 workers were enrolled in federally funded classroom or on-the-job training programs—at a cost of close to $2,000 per trainee on the average. One need not be a hard-bitten cynic to ask the question, "Are these programs worth their cost?" At times the answer seems to be a clear-cut "No."

During the 1960s, one government training program was aimed primarily at blacks in the poverty-stricken Mississippi-delta area. When delta training programs were geared to produce more than 8,000 trainees a year, available jobs for trainees were opening up at a rate of 3,000 per year.[23] Given this lack of job openings the programs became, in effect, welfare programs—valued for the stipend they paid trainees rather than their future benefits. Trainees had no incentive to graduate and tried to stay in the program as long as possible.

While it can be argued that enhancing the incomes of poor delta blacks is itself a worthy enterprise, it must be pointed out that training programs are not efficient means of doing this. They require society to pay the salaries of instructors (who are not poor) and to purchase capital equipment—funds which might better be used if they were given directly to the poor.

The intent of a properly conceived job-skills training program is to enhance private and social productivity by training workers to do jobs that are in demand. Some policymakers have followed a *personnel planning* approach in deciding how many workers—in what fields—to train. This personnel-planning approach asks employers how many persons with certain kinds of qualifications they will need, projects the numbers likely to be supplied by other sources, and recommends filling the gap with government training programs. While this method, if successfully used, should avoid the problems mentioned in the case of delta trainees, it does suffer the fatal flaw of ignoring *costs:*

> The manpower planner who plans supply to match demand asks the *wrong* questions. He asks, "What is the absorptive capacity of the economy for persons with

---

[23]Michael J. Piore, "Negro Workers in the Mississippi Delta: Problems of Displacement and Adjustment," in *Perspectives on Poverty and Income Distribution,* ed. James G. Scoville (Lexington, Mass.: D.C. Heath, 1971), pp. 151–57.

different skills and educational attainments?'' and does not consider the costs of schooling at all. If employers say (or his calculations lead him to believe) that an extra graduate would be hired, the manpower planner directs the education system to produce an extra graduate. He does not ask, ''What is the nature of the work the graduate will perform and what benefits will he confer on society?'' Nor does he ask, ''How much will it cost society to educate another graduate? Do the benefits justify the costs?''[24]

The only way in which one can be sure that investments in training programs are socially productive is to weigh their costs against the increases in productivity they permit. Since theory implies that marginal productivity and wages are roughly equal, one can look at the wage increases of trainees to obtain an approximation of productivity increases. For example, if a worker would have earned $8,000 per year had she not had training, and earns $8,600 a year after training, the program has pretty clearly increased her productivity by $600 per year. This yearly benefit to her (and society) must then be weighed against the cost of training in order to see if the rate of return is as large as it would be if the funds had been invested elsewhere.

Weighing costs against returns is not an easy job, primarily because one must find some way of estimating what trainees would have earned in the absence of the program. One way to make such an estimate is to project the earnings based on past earnings trends, taking note of earnings trends among comparable workers who did not enter the training program. A comprehensive study of 13,000 people who received training in 1964 under the federal Manpower Development and Training Act (MDTA) found that, for males, yearly increases in earnings were in the $150–$500 range, with the effects declining by half over a five-year post-training period. For females, the gains were in the $300–$600 range, with no decline over time.[25]

Do these returns justify the costs? The costs per student in this program were $1,800. If a 10 percent rate of return on this investment were to be earned indefinitely, the gains would have to amount to $180 a year. The results for males roughly meet this standard, while those for females clearly exceed it. Thus, the MDTA program appears to have been a good investment, in 1964, although the results do indicate that training for females was a better investment and should, therefore, have been expanded. (Later classes of trainees, it should be pointed out, did not experience as high a rate of return as did the 1964 class.)

APPLICATIONS OF HUMAN CAPITAL THEORY

The theory of human capital can be used to explain several interesting phenomena found in the labor market. This section will apply the theory to post-school investments in training, the labor-force behavior of women, and the distribution of earnings.

---

[24]Gary S. Fields, ''Private and Social Returns to Education in Labour Surplus Economies,'' *Eastern Africa Economic Review* 4, 1 (June 1972): 43.

[25]Orley Ashenfelter, ''Estimating the Effect of Training Programs on Earnings,'' *Review of Economics and Statistics* 60, 1 (February 1978): 47–57.

Example 9.3
Communists or (Human) Capitalists?

The concepts of human-capital theory are neither unknown nor ignored in the Soviet Union. A study of wages in the American, German, Dutch, Italian, and Russian steel industries, for example, found that the wage premiums skilled workers in Russia command over unskilled workers are much larger than in the other countries. In fact, the range of wages paid to blast-furnace and open-hearth workers in the Soviet Union is roughly twice the range paid to comparable American workers. Why do these large wage differentials exist in a country supposedly dedicated to the ideal of equality?

According to the Soviet managers, the Soviet Union places extraordinary emphasis on the education and training of their workers:

> The Soviet government recognizes that such training costs the individual effort and time, and it is willing to reward him by promotion to distinctly higher-paying jobs. . . . In other words . . . the big wage-rate differentials are part and parcel of a tremendous effort to raise the qualifications and performance of workers in the Soviet iron and steel industry.

SOURCE: M. Gardner Clark, "Comparative Wage Structures in the Steel Industry of the Soviet Union and Western Countries," *Proceedings of the Thirteenth Annual Meeting, Industrial Relations Research Association* (Madison, Wis.: IRRA, 1961), pp. 266–88.

Post-Schooling Investments and Age/Earnings Profiles

Schooling is largely a full-time, formally organized activity. However, there are less formal kinds of human-capital investments that are more difficult to observe. These investments take the form of training that normally occurs in the workplace. Some of this "training" is *learning-by-doing* (as one hammers nails month after month, one's skills naturally improve), but much of it takes place on the job, under close supervision, or consists of a formal program in the workplace. All forms of training are costly in the sense that the productivity of learners is low, and all represent a conscious *choice* on the part of the employer to accept lower current productivity in exchange for higher output later. It has been estimated that the average worker acquires the equivalent of at least two years of college in on-the-job training and that the annual cost of such training amounts to 3 percent of gross national product![26]

Who bears the cost of on-the-job training? You will recall that Chapter 5 argued that the cost of *specific training*—training of use *only* to one's employer—would be shared by the worker and firm. The employee might be paid a wage greater than marginal product *(MP)* during the training period, but after training the employee's wage is below *MP* (but above what the employee could get else-

---

[26]Jacob Mincer, "On-the-Job Training: Costs, Returns, and Some Implications," *Journal of Political Economy* (Supplement 1962), pp. 50–79.

where). In the case of general training, where employees acquire skills they can use elsewhere, it is they alone who pay for the training costs.

How do employees pay the costs of general training provided by their employer? They work for a wage lower than they would get if they were not receiving training. Their wage is equal to their *MP*—which is, of course, decreased during the training period when trainees require close supervision or time off the job to engage in classroom learning. Why do employees accept this lower wage? They accept it for the same reason that some decide to obtain schooling: in the expectation of improving the present value of their lifetime earnings. In other words, employees incur current investment costs (lower wages) in order to obtain increased earnings later.

The timing of post-schooling investments.   This chapter has demonstrated that if people are going to invest in themselves they will tend to undertake most of the investment at younger ages for two reasons:

1. Investments made at younger ages have a longer period over which to capture returns and thus will tend to have higher total benefits.
2. One big cost of investing in education and training is forgone earnings— and this cost rises as one gets older and earnings become higher (if, for no other reason, because of learning-by-doing).

Consequently, putting off human-capital investments will lower the returns to such investments.

It is not surprising to find, then, that schooling—largely a full-time activity— is followed by on-the-job training, which is normally a part-time activity. Further, we should also find that job training declines with age, being most heavily concentrated in one's early years on the job when opportunity costs are lower. However, in the case of job training, where scholarships and loans are not available and where the training is part-time, investment will not take place all at once. Too much current consumption would have to be forgone by the ordinary worker if one's entire lifetime amount of job training were acquired completely in the first two years (say) of one's career. Thus, employees will tend to parcel out their job training over a number of years but will gradually reduce such training as time goes by.

Timing of investment and age/earnings profiles.   The above theory of post-schooling investments helps to explain why age/earnings profiles are concave: rising more rapidly at first, then flattening out, and ultimately falling (see Figure 9.12). Earnings, low at first because of training investments, rise quickly as new skills are acquired. However, as workers grow older, the pace of training investment slows and so does the rate at which productivity increases. At the end of one's working life skills may have depreciated—due to lack of continued investment and the aging process—to the extent that retirement, semiretirement, or a change in jobs is necessary for many workers. This depreciation contributes to the downturn in *average* earnings near retirement age.

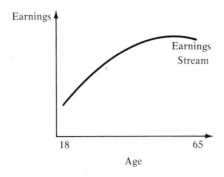

FIGURE 9.12 Age/Earnings Profile

The fanning out of age/earnings profiles by education.   As noted earlier in this chapter, the differences in average earnings between people of the same age, but with different educational levels, increase over time (see Figure 9.11). This phenomenon is also consistent with what human-capital theory would predict.

The answer to the question, "Who will invest most in post-school training?" should be familiar by now. Those who expect the highest benefits and workers who learn most quickly will do the most investing in job training. The fact that they learn rapidly shortens the training period, which both reduces investment costs and increases the duration of benefits. But who are these fast learners? They are most likely the people who, because of their abilities, were best able to reap benefits from formal schooling! Thus, human-capital theory leads us to expect workers who invested more in schooling to also invest more in post-schooling job training.

The tendency of the better-educated workers to invest more in job training explains why their age/earnings profiles start low, rise quickly, and keep rising after the profiles of their less-educated counterparts have leveled off. Their earnings rise more quickly because they are investing more heavily in job training, and they rise for a longer time for the same reason. In other words, people with the ability to learn quickly select the ultimately high-paying jobs where much learning is required and thus put their abilities to greatest advantage.

Females and the Acquisition of Human Capital

As implied in Chapters 6–7, the career pattern of many married women tends to consist of distinct stages. First, there is a period of employment preceding childbirth. Following the birth of the first child is a period of nonparticipation in the labor force, and then there is a return to labor market participation, often on a part-time or temporary basis. A study conducted on data collected in the 1960s found that the first stage of participation usually lasted 3–4 years and that the second stage of nonparticipation usually lasted 7 years,[27] although since the 1970s it is likely that the former lengthened and the latter shortened.

---

[27]These data are taken from Jacob Mincer and Solomon Polachek, "Family Investments in Human Capital: Earnings of Women," *Journal of Political Economy* 82, 2 (March/April 1974): S76–S108.

The interrupted nature of many women's careers has profound implications for the acquisition of education and training. First, because women's careers are usually shorter than men's, they have less time over which to reap the rewards of investments in human capital. This lowers the benefits of such investments as schooling and training, rendering women less likely than men to invest.

Second, the interrupted nature of women's work experience adds additional incentives to avoid costly investments. The period of nonparticipation in the labor market is one in which skills depreciate and the continuity of experience is broken. Previous investments in human capital may become almost useless—especially in highly technical, ever-changing fields such as law, medicine, engineering, and research. Thus, many women in the prematernal years will avoid investments that will lose their value during the years of child rearing, thereby taking themselves out of occupations that require continuity of experience or training to be successful.

Human-capital theory therefore predicts that women will acquire less schooling and less training than men. The evidence is consistent with these predictions, as we shall see below. Before reviewing the evidence, however, we must point out that these predictions of human-capital theory are for a "traditional" woman—one who has, *and expects to have,* an interrupted labor-market career. The predictions do not apply to women who expect to have uninterrupted lifetime careers in the labor market—whose behavior (if we had good enough data to observe it) would be expected to parallel that of the typical male.

Women and schooling.   When one considers the reduced benefits women typically receive (compared with men), it is not surprising to find that a lower percentage of women have tended to enroll in college. For example, in 1979 29.6 percent of all female high-school graduates between the ages of 18 and 24 were enrolled in college compared to 32.9 percent of males the same age. Moreover, females of high ability are apparently much more responsive than males of similar ability to the availability of a hometown college in deciding whether or not to attend.[28] As argued in the first section of this chapter, this greater responsiveness to cost considerations—seen also in males of moderate ability—is indicative of a greater likelihood of being "at the margin" (closer to deciding not to go).

Note: The percentage of women high-school graduates attending college is rising very quickly, while that of men is falling. It appears that in the early 1980s the percentages may equalize—a circumstance undoubtedly influenced by the lengthening expected career lives of women and by associated changes in their choice of occupations. Thus, the generalizations about women and schooling made above hold only as long as a significant number of women expect substantially shorter careers than men; as expected durations of work life equalize, so will college enrollment behavior.

---

[28]C. A. Anderson, M. J. Bowman, and V. Tinto, *Where Colleges Are and Who Attends* (New York, McGraw-Hill, 1972).

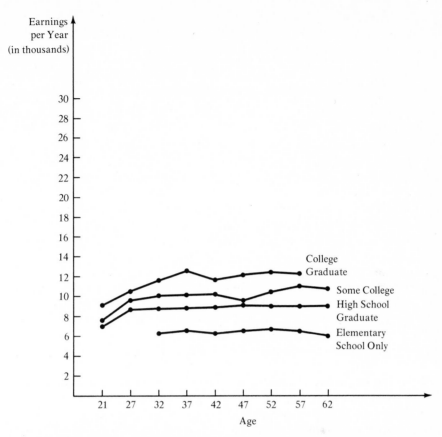

FIGURE 9.13 Total Money Earnings (mean), Full-Time Females, 1977

SOURCE: U.S. Bureau of the Census, *Money Income in 1977 of Families and Persons in the United States,* Current Population Reports, Series P-60, No. 118 (March 1979), Table 48.

Women and job training. Besides reduced incentives to invest in schooling, women have fewer incentives than men to invest in job training. As a result, women do not typically find themselves in jobs with steep age/earnings profiles. While we lack the data necessary to track the earnings of individual women through time, we can plot (as we did for males) average earnings of each age group. As Figure 9.13 shows, the age/earnings profiles for women are very flat: older women do not appear to earn much more than younger women. We can conclude from this that experience-related increases in productivity are not a big influence on women's wages—which implies that the acquisition of job training is not very widespread among women.

One reason for the lack of job training among women may be their shorter and more interrupted careers, which reduces both their incentives and the incentives of their employers to engage in such training. Another reason, however, may be various forms of discrimination (see Chapter 14, ''Discrimination,'' for further discussion of women's earnings). Nevertheless, at least some of the differences

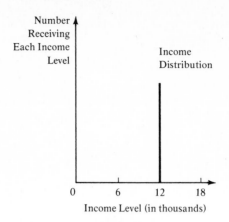

FIGURE 9.14 Income "Distribution" with Perfect Income Equality

between the earnings of men and women are due to differences in the acquisition of human capital. The magnitude of these differences will be addressed in Chapter 14.

Human Capital and the Distribution of Earnings

Society is often as interested in the *distribution* of income as it is in the average *level* of income. For example, it is frequently asserted that the United States is a rich country but one in which advantaged workers are rewarded handsomely while those less fortunate receive a very small portion of the national wealth. To evaluate this assertion that the outcome of our market system is "unfair" requires data on the *distribution* of income. Such distribution data are needed to answer questions like, "How much more does the top 10 percent of the population make than the bottom 10 percent?"

This section presents a few basic facts about the distribution of both family *income* and individual *earnings* in the United States and uses human-capital theory to explain certain characteristics of the distribution of *earnings*. Earnings are considered separately from income, because income can include rents, dividends, interest, and income-maintenance payments that are not the result of labor-market transactions and are therefore not the subject of human-capital theory.[29]

Statistical concepts. To understand certain basic concepts related to the distribution of income (or the distribution of earnings) it is helpful to think in graphical terms. Consider a simple plotting of the number of people receiving each given level of income. If everyone made the same income—say, $12,000 per year—there would be no dispersion or disparities in income. The graph of the income distribution would look like Figure 9.14.

---

[29]Because the availability of loans for human-capital investments is imperfect, students from wealthy families face fewer constraints in making such investments than others. Thus, financial and human wealth are interconnected to some extent.

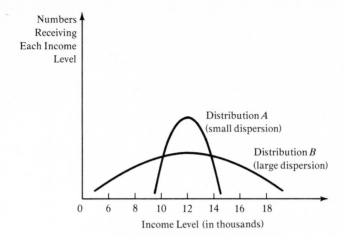

**FIGURE 9.15 Symmetric Distributions
of Income with Different
Degrees of Dispersion**

If there *were* disparities in the income people received, these disparities could
be relatively large or relatively small. If the average level of income received was
$12,000, and virtually all people received incomes very close to the average, the
dispersion of incomes would be small. If the average was $12,000, but some
made much more and some much less, the dispersion of incomes would be large.
In Figure 9.15, two hypothetical income distributions are illustrated together. Distribution *A* exhibits smaller dispersion than distribution *B*. Incomes in *A* are more
closely "bunched" and do not show wide differences. We could conclude that
because of its smaller dispersion, distribution *A* exhibits a *greater degree of
equality*.

While for most purposes the degree of income dispersion is of most importance in judging equality, it is also interesting to inquire if the distribution of
incomes (or earnings) is *symmetric* or not. If the distributions are symmetric, as
in Figure 9.15, then as many people earn $X less than average as earn $X more
than average. Put differently, the dispersion of incomes for the poorest half of
society mirrors the dispersion for the richest half if the distribution is symmetric.
If the distribution is not symmetric, we say it is *skewed*—meaning that one part
of the distribution is bunched together and the other part is relatively dispersed
(see Figure 9.16). In fact, the actual distributions of income and earnings in the
United States are "skewed to the right"—meaning that they are bunched at the
left (at the lower levels of income) and widely dispersed at the higher income
levels.

Skewness is an important characteristic of the distribution of income or earnings, because the concept suggests another dimension of "fairness." For example,
many less developed countries do not have a sizable middle class. Such countries
have a huge number of very poor families and a tiny minority of very wealthy
families. Thus, the distribution of income in these countries—normally considered unfair—is highly skewed to the right.

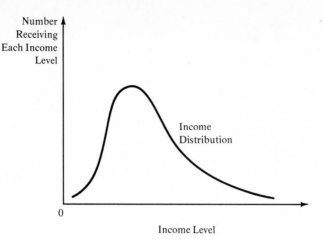

FIGURE 9.16 Skewed Distribution
of Income

While dispersion and skewness in the distribution of earnings are indicators of inequality in labor-market outcomes, their presence can be at least partially explained by investments in human capital.

Dispersion. Although incomes in the United States are disparate, there is no evidence of a recent trend toward greater equality. Note from Table 9.2 that the 20 percent of families that have the lowest incomes obtain 4–5 percent of the total income received, while the top 20 percent obtains more than 40 percent of the total income. Neither figure has changed very much since 1947. This pattern of income dispersion is not unique to the United States; Table 9.3 gives similar data on the percentage of national income received by the lowest and highest 20 percent of families in seven other countries.

TABLE 9.2.   **Distribution of Income among Families at Different Income Levels, 1947–1978**

Income Level	Percent of Aggregate Income Received						
	1947	*1957*	*1967*	*1972*	*1974*	*1975*	*1978*
Total families	100.0	100.0	100.0	100.0	100.0	100.0	100.0
Lowest fifth	5.1	5.0	5.5	5.4	5.5	5.4	4.3
Second fifth	11.8	12.6	12.4	11.9	12.0	11.8	10.3
Third fifth	16.7	18.1	17.9	17.5	17.5	17.6	16.9
Fourth fifth	23.2	23.7	23.9	23.9	24.0	24.1	24.7
Highest fifth	43.3	40.5	40.4	41.4	41.0	41.1	43.9
Top 5 percent	17.5	15.8	15.2	15.9	15.5	15.5	16.8
Median family income (in 1975 dollars)	$7,303	$9,496	12,788	14,301	14,081	13,719	12,438

Note: The income (before taxes) boundaries of each fifth of families, arranged by income in 1978, were: lowest fifth, under $6,391; second fifth, $6,392 to $11,955; third fifth, $11,956 to $18,121; fourth fifth, $18,122 to $26,334; highest fifth, over $26,334; top 5 percent, over $42,055. Detail may not add to totals because of rounding.

SOURCE: Department of Commerce, Bureau of the Census.

not Wealth

**TABLE 9.3. Percentage of National Income Received
by the Lowest- and Highest-Income Families
in Seven Countries, 1973**

| | Percentage of National Income Received by | |
Country	Lowest 20 Percent	Highest 20 Percent
Australia	6.8	39.7
Denmark	5.6	44.5
France	5.1	42.5
Germany	6.0	46.7
Japan	3.8	46.2
Sweden	6.0	40.5
United Kingdom	5.6	40.2

SOURCE: Paolo Roberti; "Income Inequality in Some Western Countries: Patterns and Trends," *International Journal of Social Economics* 5 (1978): 22–41.

Another way to measure inequality is by comparing the incomes of those whose income ranks at the 20th percentile (where 80 percent of the population has a higher income) with those whose income ranks at the 80th percentile (where only 20 percent of the population has a higher income). In 1978, those families at the 80th percentile received an income of $26,334—4.1 times higher than the $6,391 received by those at the 20th percentile. The absolute difference in income between the two groups was almost $20,000.

As noted earlier, this chapter is interested *not* in the distribution of *income* but in the distribution of *earnings*. There are three major factors that could cause the distribution of income to be different from that of earnings:

1. The owners of financial capital (stocks, bonds, real estate) are probably people who also have high earnings, a situation that would cause the distribution of income to be even more unequal than the distribution of earnings.
2. Many income-maintenance programs redistribute income in favor of those with low earnings—this time making the distribution of income more equal than the distribution of earnings.
3. Many families have more than one wage earner. If high-earning males tend to marry high-earning women, the distribution of family income would tend to be more unequal than the distribution of earnings.

The 1978 distribution of earnings for males, aged 25–64, is graphed in Figure 9.17. (The distribution of earnings for males of this age group is less affected by variations in hours of work and labor-force-participation status than the earnings of any other group.) It is obvious from Figure 9.17 that there is considerable dispersion (as well as skewness) in the earnings of this group. However, this dispersion turns out to be slightly less than that noted above for family income. For example, the ratio of *incomes* at the 80th percentile to those at the 20th percentile was 4.1 to 1, while the corresponding ratio for male *earnings* is 2.5 to 1. The absolute difference in earnings between males at these two percentiles— $22,850 at the 80th and $9,100 at the 20th percentile—is also smaller. It would

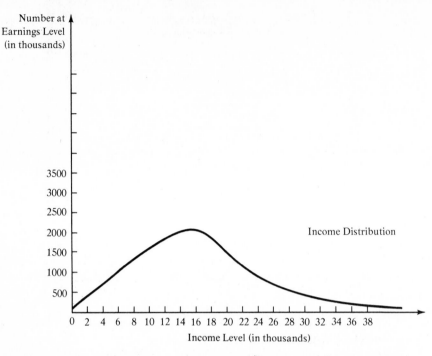

FIGURE 9.17   Distribution of Earnings, Males 25-64, 1978

appear, therefore, that the forces tending to make earnings *more* equal than incomes are somewhat dominant.

It is not surprising, of course, that earnings vary. This chapter, for example, has shown that much of the higher earnings received by the well educated and highly trained is a return to their investments in human capital. In fact, in any society where people can make themselves more productive—but only through a costly investment of time and money—we would expect to observe earnings differentials. Not *all* of the observed dispersion in earnings is related to the normal returns on human-capital investments, but *some* dispersion is to be expected in a situation where these investments are being made by some people and not others.

A portion of the overall dispersion in earnings among males aged 25–64 is the result of combining men of different ages in the same distribution. We know that productivity increases over time, so that older men typically earn more than younger men. This source of dispersion is probably not of too much concern to society because everyone's income follows the pattern of being relatively low in their younger years.

What may be of more concern is the dispersion of earnings *within* age groups. Here, human-capital theory offers a clear-cut prediction. When people are young, the job training in which some people are investing keeps their earnings close to (or below) what those who are not investing receive. As time passes, however, the earnings of those who have invested are raised considerably above the earnings of others. We noted this phenomenon when we examined age/earnings profiles: earnings ''fan out'' with age. Hence, due to the acquisition of more human capital by some than others, the dispersion of earnings among older workers is expected to be greater than among younger workers.

Human-capital theory can thus help to explain the presence and patterns of dispersion in earnings. Can it also help explain why the earnings distribution is skewed?

Skewness. It has long been a puzzle to people why the distribution of earnings is skewed. *If* ability is distributed symmetrically, and if ability is reflected in productivity, it would seem that earnings should be symmetrically distributed. Human-capital theory suggests at least two reasons why even if there *were* a symmetric distribution of ability one would expect to find earnings skewed to the right.

First, it is true that *if* ability were symmetrically distributed and no one invested in education or training in order to enhance their productivity, the earnings distribution would be symmetric. However, the people who make investments that increase their earnings later in life tend to be the high-ability people. Thus, while the low-ability people tend to go through their careers with their productivity relatively unchanged by investment, the high-ability people augment their productivity by investments. The more ability they have, the more they tend to invest. Thus, education and training tend to increase the earnings of workers in some rough proportion to their abilities, which extends—or *skews*—the distribution at the upper earnings levels.

Second, the discounting process aids the above forces in skewing the distribution of earnings. A person attending graduate school for one year after graduating from college incurs a greater cost and has a shorter time over which to obtain benefits than a person deciding to attend two years of college rather than one. The graduate student has higher opportunity costs and is also older and just that much closer to retirement. Therefore, those considering ever-larger investments in schooling will require ever-larger payoffs per year (in the form of earnings increments). This need for ever-larger payoffs in order to encourage greater investments in human capital tends to skew the distribution of earnings. In effect, the larger costs and smaller remaining career life discourages most people from continuing to invest—which serves to handsomely reward those who do undertake the investment (since they are "scarce"). Since these latter people tend to be those of highest ability (they are the ones who can learn with the most ease), the "rich get richer" and the distribution becomes skewed.

While one may be tempted to conclude from this analysis that human-capital investments make the distribution of earnings more unequal than it would otherwise be, one must first consider two mitigating factors. First, human-capital theory suggests that some of the inequality observed in earnings is a normal return on a prior investment—that is, it is compensation for an earlier period in one's life when earnings were low due to the acquisition of human capital. Second, if access to colleges (say) were severely limited, the lucky few able to advance themselves would reap very large rewards. This limitation on opportunities would impart an extreme skewness to the earnings distribution (very few would get a lot, and most would earn very little). Thus, although human-capital acquisitions will impart a rightward skew, widespread availability of educational and training opportunities serves to reduce the skewness relative to what it would be with only limited access to these opportunities.

Policy Application: Human Capital and Earnings in Regulated Industries

Human-capital theory can be useful in analyzing policy issues related to employee earnings. One such issue arises in the state regulation of monopolies. State commissions that regulate public utilities (such as telephone, electric, and gas companies) must decide whether all the costs that the utilities incur should be legitimately charged to consumers. It would be obvious to the commission that some costs should not be charged to consumers. For example, if an executive of a company had chartered a plane to take his family on a winter vacation to the Bahamas, surely that cost would be disallowed. Or, if a construction contract were awarded to the friend of the president of a local utility without being submitted to competitive bidding, a commission might want to examine that contract closely to make sure the price charged was comparable to what other contractors in the area would have charged.

Deciding whether or not labor costs should be charged to consumers is more difficult. On the one hand, it is often conjectured that employers in regulated industries have less of an incentive to "bargain tough" with the unions that represent their employees than do employers in nonregulated industries, because historically regulatory commissions have allowed utilities to pass all labor-cost increases on to consumers (in the form of higher utility prices). If such an argument is valid, it would indicate the need for commissions to carefully scrutinize utilities' wage settlements. On the other hand, it is difficult to decide upon what wage rates a commission should consider "just and reasonable." A utility's work force consists of a number of different skill categories, as does the work force of other employers in an area, and making simple comparisons using raw wage-rate data would fail to take into account any qualitative differences among work forces.

The human-capital framework suggests a more appropriate comparison. According to this framework, better educated workers will receive higher wages than less educated workers, and more experienced workers will get paid more than less experienced workers. By statistically controlling for such worker characteristics as education and experience, it should be easier to see if employees in a regulated industry are paid more than employees in other firms. When such a comparison was made for telephone workers in New York State, it was found that the utility's employees were paid approximately 9–12 percent more than were other employees with comparable education and experience levels in the state in 1970.[30]

Such evidence in itself does not imply that a public commission should prevent a utility from passing all of its labor-cost increases on to consumers in the form of higher prices. For example, the wage premium might in some cases be seen as a compensating differential paid to the utility's employees for more diffi-

---

[30]Ronald G. Ehrenberg, *The Regulatory Process and Labor Earnings* (New York: Academic Press, 1979).

cult jobs or less favorable working conditions, as discussed in Chapter 8. Nevertheless, the human-capital framework does provide a useful starting point for public-utility commissions seeking to address the labor-cost issue. In the particular case mentioned above, the commission decided not to limit the permissable wage increase but did reserve the right to limit future wage "pass-throughs" if similar comparative studies illustrated the need for such limits.

REVIEW QUESTIONS

1. Why do women receive lower wages, on average, than men of equal age? Why does the discrepancy between male and female earnings grow with age? ·
2. How would college enrollments be affected if
   a. income-tax rates were substantially cut for higher-income workers but only modestly reduced for lower-income employees?
   b. the real rate of interest increased?
   c. government subsidies for college students were reduced?
   d. young people became more present-oriented?
   e. the *work* life of employees became longer (that is, if people retired at a later age)?
3. Many crimes against property (burglarly, for example) can be thought of as acts that have immediate gains but that entail long-run costs (sooner or later the criminal may be caught and imprisoned). If imprisoned, the criminal loses income from both criminal and noncriminal activities. Using the framework for occupational choice in the long run, analyze what kinds of people are most likely to engage in criminal activities. What can society do to reduce crime?
4. Suppose education provides no *social* benefits of any kind; that is, it does not enhance worker productivity and it does not accurately "signal" who is already more productive. What conditions would have to hold for there to be a positive *individual* return to education in this circumstance?
5. Why do those who argue that more education "signals" greater ability believe that the most able people will obtain the most education?

SELECTED READINGS

Becker, Gary. *Human Capital*. New York: National Bureau of Economic Research, 1975.

Berg, Ivar. *Education and Jobs: The Great Training Robbery*. New York: Praeger Publishers, 1970.

Blaug, Mark. "Human Capital Theory: A Slightly Jaundiced Survey." *Journal of Economic Literature* 14 (September 1976):827–55.

Freeman, Richard B. *The Overeducated American*. New York: Academic Press, 1976.

Mincer, Jacob. "On-the-Job Training: Costs Returns, and Some Implications." *Journal of Political Economy* (Supplement 1962), pp. 50–79.

Mincer, Jacob. *Schooling, Experience and Earnings*. New York: National Bureau of Economic Research, 1974.

Mincer, Jacob. "The Distribution of Labor Incomes: A Survey with Special Reference to the Human Capital Approach." *Journal of Economic Literature* (March 1970), pp. 1–26.

Mincer, Jacob and Solomon Polachek. "Family Investments in Human Capital: Earnings of Women." *Journal of Political Economy* 82 (March/April 1974): S76-S108.

Schultz, Theodore. *The Economic Value of Education*. New York: Columbia University Press, 1963.

Spence, Michael. "Job Market Signalling." *Quarterly Journal of Economics* 87 (August 1973):355–74.

"Signaling" in the Labor Market

Chapter 9 discussed both the private and social benefits of education and stressed that individuals will undertake an educational investment if the long-run gains to them outweigh the monetary and psychic costs. *Societal* decisions to invest in education should likewise be made only if the social gains outweigh the social losses; however, Chapter 9 noted that there is a rather lively debate about the nature and extent of the social benefits of formal education. Some believe that education *enhances* worker productivity, while others believe that, at best, education simply *reveals*—or "signals"—the inherent productivity of workers.

This appendix will delve into the signaling aspect of formal education in greater depth.[1] It will analyze the benefits and costs of educational signaling to workers and firms in an example where it is assumed that education does *not* enhance productivity. Initially, however, it is important to carefully explain just what *signaling* is and why it exists.

An employer seeking to hire workers is never completely sure of the actual productivity of any applicant, and in many cases the employer may remain unsure long after an employee is hired. What an employer *can* observe are certain *indicators* that firms have found (or otherwise believe) to be correlated with productivity: age, race, sex, experience, education, and other personal characteristics. Some of these indicators—such as age, race, and sex—are immutable. Others, like formal schooling, can be *acquired* by workers. Indicators that can be acquired by individuals can be called *signals;* our analysis will focus on the signaling aspect of formal education.

THE FIRM'S DESIRE FOR SIGNALS

Let us suppose that firms trying to hire new employees in a particular labor market know there are two groups of applicants that exist in roughly equal proportions. One group has a productivity of 2, let us say, and the other group has a produc-

---

[1]This appendix is based on Michael Spence, "Job Market Signaling," *Quarterly Journal of Economics* 87 (August 1973): 355–74.

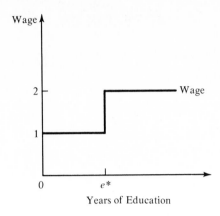

**FIGURE 9A.1   The Benefits to Workers
of Educational Signaling**

tivity of 1. In the absence of screening or applicant signaling, firms would be forced to assume that workers in this market had average productivities of 1.5 and would offer wages up to 1.5.

While workers in this simple example would be receiving what they are worth on *average,* any one firm could increase its profits if it were possible (at no cost) to distinguish between the two groups of applicants. When wages equal 1.5, some workers (those with productivities equal to 1) are receiving more than they are worth. If these applicants could be identified, a firm could increase profits by rejecting their applications and hiring only those with productivity 2. These gains might be short-lived if other firms do the same and drive the wage for the more productive workers up to 2. However, the individual firms in a competitive market cannot control or affect the behavior of competitors, and screening will occur as each seeks to obtain maximum profit.[2]

WORKER SUPPLY OF SIGNALS

To continue with our example, suppose that firms believe that if an applicant has acquired e^* or more years of schooling, he or she has productivity of 2. If the applicant has less than e^* years of formal education, it is believed he or she has productivity 1. Let us also assume that education does *not* enhance productivity. In what situations, if any, could this use of schooling as a screening device be productive? The answer is that educational signaling can only be useful if the costs to the worker of acquiring the signal are negatively related to productivity.

If firms use e^* as a hiring standard, applicants with schooling of e^* or greater will be preferred if wages for all workers are equal; their wage will eventually be driven up to 2, while those with less than e^* will obtain wages of 1 (see Figure 9A.1). If all applicants could acquire e^* at no cost, they would obviously do so

---

[2]The phenomenon here is very similar to the entry of firms into markets with excess profits. The gains from entry are short-lived because the entry of others will drive profits down to the normal level. Individual firms, however, react to the presence of excess profits nevertheless, expecting to catch "a piece of the action" and hoping no one else will be quite as smart as they are!

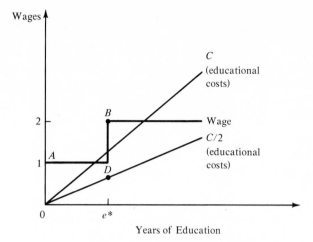

**FIGURE 9A.2   The Benefits and Costs
to Workers of Education
Signaling**

and this screening device would fail; workers of both productivity levels would have at least e^* years of schooling. As we argued in Chapter 9, however, formal schooling is not costless. Furthermore, we also argued that the *psychic* costs of education are probably inversely related to one's ability: those who learn easily can acquire the educational signal (of e^* in this case) more cheaply than others. *If*—and this is crucial—those who have *lower* costs of acquiring education are *also* more productive on the job, then educational signaling can be useful.

To understand the role of costs in signaling, refer to Figure 9A.2, in which the reward structure from Figure 9A.1 is reproduced. If we assume that each year of education costs those with lesser productivity C and those with greater productivity $C/2$, the fundamental influences on worker choices concerning education are easily seen. Workers will want to choose a level of education where the difference between benefits (wages) and educational costs are maximized. For those with productivity of 1 and educational cost of C, the difference between wages and costs is greatest where years of schooling equal zero (distance $0A$). For those whose educational costs are $C/2$, this difference is maximized at e^* (where it equals BD—which is greater than $0A$). Thus, only those with costs of $C/2$—the workers with productivities of 2—acquire e^* years of school.

THE USEFULNESS OF EDUCATIONAL SIGNALING

Several points should be made about our simple example of signaling above. First, workers may not think of themselves as acquiring a signal if they attend school, even though in our example they are. All most workers will know is that by obtaining more education they can increase their wages—and their decision about how much education to acquire depends on the costs and returns to them.

Second, our simple example demonstrated how education could have signaling value even if it did not directly enhance worker productivity. It is necessary to stress, though, that for education to have signaling value in this case, on-the-job productivity and the costs of education must be *negatively* related. This negative relationship is by no means universally accepted, and there are even those who assert that better-educated workers are actually *less* productive.[3] However, if education is *not* a good signal for productivity firms should eventually find this out and stop using formal schooling as a screening device! (The argument that education will survive as a signal for productivity only if it is an accurate indicator does not suggest, of course, that firms will learn about signaling errors immediately.)

Third, if the signal required by firms were reduced from e^* to e' (in Figure 9A.3) the signaling value of education would be lost. Workers of both productivity levels would find it beneficial to acquire the signal of e', because the distance $0A$ is exceeded by GD for the less productive and by BD for the more productive. Education would cease to be a good screening device for employers to use. A signal of e' could not be an equilibrium signal in the long run, because employers would eventually learn that not all workers with e' years of education have a productivity of 2. They would either have to give up on screening and pay a wage of 1.5 or increase hiring standards.

Fourth, increases in the educational signal beyond e^* in our example are not productive. A look back at Figure 9A.2 indicates that individual workers with educational costs of $C/2$ have no incentives to obtain more schooling than e^*, because such schooling is costly but results in no higher wage offer. Moreover, if firms increased their minimum hiring standard from e^* to e'' (Figure 9A.3) the signaling value of education would again be lost. Even the more productive workers would not have incentives to acquire an education (because $0A$ exceeds EF), and firms could not distinguish between the two kinds of workers.

Finally, there *is* an optimum educational signal in our example. This optimum educational hiring standard is the minimum schooling level that successfully distinguishes between the two types of workers. Optimality is reached *just to the right* of e^{**} in Figure 9A.4. A required signal of just beyond e^{**} is one that will be acquired by workers of productivity 2, but it will not be acquired by those with productivity 1. If the required signal were reduced below e^{**}, both kinds of workers would acquire it and signaling value would be lost. If the required signal were increased much beyond e^{**}—to e^* say—the signal would still be accurate, but would cost more than necessary. Put differently, if e^* were required, the more productive workers would acquire it and the less productive ones would not. However, the extra e^*-e^{**} years in school would entail social costs for which there are no benefits, because e^{**} distinguishes between the two types of workers just as well as e^*. The critics of education, mentioned in Chapter 9, argue that the escalation of educational standards occurs for jobs in which work requirements are largely unchanged. These critics can be understood as saying that firms require e^* when e^{**} would distinguish between workers just as well and be much less costly![4]

---

[3]See Ivar Berg, *Education and Jobs: The Great Training Robbery* (New York: Praeger Publishers, 1970), pp. 85–104, which questions the social value of educational investments.

[4]See Berg, *Education and Jobs,* pp. 38–60.

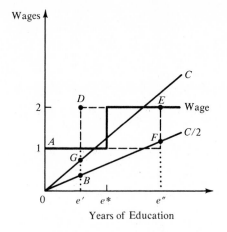

FIGURE 9A.3   Signaling Failures

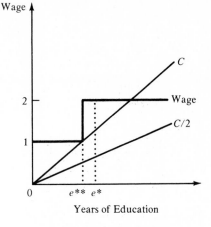

FIGURE 9A.4   The Optimum
Educational Signal

Are there market forces pushing the required signal toward e^{**}? We have argued that a required signal below e^{**} would be unsuccessful in discriminating between applicants and would eventually be abandoned by employers. However, if the required signal were initially e^*, there would *also* be forces pushing it back to e^{**}, although these influences take us outside of our simple model with its fixed wages. Workers who have acquired e^* years of education will be more costly to hire than workers acquiring e^{**}, because they will want to recoup their educational costs. Noting their higher asking wage, some firms may experiment and hire applicants with only e^{**} years of schooling. If these latter workers proved to be just as productive as those with e^* years of schooling, the firms that experimented would be rewarded with extra profits. Other firms would eventually follow, and e^{**} would become the equilibrium hiring standard.

10

Worker Mobility:
Turnover and Migration

A salient fact about the U.S. economy is the high degree of mobility among its workers. As noted in Chapter 8, the monthly quit rate in manufacturing industries is 1-2 percent per *month*—which implies a yearly turnover rate of 12-24 percent. Chapter 8 also noted that 20 percent of male, semiskilled workers over age 25 in 1965 were employed in a *completely different* occupation by 1970—and the figure jumps to 43 percent for *all* males over 20. Roughly 25 percent of all workers change the industry in which they work over a three-year period.[1] Moreover, in many cases job mobility is accompanied by geographic mobility. Between 1975 and 1978, for example, 9 million people over 20 years of age—6.4 percent of the total—moved between states; 11 million more (7.6 percent) moved to a different county within a state. Thus, one seventh of the adult population made a major move in just a three-year period—and the fraction rises to one-fourth when focusing only on those in their twenties. Finally, the United States receives roughly 400,000 legal immigrants each year—and the discrepancy between the numbers who want to come and the numbers permitted by law is so great that thousands more enter illegally. As of 1980, most experts believe that there are at least 4 million illegal immigrants living permanently in the country.

The mobility cited above is not without its costs. There is sometimes a temporary loss of income that occurs between the time one job is given up and a new one—perhaps in a new place—is obtained. There are direct moving costs when migration occurs. There are the psychic costs of leaving a familiar job or a familiar place and having to become acquainted with a new environment. There can be no doubt, then, that rather large monetary and psychic costs are borne each year by large numbers of people wanting to improve their lot in life. In this sense mobility represents a significant investment in human capital. Costs are borne in

---

[1]Lowell E. Gallaway, *Interindustry Labor Mobility in the United States, 1957 to 1960,* Social Security Administration Research Report No. 18 (Washington D.C.: U.S. Government Printing Office, 1967), p. 29.

the short run in order that benefits will be possible in the long run. The human-capital model of mobility described in this chapter offers some clear-cut implications about who invests in mobility and where they go.

The basic human-capital model of mobility is a model of "voluntary" mobility undertaken by workers who perceive mobility to be in their self-interest. The factors influencing employer-initiated mobility—layoffs, for example—are quite different, as discussed in Chapter 5. The determinants of voluntary mobility are discussed first, and later in the chapter the testable implications of human-capital theory for both migration and job-quitting behavior are analyzed. The chapter will conclude with an economic analysis of immigration and its implications for national policy.

THE DETERMINANTS OF MOBILITY

The human-capital model presented in Chapter 9 can be used to understand and predict worker-initiated mobility. This model views voluntary mobility as an investment, wherein costs are borne in some early period in order to obtain returns over a longer period of time. If the present value of the benefits associated with mobility exceeds the costs—both monetary and psychic—we assume that people will decide to change jobs or move or both. If the discounted stream of benefits is not as large as the costs, then people will decide against such a change.

What determines the present value of the net benefits of mobility—that is, the benefits minus the costs—determines the mobility decision. These factors can be better identified by writing out the formula one would use if one were to precisely calculate these net benefits:

$$\text{Present Value of Net Benefits} = \sum_{t=1}^{T} \frac{B_{jt} - B_{ot}}{(1 + r)^t} - C \qquad (10.1)$$

where:

B_{jt} = the utility derived from the new job (j) in the year t;
B_{ot} = the utility derived from the old job (o) in the year t;
T = length of time (in years) one expects to work at job j;
r = the rate of discount;
C = the utility lost in the move itself (direct and psychic costs); and
Σ = a summation—in this case the summation of the yearly discounted net benefits over a period running from year 1 to year T.

Clearly, the present value of the net benefits of mobility will be larger (a) the greater the utility derived from the new job, (b) the less happy one is in the job of origin, (c) the smaller are the immediate costs associated with the change, and (d) the longer one expects to be in the new job or live in the new area (that is, the greater is T). These observations lead to some clear-cut predictions about which groups in society will be most mobile and about the *patterns* of mobility one would expect to observe. These predictions are analyzed in the following sections on migration and quit behavior.

GEOGRAPHIC MOBILITY

When people are asked about the reasons for their geographic-mobility decisions, about 75 percent mention job change as a *critical* factor, and 60 percent mention it as the *exclusive* factor motivating their move. This emphasis on job change suggests that the implications of the human-capital theory for migration can be tested in the labor market.

Comparing Wages and Employment Opportunities

If job changes are the most dominant factor motivating mobility, then we should observe people migrating from areas where wages and employment opportunities are relatively poor to areas where they are relatively good. Three interrelated patterns of internal migration can be observed in the United States over the recent decades: 1. rural-to-urban shifts, 2. the movement of blacks, and 3. the interregional flows of people.

Rural-to-urban movements.   Huge movements of people from rural to urban areas have occurred in this century as farming jobs have diminished in number.[2] In 1910, 54 percent of the U.S. population lived in rural areas—that is, areas with less than 2500 inhabitants. In 1970 this percentage had fallen to 26 percent. In the 1960s alone, farming employment fell by 40 percent, and the rural areas of California, the Dakotas, Nebraska, and Kansas experienced population losses of 10-16 percent. Interestingly enough, the *overall* rural population fell by only 0.3 percent during the 1960s because of rural population increases in New England, the mid-Atlantic states, and the eastern north-central states. This growth reflects, to a large degree, the extension of suburban areas into neighboring rural counties and thus does not contradict our observation that people move to where the jobs are.

Migration of blacks.   A dramatic characteristic of rural-urban migration in this century has been the massive movement of blacks out of the rural South to urban areas in the non-South.[3] This movement began during World War I, when wartime production created jobs in the urbanized, industrial states in the North. In the 1920s this migration continued as 800,000 blacks left the South, headed primarily for big cities in the North. This flow was cut in half during the 1930s, when the Great Depression diminished job opportunities in the industrial sector, but it rose to 1.6 million during the war-dominated 1940s. In the essentially prosperous decades of the 1950s and 1960s, 2.9 million more blacks left the South.

Undoubtedly part of the migration of blacks reflects the decline in farming employment. Many southern states have also experienced outflows of whites. More whites left the states of Alabama, Kentucky, Oklahoma, and West Virginia

---

[2] Data in this section are from the *Manpower Report of the President* (Washington, D.C.: U.S. Government Printing Office, 1974), pp. 77–78.

[3] Data in this section were obtained from the *Manpower Report of the President,* 1974, pp. 90–97 and U.S. Bureau of the Census, *Statistical Abstract of the U.S.,* 99th ed. (Washington, D.C.: U.S. Government Printing Office, 1978), Table 26.

during the 1950s and 1960s than entered them, while Arkansas, the Carolinas, Georgia, Mississippi, and Tennessee experienced out-migration of whites in the 1950s but net in-migration of whites during the 1960s.

That the migration of blacks out of the South is not completely due to the decline in agricultural jobs is clearly indicated by the fact that while blacks were *leaving* the South during the 1960s, whites were, on balance, *flowing into* the South as jobs there expanded. Because basic federal civil-rights laws concerning segregation and voting were not passed until the mid-'60s and programs aimed at eliminating job discrimination were not implemented until the late '60s, it is not farfetched to speculate that much of the black migration out of the South was induced by perceptions of greater freedom and opportunities elsewhere. As discrimination lessened in the 1970s, however, and as blacks began to share in the general economic expansion underway in the South, there has been, on balance, a movement of blacks *into* the South. Between 1970 and 1975 there was a net influx of 44,000 blacks into the South—the first time this has occurred in the 20th century.

Regional migration.   Further evidence that tends to support the view that people move from regions where opportunities are poor to regions where they are better can be found by examining regional migration. The older, slow-growing industrial states of New York, Pennsylvania, Ohio, Illinois and Michigan are experiencing outmigration, while the faster-growing states in the South and West are the recipients of an influx of migrants. During 1975-1978, for example, the northeast and north-central states had a net outflow of 1.4 million people, while the South and West had net inflows of 1 million and 400,000 respectively. The net inflow to the South is a complete turnaround from the 1950s, when the region was largely rural and offered relatively few job opportunities. As the South has industrialized and opportunities have improved, it has become the region with the most net in-migration.

Human-capital theory predicts that people will tend to move from areas of relatively poor earnings possibilities to places where opportunities are better. While the general regional flows of people support this prediction, it is important to note that the prediction can also be tested by looking at the characteristics of more specific areas from which and to which people move. In general the results of such studies suggest that the "pull" of good opportunities in the areas of destination are stronger than the "push" of poor opportunities in the areas of origin. In other words, while people are more attracted to places where earnings are expected to be better, they do not necessarily come from areas where the opportunities are poorest.

The most consistent finding in these detailed studies is that people are attracted to areas where the real earnings of full-time workers are highest. One might also expect that the chances for obtaining work in the new area would also affect that area's attractiveness. One way to measure job availability in an area is to use the unemployment rate, but the studies find no consistent relationship between unemployment and in-migration—perhaps because the number of people moving with a job already in hand is three times as large as the numbers moving *to look* for work.[4] If one already has a job in a particular field, the *overall* unemployment rate is irrelevant.

Most studies have found that, contrary to what human-capital theory implies, the characteristics of the place of origin do not appear to have much influence on migration. One reason for this finding is that while those in the poorest places have the greatest *incentives* to move, the very poorest areas also tend to have people with lower levels of education and skills—the very people who seem least *willing* (or able) to move. To understand this last phenomenon, we must turn from the issue of *where* people go to a discussion of *who* is most likely to move.

Personal Characteristics of Movers

Migration is highly selective in the sense that it is not an activity in which all people are equally likely to be engaged. To be specific, mobility is much higher among the young and the better-educated—as human-capital theory would suggest.

Age.   Age is the single most important factor in determining who migrates. The peak years for mobility are the ages 22-24, when nearly 20 percent of the population migrates across county or state lines. By age 32, the rate of migration is half what it was in the early twenties, and by age 42 migration is only one fourth as likely as it was in the twenties.

There are two explanations for the fact that migration is an activity primarily for the young. First, the younger one is, the greater the potential returns from any human-capital investment. As noted earlier, the longer is the period over which benefits from an investment can be obtained, the larger is the present value of these benefits.

Second, a large part of the costs of migration are psychic—the losses associated with giving up friends, community ties, and the benefits of knowing one's way around. When one is starting out as an adult, these losses are comparatively small because one is not well-established in the adult world. However, as one grows older, community ties become stronger, and the losses associated with leaving loom larger—thus inhibiting mobility. This line of reasoning is underscored by the fact that, within age groups, unmarried people are more likely to migrate than married ones, and that married people without children are more mobile than those with children.[5]

Education.   While age is probably the best predictor of who will move, education is the single best indicator of who will move *within* an age group. As can be seen from Table 10.1, strictly speaking, more education does not make one more likely to move; it is a *college* education that makes migration more likely. The labor markets for college-educated workers are more likely to be regional or national in character than are the labor markets for those with less education.

[4]John B. Lansing and Eva Mueller, *The Geographic Mobility of Labor* (Ann Arbor, Mich.: Survey Research Center, University of Michigan, 1967), p. 37.

[5]See Jacob Mincer, "Family Migration Decisions," *Journal of Political Economy* 86,5 (October 1978):749–73.

Example 10.1
Indentured Servitude and Human
Capital Investments

Obtaining the funds necessary to make an investment is a common problem for would-be investors. The problem is especially formidible for those who would invest in human capital, because loans for human-capital investments are not widely made. Unlike loans for investments in physical capital (cars, homes, machines)—which can be secured by the asset purchased—loans for human-capital investments must generally be unsecured and thus are more risky to the creditor.

In the colonial days, indentured servitude was an institution that permitted poor immigrants to obtain passage to the New World using funds provided by a creditor and to secure this "loan" with all they had: their labor. British emigrants would sign an indenture with a British merchant or sea captain that specified the colony to which they would be sent and the length of time they would be bound to their master. The merchant or sea captain was then responsible for feeding, clothing, and transporting the servant to the colony. Upon arrival at the colony, the contract would be sold to a colonial farmer or planter, and the servant would be bound to this employer for the specified length of time—a length of time presumably long enough to pay back the expenses connected with immigration, plus interest.

The market for indentures was apparently competitive. There were enough British agents selling these indentures, and the potential servants were well-enough informed, that genuine bargaining took place. The "price" of an indenture was its length, which varied from 2 to 10 years. A long indenture was obviously costly to the servant, but it could bring a high price in the colonies to the agent. A short indenture was less profitable to the agent and a better deal for the servant.

Looking at the length of British indentures during the period 1718–1759 offers striking confirmation of the general implications of human-capital theory presented in Chapter 9. Literate and experienced workers were able to obtain the shortest indentures—while younger, less experienced, or illiterate workers had to sign for longer periods of indenture. (Women were able to obtain slightly shorter indentures than men, other things equal—a fact that the reader is free to interpret.) There is also evidence of compensating differentials. Indentures to be sold in the West Indies were shorter than those to be sold in the mainland colonies, where environmental conditions were more healthy and post-servitude opportunities were considered better.

SOURCE: David Galenson, "Immigration and the Colonial Labor System: An Analysis of the Length of Indenture," *Explorations in Economic History* 14(1977):360–77.

One of the costs of migration is that of ascertaining *where* opportunities are and *how good* they are likely to be. If one's occupation has a national labor market, for example, it is relatively easy to find out about opportunities in distant

TABLE 10.1. Migration Rates for Men and Women 25–29 By Educational Level, 1965–1971

| Educational Level (in years) | Percent Moving Each Year | | | |
| | Between Counties within States | | Between States | |
	Men	Women	Men	Women
0–7	6.7	4.9	5.2	4.3
8	6.9	4.9	5.7	6.3
9–11	6.4	4.3	5.2	4.8
12	5.5	4.8	5.2	5.2
13–15	6.1	6.4	6.9	8.0
16	9.2	7.0	11.3	11.0
17 or more	8.3	8.1	15.6	13.5

SOURCE: *Manpower Report of the President,* 1974, p. 84.

places. Jobs are advertised in national newspapers. Recruiters from all over visit college campuses. Employment agencies make nationwide searches. In cases such as these, people usually move with a job already in hand.

However, if the relevant labor market for one's job is localized, it is difficult to find out where better opportunities in other areas might be. For a janitor in Beaumont, Texas, to find out about employment opportunities in the north-central region is like looking for the proverbial needle in a haystack. That such moves occur at all, let alone in reasonably large numbers, is testimony to the fact that people are able to acquire information despite the obstacles.

The Role of Distance

Human-capital theory clearly predicts that as migration costs rise, the flow of migrants will fall. The costs of moving increase with distance for two reasons. First, as noted above, for people in local labor markets, acquiring information on opportunities elsewhere can be very difficult (costly). Surely it is easier to find out about employment prospects closer to home than farther away: newspapers are easier to obtain, phone calls are cheaper, friends and relatives are more useful contacts, and knowledge of employers is greater. Second, the money costs of transportation—both for the move and for trips back to see friends and relatives— obviously rise with distance. Thus, one would clearly expect to find that people are more likely to move short distances than long distances.

In general, people *are* more likely to move shorter than longer distances. One study published in the late 1960s found that 34 percent of all moves were of less than 100 miles and 51 percent were of less than 200 miles. In contrast, only 17 percent were of distances between 200–400 miles and only 10 percent were between 400 and 600 miles in length.[6] Thus, moves over 600 miles accounted for

---

[6]Lansing and Mueller, *The Geographic Mobility of Labor,* p. 28. Some of the moves of less than 100 miles may not have been accompanied by a job change; the explanation for these moves lies outside the realm of human-capital theory.

only 22 percent of all moves. Clearly, the propensity to move far away is smaller than the propensity to stay close to home.

Related to the desire to minimize psychic and informational costs is the fact that people tend to migrate to areas where friends or relatives have previously migrated. This *chain migration* is especially evident in the stream of migration from Puerto Rico to the mainland: most Puerto Ricans go to Chicago and to the tristate area of New York-New Jersey-Connecticut.

The Individual Returns to Migration

The previous section discussed the fact that the people most likely to move are the ones with the most to gain and the least to lose by migration—and that they move to areas where their net gains are likely to be largest. Another way to test our human-capital theory of migration is to see if the incomes of people who migrate are higher than they would have been in the absence of migration.

One interesting study that analyzed the earnings of foreign-born males found that these immigrants had, on the average, fewer skills and less education than native men, and initially earned much less than Americans of comparable skills and education.[7] After five years they still earned 10 percent less, but after 10-15 years their earnings were equal to comparable native males. Interestingly, after 20 years foreign-born males earned 6 percent more than native men. This earnings pattern suggests that hiring newcomers is regarded as a risky proposition by employers, either because they find it hard to evaluate their background or because their productivity is lowered by language and cultural problems. During this period, in effect, immigrants are investing heavily in themselves by acquiring experience in the culture and facility in the language.

Eventually, however, immigrants surpass the average native-born male (of the same educational background) in earning ability—primarily because immigrants are not average people. They are people with enough drive to accept the high costs of immigration in order to "get ahead." Interestingly, the high ability and work motivation of immigrants is also seen in the fact that white native-born sons of immigrants have earnings that are 5 percent higher than white sons of native-born parents with the same educational characteristics living in the same area.[8]

Given the poverty of the countries from which immigration of less skilled workers generally comes, the fact that they do well here clearly implies eventual gains from immigration for them as individuals. Can the same conclusion be reached concerning migrants *within* the United States? Studies have found that, as a general rule, migrants do earn more than they would have earned if they had not moved. The exact size of the typical earnings differential is unclear, but earnings increases in the 10-20 percent range have been found for blacks moving out of the South.[9] There may be no *immediate* increases in income for migrants within the

[7]Barry Chiswick, "The Effect of Americanization on the Earnings of Foreign-Born Men," *Journal of Political Economy* 86 (October 1978): 897–921.

[8]Barry Chiswick, "Immigrants and Immigration Policy," in *Contemporary Economic Problems,* ed. William Fellner (Washington, D.C.: American Enterprise Institute, 1978).

[9]Michael J. Greenwood, "Research on Internal Migration in the United States: A Survey," *Journal of Economic Literature* 8, 2 (June 1975):397–433.

United States, but increases after five years are found and turn out to be large—a finding more or less consistent with the finding for foreign-born migrants. Thus, the studies of returns accruing to *individual* moves confirm the findings of research on the relationship between area-wide incentives and the *general flow* of migrants.

One other finding regarding the individual returns to migration is that the gains to *wives* from migration are much lower than the gains to husbands. For example, one study of husband-wife families who moved across state lines in 1971–72 found that the changes in present value of earnings over the next four years were $4254 for husbands and −$1716 for wives. (These figures compare to increases of $1648 and $160, respectively, for nonmovers.)[10] The reason for this disparity between husbands and wives is found in the way that family migration decisions have traditionally been made. The husband's earnings opportunities have probably been given primary weight in the decision about whether (and where) to move. The husband is thus free to move where his earnings potential is best, and it would only be by coincidence that this same place would be optimal for his wife (in terms of earnings). Thus, while *family* income seems to rise after a move, it is the husband's income that increases the most. The wife's earnings, as shown by this one study, may actually decline when migration takes place.

Return Migration

To say that, on average, migration is a good investment for those who decide to undertake it does not imply that it is a good investment for all. Clearly, most people *do not* migrate in any given year—presumably because they believe that, for them, it would not be a good investment. It is equally clear, however, that some migrants find out they have made a mistake. What they thought would be a good investment may turn out not to be. In these cases people will seek to leave where they are and move elsewhere—and it is understandable that they might seek to minimize costs by moving back to an area with which they are familiar.

Twenty percent of all moves are to an area in which the person had *previously* lived—and about half of these are back to one's birthplace.[11] Thus, *return migration*—migrating to a place from which one originated in some sense—is an important phenomenon of geographic mobility. Not all of return migration may be the result of a failed investment. After all, people do leave home to acquire training or experience with the intent to return. However, much of return migration may be a response by those who find that job opportunities were not what they had expected or that the psychic costs of living in strange surroundings are higher than they had anticipated. Return migration, then, serves to remind us that—as with other forms of investments—investments in human capital can also fail to be profitable.

---

[10]Solomon W. Polachek and Francis W. Horvath, "A Life-Cycle Approach to Migration: Analysis of the Perspicacious Peregrinator," in *Research in Labor Economics,* ed. Ronald Ehrenberg (Greenwich, Conn.: JAI Press, 1977), pp. 128–29.

[11]Lansing and Mueller, *The Geographic Mobility of Labor,* p. 34.

VOLUNTARY TURNOVER

While most workers who experience geographical mobility also change jobs (although perhaps not employers), these migrants are but one part of a wider group of workers who change jobs each year with or without a change of residence. Some of this job changing is "voluntary" in the sense that it is initiated by the employee; the remainder is said to be "involuntary" because it is employer-initiated. Voluntary separations are defined as *quits* and involuntary separations as *layoffs*. Layoffs can be temporary separations for economic reasons or permanent discharges—whether for cause (firing) or for economic reasons.

The human-capital model outlined in this chapter focuses on *worker-initiated* mobility and contains the same types of implications for this wide class of voluntary job mobility as it did for geographical mobility. This section will focus on *voluntary* turnover—deciding whether or not to quit; some of the major determinants of employer-initiated turnover have already been discussed in Chapter 5. The related decision of *how long to search* for a new job once one has quit his or her former job is discussed in Chapter 15.

Human-capital theory predicts that, *other things equal,* a given worker will have a higher probability of quitting a low-wage job than a higher-paying one. That is, workers employed at lower wages than they could obtain elsewhere are those most prone to quitting. Indeed, a very strong and consistent finding in virtually all studies of worker quit behavior is that, holding worker characteristics constant, employees in industries with lower wages have higher quit rates.[12]

Another implication of the theory is that workers will have a higher probability of quitting when it is relatively easy for them to obtain a better job quickly. Thus, when labor markets are *tight* (jobs are more plentiful relative to job seekers) one would expect the quit rate to be higher than when labor markets are *loose* (few jobs are available and many are being laid off). This prediction is confirmed in studies of time-series data.[13] Quit rates tend to rise when the labor market is tight and fall when it is loose. One measure of tightness is the unemployment rate; the negative relationship between the quit rate and unemployment can be readily seen in Figure 10.1. Another measure of labor-market conditions is the layoff rate, which tends to rise in recessions and fall when firms are expanding production. It, too, is inversely correlated with the quit rate (see Figure 10.1).

Finally, while human-capital theory predicts that, on average, workers will flow from jobs with lower wages to those with higher wages (other things equal), it does not imply that mistakes are never made. Like other investments, human-capital investments involve a substantial element of risk. A person might quit a job thinking better opportunities are abundant only to find out that he or she was misinformed. The risk of turnover, however, can be decreased if a worker who intends to quit lines up another job first. One study of "quitters" in 1966–67

---

[12]Donald O. Parsons, "Models of Labor Market Turnover: A Theoretical and Empirical Survey," in *Research in Labor Economics,* ed. Ronald Ehrenberg (Greenwich, Conn.: JAI Press, 1977), pp. 185–223.

[13]Parsons, "Models of Labor Market Turnover," pp. 185–223.

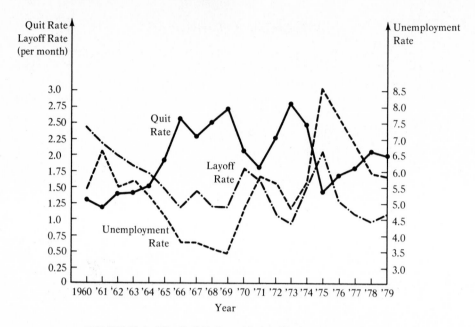

FIGURE 10.1   The Quit Rate and Labor Market "Tightness"

SOURCE: U.S. Department of Labor, Bureau of Labor Statistics, *Handbook of Labor Statistics,* Bulletin 2070 (Washington, D.C.: U.S. Government Printing Office, December 1980).

found that those who quit only after another job had been obtained—about 50–60 percent of all quitters—increased their wages by 10.7 percent on average.[14] This same study found that for those who quit one job and were unemployed for a while, the average wage increase was almost nil. While the utility of the latter group of "quitters" could still have been increased by *nonwage* factors, it does seem likely that at least some of this group received returns below what they expected.

Earlier this chapter argued that people tend to invest more heavily in human capital early in their careers. In many cases younger people have lower opportunity costs, and they have a longer period over which to recoup such costs. The data on all forms of job mobility clearly indicate that turnover falls as age rises, but is this true for *voluntary* mobility? The answer appears to be yes. Studies that have investigated the differences in quit rates among various industries have generally found that, other things (wages, for example) equal, quit rates are higher where the proportion of younger workers is greater.[15]

Another prediction of human-capital theory is that quit rates will be higher when the costs of quitting are lower. For example, workers in rural areas who change employers may well have to move their residence if they want to find a

[14]J. Peter Mattila, "Job Quitting and Frictional Unemployment," *American Economic Review* 64 (March 1974): 235–39.

[15]Parsons, "Models of Labor Market Turnover," p. 209; Farrell E. Bloch, "Labor Turnover in U.S. Manufacturing Industries," *Journal of Human Resources* 14 (Spring 1979): 236–46.

Example 10.2
A Positive and Normative Theory of Quitting
in 19th-Century Japan

Is modern labor economics, in both its positive and normative modes, culture-bound. Does the theory presented in this book pertain only to circumstances as they now are in the United States? Despite our emphasis on the analysis of current American policy issues, economic behavior is so general, and the need for markets so pervasive, that the theory presented here as *modern labor economics* is neither American nor necessarily modern.

For example, in the years just before 1900 when Japan was just beginning to industrialize, labor turnover rates (as noted in Example 5.1) were very high owing to persistent labor shortage. In 1898 a conference of business and government leaders was held to discuss the problems underlying this high turnover and the need for legislation concerning it. In the course of those discussions, Shoda Heigoro, a Mitsubishi executive, articulated the "modern" theory of job quitting behavior—in both its positive *and* normative aspects:

> Since it is the nature of man to be tempted by better opportunities, it is impossible to keep workers without adequate provisions. That is, if a worker desires to go to another factory because of better pay there, his present employer should allow him to go. If the employer wanted to keep the worker, he should raise wages so that the worker would see no reason to move. Were I censured for this statement on the ground that the competitive spiraling of wages would damage the profits of factory owners and retard industrial progress, I would rebut by calling attention to the simple logic of demand and supply in the market. Factory operatives, engineers, machinists, and other workers in modern industries are scarce in Japan today, because these occupations unlike the traditional crafts emerged only recently. It is true that their relative scarcity enables them to command relatively higher wages than other types of labor. But this very fact of high wages also induces more workers to flow into these occupations. . . .
>
> Therefore, if the forces of demand and supply worked normally, the increase in their number would in time reduce their wages. But this subsequent decrease in their wages would spell no hardship for them, because workers would move into these occupations only insofar as the advantages there were sufficient to make them willing to move. . . . Thus, in my opinion, it is highly necessary that factory owners should acquiesce in the economic motives of workers in seeking high wages and better occupations. . . .

SOURCE: Koji Taira, *Economic Development and the Labor Market in Japan* (New York: Columbia University Press, 1970), p. 118.

job in the same industry or occupation. Job changers who live in large cities have a much wider choice of jobs in their field and have a much lower probability of having to move. Because job changing is thus less costly for residents of large cities, one would expect turnover to be higher in these large cities. Indeed, we do

TABLE 10.2.   Officially Recorded Immigration: 1820 to 1977

Period	Number (in thousands)	Annual Rate (per thousand of U.S. population)	Year	Number (in thousands)	Annual Rate (per thousand of U.S. population)
1820–1978	48,664	3.5			
1820–1830	152	1.2	1965	297	1.5
1831–1840	599	3.9	1966	323	1.6
1841–1850	1,713	8.4	1967	362	1.8
1851–1860	2,598	9.3	1968	454	2.3
1861–1870	2,315	6.4	1969	359	1.8
1871–1880	2,812	6.2	1970	373	1.8
1881–1890	5,247	9.2	1971	370	1.8
1891–1900	3,688	5.3	1972	385	1.8
1901–1910	8,795	10.4	1973	400	1.9
1911–1920	5,736	5.7	1974	395	1.9
1921–1930	4,107	3.5	1975	386	1.8
1931–1940	528	0.4	1976	399	1.9
1941–1950	1,035	0.7	1977	462	2.1
1951–1960	2,515	1.5	1978	601	2.8
1961–1970	3,322	1.7			

SOURCE: U.S. Immigration and Naturalization Service, *Annual Report.*

find that industries in which employment is more concentrated in larger cities have higher quit rates, other things (wages and age of worker, for example) equal.[16]

NATIONAL IMMIGRATION POLICY

Nowhere are the analytical tools of the economist more important than in the area of immigration policy; the lives affected by immigration policy number in the millions each year. After a brief outline of the history of U.S. immigration policy, this section will analyze in detail the consequences of illegal immigration—a problem currently attracting widespread attention.

U.S. Immigration History

The United States is a rich country—a country whose wealth and high standard of living make it an attractive place for immigrants from nearly all parts of the world. For the first 140 years of our history as an independent country, the United States followed a policy of essentially unrestricted immigration (the only major immigration restrictions were placed on Orientals and convicts). The flow of immigrants was especially large after 1840, when industrialization here and political and economic upheavals in Europe made immigration an attractive investment for millions. As one can see from Table 10.2, officially recorded immigration peaked in the first decade of the 20th Century, when the *yearly* flow of immigrants was more than 1 percent of the population.

In 1921, however, Congress adopted the Quota Law, which set annual quotas

---

[16]Parsons, ''Models of Labor Market Turnover''; Bloch, ''Labor Turnover in U.S. Manufacturing.''

on immigration on the basis of nationality. These quotas had the effect of reducing immigration from eastern and southern Europe. This act was followed by other laws in 1924 and 1929 that further restricted immigration from southeastern Europe. These various revisions in immigration policy were motivated, in part, by widespread concern over the alleged adverse impact on native employment caused by the arrival of unskilled immigrants from eastern and southern Europe.

In 1965, the passage of the Immigration and Nationality Act abolished the quota system based on national origin that so heavily favored northern and western Europeans. Under this new law, overall ceilings were established for the eastern and western hemisphere, with no more than 20,000 coming from any one country. Within these limits, however, first preference is given to family reunification (74 percent of all immigrant visas). Sixteen percent of visas are reserved for professionals or artists of exceptional ability and for workers in occupations for which labor is scarce. Immigrants in the latter categories must obtain a labor certificate approved by the U.S. Department of Labor after an investigation to verify that the applicant is qualified for the job, to verify that there is a shortage of workers for that job in the area, and to verify that the terms of employment are average or better.

While the 1965 change in immigration policy did achieve its goal of making immigration less overtly discriminatory, the policy still imposes a ceiling on immigrants that is far below the numbers who wish to come. The fact that immigration to the United States is viewed as a very worthwhile investment for many more people than are allowed to take advantage of it has created incentives for people to enter the country illegally.

One way in which entry is made illegally is for the immigrant to come to this country as a student or visitor. Once here, the foreigner can look for work—although it is illegal to work at a job under a student's or visitor's visa. If the "student" or "visitor" is offered a job, he or she can apply for an "adjustment of status" to become a permanent resident (based on the existence of a labor certificate). Emigrants from the eastern hemisphere are allowed to remain in the United States while their adjustment-of-status application is being evaluated. Because *employers* of illegal immigrants are not subject to punishment (as of 1981), many are able to find jobs during the interim period.

Residents from the western hemisphere are required to return home while their adjustment-of-status application is being processed. The backlog of people awaiting entry is such that, as of the late 1970s, the delay in re-entering the United States as a legal permanent resident was two and one-half years. Since most job offers will not wait that length of time, the affected immigrants understandably take the jobs and work here illegally while awaiting approval of their status change.

Roughly 7 million people enter the United States every year under nonimmigrant visas. Since many leave without informing U.S. officials, it is impossible to say how many of these 7 million overstay their period of admission, but government officials believe that the numbers range from 10 to 20 percent.[17] If (say) half

---

[17]Walter Fogel, "Illegal Alien Workers in the United States," *Industrial Relations* 16, 3 (October 1977):250.

of these visa abusers intend to immigrate illegally, the number of illegal immigrants would at least be equal to—and perhaps double the size of—the number of legal immigrants.

Moreover, there are other ways of illegally immigrating to the United States. Immigrants from the Caribbean often enter through Puerto Rico, whose residents are U.S. citizens and thus allowed free entry to the mainland. Others walk across the Mexican border. Still others are smuggled in the United States or use false documents to get through entry stations. The value of immigration as a human-capital investment is indicated by the fact that *coyotes,* people who help illegal aliens to cross the border and to find jobs, could command $300 per head in 1978[18]—or roughly 8 months of pay for the average Mexican peasant.

No one knows how many illegal immigrants are in the United States. In 1977, the Immigration and Naturalization Service apprehended and deported more than 1 million illegal aliens, and many believe that for every person apprehended two make it into the country successfully.[19] The report of the Select Commission on Immigration and Refugee Policy submitted in 1981 places the total number of illegal residents at below 6 million, possibly in the range of 3.5–5 million.[20] While not all "illegals" are in the labor market, the profile of the typical illegal alien is that of a young, unattached male who is seeking work and unaccompanied by nonworking family members.

Despite the lack of precise knowledge about the dimensions of illegal immigration, the fact remains that by the early 1980s it had become a very prominent policy issue. The Secretary of Labor estimated in late 1979 that if only *half* of the jobs held by illegal aliens were given to U.S. citizens, the unemployment rate would drop from 6 percent to 3.7 percent. Similar beliefs have, in part at least, led the Select Commission on Immigration and Refugee Policy to recommend that the *hiring* of undocumented workers be made illegal and that offending employers be punished.[21] Some advocate allowing foreign workers in on a temporary, *guest-worker* basis only, while still others claim that permitting the flow of illegals to continue is both rational for us and humane for them. It is important to stress that the policies people advocate are based on their beliefs about the consequences of immigration. Nearly everyone with an opinion on this subject has an economic model implicitly or explicitly in mind when addressing these consequences; the purpose of the remainder of this chapter is to make these economic models explicit and to evaluate them.

Naive Views of Immigration

There are two opposing views of illegal immigration that can be considered naive. One view, which is widely held in the government, is that every illegal immigrant deprives a citizen or legal alien of a job. For example, a Department of Labor

---

[18]Edwin P. Reubens, "Aliens, Jobs, and Immigration Policy," *Public Interest* 51 (Spring 1978):126.

[19]Reubens, "Aliens, Jobs and Immigration Policy," p. 126.

[20]Select Commission on Immigration and Refugee Policy, *U.S. Immigration Policy and the National Interest* (Washington, D.C.: U.S. Government Printing Office, 1981), p. 36.

[21]Select Commission on Immigration and Refugee Policy, *U.S. Immigration Policy and the National Interest,* pp. 61–69.

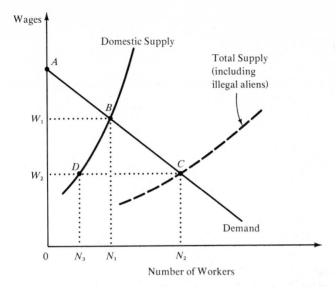

FIGURE 10.2 Demand and Supply of Rough Laborers

official told a House committee studying immigration, "I think it is logical to conclude that if they are actually employed they are taking a job away from one of our American citizens."[22] According to this view, if x illegal aliens are deported and others kept out, the number of unemployed Americans would decline by x.

At the opposite end of the policy spectrum is the equally naive argument that the illegals perform jobs no American citizen would do:

> You couldn't conduct a hotel in New York, you couldn't conduct a restaurant in New York . . . if you didn't have rough laborers. We haven't got the rough laborers anymore . . . . Where are we going to get the people to do that rough work?[23]

Both arguments are simplistic because they ignore the slopes of the demand and supply curves. Consider, for example, the labor market for the job of "rough laborer"—any job that most American citizens find distasteful. Without illegal immigrants the restricted supply of Americans to this market would imply a relatively high wage (W_1 in Figure 10.2). N_1 citizens would be employed. If illegal aliens enter the market, the supply curve would shift outward and perhaps flatten (implying that immigrants were more responsive to wage increases for rough laborers than citizens). The influx of illegals would drive the wage down to W_2, but employment would increase to N_2.

Are Americans unwilling to do the work of rough laborers? Clearly, at the market wage of W_2, many more aliens are willing to work at the job than U.S. citizens. Only N_3 citizens would want these jobs at this wage, while the remaining

[22]Elliott Abrams and Franklin S. Abrams, "Immigration Policy—Who Gets In and Why?" *Public Interest* 38 (Winter 1975):25.

[23]Abrams and Abrams, "Immigration Policy—Who Gets In and Why?" p. 26

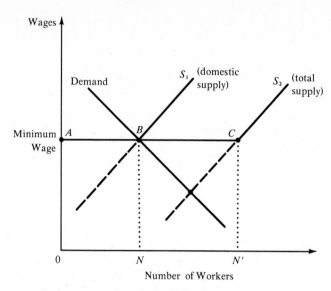

FIGURE 10.3   **Demand and Supply of Rough Laborers
with a Minimum Wage**

supply (N_2–N_3) is made up entirely of aliens. If there were no immigrants, however, N_1 Americans would be employed at wage W_1 as rough laborers. Wages would be higher, as would the prices of the goods or services produced with this labor, but the job would get done. The only "shortage" of American citizens is at the low wage of W_2; at W_1, there is no shortage (see Chapter 2 for further discussion of labor shortages).

Would deporting those illegal aliens working as rough laborers create the same number of jobs for U.S. citizens? The answer is clearly no. If the N_2–N_3 aliens working as laborers were deported—and if all other illegal aliens were kept from the market—the number of Americans employed as laborers would rise from N_3 to N_1, and their wages would rise from W_2 to W_1 (Figure 10.2). N_2–N_1 jobs would be destroyed by the rising wage rate associated with deportation. Thus, while deportation would increase the employment and wage levels of Americans in the laborer market, it would certainly not reduce unemployment on a one-for-one basis.

There is, however, one case where deportation *would* create jobs for American citizens on a one-for-one basis: the case where the federal mimimum-wage law creates a surplus of labor. Suppose, for example, that the supply of American laborers is represented by ABS_1 in Figure 10.3, and the total supply is represented by ACS_2. Because an artificially high wage has created a surplus, only N of the N' workers willing to work at the minimum wage can actually find employment. If some of them are illegal aliens, sending them back—coupled with successful efforts to deny other aliens access to these jobs—would create jobs for a comparable number of Americans. However, the demand curve would have to intersect the domestic supply curve (ABS_1) at or to the left of Point B to prevent the wage level from rising (and thus destroying jobs) after deportation. In addition, all laborers would have to be paid the minimum wage—an unlikely eventuality given the lack of compliance noted in Chapter 3.

An Analysis of the Gainers and Losers

Some claim that, while perhaps not reducing citizen-held jobs one-for-one, large immigrant flows are indeed harmful to American workers. This view is probably the dominant force behind our restrictive immigration policy and behind the consequent concern about illegal immigration.

The argument is based primarily on a single-market analysis like that contained in Figure 10.2, where only the effects on the market for rough labor (say) are examined. As far as it goes, the argument is correct. When immigration increases the supply of rough laborers, both the wage and the employment level of American citizens working as laborers are reduced. The total wage bill paid to American laborers falls from $W_1 0 N_1 B$ in Figure 10.2 to $W_2 0 N_3 D$. Thus, some American workers leave the market in response to the reduced wage, and those who stay earn less. If the Americans employed as laborers are, for example, minorities or members of some other group that is the target of antipoverty efforts, the influx of immigrants could substantially frustrate such efforts.

It would be a mistake, however, to conclude from the above analysis that because immigration is harmful to domestic *laborers* it is therefore necessarily harmful to Americans as a *whole*. First, immigration of "cheap labor" clearly benefits consumers using the output of this labor. As wages are reduced and employment increases, the goods and services produced by this labor are increased in quantity and reduced in price.

Second, employers of rough labor (to continue our example) are obviously benefited, at least in the short run. In Figure 10.2, profits are increased from $W_1 A B$ to $W_2 A C$. This rise in profitability, however, should serve to attract more people to become employers—which in the long run will reduce profits back down to normal levels. As employers or managers become more numerous, opportunities for workers who would have been neither in the absence of immigration are expanded. (For example, a supply of cheap labor may induce a cook to open up his own diner or a janitor to open her own cleaning service.)

Third, our analysis of the market for laborers assumed that the influx of immigrants has had no effect on the demand curve (which was held fixed in Figure 10.2). This is not a bad assumption when looking at just one market, because the fraction of earnings immigrant laborers spend on the goods and services produced by rough labor is probably small. However, immigrants do spend money in the United States, and this added demand may create job opportunities or higher wages (or both) for the more skilled workers (see Figure 10.4). Thus, workers who are not close substitutes for unskilled immigrant labor may benefit from immigration because of the increase in consumer demand attendant to this addition to our working population.

(Note: Recall from Chapter 3 that if the demand for skilled workers increases when the wage of unskilled labor falls, the two grades of labor would be *gross complements*. Assuming skilled and unskilled labor are substitutes in the production process, the only way they could be gross complements is if the *scale effect*

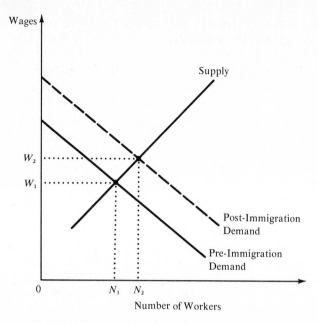

FIGURE 10.4   Market for All Labor Except Unskilled

of a decline in the unskilled wage dominated the substitution effect. In the case of immigration one may suppose the scale effect to be very large, because as the working population rises, aggregate demand is increased. While theoretical analysis cannot *prove* that the demand for skilled workers is increased by unskilled immigration if the two grades of labor are substitutes in the production process, it can offer the above observation that an increase in demand for skilled workers remains a distinct possibility. Of course, for any type of labor that is *complementary* with unskilled labor in the production process—supervisory workers, for example—immigration does represent a clear-cut gain.)

The Effect of Immigration on the "Native" Population

Thus far we have concluded that illegal immigration is harmful to the interests of native unskilled workers but increases the real incomes of owners and possibly of skilled workers as well. However, it is also interesting and important to inquire whether the *aggregate income of native Americans* is increased. If it is, the gainers (skilled workers and owners) gain more than the losers lose. There would thus be large enough gains that the losers could be compensated for their losses—by income-maintenance or job-training programs—and the gainers would still come out ahead. In this case, policymakers might choose to pursue a policy of ignoring illegal immigration.

If immigrants are paid a wage equal to the value of their marginal product (*MP*) and if they are not subsidized by native taxpayers, then the aggregate income of U.S. citizens *will* increase as a result of the immigration. Recall that total product—the area under the marginal product curve—is greater than wages paid. Only for the last unit of labor employed, where *MP* = Wage, is there no surplus or profit generated. Thus, as long as immigrants get paid a wage equal only to their *MP,* the aggregate income of the native-born population cannot be reduced.

One way in which the native-born population, taken as a whole, *can lose* from immigration is if the immigrants obtain government services or payments in excess of the payroll, income, sales, and property taxes they pay. Because many government programs are essentially aids to the poor—public health, welfare, and unemployment insurance, to name just three—there is a distinct possibility that legal immigrants could be receiving net subsidies. On the other hand, *illegal* immigrants tend to be young, unattached males—people without children in school who do not generally qualify for other government programs because they are undocumented. Moreover, the taxes these workers do pay, directly or indirectly, also serve to reduce the burden of certain "overhead" expenses to U.S. citizens— expenses, like those of national defense and road maintenance, which the presence of immigrants does not increase. Thus, illegal immigration is likely to increase the aggregate income of the native-born populace.

If the aggregate income of the resident population is increased by immigration, then the gainers gain more than the losers lose. You will recall from Chapter 1 that when the gains are larger than the losses a mutually beneficial transaction is possible. The immigrants gain from their move to this country and, on balance, the resident population gains. In fact, the gains are large enough that the beneficiaries could compensate those who lose from immigration and *still* be better off.

Whether one would in fact favor a policy of unrestricted immigration would probably depend on

1. the possibility that those hurt by it could actually receive compensation,
2. the probability that immigrants would remain unsubsidized, and
3. the desirability of programs designed to reduce or deny subsidies to immigrants.

Since many social programs are aimed at the poor, compensation to unskilled workers for their losses associated with immigration of the unskilled may be fairly automatic—coming in the form of unemployment compensation, public housing, food stamps, job retraining, and welfare payments. Compensation to skilled workers (if the immigrants are predominantly skilled) would be less automatic and might have to take the form of a special program.[24]

The reservations many have about unrestricted immigration center on points 2 and 3, especially as they relate to immigration of those most likely to receive public subsidies: the unskilled. Illegal immigrants *are* denied access to certain public-welfare programs because of their undocumented status, but they also represent what some view as an "under class" who cannot vote and who do not have full citizenship rights. An alternative used in Europe—"guest worker" programs—also denies permanent residence and citizenship rights to immigrants; in

---

[24]Such a program already exists for those hurt by foreign imports. The Trade Adjustment Assistance Program identifies those hurt and compensates them through job retraining, subsidies to move to other areas, and special unemployment-insurance payments. While this program has been criticized as generally unsuccessful in several respects, it does serve as an example of a program specifically designed to compensate those who lose as a consequence of a public policy.

addition, these workers can be required to leave the country at the government's will. Thus, ensuring that poor, unskilled immigrants remain unsubsidized means denying them the rights of other citizens and legal aliens. While the immigrants themselves are obviously willing to pay the price when they immigrate, some worry that they or their children may not be willing to pay this price indefinitely.

The Consequences of Emigration

The consequences of emigration are generally the reverse of those for immigration. The country loses a productive resource, and those remaining are deprived of the surplus (total product less wages) produced by the emigrants. The groups most competitive with the emigrants are helped by their departure, but the aggregate income of the residents who remain will be smaller—with two important exceptions.

First, if the emigrants are owners of capital and are forced by the government to leave this capital behind, the remaining population could benefit (in much the same way the Black Death benefited the survivors, as pointed out in Chapter 2). Some governments—most notably, Cuba—have permitted middle-class workers to leave under these conditions. A drawback, however, is that workers (such as doctors) with sizable amounts of financial capital may also have sizable amounts of *human* capital that *does* leave with them—making it necessary for those remaining to invest in programs to train replacements.

The second exception applies to economies where there is a permanent labor surplus. Many believe that in very poor countries the supply of labor is so large relative to demand that the equilibrium wage is below a socially acceptable minimum (perhaps the subsistence level). If the minimum must be paid, a labor surplus is created (see Figure 10.5). If surplus workers leave, the country obviously gains. These workers were not producing anything, but they had to be kept alive by transfer payments from others. Emigration is a clear-cut help to those who remain.

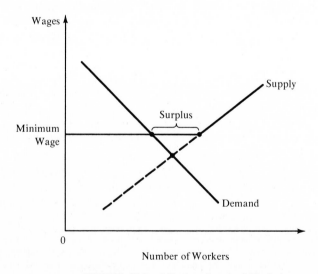

FIGURE 10.5 A "Labor-Surplus" Market

It should be noted that labor surpluses in less developed countries can also be created by the high wages paid in the industrial, urban sector. These wages are high in order to attract foreign labor with the requisite skills and must by law be paid to native workers also. Hoping to be lucky enough to obtain these jobs, migrants flock to the cities where they form a sizable group of unemployed, surplus workers. If the country were not willing to let the industrial wage for native workers fall to the point of market equilibrium, emigration would be an attractive solution to the resulting problem of a labor surplus.

REVIEW QUESTIONS

1. The following four paragraphs were taken from an Associated Press story on December 8, 1979:

   > WASHINGTON (AP)—Treasury Secretary G. William Miller said Friday that the Senate Banking Committee version of the Chrysler aid bill is "unworkable," in part because the automaker might lose many of its best workers.
   >
   > Miller said the most objectionable feature of the committee bill is a requirement that Chrysler workers accept a three-year wage freeze in exchange for $1.25 billion in federal loan guarantees for Chrysler.
   >
   > "Under the proposed bill, efforts to aid Chrysler would fail, because conditions of the bill simply could not be met," he said, adding that the wage freeze would impose "a disproportionate financing burden on the workers of the company."
   >
   > "The terms of the bill would substantially impair the operations of the Chrysler Corporation, risk loss to the company of many of its most able employees, and seriously damage the morale and productivity of the workers essential to the company's future success," he said.

   Suppose you are a staff worker for an important Senator trying to evaluate Secretary Miller's contention that a wage freeze would cause Chrysler to lose its best employees. Write an essay evaluating Miller's contention. Start with a coherent statement of the theory relevant to Miller's assertion and then analyze all the conditions necessary for Miller's assertion to be true.

2. As you know, thousands of illegal immigrants are working in the United States. Suppose the United States increases the penalties for illegal immigration to include long jail sentences. Analyze the effects of this increased penalty on the wages and employment levels of *all* affected groups of workers.

3. Suppose there are two nations, M and U. The government of U is having a problem with illegal immigration of unskilled workers from M and wants your advice on the best way to handle the problem. There are three options:

   a. The government could fine a firm that employs unskilled workers from M. (For example, the fine could be $1,000 per worker and could be collected every year.)

   b. The government could beef up border patrols in an effort to reduce migration from M to U.

   c. The government could introduce a wage subsidy to be paid only to workers from U.

   The government's goals are to both reduce migration from M to U and to raise the amount of income that unskilled workers in U obtain from an hour of work. The government of U doesn't really care what happens to workers in M—that is M's problem.

Given these goals and the following six assumptions, rank the options from best to worst, giving reasons for your ranking. Assume that at present (before any policy change),

a. market wages of unskilled labor in U are higher than market wages of unskilled labor in M. Thus, by migrating from M to U one is able to obtain a higher wage.

b. demand for unskilled labor in U is perfectly inelastic (the demand curve is vertical).

c. supply curves of unskilled labor from both M and U are upward-sloping (higher market wages lead to greater labor supply).

d. unskilled workers from M and U are perfect substitutes.

e. when workers in M migrate to U they must pay a fee to a guide. If border patrols are beefed up, these fees will rise.

f. when in U, unskilled workers from M receive the same wage as unskilled workers from U.

SELECTED READINGS

Chiswick, Barry. "The Economic Progress of Immigrants: Some Apparently Universal Patterns." In *Contemporary Economic Problems,* edited by William Fellner. Washington, D.C.: The American Enterprise Institute for Public Policy Research, 1979.

Chiswick, Barry. "The Effect of Americanization on the Earnings of Foreign-Born Men." *Journal of Political Economy* 86 (October 1978): 897–921.

Greenwood, Michael J. "Research on Internal Migration in the United States: A Survey" *Journal of Economic Literature* 8, 2 (June 1975): 397–433.

Parsons, Donald O. "Models of Labor Market Turnover: A Theoretical and Empirical Survey." In *Research in Labor Economics,* edited by Ronald Ehrenberg. Greenwich, Conn.: JAI Press, 1977, pp. 185–223.

Pencavel, John. *An Analysis of the Quit Rate in the Manufacturing Industry.* Princeton, N.J.: Industrial Relations Section, Princeton University, 1970.

Piore, Michael J. "The 'New Immigration' and the Presumptions of Social Policy." *Proceedings of the Industrial Relations Research Association* (1974), pp. 350–58.

Reder, Melvin. "The Economic Consequences of Increased Immigration." *Review of Economics and Statistics* 45, 3 (August 1963): 221–30.

11

Economic Issues
in Compensation

Chapters 6 and 7 examined factors influencing the decision to work for pay and the desired hours of work. Chapters 8 and 9 analyzed the day-to-day and human-capital aspects, respectively, of occupational choice. Chapter 10 discussed human-capital aspects of voluntary job and geographical mobility. We now turn to a discussion of yet another set of factors influencing job-choice and work-effort decisions; namely, employer compensation policies.

What ultimately matters to workers in making labor-supply decisions is the total compensation they receive per hour or month for their work. This total compensation paid to employees consists of far more than hourly, weekly, or monthly pay for time worked. There are numerous *fringe benefits* offered in varying combinations by employers, which have value to employees but are not paid to them in the form of currently spendable cash. Employers can also offer—explicitly or implicitly—different bases for computing or timing pay over one's career. These various forms of compensation affect employee behavior and labor-market outcomes in interesting ways.

This chapter will begin by describing and analyzing the consequences of fringe benefits. Of particular policy importance is the issue of pension-fund regulation by the federal government. The chapter will also discuss various ways to arrange compensation in order to provide strong incentives for employees not to be absent, not to shirk their duties, and not to perform other acts that are damaging to company interests. These forms of compensation offer different ways to *compute* current pay, but they also include a certain element of choice in *timing* a worker's pay over his or her career with a firm—choices that are particularly available in the context of an internal labor market.

THE ECONOMICS OF FRINGE BENEFITS

As noted in Chapter 5, the proportion of total compensation coming in the form of cash payments to workers has fallen over time as the use of fringe benefits has risen. According to the data presented in Table 11.1, the most common fringe benefits are paid vacations, medical insurance, maternity leaves, pensions, life

TABLE 11.1.   Fringe Benefits Available to Workers

Fringe Benefit	Percentage of Workers Reporting the Availability of the Benefit in 1977[a]
Paid vacation	80.8
Medical, surgical, or hospital insurance that covers any illness or injury that might occur *off* the job	78.1
Maternity leave will full re-employment rights	74.5
A retirement program	67.4
Life insurance that would cover a death occurring for reasons *not* connected with job	64.1
Sick leave and full pay	62.8
A training (or education) program to improve skills	49.0
Thrift or savings plan	39.8
Free or discounted merchandise	34.3
Dental benefits	29.4
Maternity leave with pay	29.4
Eyeglass or eye-care benefits	21.8
Profit sharing	19.8
Stock options	17.6
Work-clothing allowance	16.8
Free or discounted meals	16.3
Legal aid or services	10.3
Day-care facilities	2.2

[a]Includes only wage and salaried workers.

SOURCE: Robert P. Quinn and Graham L. Staines, *The 1977 Quality of Employment Survey: Descriptive Statistics, with Comparison Data from the 1969–70 and the 1972–1973 Surveys,* Research Report Series, Survey Research Center, Institute for Social Research, University of Michigan, 1979, pp. 58–59.

insurance, and paid sick leave. Less common, but still available to large numbers of workers, are company-paid education or training; discounted meals, merchandise, or work clothing; dental care, eye care, or legal benefits; stock options or savings plans; and maternity leave with pay. In addition to these private fringes, there are also publicly mandated benefits that employers must fund: social security, workers' compensation, and unemployment insurance.

One way to grasp the growth and composition of fringe benefits is to look at their cost to employers. Table 11.2 contains two sets of data on employer cost for specific benefits as a percentage of total compensation for workers in manufacturing industries. One set of data derives from Chamber of Commerce surveys, which are heavily weighted with larger firms.[1] The other data were obtained from a more representative sample of manufacturing firms.

Table 11.2 provides a number of insights. First, the proportion of total compensation devoted to fringe benefits rose about 10 percentage points from 1959 to 1976/1977 in each data set. Second, the most costly fringes are paid leave time and the government-mandated benefits, which together account for 59 percent of all fringe-benefit costs. Life and health insurance and private pension plans account for roughly 35 percent of fringe-benefit costs. Third, it is clear from the

---

[1]These data are based on information contained in Table 5.2 (see p. 119). The data in Table 5.2, however, calculated fringe benefits as a percentage of *wage and salary* payments; the data in Table 11.2 state fringes as a percentage of *total compensation*.

TABLE 11.2.   Comparisons of Employer Expenditures for Compensation, 1959–1977

| | Percentage of Employer's Total Compensation Expenditures | | | |
| | *(a)* Production and Related Workers in Manufacturing | | *(b)* All Employees in Larger Manufacturing Firms | |
Categories of Compensation	*1959*	*1976*	*1959*	*1977*
Pay for working time	85.4	75.2	82.2	72.8
Pay for leave time (vacations, holidays, sick leave, personal days)	5.4	7.4	7.7	9.3
Private pension plans	2.2	4.1⎫	5.1	9.4
Life, accident, and health insurance	2.0	5.3⎭		
Government-required contributions to Social Security, workers' compensation, and unemployment insurance	4.1	7.3	3.7	6.8
Other	0.5	0.7	1.3	1.7
Total fringe benefits	14.6	24.8	17.8	27.2
Total compensation	100.0	100.0	100.0	100.0

SOURCES: (a) U.S. Department of Labor, Bureau of Labor Statistics, *Handbook of Labor Statistics 1978,* Bulletin 2000 (Washington, D.C.: U.S. Government Printing Office), 1979.

(b) U.S. Chamber of Commerce, *Fringe Benefits and Employee Benefits* (1959, 1977).

data in Table 11.2 that fringe benefits are a greater proportion of total compensation in large firms than in small ones.

Table 11.3, which compares office and nonoffice employees of all but the smallest firms in the private sector, illustrates another interesting fact: fringe benefits as a percentage of compensation are slightly, but not markedly, higher for office than nonoffice workers. Further, government-required fringes and pay for nonworking time comprise the largest two components of the fringe package in both cases.

TABLE 11.3.   Employee Compensation for Private, Nonagricultural Workers, 1976 (in percent)

| | Percentage of Employer's Total Compensation Expenditures | |
	Office Workers	*Nonoffice Workers*
Pay for working time	75.7	77.4
Pay for leave time (vacations, holidays, sick leave, personal days)	7.9	6.3
Private pension plans	5.1	3.7
Life, accident, and health insurance	3.6	4.4
Government-required contributions to Social Security, workers' compensation, and unemployment insurance	5.2	7.4
Other	2.5	0.8
Total compensation	100.0	100.0

Note: The data are for workers in plants with 20 or more employees.

SOURCE: U.S. Department of Labor, Bureau of Labor Statistics, *Handbook of Labor Statistics 1978,* Bulletin 2000 (Washington, D.C.: U.S. Government Printing Office), 1979.

What accounts for the growth and size of fringe benefits? What are the consequences of this growth and size? To answer these questions we must examine both the employee and employer sides of the market.

Employee Preferences

The distinguishing feature of all fringe benefits is that they compensate workers in a form *other* than currently spendable cash. In general, there are two broad categories of such benefits. First and largest are *payments-in-kind*—that is, compensation in the form of some commodity. As we have seen, it is very common for employers to buy, or at least partially buy, insurance policies of one kind or another on behalf of their employees. Slightly less obvious as payments-in-kind are paid vacations and holidays. A woman earning $15,000 per year for 2,000 hours of work can have her hourly wage increased from $7.50 to $8.00 by either a straightforward increase in current money payments or by a reduction in her working hours to 1,875 with no reduction in yearly earnings. If her raise comes in the form of an increase in money payments she will receive $1000 (before taxes) more in yearly income that she can use to buy a variety of things (she could even buy time off by giving money back to her employer in exchange for days off). However, if she receives her raise in the form of paid vacation time she is in fact being paid in the form of a commodity: leisure time.

The second general type of fringe benefit is *deferred compensation*—compensation that is earned now but that will be paid in the form of money later on. Pension benefits are the largest proportion of these fringes.

Payments-in-kind.   It is a well-established tenet of economic theory that, *other things equal,* people prefer to receive $X in cash to receiving a commodity that costs $X. The reason is simple. With $X in cash the person can choose to buy the particular commodity, but he or she can also buy a variety of other things. Cash is thus the form of payment that gives the recipient the most discretion and the most options in maximizing utility. In-kind payments are inherently more restrictive, and while they generate utility, they do not ordinarily generate as much as cash payments of equal monetary value.

As might be suspected, however, "other things" are not equal. Specifically, in-kind payments offer employees a sizable tax advantage because, for the most part, they are not taxable under current income-tax regulations. The failure to tax important in-kind payments is a factor that tends to offset their restrictive nature in affecting employee demand for in-kind payments. A worker may prefer $1000 in cash to $1000 in some in-kind payment, but if his or her income- and payroll-tax rates total 25 percent, the comparison is really between $750 in cash and $1000 in the in-kind benefit.

Deferred compensation.   Like payments-in-kind, deferred compensation schemes enjoy a tax advantage as compared to current cash payments. With deferred payments the tax advantage is that the compensation is not taxed until it is received by the worker. In the case of pensions, for example, employers contribute currently to a pension fund, but employees do not obtain access to this fund until they retire. Neither the pension fund *contributions* made on behalf of employees by employers nor the *interest* that compounds when these funds are invested are subject to the personal income tax. Only when the retirement benefits are received does the ex-worker pay taxes, but because of lower income and special tax advantages given to the elderly, the tax rates actually paid are relatively low.

Because of the above-noted tax advantages accorded to pension-fund contributions, employees wishing to save for old age have incentives to do so through a pension fund rather than receiving cash payments and saving from that. In this latter case, all of their compensation would be taxed at the relatively high rates that prevail during their working years, as would the interest they earn on their *savings* toward retirement. Saving through a pension fund defers the taxation of part of one's compensation (the pension-fund contributions) until old age and permits funds for retirement to accumulate on a tax-free basis. What one *loses* with saving through a pension fund is the ability to currently control one's assets: by putting money into a pension fund, one is forgoing the ability to use that money now for routine or emergency needs.

Again, then, two opposing forces are at work on the demand for fringe benefits by employees. With both kinds of benefits there is a loss of discretion in spending one's total compensation—which tends to render fringes inferior to cash payments in generating utility. On the other hand, special tax advantages are accorded to both kinds of benefits as compared with cash payments, which tends to increase the demand for fringes.

Employer Preferences

Suppose employers are totally indifferent between spending $X on wages or $X on fringes. Both expenditures are of equal sums of money and both are equally deductible as a business expense. If so, the composition of total compensation is a matter of indifference to them; only the level of compensation is of concern.

The easiest way to depict the willingness of a firm to offer fringe benefits is through the use of isoprofit curves (introduced in Chapter 8). Suppose that a firm offers a certain type of job for which it must pay at least $X in total compensation in order to attract workers. Let us also suppose that if it paid more than $X its profits would fall below zero. Thus, it must compensate its workers $X per year in order to remain competitive in both the labor and product markets. However, if the *composition* of total compensation is a matter of indifference to the firm, it will be willing to offer any combination of wages and fringes that totals $X in value. The various compensation packages a firm is willing to offer fall along the zero-profit isoprofit curve drawn between wages and fringes (see Figure 11.1).

Any combination of wages and fringes along the isoprofit curve shown in Figure 11.1 would yield the firm equal profits (assuming it could recruit workers). Thus, it is willing to offer $X in wages and no fringe benefits, fringes that cost (say) $300 and wages that equal $(X − 300), or any other combination totaling $X in cost. The slope of the isoprofit curve is *negative,* reflecting the fact that the firm can only increase fringes if it reduces wages (again, because of competitive pressures). Further, in this case the isoprofit curve has a slope of −1, which

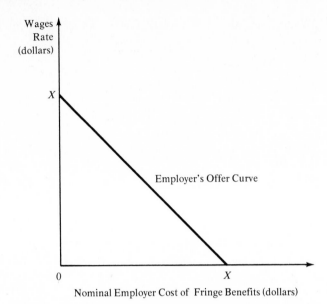

FIGURE 11.1   An Isoprofit Curve Showing the Wage/Fringe
Offers a Firm Might Be Willing to Make
to Its Employees: A Unitary Trade-off

reflects employer indifference about the composition of compensation. If employees want a health-insurance policy costing $300, it will cost them $300 in wages.

There are some reasons to expect that firms might offer fringe benefits to their employees on something other than the dollar-for-dollar basis assumed above. One of the more obvious reasons is that by increasing compensation in the form of fringes rather than wages employers can often avoid taxes and required insurance payments that are levied as a fraction of payroll. Social-security taxes and workers' compensation premiums are examples of costs that generally increase with salaries and wages but not with fringe benefits—thus making it more costly for an employer to increase compensation by increasing salaries than to do it by increasing benefits.[2] Payroll taxes thus tend to flatten the offer curve shown in Figure 11.1 (a $300 increase in fringes could be accompanied by a $280 reduction in wages, say, and the firm would be equally profitable).

There are also more subtle factors that might cause firms to offer fringes to their employees on something other than the dollar-for-dollar basis in Figure 11.1. Some fringe benefits allow firms to attract a certain kind of worker in situations where the use of wage rates would be of questionable legal validity. For example, suppose a firm prefers to hire mature adults, preferably those with children, in the hopes of acquiring a stable, dependable work force. An employer attempting to attract these people by offering them higher wages than single, younger, or much

---

[2]The argument that the presence of social-security taxes levied on the employer increases the costs of granting salary increases holds only for workers who earn less than the maximum taxable earnings base—which in 1981 was $29,000. Earnings beyond $29,000 in 1981 were not subject to the social-security tax.

older adults would risk charges of discrimination. Instead, the firm can accomplish the same effect by offering its employees fringe benefits that are of much more value to the group it is trying to attract than to others. For example, offering *family* coverage under a health-insurance plan has the effect of compensating those with families more than others, because single or childless people cannot really take advantage of the full benefit. Offering dental insurance covering orthodontic work—or tuition assistance for children who attend college—accomplishes similar purposes. Thus, at times fringe benefits allow the firm to give preferential treatment to a group it wants to attract without running afoul of discrimination laws.

The preferential treatment given to some groups of workers, however, has become of increasing concern to employees as fringes have grown in importance. Many families, for example, have dual earners—and have no need of two family medical-insurance policies. In a move to take into account employee dissatisfaction concerning the biases in fringe benefits, some firms have adopted a *cafeteria plan* whereby workers are free to elect their own fringe benefits up to some dollar limit. Instead of receiving a redundant medical insurance policy, for example, a worker already covered by a spouse's insurance policy could elect to receive a longer paid vacation. One firm implementing such a plan found that only 10 percent of its employees elected to receive the same benefits offered by its old program.[3]

Another subtle reason why a firm may prefer to put an extra dollar of compensation into fringe benefits rather than wages (and thus have a flatter offer curve than is shown in Figure 11.1) is found whenever the government regulates profits or controls wages. Regulated monopolies, for example, fearing that the granting of large wage increases would call forth an investigation or outrage public opinion, could hide an increase in compensation by granting increases in fringe benefits that are difficuilt to cost out: a nicer work environment, shortened days in the summer, time off for religious observances, top quality food in the company cafeteria for bargain prices, low-cost loans to employees for buying a home, and so forth.[4] Similar behavior will occur among firms that are having trouble recruiting employees during a period when the government is attempting to control wages for the purposes of fighting inflation. Wages are easy to observe and measure. Many fringe benefits are very difficult to observe and quantify, and they can thus be used to increase compensation without violating wage controls.[5] Examples of fringes that are difficult for wage-control boards to monitor are increased rest times on the job, rules increasing crew sizes in dangerous activities, and better recreational facilities for employees.

On the other hand, some fringe benefits could conceivably increase absenteeism—thus reducing, rather than increasing, the firm's profitability. Life insurance, health insurance, and pensions, for example, are all awarded to current

---

[3] "Making Job Benefits Flexible," *The New York Times,* March 13, 1981, pp. D1, D3.

[4] For further arguments along this line *see* Armen Alchian and Reuben Kessel, "Competition, Monopoly, and the Pursuit of Money," *Aspects of Labor Economics,* ed. H. G. Lewis (Princeton, N.J.: Princeton University Press) 1962.

[5] For a brief discussion of the difficulties inherent in controlling fringe benefits, *see* John Dunlop, "Wage and Price Controls as Seen by a Controller," *Proceedings of the Industrial Relations Research Association,* May 1975, pp. 457–63.

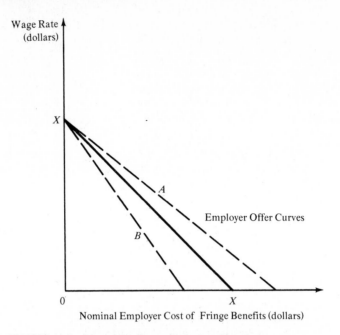

**FIGURE 11.2   Alternative Isoprofit Curves Showing
the Wage/Fringe Offers a Firm Might Be Willing
to Make to Its Employees: Nonunitary Trade-offs**

employees regardless of their actual hours of work during the year (assuming they work enough to keep their jobs). If an increase in compensation comes in the form of increasing one of these benefits, workers' *incomes* are increased—in the sense that they need to save less for "rainy days" and are thus freer to spend their cash income. However, this increase in income is accomplished without an increase in the price of leisure, because the hourly wage has not risen. Recall from Chapter 6 that an increase in income with no change in the price of leisure causes people to want to work less. In this case, workers will not quit their jobs, but they may be absent from work more often.[6] The connection between absenteeism and a fringe benefit is even more obvious in the case of paid sick leave.[7]

Aside from the possibility of contributing to absenteeism, some fringe benefits compress the differentials in compensation between skilled and unskilled workers, thereby reducing the incentives of employees to obtain training for skilled positions.[8] Fringes such as medical insurance and free or discounted mer-

[6]Although there has not been much empirical work on this issue, a study of absenteeism in the paper-and-box industry found it was positively related to pensions and negatively related to wage rates. *See* Steven G. Allen, "Compensation, Safety, and Absenteeism: Evidence from the Paper Industry," *Industrial and Labor Relations Review,* 34 (January 1981): 207–18. *See also,* his "An Empirical Model of Work Attendance," *Review of Economics and Statistics* 63 (February 1981): 77–87.

[7]For evidence on teacher absenteeism, *see* Donald R. Winkler, "The Effects of Sick-Leave Policy on Teacher Absenteeism," *Industrial and Labor Relations Review* 33, 2 (January 1980): 232–40.

[8]See Chapter 9 for the complete argument on how wage differentials affect the incentives of workers to acquire human capital.

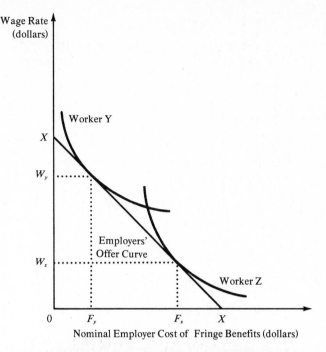

FIGURE 11.3 **Market Determination of the Mix
of Wages and Fringes**

chandise are of equal value to people of similar-sized families, no matter how much they earn. Because their value thus represents a larger percentage of a low-wage worker's compensation, such benefits tend to compress earnings differentials between skilled and unskilled workers.

The major point of our analysis of fringes from the employer's perspective is that a dollar spent on fringes could cost employers more or less than a dollar nominally spent on wages or salaries.[9] In cases where fringes enhance productivity more than a similar expenditure on wages would, the isoprofit curve in Figure 11.1 will flatten. Figure 11.2 shows this as isoprofit curve A. In cases where fringes increase costs or reduce productivity, the isoprofit curve will steepen. In this case—curve B in Figure 11.2—a $300 fringe benefit would have to be accompanied by a $320 fall in wages, say, to keep profits constant.

The Joint Determination of Wages and Fringes

The offer curve in a particular labor market can be obtained by connecting the relevant portions of each firm's zero-profit isoprofit curve, as done in Chapter 8 (see Figure 8.5 on p. 214). In the case where all firms have isoprofit curves with a slope of -1 (see Figure 11.3), the offer curve is a straight line with a negative

---

[9]Many fringe benefits, like pensions and paid vacations, become more generous as the worker's tenure with the firm increases. In fact, in most firms, workers are not even eligible to receive retirement benefits unless they have worked at least 10 years for the firm. These policies are clearly designed to reduce costly turnover, but they are more a matter of the *timing* of compensation than anything else. We will discuss issues regarding the timing of compensation later in this chapter.

Example 11.1
The Wage/Fringe Trade-Off
in the Collective-Bargaining Process

At times, the wage/fringe trade-off can be directly observed in the collective bargaining process, although management and unions are usually reluctant to explicitly acknowledge that workers might be paying for their own fringe benefits. In 1950, however, the United Automobile Workers (the UAW) called a strike against Chrysler over the issue of pensions. Chrysler had promised a pension benefit to its workers for the first time, but it had not promised to put aside current funds to *guarantee* retirees that they would obtain benefits in the future. Fearing that Chrysler could become bankrupt in the future, the UAW wanted this pension promise to be backed up with current funding, and it called a strike. (As of 1981, Chrysler was teetering on the edge of bankruptcy.) The unions last offer to Chrysler before the strike is an excellent illustration of a wage/fringe trade-off: it asked Chrysler either to pay 6 cents per hour (per worker) to a pension fund and 4 cents to buy medical insurance or to give workers a 10 cents per hour raise in wages!

SOURCE: *The Daily Labor Report,* January 17, 1950, p. A–17.

---

and unitary slope along which employees will locate. Those employees (like *Y* in Figure 11.3) who attach relatively great importance to the availability of currently spendable cash will choose to accept offers where total compensation comes largely in the form of wages. Other employees, who may be less worried about current cash income but more interested in the tax advantages of fringe benefits, will accept offers where fringe benefits form a higher proportion of total compensation (see the curve for Worker Z in Figure 11.3).[10]

Figure 11.3 shows that workers receiving more generous fringe benefits pay for them by receiving lower wages, other things being equal. Further, if employer isoprofit curves have a unitary slope, a fringe benefit that costs the employer $1 to provide will cost workers $1 in wages. In other words, economic theory suggests that workers pay for their own fringe benefits!

Actually observing the trade-off between wages and fringe benefits is not an easy matter. Because firms that pay high wages usually also offer very good fringe benefits, it often appears to the casual observer that wages and fringes are *positively* related. Casual observation in this case is misleading, however, because it does not allow for the influences of *other factors*—such as the demands of the

---

[10]The indifference curves in Figure 11.3 are drawn with the typical convexity. One assumption underlying this convexity is that as *fringes* increase, the decrease in currently spendable cash that one is willing to bear declines owing to the loss of discretionary control in spending one's income. The other assumption is that as *current wages* increase and workers advance into higher income-tax brackets, the tax advantages offered by fringe benefits become ever more attractive (which causes the indifference curves to steepen).

job and the quality of workers involved—that influence total compensation. The other factors are most conveniently controlled for statistically, and the few statistical studies on this subject *do* tend to support the prediction of a negative relationship between wages and fringe benefits.[11]

The policy consequences of a negative wage/fringe trade-off are enormously important, because government legislation designed to improve fringe benefits might well be paid for by workers in the form of lower future wage increases.

Policy Application: Pension Reform Legislation

Pension plans provided by employers are of two general types: 1. the *defined-contribution* plan and 2. the *defined-benefit* plan. The least common is a *defined contribution* plan, where the employer merely promises to contribute a certain amount each year to a fund to which the employee has access upon retirement. The fund is increased each year by employer—and also perhaps by employee—contributions and by returns from investments made by the fund's managers. One's retirement benefits depend solely on the size of the fund at the age of retirement.

More common are *defined benefit* pension plans where the employer promises employees a certain benefit upon retirement. This benefit may be a fixed sum per month or it may be a fixed fraction of one's earnings prior to retirement. In either case, employers guarantee the size of the pension benefit—and it is up to them to make sure that the funds are there when the promised benefits need to be paid.

The *vesting* provision of any pension plan is the rule about who becomes eligible to receive a pension. If a plan is unvested, any worker who quits the company before retirement age loses all rights to a pension benefit. If workers are vested, they can receive a pension from Company X even if they quit X before retirement age and work elsewhere. How much they receive from X at retirement, of course, depends on their length of service with X and their preretirement earnings; however, the point is that they receive *something* from X upon retirement if they are vested.

In 1974 Congress passed the Employee Retirement Income Security Act (ERISA) that, among other things, required private-sector employers to adopt liberalized vesting rules. The intent of the legislation was to help employees by making it more likely that they will receive pensions in their old age. However, as we have seen with other programs designed to help workers, good intentions can sometimes be undone by unintended side effects. What are the side effects of ERISA's vesting provisions?

From the employees' perspective, rules that entitle them to become vested, or vested sooner, enhance their welfare if nothing else in the compensation package

---

[11]Empirical studies of the trade-offs between wages and pensions are as yet few in number. However, the studies that do exist indicate workers pay—perhaps dollar-for-dollar—for their pensions in the form of lower wages. For a review of these studies, see Ronald Ehrenberg and Robert Smith, "A Framework for Evaluating State and Local Government Pension Reform," in *Public Sector Labor Markets,* eds. Peter Mieszkowski and George E. Peterson (Washington, D.C.: The Urban Institute, 1981). For a discussion of data requirements for estimating these trade-offs—and estimated wage trade-offs for both pensions and paid holidays—see Ehrenberg and Smith, "Who Pays for Pension Reform?" in *Coming of Age: Toward a National Retirement Income Policy,* issued in conjunction with the report of the President's Commission on Pension Policy, 1981.

is changed. They are not penalized as much for voluntarily leaving an employer—nor are they as economically vulnerable to being fired. However, the value different workers attach to liberalized vesting may vary widely. Suppose ERISA forced a plant to vest its employees after 10, rather than 15, years of work. Employees who plan on working for a given employer less than ten years do not benefit at all from the liberalized vesting mandated by ERISA; neither do workers who have more than 15 years of service with the company. On the other hand, workers who might want to change employers after 10–15 years of service—or who might be fired during that period—stand to gain from liberalized vesting.

From the employers' perspective, ERISA's vesting rules impose costs, because they make it possible for more workers to qualify for pensions. For example, it was estimated that the pension costs of nonvesting employers would rise by 3–26 percent as a result of ERISA's vesting rules.[12] Will firms simply absorb these costs, or will they force workers to pay for their more liberal pension benefits in the form of lower wages?

Our theory suggests that employers will not—and in a competitive market, cannot—absorb the added pension costs. Those firms for which pension costs are increased will have to hold the line on future wage increases in order to remain competitive in the product market, and over time the wages they pay will fall below the level that would have held had it not been for the pension-reform legislation.[13]

Unfortunately, the decline in wages that will occur in the firms affected by ERISA's vesting rules does *not* simply mean that worker welfare is unchanged. Indeed, it can be shown (see Figure 11.4) that *if* the workers employed by firms with illiberal vesting are both *informed* and *mobile,* their utility will be negatively affected by the ERISA vesting regulation. Suppose, for example, that before ERISA Person A worked for a nonvesting employer, receiving the relatively high wage of W_1 and a low level (P_0) of expected retirement benefits owing to the slim chances of receiving a pension. Person B, who obviously cares more than A about pensions—as can be seen by the different-shaped indifference curve—takes a job promising a relatively large and secure pension (P_1) but paying a lower current wage (W_0). Suppose also that ERISA in effect makes all levels of expected pension benefits below P_1 illegal by forcing employers with pension plans to provide vesting after 10 years.

Competitive pressures force all wage/pension offers to lie along the zero-profit curve, *XX,* in Figure 11.4. Thus, when the pension promises of A's employer are forcibly increased to P_1, the wage offer in that firm will eventually fall to W_0. For Person A—a person who is not willing to give up much in the way of current compensation to obtain a better pension—utility is reduced from A_1 to A_0. In other words, the effect of a law that increases pension benefits may well be to

[12]Norman Ture, *The Future of Private Pension Plans* (Washington, D.C.: The American Enterprise Institute for Public Policy Research, 1976), p. 89.

[13]The two studies that have looked at the effects of vesting on wages have both found that nonvesting (public) employers pay higher wages, other things equal, than ones who vest. See Ehrenberg and Smith, "A Framework for Evaluating State and Local Government Pension Reform," for more details.

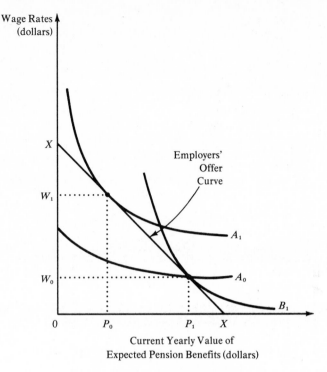

Wage Rates (dollars)

Current Yearly Value of
Expected Pension Benefits (dollars)

**FIGURE 11.4   The Effects of ERISA in a Properly
Functioning Market**

reduce wages—with the consequence that it reduces the utility of people who
have the strongest preferences for current, as opposed to deferred, income.

Under certain circumstances, however, the ERISA vesting rules would enhance worker welfare. For example, take the case where people with preferences
like Person C in Figure 11.5 *thought* they were working for an employer who,
while perhaps not vesting their pension rights, would in fact employ them until
they retired. Later, they find out that this employer is likely to fire them before
retirement and that, if so, they will lose their entire pension. These people *believed* themselves to be at point L, receiving P_1 in expected pensions, W_1 in
wages, and C_2 in utility. In actuality, they are, at point M, receiving P_0 in pension
benefits and C_0 in utility. If ERISA forces the expected pension level to rise to P_1
by requiring vesting, their *actual* utility will increase from C_0 to C_1, despite the
fact that their wages fall from W_1 to W_0 (they move in actuality from point M to
N in Figure 11.5). ERISA would also improve the welfare of people like C if they
were at point M and, because of a lack of mobility, could not find a job with
another employer that would place them at point N.

The major point of this discussion is that if product markets are competitive—
and firms are forced to operate on their zero-profit isoprofit curves—workers will
pay for ERISA-mandated increases in pension benefits in the long run. Workers
immobilized by ignorance or lack of choice may be better off with government-
mandated floors on pension benefits, despite the downward pressure on their

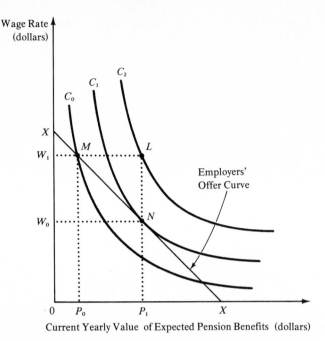

FIGURE 11.5 Effects of ERISA in an Uninformed Market

wages. However, there are also circumstances in which workers would be made worse off by the mandated increases in expected pension benefits. Careful study in advance of reform legislation may be desirable to avoid hurting the people government is intending to help.

MOTIVATING WORKERS: INCENTIVE PAY

Beginning in Chapter 1, this book has repeated the theme that unless workers are ignorant or immobile, the contracts they make with employers represent a mutually beneficial transaction. However, as in any transaction, each side will try to get the most it can while giving as little as it must. Employees may find that supervisors who were pleasant to them during job interviews are not quite as pleasant or easygoing after they take the job, that overtime is expected of them on a regular basis, or that their duties include more than they were told. If things get too bad they can quit—or, if they are in a union, they can protest through union channels. However, because both of these courses of action entail time and effort, employees may just decide to put up with unexpected disadvantages if they are not too serious.

Employers are faced with another set of problems. Work, by its very nature, is unpleasant to one degree or another. Some employees will try to do as little of it as possible, while still retaining their jobs. This behavior, called *shirking*, may take the form of not putting forth maximum work effort, doing poor quality work, or being absent a lot. Shirking can be minimized by close supervision, but it is not always easy to closely monitor the work of employees. Thus, it is often necessary to find other ways to induce workers not to shirk. Several kinds of compensation schemes have been designed to motivate employees to work industriously.

Firms can offer financial rewards for hard work in two ways. 1. They can offer *incentive pay*—that is, they can pay workers directly for the desired outcome; or 2. they can reward those employees who have been consistently industrious and reliable with high future compensation.

The Basis of Pay

The agreements between employers and employees concerning job duties and compensation can be considered as *contracts,* whether or not they are formally written. As mentioned briefly in Chapter 1, there are two basic types of pay provisions in labor contracts. One rewards employees for the *time* they work, and the other rewards them for some *result* of their work.[14] Some contracts, however, contain a hybrid system of rewards.

The most common reward structure is payment for time worked, with about 86 percent of U.S. employees paid either by the hour or by the month. When employees are paid for time at work, it becomes management's challenge to motivate them not to shirk during that time. An alternative that would appear to alleviate the problem of shirking is payment by results, or incentive pay. In some industries—particularly the garment industry—workers are paid for each piece of output produced. In other firms, a *standard time*—60 minutes, say—is allowed for a given task. If the task is completed *within* that time the employee is paid for the full 60 minutes regardless of the actual time spent on the task; however, if the worker takes longer than 60 minutes to complete the job, he or she is paid for the *actual* time spent. In still other instances, workers share in the profits of the firm or receive a fraction of the value of the items they sell *(commissions)*. In all these cases, workers are paid at least somewhat proportionally to their output or to the degree their employer prospers. Because such payment schemes serve as an obvious incentive to work industriously, one is led to wonder why only 14 percent of U.S. workers are paid on an incentive basis. Selecting the basis for pay is ultimately a matter of satisfying the interests of both employer and employee.

Employee preferences.   If employees were told that their average earnings over the years under a time-payment system would be equal to their earnings under an individual incentive-pay scheme, they would probably choose to be paid on a *time* basis. Why? Earnings under a piece rate or commission system depend on the thought and energy one is able to bring to the job. There are days and even weeks in any person's life when one is depressed, preoccupied, tired, or otherwise distracted from maximum work effort. There are other periods when one is exceptionally productive. If employees are paid on a piece-rate basis, their earnings

---

[14]This distinction concerning labor contracts is analyzed in Herbert A. Simon, "A Formal Theory of the Employment Relationship," *Econometrica* 19, 3 (July 1951): 293–305; and more recently in Joseph E. Stiglitz, "Incentives, Risk, and Information: Notes Towards a Theory of Hierarchy," *Bell Journal of Economics* 6 (Autumn 1975): 552–79.

could be highly *variable* over time because of the somewhat uncontrollable swings in productivity. The variability in their income could cause anxiety owing to the possibility that several low-productivity months could be strung together, making it difficult to meet mortgage payments and other obligations.

Because of this anxiety about less productive periods of time, employees prefer the certainty of time-based pay to the uncertainty of piece-rate pay if both schemes pay the same average wage over time. In order to induce employees to accept piece-rate pay, employers would have to pay higher average wages over time—that is, a compensating differential would have to exist to compensate workers for the anxiety associated with variations in their earnings. Conversely, to obtain more certainty in their stream of earnings, employees would probably be willing to accept a somewhat lower average wage.

Employer considerations.   The willingness of employers to pay a premium in order to induce employees to accept piece rates depends on the costs and benefits to employers of incentive-pay schemes. If workers are paid on a *time* basis, the *employer* accepts the risk of variations in their productivity. When they are exceptionally productive, profits increase; when they are less productive, profits decline. Employers, however, may be less anxious about these *variations* than employees are. They typically have more assets and can thus weather the lean periods more comfortably than can individual workers. More important, perhaps, employers usually have several employees, and the chances are that not all will suffer the same swings in productivity at the same time (unless there is a morale problem in the firm). Thus, employers may not be as willing to pay for income certainty as are workers.

Employers must also consider, however, that incentive-pay schemes—such as piece rates—may reduce the variations in profits over time, but they will also increase the *level* of productivity. Because workers directly benefit from their own diligence in a piece-rate system, they may work much harder. A full analysis of these productivity-related incentives and the costs of implementing them must take into account differences between *individual* and *group* incentive-pay plans.

Individual Rewards: Piece Rates and Commissions

The Bureau of Labor Statistics found in 1973 that nearly half of the production workers in U.S. auto-repair shops were paid incentive rates.[15] Roughly one-quarter received some fraction of the labor costs charged to the customer (they were paid by *commission,* in essence), and the other quarter were paid a flat rate *(piece rate)* for each kind of repair performed. The big advantage of these compensation schemes from the employer's perspective is that they induce employees to adopt a set of work goals that are consistent with those of their employer. Employees paid a piece rate are motivated to work quickly, while those paid by commission are induced to very thoroughly evaluate the servicing needs of the firm's customers. Morever, these inducements exist without the need for, and expense of, close monitoring by the firm's supervisors. Auto-repair shops, however, provide a spe-

---

[15]Sandra King, ''Incentive and Time Pay in Auto Dealer Repair Shops, *Monthly Labor Review* 98, 9 (September 1975): 45–48.

cific example of several general disadvantages to individually based incentive-pay schemes. These general problems include 1. maintaining quality standards, 2. misusing equipment, 3. setting the rate, and 4. measuring output.

— cheating?

Maintaining quality standards. Workers paid by the job are motivated to work quickly, but they are also motivated to have minimal regard for quality. Workers paid by commission are motivated to be so thorough in ferreting out servicing needs that they may fix things that are not broken. Both bases for compensation thus create a need for close supervisory attention to the quality of work performed—a need and an expense that in many cases will offset the supervisory savings associated with incentive pay.

Equipment misuse. Allied to the problem of work quality is the problem of equipment misuse. Workers receiving incentive pay are motivated to work so quickly that machines or tools are often damaged or otherwise misused. It is often asserted, for example, that piece-rate workers disengage safety devices on ma-

---

Example 11.2
Incentive Pay and Output—or "You Get What You Pay For"

Paying workers for a given output can lead to unexpected uses of employee resources and time. As noted in this chapter, piece rates tend to induce workers to emphasize quantity over quality, but the total effects of piece-rate schemes also depend on just what "output" is being paid for.

There is a (probably apocryphal) story that when Soviet farm labor was compensated according to the number of acres planted, plowing was done too hastily and seeds were sown too far apart for high productivity. In an effort to improve output, the Soviet Union began to compensate farm workers on the basis of yield per acre. This caused farmers to invest too many resources (time, fertilizer) per acre and not plant extensively enough, and costs rose. Only when they seized upon the idea of paying farmers on the basis of the difference between the value of output and the costs of production (that is, *profit*) did farmers have the incentives to take into account output and costs.

Another example of the importance of understanding how incentive pay can affect output comes from Great Britain. Instead of compensating dentists on the basis of "contact hours" with patients, The British National Health Service decided (for a while) to compensate dentists on the basis of cavities filled. The result was that the incidence of tooth decay identified by dentists increased substantially and the time it took to fill cavities dropped from 18 minutes to six minutes per filling! It is obvious that this new basis for compensation was of questionable benefit to the patient.

SOURCES: Assar Lindbeck, *The Political Economy of the New Left* (New York: Harper & Row, 1971), p. 71; John Pencavel, "Piecework and On-the-Job Screening" (New York: Department of Economics, Stanford University, June 1975), p. 4.

chinery in their desire to maximize output. This problem is mitigated to the extent that equipment damage causes *downtime* that results in lost employee earnings.

Setting the rate.   A third problem, probably more associated with piece rates than with commissions, is setting the rate. For example, it may be standard practice in the auto-repair industry to assume that an engine tune-up will require two hours of work and to translate this time requirement into a "per job" piece rate. Suppose, however, some new tool or electronic device is adopted that reduces the time required for a tune-up. A new piece rate will have to be adopted, but how do the shop's owners determine the standard time requirement for tune-ups now? The best way may be to observe mechanics using the new devices, but if these workers know they are being observed for purposes of setting a new rate they will deliberately work slowly so that the time requirement is overestimated—in order to drive up the piece rate. The problem is compounded in industries facing frequent changes in products or technology. In the women's apparel industry around the turn of the century, for example, it was common to have seasonal strikes— coinciding with seasonal changes in fashions—over piece rates.[16]

Measuring output.   A fourth reason why individual incentive-pay schemes are not more widely used is the problem of measuring and motivating individual *output*. The output of an auto mechanic, salesperson, or a dressmaker is relatively easy to measure in terms of quantity, but what about that of an office manager or auto assembly-line worker? The manager has a number of duties and deals with a multitude of problems—combining them into a single index of output would be next to impossible. Assembly-line workers, on the other hand, may have an easily-counted output, but this output is not individually controlled. In both cases, *individual* incentive pay would be arbitrary or useless; however, *group* incentives might be attractive in these situations.

Group Incentive Pay

In situations where individual output is hard to monitor or control, group incentive-pay schemes have sometimes been adopted. Their intent, like that of individual incentive-pay systems, is to bring the interests of workers in line with those of the employer. The form these pay systems take are analogous to the schemes discussed above. In some cases, work groups will be paid by the piece for output produced *by the group*. In other cases, the employees will share in the profits of the firm each year—a close analogue to the commission basis for individual pay. In still other cases, the workers might *own* the firm and split the profits among themselves.[17]

---

[16]Louis Levine, *The Women's Garment Workers* (New York: B. W. Huebsch, 1924), p. 42. The observation that a stable technology is important for the success of an incentive-pay system is also made by Sumner H. Slichter, James J. Healy, and E. Robert Livernash, *The Impact of Collective Bargaining on Management* (Washington: The Brookings Institution, 1960), p. 519.

[17]For a detailed treatment of worker-owned enterprise—the most widespread example of which is in Yugoslavia—see Jaroslav Vanek, *The General Theory of Labor-Managed Market Economies* (Ithaca, N.Y.: The Cornell University Press, 1970).

The drawback to group incentives is that groups are composed of individuals, and it is at the individual level that decisions about shirking are ultimately made. A person who works very hard to increase group output or firm profits winds up splitting the fruits of his or her labor with everyone else in the firm. Very little of the person's extra efforts are captured by him or her—most go to other people, who may not have put out extra effort. Group incentives, then, are sometimes no incentive at all. People come to realize that they can reap the rewards of someone else's hard work without doing any extra work of their own, and that if they do put out extra work, the rewards mainly go to others. Such schemes thus give workers incentives to cheat on their fellow employees by shirking.

In very small groups, however, cheating may be easy to detect, and group punishments—such as ostracism—can be effectively used to eliminate it. In these cases, group incentive-pay systems can accomplish their aims (subject, of course, to all the drawbacks of individual incentive-pay systems noted above). However, if the group of workers receiving incentive pay is large, cheating (shirking) probably cannot be effectively handled. Group incentive-pay schemes thus become less effective as group size increases.

Earnings Under Piece and Time Rates

Two observations lead to the prediction that workers on incentive pay earn more per hour than comparable workers paid on a time basis. First, if workers have a preference for being paid on a time basis, employers will have to pay a premium—a compensating wage differential—to induce them to accept an incentive-pay scheme. This earnings differential would compensate workers for accepting the risks associated with incentive pay. Second, the workers most likely to accept a job with incentive pay are those most likely to be successful at it: the fastest, most intense workers.

Although there are few studies of this issue, the prediction that incentive-pay workers earn more appears to hold up. A 1960s study of punch-press operators in Chicago found that piece-rate workers earned about 9 percent more per hour of work than did those paid an hourly wage.[18] More recent research by the Bureau of Labor Statistics found that auto repair workers paid on an incentive basis earned 20–50 percent more per hour than those paid on a time basis.[19]

Other Kinds of Incentive Pay

Although used relatively infrequently, firms have also devised incentive pay schemes other than piece rates, commissions, and profit sharing in order to solve particular production problems. These plans usually provide for the payment of some kind of bonus if a desired outcome is achieved. For example, a firm attempting to induce employees to avoid injuries on the job might give a quarterly bonus to any worker who remains uninjured during that quarter.

---

[18]John Pencavel, "Work Effort, On-the-Job Screening, and Alternative Methods of Remuneration," in *Research in Labor Economics*, vol. 1, ed. Ronald Ehrenberg (Greenwich, Conn.: JAI Press, 1977), pp. 225–58.

[19]King, "Incentive and Time Pay in Auto Dealer Repair Shops," p. 46.

Some of the most imaginative incentive pay systems have been directed at the problem of absenteeism. There are two in particular that have achieved notice in the oral tradition of labor economics. A manufacturing plant during the 1940s coped with absenteeism by holding a daily raffle. The prizes were various consumable and durable items of special value to householders during those shortage-prone years. However, to have a chance to win, a worker had to be present. Absenteeism apparently fell dramatically.

Another scheme to reduce absenteeism was adopted by an automobile manufacturer. This involved awarding daily points to each employee who was present for work—points which could be accumulated and redeemed for prizes, such as tickets to popular vacation attractions. The wrinkle in this plan was that the points were not given to the worker, but were instead given to the worker's spouse! With the spouse helping to monitor work behavior it is said that absenteeism problems were greatly reduced.[20]

INTERNAL LABOR MARKETS AND THE TIME PATTERN OF COMPENSATION

Given the difficulties and disadvantages of implementing the common forms of individual or group incentive pay, firms have generally sought methods of motivating workers using a time-based pay system. Time-based approaches to motivation usually offer delayed rewards to workers only *after* diligent effort has been expended by the worker and observed by the employer over a long period. The prospect of these rewards gives workers incentives to work hard. The rewards may come either in the form of a bonus after years of loyal effort or in the form of a promotion. However, a common requirement for both forms of rewards is a *long-term relationship* between employer and employee. One way to encourage a long-term relationship is for firms to adopt *internal labor markets*, wherein promotions are exclusively or primarily done from within the organization.

Internal Labor Markets and Delayed Rewards

Recall from Chapter 5 that firms sometimes create an *internal labor market*, wherein hiring is done only at certain *entry-level jobs*, and all other jobs are filled from within the firm. This hiring and promotion system serves in part as a substitute for the careful screening of job applicants. Workers are hired at low levels of responsibility and then observed over time to determine their actual productive characteristics. Internal labor markets, however, can also be useful in constructing a system of deferred compensation for the purpose of motivating employees. The long-term association between employer and employee fosters opportunities for both deferred payments and the long-term monitoring of employee behavior necessary to make the system work.

---

[20]We are grateful to Walter Oi for this example. This fringe benefit is an excellent illustration of how such benefits can be tailored to attract certain groups of workers. Giving points to spouses is only of benefit to married workers—and if married workers tend to be more dependable, absenteeism could be reduced by attracting members of this group to the plant.

Example 11.3
Compensation Schemes to Modify Worker Behavior in Other Times and Places

Employers, like psychologists, confront the problem of whether positive or negative incentives—rewards or punishments—are the better approach to changing behavior. Farmers in colonial America, for example, faced the problem of inducing their indentured servants not to run away before the end of their contractual period (and thus before the farmers' investment costs had been recouped). They adopted several negative incentives for runaways; extension of the indenture period or corporal punishment were the most common forms of penalty. However, they also used the positive incentive of *freedom dues*—a lump-sum payment of cash or property paid to servants at the end of their indenture period—that would be forfeited if the servant ran away. The use of freedom dues illustrates how deferred compensation can be used to motivate employee cooperation over long periods of time.

The same dilemma of whether to use positive or negative incentives also confronted Japanese employers in the early 1900s, when they were faced with the vexing problem of absenteeism. At times, absent employees were sought out and subjected to physical torture; in other cases, wages were confiscated unless a certain consecutive number of days were worked. As argued in Chapter 8, however, employers offering disagreeable conditions of employment will have more difficulties attracting workers in a competitive labor market than will employers offering comparable jobs without the unpleasant conditions. Thus, harsh penalties for *unwanted* behavior are not costless for employers, which has often led them to adopt positive rewards for *wanted* behavior. In Japan, for example, payments in addition to regular wages were frequently made to workers who had worked without absence for an entire month. Sometimes the bonuses were sent to the workers' families in an attempt to induce parents to encourage regular work attendance among their children. At other times the bonuses were paid to *groups* of workers with good group attendance records; often these bonuses took the form of improved worker dormitory facilities for the work group.

These compensation schemes in other times and other places indicate that the careful structuring of pay for the purpose of changing worker behavior is not the exclusive invention of modern management science.

SOURCES: David Galenson, ''The Market Evaluation of Human Capital: The Case of Indentured Servitude,'' *Journal of Political Economy* 89, 3 (June 1981): 446–67; Koji Taira, *Economic Development and the Labor Market in Japan* (New York: Columbia University Press, 1970), pp. 120–121.

If employees are hired with the expectation that they will spend an entire career with a firm—an expectation that is certainly encouraged by a policy of promoting only from within—then the critical element in their choice of an employer is the *present value of their career earnings*. That is, they will be concerned about their likely earnings over their entire *career* and not just the pay on the job for which they are initially hired. A firm with an internal labor market must offer a *stream* of earnings over time whose overall present value is equivalent to that offered by other firms competing in the same labor market.

To say that the present value of an earnings stream must be equivalent to that paid elsewhere does *not* imply that the wages offered for each job or at each stage in one's career must be exactly equal to those paid by other firms. Firms that pay low wages initially, but offer high earnings later on, may be very competitive with firms offering initially higher wages but not raising them much over time.

For example, suppose a firm offered a 10-year job sequence where the workers were paid $15,000 in each of the first five years and $18,000 for the next five years. Using a discount rate of 7 percent, an income stream with the same present value could be achieved by a labor-market competitor who offered $10,000 for each of the first five years and paid $25,000 per year for the last five! Thus it should be clear that firms offering workers *careers,* and not just jobs, have a fairly wide latitude in the way they sequence compensation within the constraint of having to offer career earnings whose present value is comparable to that paid by other firms for the same type of worker. It is this latitude, of course, that allows these firms to defer some of a worker's compensation until the end of his or her career.

The advantages of being able to defer rewards to the worker are captured by both employer and employee. The employer need not devote as many resources to supervision each year as would otherwise be the case, because the firm has several years in which to identify shirkers and withhold from them the reward. Workers are less likely to take chances and shirk their responsibilities because the penalties for being caught and fired are forfeiture of a large reward. Because all employees work harder than they otherwise would, their total compensation tends to be higher also.

Employment Contracts and the Sequencing of Pay

We have just argued that employers with internal labor markets have options for *sequencing* workers' pay while still offering jobs with the same *present value* of career compensation as paid by the market generally.[21] In such a setting, it may be beneficial to both employer and employee to arrange workers' pay over time so that employees are "underpaid" early in their careers and "overpaid" later on. This sequencing of pay will increase worker productivity and enable firms to pay higher present values of compensation than otherwise.

A company that pays low to begin with but pays well later on increases the incentives of its employees to work industriously. Once in the job, an employee has incentives to work diligently in order to qualify for the overpayment later on. One feasible compensation sequencing scheme would pay workers *less* than their marginal product early in their careers and *more* than their marginal product later on. This scheme, however, must satisfy two conditions. First, the present value of the earnings streams offered to employees must at least be equal to alternative streams offered to workers in the labor market; if not, the firm cannot attract the workers it wants. Since pay that is deferred into the future is discounted, deferred

---

[21] Our discussion here draws on Edward Lazear, "Why Is There Mandatory Retirement?," *Journal of Political Economy* 87, 6 (December 1979): 1261–84.

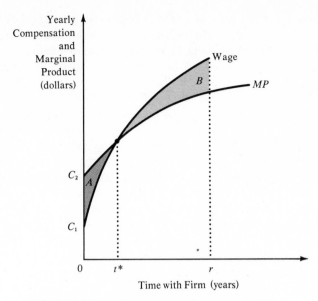

**FIGURE 11.6   A Compensation Scheme Designed
to Increase Worker Motivation**

sums must be larger the higher is the discount rate (or *present-orientedness)* of
workers (see Chapter 9). Second, the scheme must also satisfy the equilibrium
conditions that firms maximize profits and do not earn supernormal profits. If
profits are not maximized the firm's existence is threatened; if firms make supernormal profits, new firms will be induced to enter the market. Thus, in neither
case would equilibrium exist.

The above two conditions will be met if hiring is done until the present value
of one's career-long marginal product *(MP)* equals the present value of one's
career earnings stream. (This career-long condition is the multiyear analogue of
the single-year profit conditions discussed in Chapter 3 and the two-year profit-
maximization criteria discussed in Chapter 5.) Thus, for firms choosing the "underpayment now, overpayment later" compensation scheme to be competitive in
both the labor and product markets, the present value of the yearly amounts by
which *MP exceeds* compensation early on must equal the present value of the later
amounts by which *MP falls short* of pay.

The above compensation plan is diagrammed in Figure 11.6. We assume that
MP rises slightly over one's career but that in the first *t** years of employment,
compensation remains below *MP*. At some point in one's career with the firm—
year *t** in the diagram—compensation begins to exceed *MP*. From *t** onward are
the years in which diligent employees are rewarded by receiving compensation in
excess of what they could receive elsewhere (namely, their *MP*). For the firm to
be competitive in both the labor and product markets, the *present value* of area *A*
in the diagram must equal the *present value* of area *B*. (Area *B* is larger than area
A in Figure 11.6 because values received farther in the future are subjected to
heavier discounting when present values are calculated.)

To be sure, there are risks to both parties in making this kind of agreement. Employees agreeing to this compensation scheme take a chance that they may be fired without cause or that their employer may go bankrupt before they have collected their reward in the years beyond t^*. It is easy to see that employers will have some incentives to renege since older workers are being paid a wage that exceeds their immediate value (at the margin) to the firm.

On the other hand, employers who do not wish to fire people face the risk that older, "overpaid" employees will stay on the job longer than is necessary to collect their reward—that is, they will stay on longer than time r in Figure 11.6. Knowing that their current wage is greater than the wage they can get elsewhere—since it reflects payment for more than current output—older employees will have incentives to keep working longer than is profitable for the firm.

A partial solution to these problems of risk is to agree on a formal employment contract that has two elements. One element protects older employees from arbitrary discharge by (a) stipulating the grounds under which employees can be discharged and (b) guaranteeing "seniority rights" for older workers. According to these seniority provisions, workers with the shortest duration of employment with the firm are usually laid off first when the firm cuts back its work force. Without these seniority rights, firms might be tempted to lay off older workers, whose wage is greater than MP, and keep the younger ones (who are paid less than MP at this point in their career).

The second element of a formal employment contract designed to reduce the risk inherent in this compensation plan is some form of retirement clause. Unless firms can induce workers to retire before the present value of area B in Figure 11.6 exceeds that of A—or unless they can force older employees to accept wage cuts so that after year r their wage equals MP—employers will not agree to the compensation-sequencing plan under discussion.

In some instances, formal employment contracts have included a mandatory retirement age, which prior to 1978 was normally set at age 65. Under these agreements, employees would have to retire at age 65 whether they wanted to or not. In other cases there may be inducements offered for voluntary early retirement. For example, the 1965 contract between the automakers and the United Automobile Workers permitted workers to retire as early as age 55—assuming they had 30 years of service. Moreover, the monthly pension benefit before age 65 was much larger than after 65, yielding an average present value of early retirement benefits equal to $18,365—compared to a present value of $9,700 associated with retirement at age 65.[22]

In making an early retirement decision, one must compare the utility generated by one's income and leisure streams if retirement occurs at 65 (say) with that generated by early retirement and its associated streams of leisure and pension income. When the stream of pension income associated with early retirement is increased in some way, the utility associated with early retirement is enhanced. Inducing early retirement by essentially bribing people to retire makes economic

---

[22]See Richard Burkhauser, "The Pension Acceptance Decision of Older Workers," *Journal of Human Resources* 14 (Winter 1979): 63–75.

sense in the case where older employees are paid more than they are currently worth.

Formal agreements cannot remove risks altogether, however. There is, on the employee side, no assurance that the firm will be in business during the employee's older years. Even large, once-profitable firms go bankrupt, close down plants, or are bought out by other firms—all of which can have the effect of reducing jobs or wage opportunities for older workers in the firm. Whereas most *pension* promises are backed up by a separate fund that remains even if the employer goes bankrupt, there is really nothing to back up a promise of future pay increases. On the employer side, mandatory retirement agreements can be, and have been, voided by federal legislation. Amendments made to the Age Discrimination in Employment Act in 1978, for example, outlawed agreements that contained age 65 as the minimum age of mandatory retirement. Age 70 is now the earliest anyone can be forced to retire.

Thus, *formal* contracts safeguarding the deferral of earnings to late in one's career are not riskless. Even more risky are *implicit contracts*—contracts that are understood to exist but that have not been formally written and signed by both parties. In these contracts, the employee is protected from arbitrary dismissal only by the need for the employer to recruit *other* workers. If a certain employer gains a reputation for firing older workers, despite an implicit agreement not to do so, that employer will have trouble recruiting new employees (as noted earlier)— which is some incentive to adhere to the implicit contract. However, if the company is in permanent decline, if it faces an unusually adverse market, or if information on company employment policies is not easily or accurately available to applicants, the incentives to renege on implicit contracts are probably very strong.

Pensions as Deferred Payments

One way to assure employees of receiving their delayed reward is to provide a pension. According to statistics published by the American Council of Life Insurance, the average yearly retirement benefit paid by private pension plans in 1978 was $1,752.[23] While this sum does not strike one as overwhelmingly large, a yearly payment of this size beginning at age 65 and lasting 15 years (the average life expectancy of a 65-year-old) requires a fund of $16,000 to finance it at a 7 percent rate of interest. Thus, giving pensioners $1,752 per year from age 65 until death is equivalent to giving the average retiree a lump-sum payment of $16,000. If the pension benefits were more generous, the lump-sum equivalent increases proportionately. For example, the average city employee in Pennsylvania receives $3,800 per year in retirement benefits, implying a lump-sum equivalent of $34,700 (at a 7 percent interest rate).

It is obvious, then, that pensions represent the equivalent of a deferred payment paid to workers at the end of their careers. Under ERISA, the money to finance this payment must be set aside each year by the employer in a separate fund so that employees have some assurance of receiving their reward even if the

---

[23]American Council of Life Insurance, *Pension Facts 1978–1979* (Washington, D.C.: American Council of Life Insurance, 1979), p. 15.

firm goes bankrupt. As discussed in this chapter, firms offering their employees pensions must pay lower wages, other things equal, in order to remain competitive. Thus, pensions offer a mechanism whereby spendable pay is "low" during one's working years but a reward is received later on.

The strongest incentives for diligence under a pension scheme would exist if the pension were not vested. Nonvested employees can be threatened with loss of a pension up to the day before retirement. Vesting, however, modifies the incentive effects of this compensation scheme somewhat. Most private-sector employees with pensions become vested after 10 years, so that the threat of losing all rights to their pension is, strictly speaking, only there for the first 10 years. This in itself may be a long enough time to motivate and observe reliable work habits, but even being fired after becoming vested entails loss. A vested worker fired by Firm X may be able to obtain a pension from X at retirement, but this pension will be smaller to the extent that one's tenure with X is shorter. To receive a *full* pension benefit would require the worker to qualify for a pension with *another* firm—a process that will normally take 10 more years in itself. Thus, while vesting softens the threat of being fired for cause after 10 years, it does not remove all of the incentive to work honestly and diligently throughout one's career.

Promotion Lotteries

Another form of worker motivation within the context of internal labor markets might best be called a *promotion lottery*. Suppose a group of entering management trainees were hired with the expectation that *one* of them would become a high-ranking corporate officer and make an extraordinary sum of money each year. The employees who did not make it to the top would be guaranteed a spot in the firm somewhere, but they would not achieve such high earnings.

Now if everyone knew in advance who would be promoted, this scheme would be neither incentive-producing nor would it have aspects of a lottery. However, if no one knew in advance who would "win" but all were told that winning the top job depended on hard work, then all would be attracted by the large salary (or prestige) and work hard to get it. Here, as in the previous schemes, the prospect of obtaining large sums towards the end of one's career offers incentives for diligent work throughout earlier years.

In this scheme, however, not all diligent workers get the prize at career's end; only the winner does. Further, once the prize has been awarded and the losers are known, they no longer have the same strong incentives to work hard. Moreover, the employer—knowing the "losers" have reduced incentives—has every reason to want to get rid of them. Dangling a lucrative job in front of everyone increased the incentives of all—even the eventual losers—to work hard; once the prize has been awarded, the losers are of substantially less value to the firm.

The problem for the employer is that employees may not be willing to enter this lottery unless even the losers are treated relatively well. A firm known for firing older mid-level managers may not be able to attract a large enough group of young management trainees from which to produce an excellent corporate officer in the future. For this reason, a firm may be tempted to agree to essentially guarantee the losers a job somewhere in the organization.

Since workers whose wages are less than or equal to their marginal product do not need any guarantee of job security, it is most likely true that the losers of promotion lotteries have wages or salaries that *exceed* marginal product. If this is the case, the employer will obviously want to offer strong incentives for these employees to retire at a certain point. Again then, a mandatory retirement clause may be an essential ingredient in the running of a promotion lottery.

Hypothesizing that promotion lotteries exist helps explain three phenomena that are widely observed in the labor market. First, it helps explain why—after carefully considering a number of candidates for a top executive job—one is selected and paid perhaps three times what the others receive. Is it because he or she is three times as productive as the others? If so, the others would not have been serious contenders for the job. The huge pay differential most likely exists to serve as an incentive for younger employees to work hard so they can win the next lottery.[24]

Second, the existence of promotion lotteries helps explain why corporations sometimes tolerate *deadwood*—the older employee who obviously is not going to be promoted and who clearly is not as productive as he or she used to be—in the ranks. Such deadwood is the unfortunate cost to the firm of running a successful lottery. Third, because deadwood can be tolerated for a while but not indefinitely there have arisen mandatory-retirement rules or other inducements for employees to retire before they might otherwise decide to do so.

Federal Policy on Mandatory Retirement Reconsidered

This chapter has argued that "underpaying" employees in the early stages of their careers and "overpaying" them later serves as an incentive for employees to work industriously. Because workers are more productive, employers can offer them an income stream whose present value is increased over what it would otherwise be. While employees can command more compensation because they, as individuals, work harder, they benefit *additionally* by a system that causes *other* employees to also work more diligently.

As we have pointed out, however, overpaying workers is something a firm cannot tolerate indefinitely. Thus, for this payment scheme to work—and it must work for both parties in order for each to have incentives to agree to it—firms must be able to terminate the overpayment at the point where it is no longer profitable in the long run.

One way to end the overpayment is to reduce the wage rate of older workers after a certain age to a wage that more closely corresponds to their marginal product. Reducing the wage rate in this way would almost surely raise charges of age discrimination—reflect a prevailing social value that workers' nominal wages should not be reduced under any but the most extraordinary circumstances. Why society has adopted this particular value is an interesting—and open—question.[25]

A social "rule" against wage cutting suggests that the "underpay now, overpay later" scheme will be adopted only if older workers can be fired—or, more

---

[24]This argument is advanced by Edward Lazear and Sherwin Rosen, "Rank-Order Tournaments As Optimum Labor Contracts" (Chicago: University of Chicago, Economics Department, 1979).

[25]Chapter 15 discusses the related question of why employers react to decreases in demand by laying off workers rather than cutting their wages.

politely, subjected to mandatory retirement—by their employers. In most cases such retirement will mean no work at all; in other cases, the employees might be able to find work at a lower wage rate with some other employer. In either case, the affected employees have absorbed wage cuts, and because these cuts—when seen from the workers' perspective in old age—have been forced on them they are likely to feel worse off. They may even ask for and support legislation to outlaw mandatory retirement—which is exactly what happened with the 1978 amendments to the Age Discrimination in Employment Act, which raised the minimum age for mandatory retirement from 65 to 70.

Who gains and who loses from this mandated increase in the age for mandatory retirement? It is clear that employers lose, but is it equally clear that employees gain? Surely people who are currently near retirement gain. However, their gain lies in the fact that governmental authority has been used to break a key element of a contract from which they benefited in the past. The fact that firms can no longer enforce a critical element of their old contracts removes from them the incentive to agree to future contracts of the same type. Thus, younger employees may be harmed by the provisions of the 1978 Act. In fact, the gains to older employees only occur *once*—to the group that is allowed to break its contract. Future generations of older workers do not gain, since their employment contracts and compensation schemes will be made under the new rules of the game.[26]

REVIEW QUESTIONS

1. There is a law saying that compensation of federal-government employees must be comparable to that of private-sector employees of similar skills who perform similar duties. Suppose that comparing pay in the two sectors is done by measuring salaries or wages of a ''typical'' worker in each sector (one, say, with 10 years of experience). In what respects would this approach be deficient?

2. The President's Commission of Pension Policy has proposed that every employee in the country be covered by a Minimum Universal Pension (MUP). This pension would vest immediately and would be fully *portable*. (That is, all workers would qualify for a pension no matter how many employers they worked for in their lifetime or how long they worked for each. Currently, employees are not eligible to receive any private-pension benefits at age 65 unless they work for an employer 10 years.) What impact would an MUP have on labor costs and productivity in this age of inflation?

3. Suppose mandatory retirement laws were abolished and firms undertook various strategies to induce *voluntary* retirements at age 65. Some of these possible strategies are listed below. The firm's objectives are to unambiguously increase the incentives for people over 65 to retire, but to do so in a way that offers the strongest incentives to the *least productive* of the older workers to retire. (For our purposes, the least productive

---

[26]For further analysis of the winners and the losers, see Ronald G. Ehrenberg, ''Retirement Policy, Employment, and Unemployment,'' *American Economic Review* 69, 2 (May 1979): 131–36.

will be defined as the workers no other firm would want at anything close to their current wage. Productive workers, even though elderly, could get jobs elsewhere at close to their current wage.) Evaluate each of the following strategies to determine whether it will accomplish the firm's objectives:

a. Cut the wages of all workers after the age of 60.
b. Provide a large lump-sum payment to anyone who quits his or her employment *at the firm* at age 65.
c. Increase the monthly pension benefit of anyone who *retires* (and does not work elsewhere) at age 65.

SELECTED READINGS

Alchian, Armen and Reuben Kessel. "Competition, Monopoly, and the Pursuit of Money." *Aspects of Labor Economics,* edited by H. G. Lewis. Princeton, N.J.: Princeton University Press, 1962.

Allen, Steven G. "Compensation, Safety and Absenteeism." *Industrial and Labor Relations Review* 34 (January 1981): 207–18.

Doeringer, Peter and Michael Piore. *Internal Labor Markets and Manpower Analysis* Lexington, Mass.: D. C. Heath and Company, 1971.

Ehrenberg, Ronald and Robert Smith. "A Framework for Evaluating State and Local Government Pension Reform." In *Public Sector Labor Markets,* edited by Peter Mieszkowski and George E. Peterson. Washington, D.C. The Urban Institute, 1981.

Lazear, Edward. "Why Is There Mandatory Retirement?" *Journal of Political Economy* 87 (December 1979): 1261–84.

Pencavel, John. "Work Effort, On-the-Job Screening, and Alternative Methods of Remuneration." In *Research in Labor Economics,* Vol. 1, edited by Ronald Ehrenberg. Greenwich, Conn.: JAI Press, 1977, pp. 225–58.

Simon, Herbert A. "A Formal Theory of the Employment Relationship." *Econometrical* 19, 3 (July 1951): 293–305.

Stiglitz, Joseph E. "Incentives, Risk and Information: Notes Toward a Theory of Hierarchy." *Bell Journal of Economics and Management Science* 6 (Autumn 1975): 552–79.

12

Unions
and Collective Bargaining
in the Private Sector

Our analysis of the workings of labor markets has, for the most part, omitted any mention of the role of labor unions and collective bargaining. Because many people have strong and conflicting opinions about the role of unions in our society, it is often difficult to remain objective when discussing them. Some individuals view labor unions as forms of monopolies that, while benefiting their members, impose substantial costs on other members of society. In contrast, other individuals view unions as *the* major means by which working persons have improved their economic status and as important forces behind much social legislation.

In recent years approximately 20 percent of all individuals in the labor force and 25 percent of all employees on nonagricultural payrolls were union members (see Table 12.1). This percentage is considerably lower than that found in most western countries. In addition, the United States is one of the few western countries in which labor unions are not intimately and uniformly associated with one political party (such as the Labour Party in England, which is dominated by trade unionists). While unions play an important role in our society, their influence is probably not as pervasive as either their supporters or opponents would have us believe.

This chapter initially presents a brief discussion of the nature of unions and the collective-bargaining process and the major pieces of labor legislation that have shaped collective bargaining in the private sector in the United States. (Public-sector labor markets and collective bargaining will be discussed in Chapter 13.) The chapter then presents a simple conceptual model of the forces that influence the level of unionization and shows how this model can be used to explain the historical pattern of union membership in the United States.

The chapter will then discuss how unions seek to achieve their bargaining goals. After reviewing the Hicks-Marshall laws of derived demand, initially discussed in Chapter 4, to analyze the factors that limit a union's ability to improve the economic well-being of its members without causing a substantial fraction of

Table 12.1   Union and Association Membership in the United States, 1930–1978

	Union Membership Only			Union and Association Membership		
Year	Total (in thousands)	Percentage of Labor Force	Percentage of Nonagricultural Employment	Total (in thousands)	Percentage of Labor Force	Percentage of Nonagricultural Employment
1930	3,401	6.8	11.6			
1932	3,050	6.0	12.9			
1934	3,088	5.9	11.9			
1936	3,989	7.4	13.7			
1938	8,034	14.6	27.5			
1940	8,717	15.5	26.9			
1942	10,380	17.2	25.9			
1944	14,146	21.4	33.8			
1946	14,395	23.6	34.5			
1948	14,300	23.1	31.9			
1950	14,300	22.3	31.5			
1952	15,900	24.2	33.3			
1954	17,022	25.4	33.7			
1956	17,490	25.2	33.2			
1958	17,029	24.2	33.2			
1960	17,049	23.6	31.5			
1962	16,586	22.6	29.9			
1964	16,841	22.2	28.9			
1966	17,940	22.7	28.1			
1968	18,916	23.0	27.9	20,721	25.2	30.5
1970	19,381	22.6	27.3	21,248	24.7	30.0
1972	19,435	21.8	26.4	21,657	24.3	29.4
1974	20,119	21.7	25.8	22,809	24.5	29.1
1976	19,634	20.3	24.5	22,662	23.4	28.3
1978	20,246	19.7	24.0	22,880	22.3	27.1

SOURCE: U.S. Bureau of Labor Statistics, *Directory of National Unions and Employee Associations, 1979*, Bulletin 2079 (Washington, D.C.: U.S. Government Printing Office, 1980) for 1958–1978 data; U.S. Bureau of the Census, *Historical Statistics of the United States: Colonial Times to 1970* (Washington, D.C.: U.S. Government Printing Office, 1975) for 1930–1956 data.

them to lose their jobs, the chapter will turn to a discussion of how, given such constraints, unions can translate their bargaining goals into actual outcomes.

The chapter also examines the effects unions have had on wage *and* nonwage outcomes. Neoclassical economists have traditionally focused on estimating the amount by which unions have increased the wages of their members *relative* to the wages of comparable nonunion workers—and the conclusion that unions have a negative effect on society is based on these estimates. Recently, however, analytical labor economists have begun to rediscover the variety of roles that unions play and concluded that unions may play many positive roles that leave society as a whole better off.[1]

Returning to our earlier example (in Chapter 9) of wage determination in a heavily unionized regulated industry, we will conclude the chapter by noting that there may be a fundamental inconsistency between a policy that seeks to promote the collective-bargaining rights of workers and one that seeks to minimize the

---

[1]This "new" view of unions is summarized by two of its exponents in a nontechnical fashion in Richard B. Freeman and James L. Medoff, "The Two Faces of Unionism," *Public Interest* 57 (Fall 1979): 69–93.

prices paid by consumers for products produced in regulated industries, such as public utilities. Policymakers often face the dilemma that different policy goals may be mutually inconsistent.

UNIONS AND COLLECTIVE BARGAINING

Labor unions are collective organizations whose primary objectives are to improve the pecuniary and nonpecuniary conditions of employment of their members. Unions can be classified into two types: 1. an *industrial* union represents most or all of the workers in an industry or firm regardless of their occupations; and 2. a *craft* union represents workers in a single occupational group. Examples of industrial unions are the unions representing automobile workers, steel workers, bituminous coal miners, and rubber workers; while examples of the craft unions are the unions representing the various building trades, printers, and dock workers.

Although most unions are members of the American Federation of Labor–Congress of Industrial Organizations (AFL-CIO), this federation of unions is not involved in the collective-bargaining process *per se*.[2] In some industries—for example, automobile and steel—bargaining is done primarily at the *national* level. In others—such as construction—bargaining is done at the *local* level. In either case, bargaining can be *multiemployer,* in which case an agreement is reached simultaneously with a number of employers, or bargaining can take place separately with individual employers. The structure of bargaining in our economy influences both the ability of unions to accomplish their objectives and the inflationary process.

Collective bargaining typically covers a much wider range of issues than simply the issue of wage rates. Among the issues usually included are other pecuniary conditions of employment (such as vacation pay, health insurance, pensions, and the like) as well as nonpecuniary conditions of employment, including job-security provisions (such as seniority rules or rules governing layoffs) and working conditions (such as workplace safety, rights to refuse overtime, and methods of production). Unions also help employers to administer the provisions of union contracts during the time collective-bargaining agreements are in effect and provide individual employees with a means of communicating their concerns to management. The tendency of some observers to focus on the pecuniary aspects of collective-bargaining agreements—to the neglect of the nonpecuniary aspects and the roles unions play while a contract is in effect—can lead to an incomplete analysis of the effects of unions.

Modern Labor Legislation in the United States

Public attitudes and federal legislation have not always been favorably disposed toward labor unions and the collective-bargaining process. For example, during the early part of the twentieth century, employers were often able to claim that

---

[2]The United Automobile Workers (UAW) and Teamsters were the major large national unions not in the AFL-CIO during the early 1980s.

Table 12.2   Major Pieces of Federal Labor Legislation Governing Collective Bargaining in the Private Sector

Date	Law	Some Salient Provisions
1932	Norris-LaGuardia Act	1. Restricted employers' uses of court orders and injunctions as weapons to combat union-organizing drives. 2. Prohibited "Yellow-Dog" contracts—contracts in which potential employees had to agree *not* to join a union as a condition of employment.
1935	National Labor Relations (Wagner) Act	1. Defined unfair labor practices, both for employers and employees. In particular, employers are required to bargain with unions representing the majority of their employees, and it is an unfair labor practice to interfere with employees' right to organize. 2. The National Labor Relations Board (NLRB) was established to settle many labor-management disputes. The NLRB was given power to investigate alleged unfair labor practices, to order violators to cease and desist, and to have its orders enforced by the courts. The NLRB was also given the rights to conduct elections to see which unions, if any, employees wanted.
1947	Taft-Hartley Act	1. Restricted some aspects of union activity. Section 14B permits states to pass right-to-work laws; these prohibit the requirement that persons become (or refrain from becoming) a union member as a condition of employment.
1959	Landrum-Griffin Act	1. Designed to protect the rights of union members, it increases union democracy. It includes provisions for periodic reporting of union finances and provisions that regulate union elections.

unions acted like monopolies in the labor market and hence were illegal under existing antitrust law. Such employers were often able to get court orders or injunctions that prohibited union activity and aided them in stopping union-organization drives. In addition, employers were often able to require potential employees to sign *yellow dog contracts*—contracts in which employees agreed not to join a union as a condition of accepting employment. Given this environment, it is not surprising that the fraction of the labor force that were union members stood at less than 7 percent in 1930 (see Table 12.1).

Since that date, four major pieces of federal labor legislation have shaped the collective-bargaining process in the private sector, the ability of unions to increase their membership, and the way unions operate. These laws and some of their salient provisions are listed in Table 12.2.

Two laws were products of the Depression. The *Norris-LaGuardia Act,* enacted in 1932, for all practical purposes outlawed the antiunion practices of employers discussed above. The *National Labor Relations Act* (NLRA), or *Wagner Act,* of 1935 went far beyond the earlier act by requiring employers to bargain with unions that represented the majority of their employees and by asserting that it was illegal for employers to interfere with their employees' right to organize collectively. The National Labor Relations Board (NLRB) was established by the NLRA and given power both to conduct elections to see which union, if any, employees wanted to represent them and to investigate claims that employers were either violating election rules or refusing to bargain with elected unions.[3] In the event violations were found, the NLRB was given further power to order violators to "cease and desist"; these orders were to be enforced by the courts.

After World War II, the pendulum shifted decidedly in an antiunion direction. The *Taft-Hartley Act* of 1947 restricted some aspects of union activity. Perhaps its most famous provision is Section 14B, which permits individual states to pass *right-to-work laws*. These laws prohibit the requirement that a person become, or promise to become, a union member as a condition of employment. By 1980, some 20 states, located primarily in the south, southwest, and plains areas, had passed such laws.

Finally, in 1959 Congress passed the *Landrum-Griffin Act*. This law, which was designed to protect the rights of union members in relation to their leaders, contained provisions that increased union democracy. As argued below, such provisions may well have had the side effect of increasing the level of strike activity in the economy.

A Model of the Level of Unionization

Table 12.1 presents data on union membership from 1930 through the late 1970s. For the last decade the table also includes data on membership in employee associations, such as the National Education Association (NEA). The primary purposes of employee associations historically have not related to collective bargaining; for example, the NEA has long been primarily concerned with professional standards and improving the quality of education students receive. However, these associations have become increasingly involved in the collective-bargaining process.

Data on union membership are notoriously poor; nevertheless, Table 12.1 yields some striking patterns. First, union membership, in both absolute terms and as a percentage of the labor force (and of nonagricultural employment), grew steadily during both the 1930s and through World War II. The former result was somewhat surprising to analysts since prior to the 1930s periods of high unemployment were typically associated with declining union strength.[4] After a slight dip in the immediate postwar period, union strength reached a peak of 25 percent of the labor force in the mid-1950s. However, since that time, the share of union members in both total nonagricultural employment and the labor force has declined steadily. Indeed, by 1978 union membership stood at about 20 percent of the labor force—a 30-year low. While inclusion of employee association members in Table 12.1 raises this estimate somewhat, it does not alter the underlying trend.

Further evidence of this trend can be found in the National Labor Relations Board union election and decertification vote data for the decade of the '70s,

---

[3]Actually, the NLRA was much less pro-labor than our brief discussion indicates; the NLRA also gave the NLRB power to investigate employers' claims that their employees, or unions, were violating provisions of the act.

[4]For evidence and a discussion of the pre-1930s view, see John R. Commons, *The History of Labor in the United States,* vol. III (New York: Macmillan, 1918).

Table 12.3   Results of Representation Elections and Decertification
Polls Supervised by the National Labor Relations Board

Fiscal Year	Union Elections	Percent Won By Union	Decertification Votes	Percent Lost By Union
1970	8,074	55.2	301	69.8
1971	8,362	53.2	401	69.6
1972	8,923	53.6	451	70.3
1973	9,369	51.1	453	69.5
1974	8,858	50.0	490	69.0
1975	8,577	48.2	516	73.4
1976	8,638	48.1	611	72.8
1977	9,484	46.0	849	76.0
1978	8,240	46.0	807	73.6
1979	8,043	45.0		

SOURCE: *Annual Report of the National Labor Relations Board,* Appendix Tables (various years).

which are found in Table 12.3. These data indicate that while the number of elections in which unions have sought to win the right to represent unorganized workers has fluctuated between 8000 and 9500 a year, the *share* of the elections that the unions actually won has fallen steadily during the period, from 55 to 45 percent. Furthermore, the annual number of *decertification votes*—votes in which union claims to represent a majority of workers in a firm were challenged—more than doubled, with the share of these votes lost by unions increasing slightly to more than 70 percent during this period.

A simple model of the demand and supply of union activity can be used to explain the forces that influence union strength.[5] On the demand side, employees' demand to be union members will be a function of the "price" of union membership; this price includes monthly dues, initiation fees, the value of the time an individual is expected to spend on union activities, etc. Other things equal, the higher the price, the lower the fraction of employees that will want to be union members—as represented by the demand curve D_0 in Figure 12.1.

It is costly to represent workers in collective-bargaining negotiations and to supervise the administration of union contracts. Moreover, union-organizing campaigns require resources, and as unions move from organizing workers who are the most favorably inclined towards unions to those who are the least favorably inclined, the cost of making a sufficiently strong case to win a union-representation election increases. As such, it is reasonable to conclude that, other things equal, on the supply side of the market the willingness of unions to provide union services is an upward-sloping function of the price of union membership—as represented by the supply curve S_0 in Figure 12.1. The intersection of these demand and supply curves yields an equilibrium percentage of the work force that is unionized (U_0) and an equilibrium price of union services (P_0).

---

[5]This model is based upon the approach found in Orley Ashenfelter and John Pencavel, "American Trade Union Growth, 1900–1960," *Quarterly Journal of Economics* 83 (August 1969): 434–48; and John Pencavel, "The Demand for Union Services: An Exercise," *Industrial and Labor Relations Review* 24 (January 1971): 180–91.

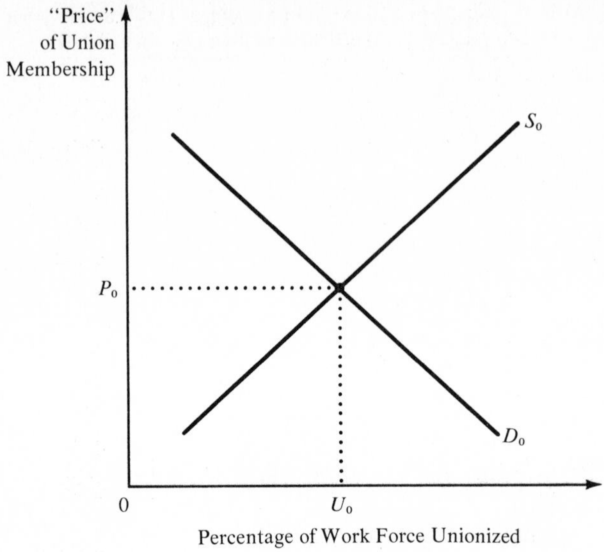

"Price" of Union Membership

S_0

P_0

D_0

0

U_0

Percentage of Work Force Unionized

**FIGURE 12.1   The Demand and Supply
of Unionization**

What are the forces that determine the *positions* of the demand and supply curves? Anything that causes either the demand curve *or* the supply curve to shift to the right will increase the level of unionization in the economy, other things equal. Conversely, if either of these curves shifts to the left, other things equal, the level of unionization will fall. Identifying the factors that shift these curves enables one to explain *changes* in the level of unionization in the economy over time.

On the demand side, it is likely that individuals' demand for union membership is positively related to their perceptions of the *net benefits* from being union members. For example, the larger the wage gain they think unions will win for them, the further to the right the demand curve will be and the higher the level of unionization. Another factor is *tastes;* if individuals' tastes for union membership increase—perhaps because of changes in social attitudes or the introduction of labor legislation that protects the rights of workers to join unions—the demand curve will also shift to the right.

On the supply side, anything that changes the *costs* of union-organizing activities will affect the supply curve. Introduction of labor legislation that makes it easier (harder) for unions to win representation elections will shift the supply curve to the right (left). Changes in the industrial structure that make it more difficult to organize the work force will also shift the curve to the left and reduce the level of unionization.

The rapid growth in unionization that took place during the 1930s was a product of both the changing legal environment (Norris-LaGuardia and Wagner Acts) and changing social attitudes towards unions induced by the Great Depression—changes that shifted both the demand and supply curves to the right.[6] The growth continued during the World War II years as low unemployment rates reduced workers' fears of losing their jobs if they indicated pro-union sentiments (shifting the demand curve to the right). Unemployment increased after the end of World War II, shifting the demand curve back to the left, while the passage of the Taft-Hartley Act made it more difficult for unions to increase membership in right-to-work states and shifted the supply curve further to the left. Both of these shifts served to decrease the percentage unionized.

The decline in union membership since the mid-1950s can be at least partially explained by two factors, already discussed in earlier chapters. First, the fraction of the labor force that is female has increased substantially (see Chapter 6), and females historically have tended not to join unions. The benefits from union membership are a function of individuals' expected tenure with firms; seniority provisions, job-security provisions, and retirement benefits are not worth much to individuals who expect to be employed at a firm for only a short while. *In the past,* females tended to have shorter expected job tenure than males and to have more intermittent labor-force participation. As a result, their expected benefits from joining unions were lower; an increase in their share in the labor force would shift the aggregate demand curve for union membership to the left.[7]

The second factor in the decline of union membership is the shift in the industrial composition of employment, discussed in Chapter 2. The last 25 years have seen a substantial decline in the relative employment shares of manufacturing, mining, construction, transportation, and public utilities and, conversely, a substantial increase in the share of employment in wholesale and retail trade, finance, insurance, real estate, and the service industries. Indeed, the former group fell from 48.7 percent of nonagricultural payroll employment in 1955 to 35.3 percent by 1978. During the same period the latter group rose from 37.6 to 46.7 percent.[8] As Table 12.4 indicates, the industries in the former group are the most heavily unionized in the private sector, while the industries in the latter group are the ones that are least unionized. The shifting industrial composition of employment has led to a distribution that is weighted more heavily towards industries that are not heavily unionized.

Why does the latter set of industries tend not to be unionized? These industries tend to be highly competitive ones, with high price elasticities of demand.

---

[6]It is difficult to identify the effect of the laws per se, as they are determined by societal attitudes themselves. However, as noted both above and also below, prior to and after the Depression, periods of high (low) unemployment have been associated with weakening (growing) union membership, which leads one to suspect that the changing legal environment induced by the Depression, which reduced employees' fears of being fired for union activities, did have a substantial effect on union growth during the 1930s.

[7]We emphasize "in the past" here. Changing labor-force patterns, with a greater share of females now having permanent attachment to the labor force, will likely increase their propensity to become union members in the future.

[8]U.S. Department of Labor, *1979 Employment and Training Report of the President* (Washington, D.C.: U.S. Government Printing Office, 1979), Table C-1. We defer discussion of government employment until Chapter 13.

Table 12.4   Union and Association Membership by Industry in 1976

Industry	Number of Union Members (in thousands)	Number of Employees on Payrolls (in thousands)	Percentage of Employees that Are Union Members
Manufacturing	8,568	18,956	45.2
Mining	401	783	51.2
Construction	2,694	3,594	75.0
Transportation and public utilities	3,213	4,509	71.3
Wholesale and retail trade	1,314	17,694	7.4
Finance, insurance, and real estate	49	4,316	1.1
Service	1,665	14,644	11.3
Federal government	1,334	2,733	48.8
State and local government	4,528	12,215	37.1

SOURCE: U.S. Bureau of Labor Statistics, *Directory of National Unions and Employee Associations,* Bulletin 2044 (Washington, D.C.: U.S. Government Printing Office, 1979), Table 16; U.S. Bureau of Labor Statistics, *Handbook of Labor Statistics, 1978,* Bulletin 2000 (Washington, D.C.: U.S. Government Printing Office, 1979).

As discussed in Chapter 3, other things equal, industries with high price elasticities of demand will also have high wage elasticities of demand. High wage elasticities limit unions' abilities to increase their members' wages without substantial employment declines also occurring. As such, the net benefits individuals perceive from union membership may be lower in these industries, and an increase in their importance in the economy would shift the demand for union services to the left in Figure 12.1, thereby reducing the percentage of the work force that is unionized.[9]

One additional factor that may have contributed to the decline in union strength is the movement in population and employment that has occurred since 1955 from the industrial northeast and midwest—the "snow belt"—to the "sun belt" of the south. As noted earlier, the Taft-Hartley Act permitted states to pass right-to-work laws. Such laws raise the costs of increasing union membership since individuals who accept employment with a firm cannot be compelled to become union members as a condition of employment. In terms of Figure 12.1, these laws shift the supply curve of union services to the left, thereby reducing the level of unionization. It so happens that most sun-belt states do have right-to-work laws.

Table 12.5 presents data on the extent of unionization that existed in 1978 in right-to-work and other states. The data indicate quite clearly that right-to-work

[9]These industries also tend to be populated by small establishments. The demand for unionization is thought to be lower for employees who work in small firms, since they often feel less alienated from their supervisors. Similarly, since it is more costly to try to organize 1000 workers spread over 100 firms that it is to organize 1000 workers at one plant, it is often thought that the supply of union services would shift down as the share of employment going to small firms increases. Both of these factors tend to suggest (in terms of Figure 12.1) that unionization will decline as the share of employment occurring in small establishments increases, providing another reason why the shift in industrial distribution of employment has affected the extent of unionization.

Table 12.5   Percent of Nonagricultural Employees That Are Union or Association Members, 1978

Right-to-Work States	Union or Association Members (percent)	Other States	Union or Association Members (percent)
Alabama	24.6	Alaska	32.3
Arizona	18.0	California	28.8
Arkansas	17.6	Colorado	18.1
Florida	13.2	Connecticut	26.4
Georgia	15.8	Delaware	23.9
Iowa	22.6	Hawaii	35.9
Kansas	15.8	Idaho	19.1
Louisiana	17.0	Illinois	33.4
Mississippi	15.0	Indiana	32.0
Nebraska	19.3	Kentucky	25.4
Nevada	27.2	Maine	24.7
North Carolina	10.7	Maryland-D.C.	25.0
North Dakota	19.4	Massachusetts	27.7
South Carolina	8.9	Michigan	38.5
South Dakota	14.6	Minnesota	27.6
Tennessee	21.0	Missouri	31.0
Texas	13.3	Montana	29.9
Utah	19.6	New Hampshire	16.8
Virginia	15.3	New Jersey	27.3
Wyoming	19.6	New Mexico	14.8
		New York	41.0
		Ohio	33.6
		Oklahoma	17.2
		Oregon	29.4
		Pennsylvania	37.3
		Rhode Island	29.9
		Vermont	22.7
		Washington	36.5
		West Virginia	40.4
		Wisconsin	30.5

SOURCE: U.S. Bureau of Labor Statistics, *Directory of National Unions and Employee Associations, 1977*, Bulletin 2079 (Washington, D.C.: U.S. Government Printing Office, 1980), Table 19.

states are the ones in which union strength is the lowest. In 16 of the 20 right-to-work states, the proportion of nonagricultural employees that were union or employee-association members was less than 20 percent. In contrast, in 22 of the other 30 states, the proportion exceeded 25 percent. While right-to-work states are not uniformly identical to those in the sun belt, there is considerable overlap. As a result, between 1955 and 1978 the proportion of employees working in right-to-work states increased from 24.1 to 30.6 percent. This shifting geographic distribution of the work force, coupled with the existence of these laws, undoubtedly had a depressing effect on union membership.

It is not at all obvious, however, that the decline in unionization, occasioned by the move to the sun belt, can be attributed to right-to-work laws *per se*. The extent of unionization in right-to-work states tended to be lower than that in other states even prior to the passage of the laws. These laws may only reflect attitudes towards unions that already exist in these communities.[10] The increasing influx of "snowbelters" into the sunbelt may eventually lead to a change in public attitudes *and* the repeal of some of these laws.

Two lessons follow from this discussion. First, population shifts to the sunbelt may not imply a permanent weakening of the union movement in the United States. Second, and more generally, the effects of legislation may be more political than economic; the environmental factors that shape legislation might also cause the same economic outcomes to occur (in this case union strength) even in the absence of the legislation.

HOW UNIONS ACHIEVE THEIR OBJECTIVES

Union Policies to Ease Market Constraints

Many theories of union behavior attempt to formalize the view that unions are organizations that seek to maximize some well-defined objective function.[11] Indeed, recently several studies have even attempted to econometrically estimate the parameters of such an objective function.[12] As noted above, unions play many roles in addition to negotiating wage rates for their members; hence, it is not surprising that there is no widespread agreement as to what specifically is a union's objective function. Nevertheless, it is generally agreed that in most cases unions value 1. the wage and fringe benefits they can achieve for their members *and* 2. their members' employment levels. Therefore, the position and wage elasticity of the labor-demand curve are the fundamental *market constraints* that limit the ability of unions to accomplish their objectives.

Figure 12.2 shows two demand curves, D_e^0 and D_i^0, that intersect at an initial wage W_0 and employment level E_0. Suppose a union seeks to raise the wage rate of its members to W_1. To do so would require employment to fall to E_e^1 if the union faced the relatively elastic demand curve D_e^0, or to E_i^1 if it faced the rela-

---

[10]Numerous econometric studies have sought to estimate the effect of right-to-work laws on union strength, wages, and industrial conflict. Studies that conclude that these laws have little or no effect on union-membership levels include Keith Lumsden and Craig Peterson, "The Effect of Right-to-Work Laws on Unionization in the United States," *Journal of Political Economy* 83 (December 1975): 1237–48; William Moore and Robert Newman, "On the Prospects for American Trade Union Growth: A Cross-Section Analysis," *Review of Economics and Statistics* 57 (November 1975): 435–45; and Barry T. Hirsch, "The Determinants of Unionization: An Analysis of Interarea Differences," *Industrial and Labor Relations Review* 33 (January 1980): 147–61.

[11]See Wallace Atherton, *Theory of Union Bargaining Goals* (Princeton, N.J.: Princeton University Press, 1973) for an extensive discussion of the various theories. A classic debate took place more than 35 years ago between John Dunlop, *Wage Determination Under Trade Unions* (New York: Macmillan, 1944) and Arthur Ross, *Trade Union Wage Policy* (Berkeley, Calif.: University of California Press, 1948) with respect to whether it was meaningful to analyze unions in terms of how they maximize well-defined objective functions. Dunlop argued yes, and Ross no, the latter articulating an alternative political model of union behavior. Here we will follow in Dunlop's footsteps, although we will return to the Ross view later.

[12]See Henry Farber, "Individual Preferences and Union Wage Determination: The Case of the United Mine Workers," *Journal of Political Economy* 86 (October 1978): 923–42; and J. N. Dertouzos and J. H. Pencavel, "Wage and Employment Determination Under Trade Unionism: The International Typographical Union" (Stanford University Workshop on the Microeconomics of Inflation Discussion Paper No. 27, April 1980).

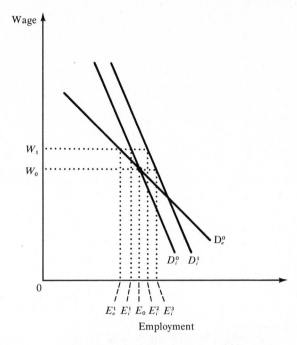

FIGURE 12.2 Effects of Demand Growth and Wage Elasticity of Demand on Market Constraint Faced by Unions

tively inelastic demand curve D_i^0. Other things equal, the more elastic the demand curve for labor is, the greater the reduction in employment that will be associated with any given increase in wages.

Suppose now that the demand curve D_i^0 shifts out to D_i^1 while the negotiations are under way, due perhaps to growing demand for the final product. If the union succeeds in raising its members' wage to W_1, there will be no absolute decrease in employment in this case. Rather, the union will have only slowed the rate of growth of employment to E_i^2 instead of E_i^3. More generally, other things equal, the more rapidly the labor demand curve is shifting out (in) the smaller (larger) will be the reduction *in employment* or the reduction *in the rate of growth of employment* that will be associated with any given increase in wages. Hence, the unions' ability to raise their members' wages will be strongest in rapidly growing industries with inelastic labor-demand curves. Conversely, unions will be weakest in industries in which the wage elasticity of demand is highly elastic and in which the demand curve for labor is shifting in.

Many actions that unions take are direct attempts to relax the market constraints that they face: either to increase the demand for union labor or to reduce the wage elasticity of demand for their members' services. The laws of derived demand discussed in Chapter 4 implied that three important determinants of the wage elasticities of demand were the price elasticity of demand for the final product, the ease of substituting other inputs for union members in the production process, and how responsive the supply of other inputs is to their prices. Other things equal, if price elasticities of demand for the final product are less elastic, if it is difficult to substitute other inputs for union labor, and if the supply schedules of other inputs are unresponsive to their prices, a more inelastic demand for union labor will result.

As noted in Chapter 4, the wage elasticity of demand for labor is more elastic in the long run than in the short run. In the short run there may be only limited foreign competition in the output market while, as American automobile manufacturers realized in the late 1970s and early 1980s, in the long run foreign competition may increase, increasing the price elasticity of demand for output. In the short run, production technologies may be fixed; in the long run labor saving technologies may be introduced. Finally, in the short run, the supplies of alternative inputs may be fixed, while in the longer run—due to immigration, the training of other nonunion workers, or the production of new capital equipment—they may be more responsive to price. As a result, the market constraints unions face are more severe in the long run than in the short run; large wage gains won today may lead to substantial employment losses in the future. Such constraints are the primary reason why the economic gains that unions have won for their members are, in fact, relatively modest.

Altering the Demand for Union Labor

Attempts by unions to shift the demand curve for union labor to the right and to reduce the wage elasticity of demand have taken many forms. Many of these attempts have *not* occurred through the collective-bargaining process per se. Rather, they have occurred through union support of legislation that, at least indirectly, achieved union goals and through direct public-relations campaigns to increase the demand for products produced by union members.

Turning first to policies to shift the demand for the final product, at times unions have lobbied for quotas or tariffs on foreign-produced goods that would limit the amount of these goods sold in the United States. Both the steel workers and the automobile workers sought such forms of protection during the late 1970s and early 1980s. Other unions have sought to directly influence people's tastes for the products they produce. The International Ladies Garment Workers' Union (ILGWU) continually seeks to encourage people to "Buy American," featuring the song "Look For the Union Label" in some of its television ads.

Unions have also sought, by means of legislation, to pursue strategies that increase the costs of other inputs that are potential substitutes for union members. For example, as noted in Chapter 3, labor unions have been among the primary supporters of higher minimum wages.[13] While such support may be motivated by their concern for the welfare of low-wage workers, increases in the minimum wage *do* have the effect of increasing the relative costs to employers of low-

---

[13]For evidence that union support for minimum wage legislation is often transformed into pro-minimum wage votes by members of Congress, see James Kau and Paul Rubin, "Voting on Minimum Wages: A Time-Series Analysis," *Journal of Political Economy* 86 (April 1978): 337–42; Jonathan Silberman and Garey Durden, "Determining Legislative Preferences on the Minimum Wage," *Journal of Political Economy* 84 (April 1976): 317–30; and James Cox and Ronald Oaxaca, "The Determinants of Minimum Wage Levels and Coverage in State Minimum Wage Laws" in *The Economics of Legal Minimum Wages* (Washington, D.C.: American Enterprise Institute for Public Policy, 1981).

Example 12.1
The Davis-Bacon Act

The Davis-Bacon Act was passed in the midst of the Depression in 1931. Its goal was to maintain local wage standards by requiring subcontractors and contractors on federally financed projects to pay employees wage rates established by private industry in the locality. The legislation was enacted in response to a situation in which federal construction contracts to help offset unemployment in depressed areas were being won by contractors from other areas who were underbidding local builders by importing low-wage workers. The act was designed to assure that the federal funds would go to the unemployed workers in the targeted areas.

The Davis-Bacon Act undoubtedly served a useful function during the 1930s. However, since that time almost 100 statutes have been passed, in fields such as education, health, housing, and transportation, that include similar *prevailing-wage* clauses for federally assisted projects as well. Furthermore, 35 states have passed "little Davis-Bacon statutes" covering state construction expenditures as well. As noted above, the net effect of these provisions today is to increase the labor costs on school construction, public-housing projects, hospitals, and mass-transit projects because these provisions effectively preclude nonunion contractors from bidding on such projects.

This example illustrates how social legislation that is desirable at one point in time may prove to be undesirable at a later date. For this reason, social legislation and programs should be continually reexamined and evaluated to make sure that their social benefits continue to exceed their social costs.

skilled nonunion workers, thereby increasing the costs of the products they produce and reducing employers' incentives to substitute nonunion workers for more skilled union workers.

An example of such a strategy is union support for the Davis-Bacon Act and other forms of prevailing-wage legislation that require that wages paid to construction workers on projects that are federally financed, federally assisted through loans, or whose financing is insured by the federal government, be set at least equal to the prevailing wage in the area as determined by the Secretary of Labor. Since typically the prevailing wage has been set equal to the union wage scale, the net effect is to eliminate any cost advantage that nonunion construction workers may have, thereby increasing the demand for union labor.[14]

A final example of how unions can influence the demand for union labor is the union position on immigration policy. The AFL-CIO has been quite explicit,

---

[14]John Gould, *Davis-Bacon Act: The Economics of Prevailing Wage Laws* (Washington, D.C.: American Enterprise Institute, 1971) and Armand Thieblot, Jr., *The Davis-Bacon Act* (Philadelphia, Pa.: Industrial Research Unit, Wharton School, 1975) contain more complete descriptions of the act and its administration.

both historically and in recent years, about its concern that immigrants depress wages and provide competition for unionized American workers. Indeed, with respect to the problem of illegal immigration in the early 1980s, the AFL-CIO asserted that

> while the nation should continue its compassionate and humane immigration policy, it is apparent that large numbers of illegal immigrants are being exploited by employers, thus threatening hard-won wages and working conditions. U.S. immigration policy should foster re-unification of families and provide haven for refugees from persecution, while taking a realistic view of the job opportunities and the needs of U.S. workers.[15]

It is not surprising then, that unions have historically supported legislation restricting immigration, especially during recessionary periods.[16]

Union attempts to restrict the substitution of other inputs for union labor typically occur by means of the collective-bargaining process. Some unions, notably those in the airline, railroad, and printing industries, have sought and won guarantees of minimum crew sizes (for example, at least three pilots are required to fly certain jet aircrafts). Such *staffing requirements* prevent employers from substituting capital for labor.[17] Other unions have won contract provisions that prohibit employers from *subcontracting* for some or all of the services they provide. For example, a union representing a company's janitorial employees may win a contract provision preventing the firm from hiring external firms to provide it with janitorial services. Such provisions may limit the substitution of nonunion for union workers. Craft unions, especially those in the building and printing trades, often negotiate specific contract provisions that restrict the functions that members of each individual craft can perform, thereby limiting the substitution of one type of union labor for another. Finally, craft unions also limit the substitution of unskilled union labor for skilled union labor by establishing rules about the maximum number of *apprentice* workers—workers who are learning the skilled trades—that can be employed relative to the experienced *journeymen* workers.

Apprenticeship rules also serve to limit the supply of skilled workers to a craft. Indeed, they represent only one of several ways in which unions or employee associations may restrict entry into an occupation. Another way is to control the accreditation of outside institutions that provide training; the American Medical Association's accreditation of medical schools is an example of this. A final way of restricting entry into an occupation is to lobby for state occupational licensing laws.[18]

---

[15]*The AFL-CIO Platform Proposals: Presented to the Democratic and Republican National Conventions 1980* (Washington, D.C.: AFL-CIO, 1980), p. 14.

[16]F. Ray Marshall, Allan King, and Vernon Briggs, *Labor Economics: Wages, Employment, and Trade Unionism*, 4th ed. (Homewood, Ill.: Richard D. Irwin, 1980), p. 196.

[17]In cases in which these requirements call for the employment of employees whose functions are redundant—for example, fire stokers in diesel operated railroad engines—*featherbedding* is said to take place. For an economic analysis of this phenomenon, see Paul Weinstein, "The Featherbedding Problem," *American Economic Review* 54 (May 1964): 145–52.

[18]See, for example, Alex Maurizi, "Occupational Licensing and the Public Interest," *Journal of Political Economy* 82 (March/April 1974): 399–413.

From Market Constraints to Bargaining Power

How do unions convince employers to agree to changes that reduce the wage elasticity of demand or shift the demand curve for union labor to the right? Given the elasticity and position of demand curves, how are unions able to bargain for, and win, real wage increases, when in most cases an increase in the price of an input reduces a firm's profits?[19]

In some cases a union and an employer may agree to a settlement in which real wages are increased in return for the union's agreeing to certain work-rule changes that will result in increased productivity. If such an agreement is explicit and tied to the resulting change in productivity, the process is often referred to as *productivity bargaining.*[20] More typically, however, unions are able to win management concessions at the bargaining table because of the unions' ability to impose costs on management. These costs typically take the form of work slowdowns and strikes. A *strike* is an attempt to deny the firm the labor services of all union members. Craft unions often have the added weapon of explicitly controlling the labor-supply curve that firms face, by means of previously negotiated or legislated entry restrictions, described above.

Whether a strike, or a threat of a strike, will enable a union to win a concession from management depends upon

1. the profitability of the firm and its ability to raise prices without losing its market (clearly unions in concentrated industries will be better off than those in competitive industries on this score);
2. the ability of the union to impose costs on the firm—which depends on whether the firm can stockpile its product in anticipation of a strike, thus avoiding the loss of customers during a strike, and whether nonunion supervisory employees can operate a plant during a strike;
3. whether the firm has the financial resources to withstand the losses it would incur during a strike; and
4. whether the union members have the financial resources to withstand their loss of income during a strike.[21]

If strikes involve costs to both union members and employees, why do they ever occur? It would seem that if both parties were aware of these costs, they would have an incentive to reach a settlement before a strike results. In fact, most models of the collective-bargaining process focus on the likely division of the spoils between management and employees and ignore the determinants of strike activity.

The first, and also simplest, model of the bargaining process was developed

---

[19]It is easy to show in the context of a simple textbook model of firm behavior that an increase in the price of labor will reduce a firm's profits. However, this conclusion takes the firm's production function as given and does not consider other ways in which unions may increase productivity.

[20]See Allan Flanders, ed., *Collective Bargaining* (Baltimore, Md.: Penguin Books, 1969), pp. 317–68, for a description of productivity bargaining.

[21]In this regard, it is often alleged, although there is no strong empirical evidence on this point, that the level of strike activity is higher in the two states, New York and Rhode Island, that allow workers on strike to collect unemployment-insurance benefits (after a waiting period) than would otherwise be the case.

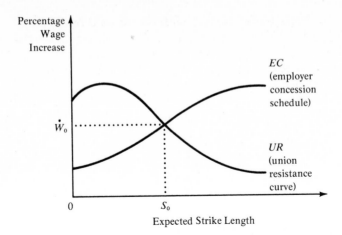

**FIGURE 12.3   Hicks' Bargaining Model
and Expected Strike Length**

by Sir John Hicks.[22] Suppose that management and labor are bargaining over only one issue—the size of the wage increase to be granted. How would the percentage increase that the union demands and the increase that the employer is willing to grant vary with the expected duration of a strike?

On the employer side of the market, the longer a strike lasts, the more costly it becomes in terms of lost customers. This increasing cost suggests that, as a strike progresses, an employer should be willing to increase the wage offer; this willingness is denoted by the upward-sloping *employer concession schedule, EC,* in Figure 12.3.

On the employee side of the market, initially union members' attitudes may harden, and they may actually increase their wage demands during the early part of a strike. However, after some point the loss in income they are suffering begins to color their attitudes, and they should begin to reduce their wage demands. This reduction is indicated by the *union resistance curve, UR,* in Figure 12.3, which eventually becomes downward-sloping.

As the strike proceeds, the union's demands decrease and the employer's offer increases until at strike duration, S_0, the two coincide. At this point a settlement can be reached, the parties would agree upon a wage increase of $\dot{W}_0$, and the strike would be terminated. Of course, *if* each party were aware of the position and shape of the other party's curve, each would know in advance of the strike what the size of the ultimate settlement would be. As such, it would make sense to agree to a settlement of $\dot{W}_0$ *prior* to the strike so that *both* parties could avoid incurring the costs associated with the strike.

If such a settlement could be made in advance, why would strikes ever occur? One reason is that information is imperfect; one or both sides in the negotiation could fail to convey the true shape and position of their schedule to the other

---

[22]John R. Hicks, *The Theory of Wages,* 2nd ed. (New York: St. Martin's Press, 1966), pp. 136–57.

Table 12.6 Work Stoppages in the United States, 1953–1977

| | | Workers Involved | | Estimated Percentage | |
Year	Number of Strikes	Number (in thousands)	As Percentage of Employed	of Working Time Lost	Unemployment Rate
1953	5,091	2,400	4.7	0.22	2.9
1954	3,468	1,530	3.1	0.18	5.5
1955	4,320	2,650	5.2	0.22	4.4
1956	3,825	1,900	3.6	0.24	4.1
1957	3,673	1,390	2.6	0.12	4.3
1958	3,694	2,060	3.9	0.18	6.8
1959	3,708	1,880	3.3	0.50	5.5
1960	3,333	1,320	2.4	0.14	5.5
1961	3,367	1,450	2.6	0.11	6.7
1962	3,614	1,230	2.2	0.13	5.5
1963	3,362	941	1.1	0.11	5.7
1964	3,655	1,640	2.7	0.15	5.2
1965	3,963	1,550	2.5	0.15	4.5
1966	4,405	1,960	3.0	0.15	3.8
1967	4,595	2,870	4.3	0.25	3.8
1968	5,045	2,649	3.8	0.28	3.6
1969	5,700	2,481	3.5	0.24	3.5
1970	5,716	3,305	4.7	0.37	4.9
1971	5,138	3,280	4.6	0.26	5.9
1972	5,010	1,714	2.3	0.15	5.6
1973	5,353	2,251	2.9	0.14	4.9
1974	6,074	2,778	3.5	0.24	5.6
1975	5,031	1,746	2.2	0.16	8.5
1976	5,648	2,420	3.0	0.19	7.7
1977	5,600	2,300	2.8	0.17	7.0

SOURCE: U.S. Bureau of Labor Statistics, *Handbook of Labor Statistics, 1978,* Bulletin 2000 (Washington, D.C.: U.S. Government Printing Office, 1979), Tables 56 and 151.

party.[23] A second reason is that to enhance their bargaining positions and retain the credibility of the threat of a strike, unions may have to periodically use the weapon; a strike may be designed to influence *future* negotiations.[24] Finally, strikes may be useful devices by which the internal solidarity of a union can be enhanced against a common enemy—the employer.[25]

The major problem with these explanations of when a strike will occur is that they do not enable one to predict whether a strike will occur in a particular contract negotiation and, more important, they do not offer any insights about why the aggregate level of strike activity should vary over time. Table 12.6 presents data on work stoppages in the United States during a recent 25-year period. These data suggest that strike activity, as measured either by the percentage of workers involved in strikes or the percentage of estimated working time lost, is cyclical, increasing when unemployment rates are low and decreasing when unemployment

---

[23]In the words of Hicks, "The majority of strikes are doubtless the results of faulty negotiations," Hicks, *The Theory of Wages,* p. 146.

[24]Lest one carry this "rusty weapon" argument too far, the reader should consider its implication for the use of nuclear weapons.

[25]Richard Walton and Robert McKersie, *A Behavioral Theory of Labor Negotiations* (New York: McGraw-Hill, 1965), p. 32.

rates are high. To be useful a model of strike activity should be able to explain this observed pattern of behavior.

A Political Model of Strike Activity

Although there is no universally accepted model of strike activity, Orley Ashenfelter and George Johnson have recently built upon Arthur Ross's earlier work and developed what is essentially a political model of strike activity.[26] Their approach illustrates how the maximization models of economists can be generalized to incorporate noneconomic variables and allows us to analyze the effects of the Landrum-Griffin Act on the level of strike activity.

The Ashenfelter-Johnson model is based upon the premise that it is inappropriate to view the collective-bargaining process as involving only two parties, an employer and a union. Rather, they acknowledge that different members of the union will have different, and sometimes conflicting, objectives. Their focus is on the divergence in objectives between union members and union leaders. While union members are concerned primarily with their pecuniary and nonpecuniary conditions of employment, union leaders are also concerned about the survival and growth of the union *and* their own personal political survival.

Union leaders, who have been actively involved with management in the bargaining process, have much better information than rank-and-file union members about the employer's true financial position and the maximum wage settlement the union will be able to extract. If this settlement is smaller than the settlement that the membership wants, the union leaders face two options.

On the one hand, union leaders can return to their members, try to convince them of the employer's true financial picture, and recommend that management's last offer (the maximum that they know they can achieve) be accepted. The danger they face with this option is that the members may vote down the recommendation, accuse the leaders of selling out to management, and ultimately vote them out of office.

On the other hand, union leaders can return to their members and recommend that the members go out on strike. This recommendation will allow them to appear to be strong, militant leaders, even though the leaders themselves know that the strike will not lead to a larger settlement. However, after a strike of some duration, in accordance with the notion of the union resistance curve in Figure 12.3, union members will begin to moderate their wage demands and ultimately a settlement—for which the union leader will receive credit—will be reached. Since the latter strategy is the one that is more likely to maintain the union's strength *and* keep the leaders in office, it is the strategy leaders may opt for even though it is clearly not in their members' best interests in the short run (the members have to bear the costs of the strike).

This model can provide insights about the forces that affect the frequency and

---

[26]Arthur Ross, *Trade Union Wage Policy* (Berkeley, Calif.: University of California Press, 1948), and Orley Ashenfelter and George Johnson, "Bargaining Theory, Trade Unions, and Industrial Strike Activity," *American Economic Review* 59 (March 1969): 35–49. A more recent test of the model is found in Henry Farber, "Bargaining Theory, Wage Outcomes, and the Occurrence of Strikes," *American Economic Review* 68 (June 1978): 262–71.

(a) Union Members' Acceptable Wage Increase

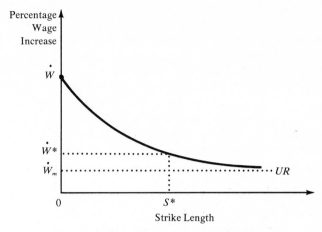

(b) Employer Present Value of Profit Function

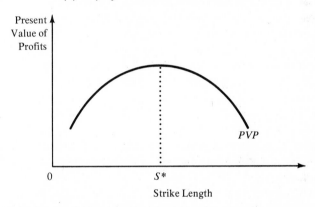

FIGURE 12.4 Graphic Representation of Ashenfelter-Johnson Model of Strike Activity

duration of strike activity. In panel (a) of Figure 12.4, curve *UR* represents union members' minimum acceptable percentage wage increase *($\dot{W}$)* as a function of the length of a strike; this curve is nothing more than the Hicks' union-resistance curve. To simplify the discussion, we have assumed that curve *UR* always declines with strike length. In this diagram $\dot{W}$ is the union members initial wage demand (the amount they would settle for without a strike), and $\dot{W}_m$ is the minimum amount they would ever settle for. Depending upon economic conditions and the members' hostility to management, $\dot{W}_m$ may be positive, zero, or even negative—the last possibility would occur if union members felt that they had to take a pay cut to preserve their jobs.

Panel (b) of Figure 12.4 plots the employer's present value of profits *(PVP)* as a function of the length of a strike. An increase in strike duration has two offsetting effects. In the immediate period, the employer loses profits because the firm loses some sales. However, in the future the firm's profits may be higher because the longer strike means that the employees will be willing to settle for smaller wage increases [from panel (a) of Figure 12.4]. In panel (b), initially the first effect dominates and then, ultimately—since the union wage demands fall less rapidly (in absolute terms) and lost sales begin to mount up—the latter effect dominates. That is, the employer's present value of profits first increases and then decreases with strike duration.

Suppose the employer's goal is to maximize the firm's present value of profits, and suppose the employer knows the position and shape of the curves in Figure 12.4. The employer can maximize the firm's present value of profits by offering the union a wage increase of $\dot{W}^*$ after a strike of length S^*. At that point, the union members will accept the offer and the strike will end. If the *PVP* curve in Figure 12.4 were always negatively sloped, the employer would either settle prior to a strike or go out of business if paying $\dot{W}$ would cause the firm to suffer losses.

Changing the model's parameters influences the probability of occurrence and expected duration of a strike. For example, if the union's initial wage demand $(\dot{W})$ increases, other things equal, a strike will have a greater payoff to the employer and the expected duration will increase. Similarly, an increase in the rate at which the union's wage demands decline over time, other things equal, will increase the employer's payoff from prolonging the strike. In contrast, an increase in the union members' minimum acceptable wage demand $\dot{W}_m$ (sometimes called the union's *resistance point*) will reduce the employer's gain from incurring a strike, other things equal, and will reduce the probability of a strike occurring.

The Ashenfelter and Johnson model—which assumed that the above parameters are influenced by the unemployment rate in the economy, by past changes in wage rates and prices, and by the profit rates of corporations—is able to explain why increases in the unemployment rate lead to reduced strike activity.[27] In the context of their model, an increase in the unemployment rate reduces the initial wage demands of unions, $\dot{W}$.

Ashenfelter and Johnson also found that after statistically controlling for the unemployment rate, profits, and past wage and price changes, the level of strike activity (as measured by the number of strikes per year) tended to decline during the 1952–1967 period. However, the decline took a particular form: while the pattern was downward from 1952 to 1959, the number jumped up in 1959 before resuming its downward trend (see Figure 12.5).[28]

The general decline in strike activity in the U.S. economy has been attributed by many observers to the maturation of industrial relations in the United States; fewer strikes are now caused by the parties misunderstanding each other's intensions or by the need to use a strike today to enhance bargaining power tomorrow.[29] The increase in 1959 coincided with the passage of the Landrum-Griffin Act. By

---

[27] Ashenfelter and Johnson, "Bargaining Theory," pp. 42–46.

[28] Ashenfelter and Johnson, "Bargaining Theory," p. 47.

[29] It is hard to discern a trend in any of the measures of strike activity over the 1953–78 period in the *raw* data presented in Table 12.6. One must remember, however, that during the period all of the other variables (unemployment, wage and price changes, profits) were changing. The trends Ashenfelter and Johnson observe are found after one statistically controls for these other factors.

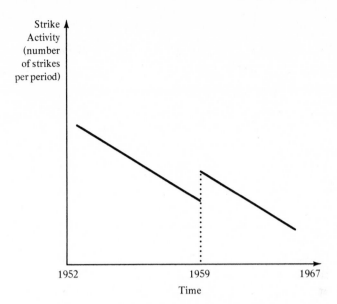

FIGURE 12.5 Ashenfelter and Johnson's Estimated Time Trend
in Strike Activity

increasing union democracy this act increased the chances that union leaders
would be voted out of office if they failed to satisfy union members' expectations
at contract-negotiation time. In the context of the model presented here, making
union leaders more accountable to membership would increase the probability that
leaders would recommend going on strike to their members, rather than trying to
sell the rank and file on an unacceptable contract. To return to a previous theme,
social programs and legislation often have unintended side effects; the Landrum-
Griffin Act may well have unintentionally led to an increase in the level of strike
activity in the economy.

The model presented in this section does not pretend to be the ultimate model
of strike activity. It focuses only on strikes that result due to disagreements over
economic issues and ignores strikes that may result from conflict over recognition
procedures, grievance procedures, unsafe working conditions, and the like. It also
makes certain assumptions that, while sometimes plausible, are unlikely to always
be true. For example, in essence this model suggests that union leaders and management implicitly collude to the detriment of union members. Union leaders are
assumed to be willing to recommend a strike that will impose costs (in the form
of lost income) on members, even though they know that the strike will not increase management's ultimate wage offer. Management is assumed to fully know
union members' resistance curve. Finally, union members are assumed to be ignorant, in the sense that they never learn how the bargaining process is actually
working. Nonetheless, the model provides useful insights into the bargaining process and an explanation of why the Landrum-Griffin Act and the unemployment
rate should be expected to influence the level of strike activity.

THE EFFECTS OF UNIONS

The Theory of Union Wage Effects

Suppose one had data on the wage rates paid to two groups of workers who were identical in every respect except for the fact that one group was unionized and the other was not.[30] Let W_u denote the wage paid to union members and W_n the wage paid to nonunion workers. If the difference between the two could be attributed solely to the presence of unions, then the *relative-wage advantage* that unions would have achieved for their members would be given, in percentage terms, by

$$R = (W_u - W_n)/W_n \tag{12.1}$$

Contrary to what one might expect, this relative-wage advantage does *not* represent the absolute amount, in percentage terms, by which unions would have increased the wages of their members because unions both directly and indirectly affect *nonunion* wage rates also. Moreover, one can not *a priori* state whether estimates of R will overstate, or understate, the absolute effect of unions on their members' real wage levels. (This chapter, as noted before, focuses on the union effects on wage *levels;* Chapter 16 will discuss union effects on the *rate of wage change.*) Figure 12.6 presents a simple two-sector model of the labor market. Except for the fact that the labor-supply curves are upward-sloping in both sectors, this model is identical to the one used in Chapter 3 to analyze the effects of the minimum wage in the presence of incomplete coverage; the analyses here will proceed along similar lines.

Panel (a) is the union sector and panel (b) is the nonunion sector. Suppose initially, however, that both sectors are unorganized. If mobility is relatively cost-less, workers will move between the two sectors until wages are equalized between them. With demand curves D_u and D_n, workers will move between sectors until the supply curves are S_u^0 and S_n^0, respectively. The common equilibrium wage will be W_0, and employment will be E_u^0 and E_n^0 respectively in the two sectors.

Now suppose a union succeeds in organizing the workers in the first sector and also succeeds in raising their wage to W_u^1. This increased wage will cause employment to decline to E_u^1 workers in the union sector, resulting in $L_u^1 - E_u^1$ unemployed workers in that sector. These workers have several options; one is to seek employment in the nonunion sector. If all of the unemployed workers *spill over* into the nonunion sector, the supply curves in the two sectors will shift to S_u^1 and S_n^1 respectively. Unemployment will be eliminated in the union sector; however, in the nonunion sector an excess supply of labor would exist at the old market-clearing wage, W_0. As a result, downward pressure would be exerted on the wage rate in the nonunion sector until the labor market in that sector cleared at a *lower* wage W_n^1 and a higher employment level E_n^1.

In the context of this model, the union has succeeded in raising the wages of its members who kept their jobs. However, it has done so at the expense of shifting some of its members to lower-wage jobs in the nonunion sector and, because of this spillover effect, at the expense of actually lowering the wage rate

---

[30]Much of the discussion in this section is based upon the pioneering work by H. G. Lewis, *Unionism and Relative Wages in the United States* (Chicago: University of Chicago Press, 1963).

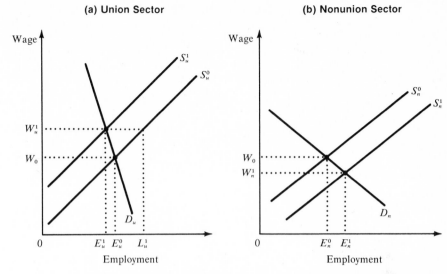

(a) Union Sector   **(b) Nonunion Sector**

FIGURE 12.6   Spillover Effects of Unions on Wages and Employment

paid to individuals initially employed in the nonunion sector. As a result, the observed union *relative-wage* advantage (R_1), computed as

$$R_1 = (W_u^1 - W_n^1)/W_n^1, \qquad (12.2)$$

will tend to be greater than the true *absolute* effect of the union on its members' real wage. This true absolute effect (A_1), stated in percentage terms, is computed as

$$A_1 = (W_u^1 - W_0)/W_0 \qquad (12.3)$$

The relative effect will not necessarily be larger than the absolute effect however, because there are several other responses that employees or employers can make. Employers in the nonunion sector may be concerned that unions will subsequently try to organize their employees—employers may view a union as undesirable if unionization both increases their wage costs and limits their managerial flexibility. As such, they may try to "buy off" their employees by offering them wage increases to reduce the probability that the employees will vote for a union.[31] Because of the costs associated with union membership, noted earlier, some wage less than W_u^1, but higher than W_0, would presumably be sufficient to assure employers that the majority of their employees would not vote for a union (assuming that the employees are happy with their nonwage conditions of employment).

The implications of such *threat effects*—nonunion wage increases resulting from the threat of union entry—are traced in Figure 12.7. The increase in wage in the union sector, and resulting decline in employment there, is again assumed to cause the supply of workers to the nonunion sector to shift to S_n^1. However, in

---

[31]For a more formal discussion of this possibility, see Sherwin Rosen, "Trade Union Power, Threat Effects, and the Extent of Organization," *Review of Economic Studies* 36 (April 1969): 185–96.

Nonunion Sector

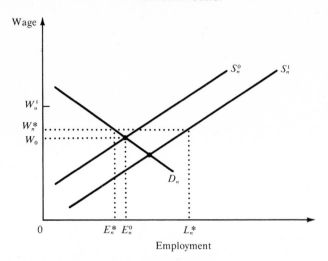

**FIGURE 12.7   Threat Effects of Unions on Wages
and Employment**

response to the threat of union entry, nonunion employers are assumed to *increase* their employees' wages to W_n^*, which lies between W_0 and W_u^1. This wage increase causes employment to decline to E_n^*; at the higher wage nonunion employers demand fewer workers. Moreover, since the nonunion wage is now not free to be bid down, an excess supply of labor, $L_n^* - E_n^*$, exists, resulting in unemployment. Finally, because the nonunion wage is now higher than the original wage, the observed union relative-wage advantage,

$$R_2 = (W_u^1 - W_n^*)/W_n^*, \qquad (12.4)$$

is smaller than the absolute effect of unions on their members' real wages.

One might question whether workers who lose their jobs in the union sector, as a result of the union's increasing the wage rate, will necessarily seek jobs in the nonunion sector. Even with a fixed employment level in the union sector, job vacancies occur due to retirements, deaths, and voluntary turnover (including quits to take other jobs in the same area, geographic migration, and individuals who are temporarily leaving the labor force). It may pay union members to remain attached to the union sector *and* temporarily unemployed if they believe that they will ultimately obtain a job in the union sector. Indeed, it may actually pay some employed nonunion workers to quit their jobs and move to the union sector in the hopes that they will obtain a relatively higher-paying union job in the future. Such decisions lead to *wait unemployment:* workers rejecting lower-paying nonunion jobs and waiting for higher-paying union jobs to open up.[32]

---

[32]See Jacob Mincer, "Unemployment Effects of Minimum Wages," *Journal of Political Economy* 84 (July/August 1976, Part 2): S87-S104. Although Mincer discusses minimum-wage effects, union-imposed "minimum wages" can be analyzed analogously.

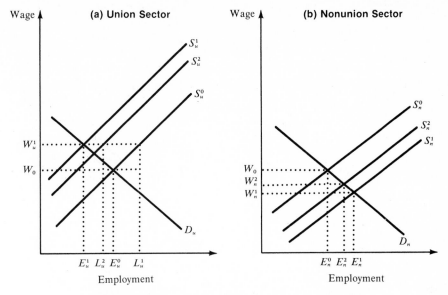

FIGURE 12.8 Wait Unemployment (nonunion wage falls)

Workers will move between the union and nonunion sector until their *expected earnings* in each are equal. If one ignores complications such as the costs of union membership, the presence of unemployment-insurance benefits for some unemployed workers, fringe benefits, and the like, expected earnings will be equal when the wage rate paid in each sector multiplied by the fraction of each period (F) that individuals in the sector expect to be employed are equal—or when

$$W_u F_u = W_n F_n. \tag{12.5}$$

Figure 12.8 illustrates the process. If threat effects are ignored, the consequences of an increase in the union wage to W_u^1 would be a decline in employment in the union sector to E_u^1, a shift in the supply curves to S_u^1 and S_n^1, and a resulting decrease in nonunion wages to W_n^1 and increase in nonunion employment to E_n^1. Since there is no unemployment in this situation, F_u and F_n are both equal to unity. Hence, labor-market equilibrium, as indicated in equation (12.5), would require that wages be equal in the two sectors. But they are *not;* W_u^1 is greater than W_n^1; hence, individuals' expected earnings are higher in the union sector.

The above difference in expected earnings would induce some individuals to move from the nonunion sector to wait for jobs in the union sector. This movement leads to an increase in the expected earnings in the nonunion sector (as supply decreases there, wages are bid up) and and a decrease in expected earnings in the union sector (as supply increases there, the probability of obtaining a job in that sector decreases). Eventually expected earnings are equalized between the two sectors by this process.

We have *assumed* that expected earnings are equalized in Figure 12.8 at the points at which the supply curves in the two sectors are S_u^2 and S_n^2, respectively.

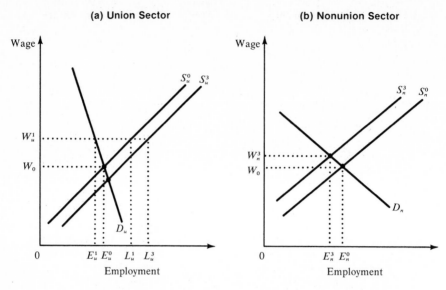

FIGURE 12.9 Wait Unemployment (nonunion wage increases)

The resulting wage in the nonunion sector is W_n^2, and the resulting employment level is E_n^2. *Wait unemployment* now exists in the union sector; its level is given by $L_u^2 - E_u^1$. Finally, although W_n^2 is greater than W_n^1, W_n^2 is less than W_0. Thus, if the union relative-wage advantage is measured as

$$R_3 = (W_u^1 - W_n^2)/W_n^2, \tag{12.6}$$

it will again be larger than the true absolute effect of the union on its members' real wage levels.

Of course, we have assumed that the expected earnings would be equalized as indicated in Figure 12.8. Under certain assumptions, the equalization may not occur until after the supply of labor to the union sector has shifted to the *right* of its initial position and after the supply of labor in the nonunion sector has shifted to the *left* of its initial position. This situation is more likely to occur if the demand curve in the union sector is inelastic. An inelastic demand curve would cause *expected earnings* $(W_u^1 F_u)$ in the union sector to increase immediately after the increase in the union *wage,* because employment losses are so small. This immediate rise in expected earnings induces employees to migrate from the non-union to union sector.[33] As Figure 12.9 indicates, supply in the union sector shifts right (to S_u^3) and supply in the nonunion sector shifts left (to S_n^3). In this situation wait unemployment would increase to $L_u^3 - E_u^1$, and the nonunion wage would

[33]See Mincer, ''Unemployment Effects of Minimum Wages'' and Edward Gramlich, ''The Impact of Minimum Wages on Other Wages, Employment, and Family Incomes,'' *Brookings Papers on Economic Activity,* 1976–2, pp. 409–51, for a more complete discussion of when this is likely to occur.

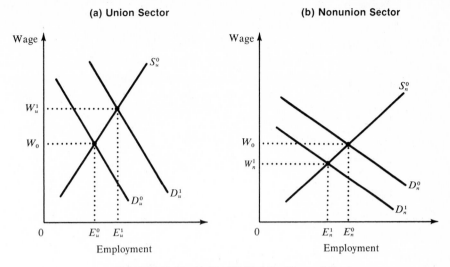

FIGURE 12.10 Union "Shifts" the Demand Curve

increase to W_n^3, which is greater than W_0. The union relative-wage advantage in this case, which is computed as

$$R_4 = (W_u^1 - W_n^3)/W_n^3, \qquad (12.7)$$

would be less than the absolute effect of unions on their members' real wages.

One final case will complete our discussion. Suppose the union increases its members' wages by means of increasing the demand for union labor—using any of the methods discussed in the previous section. Figure 12.10 illustrates an increase in the demand for labor in the union sector to D_u^1. If this increase comes at the expense of the demand for labor in the nonunion sector, the latter curve will fall—say, to D_n^1. Initially, the effect is to increase both wages (W_u^1) and employment (E_u^1) in the union sector and decrease wages (W_n^1) and employment (E_n^1) in the nonunion sector. The ultimate change in the nonunion wage, however, will depend upon the extent to which threat effects or wait unemployment are important. So again, estimates of the union *relative*-wage effects alone tell us little about the *absolute* effects of unions on their members' real wage levels.

Because unions *are* present in the economy, at any point in time all one can observe are the union and nonunion wage rates (W_u and W_n). One can *not* observe the wage that would have existed in the absence of unions, W_0. Hence, direct estimates of a union's effects on the absolute level (A_1) of its members' real wages—refer back to equation (12.3)—can not be obtained. Care must be taken not to mistake relative-wage effects for absolute-wage effects.[34]

---

[34]This discussion has assumed a partial-equilibrium model. Once one considers a general-equilibrium framework and allows capital to move between sectors, even more possibilities may exist. On this point, see Harry Johnson and Peter Mieszkowski, "The Effects of Unionization on the Distribution of Income: A General Equilibrium Approach," *Quarterly Journal of Economics* 84 (November 1969): 539–61.

Evidence of Union Wage Effects

In recent years, economists have expended considerable effort to estimate the extent to which unions have raised the wages of their members relative to the wages of comparable nonunion workers in the private sector.[35] These studies have tended to use data on large samples of individuals and have attempted to separate wage differentials due to unionization from wage differentials due to differences in personal characteristics and differences in industry and occupation of employment. That is, these economists have sought to ascertain how much more union members get paid than nonunion workers, after controlling for any differences between the two groups in other factors that might be expected to influence wages.[36]

The various studies use several different data bases that span various years, and they often employ different statistical methodologies. As such, they do not yield a single unambiguous estimate of the extent to which union members' wages exceed the wages of comparable nonunion workers in the private sector. Perhaps the best estimate is that the union relative-wage advantage, on average, has fallen to the range of 10 to 20 percent in recent years. These union wage effects, however, are neither constant over time nor constant across groups.

A recent study by Orley Ashenfelter, summarized in Table 12.7, suggests that the estimated union relative-wage advantage rose substantially between 1967 and 1975, from 11.6 to 16.8 percent. The year 1967 was one of low unemployment; the year 1975 was one of high unemployment. Since unionized workers' wages tend to be less responsive to labor-market conditions than nonunion workers' wages (see Chapter 16), this result is not surprising; the union relative-wage advantage tends to be larger during recessionary periods.[37]

The estimates in Table 12.7 also suggest that unions have helped improve the relative economic positions of black males. On the one hand, the estimated relative-wage effects are larger for black males than white males; being a union member enhances black males' earnings by more than it does white males' earnings. On the other hand, the percentage of black males that are union members also appears to be slightly larger than the comparable percentage for white males. On balance then, in spite of well-publicized conflicts between some unions and civil-rights organizations over union seniority rules and the use of racial quotas, unions appear to have improved the economic well-being of black males relative to white males.

In contrast, Table 12.7 emphasizes that female workers are considerably less likely to be union members than are male employees. Although in some years females who are union members appear to have gained as much as *white* males

---

[35] See C. J. Parsley, "Labor Unions and Wages: A Survey," *Journal of Economic Literature* 18 (March 1980): 1–31; and for an earlier survey, George E. Johnson, "Economic Analysis of Trade Unionism," *American Economic Review* 65 (May 1975): 23–28.

[36] Some of the more ambitious studies also attempt to control for the fact that unionization and wages may be simultaneously determined; as noted earlier, workers' decisions to join a union are partially based on the expected gains from union membership. See for example, Lung-Fei Lee, "Unionism and Wage Rates: A Simultaneous-Equations Model with Qualitative and Limited Dependent Variables," *International Economic Review* 19 (June 1978): 415–33.

[37] Lewis, *Unionism and Relative Wages,* provides evidence that this relationship appeared to hold during the 1930-1960 period as well.

Table 12.7   **Estimated Union/Nonunion Relative Wage Effects,**
1967, 1973, and 1975

	Percentage Union Wage Effect			*Percentage Unionized*		
	1967	*1973*	*1975*	*1967*	*1973*	*1975*
All workers	11.6	14.8	16.8	23	26	25
White males	9.6	15.5	16.3	31	33	31
Black males	21.5	22.5	22.5	32	37	37
White females	14.4	12.7	16.6	12	14	14
Black females	5.6	13.2	17.1	13	22	22

SOURCE: Orley Ashenfelter, "Union Relative Wage Effects: New Evidence and a Survey of Their Implications for Wage Inflation," in *Econometric Contributions to Public Policy*, eds. R. Stone and W. Peterson (New York: St. Martin's, 1979), Tables 2.1 and 2.2.

who are union members vis-a-vis their nonunion counterparts, on balance the *overall* effect of unions is to reduce female wages relative to male wages—perhaps by as much as 2.9 percent in 1975.[38]

The estimates cited above are of the relative-wage advantage (*R*) that unions have achieved for their members in comparison to nonunion workers. These estimates do not indicate what effects unions have had on the absolute real wage levels of their members. In other words, the estimates do not reveal how unions have influenced *nonunion* workers' wages. The limited evidence on this point, although ambiguous, suggests that unions may well depress the wages of nonunion workers; the *spillover effect* described in Figure 12.6 appears to dominate over the *threat* and *wait-unemployment effects* described in Figures 12.7 and 12.9.[39] That is, other things equal, the wages of nonunion workers are lower in cities in which the percent of workers in the city who are union members is high. Thus, estimates of the relative-wage effects of unions may well be greater than their effects on the absolute level of their members' real wages.

One might think that the above evidence suggests that unions increase the dispersion of labor earnings, increasing the wages of high-paid union members and decreasing the wages of lower-paid nonunion workers. In fact, however, several studies indicate that unions actually tend on balance to *decrease* the dispersion of labor earnings. For example, it is now well known that rates of return to education and job training are lower in the union than nonunion sector; these lower payoffs in the union sector cause the earnings there to be more equal among workers with different human-capital investments than would otherwise be the case.[40] Other studies find 1. that union wage policies designed to standardize wage rates within and across establishments significantly reduce the extent of wage dispersion among workers covered by union contracts, and 2. that unions also reduce the relative-wage advantage of white-collar workers vis-a-vis blue-collar workers.

---

[38]Ashenfelter and Johnson, "Bargaining Theory."

[39]Lawrence Kahn, "The Effect of Unions on the Earnings of Nonunion Workers," *Industrial and Labor Relations Review* 31 (January 1978): 205–16.

[40]Farrell Bloch and Mark Kuskin, "Wage Determination in the Union and Nonunion Sectors," *Industrial and Labor Relations Review* 31 (January 1978): 183–92; and Greg M. Duncan and Duane E. Leigh, "Wage Determination in the Union and Nonunion Sectors: A Sample Selectivity Approach," *Industrial and Labor Relations Review* 34 (October 1980): 24–35.

Example 12.2
Codetermination and Union Relative-Wage Gains in West Germany

Since the early 1950s, legislation has encouraged greater employee participation in management in West Germany. These *codetermination laws* give employees in the German iron-steel and mining industries one-half of the seats on company Boards of Directors and give employees in all other industries (save for shipping and air transport) one-third of the seats. The position of labor director has also been established on Management Boards in the steel and mining industries; this director cannot be approved, or dismissed, without a majority vote of the employee representatives to a company's Board of Directors.

German employee representatives on Boards of Directors participate in decisions about industrywide collective-bargaining agreements. One might expect that these laws have increased labor's bargaining power, especially in the iron-steel and mining industries, and have thus increased the size of observed wage differentials between unionized workers in these industries and other employees in the economy. A recent study concluded that codetermination has increased the earnings of the average unionized German iron-steel and mining employee by roughly 6.2 percent relative to the earnings of primarily nonunion employees in the textile industry. The effects of unions on relative wages clearly depend upon the prevailing institutional arrangements.

SOURCE: Jan Svejnar, "Relative Wage Effects of Unions, Dictatorship, and Codetermination: Econometric Evidence From Germany," *Review of Economics and Statistics* 63 (May 1981): 188–97.

Indeed, one study suggests that these effects dominate over the more widely known union effects on union/nonunion worker wage differentials, in the sense that on balance unions appear to reduce wage dispersion in the United States.[41] Finally, another study suggests that other things equal, inequality of earnings within metropolitan areas tends to be less widespread in areas in which the extent of unionization is high.[42]

Evidence of Union Total Compensation Effects

Estimates of the extent to which the wages of union workers exceed the wages of otherwise comparable nonunion workers may prove misleading for two reasons. First, such estimates ignore the fact that wages are only part of the compensation package. It has often been argued that fringe benefits, such as paid holidays, vacation pay, sick leave, and retirement benefits will be higher in firms that are unionized than in nonunion firms. The argument states that because tastes for the various fringe benefits differ across individuals, and because there is no easy way

[41]Richard Freeman, "Unionism and the Dispersion of Wages," *Industrial and Labor Relations Review* 34 (October 1980): 3–23.

[42]Thomas Hyclak, "The Effects of Unions on Earnings Inequality in Local Labor Markets," *Industrial and Labor Relations Review* 33 (October 1979): 77–84.

to communicate the preferences of the average employee to the employer in a nonunion firm, nonunion firms will tend to pay a higher fraction of total compensation in the form of money wages.[43] Recent empirical evidence tends to support this contention; fringe benefits and the share of compensation that goes to fringe benefits do appear to be higher in union than in nonunion firms.[44] Ignoring fringes may therefore understate the true union/nonunion total compensation differential.

In contrast, ignoring nonpecuniary conditions of employment may cause one to overstate the true effect of unions on their members' total compensation vis-a-vis nonunion workers. For example, two recent studies have shown that for blue-collar workers, unionized firms tend to have more structured work settings, less flexible hours of work, faster work paces, and less employee control over the assignment of overtime hours than do nonunion firms.[45] This situation may arise because production settings that give rise to interdependence among workers and the demand for specific work requirements by employers also give rise to unions. That is, the decision to vote for unions may be heavily influenced by these nonpecuniary conditions of employment. While unions often strive to affect these working conditions, they do not always succeed. Part of the estimated union/nonunion earning differential may be a premium paid to union workers to compensate them for these unfavorable working conditions. Indeed, one study estimates that two-fifths of the estimated union/nonunion earnings differential reflects such compensation—suggesting that the observed union/nonunion earnings differential may overstate the true union/nonunion total compensation differential.[46]

The Traditional View of Union Effects on Productivity and Output

According to the traditional neoclassical view of unions, although they may improve the welfare of their members by improving their pecuniary and nonpecuniary conditions of employment, on balance their effects on the economy at large are negative. Three reasons are given to support this view.

First, to the extent that unions do succeed in driving a wedge between the wage rates of comparable quality workers who are employed in the union and nonunion sectors, there is a loss of output. Recall from Chapter 3 that the demand curves for labor reflect the marginal product of labor. If the "spillover" model in Figure 12.6 holds, the union wage, W_u, exceeds the nonunion wage, W_n—and the marginal product of labor is higher in the union sector than in the nonunion sector. Consequently, output could be increased if labor were reallocated from the nonunion sector to the union sector where its marginal product is higher. Put another way, unions cause a misallocation of workers: too many workers are employed in the nonunion sector and too few in the union sector. Of course, if the

[43]This line of reasoning goes back at least as far as Richard Lester, "Benefits as a Preferred Form of Compensation," *Southern Economic Journal* 33 (April 1967): 488–95.

[44]Richard Freeman, "The Effect of Trade Unions on Fringe Benefits," *Industrial and Labor Relations Review* 34 (July 1981): 489–509.

[45]Greg Duncan and Frank Stafford, "Do Union Members Receive Compensating Wage Differentials?" *American Economic Review* 70 (June 1980): 355–71; and Ronald G. Ehrenberg and Paul L. Schumann, "Compensating Wage Differentials for Mandatory Overtime" (paper presented at the Econometric Society Meetings, September 1980).

[46]Duncan and Stafford, "Do Union Members Receive Compensating Wage Differentials?"

union wage gain also induces some unemployment (see Figures 12.7, 12.8, and 12.9), the loss of output due to these idled resources must also be considered.

Second, union-negotiated contract provisions that establish staffing requirements or other restrictive work practices, limit firms from employing capital and labor in the most efficient ways and may cause output losses. Several examples of such provisions include minimum crew sizes in jet aircrafts, maximum apprentice/journeymen ratios in construction, provisions limiting subcontracting or mandatory assignment of overtime, and requirements that redundant employees be employed (fire stokers in diesel-operated railroad engines, typesetters in printing plants where type is set by computer). By limiting substitution possibilities or forcing firms to use redundant inputs, unions reduce output below its maximum achievable level.

Third, unions are thought to reduce output because strikes called either at the time that collective-bargaining is occurring (to influence the settlement) or during the term of a contract (to protest the way the contract is being administered) result in lost work days. In this view, if strikes were eliminated, output would increase.

Actual empirical estimates of the magnitudes of these alleged losses are few and far between. In an often cited study, Albert Rees estimated that society lost no more than 0.3 percent of gross national product because of the creation of wage differentials between comparable quality union and nonunion workers.[47] Rees also estimated that the loss of output due to restrictive work practices was at least as large. Finally, Table 12.6 indicated that the estimated percentage of working time lost due to strikes over the 25-year period from 1953–1977 averaged 0.2 percent. Summing these three figures yields a ballpark estimate of a loss in output of less than 0.8 percent due to these three factors. Of course, whether one considers this an acceptable or unacceptable cost depends upon the benefits that one believes society as a whole receives from unionization.

An Alternative View of Union Effects on Productivity and Output

Recently labor economists have begun to rediscover the possibility that unions may also have positive influences on productivity.[48] The analyses of Richard Freeman and James Medoff and their associates are based heavily upon the assumption that unions function as institutions of *collective voice* operating within structured internal labor markets.[49] That is, because unions can communicate the preferences

---

[47]Albert Rees, "The Effects of Unions on Resource Allocation," *Journal of Law and Economics* 6 (October 1963): 69–78. Rees's estimate also included consideration of output losses due to union effects on intra-industry wage differentials—for example, requiring all unionized firms in an industry to pay the same wage.

[48]For a discussion of the evidence supporting this view, see Richard B. Freeman and James L. Medoff, "The Two Faces of Unionism," *Public Interest* 57 (Fall 1979): 69–93. A more detailed discussion is found in their *What Do Unions Do?* (New York: Basic Books, 1982).

[49]Albert Hirschman, *Exit, Voice and Loyalty* (Cambridge: Harvard University Press, 1973), and Richard Freeman, "Individual Mobility and Union Voice in the Labor Market," *American Economic Review* 66 (May 1976): 361–68 provide discussions of unions' role as institutions of collective voice. Oliver Williamson, Michael Wachter, and Jeffrey Harris, "Understanding the Employment Relation: Analysis of Idiosyncratic Exchange," *Bell Journal of Economics* 6 (Spring 1975): 250–80, emphasize the interrelationship between unions and internal labor markets.

of workers on various issues directly to management and can help establish work rules and seniority provisions in the context of structured internal labor markets, they can contribute to increases in productivity in a number of ways.

First, by providing workers with a direct means to voice their discontent to management and by establishing job rights based upon seniority, unions may reduce worker discontent—thus reducing voluntary turnover (quit rates). As discussed in Chapter 5, reductions in job turnover increase employers' incentives to provide their employees with *firm-specific training,* which will lead to increased productivity. Considerable evidence suggests that unions do in fact reduce quit rates.[50] Moreover, seniority systems weaken the extent of rivalry between inexperienced and experienced employees and consequently increase the amount of informal on-the-job training that the latter are willing to give to the former.[51]

Second, by increasing the economic rewards to employment and providing grievance mechanisms, unions may directly enhance productivity by increasing worker morale, motivation, and effort. Third, unions provide an explicit mechanism by which labor can point out possible changes in work rules or production techniques that will benefit both labor and management.

Several studies have been undertaken in recent years that attempt to estimate the net effect of unions on productivity. These studies are summarized in Table 12.8. The methodological approach used in all but the Clark study is to estimate the extent to which value of output per worker (the *value added*) is associated with the level of unionization in an industry or establishment at a point in time, after controlling for other factors expected to influence productivity.[52] (The Clark study uses data on the physical volume of output and also looks at how productivity changes after a plant becomes unionized.)

These studies suggest that union workers are more productive than nonunion workers in manufacturing. Indeed, the size of the productivity differential appears to be large enough to offset the estimated union/nonunion wage differential; that is, the unit labor cost of unionized manufacturing workers does not appear to exceed the unit labor cost of nonunion workers. This result provides an explanation of how high-wage union firms and lower-wage nonunion firms can co-exist in the same competitive industry.

In the bituminous coal industry, positive union productivity differentials are found in 1965, but substantial negative ones appear in 1975. Indeed, in 1975 unionized workers were estimated to be 20 to 25 percent *less* productive than nonunion workers in the industry. This decline in relative productivity has been attributed to the well-known breakdown of the United Mine Workers' (UMW) national leadership that occurred in the late 1960s and early 1970s, which resulted in deteriorating industrial-relations practices, including increased occurrence of

---

[50]See Richard B. Freeman, "The Exit-Voice Trade-off in the Labor Market: Unionism, Job Tenure, Quits, and Separations," *Quarterly Journal of Economics* 94 (June 1980): 644–73; and James Medoff, "Layoffs and Alternatives Under Trade Unions in United States Manufacturing," *American Economic Review* 69 (June 1979): 380–95.

[51]See Peter Doeringer and Michael Piore, *Internal Labor Markets and Manpower Analysis* (Lexington, Mass.: D.C. Heath, 1971).

[52]Value added is the difference in dollar terms between the sales price of a product and the value of the materials that went into making it.

wildcat (unauthorized) strikes over local issues.[53] These results emphasize that the effects of unions on productivity are neither constant nor always positive; they vary across industries and time periods as industrial-relations practices vary.

The Allen study cited in Table 12.8 finds surprisingly large union productivity differentials in construction—surprising because in the construction industry unions were widely thought to have adverse effects on productivity owing to their restrictive work rules (limits on apprentice/journeymen ratios, limits on the jobs members of each craft can do, etc.).[54] Because of some statistical problems associated with the Allen study, however, his results should be considered only tentative.[55]

On balance, then, the studies summarized in Table 12.8 suggest that unions have *increased* productivity in certain industries. There is no consensus yet, however, as to whether these increases more than offset the losses of gross national product caused by union effects on wage structures and union strike activity. These studies suggest, however, that like most questions in economics, whether unions have had a net positive or negative effect on output is an empirical question. The answer is not as obvious as either the supporters or opponents of unions would have one believe.

UNIONS IN REGULATED INDUSTRIES: CONFLICTING POLICY GOALS

This chapter concludes by returning to a policy issue originally discussed in Chapter 9; namely, whether wage increases negotiated by unions in regulated industries should automatically be passed on to consumers in the form of higher utility prices.[56] Chapter 9 used the human-capital framework to derive a standard by which public utility commissions could judge wage levels to be "just and reasonable." In particular, it was suggested that a reasonable standard would be to ask, after controlling statistically for the worker characteristics that are expected to influence earnings, if the unionized employees in the regulated industries are paid more than otherwise comparable workers employed elsewhere. This chapter will try to show how fraught with difficulties such comparisons would be.

Part of any estimated wage premium paid to unionized workers in regulated industries may be justified as a differential to compensate them for having relatively unfavorable working conditions or more difficult jobs than employees in other industries. Wage comparisons may not accurately reflect total compensation

---

[53]Richard Freeman, James Medoff, and Marie Connerton, "Industrial Relations and Productivity: A Case Study of the U.S. Bituminous Coal Industry" (Cambridge, Mass: Harvard University mimeo, 1979).

[54]Steven Allen, "Unionized Construction Workers Are More Productive" (Washington, D.C.: Center to Protect Workers' Rights, November 1979).

[55]Suppose union workers succeed in raising their wages. To cover the increased costs, employers may increase their product prices; however, this action increases value added. Thus, the association between unions and value added may reflect the effects of unions on wages and prices, not on productivity. This problem is particularly acute in construction since the market for construction products is in the main a local one and output prices are therefore set locally.

[56]Our discussion again draws heavily on Ronald G. Ehrenberg, *The Regulatory Process and Labor Earnings* (New York: Academic Press, 1979).

Table 12.8 Estimates of the Impact of Unionism
on Productivity in U.S. Industries

Industry	Estimated Impact of Unions on Productivity (percent)
(a) All U.S. Manufacturing, 1972	20 to 25
(b) Wooden Household Furniture, 1972	15
(c) Cement, 1953–76	6 to 8
(d) Underground Bituminous Coal, 1965	25 to 30
(e) Underground Bituminous Coal, 1975	−20 to −25
(f) Construction	29 to 38

SOURCES OF ESTIMATES: (a) Charles Brown and James Medoff, "Trade Unions in the Production Process," *Journal of Political Economy* 86 (June 1978): 355–78. (b) John Frantz, "The Impact of Trade Unions on Productivity in the Wood Household Furniture Industry," (Honors Thesis, Harvard University, 1976). (c) Kim Clark, "The Impact of Unionization on Productivity: A Case Study," *Industrial and Labor Relations Review* 33 (July 1980): 451–69. (d)-(e) Richard Freeman, James Medoff, and Marie Connerton, "Industrial Relations and Productivity: A Case Study of the U.S. Bituminous Coal Industry" (mimeo, Harvard University, 1979). (f) Steven Allen, "Unionized Construction Workers Are More Productive" (Washington, D.C.: Center to Protect Workers Rights, November 1979).

comparisons because they ignore fringe benefits. They also may neglect the potential positive effects that the union and a high-wage policy might have. These positive effects include, as noted earlier, reduced employee turnover (and, hence, reduced training costs), reduced loss of output since strike activity will be lower, and, in general, increased productivity. To accurately judge whether any union-negotiated wage increase should be passed on to consumers in the form of higher prices one must evaluate all of the above factors, which is no easy task. It has been suggested that it would be better to establish a set of incentives to encourage utilities to keep their costs down than to do "after-the-fact" statistical studies to ascertain if wage increases negotiated by utilities are acceptable.[57]

This policy issue poses a rather fundamental dilemma. On the one hand, ever since the National Labor Relations Act the explicit intent of the federal government has been to encourage free collective bargaining. In fact, the NLRA forbids any interference by states into the collective-bargaining process that has the effect of influencing the terms of the settlement. On the other hand, state utility commissions have the explicit goal of holding down consumers' utility costs.

A commission decision to disallow part of any collectively bargained wage settlement from being passed on to consumers would not violate the NLRA since it would not affect the terms of the settlement.[58] However, it would undoubtedly affect management willingness to grant the union large wage increases in the future; if the commission refuses to grant price increases to cover cost increases, the firms' profits must fall. In other words, the commission intervention would affect the environment in which bargaining takes place and the relative bargaining power of the union. Thus, implicitly, the commission action would affect future wage settlements.

We should also note, however, that commissions which uncritically allow all labor-cost increases to be passed on to consumers will also affect the environment

[57]Ehrenberg, *The Regulatory Process,* chapter 4. See Chapter 16 for further discussion of such incentive schemes.

[58]Ehrenberg, *The Regulatory Process,* pp. 118–22.

in which bargaining takes place—by increasing the relative bargaining power of unions. This outcome, which corresponds closely to the status quo in most states, is not necessarily more desirable. In any case, it should be clear that it is difficult for government to remain neutral; its mere presence—whether or not it takes any action—affects labor markets.

REVIEW QUESTIONS

1. Suppose that a proposal for tax reductions associated with the purchase of capital equipment is up for debate. Suppose, too, that union leaders are called upon to comment on the proposal from the perspective of how it will affect the welfare of their members as workers (not consumers). Will they all agree on the effects of the proposal? Explain your answer.
2. The head of a large national union is trying to decide where he should concentrate his efforts at organizing a union. He perceives three options: Firm A, Firm B, or Firm C. The three firms are identical except that:
   a. Firm A faces a perfectly elastic (horizontal) supply curve of labor and a rather inelastic demand curve for its output.
   b. Firm B behaves as a monopsonist (faces an upward-sloping supply curve of labor) and faces a perfectly elastic (horizontal) demand curve for its output.
   c. Firm C faces a perfectly elastic supply curve of labor and a perfectly elastic demand curve for its output.
   This union head would like to know where a new union will pay off in large wage gains and small reductions in numbers of workers. Rank the three options from best to worst giving reasons for your ranking.
3. Is the following statement true, false, or uncertain? "The host of empirical studies that indicate that unions raise the wages of their members by 10 to 15 percent relative to the wages of comparable nonunion workers imply that unions have a negative effect on national output." Explain your answer.
4. Unionized plumbers are in unions that control the size of their membership. Wages are kept high by keeping membership highly qualified and therefore small. Employers needing or wanting to employ union labor must hire from the ranks of union membership. Suppose there is a plumbers' union in each of two cities. City A has an ordinance that states that all plumbing installations and repairs must be performed by union members. City B has no such ordinance. Analyze as completely as you can the effects of City A's ordinance on workers, consumers, and the general well-being of society. (*Hint:* you can gain insight into this question by comparing Cities A and B.)
5. The Jones Act mandates that at least 50 percent of all U.S. government-financed cargo must be transported in U.S.-owned ships and that any U.S. ship leaving a U.S. port must have at least 90 percent of its crew composed of U.S. citizens. What would you expect the impact of this act to be on the demand for labor in the shipping industry and the ability of unions to push up the wages of their members?

SELECTED READINGS

Ashenfelter, Orley. "Union Relative Wage Effects: New Evidence and a Survey of Their Implications for Wage Inflation." In *Econometric Contributions to Public Policy,* edited by Richard Stone and William Peterson. New York: St. Martin, 1979.

Ashenfelter, Orley and George Johnson. "Bargaining Theory, Trade Unions, and Industrial Strike Activity." *American Economic Review* 59 (March 1969): 35–49.

Ashenfelter, Orley and John Pencavel. "American Trade Union Growth, 1900–1960." *Quarterly Journal of Economics* 83 (August 1969): 434–48.

Atherton, Wallace. *Theory of Union Bargaining Goals.* Princeton, N.J.: Princeton University Press, 1973.

Brown, Charles and James Medoff. "Trade Unions in the Production Process," *Journal of Political Economy* 86 (June 1978): 355–79.

Freeman, Richard B. and James L. Medoff. "The Two Faces of Unionism." *Public Interest* 57 (Fall 1979): 69–93.

Lewis, H. G. *Unionism and Relative Wages in the United States: An Empirical Inquiry.* Chicago: University of Chicago Press, 1963.

Parsley, C. J. "Labor Unions and Wages: A Survey," *Journal of Economic Literature* 18 (March 1980): 1–31.

13

Public-Sector
Labor Markets

Federal, state, and local governments are differentiated from most (but not all) private-sector employers in that profit maximization is unlikely to be an objective of governmental units.[1] As such, a labor-market model based upon the assumption of profit maximization is clearly inappropriate for the government sector. As this chapter will show, it is *not* necessary to assume profit maximization in order to deduce that the demand for public employees is a downward-sloping functon of their wage rate.

Employment expanded more rapidly between 1950 and 1975 in the *state and local government* (SLG) *sector* than in any other sector of the economy. While civilian employment by the federal government (when expressed as a percentage of total nonagricultural employment) actually declined slightly during the period, SLG employment rose from 9.1 percent to 15.5 percent of total nonagricultural payroll employment (see Table 13.1). Indeed, the absolute number of state- and local-government employees almost tripled during this period, rising from 4.1 to 11.9 million. Although the share of SLG employment in total employment has declined slightly since 1975, the absolute number of SLG employees has continued to rise.

The public sector is also the sector of the economy in which the extent of unionization is growing most rapidly. Although Chapter 12 discussed the declining fraction of private-sector workers who are union members, union membership is growing rapidly in the public sector in both absolute and percentage terms. For example, between 1963 and 1977, the proportion of federal employees in the executive branch covered by collective-bargaining agreements rose from 48 to 88 percent.[2] Similarly, the proportion of SLG employees belonging to unions rose

---

[1] For an interesting analysis of the *private* not-for-profit or voluntary sector, see Burton Weisbrod, *The Voluntary Nonprofit Sector: An Economic Analysis* (Lexington, Mass.: Lexington Books, 1977).

[2] John F. Burton, Jr., "The Extent of Collective Bargaining in the Public Sector," in *Public Sector Bargaining,* eds. Benjamin Aaron et al. (Washington, D.C.: Bureau of National Affairs, 1979), Table 3.

Table 13.1 Government Employment in the United States

Year	Total Nonagricultural-Payroll Employment (in thousands)	Federal Civilian Employment (in thousands)	State and Local Government Employment (in thousands)	Federal Employment as Percentage of Total	SLG as Percentage of Total	Public-Employment-Program Enrollments (in thousands)	Public-Employment-Program Enrollments as Percentage of SLG
1950	45,196	1,928	4,098	4.3	9.1		
1952	48,794	2,420	4,188	5.0	8.6		
1954	48,989	2,188	4,563	4.5	9.3		
1956	52,369	2,209	5,069	4.2	9.7		
1958	51,322	2,191	5,648	4.3	11.0		
1960	54,189	2,270	6,083	4.2	11.2		
1962	55,550	2,340	6,550	4.2	11.8		
1964	58,282	2,348	7,248	4.0	12.4		
1966	63,901	2,564	8,220	4.0	12.9		
1968	67,896	2,737	9,102	4.0	13.4		
1970	70,879	2,731	9,823	3.9	13.9		
1972	73,675	2,684	10,649	3.6	14.5	138	1.3
1974	78,265	2,724	11,446	3.5	14.6	60	0.5
1975	76,945	2,748	11,937	3.6	15.5	310	2.6
1976	79,382	2,733	12,138	3.4	15.3	328	2.7
1977	82,256	2,727	12,352	3.3	15.0	416	3.4
1978	85,763	2,753	12,723	3.2	14.8	569	3.3

SOURCES: *1979 Employment and Training Report of the President* (Washington, D.C.: U.S. Government Printing Office, 1979), Tables C1 and F1; and unpublished data on public-employment-program statistics provided us by the U.S. Department of Labor.

from 7.7 percent in 1964 to 17.4 percent in 1978 (see Table 13.2). If one includes membership in bargaining organizations—which include professional organizations such as the National Education Association (NEA) that over time have behaved more and more like unions—an even more rapid increase is observed. As Table 13.2 indicates, the percentage of SLG employees who belong to bargaining organizations rose from 27 to 36 percent, while their absolute membership increased from 2.5 to 4.7 million between 1968 and 1978.

One factor that continued to affect this growth in public-sector unionization was changing public attitudes and legislation governing bargaining in the public sector. Unlike the private sector in which the rights of workers to organize and bargain collectively have been guaranteed since the National Labor Relations Act, laws governing bargaining in the public sector are of much more recent vintage. For example, Executive Order 10988 issued by President John F. Kennedy in 1962 legitimized collective bargaining in the federal sector for the first time, providing federal workers with the rights to join unions and bargain over working conditions—but *not* wages. While this executive order has been modified several times since then, in the early 1980s most federal employees' wages were still not determined by the collective-bargaining process.[3]

---

[3]There were some major exceptions—namely, postal workers and employees of federal-government authorities, such as the Tennessee Valley Authority (TVA). In each of these cases the prices of the products or services produced (mail delivery, hydroelectric power) can be raised to cover the cost of the contract settlement, unlike other federal agencies where salaries are paid out of general revenues.

Table 13.2   State and Local Government Employees Belonging to Unions or Bargaining Organizations or Covered by Union Contracts

Year	SLG Employees Belonging to Unions Number (in thousands)	Percent	SLG Employees Belonging to Bargaining Organizations Number (in thousands)	Percent	Percentage of SLG Employees Covered By a Formal Contract
1964	556	7.7			
1966	664	7.8			
1968	804	8.8	2,466	27.1	
1970	947	9.6	2,668	27.1	
1972	1,105	10.4	3,137	29.4	
1974	1,529	13.4	3,911	34.1	
1976	1,710	14.0	4,521	37.0	27.7
1978	2,243	17.4	4,674	36.2	

SOURCE: John F. Burton, Jr., "The Extent of Collective Bargaining in the Public Sector" in *Public Sector Bargaining* eds. Benjamin Aaron et. al. (Washington, D.C.: Bureau of National Affairs, 1979), Tables 2 and 4; and U.S. Bureau of Labor Statistics, *1979 Directory of National Union and Employee Associations* (Washington, D.C.: U.S. Government Printing Office, 1980).

Favorable state legislation for SLG-employee collective-bargaining began with a 1959 state law in Wisconsin; prior to that date collective bargaining was effectively prohibited in the state and local sector. By the late 1970s most industrial states had adopted statutes that permitted SLG employees to participate in the determination of their wages and conditions of employment, although not all em-

Table 13.3   Private- and Government-Employee Earnings Comparisons

Year	(1)	(2)	(3)	(4)	(5)
1954	1.65	1.78	306	1.03	1.11
1956	1.80	1.95	334	1.03	1.11
1958	1.95	2.11	365	1.04	1.12
1960	2.09	2.26	398	1.06	1.14
1962	2.22	2.39	440	1.10	1.19
1964	2.36	2.53	470	1.11	1.19
1966	2.56	2.72	515	1.14	1.21
1968	2.85	3.01	603	1.20	1.27
1970	3.23	3.35	693	1.24	1.28
1972	3.70	3.82	764	1.20	1.24
1974	4.24	4.42	894	1.21	1.27
1976	4.86	5.22	1,016	1.17	1.25
1978	5.69	6.17	1,132	1.10	1.19

(1) Average hourly earnings of private nonagricultural nonsupervisory workers during the year (in dollars).
(2) Average hourly earnings of manufacturing production workers during the year (in dollars).
(3) Average monthly earnings of full-time state- and local-government (SLG) employees in October of the year (in dollars).
(4) Average *annual* earnings of SLG workers divided by average annual earnings of private nonagricultural nonsupervisory workers.
(5) Average *annual* earnings of SLG workers divided by average annual earnings of manufacturing production workers.

SOURCE: Based on U.S. Department of Labor, *Employment and Earnings* (various issues); and U.S. Bureau of Census, *Public Employment in (Year)* (various issues).

ployees in each state were covered by the laws.[4] Nevertheless, by 1976 27.7 percent of all SLG employees were covered by a formal union contract (see Table 13.2).

At the same time that employment and unionization were growing in the SLG sector, SLG employees' earnings also started to rise relative to the earnings of private-sector employees. Table 13.3 presents data for the 1954–1978 period on the average hourly earnings of both private nonagricultural nonsupervisory workers and manufacturing production workers, as well as on average monthly earnings of full-time SLG employees. After converting each measure to an annual figure (by multiplying the first two by 2000 and the latter by 12), one can observe how the earnings of SLG employees compared to those of private-sector employees during the period. The data make it quite clear that from the mid-1950s to 1970, SLG employees' earnings grew relative to those of private employees; indeed by 1970, their relative-earnings position had improved by some 15 to 20 percent [see Table 13.3, columns (4) and (5)].[5] However, during the 1970s the trend was reversed, and SLG employees' earnings fell relative to those of their private-sector counterparts.[6]

The growth in the relative-earnings position of SLG employees during the 1960s, coupled with the growing strength of public-employee unions, their increased militancy, and the trend towards allowing SLG employees to bargain over wage issues, led to fears that inflationary wage settlements would continue in the sector and aggravate the financial problems faced by state and local governments. These fears were explicitly based upon the belief that many public services are both essential and produced under monopoly conditions, which implies that the wage elasticity of demand for public employees is very inelastic. To many, the logical conclusion was that, in the absence of market constraints that would limit the wage demands of public employees, limitations should be placed on the collective-bargaining rights of these groups.[7]

Although by the late 1970s eight states did grant the right to strike in one

---

[4]See B. V. H. Schneider, "Public-Sector Labor Legislation: An Evolutionary Analysis" in *Public Sector Collective Bargaining,* eds. Benjamin Aaron et al. (Washington, D.C.: Bureau of National Affairs, 1979) for a more complete discussion of the evolution of legislation governing bargaining in the public sector.

[5]Note that 1.24 divided by 1.03 equals 1.20—column (4)—and 1.28 divided by 1.11 equals 1.15—column (5), which implies 20 percent and 15 percent increases, respectively.

[6]The comparisons in Table 13.3 are subject to a number of qualifications. On the one hand, they focus only on wages and ignore fringe benefits and differences in working conditions. On the other hand, they do not control for differences in skill level or occupational mixes between the public and private sectors. When the average earnings of workers in the two sectors are compared, we find that in 1954 the average annual earnings of SLG employees exceeded that of manufacturing production workers by 11 percent [column (5)]. This percentage tells us nothing about how the earnings of a worker with a *given* skill level would compare in the two sectors. Average earnings in the SLG sector might exceed those in the private sector—even if the wage rate paid in each occupation were the same in both sectors—simply because the public sector tends to employ relatively more high-skilled workers. Similarly, when we observe changes in the ratios in columns (4) and (5), one should be aware that they may reflect changes in the relative occupational mixes across the two sectors, as well as changes in the relative compensation levels.

[7]See, for example, H. Wellington and R. Winter, "The Limits of Collective Bargaining in Public Employment," *Yale Law Journal,* 69 (June 1969): 1107–27.

form or another to selected employee groups, most continued historic prohibitions against strikes.[8] The states that prohibited strikes, however, often provided assistance to local governments and unions in settling contract disputes, with a number of states adopting forms of binding arbitration as the terminal stage in their impasse procedures.[9]

At the federal level, *comparability legislation* was first passed in 1962 and now ties the wages of federal white-collar workers to the results of a government survey of wages of "comparable" private workers, subject to possible presidential or congressional modification.[10] The influence of federal unions on wages operates, then, primarily through the political pressure they can exert on the President and Congress to approve wage increases that the surveys suggest they deserve. The wage-determination process under collective bargaining in the public sector clearly differs in many ways from wage determination under collective bargaining in the private sector.

Public-sector labor markets also warrant separate treatment because they represent an area toward which much of our public policy has recently been directed. To take one example, during the decade of the '70s attempts were made to reduce unemployment by means of *public-employment programs*. Starting with the *Emergency Employment Act of 1971* and then continuing under the *Comprehensive Employment and Training Act* (CETA), the federal government provided funds to state and local governments to increase their employment levels, in the hope that the availability of extra public-sector jobs would provide job opportunities for the unemployed. By 1978, 569,000 individuals were *reported* employed on public-employment-program funds; these employees comprised some 3.3 percent of total SLG employment (see Table 13.1). To take another example, growing concern over the fiscal condition of state and local governments and the increased state and local tax burden borne by taxpayers led to the passage of expenditure- and tax-limitation legislation in a number of states in the late 1970s. The most notable was the enactment of Proposition 13 in California, which drastically reduced local property taxes and limited the ability of all governmental units in the state to increase their revenues.

The objective of this chapter is to present a simple analytical framework that

---

[8]For more details on dispute resolution in the public sector, see Thomas Kochan, "Dynamics of Dispute Resolution in the Public Sector" in *Public Sector Bargaining*, eds. B. Aaron et al. (Washington, D.C.: Bureau of National Affairs, 1979).

[9]Some definition of terminology may be useful. An *impasse* is a situation in which the parties cannot agree on the terms of a collective-bargaining agreement. State public-employment-relations agencies provide three types of assistance to the parties. *Mediators* are individuals who attempt to assist the parties to negotiate with each other, by serving as intermediaries in situations when personal conflicts prevent negotiations from occurring or by making suggestions that both parties may find acceptable. *Factfinders*, after hearing both parties' positions, issue oral or written statements to the parties about the types of settlements they believe are justified by the evidence (facts). Such positions taken by impartial third parties often influence the positions taken by the parties in the negotiations. Finally, *arbitrators* issue formal rulings about what they believe the settlement should be; in many cases state laws or prior agreement by the parties dictate that if the negotiations go to arbitration, the arbitrator's decision will be *binding*.

[10]See Sharon Smith, *Equal Pay in the Public Sector: Fact or Fantasy* (Princeton, N.J.: Princeton University, 1977) for a more complete description of the comparability process in the federal sector. Federal blue-collar workers' wages are also determined, in the main, by the comparability process, with comparisons in this case being made at the local labor-market level.

can be used to discuss public-sector labor markets and to then use the framework to analyze:

1. why SLG employment grew so rapidly between 1950 and 1975.
2. why the relative earnings of SLG employees increased during most of the same period.
3. why the growth of unionization has been so rapid in the sector.
4. what the effects of unions have been on wage and nonwage outcomes in the SLG sector.
5. what the effects of comparability legislation have been on federal employees' wages.
6. whether the form of impasse procedure used affects the size of wage settlements in the SLG sector.
7. what the likely effects of expenditure- and tax-limitation legislation on public sector-labor markets will be.
8. what the net job-creation effects of public-employment programs have been.

A MODEL OF A PUBLIC-SECTOR LABOR MARKET

What are the forces that affect the level of employment and wages in a given governmental unit? Turning first to the demand side of the market, we have already indicated that profit maximization is an untenable assumption to make when analyzing the public sector. Suppose instead that there is a single decision maker (or group of decision makers) who makes decisions on the level and cost of governmental services in accordance with the wishes of voters who elect him or her to office.[11] Presumably voters are concerned both with the level of public services they receive and the resources left to them, after paying for these services through taxes or user charges, that can be used to consume private goods and services. Assume also, for simplicity, that the level of public services is proportional to the number of public employees who are hired.[12]

Decisions made by the representative public decision maker in an effort to maximize a utility function form the basis for the demand for public employees. The decision maker weighs the level of public services provided against the burden financing this level places on taxpayers, subject to a budget constraint that takes into account the prices of both public and private goods and services and the total resources available to the community. Without going through the details of such a maximization problem, it should be obvious that an increase in the cost of

---

[11]There is extensive literature in economics on how decisions are made in the public sector. Under certain conditions in an open democratic political system, the preferences of the median voter on an issue will become the preferences of the decision makers. See Anthony Downs, *An Economic Theory of Democracy* (New York: Harper & Row, 1957), and Gordon Tullock, *Towards A Mathematics of Politics* (Ann Arbor, Mich.: University of Michigan Press, 1967). However, not all economists believe that public-sector decision making can be modeled in such a way. See, for example, Melvin Reder, "The Theory of Employment and Wages in the Public Sector" in *Labor in the Public and Private Nonprofit Sectors,* ed. Daniel Hamermesh (Princeton, N.J.: Princeton University Press, 1975).

[12]Such an assumption, which ignores the possibility of substituting capital for labor in producing public services, is made only for expository purposes and does not affect our final conclusion.

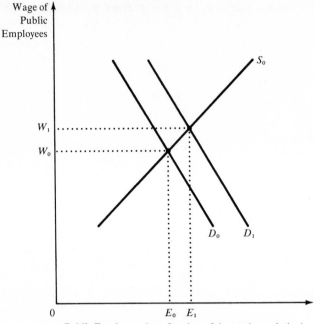

**FIGURE 13.1   The Public-Sector Labor Market
and the Growth of Public Employment**

public services should reduce the quantity of services demanded (other things equal), just as an increase in the price of a consumer good leads a consumer to reduce his or her purchase of that good. Hence, an increase in the wage rate of public employees should lead governmental employers to demand fewer of them. Put another way, other things equal, the demand for public employees *is* a downward-sloping function of their wage rate despite its departure from an assumption of profit maximization.

Figure 13.1 shows a representative public-sector labor-demand curve (D_0). This curve has been drawn in *per capita* terms (public employees as a percentage of the population) in recognition of the fact that the flow of public services that an individual citizen receives from a given number of public employees depends upon the number of other individuals in the community that he or she has to "share" these public services with.[13] The position of the demand curve depends on a number of factors. Increases in the total resources available in the community, as measured perhaps by per capita family income or per capita grants from higher levels of governments, will shift the demand for public employees to the right.

---

[13]In the case of some government goods or services, however, one citizen's consumption does not reduce the amount available to others. National defense is an example of such a *pure public good.*

Similarly, factors that increase the community's tastes for public services, such as a rise in the school-age population, will also shift the demand curve to the right.

Turning to the supply side, one can treat the supply of individuals to public-sector jobs in the same framework used in Chapters 2 and 8 to analyze labor supply to other occupations or industries. Other things equal, the higher the wage paid to public employees, the greater the fraction of the population that would be willing to work for the local government, as indicated by the upward-sloping labor-supply curve (S_0) in Figure 13.1. The position of this curve is presumably determined by individuals' tastes for jobs in the public sector, by the wages and nonwage conditions of employment that are offered by other governmental and private employers, and by the nonwage conditions of employment offered by the particular governmental units. One important condition of employment, to which we will return later, is job security. If the probability of being laid off in the future were to increase, for example, one would expect fewer people to be willing to work for the governmental employer—in which case the labor-supply curve would shift to the left.[14]

Given the demand curve, D_0, and the supply curve, S_0, E_0 public employees per capita are hired and are paid a wage of W_0. At any wage less than W_0, the demand for public employees would exceed the supply, governmental units would have unfilled positions (job vacancies), and pressure would be exerted to raise the wage to attract more applicants. At any level of wages above W_0, there would be an excess supply of applicants, and astute public employers would realize that they could attract the desired work force at a lower real wage. Since funds used to hire public employees have alternative uses in the public and private sector, this excess supply would create downward pressure on the real wage. Hence, the wage/employment combination (W_0, E_0) would be an equilibrium one.[15]

Suppose the demand curve for public employees were to shift out to D_1 in Figure 13.1. As indicated there, *both* public employees' wages and their per capita employment levels would increase. Between 1950 and 1970 median family income, measured in 1974 dollars, increased substantially in real terms from $6,800 to $12,531, as did per capita federal grants to state and local governments (from $33 to $137). Both of these factors should have increased the demand for SLG employees. Similarly, the proportion of the population that was of elementary-school age through college age (5 through 21) increased from 26.1 to 32.9 percent during the period, which should have increased the demand for SLG educational

---

[14]See Orley Ashenfelter, "Demand and Supply Functions for State and Local Government Employment" in *Essays in Labor Market Analysis,* eds. Orley Ashenfelter and Wallace Oates, (New York: Halstead Press, 1979).

[15]As noted in Chapter 3, there is some evidence that, *outside* of metropolitan areas, a monopsony model of public-sector labor markets may be the relevant one to use. In general, however, the simple demand-and-supply model presented in the text is sufficient for our purposes. In major metropolitan areas in which scores of different local governments may employ workers in the same occupation (such as teachers), it is clear that the monopsony model is not relevant. Later the chapter does consider the possibility that the existence of excess supplies of applicants will not put downward pressure on public-sector wages.

employees.[16] Together, these three forces were undoubtedly largely responsible for most of the growth of employment and relative wages of SLG employees that occurred during the period (see Tables 13.1 and 13.3). However, during the mid- and late-1970s, the school-age population declined as a proportion of the population and real family incomes did not increase substantially. In retrospect, then, it is not surprising that the employment level and relative wages of SLG employees both declined during this latter period.

THE GROWTH AND EFFECTS OF PUBLIC-SECTOR UNIONS

The simple demand and supply model of union membership presented in Chapter 12 (see Figure 12.1 on p. 334) can be used retrospectively to provide some insight into why unionization in the public sector has grown so rapidly since the 1960s. On the one hand, changing public attitudes and the evolution of labor legislation relating to collective bargaining in the public sector, which were described earlier in the chapter, reduced the costs of organizing public employees (shifting the supply of union services to the right) and probably increased the benefits public employees perceived from union membership (shifting the demand for union membership to the right). Both forces would lead to an increase in union strength. On the other hand, the decline in the relative-earnings position of SLG employees that occurred in the mid-1970s, along with the slowdown in the rate of growth of employment and the imposition of expenditure- and tax-limitation legislation in several states, may have strengthened the desires of public employees to turn to unions in the hopes of regaining their former relative-earnings positions and winning job-security clauses in their contracts. Because these forces all increased the net benefits public employees perceived from union membership, they shifted the demand for unions further to the right.

This analysis naturally leads one to wonder what the effects of unions have been on wages and nonwage contract outcomes in the SLG sector. As in the private sector, a key determinant of public-sector unions' ability to raise their members' wages is the wage elasticity of demand for SLG employees. If a public-sector union succeeds in raising wages above the market-clearing level (W_0) to W_u in Figure 13.2, the result will be a loss of jobs of $E_0 - E_u$; the magnitude of this loss will depend upon the wage elasticity of demand. The larger this loss, the less likely that those unions which value both the wages and employment levels of their members will push for large wage gains. Of course, if the demand for labor were shifting out rapidly in the SLG sector, as it was through the mid-1970s, fear of job loss would be less likely to constrain the wage demands of SLG employees' unions.

As noted earlier, the "conventional wisdom" has been that because many forms of public services are both "essential" and monopolized, the demand for public employees was wage inelastic. This supposed wage inelasticity of demand implies that market forces would not constrain public employees' wage demands. However, one can easily think of possibilities for substituting capital for labor in

---

[16]These data come from the U.S. Bureau of the Census, *Statistical Abstract of the United States, 1975* (Washington, D.C.: U.S. Government Printing Office, 1975).

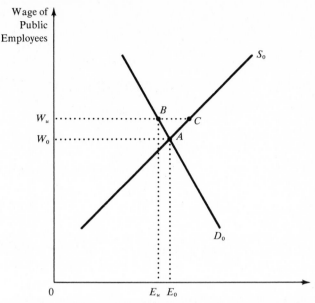

FIGURE 13.2   The Effects of Unions in the Public Sector: Excess Applicants

the provision of public services (for example, police patrol cars could be substituted for officers on the beat, or snowblowers could be substituted for snow-removal workers with shovels). Further, private firms can provide the same services as now provided publicly (for example, garbage pick-up could be subcontracted to private employers, or private companies could be hired to handle janitorial services in public buildings). Moreover, given the limited resources that state and local governments can command, an increase in the relative price of one service should lead a government to substitute other services that would become relatively cheaper (for example, minimally supervised playground programs could be substituted for summertime instructional programs in sports or crafts). In other words, while a local government does not have the option of moving its plant to a nonunion area (that is, fleeing to the sunbelt), it can substitute capital for labor, change its services, or subcontract with private firms if it feels its labor costs are too high. Hence, it is *not* obvious *a priori* that the wage elasticities of demand for all categories of state- and local-government employees are inelastic.

Three studies have presented estimates of the wage elasticities of demand for 11 functional categories of state- and local-government employees, and these studies are summarized in Table 13.4.[17] In the main, these estimates do suggest that

[17]Orley Ashenfelter and Ronald G. Ehrenberg, ''The Demand for Labor in the Public Sector'' in *Labor in the Public and Nonprofit Sectors,* ed. Daniel Hamermesh (Princeton, N.J.: Princeton University Press, 1975); Ronald G. Ehrenberg, ''The Demand for State and Local Government Employees,'' *American Economic Review,* 63 (June 1973): 366–79; and Robert Thornton, ''The Elasticity of Demand for Public School Teachers,'' *Industrial Relations* 18(Winter 1979): 86–91.

**Table 13.4   Estimates of Wage Elasticities of Demand
for Labor in the State and Local Sector**

Category	(1)	(2)	(3)
Education	−1.06	−0.08 to −0.57	−0.57 to −0.82
Noneducation	−0.38		
Streets and highways	−0.09	−0.44 to −0.64	
Public welfare	−0.32	−0.33 to −1.13	
Hospitals	−0.30	−0.30 to −0.51	
Public health	−0.12	−0.26 to −0.32	
Police	−0.29	−0.01 to −0.35	
Fire	−0.53	−0.23 to −0.31	
Sanitation and sewage	−0.23	−0.40 to −0.56	
Natural resources	−0.39	−0.39 to −0.60	
General control and financial administration	−0.28	−0.09 to −0.34	

SOURCES:
(1) Orley Ashenfelter and Ronald Ehrenberg, "The Demand for Labor in the Public Sector" in *Labor in the Public and Nonprofit Sectors,* ed. Daniel Hamermesh (Princeton, N.J.: Princeton University Press, 1975), Table 6.
(2) Ronald G. Ehrenberg, "The Demand for State and Local Government Employees," *American Economic Review* 63 (June 1973): 366–79.
(3) Robert J. Thornton, "The Elasticity of Demand for Public School Teachers," *Industrial Relations* 18 (Winter 1979): 86–91.

demand curves for labor in the SLG sector *are* inelastic. However, the estimated elasticities do not appear substantially lower in absolute value than the private-sector wage elasticities of demand that were summarized in Table 4.1 (see p. 98). Regardless of these estimates, one should remember that public employees are also voters and, through the political process, seek to increase (shift) the demand for their own services.[18] To the extent that they are successful, the employment loss that would be associated with any wage increase would be smaller than if the demand curve had not been shifted out.

Numerous studies have attempted to estimate what the effect of SLG-employee unions has been on their members' wages relative to the wages of otherwise comparable nonunion public employees. A detailed study using data from 1967 for noneducational municipal employees suggested that average monthly earnings of municipal employees represented by unions or employee associations exceeded those of otherwise comparable nonorganized employees by between 2 and 16 percent.[19] These estimates are no higher, and are perhaps even lower, than

---

[18]For a recent treatment of this point see Paul Courant, Edward Gramlich, and Daniel Rubinfeld, "Public Employee Market Power and the Level of Government Spending," *American Economic Review,* 69 (December 1979): 806–17.

[19]Ronald G. Ehrenberg and Gerald S. Goldstein, "A Model of Public Sector Wage Determination," *Journal of Urban Economics* 2 (April 1975): 223–45. This study also showed that the magnitude of the union relative-wage effect for a given category of municipal employees (such as police) depended upon the extent of unionization of other categories of municipal employees (such as firefighters) in the city *and* the extent of organization of municipal employees in neighboring cities. That is, both occupational and geographic wage spillovers appear to occur. In the context of our public-sector labor-market model, one can explain these results by noting that the supply curve of, say, police to City A will shift to the left as the wages of police in a neighboring city, or the wages of other categories of municipal employees in City A, increase. This shift would, other things equal, increase the wages of police in City A. These occupational and geographic spillovers may result, then, from the impact of other unions on the supply of police in City A.

Example 13.1
Pension Underfunding in the Government Sector

The assertion that government officials tend to concentrate on labor costs in the short run—as opposed to the long run—can be illustrated by the extent to which public-employee retirement systems are underfunded (that is, these systems lack the assets to meet their accrued liabilities). Pension funds in the *private* sector must (by law) be fully funded in advance, which means that private employers must put enough money per worker into their pension funds each year so that, when invested, these funds grow large enough to finance the expected pension liability of the worker upon retirement. These funds are necessary to guarantee the pension promises made to workers in the event employers became insolvent. Although most public-sector pension systems nominally require advance funding, the typical public-employee pension fund had only *half* of the assets it should have had to be fully funded in 1975. In other words, the typical public-sector pension system would have had to receive a one-time contribution equal to about $12,000 per employee to become fully funded in 1975—implying an overall level of underfunding amounting to more than $120 billion in the state- and local-government sector.

How did this state of affairs arise? In some cases, the contributions required to fund pension promises have been deliberately understated. For example, many public-sector pensions funds have not taken into account the fact that pension benefits will increase as *salaries* increase; they have, in effect, assumed salaries will remain constant over the preretirement years of each worker.

A 1975 investigation of the New York City Employees' Retirement System found that the actuarial assumptions being used about retirees' life expectancy came from New York City's records of experience during the *1908–1914* period. Since life expectancy has increased substantially over the last 70 years, it is not surprising that in 1970 the actual mortality rates of male and female retirees were only 74 percent and 62 percent, respectively, of what the system projected they would be. This underestimate of retirees' life expectancy led to an underestimate of the revenue necessary to pay for their pensions—and thus to underfunding of the system.

The two sources of underfunding mentioned above cause an understatement of the officially reported liabilities (obligations) of public-sector pension funds. If these errors were corrected, it is estimated that reported unfunded pension liabilities in the state and local government sector would be closer to $175 billion than to $120 billion. The other major source of underfunding is the simple refusal of employers to contribute sufficient funds to the pension systems. Underfunding is clearly used as a means of balancing current operating budgets, suggesting that short-term considerations take priority over long-run consequences when government employers put together compensation packages.

SOURCES: U.S. House of Representatives, *Pension Task Force Report on Public Employee Retirement Systems* (Washington, D.C.: U.S. Government Printing Office), March 15, 1978 and the *Report of the Permanent Commission on Public Employee Pension and Retirement Systems—Financing the Public Pension Systems Part I: Actuarial Assumptions and Funding Policies* (New York, 1975).

the union relative-wage effects observed in the private sector. Numerous studies, which use data from later periods and include analyses of educational employees' earnings, confirm this result. That is, unions in the SLG sector appear to have had more moderate effects on the relative wages of their members than unions in the private sector.[20]

As emphasized, however, wages are not identical to total compensation. In addition to those reasons presented in the previous chapter, there are other reasons to believe that the effects of public-sector unions on nonwage benefits may well exceed their effects on wages. On the one hand, public employees' wages are much more visable to the public than are their fringe benefits. The public may be more aware of the cost of a $200 increase in annual starting salaries, which is well publicized, than they are of the cost of an improvement in health-insurance benefits that will also cost $200 per employee. As such, it may be politically easier for governmental negotiators to make concessions on fringe-benefit items than on wages.

On the other hand, while the costs of increased wages must be borne in the present, the costs of improved fringe benefits are often not known at the time of settlement or are borne in the future. For example, the true cost of agreeing to pay 100 percent of employees' health-insurance costs depends upon future increases in health-insurance rates. To take another example, if public-employee pension plans are not fully funded, the costs of agreeing to more generous retirement provisions today will become evident only in the future when employees begin to take advantage of these provisions.[21] Since government officials' tenure in office is often short, and since they typically will depart from office well before the true costs of such fringe benefits become known, it is in their *short-run* political interests to win favor with public-employee unions by agreeing to increased fringes since the short-run costs of such agreements to taxpayers may well be small.[22]

For both of these reasons then, one might expect that the effect of public-sector unions on fringe benefits would be larger than their effects on wages. Although the limited empirical evidence on this point is somewhat ambiguous, it does suggest that this has occurred.[23]

---

[20]See Daniel J. B. Mitchell, "The Impact of Collective Bargaining on Compensation in the Public Sector" in *Public Sector Bargaining,* eds. B. Aaron et al. (Washington, D.C.: Bureau of National Affairs, 1979) for a survey of the recent studies.

[21]That most public retirement systems are not fully funded (that is, they do not have assets sufficient to meet their accrued liabilities) is well known. For example, one study found that in 1975 state- and local- government pension funds had assets equal only to 38 percent of their accrued liabilities. See U.S. House of Representatives, *Pension Task Force Report on Public Employee Retirement Systems* (Washington, D.C.: U.S. Government Printing Office, 1978). See Example 13.1

[22]We say short run because in the long run facts become known. The best example of this occurred in New York City where Mayor Lindsey agreed to generous fringe-benefit packages for New York City employees during the late 1960s and early 1970s. Many people subsequently blamed him for all of the financial problems that the city experienced in the mid-1970s, and when he ran for U.S. Senator in the Democratic primary in 1980 he finished well behind the winner.

[23]See Casey Ichniowski, "Economic Effects of the Firefighters' Union," *Industrial and Labor Relations Review* 33(January 1980): 198–211; and David Rogers, "Municipal Government Structure, Unions, and Wage and Nonwage Compensation in the Public Sector" (unpublished Cornell University M.S. thesis, 1979).

THE EFFECTS OF ARBITRATION STATUTES ON THE WAGES OF STATE AND LOCAL-GOVERNMENT EMPLOYEES

One reason why the effect of SLG employee unions on their members' wages is not substantially larger may be that SLG employees' rights to strike are seriously limited. Many states explicitly prohibit strikes by SLG employees, substituting instead alternative forms of impasse resolution. Some states have adopted *binding arbitration* as the final stage of their impasse procedure for some categories of public employees, most notably those in the "essential" police and firefighter areas.[24]

Such binding-arbitration legislation is typically opposed by municipal-government officials who argue that arbitration takes the final decision over public employees' wages out of the hands of elected officials and leads to inflated wage settlements. Several studies have analyzed the consequences of arbitration statutes and have concluded that 1. the use of arbitration may compress differentials across cities (since arbitrators tend to award larger increases in cities in which public employees are paid relatively low wages than they do in cities in which public employees' wages are relatively high), but that 2. on average the wage settlements that go to the arbitration stage are no higher than the wage settlements in otherwise comparable cities that do not go to arbitration.[25] That is, if the average percentage wage settlement in cities that went to arbitration, $\dot{W}_A$, in a particular bargaining round is compared to the average percentage wage settlement in otherwise comparable cities that did not go to arbitration, $\dot{W}_N$, the difference *(D)* is roughly zero:

$$D = \dot{W}_A - \dot{W}_N = 0 \tag{13.1}$$

One might be tempted to conclude that the arbitration process *per se* has had no effect on the size of the average wage settlement in the public sector. However, this conclusion assumes that the rates of wage increase in cities in which negotiations did not go to arbitration $(\dot{W}_N)$ are the same as they would have been in the absence of the arbitration statute—which is not necessarily correct. The existence of the arbitration statute *per se* may well alter the size of wage settlements even in cities that do not go to arbitration.

For example, if municipal-government labor negotiators fear that there is some chance that arbitrators will award settlements that are substantially more generous than would otherwise occur, they may try to induce a settlement prior to the arbitration stage by voluntarily offering their employees a wage package in excess of what they would have offered in the absence of the statute.[26] Such an

---

[24]By 1979, at least 18 states had adopted some form of binding arbitration for police and firefighters contract-dispute resolution. See Thomas Kochan, "Dynamics of Dispute Resolution in the Public Sector" in *Public Sector Bargaining,* eds. B. Aaron et al. (Washington D.C.: Bureau of National Affairs, 1979).

[25]See, for example, Thomas Kochan et al., *Dispute Resolution Under Factfinding and Arbitration* (New York: American Arbitration Association, 1979), and James Stern et al., *Final Offer Arbitration* (Lexington, Mass.: Lexington Books, 1975).

[26]The union might agree to such a settlement even if they expected that, on average, an arbitrated settlement would be higher because of their uncertainty about how the arbitrator would rule (that is, there is some chance that his settlement would be lower). Put another way, "a bird in the hand may well be worth two in the bush."

action would cause the estimated differential D to *understate* the effect of the arbitration statute on wages. Conversely, if public employers believed, and public employee unions concurred, that arbitrators were likely to award low settlements, management might offer—and unions might accept—an offer less than what management would have offered in the absence of the statute. While we can not ascertain *a priori* whether the existence of the arbitration statute *per se* increases or decreases the size of wage settlements in cities that do not go to arbitration, it is very likely that the presence of an arbitration statute *does* affect the negotiations where settlement is made prior to arbitration.[27]

PUBLIC VS. PRIVATE PAY COMPARISONS

As noted early in the chapter, the pay of most federal-government white-collar workers is determined through a comparability process that ties their wages to the results of a government survey of wages of "comparable private workers," subject to possible presidential and congressional modification. As a result of this process, however, do comparably qualified workers performing comparable work in the public and private sectors receive equal total compensation?[28] This question is difficult to answer because the comparability survey currently focuses on wages and ignores both nonwage benefits and nonpecuniary forms of compensation. Moreover, the jobs performed in the public and private sectors are not always directly comparable, and subjective decisions must often be made as to how a job should be classified.

Instead of focusing on the earnings of workers with comparable *job characteristics,* which (as noted above) is often impossible to do, one could focus on the earnings paid to workers who have comparable *measured personal characteristics*—such as education and experience—in the public and private sectors. In the most detailed empirical study on the subject to date Sharon Smith used a framework analogous to the one noted in Chapter 9 that contrasted earnings in regulated and nonregulated industries.[29] Smith's comparisons, which pertain to state- and local-government employees as well as federal employees, are summarized in Table 13.5. Quite strikingly, as of 1975 individuals who worked for the federal government appeared to receive wages that were some 13 to 20 percent higher than the wages received by private sector workers with comparable personal characteristics. The differentials for state- and local-government employees in relation to private-sector employees were much more modest, and, in the case of white males, the differentials were actually negative. That is, white males employed in the state and local sector appeared to receive lower wages than workers with comparable measured personal characteristics in the private sector.

---

[27]For a more complete discussion of this point in the context of a simple bargaining model, see Henry S. Farber and Harry C. Katz, "Interest Arbitration, Outcomes, and the Incentive to Bargain," *Industrial and Labor Relations Review* 33 (October 1979): 55–63.

[28]This discussion draws heavily on Sharon P. Smith, *Equal Pay in the Public Sector: Fact or Fantasy* (Princeton, N.J.: Princeton University, 1977).

[29]Smith, *Equal Pay in the Public Sector.*

**Table 13.5   Implied Estimated Percentage Differences Between the Wages of Government-
and Private-Sector Employees in 1975**

	Percentage Difference Between Wages of		
Category	Federal and Private Employees	State and Private Employees	Local-Government and Private Employees
By Sex:			
Male	13 to 15	−3 to −11	−4 to −9
Female	18 to 20	6 to 7	1 to 2
By Race and Sex:			
White Male	16	−4	−7
Nonwhite Male	17	12	3
White Female	25	7	1
Nonwhite Female	21	9	4

SOURCE: Based on Sharon P. Smith, *Equal Pay in the Public Sector: Fact or Fantasy* (Princeton, N.J.: Princeton University, 1977), Tables 3.7 and 6.4.

As noted in our discussion of the relative earnings in regulated and nonregulated industries (see Chapter 9) earnings comparisons like those in Table 13.5 may not accurately reflect total-compensation comparisions because they ignore fringe benefits and other nonpecuniary conditions of employment. For example, they do not take into account the possibility that public employees may have more (or less) difficult jobs, better (or worse) fringe benefits, and higher (or lower) job stability than do their private-sector counterparts.[30] Furthermore, they do not take into account the possibility that public employers may deliberately pursue a high-wage policy to reduce turnover and increase productivity.

Nevertheless, it is interesting to ask why the wage premium paid to public employees in relation to private-employees appears to be larger in the federal than in the state and local sectors. One possible explanation is that taxpayer information about the effect on tax rates of a wage increase for public employees is much more easily obtained and understood at the state and local level than at the federal level. It may also be easier to hold local politicians accountable for such financial decisions; each federal legislator is just one out of hundreds of representatives who vote on scores of issues besides federal pay legislation. Pressure to hold down public-employee wage scales may thus be greater at the state and local level than it is at the federal level.

One may also ask whether equal pay for equal work in the public and private sectors is a reasonable criterion upon which to base federal-employee compensation. If one defines *pay* to include all current and expected future wage and non-wage benefits and all conditions of employment, it is likely that with free mobility of labor, workers will allocate themselves across sectors until pay is equalized.

---

[30]As of the mid-1970s, the limited evidence available suggested that, other things equal, both fringe benefits and job stability were higher in the government than private sectors. See Smith, *Equal Pay in the Public Sector;* Farrell Bloch and Sharon Smith, "Human Capital and Labor Market Employment," *Journal of Human Resources* 12 (Fall 1977): 550–560; and Joseph F. Quinn, "Wage Differentials Among Older Workers in the Public and Private Sectors," *Journal of Human Resources,* 14 (Winter 1979): 41–62; for the evidence. Thus, the comparisons in Table 13.5 may *understate* the public/private total-compensation differentials.

However, it does not follow that *current wage rates* should thus be equalized. Indeed, if public employees received equal (or higher) wages than private employees and had more desirable nonwage benefits and conditions of employment, one should expect to see queues of applicants lined up for public-sector jobs and very low quit rates for existing public employees. Although occasionally there are reports of job vacancies in the public sector, in the main one's impression is that there are fairly long lists of applicants for most public-sector jobs.[31] Furthermore, there is some evidence that quit rates in the federal sector are substantially lower than quit rates in the private sector.[32] Long queues of applicants and very low quit rates are both consistent with the notion that government workers receive higher pay than comparable private-sector workers.

THE EFFECT OF EXPENDITURE- AND TAX-LIMITATION LEGISLATION

In June of 1978, California voters overwhelmingly adopted Proposition 13, a state constitutional amendment that rolled back property taxes and drastically limited the ability of all levels of government in the state to increase their tax revenues in the future. Since that date attempts to limit state and local government spending or taxing have proliferated and, in a number of cases, these attempts have been successful.[33]

The simple demand and supply model developed in this chapter can help illustrate the likely effects of such legislation on public-sector labor markets.[34] Suppose that initially the demand and supply of public employees were D_0 and S_0, respectively, in Figure 13.3. In this case, ignoring for the moment the effect of union-won increases in wages (and queues for public jobs), equilibrium would be at point A, with the wage/employment combination (W_0, E_0).

The first-round effect of expenditure- or tax-limitation legislation is no different than the effect of any other decline in a community's ability, or willingness, to pay for public employees. The demand for public employees will decline to say D_2; if nothing else occurred equilibrium would be reached at point B with the lower wage and employment combination (W_2, E_2).

This is not the end of the story, however. Expenditure- and tax-limitation legislation undoubtedly reduces public employees' expectations about the level of their *future* wages and also increases the probability that they will be laid off for

---

[31]For example, Sharon Smith in *Equal Pay in the Public Sector* reports that in September of 1974 over 42,000 individuals had passed tests to become police officers in New York City and were awaiting assignment (p. 20). To take another example, the *New York Times* reported that more than 10,000 people lined up to apply for 70 Social Security Administration jobs in Baltimore in September of 1980 ("10,000 Line Up in Baltimore Seeking 70 Federal Jobs," *New York Times*, September 16, 1980). Finally, the *Wall Street Journal* reported on March 24, 1981 that the New York City Postmaster had received 225,000 applications for 2,500 jobs that paid starting salaries of $9.05 an hour.

[32]See Douglas Adie, *An Evaluation of Postal Service Wage Rates* (Washington, D.C.: American Enterprise Institute, 1977), p. 64.

[33]For a discussion of the causes and effects of such legislation, see "Proceedings of a Conference on Tax and Expenditure Limitations," *National Tax Journal* 32 (June 1979).

[34]See Ronald G. Ehrenberg, "The Effect of Tax Limitation Legislation on Public Sector Labor Markets," *National Tax Journal* 32 (June 1979): 261–66, for a more complete discussion.

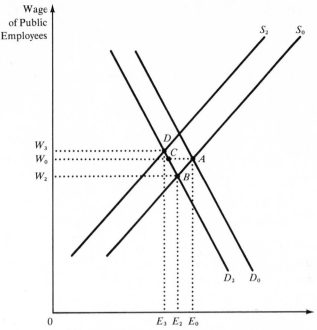

FIGURE 13.3   **The Effect of Expenditure- or Tax-Limitation Legislation on Employment and Wages in the Public Sector**

financial reasons in the future. These changes reduce the desirability of being a state- or local-government employee. As a result, the supply curve shifts to S_2; equilibrium now occurs at point D, with the wage/employment combination (W_3, E_3). Although employment has *fallen* still further, public employees' wages have now *risen* above W_2.

Whether the final wage W_3 is greater or less than the initial wage W_0 is an open question and depends upon whether the shift in supply dominates the shift in demand. If the supply shift does dominate, as in Figure 13.3, public employees' wages will actually rise above their initial level; their employment, however, would fall by more than the shift in the demand curve (point D lies to the left of point C). Although the legislation *may* serve to reduce public employees' wages, it unambiguously reduces their employment levels and the flow of public services.[35]

Figure 13.4 introduces public-employee unions into the analysis. Suppose, at the outset, that a public-employee union had succeeded in keeping the wage rate at W_u, which lies above the equilibrium level. In this case employment would initially be E_u^0. The fall in demand to D_2 caused by the expenditure- or tax-limitation legislation would cause public employment to fall to E_u^1, but unless the union agreed to a reduced wage scale, wages would remain at W_u. As drawn, the

---

[35]This last statement ignores the possibility that public-employee productivity might increase in response to the legislation. See Ehrenberg, "The Effect of Tax Limitation Legislation," for a discussion of why this might occur.

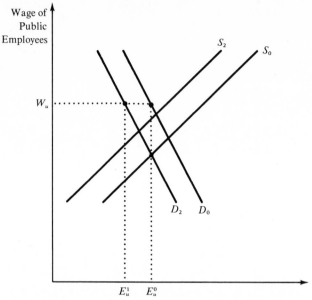

**FIGURE 13.4   The Effect of Expenditure- or Tax-Limitation
Legislation with Unions in the Analysis**

reduction in labor supply to S_2 would have *no* effect on wages or employment; it would serve only to reduce the excess supply of labor. Of course, if the leftward shift in supply were large enough, employment would fall still further and wages would rise above the level set by the union.

While public-employee unions could still push for higher wages, at the expense of lower employment levels, the expenditure- or tax-limitation legislation would reduce their ability to use the political process to shift out the demand for public employees.[36] One could reasonably project, then, that an additional effect of such legislation may be to reduce the size of the union relative-wage effects observed in the state and local sector.

PUBLIC-SECTOR EMPLOYMENT PROGRAMS

The final focus of this chapter is on the *net job-creation effects* of public-employment programs, or the extent to which funds provided to state and local governments by the federal government to increase their employment levels actually serve to expand employment. As noted earlier, these funds were provided during the decade of the 1970s, first under the *Emergency Employment Act of 1971* and then under the *Comprehensive Employment and Training Act* (CETA).

---

[36]Not surprisingly, public employees are overwhelmingly against expenditure- and tax-limitation legislation. See Paul Courant et al., "Tax Limitation and the Demand for Public Service in Michigan," *National Tax Journal* 32 (June 1979): 147–58.

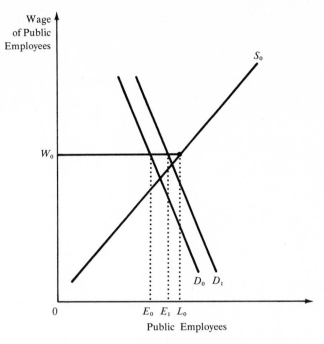

FIGURE 13.5   A Public-Sector Employment Program

Ignoring for a moment private-sector labor markets, suppose that all of the unemployed workers in the economy have attached themselves to the public-sector labor market and that the wage in that market is rigid downward in the *short run*; Figure 13.5 shows that at the prevailing SLG employee wage (W_0), the supply of workers to the SLG sector exceeds the demand for SLG employees; employment is E_0, and $L_0 - E_0$ individuals who want work cannot find it. If, through a public-employment program, such as that administered under CETA, the federal government provides funds to SLGs to expand their employment, the demand for labor will shift to the right (to, say, D_1). SLG employment will expand to E_1, and unemployment will be reduced.[37]

The key issue in evaluating such a program is the extent to which the demand curve actually shifts to the right in response to the program. If, given the prevailing public-sector wage, W_0, funds are provided to create 100 new SLG positions, will the demand curve actually shift to the right by 100 positions? The answer in general is no. Since SLG decision makers have other goals in addition to increasing public-employment expenditures—goals such as increasing other government expenditures, reducing local taxes, and reducing local debt—it is logical to hypothesize that they will use at least a portion of the public-employment-program

---

[37]If the demand curve should shift horizontally by more than $L_0 - E_0$, or if the initial SLG employee wage were a market-clearing one, the reader should be able to show that the SLG employee wage would also increase. Surprisingly, only one study has attempted to analyze the effect of these programs on public-sector wage levels, and that study proved inconclusive. See Lauri Bassi, "Estimating the Impact of Job Creation Programs on Public Sector Wages" (Princeton University Working Paper, 1979).

funds to hire people they would have hired even in the absence of the program (thus freeing up their own resources for the above-mentioned alternative uses). Put another way, the public-employment-program funds might at least partially *displace* regular SLG expenditures on public employees, thereby reducing the net job-creation effect of the program.[38]

One may wonder how such a *displacement effect* (or *fiscal substitution*) could occur, if by law the public-employment-program funds can be used only to expand SLG employment levels. The answer is that as long as SLG officials would have planned to expand their employment even in the absence of the program, program monitors have no direct way of ascertaining whether the jobs "created" by the program would have been created in its absence.[39] Since the annual growth of SLG employment exceeded the increase in the number of public-employment-program positions in every year covered by Table 13.1, it is possible that such displacement or fiscal substitution occurred.

Numerous attempts have been made to estimate the displacement effects of public-employment programs. A number of empirical studies have used either aggregate time-series data or cross-section data on local-government employment to estimate the effects of various factors on the demand for SLG employees— including such factors as public-employee wage rates, community income levels, *and* the number of public-employment positions funded. Although the estimated effects of the program vary widely with the models and data used in these studies, a reasonable consensus would be that at least 30 to 50 percent of program funds ultimately displace local-government funds.[40] That is, no more than 50 to 70 percent of these funds actually go towards increasing SLG employment.[41]

---

[38]Even if such displacement is complete, program funds will still have a stimulative impact even if they are implicitly spent on nonlabor items, used to retire a local debt, or used to reduce local taxes. If the funds have this stimulative impact, the effects of the program will be similar to any other general increase in government spending or decrease in taxes. However, they will not necessarily benefit the unemployed workers at which such programs are targeted.

[39]There are literally thousands of state and local governments in the United States, and it would be nearly impossible to obtain direct information on their planned employment levels in the absence of the public-employment programs. Clearly, local officials have no incentive to report that they planned to expand employment; such an action would limit their ability to implicitly shift public employment funds to other uses.

[40]See for example, George Johnson and James Tomola, "The Fiscal Substitution Effects of Alternative Approaches to Public Service Employment," *Journal of Human Resources* 12 (Winter 1977): 3–26; Michael Borus and Daniel Hamermesh, "Estimating Fiscal Substitution by Public Service Employment Programs," *Journal of Human Resources* 13(Fall 1978): 561–65; and Lauri Bassi and Alan Fechter, "The Implications for Fiscal Substitution and Occupational Displacement Under an Expanded CETA Title VI" (Final Report submitted to the U.S. Department of Labor, 1979). The Johnson-Tomola paper provides an interesting case study of how research affects public policy. Later studies (such as Borus and Hamermesh) showed its precise estimates of displacement to be incorrect. However, the study was well publicized in Washington and the mere fact that Johnson and Tomola raised the displacement issue provoked Congress to redesign the CETA program in an effort to minimize displacement (essentially by limiting individuals' participation in part of the public-employment program to a fixed term). As this example demonstrates, the publicity that a study gets is often as important as its scientific substance.

[41]Researchers using alternative methodologies have concluded that the net job-creation effects may be larger. See for example, Richard Nathan et al., "Monitoring the Public Service Employment Program: The Second Round" (report prepared for the National Commission for Employment Policy, March 1979). These estimates are based on subjective estimates of what local government employment would have been in the absence of the program

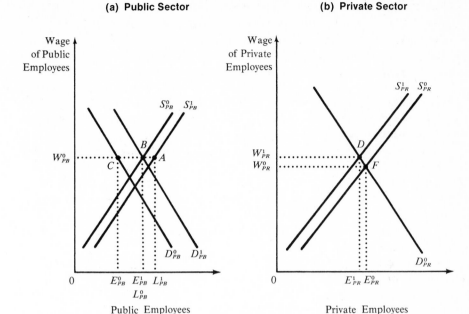

FIGURE 13.6   An Analysis of the Effects of a Public-Employment Program: Responsive Supply in the Private Sector

So far, however, our analysis of the net employment-creation effects of a public-employment program has ignored the private sector. After considering the interaction between public and private labor markets, one can see that the net job-creation effects may be even less than the 50 to 70 percent figure cited above. Our analysis of this issue assumes the existence of an above-equilibrium, downward-rigid wage in the public sector and the accompanying presence of "wait unemployment" there.

In Figure 13.6, simple demand and supply models have been drawn for private- and public-sector labor markets. Suppose that the demand and supply curves in the private sector are initially given by D_{PR}^0 and S_{PR}^0, respectively, and that equilibrium occurs at the market-clearing wage-employment combination (W_{PR}^0, E_{PR}^0). Suppose also that the public-sector demand and supply curves are given by D_{PB}^0 and S_{PB}^0, respectively. The public-sector wage rate, however, is again assumed to be fixed in the short run at the level W_{PB}^0. As a result, employment will initially be E_{PB}^0 in the public sector, and the excess supply of labor to the public sector is given by $L_{PB}^0 - E_{PB}^0$.

In order to have an equilibrium situation—in the sense that unemployed workers in the public sector have no incentive to search for jobs in the private sector—the expected level of earnings (ignoring all nonwage forms of compensation) must be the same in both sectors. Therefore, the wages in each sector multiplied by the fraction of time that individuals attached to each sector (F) expect to be employed must be equal:

$$W_{PB}^0 F_{PB}^0 = W_{PR}^0 F_{PR}^0. \tag{13.2}$$

Since there is an excess supply of labor in the public sector, F_{PB}^0 is less than one, while the market-clearing assumption in the private sector guarantees (in this framework) that F_{PR}^0 is equal to one. As a result, it must be initially true that the public-sector wage exceeds the private-sector wage:

$$W_{PB}^0 > W_{PR}^0. \tag{13.3}$$

Suppose that the federal government now provides funds to SLGs to expand their employment levels and that the result of this public-employment program is to shift the demand curve in the public sector to D_{PB}^1. The first-round effect of the program is to increase SLG employment to E_{PB}^1, eliminating the excess supply of labor. This shift, however, also eliminates the equality in equation (13.2). Since the elimination of the excess supply of labor in the public sector increases the fraction of time that workers attached to that sector expect to be employed, it must now be true that

$$W_{PB}^0 F_{PB}^1 > W_{PR}^0 F_{PR}^0, \tag{13.4}$$

where F_{PB}^1 is the fraction of time employees attached to the *SLG* sector now expect to be employed. (In our simple model where there is no unemployment when demand equals supply, F_{PB}^1 would equal one.)

The situation depicted in equation (13.4) is not an equilibrium; the expected earnings level is now higher in the public than in the private sector. Therefore, some *employed* private-sector workers have an incentive to quit their jobs to search for the now relatively more attractive public-sector jobs. This quitting behavior is reflected by a leftward shift in the supply curve of labor to the private sector and a rightward shift in the supply curve to the public sector. As a result, an excess demand for labor in the private sector now exists at W_{PR}^0, and employers there are forced to bid up wages and to reduce employment levels. The shift out in the labor-supply curve to the public sector creates an excess supply of labor there, reducing the expected fraction of the period that workers attached to the public sector will find employment. These shifts continue until equilibrium is restored and expected earnings are again equal in the two sectors.

$$W_{PB}^0 F_{PB}^2 = W_{PR}^1 F_{PR}^1 \tag{13.5}$$

This equilibrium is shown in Figure 13.6 as occurring when the supply curves are S_{PB}^1 and S_{PR}^1 in the two sectors.

Note that the increase in *total* (public plus private) employment that results is less than the increase in SLG employment because some private-sector employees have quit their jobs to search (or wait) for jobs in the SLG sector. The net-employment effects of the program are overestimated, then, if one focuses only on what happens to SLG employment and fails to measure employment changes in the private sector that are induced by the program. Note also that the market reactions to the program have induced higher private-sector wages. Is it at all surprising, then, that business organizations—especially those that represent employers whose work forces might find public-employment-program positions desirable—are vocal opponents to such legislation? Such programs are simply not in these employers' self-interest.

REVIEW QUESTIONS

1. Explain why the demand curve for public-sector employees slopes downward. Do your explanations hold for both the long run and short run?
2. You have been asked to oversee a study of the comparability of federal-government and private-sector employee compensation. List and explain the factors this study should take into account.
3. Referring to the four factors influencing the elasticity of demand for labor, spell out why the labor-demand curve in the public sector is likely to be more or less elastic than demand curves in the private sector.
4. Congresswoman X states, "I support the granting of federal funds to our cities for the purpose of hiring additional city workers. Last year, the federal government authorized payments to support 200 additional police officers in City Y, bringing its total force to 2200. This can only mean that City Y's residents were being given 10 percent more protection than they would otherwise have received—and that 200 more people were employed in City Y than would otherwise have been employed." Analyze Congresswoman X's conclusions about the effects of federal grants.

SELECTED READINGS

Ehrenberg, Ronald G. "The Demand For State and Local Government Employees." *American Economic Review* 63 (June 1973): 366–79.

Ehrenberg, Ronald G. and Gerald S. Goldstein. "A Model of Public Sector Labor Markets." *Journal of Urban Economics* 2 (April 1975): 223–45.

Farber, Henry S. and Harry C. Katz. "Interest Arbitration, Outcomes, and the Incentive to Bargain." *Industrial and Labor Relations Review* 33 (October 1979): 55–65.

Johnson, George and James Tomola. "The Fiscal Substitution Effects of Alternative Approaches to Public Service Employment." *Journal of Human Resources* 12 (Winter 1977): 3–26.

Smith, Sharon, *Equal Pay in the Public Sector: Fact or Fantasy*. Princeton, N. J.: Industrial Relations Section, Princeton University, 1977.

14

The Economics of Discrimination

We have learned that wages differ across individuals or jobs for numerous reasons. They vary with the amount of general or specific training, with job and locational characteristics, and by age. They also vary with fringe benefits and compensation schemes, and, of course, they vary with the extent of unionism. Many of these sources of wage differentials may be regarded either as necessary in the allocation of labor or as socially legitimate on other grounds. There are, however, sizable wage differentials that appear to be associated solely with race and sex, and these differentials are often thought to be synonymous with widespread discrimination against minorities—especially blacks and Hispanics—and women. This chapter discusses the evidence and theories of discrimination and concludes with an analysis of government policy in this area.

WHAT IS DISCRIMINATION?

The term discrimination is often used imprecisely because the relationship between *prejudice* and discrimination often is unclear. One might assert, for example, that a firm with two racially segregated branch offices is discriminating by failing to integrate both offices, even if workers in both branches are paid the same wages and have the same opportunities for advancement. This assertion raises the question of whether discrimination is always present where there is prejudice or just when some harm comes from this prejudice. Conversely, some people allege discrimination exists in cases where prejudice may not. For example, a firm offering specific training may prefer to hire younger workers who will stay with the firm long enough for it to recoup training costs. Is this age discrimination or good business?

TABLE 14.1 Mean Annual Salaries of Full-Time College Faculty in the
Humanities, 1972 and 1973

	Black		White	
	Number	*Salary (dollars)*	*Number*	*Salary (dollars)*
All full-time faculty	2,177	15,034	85,904	15,572
Doctorate from distinguished university	89	20,259	9,765	16,832
Doctorate from other universities	173	17,262	17,894	15,790
No doctorate	1,915	14,590	58,245	15,293

SOURCE: Thomas Sowell, *Affirmative Action Reconsidered: Was It Necessary in Academia?* (Washington, D.C.: The American Enterprise Institute for Public Policy Research, 1975), p. 20.

Another confusing issue is whether discrimination can be identified by in-equality of *achievement* or inequality of *opportunity*. Is an accounting firm located in a small, mostly white town guilty of discrimination if it has no black auditors on its staff? Would the answer change if the firm could show it had advertised job openings widely and had made the same offers to blacks as to whites but that the offers to blacks had been rejected?

Finally, just what standards are to be used to judge equality? Consider the data on college teachers in the humanities contained in Table 14.1. The overall average salary paid to black professors is slightly below the salaries paid to whites for at least two reasons. First, a lower proportion of blacks have received doctor-ate degrees, and, of those who have, fewer were obtained at distinguished univer-sities. The relatively lower levels of educational attainment among blacks thus holds down their average salary. Second, among those teachers without doctor-ates, blacks receive lower salaries than whites. However, if one looks at salaries among professors with doctorates in the humanities from distinguished universi-ties, we see that blacks earn *more* than whites. The same is true among those with doctorates from less distinguished universities.

Do the data in Table 14.1 suggest that blacks in academia are discriminated against? One could answer yes, because they earn less overall, because they have lower levels of preparation for their jobs, or because there are so few blacks in college teaching (2.5 percent of college professors are black, whereas blacks con-stitute about 8 percent of the overall employed population at large). Others might argue that there is no evidence of discrimination against blacks with doctorates, once one controls for the quality of preparation.

It is obvious from the questions raised by Table 14.1 that discrimination can occur in many forms and places. If it occurs in the labor market, workers with equal preparation and productivity receive different wages. If it occurs among educational institutions, students of equal ability are treated differently and emerge from formal schooling with unequal educations. If it occurs in childhood, young children with equal potential are raised with quite different aspirations and attitudes. Discrimination can also occur in a variety of other places: the housing market, various product markets, and treatment under the law.

The kind of discrimination this chapter will analyze in most depth is discrimination in the labor market. This emphasis should not imply that other forms of discrimination are unimportant or unrelated to labor-market discrimination. Indeed, *past* labor-market discrimination may have been instrumental in causing the poverty or attitudes that are *now* manifest in child-rearing practices, school-achievement levels, and career or sex-role aspirations. However, since the focus of our analysis is on *current labor-market discrimination,* we will lump all *other* forms of discrimination into a more general category we will call *premarket differences.*

An operational definition of *current labor-market discrimination* is ''the valuation in the labor market of personal characteristics of the worker that are unrelated to productivity.''[1] This definition recognizes that one's value in the labor market depends on all the demand and supply factors affecting marginal productivity. However, when factors that are *unrelated* to productivity acquire a positive or negative value in the labor market, discrimination can be said to occur. Race and sex are currently the most prominent of these factors alleged to be unrelated to productivity, but physical handicaps, religion, sexual preferences, and ethnic affiliations are also on the list.

Three points should be noted about the above definition. First, the emphasis in identifying discrimination is on measurable market outcomes, such as earnings, wages, occupational attainment, or employment levels. While prejudicial attitudes may be felt by members of one group towards those of another, these feelings must be accompanied by some *action* that results in a different market outcome for us to assert that discrimination is present.

Second, we are not concerned with the routine random differences in outcomes that are matters of luck. Rather, the concept of discrimination encompasses only those differences that are so systematic that they do not cancel each other out within large groups.

Finally, our definition of labor-market discrimination suggests an operational way to distinguish between *labor-market* and *premarket* factors that cause earnings differentials. Differentials that derive from differences in average *productivity* levels across race or sex groups, for example, can be categorized as *premarket* in nature. Differentials that are attributed to race or sex, *holding productivity constant,* can be said to be evidence of labor-market discrimination.

It is very important for policy purposes to measure the relative size of labor-market and premarket factors that lead to systematic earnings differences among various population groups. Any attempts to combat discrimination must be grounded in accurate information concerning the *source* of that discrimination; otherwise, effective antidiscrimination programs cannot be formulated. If the evidence points to a significant amount of labor-market discrimination, programs aimed at employers and the hiring/promotion process may be effective. If, how-

---

[1]Kenneth J. Arrow, ''The Theory of Discrimination,'' *Discrimination in Labor Markets,* eds. Orley Ashenfelter and Albert Rees (Princeton, N.J.: Princeton University Press, 1973), p. 3.

TABLE 14.2   Black/White Ratio of Median Wage and Salary Income for Full-Time, Year-Round Workers

Black/White Income Ratio		
Year	Males	Females
1959	0.61	0.66
1961	0.66	0.67
1963	0.66	0.64
1965	0.64	0.71
1967	0.64	0.74
1969	0.66	0.80
1971	0.68	0.88
1973	0.67	0.85
1975	0.77	0.99
1977	0.73	0.95

SOURCES: U.S. Bureau of the Census, *Current Population Reports: Consumer Income,* Series P-60 (relevant years).

ever, most of any systematic earnings differences related to race or sex appear to be rooted in premarket factors, then programs aimed at education, training, and the process of socializing children will be required.

EARNINGS DISPARITIES BY RACE AND SEX

There have been, and continue to be, strikingly large income disparities between most minorities and whites and between men and women. These differences are a cause of widespread social concern about discrimination, its sources, and possible remedies. This chapter will analyze various theories and their consequences for antidiscrimination policies after first describing the race and sex differences in earnings that actually exist.

Racial Differences

Blacks.   In 1977, labor market earnings of the typical black male were 73 percent of those earned by white males. While the disparity is obviously large, it appears to be declining over time. As indicated in Table 14.2, the 1977 ratio was 7–9 percentage points higher than in the 1960s, and 5–6 points higher than in the early 1970s. A similar but much more pronounced trend for females appears in Table 14.2. Black and white women had virtually the same earnings ratios as did men in the early 1960s (around 0.65). However, in the mid-1960s the ratio for women began to rise until by 1977 black women who worked full time earned, on average, 95 percent as much as full-time white women workers.

While these ratios and their trends are very interesting and important, they do not help us identify the immediate *source* of the disparities. Are the differences primarily due to *current labor-market discrimination,* or are they the result of *premarket factors?* Blacks, for example, tend to be younger and less educated, on average, than whites.[2] Further, it may well be that the average *quality* of schooling received by blacks is lower than the average for whites.[3] We know that earnings rise with both education and experience, so that *some* of the black/white earnings differences are surely attributable to these characteristics. How much of the overall differential in average earnings is due to differences in the characteristics that affect productivity, and how much is due to labor-market discrimination?

To measure the extent of market discrimination one must answer the following question: "What would be the black/white earnings ratio if blacks and whites had the same productive characteristics?" In other words, if blacks (on average) had the same education, training, experience, turnover rate, health and marital status, and region of residence as whites, what would be the ratio of their earnings to those of whites? One study that asked this question for males in 1966 found that 67–75 percent of the overall black/white disparity in wage rates was attributable to premarket differences;[4] another study found that 53 percent of the disparity was due to premarket factors;[5] a third estimated that 60 percent of the wage differences were rooted in premarket differences.[6] Thus, it would appear that from half to three-quarters of the disparity in black/white earnings can be attributed to premarket differences.

The finding that from 50–75 percent of the difference in average earnings can be explained by differences in productive characteristics implies that current labor-market discrimination *may* account for 25–50 percent of the overall differential— suggesting a rather significant role for antidiscrimination programs or policies in the labor market. However, the figures of 25–50 percent are really upper-bound estimates of the extent of labor-market discrimination, because researchers simply do not have complete data on the productive characteristics of individuals or groups. Researchers can measure age, education, and, in many cases, experience, but they rarely have data on school quality, work habits, aspirations, degree of alienation, and other intangibles that clearly affect one's productivity. These intangibles, moreover, *may* vary across race (or sex) owing to such premarket factors as social treatment, socioeconomic status of one's parents, and cultural background. If the unmeasured characteristics tend to depress the productivity of minorities or women relative to white males, attributing all of the unexplained

---

[2]As noted in Chapter 9, one's choice of education is influenced by expected labor-market earnings over the life cycle. Hence, ensuring that market discrimination against blacks is reduced or eliminated should serve as an incentive for blacks to stay in school longer.

[3]See Finis Welch, "Education and Racial Discrimination," in *Discrimination in Labor Markets*, eds. Orley Ashenfelter and Albert Rees (Princeton, N.J.: Princeton University Press, 1973), pp. 43–81.

[4]Robert J. Flanagan, "Labor Force Experience, Job Turnover, and Racial Wage Differentials," *Review of Economics and Statistics* 56 (November 1974): 521–29.

[5]Mary Corcoran and Greg Duncan, "Labor History, Labor Force Attachment, and Earnings Differences Between the Races and Sexes," *Journal of Human Resources* 14, 1 (Winter 1979): 3–20.

[6]A. S. Blinder, "Wage Discrimination—Reduced Form and Structural Estimates," *Journal of Human Resources* 8 (Fall 1973): 436–55.

difference in average earnings to current labor-market discrimination will clearly overstate the extent of that discrimination. *Some* of the unexplained 25–50 percent may be the result of unmeasured productive characteristics and thus more appropriately labeled *premarket* in nature.

After estimating the portion of the *average* race/sex earnings differential that is explained by differences in average productive characteristics, one is left with a residual, or unexplained, portion. One part of the residual may be the result of current labor-market discrimination, but the effects of any unmeasurable (or at least unmeasured) differences in average productive characteristics show up in the residual also. Because of this methodological defect—which is mainly the result of the difficulties of measuring all characteristics that affect productivity—accurate measures of the extent of labor-market discrimination do not exist. Assuming *all* of the unexplained residual is due to discrimination, we can make estimates of the *maximum possible* effects discrimination might have; however, we are unable to say if actual labor-market discrimination is close to this maximum or not.

Hispanics.   Labor-market discrimination against Hispanic workers has not been extensively studied. To control for differences in productive characteristics requires, in addition to the usual data on education and experience, information on proficiency in English—and such information is rarely available. A recent study that did make use of language proficiency data, however, suggests that discrimination against Hispanics is not as severe as against blacks.[7]

In 1975, ratios of the average earnings of male Hispanics to those of non-Hispanic white males were as follows:

—Mexicans: 0.69
—Puerto Ricans: 0.73
—Central and South Americans: 0.81
—Cubans: 0.83

However, differences in productive characteristics accounted for about 75–80 percent of the earnings gap for Mexicans and Puerto Ricans and 36 percent of the gap for Central and South Americans. Thus, if differences in average productive characteristics were eliminated, the foregoing earnings ratios would rise to 0.95, 0.93, and 0.88 for Mexicans, Puerto Ricans, and Central/South Americans, respectively. The earnings of Cuban males do not appear to be adversely affected by labor-market discrimination; if they acquired the same measured productive characteristics, on average, as non-Hispanic white males, it is estimated that they would earn about 5 percent more.

---

[7]The findings in this section are from Cordelia W. Reimers, "Sources of the Wage Gap Between Hispanic and Other White Americans" (Working Paper #139, Industrial Relations Section, Princeton University, 1980). The findings are generally corroborated by an earlier study by James D. Gwartney and James E. Long, "The Relative Earnings of Blacks and Other Minorities," *Industrial and Labor Relations Review* 31 (April 1978): 336–46. See also Geoffrey Carliner, "Returns to Education for Blacks, Anglos, and Five Spanish Groups," *Journal of Human Resources* 11 (Spring 1976): 172–84.

Sex Differences

Differences in earnings between female and male workers are large. The average white, female, full-time worker earns roughly 58 percent of what her male counterpart earns. As one can see from Table 14.3, this ratio is down from what it was in 1955 and essentially unchanged since 1964. Further, women earn substantially less than men in each of the major occupational categories, with the ratios running from 42 percent in sales work to 76 percent among professionals. Not even in government work do female incomes rise above 70 percent of male incomes, and among the self-employed the ratio is at its lowest (38 percent).

There are several factors other than labor-market discrimination that could cause these large disparities. First, because the market-work life of a woman is normally shorter than that of a man, women have fewer incentives to invest in schooling and post-schooling training that is specifically oriented to the labor market. (They, in essence, prepare for two careers—one at home and one in the labor market—and are thus typically less specialized than men.) The lack of on-the-job training, as noted in Chapter 9, is one reason why the age/earnings profiles for women are so flat, creating a greater disparity between female and male earnings as they grow older. Shorter working lives also mean that within each occupational grouping, women are likely to be less experienced than men. One survey, for example, found that in 1966 the average male, aged 30–44, had 19.4 years of

TABLE 14.3   Ratio of Female/Male Wage and Salary Income for Year-Round, Full-Time, White Workers

Year	Ratio of Female/Male Income
1955	0.65
1964	0.59
1967	0.58
1970	0.59
1973	0.56
1977	0.58
Private sector (1977):	
Professional-technical workers	0.76
Managerial	0.52
Sales	0.42
Clerical	0.64
Craft	0.59
Operatives	0.58
Laborer	0.64
Service	0.63
Government workers (1977):	
Federal—public administration	0.66
Federal—professional	0.68
State and local—public administration	0.60
State and local—professional	0.70
Self-employed, nonagricultural (1977)	0.38

SOURCES: 1955: U.S. Bureau of the Census, *Current Population Reports, Consumer Income*, Series P-60, No. 22 (September 1956), Table 7; 1964: U.S. Bureau of the Census, *Current Population Reports: Consumer Income, Income in 1964 of Families and Persons in the United States*, Series P-60, No. 47 (September 1965), Table 18; 1967–1973: U.S. Bureau of the Census, *Current Population Reports, Consumer Income: Money Income in 1973 of Families and Persons in the United States*, Series P-60, No. 97 (January 1975), Table F; 1977: U.S. Bureau of the Census, *Current Population Reports, Consumer Income: Money Income in 1977 of Families and Persons in the United States*, Series P-60, No. 118 (March 1979), Table 55.

work experience; the average work history for married women of the same age was 9.6 years.[8]

Second, because of traditional home responsibilities, women are less likely than men to work overtime or to choose occupations that offer jobs with high pay but long hours.[9] Home responsibilities also mean that women usually work closer to home than do men, a fact (as argued in Chapter 8) that implies lower wages.

Finally, historically women have tended to "follow" husbands when the husbands decided on the geographical location of their jobs (a fact noted in Chapter 10). Husbands, in effect, have been relatively free to choose their best offer, while wives have usually done the best they can *given* their geographical location. This sort of family decision-making behavior has also tended to reduce female earnings.[10]

While the above *premarket* differences are not immediately generated by *labor-market* discrimination, they will be *affected* by the presence of such discrimination. If current market discrimination exists, the resulting lower wage for women strengthens incentives for them to be the ones who engage in *household production*. The expectation that women will be the ones to stay home with children, for example, is probably the major reason behind each of the three premarket forces above. Anything that reduces the disproportionate share of women in household production will tend to increase their incentives to acquire human capital, work longer hours for pay, and select their jobs from a wider area. Thus, even though premarket differences are clearly important and deeply rooted in factors other than current labor-market discrimination, measuring the extent of labor-market discrimination and taking steps to end it is of obvious importance.

One way to obtain a sense of the extent of market discrimination is to look at the relative earnings of women who have never married. These women are not engaged in raising children and, unless involved in caring for a parent or sibling, do not have the household duties that usually befall married women. They tend to work almost as many hours per year as the average man, and they also exhibit concave age/earnings profiles.[11] Despite these closer similarities to men, however, the average income of never-married women aged 25–64 is just 65 percent of that earned by the average man in that age group (as compared to 56 percent for married women).[12]

---

[8]See Jacob Mincer and Solomon Polachek, "Family Investments in Human Capital: Earnings of Women," *Journal of Political Economy* 82 (March/April 1974): S76–S108.

[9]"Protective" labor legislation at the state level until recently often limited the maximum hours per week a woman could work—thus closing women out of overtime opportunities available to men.

[10]Evidence that geographic migration usually causes husbands' earnings to rise but wives' earnings to fall was cited earlier (Chapter 10) based on Polachek and Horvath, "A Life Cycle Approach to Migration," *Research in Labor Economics* (Greenwich, Conn.: JA1 Press, 1977). Other articles on the same topic are Robert H. Frank, "Why Women Earn Less: The Theory and Estimation of Differential Overqualification," *American Economic Review* 68 (June 1978): 360–73; and Mincer and Polachek, "Family Investments in Human Capital." Of course, increased female labor-market attachment suggests that such patterns will not necessarily persist in the future.

[11]Victor Fuchs, "Differences in Hourly Earnings Between Men and Women," *Monthly Labor Review* 94, 5 (May 1971): 9–15.

[12]These ratios are for full-time, year-round whites, aged 25–64 in 1977. See U.S. Bureau of the Census, *Current Population Reports: Money Income in 1977 of Families and Persons in the United States,* Series P–60, No. 118 (March 1979), Table 45.

Before concluding that market discrimination is immediately responsible for most of the earnings gap between men and women, however, it is important to remember that the typical never-married person, aged 25–64, is probably younger and thus less experienced than the typical married person. It is also important to realize that human-capital decisions are based on *expected* career life—and many never-married women may have expected to become married when basic schooling or occupational decisions were made. In short, previously prevailing social expectations about women's role in household production may also have influenced the human-capital decisions of women who ultimately decide not to marry, causing their earnings to be lower than otherwise. Finally, the group of never-married adults is likely to contain a higher proportion of disabled persons than is found in the married group. Thus, while *some* of the 35 percent earnings differential for never-married women may be due to current labor-market discrimination, it is unlikely that *all* of the difference can be so attributed.

The best way to estimate the upper-bound effects of market discrimination on the basis of sex is to perform the same kind of analysis reported earlier for black and white males. Thus we must ask, "What would the female/male earnings ratio be, on average, if women had the same education, training, experience, hours of work, commuting distance, turnover rate, and other productive characteristics as their male counterparts?" Studies that have attempted to answer this question have generally concluded that differences in education, training, turnover, and experience—but primarily experience—account for one-third to two-thirds of the earnings differences between men and women.[13] Thus it appears that *labor-market* discrimination can account for no more than two-thirds of the earnings gap between men and women.

One aspect of alleged labor-market discrimination against women is *occupational segregation*—the reservation of some jobs for men and others (mostly lower-paying ones) for women. Some dimensions of this segregation and its effects can be seen in Table 14.4, which presents for 1970 the share of women in a variety of high-paying and low-paying occupations. Very few of the high-paying occupations employed women to an extent even close to their overall proportion among all employed workers (37.7 percent in 1970). On the other hand, women were heavily *over*-represented in the low-paying occupations.

How much of the market discrimination against women takes the form of occupational segregation and how much takes the form of different wages *within* given occupations? A crude answer to this question can be obtained by estimating the wage women would make if they had productive characteristics similar to the average male. Comparing this estimated wage to the average male wage will yield an upper-bound estimate of overall market discrimination. If we then estimate the wage women would receive if they had the same productive characteristics *and* the same *occupational* distribution as men, we can calculate the wage disparities caused solely by occupational differences. The most widely quoted study of the effects of occupational segregation suggests that equalizing the occupational dis-

---

[13]Corcoran and Duncan, "Work History, Labor Force Attachment, and Earnings Differences Between the Races and Sexes"; Mincer and Polachek, "Family Investments in Human Capital: Earnings of Women;" and Sharon P. Smith, *Equal Pay in the Public Sector: Fact or Fantasy* (Princeton, N.J.: Industrial Relations Section, Princeton University, 1977).

TABLE 14.4   **Representation of Women in Ten High-Paying and Ten Low-Paying Occupations, 1970**

Occupation	Percent Female 1970
High-Paying:	
Stock and bond sales agents	8.6
Managers and administrators, n.e.c.[a]	11.6
Bank officials and financial managers	17.4
Sales representatives, manufacturing	8.5
Real-estate appraisers	4.1
Designers	23.5
Personnel and labor-relations workers	31.2
Sales representatives, wholesale	6.4
Computer programmers	22.7
Mechanical-engineering technicians	2.9
Low-Paying:	
Practical nurses	96.3
Hairdressers and cosmetologists	90.4
Cooks, except private household	62.8
Health aides, except nursing	83.9
Nurses' aides	84.6
Sewers and stitchers	93.8
Farm laborers	13.2
Dressmakers and seamstresses	95.7
School monitors	91.2
Childcare workers, except private household	93.2
All occupations	37.7

[a]The initials n.e.c. mean "not elsewhere classified."

SOURCE: Sharon Smith, "Men's Jobs, Women's Jobs and Differential Wage Treatment," *Job Evaluation and EEO: The Emerging Issues,* papers presented at the Industrial Relations Counselors Colloquium, September 14–15, 1978, Atlanta, Georgia (New York: Industrial Relations Counselors, 1979), pp. 67–84.

tribution of men and women with the same education and years of experience would reduce the earnings gap by 9 percentage points.[14]

It would appear, then, that perhaps half of the overall 40 percent differential between the earnings of men and women is due to premarket factors. Of the remaining 20 percent—which could be due to current market discrimination—roughly half again (9 percentage points) appears to be the consequence of occupational segregation. The effect of occupational segregation *could* be larger than this, however, because the "occupations" referred to in the study are very general categories, such as professional-technical worker, manager, clerical worker, skilled craft worker, and so forth. Not captured in the analysis, then, are the effects of segregation *within* these broad groupings. For example, an insurance company that was later the object of a sex-discrimination lawsuit had, between 1964 and 1970, hired men and women with college degrees to be "claims adjustors" and "claims representatives." The educational requirements for each job were the same, but only men were hired as "adjustors," and almost all "repre-

---

[14]Ronald Oaxaca, "Male-Female Wage Differentials in Urban Labor Markets," *International Economic Review* 14, 3 (October 1973): 693–709.

sentatives'' were women. Claims adjustors received $2,500 more in yearly salary to begin with, and only adjustors could be promoted to higher-level supervisory positions. Both positions are in the same general occupational class, but both pay and future opportunities were much better for the male workers.[15]

One study of professional-technical employees in a large corporation found that men and women with the same job level and the same characteristics received equal pay. However, in most cases women were assigned to lower job levels than equally qualified men. While one cannot generalize from the experience of a single corporation, the results of *this* study suggest that most of sex discrimination may be due to occupational segregation.[16]

Note, however, that not all of occupational segregation is the result of current employer practices that exclude qualified women from higher-paying jobs. Pre-market forces, beginning early in childhood, instill beliefs among women and men alike that some occupations are ''women's work'' and some are ''men's work.'' These beliefs keep women out of many low-paying laborer jobs and exclude them from high-paying jobs as well. It is probably true that these notions will change over time as alternative role models become available, but not *all* of these feelings can be attributed to *current* employer practices.

THEORIES OF MARKET DISCRIMINATION

As argued in the previous section, one cannot rule out the presence of substantial discrimination against women and minorities in the labor market. Before one can design policies to end discrimination, one must understand the *sources* and *mechanisms* causing it. The goal of this section is to lay out and evaluate the different theories of discrimination proposed by economists.

Three general sources of labor market discrimination have been hypothesized, and each source suggests an associated model of how discrimination is implemented and what its consequences are.[17] The first source of discrimination is *personal prejudice*, wherein employers, fellow employees, or customers dislike associating with workers of a given race or sex.[18] The second general source is *statistical prejudgment*, whereby employers project onto *individuals* certain perceived *group* characteristics. Finally, there are models according to which the desire for, and use of, *monopoly power* is the source of discrimination. While all of the models generate useful, suggestive insights, none has been convincingly established as superior.

---

[15]Barbara Bergmann, ''Reducing the Pervasiveness of Discrimination,'' in *Jobs for Americans,* ed. Eli Ginzburg (Englewood Cliffs, N.J.: Prentice-Hall, Inc., 1976).

[16]Burton G. Malkiel and Judith A. Malkiel, ''Male-Female Pay Differentials in Professional Employment,'' *American Economic Review* 63 (September 1973): 693–705.

[17]Two of the three general models were labeled by Kenneth Boulding, ''Toward a Theory of Discrimination,'' in *Equal Opportunity and the AT & T Case,* ed. Phyllis Wallace (Cambridge, Mass.: The MIT Press, 1976).

[18]The models of personal prejudice are based on Gary S. Becker, *The Economics of Discrimination,* 2nd ed. (Chicago: University of Chicago Press, 1971).

Personal Prejudice

Employer discrimination. Let us suppose that (white male) *employers* are prejudiced against women or blacks but that (for the sake of simplicity) customers and fellow employees are not prejudiced. This prejudice may take the form of aversion to associating with women or blacks, it may be manifest as a desire to help fellow white males whenever possible, or it may be motivated by status considerations and take the form of occupational segregation. In whatever form, this prejudice is assumed to result in the discriminatory treatment of women or minorities. Further, we assume for the purposes of this model that the women and minorities in question have the same productive characteristics as white males. (This assumption directs our focus to market discrimination by putting aside pre-market factors.)

If employers have a decided preference for hiring white males in high-paying jobs despite the availability of equally qualified women or minorities, they will act *as if* the latter were less productive than the former. By virtue of our assumption that the women and minorities involved are in fact equally productive in every way, the devaluing of their productivity by employers is purely subjective and is a manifestation of personal prejudice. The more prejudicial an employer is, the more actual productivity will be discounted.

Let us suppose that *MP* stands for the actual marginal productivity of all workers in a particular labor market and that *d* represents the extent to which this productivity is subjectively devalued for minorities and women. In this case, market equilibrium for white males is reached when their wage (W_M) equals *MP*:

$$MP = W_M \tag{14.1}$$

For the women and minorities, however, equilibrium is achieved only when their wage (W_F) equals their *subjective* value to firms:

$$MP - d = W_F, \text{ or} \tag{14.2}$$

$$MP = W_F + d. \tag{14.2a}$$

Since the actual marginal productivities are equal by assumption, equations (14.1) and (14.2a) are equal to each other, and one can easily see that W_F must be less than W_M:

$$W_M = W_F + d, \text{ or} \tag{14.3}$$

$$W_F = W_M - d. \tag{14.3a}$$

What this says algebraically has a very simple economic logic: if the actual productivity of women and minorities is devalued by employers, workers in these groups must offer their services at lower wages than white males in order to compete for jobs.

This model of employer discrimination has two major implications—as illustrated by Figure 14.1, which is a graphical representation of equation (14.2a). Figure 14.1 shows that a discriminating employer faced with a wage rate of W_F

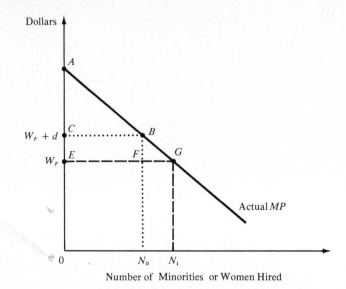

Dollars

A

$W_F + d$ *C* .... *B*

E *F* *G*
W_F

Actual *MP*

0 N_0 N_1

Number of Minorities or Women Hired

**FIGURE 14.1 Equilibrium Employment of Women
and Minorities in Firms that Discriminate**

for women and minorities will hire N_0, for at that point $MP = W_F + d$. *Profit-maximizing* employers, however, will hire N_1; that is, they will hire until $MP = W_F$. The effects on profits can be readily seen in Figure 14.1 if one remembers that the area under the *MP* curve represents total product (or total revenues) of the firm, with capital held constant. Subtracting the area representing the wage bill of the discriminating employer *(OEFN$_0$)* yields profits for these employers equal to the area *AEFB*. Profits for a nondiscriminating employer, however, are *AEG*. These latter employers hire women and minorities to the point where their marginal product equals their wage, while the discriminators end their hiring short of that point. Discriminators thus give up profits in order to indulge their prejudices.

The second implication of our employer-discrimination model concerns the size of the gap between W_M and W_F. The determinants of this gap can best be understood using a graph of the supply of jobs to women or minorities (see Figure 14.2). In a given labor market wherein workers of equal productivity are seeking jobs, the supply of job opportunities for women and minorities will be a function of the gap $(W_M - W_F = d)$ between their wages and those of white males. As shown in Figure 14.2, some employers will hire women or minorities even if their wages equaled W_M $(d = 0)$. These are the nondiscriminating (profit-maximizing) employers, and supply curve $0m_1A$ assumes they account for m_1 jobs in the market. If there are less than m_1 minorities or females seeking employment in that labor market (m' say), they would all be hired by the nondiscriminators, and no discrimination would be evident. W_F would equal W_M, and women and minorities would not have to deal with those who devalue their services.

If the supply of women and minorities were greater than the number that could be absorbed by the nondiscriminating employers (m^*, say), then a wage gap would have to arise for all of them to become employed. Curve $0m_1A$ shows that

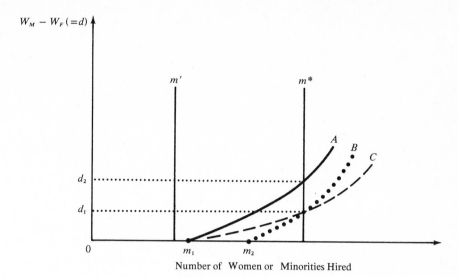

FIGURE 14.2　The Supply of Jobs to Women and Minorities

if the number of women and minorities seeking jobs were to increase from m' to m^*, the required gap would rise from zero to d_2. Thus, the gap depends in part on the sheer size of the groups against whom there is personal prejudice. If the number of women or minorities seeking jobs were to rise beyond m^*, the difference between W_M and W_F would become greater than d_2.

The equilibrium gap between W_M and W_F, however, also depends on the distribution and extent of employer prejudice against women or minorities. If the number of nondiscriminatory employers grows (or if the number of jobs offered by such employers were to grow), the supply-of-jobs curve in Figure 14.2 would shift to the right from $0m_1A$ to $0m_2B$ (say). This shift would reduce the observed wage disparity at m^* from d_2 to d_1. The same reduction in market discrimination could also occur if the number of nondiscriminators stayed constant but the *discriminatory preferences* of the others were *reduced*. If this were to happen, discriminatory employers would require less of a wage disparity to hire a given level of women or minorities, and the supply-of-jobs curve would shift to something like $0m_1C$ in Figure 14.2.

The most disturbing implication of the employer-discrimination model is that discriminators seem to be maximizing *utility* (satisfying their prejudices) instead of *profits*. This practice should immediately raise the question of how they survive. Firms in competitive labor markets *must* maximize profits just to make a normal rate of return on invested capital. Those who do not make this return will find they can earn a better return by investing some other way—a way, perhaps, that does not involve hiring workers. Conversely, since profit-maximizing (nondiscriminating) firms would normally make more money from a given set of assets than would discriminators, we should observe nondiscriminatory firms buying out others and gradually taking over the market. In short, if competitive forces are at work, employers who discriminate would be punished, and discrimination should gradually disappear.

An implication of the employer-discrimination model, then, is that wage disparities will lessen natually over time—an implication that appears to be contradicted by the facts. The figures on race and sex wage disparities in Tables 14.2 and 14.3 show a great stability over many years; recent improvements for blacks can be seen, but these improvements are coincident with the adoption of various *governmental* programs aimed at ending poverty and discrimination.

Does this apparent inconsistency with the facts mean that the employer-discrimination model is inappropriate or wrong? Some have suggested that the model really applies only to monopolistic or oligopolistic employers who are shielded from market forces. It is argued that these firms do not have to maximize profits in order to survive, so they are freer to indulge in the "luxury" of discrimination. There is some evidence that blacks are disproportionately employed in industries that are competitive and are not very well represented in large, higher-paying, oligopolistic firms.[19] However, very large firms tend to have higher skill requirements than competitive firms anyway, and that alone could explain the underrepresentation of blacks in those firms. Further, the sector most insulated from the pressures of costs and competition is the government, and, as Table 14.3 showed for women, wage disparities in this sector are less than in the private sector. Thus, serious questions must be raised about how applicable this model of employer discrimination is in explaining labor-market discrimination.

Customer discrimination.   A second personal-prejudice model stresses *customer* prejudice as a source of discrimination. Customers may have preferences to be served by white males in some situations and by minorities or women in others. If their preferences for white males extend to jobs requiring major responsibility— such as physician, stock broker, or airline pilot—and their preferences for women and minorities are confined to less skilled jobs—nurse or stewardess, say—then occupational segregation that works to the disadvantage of women and minorities will occur. Further, if women or minorities are to find employment in the jobs for which customers prefer white males, they must either receive *lower wages* or be *more qualified* than the average white male. The reason for this is that their value to the firm is in fact lower than that of an *equally qualified* white male because of customers' preferences for white males.

A major implication of the theory of customer discrimination is that women or minorities in jobs that have no customer contact or who work for employers who have no competition should face very little, if any, discrimination. Those with the most customer contact are the most vulnerable to discrimination, as manifested by unequal wages for equally qualified people or occupational segregation or both. The evidence to support this model is somewhat ambiguous. For example, the overall ratio of black-to-white earnings for full-time male workers in the private sector was 0.67 in 1977. Operatives—most of whom are factory workers with little public contact—fare better than average in the private sector (0.81), while there are so few blacks in sales jobs that comparable black/white ratios are

[19]Becker, *The Economics of Discrimination,* p. 48; Ray Marshall, "The Economics of Racial Discrimination: A Survey," *Journal of Economic Literature* 12 (September 1974): 864; and David P. Taylor, "Discrimination and Occupational Wage Differences in the Market for Unskilled Labor," *Industrial and Labor Relations Review* 21 (April 1968): 375–90.

not even published! Self-employed black males earn incomes that are 41 percent of self-employed whites.[20] Table 14.3 tells much the same story for women. Operatives and government workers do better than self-employed or sales workers; however, operatives do slightly worse than other occupations that may have more public contact.

There are obviously serious drawbacks to the above figures as measures of discrimination. Self-employed white males may own retail stores or electronics factories, and self-employed minorities or women may own magazine stands or janitorial services. Women in the sales field may be department-store clerks, while men may be involved with higher-technology sales. Black operatives may be much more heavily unionized than average.[21] It is thus obvious that the gross ratios given above do not take into account human capital or other important differences.

Studies that *do* take into account individual productive characteristics have been done for federal-government and private-sector employees of different races and sexes. These studies find that differences in productive characteristics between white males and other workers do not explain all of the earnings differentials that exist in either sector. However, as one might expect if customer discrimination is present, the "unexplained" differential tends to be smaller in the federal sector (which has no competitors and is not run for profit).[22]

The existence of unexplained race and sex earnings differentials in the federal sector, despite their smaller size than in the private sector, suggests the *possibility* of labor-market discrimination in the federal sector. Interestingly, the racial *composition* of federal employment follows a pattern that is also consistent with the *customer* discrimination model. Agencies that serve heavily minority-oriented constituencies hire greater fractions of minorities than agencies whose constituents are mainly white: employment with the Department of Housing and Urban Development is 27 percent minority, while that with the Department of Agriculture is 10 percent minority.[23] Whether this political version of the customer-discrimination hypothesis will stand up under further testing remains to be seen. While federal administrators may be sensitive to voter prejudices, the issues on which their elected superiors run are so diverse that one may legitimately wonder just how voter prejudices are communicated and enforced. At the moment, though, the existence of customer discrimination in the labor market cannot be ruled out on logical or empirical grounds.

Employee Discrimination. A third source of discrimination based on personal prejudice might be found on the supply side of the market, where white male workers may be averse to situations in which minorities or women fill certain jobs

---

[20]The ratios quoted are for 1977 and are obtained from U.S. Bureau of the Census, *Current Population Reports, Consumer Income: Money Income in 1977 of Families and Persons in the United States,* Series P–60, No. 118 (March 1979), Table 55.

[21]Orley Ashenfelter, "Discrimination and Trade Unions," in *Discrimination in Labor Markets,* eds. Orley Ashenfelter and Albert Rees (Princeton, N.J.: Princeton University Press, 1974).

[22]Smith, *Equal Pay in the Public Sector;* and James E. Long, "Employment Discrimination in the Federal Sector," *Journal of Human Resources* 11, 1 (1976): 86–97.

[23]For an analysis of this subject, see George J. Borjas, "The Politics of Racial Discrimination in the Federal Government" (Mimeo, University of California, Santa Barbara, August 1980).

they consider inappropriate. For example, they may be averse to taking orders from a woman, sharing responsibility with a minority, or working where women or minorities are not confined to menial or low-status jobs.

If white male workers have these discriminatory preferences, they will tend to quit (or avoid) employers who employ women or minorities on a nondiscriminatory basis. Employers, if they wish to hire or retain white males, will have to pay them more than they would if they confined women and minorities to their "traditional," lower-status jobs. In some cases employers may be able to avoid the higher cost of employing white males by running racially or sexually segregated plants. Segregated plants, however, are not always feasible because of the wide range of occupations required and the fact that workers of different races and sexes are not evenly distributed in each occupation.

It is interesting to note that this model of employee discrimination predicts that white males working in integrated environments will receive higher wages than those with exactly the same productive characteristics who work in segregated environments. If we could observe areas where there were no minority workers, say, we would expect to find that white male wages in these areas would be pretty much the same for people embodying comparable human capital. However, in areas where blacks are found in sufficient numbers that many whites must work in integrated plants, we should observe that the wages received by white males of equal human capital will *vary* according to whether they work in segregated or integrated firms. Thus, the theory suggests that the wages received by white males within any given human-capital category will show *greater similarity* when integrated work forces are rare than when some whites work in integrated environments and some do not. When one looks at U.S. data one does in fact find that, other things equal, white male wages are more similar in states where the minority population is small—and where, presumably, few whites work in integrated plants—than they are where the minority population is large. Moreover, this finding seems to be true of both northern and southern states considered separately.[24]

The interesting thing about the above finding is that neither the employer nor the customer models of discrimination predict that *white male* wages will become *less similar* if discrimination exists. If white males are preferred for particular, higher-paying jobs, their wages will be higher than if discrimination were nonexistent. However, the fact that their wages are *higher* does not imply they are more *dissimilar*. White males who, in the absence of discrimination, would have wages clustering around some lower level instead have wages clustering around some higher level. The point is that their wages continue to cluster. However, the above finding offers only indirect support of the employee discrimination model, and it is also consistent with predictions of the "monopoly power" model outlined below. Hence, convincing evidence for the existence of employee discrimination cannot be claimed.

---

[24]Barry R. Chiswick, "Racial Discrimination in the Labor Market: A Test of Alternative Hypotheses," *Journal of Political Economy* 81, 6 (November 1973): 1330–52. It should be noted that the inequality of *minority* earnings does not vary according to their proportion in the population—a finding that seems to rule out the existence of some other, unmeasured force causing greater inequality in high-minority states.

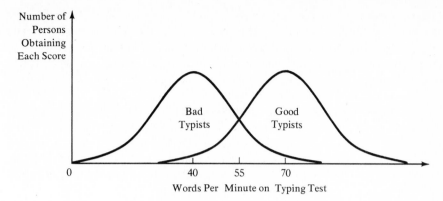

FIGURE 14.3   The Screening Problem

Statistical Discrimination

Another source of discrimination might be the kind and quality of information used in making hiring decisions.[25] Employers must try to *guess* the potential productivity of applicants, but rarely will they know what actual productivity will be. The only information available to them at the time of hire is information that is thought to be *correlated* with productivity: education, experience, age, test scores, and so forth. These correlates are imperfect predictors of actual productivity, however, and employers realize this. To some extent, then, they supplement information on these correlates with a subjective element in making hiring decisions, and this subjective element could *look* like discrimination even though it may not be rooted in personal prejudice.

Statistical discrimination can be viewed as a part of the *screening problem,* which arises when observable personal characteristics that are correlated with productivity are not perfect predictors. By way of example, suppose there are *in fact* two types of workers who apply for a secretarial job: those who can type 70 words per minute (wpm) over the long haul and those who can type 40 wpm. These actual productivities are unknown to the employer, however. All the employer observes are the results of a 5-minute typing test administered to all applicants. What are the problems created by the use of this test as a screening device?

The problems relate to the fact that some typists who can really type only 40 wpm on the job will be lucky and score higher than 40 on the test. Others who can really type 70 wpm on the job will be unlucky and score less than 70 on the test. The imperfection of the test as a predictor will cause two kinds of errors in hiring decisions: 1. some "good" applicants will be rejected, and 2. some "bad" workers will be hired.

The above screening problem is illustrated in Figure 14.3, which shows the

---

[25]The considerations developed in this section are more formally and completely treated in Dennis J. Aigner and Glen G. Cain, "Statistical Theories of Discrimination in Labor Markets," *Industrial and Labor Relations Review* 30, 2 (January 1977): 175–87. A similar theory is developed in M. A. Spence, "Job Market Signaling," *Quarterly Journal of Economics* 87, 3 (August 1973): 355–74.

test-score distributions for both groups of workers. Those who can actually type 70 wpm score 70 on average, but half score less. Likewise, half of the other group scores better than 40 on the test. If an applicant scores 55, say, the employer does not know if the applicant is a good (70 wpm) or bad (40 wpm) typist. If those scoring 55 are automatically rejected, the firm will be rejecting some good workers, and if it needs workers badly this policy will entail costs. Likewise, if it accepts those scoring 55, some bad workers will be hired.

In an effort to avoid the above dilemma, suppose the employer does some research and finds out that applicants from a particular business school are specifically coached to perform well on 5-minute typing tests. Thus, applicants who can actually type X words per minute over a normal day will tend to score *higher* than X wpm on a 5-minute test due to the special coaching (that is, they will appear better than they really are). Recognizing that students from this school are likely to have test scores above their long-run productivity, the firm might decide to reject all applicants from this school who score 55 or below (on the grounds that, for most, the test score overestimates their ability) even though some who score less than 55 really can do better.

The general lesson of this example is that, in effect, firms will use both *individual* data (test scores, educational attainment, experience) and *group* data in making hiring decisions when the former are not perfect predictors of productivity. However, this use of group data can give rise to market discrimination, because people with the same *measured productive characteristics* (test scores, education, etc.) will be treated differently on a systematic basis depending on *group* affiliation.

The relevance of the above discussion to the problem of discrimination against minorities and women is that race and sex may well be the group information used to supplement individual data in making hiring decisions. If the group data bear no relationship, on average, to actual productivity, then we really have a case of discrimination rooted in personal prejudice or monopoly power. However, we have shown that the use of group data to modify individual information may be based on nonmalicious grounds. Might these grounds legitimately apply from an employer's perspective to minorities and women?

Suppose that, *on average,* minorities with high-school educations are discovered to be less productive than white males with high-school educations owing to differences in schooling quality. Or suppose that because of shortened career lives, women with a given educational level are, *on average,* less valuable to firms than men of equal education (refer back to our discussion of women and job training in Chapter 5). Employers might employ this group information to modify individual data when making hiring decisions, just as they did in our hypothetical example of the business school above. The result would be that white males with given measured characteristics would be systematically preferred over women or minorities with the same characteristics—a condition that would be empirically identified as labor-market discrimination.

One unfortunate side effect of using group data to supplement individual data is that, while it could lead employers to the correct hiring decisions on average, it assigns a group characteristic to people who may not be typical of the group.

There are women who will have long, uninterrupted careers, just as there undoubtedly would be graduates from the business school mentioned above who do not test well and thus perform more poorly on tests than they could do on the job. There will also be minority high-school graduates of substantial ability who would have gone to college had not family poverty intervened. These atypical group members are stigmatized by the use of group data. They may have actual productivity equal to those who get hired but because of the group association do not get the job.[26]

Thus, *statistical discrimination* could lead to a systematic preference for white males over others with the same measured characteristics, and it could also create a situation where minorities or women who are the equals of white males in *actual* productivity are paid less due to the above-mentioned group stigma. Both problems are caused by the use of group data in making hiring decisions, but we have emphazised that this use need not be motivated by prejudice. The results, however, have the same appearance and effects as if prejudice were present.

An important implication of this model of statistical discrimination is that the use of group data will become a more costly screening device as members of each group become more dissimilar. For example, as greater proportions of women desire to work in full-time, year-round careers—and do not intend to drop out of the labor force to raise children—employers using sex as a handy index of labor-force attachment will find themselves making costly mistakes. They will reject many female applicants who have a permanent labor-force attachment (in whom an investment in specific training would be very worthwhile), and they may accept male applicants who are less productive. Thus, as *premarket* differences between the races or sexes narrow, the use of race or sex *group* data should lessen, and statistical discrimination should gradually disappear.

Monopoly Power Models

The persistence of large race/sex earnings disparities has led some labor economists to wonder whether the above models are really appropriate. These economists are dissenters from the orthodox view that labor markets are essentially competitive; instead, they advance *monopoly power theories* of discrimination. Inherent in these more radical views of the labor market is the assertion that discrimination exists and persists because it is *profitable* for the discriminators.

While monopoly-power theories of discrimination vary from each other in their emphasis, they tend to share the common feature that race or sex is collectively used to divide the labor force into *noncompeting* groups, creating or perpetuating a kind of worker caste system. This view clearly denies that competitive forces are at work either in the labor market or among owners.[27]

---

[26]The discussion here has obvious relevance to the "signaling" issue discussed in Chapter 9 and its appendix. Minorities, for example, may be *too poor* to acquire the necessary "signal" in many cases where their ability would indicate they should.

[27]For a summary of these views, see Glen G. Cain, "The Challenge of Segmented Labor Market Theories to Orthodox Theory: A Survey," *The Journal of Economic Literature* 14 (December 1976): 1215–1257.

Those who view labor-market discrimination as the result of noncompeting groups assert that a *dual labor market* exists.[28] These economists believe that a *secondary* labor market exists along side a *primary* labor market. Unlike the primary labor market, the secondary market offers low-wage, unstable, dead-end jobs. Workers relegated to these secondary jobs are tagged as unstable, undesirable workers and can never have much hope of acquiring a job in the primary sector. Since a large number of minorities and women are in the secondary market, discrimination against them tends to be perpetuated. Minorities and women, it is argued, are discriminated against because they tend (as a group) to have unstable work histories (which are passed on to their children) but these histories are themselves a result of being unable to break into the primary labor market.

The dual labor market description of discrimination does not really explain what initially caused women and minorities to be confined to secondary jobs. Rather, it offers an explanation of why discrimination *persists*. It calls into question the levels of competition and mobility that exist and suggests that the initial existence of noncompeting race/sex groups will be self-perpetuating. In short, the dual labor market hypothesis is consistent with any of the models of discrimination analyzed above; what it does suggest is that if any of these theories *are* applicable, we cannot count on natural market forces to eliminate the discrimination that results.

Other nonorthodox theories claim that white employers collude and become monopsonists with respect to the hiring of minority labor. Minorities are subjugated and held immobile while monopsonistic wages are forced on them.[29] One of the more cogent and complete of the *power theories* of discrimination argues that prejudice and the conflicts it creates are inherent in a capitalist society because they serve the interests of owners.[30] Even if the owners of capital did not conspire to *create* prejudice, they nevertheless find that if it continues they can enhance their profits. Workers divided by race or sex are harder to organize, and if they *are* unionized, are less cohesive in their demands. Further, antagonisms on the shop floor deflect attention from grievances related to working conditions. Hence, it is argued that owners of capital gain, while *all* workers—but particularly minorities and women—lose from discrimination.

Two pieces of evidence are cited to support this theory. First, in areas where black/white earnings differentials are largest, the income inequality among *whites* is greatest, other things equal (the greater inequality of white incomes is attributed to *owner/worker* income disparities). This kind of finding was mentioned above when we discussed employee discrimination, and there the greater inequality among whites was attributed to wage differences among white *workers*. Thus, this

---

[28]Michael J. Piore, "Jobs and Training: Manpower Policy," in *The State and the Poor,* eds. S. Beer and R. Barringer (Cambridge, Mass.: Winthrop Press, 1970).

[29]Lester Thurow, *The Economics of Poverty and Discrimination* (Washington, D.C.: The Brookings Institution, 1969.)

[30]Michael Reich, "The Economics of Racism," in *Problems in Political Economy: An Urban Perspective,* ed. David M. Gordon (Lexington, Mass.: D.C. Heath and Company, 1971), pp. 107–13.

first piece of evidence seems more or less consistent with a theory of employee discrimination as well as the power model.[31]

The second piece of evidence cited to support this power theory is that where black/white earnings differences are greatest, the percentage of the labor force that is unionized tends to be smallest. The strength of this argument decreases, however, when one realizes that the *causation* might be *reversed*. Rather than more racism causing less unionization, it could be that more unionization causes race discrimination to diminish. Indeed, Chapter 12 cited arguments to this effect.

Like the orthodox theories of discrimination, then, the monopoly power theories can muster only weak empirical support. They also share with the orthodox theories problems of logical consistency or completeness. If discrimination is created or at least perpetuated by capitalists, how does one account for its existence in precapitalist or socialist societies? It may be true that if all white employers conspire to keep women and minorities in low-wage, low-status jobs, they can all reap monopoly profits. However, if Employers A through Y adhere to the agreement, Employer Z will always have incentives to *break* the agreement! Z can hire women or minorities cheaply because of the agreement among *other* employers not to hire them, and Z can enhance profits by hiring these otherwise equally productive workers to fill jobs that A through Y are staffing with high-priced white males. Since each and every other employer has the same incentives as Z, the conspiracy will tend to break down unless cheaters can be disciplined in some way. The dual and power theorists do not tell us how the conspiracy is maintained and coordinated among the millions of U.S. employers. Thus their theories, like the orthodox ones, are less than completely satisfactory.

Evaluation of Discrimination Theories

Our analysis of the different theories of discrimination suggests that if discrimination persists, it is the result of forces that hinder *competition* or labor-market *adjustments* to competitive forces. Some theories—the "power" models—postulate the existence of noncompetitive or monopoly elements at the outset. The "orthodox" theories do not but they have trouble explaining why discrimination *would* persist. The market should punish employers who discriminate or who fail to change their screening methods as the average characteristics of minorities or women change. A competitive market should drive employers to adopt *segregated* workplaces if employee discrimination exists; if customer discrimination exists, customers who discriminate will be punished by having to pay the higher prices associated with being served only by white males.

It would thus appear that all models of discrimination agree on one thing: any

---

[31]A major difference between the Chiswick study of employee discrimination and Reich's test of the power model is that the former related white income inequality to the percentage of nonwhites in the population while the latter related it to the ratio of nonwhite to white earnings. Which is the more appropriate test is a matter beyond the scope of this text; however, we should note that observed earnings ratios can reflect human-capital differences as well as current discrimination. This issue illustrates the importance of *theoretical* analysis in both the execution and interpretation of empirical studies.

persistence of labor-market discrimination would be the result of forces or motivations that are blatantly noncompetitive or very slow to adjust to competitive forces. While no one model can be demonstrated superior to the others in explaining the facts, the various theories and the facts they seek to explain do suggest that government intervention could be useful in eliminating the noncompetitive (or sluggish) influences.

FEDERAL PROGRAMS TO END DISCRIMINATION

The federal government has enforced two sets of rules in an attempt to eliminate market discrimination. One is a *nondiscrimination* requirement made of almost all employers. The other is a requirement that federal contractors engage in *affirmative action*—that is, to actively seek out minorities and women to staff their vacancies.

Equal Pay Act of 1963

Over the years prior to the 1960s, sex discrimination was officially sanctioned by so-called *protective labor laws,* which limited women's total hours of work and prohibited them from working at night, lifting heavy objects, and working during pregnancy. Not all states placed all these restrictions on women, but the effect of these laws was to limit the access of women to many jobs. These laws were overturned by the Equal Pay Act of 1963, which also outlawed separate pay scales for men and women using similar skills and performing work under the same conditions.

The act, however, was seriously deficient as an antidiscrimination tool because it said nothing about equal opportunity in hiring and promotions. This flaw can be easily understood by a quick review of our theories of discrimination. If there is prejudice against women from whatever source, employers will treat female employees as if they were less productive or more costly to hire than equally productive males. The market response is for female wages to fall below male wages, because otherwise women cannot hope to be able to successfully compete with men in obtaining jobs. The Equal Pay Act took a step toward the elimination of wage differentials, but by so doing it tended to suppress a market mechanism that helped women obtain greater access to jobs![32] The act failed to acknowledge that if labor-market discrimination is to be eliminated, legislation must require *both* equal pay *and* equal opportunities in hiring and promotions for people of comparable productivity.

Title VII of the Civil Rights Act

Some of the defects of the Equal Pay Act of 1963 were corrected the next year. Title VII of the Civil Rights Act of 1964 made it unlawful for any employer "to refuse to hire or to discharge any individual, or otherwise to discriminate against any individual with respect to his compensation, terms, conditions, or privileges

---

[32]Some critics of the Equal Pay Act of 1973 argued that its motivation was to help men compete with lower-paid women. See Nancy Barrett, "Women in the Job Market: Occupations, Earnings, and Career Opportunities," in *The Subtle Revolution,* ed. Ralph E. Smith (Washington, D.C.: The Urban Institute, 1979), p. 55.

of employment, because of such individual's race, color, religion, sex, or national origin.'' Title VII applies to all employers in interstate commerce with at least 25 employees and is enforced by the Equal Employment Opportunity Commission (EEOC)—which has the authority to mediate complaints, encourage lawsuits by private parties or the U.S. Attorney-General, or (since 1972) bring suits itself against employers that have violated the law.

Court suits under Title VII have begun to delineate practices that are considered discriminatory. Employers, for example, may use tests and educational standards to screen applicants, but these tests must be related to job performance.[33] Employers cannot recruit applicants exclusively through current employees or other mechanisms that result in few minority or female applicants. Job-application forms must be racially and sexually neutral. They may ask, for example, about *convictions* but *not arrests* (arrest rates among minorities tend to be higher, but the courts reason that it is conviction that is important to the employer). Marital status cannot be used as a screening device unless it is applied uniformly to both sexes and is clearly a job-related requirement. Promotion systems based solely on experience (seniority) are also suspect in cases where minorities or women have been excluded from lower-level jobs in the past and are thus not now ''qualifying'' for higher-level jobs.[34]

The Federal Contract-Compliance Program

In 1965 the Office of Federal Contract-Compliance Programs (OFCCP) was established to monitor the hiring and promotion practices of federal contractors (firms supplying goods or services to the federal government). OFCCP requires contractors above a certain size to analyze the extent of their underutilization of women and minorities and to propose a plan to remedy any such underutilization. Such a plan is called an *affirmative-action plan*. Contractors submitting unacceptable plans or failing to meet their goals are threatened with cancellation of their contracts and ineligibility for future contracts, although these drastic steps are rarely taken.

Affirmative-action planning is intended to commit firms to a schedule for rapidly overcoming unequal career opportunities afforded women and minorities. Such planning affects both *hiring* and *promotion* practices, but it also raises numerous philosophical and practical questions that tend to make the planning process highly controversial.

Suppose an insurance company is attempting to construct an affirmative-action plan with regard to secretaries. Its first step in setting hiring goals is to decide on what number of minorities are ''available'' and what fraction they constitute of all available workers. If blacks, say, constitute 9 percent of the labor supply available to the firm, then it might seem to be a simple matter of setting a goal of 9 percent. However, the planner must resolve some serious questions.

First, should the pool of black secretaries be estimated based on the firm's *actual applicant* pool? The answer is probably no, since any discriminatory prac-

---

[33]*Willie S. Griggs* v. *Duke Power Company* (U.S. Supreme Court, No. 124, March 9, 1971).

[34]For a summary of discrimination law, see Arthur B. Smith, Jr., *Employment Discrimination Law* (New York: The Bobbs-Merrill Company, Inc., 1978).

tices in the past will discourage black applicants currently. Further, affirmative-action planning is intended to force companies to *change* their hiring practices. On the other hand, as was pointed out in Chapter 8, a firm's location within a city can attract more or less black applicants, depending on how far away from the firm blacks live and what the wages offered are. Thus, to some extent the potential pool of *interested* applicants is a legitimate consideration.

Should the potential pool be estimated from the fraction of all *trained secretaries* in the area who are black? If we are interested in eradicating *market* discrimination, this may be the logical measure, since it would force firms to hire black secretaries in the same proportion as they are found in the labor market. However, years of discrimination may have induced blacks to avoid training for this occupation, with the result that blacks are substantially underrepresented in the secretarial labor market.

Should firms then be compelled to hire black secretaries in proportion to their numbers in the adult *population* of the city at large? This goal implicitly sets out to eliminate all discrimination, both market and premarket, but if blacks are underrepresented in the occupation, the attainment of this goal is impractical in the short run. Firms attempting to hire more black secretaries than are available would have two choices. They could hire black high-school graduates and train them in secretarial skills. Remember, however, that such training is *general* in nature, so that the firms would not offer it unless the workers involved paid for it in some way. Without training as an option, firms would simply try to bid against each other for the services of existing black secretaries, which would drive up their wage. The higher wage rates would induce more blacks to seek secretarial training, and their underrepresentation in the occupation would disappear in the long run.

While population-based goals would appear to fight both kinds of discrimination, they might in fact fight neither. It stands to reason that if hiring goals are set beyond the immediate reach of firms, each will individually fail to meet them. Can the government reasonably punish firms for failing to hire beyond the numbers currently available? If it cannot, then failure to meet goals will not result in punishment—which seems to remove the incentive for firms to take energetic steps to integrate their work force.

A final issue in hiring has to do with how the goals are applied. If black secretaries, to continue our example, are 9 percent of the available pool, does that mean that 9 percent of all *newly hired* secretaries should be black? This goal might seem reasonable from a firm's point of view, but if labor turnover is low it would take a very long time for the 9 percent of *new hires* to accumulate to the point where blacks were 9 percent of the firm's total secretarial work force. Since the Civil Rights Act of 1964 prohibits workers of one race from being fired to make room for those of another, getting rid of employment imbalances (by race or sex) must occur through new hiring. However, only if aggrieved groups are *favored* in hiring can the effects of past discrimination be eradicated quickly. Favoritism in hiring not only raises the issue of *reverse discrimination*—wherein whites or males can assert they are being discriminated against because of race or sex—it also raises again the issue of how firms as a whole can hire women or blacks in proportions greater than their current availability.

Example 14.1
How Fast Can Discrimination Be Eradicated?

To illustrate the possible rate of progress in minority employment within a firm, let us take a numerical example. Suppose there is a job group that contains 1600 employees, 100 (6.25 percent) of whom are minorities. Suppose, further, that this is an entry-level job group (so that all replacements come from new hires) and that the yearly turnover rate is 20 percent. Finally, assume that blacks represent 12 percent of the firm's available labor pool for this job.

The firm in question must hire 320 new workers for this job group each year. If 12 percent (about 38) of those hired each year are black, how long will it take before 12 percent (192) of the 1600-person work group is black? Another, perhaps more significant, question is how fast will the racial composition of the work group change? These questions have no obvious answers, because if blacks and whites have the same turnover rate (of 20 percent), the organization is both losing and hiring blacks each year.

One way to answer the above questions is to simulate employee turnover each year. The accompanying table shows that in the first year 20 blacks quit and 38 (12 percent of the 320 new hires) are hired. The net gain in blacks raises their level of employment in the group to 118 and their percentage of employment to 7.37 (from 6.25). In year 2, 38 blacks are again hired and about 24 quit—representing a new gain of 14—and by the end of the year the work group is 8.25 percent black. As this process continues, there are net additions to the black component of the work force each year, but these additions get smaller and smaller.

Of special interest in this example is that it takes about 10 years of *nondiscriminatory hiring* for the percentage of blacks in the work group to get close to the goal of 12 percent. (The rate of progress would be approximately cut in half if the turnover rate were 10 percent instead of 20 percent.) Thus, if the proportion of blacks among new hires is equal to their proportions in the available labor pool, and if their turnover rates are no lower than those of whites, the long-run goal of employment equality will take many years to achieve once nondiscriminatory hiring is begun. This mathematical fact illustrates why those charged with administering antidiscrimination programs are simultaneously besieged by shouts of frustration and calls for patience.

Change in the Racial Composition of a 1600-Person Job Group
(20% Yearly Turnover Rate)

				Year			
	0	*1*	*2*	*3*	*4*	*5*	*10*
Number of Blacks							
Loss		20	24	26	29	31	36
New Hires		38	38	38	38	38	38
Net Gain		18	14	12	11	7	2
Cumulative Level	100	118	132	144	155	162	181
Percent Black	6.25	7.37	8.25	9.00	9.69	10.12	11.31

It is perhaps striking testimony to these difficult questions raised by affirmative-action planning that as of late 1981, no clear-cut directives for setting goals and timetables had been issued by OFCCP. What OFCCP did issue in 1974 was a list of eight factors that employers were supposed to consider in constructing their affirmative-action plans:[35]

1. the minority population of the labor area surrounding the facility;[36]
2. the size of the minority unemployment force in the labor area surrounding the facility;
3. the percentage of the minority work force as compared with the total work force in the immediate labor area;
4. the general availability of minorities having requisite skills in the immediate labor area;
5. the availability of minorities having requisite skills in an area in which the contractor can reasonably recruit;
6. the availability of promotable and transferable minorities within the contractor's organization;
7. the existence of training institutions capable of training persons in the requisite skills;
8. the degree of training that the contractor is reasonably able to undertake as a means of making all job classes available to minorities.

Factors 1, 7, and 8 seem to emphasize a *population-based* calculation of the available pool, with attention given to steps that would induce new entry of women or blacks into the occupation in question. Factors 4 and 5 suggest the pool should be calculated as the proportion of *currently available* minorities in the occupation. Factor 2 implies availability for *new hires* is appropriate, while factor 3 appears to be calling for goals to be applied to a firm's *total work force*. The government has not yet resolved the ambiguities inherent in these eight factors and has not yet given firms any directives on how to combine or weight such factors (as of 1981).

It should be added that the questions raised concerning new hires also apply to internal promotions (factor 6). If few minorities or women are at the office-manager rank in an organization, is the firm obliged to offer special managerial-training courses for them? Should such training be equally available to interested white males? What if the interest in managerial positions varies by race or sex? Are companies supposed to promote on a nondiscriminatory basis, with the result that imbalances in its *higher*-level jobs will remain for years into the future? Instead must employers hurry women and blacks along the promotional ladder faster than normal so that these higher-level imbalances will go away more quickly?

---

[35]Office of Federal Contract Compliance Programs, 1974 Revised Order No. 4, Affirmative Action Guidelines.

[36]The eight factors for women and minorities are the same except that instead of the female "proportion of the labor area surrounding the facility," employers are to consider "the availability of women seeking employment in the labor or recruitment area of the contractor."

These are the dilemmas inherent in the government's contract-compliance program.

Effectiveness of Federal Antidiscrimination Programs

A question of obvious interest is just how effective the two federal antidiscrimination programs have been in increasing the relative earnings of minorities and women. The question is not easy to answer, however, because we must make some guess as to what earnings differentials *would have been* in the absence of these programs.

As we have seen, the ratio of black to white incomes has risen since 1960 (see Table 14.2), most especially in the mid 1970s. Has this rise in the ratio been a result of government efforts, or have other forces been working to accomplish this same result? Three other forces are commonly cited. First, an improvement in the educational *attainment* of black workers relative to whites during this period is thought to have played an important role in raising the ratio of black to white income.[37] Second, the evidence that the *quality* of schooling received by blacks improved from 1960 to 1970 more than it did for whites lends further impetus to the increase in relative earnings.[38] Finally, blacks have historically experienced relative gains in periods of low unemployment and suffered disproportionately in periods of economic distress. The late 1960s was a period of very full employment, which could have helped increase the black/white earnings ratio from 1960 to 1970. However, general business conditions in the 1970s have not been as good as in the late 1960s, so the continued improvement in recent years is unlikely to be solely the result of overall business conditions.

Two types of studies have attempted to distinguish the effects of the government programs from the other factors that affect relative earnings: 1. time-series studies and 2. the analysis of federal contractors.

Time-series studies.   There seems to have been a significant upturn in the black/white earnings ratio after the EEOC was created in 1964—an upturn that is independent of both the effects of *educational* gains by blacks and changes in the *unemployment rate*.[39] However, it also appears to be true that the labor-force participation rate of blacks fell relative to whites after 1964—a year in which many income-maintenance programs began to become more generous.[40] If, as seems

---

[37]Orley Ashenfelter, "Changes in Labor Market Discrimination Over Time," *Journal of Human Resources* 5, 4 (Fall 1970): 403–30; Richard Freeman, "Changes in the Labor Market for Black Americans, 1948–72," *Brookings Papers on Economic Activity*, No. 1 (1973), pp. 67–120; Barry R. Chiswick and June A. O'Neill, eds., *Human Resources and Income Distribution: Issues and Policies* (New York: W. W. Norton, 1977), pp. 20–21.

[38]Finis Welch, "Black-White Differences in Returns to Schooling," *American Economic Review* 63, 5 (December 1973): 893–907.

[39]See Freeman, "Changes in the Labor Market for Black Americans," and (a study which updates Freeman) Richard Butler and James Heckman, "The Government's Impact on the Labor Market Status of Black Americans: A Critical Review," *Equal Rights and Industrial Relations* (Madison, Wis.: Industrial Relations Research Association, 1977), pp. 235–280.

[40]Butler and Heckman, "The Government's Impact on the Labor Market Status of Black Americans."

Example 14.2
Age and the End of Discrimination

Our discussions of investments in human capital, presented in Chapters 5, 9 and 10, suggest that if discrimination diminishes over time, it will diminish first with young adults. Job training—whether it is specific or general, whether it is on-the-job or given formally—takes place most often in one's young-adult years, so that it is this group that will be favored by any expansion of occupational opportunities. Young adults are also the group most likely to adjust to new opportunities by paying for their own education or training. Thus, human-capital theory suggests that the eradication of discrimination's effects may be a long process that will tend to favor each successive generation of new workers over their older counterparts.

Tests of the notion that young adults are helped the most by antidiscrimination programs must take into account the fact that the age/earnings profiles of women and minorities tend to be flatter than those for white males—reflecting the smaller amounts of on-the-job training offered (or induced among) these groups. Thus, the ratio of earnings among these groups to similar-aged white males tends to fall as age increases. The fact that the black/white earnings ratios in both columns of the table fall with experience reflects the more steeply sloped age/earnings profile for white male high-school graduates—not the effects of antidiscrimination efforts.

The pattern of reductions in earnings disparities can best be seen by comparing *changes* in the earnings ratios between 1960 and 1970 in the table. These comparisons can be made in two ways. First, let us follow the same groups of workers over time to see how their earnings ratios change. For example, males with 1–5 years of experience had a black/white earnings ratio of 0.714 in 1960. In 1970, this same group—then having 11–15 years of experience—had an earnings ratio of 0.749. Following the arrows in the table we can see that each age group of black males experienced improvement relative to white males as they aged over the

**Male Black/White Earnings Ratios
for High-School Graduates of Various
Experience, 1960 and 1970**

	Black/White Ratio of Average Weekly Earnings	
Years of Experience	*1960*	*1970*
1–5	0.714	0.806
6–10	0.714	0.791
11–15	0.685	0.749
16–20		0.750
21–30	0.648	0.698
31–40	—	0.690

SOURCE: James P. Smith and Finis R. Welch, "Black-White Male Wage Ratios: 1960–70," *American Economic Review* 67 (June 1977): 323–38 (Table 1).

decade of the 1960s. Although those with 1–10 years of experience in 1960 gained to a greater extent than those with 11–20 years, those with 21–30 years of experience in 1960 gained to an even greater degree. Looked at this way, the young adults do not appear to have been the biggest group of gainers among black male high-school graduates.

There is a second way of looking at the changes from 1960 to 1970, however. Instead of following the same group of workers over time, we could look to see how groups with the same experience in the two years fared. Beginning workers, for example, had an earnings ratio of 0.714 in 1960, but 0.806 in 1970. Those with 6–10 years of experience had a ratio of 0.714 in 1960, while the group 10 years behind them (with 6–10 years of experience in 1970) had a ratio of 0.791. This method suggests that the relative earnings position of the youngest blacks did improve the most.

What we can conclude from our two ways of comparing 1960 and 1970 is that while each group of black males improved in its own economic status from 1960 to 1970, the improvements were even larger for the groups 10 years their junior. To see this, look at those with 1–5 years of experience in 1960. The 1960 ratio for this group was 0.714, and in 1970 it had risen to 0.749 for the same group. However, the ratio for new workers (1–5 years of experience) in 1970 was an even higher 0.806. For those with 21–30 years of experience in 1960, the earnings ratio rose from 0.648 to 0.690; for those 10 years their junior (having 21–30 years of experience in 1970), however, the 1970 earnings ratio was 0.698.

Thus, it appears that while each age group of black males experienced relative improvement in their earnings in the 1960s, the gains made by the groups that *followed* them were larger. A sobering aspect of the way in which these changes are taking place is that overall wage equality between blacks and whites will occur some 40 years after wage parity for *new* workers is attained. (It requires 40 years to "flush" the system of discrimination's victims if discrimination is first ended among younger workers.)

---

likely, the blacks with the lowest wages were the ones who left the labor market, their exit would increase the average wage paid to blacks and give the *appearance* of improvement. Some—probably less than half—of the post-1964 improvement is due to this latter factor.[41] Thus, there seems to be at least *some* evidence that the post-1964 government efforts to lessen discrimination have helped blacks.

Analysis of federal contractors. If the contract-compliance program administered by OFCCP is effective, we should observe that the economic status of blacks improves faster among federal contractors than noncontractors. Several studies have tested this hypothesis, and some have even distinguished whether or not the contractors involved had been subjected to a compliance review by the government (the government does not have the resources to inspect the affirmative-action

---

[41]Charles Brown, ''Black/White Earnings Ratios Since the Civil Rights Act of 1964: The Importance of Labor-Market Drop-Outs'' (Cambridge, Mass.: National Bureau of Economic Research, Working Paper No. 617, 1981).

plans of *all* its contractors). The results suggest that blacks have made faster gains in contractor firms, although the gains are relatively small.[42]

One problem in assessing the *overall* effects of OFCCP, however, is that because the contract-compliance program relates only to *some* employers (contractors), the gains in black employment among these firms may come at the expense of losses among noncontractors. Eligible blacks may just be bid away from non-contractors—although it should be pointed out that anyone successfully bid away from a former employer must have experienced an expected gain in utility. Perhaps more serious is the problem that becoming or remaining a federal contractor is a voluntary decision. Firms that perceive the costs of affirmative action to be high may simply choose not to be contractors. The contract-compliance program may end up concentrating its efforts toward the firms within which discrimination is a relatively small problem.

A final reason to temper optimism about the government's efforts to end discrimination is that the one study that has attempted to look at how the contract-compliance program affects women found that the gains of blacks among contractors came at the expense of white women and other minorities, not at the expense of white males.[43] These rather discouraging results for women, however, occurred prior to 1972, when the focus of the contract-compliance program was expanded beyond minorities to include women. There are no studies that examine the post-1972 effects of the program on women.

In summary, it appears that *some* of the gains registered by blacks from 1964 on may be due to efforts by the EEOC and OFCCP, but the gains attributable to these programs are probably small. The effects of these programs on women have not been extensively studied. Since the female/male earnings ratio had made no improvements as of the late 1970s, however, one cannot be too optimistic about the effects any such studies might find.

REVIEW QUESTIONS

1. Assume that it is a fact that women live longer than men, on the average. Suppose an employer hires men and women, pays them the same wage for the same job, and contributes an equal amount per person toward a pension. However, the promised monthly pension after retirement is smaller for women than men (because the pension funds for them have to last longer). According to the *Manhart* decision by the Supreme Court, the above employer would be guilty of discrimination because of the unequal monthly pension benefits after retirement.
   a. Comment on the Court's implicit definition of discrimination. Is it consistent with the definition normally used by economists? Why or why not?
   b. Analyze the economic effects of this decision on men and women.

---

[42]For a summary of these studies, see Butler and Heckman, "The Government's Impact on the Labor Market Status of Black Americans."

[43]Morris Goldstein and Robert S. Smith, "The Estimated Impact of the Antidiscrimination Program Aimed at Federal Contractors," *Industrial and Labor Relations Review* 29, 4 (July 1976): 523–43.

2. Assume there is a central-city school district where the student population is predominantly black. Surrounding the central city are separate, predominantly white suburban school districts. Together, the central-city and suburban school districts can be thought of as a local labor market for teachers. Other things being equal, black teachers in this labor market are equally willing to work in central-city and suburban schools, but all white teachers prefer suburban schools and are reluctant to accept jobs in the central city. There are too few black teachers to completely staff central-city schools, and teachers generally have choices in the jobs they can accept.

   If federal law requires equal salaries for teachers of all races *within* a given school district—but allows salaries to vary across school districts—will black teachers earn more, less, or the same salary as they would if white teachers were not prejudiced against black students? (Note: the prejudice of white teachers extends only to students, not to black teachers as coworkers. Note also: the chain of reasoning required in this answer should be made explicit in your answer.)

3. Suppose government antidiscrimination laws require employers to disregard marital status and sex in screening and hiring workers.
   a. Disregarding the employers who are engaged in discrimination, which employers will be most affected by this ruling?
   b. What alternatives do these employers have in coping with the problems created by this decision?
   c. What are the likely consequences of each alternative on employment levels and job stability among these employers?

4. Suppose the government has two methods of awarding contracts to firms. One is competitive, with the award going to the lowest bidder (who cannot then charge more than his bid). The other is noncompetitive, with the award going to a selected contractor who is reimbursed for actual costs incurred plus a certain percentage for profits. Suppose, too, that government contractors must hire a certain quota of minorities, many of whom require general training to be fully productive. Suppose also that federal legislation prevents the employer from shifting the costs of this general training to the minority employees. If you were an already-trained minority worker, which method of contract award would you prefer? Why?

SELECTED READINGS

Aigner, Dennis J. and Glen G. Cain. "Statistical Theories of Discrimination in Labor Markets." *Industrial and Labor Relations* Review 30 (January 1977): 175–87.

Arrow, Kenneth J. "The Theory of Discrimination." In *Discrimination in Labor Markets,* edited by Orley Ashenfelter and Albert Rees. Princeton, N.J.: Princeton University Press, 1973.

Becker, Gary. *The Economics of Discrimination.* Chicago: University of Chicago Press, 1971.

Butler, Richard and James Heckman. "The Government's Impact on the Labor Market Status of Black Americans: A Critical Review." *Equal Rights and Industrial Relations.* Madison, Wis.: Industrial Relations Research Association, 1977, pp. 235–80.

Cain, Glen G. "The Challenge of Segmented Labor Market Theories to Orthodox Theory: A Survey." *Journal of Economic Literature* 14 (December 1976): 1215–1257.

Chiswick, Barry R. and June A. O'Neill, eds. *Human Resources and Income Distribution: Issues and Policies.* New York: W. W. Norton, 1977.

Freeman, Richard. "Changes in the Labor Market for Black Americans, 1948–72." *Brookings Papers on Economic Activity,* No. 1 (1973), pp. 67–120.

Fuchs, Victor. "Differences in Hourly Earnings Between Men and Women." *Monthly Labor Review* (May 1971), pp. 9–15.

Marshall, Ray. "The Economics of Racial Discrimination: A Survey." *Journal of Economic Literature* 12 (September 1974): 849–71.

Oaxaca, Ronald. "Male-Female Wage Differentials in Urban Labor Markets." *International Economic Review* 14 (October 1973): 693–709.

Reich, Michael. "The Economics of Racism." In *Problems in Political Economy: An Urban Perspective,* edited by David M. Gordon. Lexington, Mass.: D. C. Heath and Company, 1971, pp. 107–113.

Smith, James P. and Finis R. Welch. "Black-White Male Wage Ratios: 1960–1970." *American Economic Review* 67 (June 1977): 323–38.

Smith, Sharon P. *Equal Pay in the Public Sector: Fact or Fantasy.* Princeton, N.J.: Industrial Relations Section, Princeton University, 1977.

15

Unemployment

As noted in Chapter 2, the population can be divided into those people in the labor force *(L)* and those not in the labor force *(N)*. The labor force consists of those people who are employed *(E)* and those who are unemployed but would like to be employed *(U)*. The concept of unemployment is somewhat ambiguous since in theory virtually anyone would be willing to be employed in return for some extraordinarily generous compensation package. Economists tend to resolve this dilemma by defining unemployment in terms of an individual's willingness to be employed at some prevailing market wage. Government statistics take a more pragmatic approach, defining the unemployed as those who are on temporary lay-off waiting to be recalled by their previous employers or those who have actively searched for work in the previous month (of course, "actively" is not precisely defined).

Given these definitions, the unemployment rate **(u)** is further defined as the ratio of the number of the unemployed to the number in the labor force:

$$\mathbf{u} = \frac{U}{L}. \tag{15.1}$$

Much attention is focused on how the national unemployment rate varies over time, on how unemployment rates vary across geographic areas, and on how unemployment rates vary across age/race/sex groups.

It is important, however, to understand the limitations of unemployment-rate data. They *do* reflect the proportion of a group that, at a point in time, actively wants to work but is not employed. They *do not,* however, necessarily provide an accurate reflection of the economic hardship that members of a group are suffering, for a number of reasons.[1] First, individuals who are not actively searching for work, including those who searched unsuccessfully and then gave up, are not counted among the unemployed (see Chapter 7). Second, unemployment statistics

---

[1]This discussion draws heavily on the final report of the National Commission on Employment and Unemployment Statistics, *Counting the Labor Force* (Washington, D.C.: U.S. Government Printing Office, 1979); and Glen G. Cain, "Labor-Force Concepts and Definitions in View of Their Purposes" in *Concepts and Data Needs* (Appendix Volume I to the Commission's final report).

TABLE 15.1 Labor-Force-Participation, Employment, and
Unemployment Rates

Year	Unemployment Rate (U/L)	Labor-Force Participation Rate (L/POP)	Employment Rate (E/POP)
1948	3.9	58.9	56.6
1958	6.8	60.4	56.3
1968	3.6	60.7	58.5
1978	6.0	63.7	59.9

U = number of people unemployed.
L = number of people in the labor force.
E = number of people employed.
POP = total population.

SOURCE: Based on U.S. Department of Labor, *1979 Employment and Training Report of the President* (Washington, D.C.: U.S. Government Printing Office, 1979), Table A1.

tell us nothing about the earnings levels of those who are employed, including whether these levels exceed the poverty level. Third, a substantial fraction of the unemployed come from families in which other earners are present—for example, many unemployed are teenagers—and the unemployed often are not the primary source of their family's support. Fourth, a substantial fraction of the unemployed receive some income support while they are unemployed, either in the form of government unemployment-compensation payments or private supplementary unemployment benefits (*SUBs*). Finally, unemployment-rate data give us information on the fraction of the labor force that is not working but tell us little about the fraction of the population that is employed.

Table 15.1 contains data on the aggregate unemployment rate, the labor-force-participation rate and the *employment rate*—the latter being defined as employment divided by population—for 1948, 1958, 1968, and 1978. Although the unemployment rate rose from 3.9 percent in 1948 to 6.8 percent in 1958, because the aggregate labor-force-participation rate also rose during the period, the employment rate (the fraction of the population that is employed) fell only slightly. Focusing on the change in the employment rate suggests less of an economic downturn in 1958 than does focusing on the change in the unemployment rate. Similarly, while between 1968 and 1978 the unemployment rate once again rose (this time from 3.6 to 6.0 percent), the employment rate actually *rose* during the decade because of the increase in the labor-force-participation rate of 3 percentage points.

Nonetheless, the unemployment rate remains a useful indicator of labor-market conditions. This chapter will be concerned with why *anyone* is unemployed; with why the unemployment rate varies over time, regions, or age/race/sex groups; and with how various government policies affect, either in an intended or unintended manner, the level of unemployment.

The next section begins with a simple conceptual model of a labor market that emphasizes the importance of considering the *flows* between labor-market states (for example, the *movement* of people from employed to unemployed status) as well as the *number* of people in each state (for example, the *number* of the unemployed). Knowledge of the determinants of these flows is crucial to any understanding of the causes of unemployment.

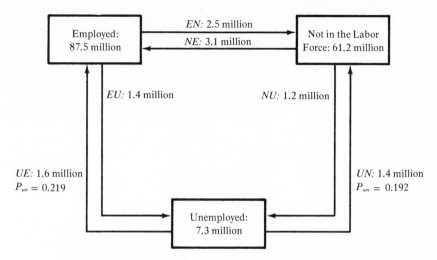

FIGURE 15.1   Labor-Market Stocks and Flows: 1976 Monthly Averages

SOURCE: Ralph E. Smith and Jean E. Vanski, "Gross Change Data: The Neglected Data Base" in National Commission on Employment and Unemployment Statistics, *Counting the Labor Force,* vol. II (Washington, D.C.: U.S. Government Printing Office, 1979), appendix.

   The chapter will then move on to discuss how unemployment arises. Economists conceptually categorize unemployment as being *frictional, structural, demand-deficient,* or *seasonal* in nature. After defining each type of unemployment and discussing its causes, we will focus on policy issues that are raised by the discussion. Among the issues that will be considered are the interrelationship between the unemployment-insurance system and unemployment, why unemployment rates vary across age/race/sex groups, why the "full-employment" unemployment rate has risen since 1960, and why firms lay off workers rather than reducing their wages in a recession. The chapter will conclude by discussing some normative issues relating to unemployment, including whether teenagers who were unemployed suffer long-run losses from such experiences.

A STOCK-FLOW MODEL OF THE LABOR MARKET

Data on the number of people who are employed, unemployed, and not in the labor force are provided each month from the national *Current Population Survey (CPS).*[2] As Figure 15.1 indicates, in 1976 (when the overall unemployment rate averaged 7.7 percent) there were 87.5 million employed, 7.3 million unemployed, and 61.2 million adults age 16 and over not in the labor force during a typical month. The impression one gets when one traces these data over short periods of time is that of relative stability; for example, it is highly unusual for the unemployment rate to change by more than a few tenths of a percentage point from one month to the next.

---

[2]The next two paragraphs draw heavily on Ralph E. Smith, "A Simulation Model of the Demographic Composition of Employment, Unemployment, and Labor Force Participation" in *Research in Labor Economics,* vol. I, ed. Ronald Ehrenberg (Greenwich, Conn.: JAI Press, 1977).

TABLE 15.2   **Categories of Unemployment**

		Percent of Unemployed Who Are:			
Year	Unemployment Rate	Job Losers	Job Leavers	Reentrants	New Entrants
1971	5.9	46.3	11.8	29.4	12.6
1973	4.9	38.7	15.7	30.7	14.9
1975	8.5	55.4	10.4	23.8	10.4
1977	7.0	45.2	13.0	28.1	13.7

SOURCE: U.S. Department of Labor, *1978 Employment and Training Report of the President* (Washington, D.C.: U.S. Government Printing Office, 1978).

Focusing only on these *labor-market stocks* and their net month-to-month changes, however, masks the highly dynamic nature of labor markets. Each month a substantial fraction of the unemployed leave unemployment status, either finding a job or dropping out of the labor force. For example, in each month of 1976 approximately 1.6 million unemployed individuals found employment (the flow denoted by *UE* in Figure 15.1), and 1.4 million of the unemployed dropped out of the labor force (the flow denoted by *UN*). These numbers represent the proportions 0.219 *(P_{ue})* and 0.192 *(P_{un})* of the stock of the unemployed, respectively; thus, one can conclude that approximately 40 percent of the individuals who were unemployed in a given month in 1976 left unemployment by the next month. These individuals were replaced in the pool of unemployed by roughly equivalent flows of individuals into unemployment from the stocks of employed individuals (the flow *EU*) and those not in the labor force (the flow *NU*).[3] The flow *EU* consists of individuals who voluntarily left or involuntarily lost their last job, while the flow *NU* consists of people entering the labor force. Finally, Figure 15.1 also indicates that each month there is considerable direct movement between employment and out-of-labor-force status.

When one thinks of the unemployed, the image of an individual laid off from his or her previous job often springs to mind. However, the view that such individuals comprise all, or even most, of the unemployed is incorrect. Table 15.2 provides some data that bear on this point for a period during the 1970s in which the unemployment rate varied between 4.9 and 8.5 percent. Only in 1975, when the unemployment rate hit 8.5 percent, were more than half of the unemployed job losers. In each of the years, more than one-third of the unemployed came from out-of-labor-force status—that is, they were individuals who were either entering the labor force for the first time *(new entrants)* or individuals who had some previous employment experience and were reentering the labor force after a period of time out of the labor force *(reentrants)*. Indeed, although the vast majority of individuals who quit their jobs obtain new jobs prior to quitting and never

---

[3]Actually, in 1976 the flows of people into unemployment from both the stocks of the employed and those not in the labor force were less than the flows out of unemployment into these stocks (see Figure 15.1). As might be expected, then, the unemployment rate was declining during most of the year.

pass through unemployment status, in each year at least 10 percent of the unemployed were voluntary job leavers.[4]

Similarly, when one thinks of an individual on layoff, one may envision an individual who has permanently lost his or her job and who finds employment with a new employer only after an exhaustive job search and long duration of unemployment. However, the evidence suggests that a substantial fraction (for example, 37 percent in 1974) of those individuals who *lost* their last job are on *temporary layoff* and ultimately return to their previous employer—many after only a relatively short spell (averaging 8.5 weeks in 1974) of unemployment.[5] Why some individuals "cycle" between employed and unemployed status, maintaining attachment to a single employer, will be discussed below.

Although ultimately public concern focuses on the level of unemployment, to understand the determinants of this level one must analyze the flows of individuals between the various labor-market states. A group's unemployment rate might be high because its members have difficulty finding jobs once unemployed, because they have difficulty (for voluntary or involuntary reasons) remaining employed once a job is found, or because they frequently enter and exit the labor force. The appropriate policy prescription to reduce the unemployment rate will depend upon which one of these labor-market flows is responsible for the high rate.

Somewhat more formally, one can show that if labor markets are roughly in balance, with the flows into and out of unemployment equal, the unemployment rate (**u**) for a group is given by

$$\mathbf{u} = \cfrac{1}{1 + \left[\cfrac{(P_{ne} + P_{nu})P_{ue} + (P_{ne})(P_{un})}{(P_{ne} + P_{nu})P_{eu} + (P_{nu})(P_{en})} \right]}. \tag{15.2}$$

P_{ij} represents the fraction of the group in labor-market state i that moves to labor market state j during the period, and the subscripts n, e, and u represent the states "not in the labor force," "employed," and "unemployed," respectively. So, for example, if there were initially 100 employed individuals in a group and 15 of them became unemployed during a period, P_{eu} would equal 0.15. [The formal derivation of equation (15.2) is found in the appendix to this chapter.]

From equation (15.2) one can see that, other things equal, increases in the proportions of individuals who voluntarily or involuntarily leave their jobs and become unemployed (P_{eu}) or leave the labor force (P_{en}) will increase a group's unemployment rate, as will an increase in the proportion of the group that enters the labor force without first having a job lined up (P_{nu}). Similarly, the greater the proportion of individuals who leave unemployment status, either to become em-

---

[4]For evidence that most quits do not involve a spell of unemployment, see J. Peter Mattila, "Job Quitting and Frictional Unemployment," *American Economic Review* 64 (March 1974): 235–39.

[5]For evidence on the magnitude of temporary layoffs, see Martin Feldstein, "The Importance of Temporary Layoffs: An Empirical Analysis," *Brookings Papers on Economic Activity*, 1975–3, pp. 725–44.

ployed *(P_{ue})* or to leave the labor force *(P_{un})*, the lower a group's unemployment rate will be. Finally, the greater the proportion of individuals who enter the labor force and immediately find jobs *(P_{ne})*, the lower a group's unemployment rate will be.[6]

The various theories of unemployment discussed in subsequent sections all essentially relate to the determination of one or more of the flows represented in equation (15.2). That is, they provide explanations for why the proportions of individuals who move between the various labor-market states vary over time, across geographic areas, or across age/race/sex groups. Equation (15.2) can help one understand why unemployment rates rise in recessions, how and why unemployment rates are influenced by the unemployment-insurance system, and why unemployment rates vary across age/race/sex groups.

Equation (15.2) and Figure 15.1 also make it clear that social concern over any given level of unemployment should focus on both the incidence of unemployment (on the fraction of people in a group who become unemployed) and the duration (or length of spells) of their unemployment. Society should be more concerned if small groups of individuals are unemployed for long periods of time than if many individuals rapidly pass through unemployment status. Up until recently, it was widely believed that the bulk of measured unemployment could be attributed to many people experiencing short spells of unemployment. However, recent evidence suggests that, while many people do pass quickly through the unemployed state, most unemployment is due to prolonged spells of unemployment for a relatively small number of individuals.[7]

TYPES OF UNEMPLOYMENT AND THEIR CAUSES

Frictional Unemployment

Suppose a competitive labor market is in equilibrium, in the sense that at the prevailing market wage the quantity of labor demanded just equals the quantity of labor supplied. Figure 15.2 shows such a labor market, in which the demand curve is D_0, the supply curve is S_0, employment is E_0, and the wage rate is W_0. Thus far the text has treated this equilibrium situation as one of full employment and has implied that there is no unemployment associated with it. However, this implication is not completely correct. Even in a market equilibrium or full-employment situation there will still be some *frictional unemployment,* because some people will be "between jobs."

Frictional unemployment arises because labor markets are inherently dynamic, because information flows are imperfect, and because it takes time for unemployed workers and employers with job vacancies to find each other. Even

---

[6]For an intuitive understanding of why each of these results holds, recall the definition of the unemployment rate in equation (15.1). A movement from one labor-market state to another may affect the numerator or the denominator, or both, and hence the unemployment rate. For example, an increase in P_{en} does not affect the number of unemployed individuals directly, but it does reduce the size of the labor force. According to equation (15.1), this reduction leads to an increase in the unemployment rate.

[7]Kim B. Clark and Lawrence H. Summers, "Labor-Market Dynamics and Unemployment: A Reconsideration," *Brookings Papers on Economic Activity,* 1979–1, pp. 13–60.

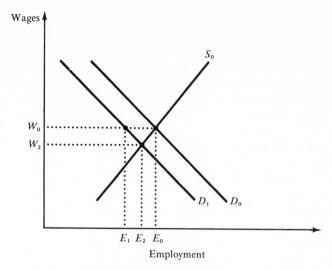

**FIGURE 15.2   The Full-Employment Rate of Unemployment:
A Decline in Demand Leads
to Increased Unemployment**

if the size of the labor force is constant, in each period there will be new entrants to the labor market searching for employment while other employed or unemployed individuals are leaving the labor force. Some people will quit their jobs to search for other employment. Moreover, random fluctuations in demand across firms will cause some firms to lay off workers at the same time that other firms will be seeking to hire new employees. Because information about the characteristics of those searching for work and the nature of the jobs opening up cannot instantly be known or evaluated, it takes time for job matches to be made between unemployed workers and potential employers. Hence, even when, in the aggregate, the demand for labor equals the supply, frictional unemployment will still exist.

The level of frictional unemployment in an economy is determined by the flows of individuals into and out of the labor market and the speed with which unemployed individuals find jobs. This speed is determined by the prevailing economic institutions, and institutional changes can influence the level of frictional unemployment. For example, instituting a computerized job-bank system, in which job applicants at the U.S. Employment Service are immediately informed of all listed jobs for which they are qualified, might reduce the time it takes them to find jobs. This system would increase the probability that an unemployed worker would become employed in any period (increase P_{ue}) and hence, as indicated by equation (15.2), would *decrease* the unemployment rate. On the other hand, one should be aware that if the time it takes unemployed workers to find jobs decreases, more employed workers may consider quitting their jobs to search for better-paying employment, thereby *increasing* P_{eu} and the unemployment rate. (This example should remind us again that well-intentioned social programs often have unintended adverse side effects.)

Structural Unemployment

Structural unemployment arises when changes in the pattern of labor demand cause a mismatch between the skills demanded and supplied in a given area—or cause an imbalance between the supplies and demands for workers across areas. *If* wages were completely flexible *and* if costs of occupational or geographic mobility were low, market adjustments would quickly eliminate this type of unemployment. However, in practice these conditions may fail to hold, and structural unemployment may result.

Our by now familiar two-sector labor-market model, represented by Figure 15.3, can be used to illustrate this point. For the moment we shall assume the sectors refer to markets for skill classes of workers; later we shall assume that they are two geographically separate labor markets. Suppose that Market A is the market for semiskilled workers in the shoe industry and that Market B is the market for skilled computer programmers—and suppose that initially both markets are in equilibrium. Given the demand and supply curves in both markets $[(D_{0A}, S_{0A})$ and $(D_{0B}, S_{0B})]$, the equilibrium wage/employment combinations in the two sectors will be (W_{0A}, E_{0A}) and (W_{0B}, E_{0B}) respectively. Because of differences in training costs and nonpecuniary conditions of employment, the wages need not be equal in the two sectors.

Now suppose that the demand for semiskilled shoe workers falls to D_{1A}, due to foreign import competition, while the demand for computer programmers rises to D_{1B} as a result of the increased use of computers. If real wages are inflexible downward in Market A because of union contract provisions, social norms, or government legislation, employment of semiskilled shoe employees will fall to E_{1A}. Employment and wages of computer programmers will rise to E_{1B} and W_{1B}, respectively. Unemployment of $E_{0A} - E_{1A}$ workers would be created in the short run.

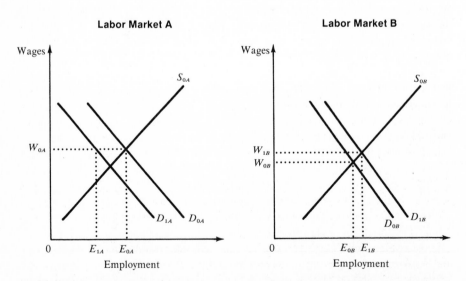

Labor Market A   **Labor Market B**

FIGURE 15.3   Structural Unemployment Due to Inflexible Wages and Costs of Adjustment

If shoe-industry employees could costlessly become computer programmers, these unemployed workers would "move" to Market B, and, since wages are assumed to be flexible there, eventually all of the unemployment would be eliminated.[8] Structural unemployment arises, however, when costs of adjustment are sufficiently high to preclude such movements. The cost to displaced individuals—many in their fifties and sixties—may prove to be prohibitively expensive, given the limited time horizons that they face. Moreover, it may be difficult for them to borrow funds to finance the necessary job training.

Geographic imbalances can be analyzed in the same framework. Suppose we now assume that Market A refers to a snowbelt city and Market B refers to a sunbelt city, both employing the same type of labor. When demand falls in the snowbelt and unemployment increases because wages are not completely flexible, these unemployed workers may continue to wait for jobs in their city for at least three reasons. First, information flows are imperfect, so that workers may be unaware of the availability of jobs thousands of miles away. Second, the direct money costs of such a move, including moving costs and the transaction costs involved in buying and selling a home, are high. Third, the psychological costs of moving long distances are substantial because friends and neighbors and community support systems must be given up. As noted in Chapter 10, such factors inhibit geographic migration, and migration tends to decline with age. These costs are sufficiently high that many workers who become unemployed, due either to plant shutdowns or to permanent layoffs, express no interest in searching for jobs outside their immediate geographic area.[9]

Structural unemployment arises, then, because of changing patterns of labor demand that occur in the face of both rigid wages and high costs of occupational or geographic mobility. In terms of Figure 15.1, structurally unemployed workers have a low probability of moving from unemployed to employed status (low P_{ue}), and any social policies that increase this probability should reduce the level of structural unemployment (other things equal). Examples of such policies include the provision of subsidized training, the provision of information about job-market conditions in other areas, and the provision of relocation allowances to help defray the costs of migration.

Each of these policies are part of the *Trade Adjustment Assistance Program,* which was initiated under the Trade Expansion Act of 1962 and expanded under the Trade Act of 1974. This program was designed to aid individuals who became unemployed because of changes in product demand brought about by foreign competition, and it also provided for an expanded form of unemployment-compensation benefits (the effects of unemployment compensation on unemployment will

---

[8]Actually, this statement is not quite correct. As Chapter 12 noted when analyzing the effects of unions using a similar model, *wait unemployment* may arise. That is, as long as the wage rate in Market A exceeds the wage rate in Market B and unemployed workers in Market A expect that normal job turnover will eventually create job vacancies in A, it may be profitable for them to remain attached to Market A and wait for a job in that sector. Wait employment is another example of a type of frictional unemployment.

[9]See, for example, Robert Aronson and Robert McKersie, *Economic Consequences of Plant Shutdowns in New York State* (Ithaca, N.Y.: New York State School of Industrial and Labor Relations, 1980).

be discussed later in the chapter). The available evidence indicates, however, that perhaps due to restrictive eligibility rules, this program has had little effect on increasing the probability that these structurally unemployed workers will find employment.[10]

On a more general level, since the early 1960s the federal government has been heavily involved in policies to reduce structural unemployment. These policies include the provision of relocation allowances to unemployed workers residing in depressed areas (under the *Area Redevelopment Act of 1959*), the provision of classroom and on-the-job training to both disadvantaged and unemployed workers (under the *Manpower Development and Training Act of 1962*), and, more recently, the provision of both training and public-sector employment opportunities (under the *Comprehensive Employment and Training Act of 1973*). Indeed, in fiscal year 1978 more than 2.5 million individuals were enrolled at some time during the year in federally funded employment and training programs.[11] Although the evidence on the effectiveness of these programs is mixed, several studies suggest that some of them have succeeded in increasing the earnings or employment probabilities of those individuals who were enrolled in the programs.[12]

Demand-Deficient Unemployment

Frictional and structural unemployment can arise even when, in the aggregate, the demand for labor equals the supply. Frictional unemployment arises because labor markets are dynamic and information flows are imperfect; structural unemployment arises because of geographic or occupational imbalances in demand and supply. *Demand-deficient unemployment* occurs when the *aggregate* demand for labor declines in the face of downward inflexibility in real wages.

Returning to our simple demand and supply model of Figure 15.2, suppose that a temporary decline in aggregate demand leads to a shift in the labor demand curve to D_1. If real wages are inflexible downward, employment will fall to E_1 and $E_0 - E_1$ additional workers will become unemployed. This employment decline occurs when firms temporarily lay off workers (increasing P_{eu}) and reduce the rate at which they replace those who quit or retire (decreasing P_{ne} and P_{ue}). That is, flows into unemployment increase while flows into employment decline.[13]

Demand-deficient (or *cyclical*) *unemployment* arises, then, when *aggregate*

---

[10]See for example, George R. Neumann, "The Labor Market Adjustment of Trade-Displaced Workers: The Evidence from the Trade Adjustment Assistance Program" in *Research in Labor Economics,* ed. Ronald Ehrenberg, vol. 2, 1978, and Walter Corson and Walter Nicholson, "Trade Adjustment Assistance for Workers: Results of a Survey of Recipients Under the Trade Act of 1974" in *Research in Labor Economics,* ed. Ronald Ehrenberg, vol. 4, 1981.

[11]*1979 Employment and Training Report of the President,* Table F2.

[12]See, for example, Orley Ashenfelter, "Estimating the Effects of Training Programs on Earnings," *Review of Economics and Statistics* 60 (February 1979): 47–57; Thomas Cooley et al., "The Estimation of Treatment Effects for Nonrandomized Samples: The Case of Manpower Training" in *Research in Labor Economics,* ed. R. Ehrenberg, Supplement I, 1979; Nicholas Kiefer, "The Economic Benefits from Four Government Training Programs" in *Research in Labor Economics,* ed. R. Ehrenberg, Supplement I, 1979; and Bradley Schiller, "Lessons From WIN: A Manpower Evaluation," *Journal of Human Resources* 13 (Fall 1978): 502–23.

[13]See Steven T. Marston, "Employment Instability and High Unemployment Rates," *Brookings Papers on Economic Activity,* 1976–1, pp. 169–203, for evidence on this point.

demand falls in the face of downward inflexibility in real wages. One appropriate government response is to pursue macroeconomic policies to increase aggregate demand; these policies include increasing the level of government spending, reducing taxes, and increasing the rate of growth of the money supply. Another policy is to use labor-market programs that focus more directly on the unemployed. Examples here include temporary employment tax credits for firms and public-sector employment programs—which were discussed in Chapters 4 and 13, respectively.

Of course, it still remains for us to explain *why* employers respond to a cyclical decline in demand by temporarily laying off some of their work force rather than reducing their employees' real wages. If the latter occurred, employment would move to E_2 and real wages to W_2 in Figure 15.2. Although employment would be lower than its initial level, E_0, there would be no measured demand-deficient unemployment because $E_0 - E_2$ workers would have dropped out of the labor force in response to this lower wage.

According to one explanation for rigid money wages, employers are not free to unilaterally cut money wages because of the presence of unions. However, this cannot be a complete explanation because less than one-quarter of American workers are represented by unions (see Chapter 12), and unions could, in any case, agree to temporary wage cuts to save jobs instead of subjecting their members to layoffs. Why they fail to make such arrangements is instructive.[14] A temporary wage reduction would reduce the earnings of all workers, while layoffs would affect—in most cases—only those workers most recently hired. Since unions represent their entire membership, not just the newly hired, and since union leaders are not likely to be drawn from the ranks of new members, unions tend to favor a policy of layoffs rather than one that reduces wages for all members.

Although layoffs occur less frequently than in union firms, they occur in non-union firms for two related reasons.[15] First, in the presence of investments in firm-specific human capital, which often lead to structured internal labor markets (see Chapter 5), employers have incentives both to minimize voluntary turnover and to maximize their employees' work effort and productivity. Across-the-board temporary wage reductions would increase all employees' incentives to quit and could lead to reduced work effort on their part. In contrast, layoffs affect only the least experienced workers—the workers in whom the firm has invested the smallest amount of resources. It is likely, then, that the firm will find choosing the layoff strategy a more profitable alternative.

Second, if potential job applicants and existing employees are aware that a firm is pursuing a temporary-layoff rather than a temporary-wage-cut strategy, they may be willing to work for a lower *average* wage rate. Individuals are typically assumed to be *risk-averse*—that is, they are assumed to prefer a constant

---

[14] See James Medoff, "Layoffs and Alternatives Under Trade Unions in United States Manufacturing," *American Economic Review* 69 (June 1979): 380–95, for the following argument and evidence.

[15] See Medoff, "Layoffs and Alternatives Under Trade Unions," for evidence that layoff rates are higher in union than nonunion firms, *ceteris paribus* (other things equal).

Example 15.1
International Unemployment-Rate Differentials

Comparisons of unemployment rates across nations are difficult because the exact definition of unemployment differs across nations. For example, in the United States "discouraged workers" who leave the labor force are not counted among the unemployed, while in Italy they are. Nevertheless it is possible to adjust the unemployment data reported by various industrial countries so that the data correspond approximately to the U.S. definition of unemployment. These adjusted unemployment rates are reported in the table below for nine industrial nations and three years during the late 1970s.

Nation/Year	1976	1977	1978
United States	7.7	7.0	6.0
Canada	7.1	8.1	8.4
Australia	4.8	5.6	6.3
Japan	2.0	2.0	2.3
France	4.7	5.0	5.4
Germany	3.6	3.6	3.4
Great Britain	5.5	6.2	6.1
Italy	3.6	3.4	3.5
Sweden	1.6	1.8	2.2

Note: The definitions of unemployment have been adjusted to approximate the U.S. concept of unemployment.

SOURCE: Joyanna Moy "Recent Labor Market Trends in Nine Industrial Nations," Monthly Labor Review 102 (May 1979): Table 1.

This table indicates that there are large differences in the adjusted unemployment rate across these nations in each year; in 1977 the adjusted unemployment rate varied from 1.8 percent in Sweden to 8.1 percent in Canada. Part of the difference results from differences in aggregate demand across nations—labor markets were tighter in Sweden than they were in Canada in 1977. Another part of the difference, however, reflects differences in social and institutional forces that affect the underlying labor-market flows.

The adjusted unemployment rate in Japan, for example, is typically lower than that in the United States. As we first saw in Chapter 5, a large sector of the Japanese labor market is characterized by a system of long-term—often lifelong—employment relations between employers and employees. Employees in this sector rarely quit their jobs voluntarily and their employers rarely lay off workers during economic downswings. As a result, the proportions of employed workers who voluntarily leave or involuntarily lose their jobs each period and enter unemployment status (P_{eu}) are low in Japan relative to the United States—as are the proportions who leave the labor force (P_{en}). As equation (15.2) indicates, the low levels of P_{eu} and P_{en} cause the Japanese unemployment rate to be lower than the American unemployment rate, other things equal.

How are Japanese employers able to maintain almost all their employees on their payrolls during economic downswings? A recent *Monthly Labor Review* article suggests one way:

> A number of Japanese enterprises with underutilized skilled labor (such as steel mills, shipbuilders, or textile producers) have adopted a novel method of maintaining employment for their regular workers. Excess workers are "loaned" for a specified period of no longer than 6 months to enterprises experiencing current labor shortages (such as automobile manufacturers). The workers maintain their affiliation with and receive their full wages from the lending company. The borrowing company usually pays temporary-worker wages, and the difference in wages plus benefits is made up by the lending employer. Thus, the borrowing company is able to temporarily increase its labor force with workers whose turnover rate is close to zero, while the lending company is able to maintain its regular work force at reduced cost.

SOURCES: Masanori Hashimoto "Bonus Payments, On-the-Job Training, and Lifetime Employment in Japan," *Journal of Political Economy* 87 (October 1979): 1086–1104 presents evidence to support the contention that P_{eu} and P_{en} are lower in Japan than in the United States; for each age group male job tenure is seen to be higher than in the United States; Joyanna Moy, "Recent Labor Market Trends in Nine Industrial Nations," *Monthly Labor Review*, 102, May 1979, p. 14.

---

earnings stream to a fluctuating one.[16] In effect, a system of layoffs in which the newest employees are laid off first provides an *implicit contract* (a guarantee or form of insurance to experienced workers) that they will be immune to all but the severest declines in demand. Put another way, after an initial period when the risk of layoff is high, earnings are likely to be very stable over time.[17] To the extent that experienced employees value stable earnings streams, they should be willing to pay for this stability by accepting lower wages in such situations—thereby reducing employers' costs. Of course, during the initial period, workers will be subject to potential earnings variability and may demand higher wages then to compensate them for these risks. However, if the fraction of the work force subject to layoffs is small, on average employers' costs should be reduced.

The incentives for both employers and employees to prefer temporary layoffs over fluctuations in real wages is magnified by two characteristics of the unemployment-insurance (UI) system: the *tax treatment of UI benefits* and the system's *method of financing benefits*.[18] The unemployment-insurance system is actually a

---

[16]This line of reasoning follows that found in Costas Azariadas, "Implicit Contracts and Underemployment Equilibria," *Journal of Political Economy* 83 (December 1975): 1183–1202; and Martin Bailey, "Wages and Employment Under Uncertain Demand," *Review of Economic Studies* 41 (January 1974): 37–50.

[17]We are ignoring here questions of real earnings growth over time.

[18]A more complete description of the characteristics of the UI system is found in Daniel S. Hamermesh, *Jobless Pay and the Economy* (Baltimore: Johns Hopkins University Press, 1977). The connection between temporary layoffs and these characteristics of the UI system was pointed out in Martin Feldstein, "Temporary Layoffs in the Theory of Unemployment," *Journal of Political Economy* 84 (October 1976): 937–58; empirical evidence on the relationship was provided in Martin Feldstein, "The Effect of Unemployment Insurance on Temporary Layoffs," *American Economic Review* 68 (December 1978): 834–40.

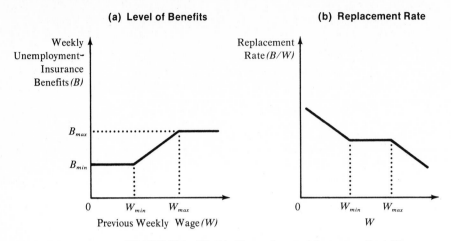

FIGURE 15.4   Weekly Unemployment-Insurance Benefits as a Function of Previous Earnings

system of individual state systems, and, although the details of the individual systems differ, one can easily sketch the broad outlines of how they operate.

Today virtually all private-sector employees are covered by a state UI system. When such workers become unemployed their eligibility for unemployment-insurance benefits is based upon their previous labor-market experience and reason for unemployment. With respect to their experience, each state requires unemployed individuals to demonstrate "permanent" attachment to the labor force, by meeting minimum earnings or weeks-worked tests during some base period, before they can be eligible for UI benefits. In all states covered workers who are laid off *and* meet these labor-market-experience tests are eligible for UI benefits. In some states workers who voluntarily quit their jobs are eligible for benefits, while in only two states (New York and Rhode Island) are strikers eligible for benefits. Finally, new entrants or reentrants to the labor force and workers fired for cause are, in general, ineligible for benefits.

After a waiting period, which is one or two weeks in most states, an eligible worker can begin to collect UI benefits. The structure of benefits is described in Figure 15.4, where it can be seen that benefits are related to an individual's previous earnings level.[19] As shown in panel (a), all eligible unemployed workers are entitled to at least a minimum benefit level, B_{min}. After previous earnings rise above a critical level, W_{min}, benefits increase proportionately with earnings—up to a maximum earnings level W_{max}, past which benefits remain constant at B_{max}. Eleven states also have dependents' allowances for unemployed workers, although in some of these states the dependents' allowance cannot increase an individual's weekly UI benefits above B_{max}.

An implication of such a benefit structure is that the ratio of an individual's

---

[19]Benefits are calculated across states in at least three different ways: as a percentage of annual earnings, as a percentage of previous weekly earnings, and as a percent of an individual's earnings during his or her "high" earnings quarter during the past year. For our purposes, such distinctions are unimportant.

UI benefits to his or her previous earnings varies according to one's past earnings—see panel (b). This ratio is often called the *replacement rate,* the fraction of previous earnings that the UI benefits replace. Over the range between W_{min} and W_{max}, where the replacement rate is constant, most states aim to replace around 50 percent of an unemployed worker's previous earnings. It is important to stress that up until 1978 *UI benefits were not subject to the federal income tax;* since then, however, UI benefits received by those whose family incomes exceed $25,000 are taxed.

Once UI benefits begin, an unemployed individual's eligibility for continued benefits depend upon his or her making continual "suitable efforts" to find employment; the definition of suitable efforts varies widely across states. In addition, there is a maximum duration of receipt of benefits that is of fixed length in some states and varies in other states with a worker's prior labor-market experience (workers with "more permanent attachment" being eligible for more weeks of benefits). Periodically Congress also passes temporary legislation that extends the length of time unemployed workers can receive benefits in states in which unemployment is high, but the maximum total duration of eligibility for benefits did not exceed 65 weeks in the 1970s.

The benefits paid out by the UI system are financed by a payroll tax. Unlike the social-security payroll tax, in all but three states the UI tax is paid solely by employers with no employee contribution required.[20] The UI tax payment *(T)* that an employer must make for each employee is given by

$$T = tW \quad \text{if } W \leq W_B \tag{15.3}$$

and

$$T = tW_B \quad \text{if } E > W_B,$$

where t is the employer's UI tax rate, W is an employee's earnings during the calendar year, and W_B is the *taxable wage base,* the level of earnings after which no UI tax payments are required. In 1980, the taxable wage base was $6,000 in most states; employers had to pay UI taxes on the first $6,000 of earnings for each employee.

The employer's UI tax rate is determined by general economic conditions in a state, the industry the employer is operating in, and the employer's *layoff experience.* This latter term is defined differently in different states; the underlying notion is that since the UI system is an insurance system, employers who lay off lots of workers and make heavy demands on the system's resources should be assigned a higher UI tax rate. This practice is referred to as *experience rating.*

Experience rating is typically *imperfect* in the sense that the marginal cost to an employer of laying off an additional worker (in terms of a higher UI tax rate) is often less than the added UI benefits that the system must pay out to that worker. Imperfect experience rating is illustrated in Figure 15.5, which plots the relationship between an employer's UI tax rate and that firm's layoff experience. (We will interpret *layoff experience* to mean the probability that employees in the

---

[20]Recall from our discussion in Chapter 3 that this fact tells us nothing about who really bears the burden of the tax.

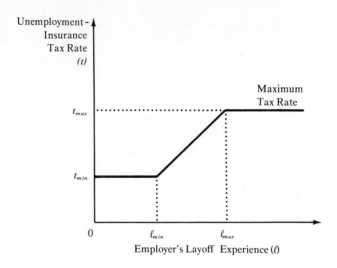

FIGURE 15.5   Imperfectly Experience-Rated Unemployment-Insurance Tax Rate

firm will be on layoff. Clearly, this probability depends both on the frequency with which the firm lays off workers and the average duration of time until they are recalled to their positions.)

Each state has a minimum UI tax rate, and below this rate—t_{min} in Figure 15.5—the firm's UI tax rate cannot fall. After a firm's layoff experience reaches some critical value, l_{min}, the firm's UI tax rate rises with increased layoff experience over some range. In each state there is also a ceiling on the UI tax rate, t_{max}, and after this tax rate is reached additional layoffs will not alter the firm's tax rate.[21] The system is *imperfectly* experience-rated because for firms below l_{min} or above l_{max}, variations in their layoff rate have no effect on their UI tax rate.[22] Further, over the range that the tax rate is increasing with layoff experience, the increase is not large enough in most states to make the employer's marginal cost of a layoff (in terms of the increased UI taxes the firm must pay) equal to the marginal UI benefits that the laid-off employees receive.

The key characteristics of the UI system that influence the desirability of temporary layoffs are the *imperfect experience rating* of the UI payroll tax and the *federal tax treatment* of UI benefits that workers receive. To understand the influence of these characteristics, suppose first that the UI system were constructed in such a way that its tax rates were perfectly experience-rated and the benefits it paid out (half of previous earnings, say) were completely taxable. A firm laying off a worker would have to pay added UI taxes equal to the full UI benefit re-

---

[21]In actuality the UI tax rate changes discretely (as a step function) over the range l_{min} to l_{max}, not continuously as we have drawn in Figure 15.5. For expository convenience, we ignore this complication.

[22]Such a system of UI financing leads to interindustry subsidies, in which industries (such as banking) with virtually no layoffs still must pay the minimum tax—and these industries subsidize those industries (such as construction) that have very high layoffs but pay only the maximum rate.

ceived by the worker, so it saves just half of the worker's wages by the layoff; the *worker's* spendable income would be cut in half if he or she were laid off.

Now suppose instead that the UI tax rate employers must pay is totally independent of its layoff experience (no experience rating) and that UI benefits are not subject to any personal income taxes. The *firm* saves the laid-off worker's *entire* wages—not just half—because its UI taxes do not rise as a result of the lay off. The worker still gets a benefit equal to half of prior earnings, but since these benefits are not taxable, his or her spendable income drops by *less* than half. Thus, compared to a UI system with perfect experience rating and completely taxable benefits, it is easy to see that the current system—which has imperfect experience rating and does not generally tax benefits—enhances the attractivensss of layoffs to both employer and employee.[23] Put differently, these characteristics of the UI system tend to increase the level of demand-deficient unemployment over what it would be if experience rating were perfect and benefits were completely taxable.

Seasonal Unemployment

Seasonal unemployment is similar to demand-deficient unemployment in that it is induced by fluctuations in the demand for labor. Here, however, the fluctuations can be regularly anticipated and follow a systematic pattern over the course of a year. For example, the demand for agricultural employees declines after the planting season and remains low until the harvest season. Similarly, the demand for construction workers in snowbelt states falls during winter months. Finally, the demand for production workers falls in certain industries during the season of the year when plants are retooling to handle annual model changes; examples here include both the Detroit automotive industry (new car models) and the New York City apparel industry (new fashion designs).

The issue remains, why do employers respond to seasonal patterns of demand by laying off workers rather than reducing wage rates or hours of work? All of the answers cited for why cyclical unemployment and temporary layoffs for cyclical reasons exist also pertain here. Indeed, one study has shown that the expansion (in the early 1970s) of the unemployment-insurance system that led to cover most agricultural employees was associated with a substantial increase in seasonal unemployment in agriculture.[24]

One may question, however, why workers would accept jobs in industries in which they knew in advance that they would be unemployed for a portion of the year. For some workers, the existence of UI benefits along with the knowledge that they will be rehired as a matter of course at the end of the slack demand season may allow them to treat such periods as paid vacations. However, since UI benefits typically replace less than half of an unemployed workers' previous gross earnings, and even smaller fractions for high-wage workers (see Figure 15.4),

---

[23]This statement is not always true since employed workers often lose fringe benefits and the ability to take advantage of on-the-job training options.

[24]Barry Chiswick, "The Effect of Unemployment Compensation on a Seasonal Industry: Agriculture," *Journal of Political Economy* 84 (June 1976): 591–602.

TABLE 15.3   **Unemployment Rates in 1978 by Demographic Groups**

Age	White Male	White Female	Nonwhite Male	Nonwhite Female	All
16–17	16.9	17.1	40.0	41.7	
18–19	10.8	12.4	30.8	36.5	
20–24	7.6	8.3	20.0	21.3	
25–34	3.7	5.8	8.8	11.2	
35–44	2.5	4.5	4.9	7.6	
45–54	2.5	3.8	5.0	5.6	
55–64	2.6	3.0	4.4	5.1	
65+	3.9	3.7	7.1	4.8	
Total	4.5	6.2	10.9	13.1	6.0

SOURCE: U.S. Department of Labor, *1979 Employment and Training Report of the President* (Washington, D.C.: U.S. Government Printing Office, 1979), Table A20.

most workers will not find such a situation desirable. To attract workers to such seasonal industries, firms will have to pay workers higher wages to compensate them for being periodically unemployed. In fact, casual observation suggests that the hourly wages of construction workers are substantially higher than the hourly wages of comparably skilled manufacturing workers who work more hours each year. More formally, a recent econometric study has confirmed that, other things held constant (including workers' skill levels), wages are higher in industries in which workers' expected annual durations of unemployment are higher.[25]

The existence of such wage differentials that compensate workers in high-unemployment industries for the risk of unemployment makes it difficult to evaluate whether this type of unemployment is voluntary or involuntary in nature. On the one hand, in an *ex ante* (or "before the fact") sense, workers have voluntarily agreed to be employed in industries that offer higher wages *and* higher probabilities of unemployment than offered elsewhere. On the other hand, once on the job (*ex post* or "after the fact"), the employee would prefer to remain employed rather than becoming unemployed. Such unemployment may be considered to be either voluntary or involuntary, then, depending upon the perspective one is taking.

THE DEMOGRAPHIC STRUCTURE OF UNEMPLOYMENT RATES

The Full-Employment Unemployment Rate

Table 15.3 presents data on unemployment rates for various age/race/sex groups in 1978. The patterns indicated in Table 15.3 for 1978 are similar to the patterns for other years: high unemployment rates for teens and young adults of each race/sex group relative to older adults in these groups; nonwhite unemployment rates roughly double white unemployment rates for most age/sex groups; and female

---

[25]John Abowd and Orley Ashenfelter, "Anticipated Unemployment, Temporary Layoffs, and Compensating Wage Differentials" (Princeton University Industrial Relations Section Working Paper, June 1980).

unemployment rates that are higher than male rates, especially for whites. The high unemployment rates of nonwhite teenagers, which ranged between 30.8 and 41.7 percent in 1978, have been of particular concern to policymakers and have led to numerous programs designed to reduce nonwhite teenage unemployment during the late 1970s and early 1980s.

Over recent decades, the age/race/sex composition of the labor force has changed dramatically due to the growing labor-force participation rates of females and to increases in the relative sizes of the teenage and nonwhite populations. Between 1960 and 1978 the proportion of the labor force that was female grew from 33.4 to 41.7 percent; the proportion that was nonwhite grew from 11.1 to 11.9 percent; and the proportion that was teenaged grew from 7.0 to 9.5 percent.[26] The increase in the relative labor-force shares of those groups that have relatively higher unemployment rates has led to an increase in the overall unemployment rate that is associated with any given level of labor-market tightness. Indeed, one investigator has concluded that demographic shifts in the composition of the labor force alone probably are responsible for the fact that the overall unemployment rate was at least 1 percentage point higher in the late 1970s and early 1980s than it was in the mid-1960s, for any given level of overall labor-market tightness.[27] The demographic changes have also led to an increase in the *full-employment* (or *natural*) *rate* of unemployment—the unemployment rate that is consistent with a zero excess demand for labor. While an aggregate unemployment rate of 4 percent was considered a reasonable unemployment goal for policymakers to aim at in the mid-1960s, policymakers and academic economists rarely referred to targets below 5.5 percent by the late-1970s.

Why Do Unemployment Rates Vary Across Groups?

Calculations such as those just referred to take the age/race/sex structure of unemployment rates as fixed, and hence it is natural to ask why this structure exists.[28] As equation (15.2) indicates, a group's unemployment rate might be high because its members have difficulty finding jobs once unemployed, because they have difficulty (for voluntary or involuntary reasons) remaining employed once a job is found, or because they frequently enter and exit from the labor force. The appropriate policy prescriptions will depend on the relative size of these monthly flows from one labor-market state to another and on which of the flows is most responsible for the high rate.

One data source that is helpful in making such a determination is the monthly *Current Population Survey (CPS)*. Since three-quarters of the individuals in the CPS sample one month are also included in the sample the next month, it is possible to compute the number of individuals in a particular age/race/sex group who move between various labor market states in a month. Since 1967, when

---

[26]U.S. Department of Labor, *1979 Employment and Training Report of the President* (Washington, D.C.: U.S. Government Printing Office, 1979), Table A3.

[27]James Tobin, "Stabilization Policy Ten Years After," *Brookings Papers on Economic Activity,* 1980–1, pp. 19–72.

[28]This section draws heavily on Ronald G. Ehrenberg, "The Demographic Structure of Unemployment Rates and Labor Market Transition Probabilities," *Research in Labor Economics* 3 (1980): 241–93.

TABLE 15.4   Average Monthly Transition Probabilities (July
1967-September 1977)

	P_{en}	P_{ne}	P_{un}	P_{nu}	P_{eu}	P_{ue}
(A) White Males						
16–19	0.114	0.150	0.308	0.072	0.041	0.301
20–24	0.036	0.192	0.153	0.069	0.026	0.322
25–59	0.003	0.072	0.100	0.032	0.010	0.321
60+	0.047	0.027	0.162	0.004	0.006	0.227
(B) White Females						
16–19	0.138	0.101	0.327	0.058	0.029	0.280
20–24	0.051	0.058	0.148	0.036	0.018	0.355
25–59	0.045	0.045	0.265	0.012	0.010	0.213
60+	0.072	0.013	0.198	0.002	0.003	0.099
(C) Black Males						
16–19	0.151	0.095	0.344	0.096	0.062	0.197
20–24	0.034	0.132	0.121	0.083	0.036	0.219
25–59	0.011	0.092	0.131	0.044	0.018	0.310
60+	0.045	0.025	0.336	0.008	0.009	0.167
(D) Black Females						
16–19	0.185	0.049	0.371	0.085	0.040	0.180
20–24	0.062	0.068	0.287	0.066	0.022	0.118
25–59	0.039	0.049	0.324	0.036	0.012	0.205
60+	0.098	0.020	0.160	0.003	0.002	0.309

Note: Each probability represents the mean proportion in each labor-market state in a month
who move to each other labor-market state in the next month. The proportions are based
upon gross-flow data that has been adjusted by researchers at the Urban Institute to correct
for errors in the data.

P_{en} = fraction of employed who leave the labor force.
P_{ne} = fraction of those not in the labor force who enter the labor force and find employment.
P_{un} = fraction of unemployed who leave the labor force.
P_{nu} = fraction of those not in the labor force who enter the labor force and become unem-
    ployed.
P_{eu} = fraction of employed who become unemployed.
P_{ue} = fraction of unemployed who become employed.

definitional changes in the CPS occurred, these monthly *gross-flow data* have
been tabulated by the Bureau of Labor Statistics (BLS), although they have not
been published. Dividing these gross flows by the size of the appropriate group in
the previous month yields estimates of the probability that an individual of a given
age, race, and sex will go from one labor-market state to another; these probabilities are called *transition probabilities*.

Table 15.4 presents estimates of the *average monthly transition probabilities*
(the proportion of individuals in each labor-market state who leave that state for
each other state by the next month) for 16 age/race/sex cohorts during the July
1967–September 1977 period. Equation (15.2) and the data in this table allow us
to estimate the extent to which a relatively high unemployment rate for a group is
caused by the values of each of its transition probabilities. Put another way, this
information can be used to determine by how much a group's relative unemployment rate would change if we replaced any one of its transition probabilities with
the comparable probability for a reference group (such as white adult males) that
has a low relative unemployment rate. Since different governmental policies will
likely affect different transition probabilities, this determination may suggest the

TABLE 15.5 Variations in Transition Probabilities and Simulated Relative
Unemployment Rates

	u_m	u_e	R	R_{en}	R_{ne}	R_{un}	R_{nu}	R_{eu}	R_{ue}
(A) White Males									
16–19	13.9	13.3	4.7	2.7	6.3	6.2	3.5	3.0	4.5
20–24	8.1	7.6	2.7	2.1	3.5	3.0	2.3	1.6	2.7
25–59	2.9	2.8	1.0	1.0	1.0	1.0	1.0	1.0	1.0
60+	3.2	3.2	1.1	0.6	0.8	1.3	3.4	1.5	0.9
(B) White Females									
16–19	14.1	14.1	5.0	2.1	5.9	6.7	3.8	4.0	4.7
20–24	8.0	7.6	2.7	1.4	2.5	2.9	2.6	2.2	2.9
25–59	4.5	4.5	1.6	0.9	1.3	2.3	2.6	1.6	1.3
60+	3.3	3.6	1.3	0.4	0.5	1.8	9.2	2.1	0.7
(C) Black Males									
16–19	28.8	27.3	9.8	5.3	10.8	12.8	6.5	6.8	7.8
20–24	14.8	14.3	5.1	4.0	5.8	5.3	4.2	2.6	3.9
25–59	5.5	5.2	1.9	1.7	1.9	2.0	1.8	1.2	1.8
60+	4.9	4.6	1.6	0.8	1.0	2.8	3.6	1.7	1.2
(D) Black Females									
16–19	34.3	33.2	11.9	4.2	10.2	15.0	7.8	10.2	9.1
20–24	17.3	16.6	5.9	3.0	5.8	8.5	4.2	4.7	3.6
25–59	7.0	6.9	2.5	1.2	2.0	3.5	2.3	2.3	1.9
60+	3.2	3.0	1.1	0.2	0.4	1.2	5.1	1.7	1.0

Note: white males, aged 25–29, are used as the reference group.

u_m = average unemployment rate during the period.
u_e* = estimated average unemployment rate using equation (15.2) and mean value of transition probabilities for that group.
R = estimated average unemployment rate of the group relative to the estimated average unemployment rate of white males 25–59.
R_{ij} = estimated value of R if P_{ij} for the group is replaced by P_{ij} for white males 25–59.

SOURCE: Based on adjusted gross-flow data.

types of policies to stress in seeking to alter the demographic structure of unemployment rates.

The first two columns in Table 15.5 present data for each demographic group on the *actual* average unemployment rate of the group over the 1967–77 period (u_m) and the *estimated* average group unemployment rate (u*) obtained when one substitutes the mean values of the group's transition probabilities from Table 15.4 into equation (15.2). Since Equation (15.2) is formally correct only in periods of labor-market balance (when the labor-market flows into each of the states roughly equal the flows out of the states), it is reassuring to note the correspondence between the two unemployment series—especially the close matches for the adult (25–59) groups.

The third column in the table presents the ratio *(R)* of the estimated average unemployment rate of each group during the period relative to the estimated average unemployment rate of the *reference* group (white males 25–59). The next six columns contain calculations of the estimated values of this ratio when the values of each transition probability are replaced, one at a time, by the equivalent probability for white males 25–59. That is, data in the last six columns indicate what the group's relative unemployment rate would be if we changed, one at a time, each transition probability to the reference group's level. Comparisons of columns (4) through (9) to column (3) indicate which transition probabilities are the major sources of difference between the unemployment rate of a particular group and that of white males, aged 25–59. If R decreases significantly when a given transition probability is replaced by its reference-group counterpart, there is room for government policies to try to alter that probability.

High teenage unemployment rates (relative to adult male unemployment rates) stem primarily from the high probability that teenagers will leave employment to move out of the labor force (P_{en}) and from the high probability that teenagers will move into unemployment from either employment (P_{eu}) or out-of-labor-force (P_{nu}) status.[29] Teens, then, move into and out of the labor force frequently and frequently lose or voluntarily leave their jobs. For nonwhite teens, low probabilities of moving from unemployment to employment (P_{ue})—that is, of finding a job— also play a role.

The primary source of high relative unemployment for white female adults is the large flow from employment to out-of-labor-force status (P_{en}); they frequently leave the labor force directly from employment status. Lower probabilities of moving into employment $(P_{ne}$ and $P_{ue})$ also increase adult female unemployment. The major cause of high nonwhite adult male (25–59) unemployment is the group's high probability of voluntarily or involuntarily leaving employment to become unemployed (P_{eu}); nonwhite adult males have difficulty holding jobs. In contrast, the relatively high nonwhite adult female unemployment rate is due primarily to the group's high probability of leaving the labor force from employment status (P_{en}) and to the low probability of unemployed group members finding employment (P_{ue})—results that are very similar to those for adult white females.

A similar simulation exercise can be performed to see why nonwhite teenage unemployment rates tend to be double those of white teenagers. (These comparisons use white teens as the reference group.) Save for P_{un}, differences in all of the transition probabilities appear to be factors, at least to a degree. For both males and females, however, lower probabilities of finding employment $(P_{ne}$ and $P_{ue})$ have the largest influence on the relative teenage unemployment rates. A key question for policymakers to answer then is, "Why do nonwhite teens have greater difficulty finding employment than white teens?"

A number of potential explanations have been offered. Some revolve around the methods of job search used. For example, it has been argued that nonwhites rely on institutions such as the Employment Service to find jobs, while white teens tend to find jobs through friends and neighbors.[30] Others focus on the growing concentration of nonwhite youths in the central cities, while employment opportunities have been moving to the suburbs and nonmetropolitan areas. However, the data indicate that nonwhite teenage unemployment rates are higher than white teenage unemployment rates in all types of geographic areas (central city, subur-

---

[29]Why high values of P_{en} should lead to high unemployment rates was discussed in footnote 6.

[30]Paul Osterman, "Racial Differentials in Male Youth Unemployment," in U.S. Department of Labor, *Conference Report on Youth Unemployment: Its Measurement and Meaning* (Washington, D.C.: U.S. Government Printing Office, 1978).

ban, and nonmetropolitan).[31] Moreover, if nonwhite youths had been reallocated across areas so that, in each, their proportionate representation relative to white youths was the same, the data suggest that the overall black/white teenage unemployment rate differential would have fallen by less than 10 percent.

Other explanations revolve around more traditional supply and demand factors. These factors include: the relative growth in the nonwhite teenage population coupled with increases in the minimum wage; the growth of income-maintenance programs that may reduce the willingness of nonwhite teens to accept low-wage jobs; the reduction in the size of the armed forces; and the possibly lower-quality education that nonwhite teens receive, especially in innercity areas, that may reduce their perceived attractiveness to employers. It is clear, however, that no single explanation is sufficient to account for the much higher rates of nonwhite teenage unemployment.

SEARCH UNEMPLOYMENT AND THE ROLE OF UNEMPLOYMENT-INSURANCE BENEFITS

As noted earlier in the chapter, because information about job opportunities and workers' characteristics is imperfect, it will take time for job matches to be made between unemployed workers and potential employers. Other things equal, the lower the probability that unemployed workers will become employed in a period (the lower is P_{ue}), the higher will be their expected duration of unemployment and the higher will be the unemployment rate.

Critics of the unemployment-insurance system often point out that the existence of UI benefits reduces the costs of being unemployed and may prolong unemployed workers' job search.[32] Supporters of the UI system respond that an explicit purpose of the UI system when it was founded in the late 1930s was to provide unemployed workers with temporary resources to enable them to turn down low-wage jobs that were not commensurate with their skill levels and to keep searching for better jobs.[33] That is, many believe that while the existence of UI benefits might prolong spells of unemployment, such benefits also might lead to higher postunemployment wages and better job matches—and better job matches might reduce subsequent job turnover, thus providing a further benefit to society.

Before turning to the empirical evidence on these points, analyzing a formal model of job search will yield implications about a variety of labor-market phenomena in addition to the role of UI benefits in the job-search process.[34] This

---

[31]U.S. Department of Labor, *1978 Employment and Training Report of the President* (Washington, D.C.: U.S. Government Printing Office, 1978), p. 73.

[32]Martin Feldstein, "The Economics of the New Unemployment," *Public Interest* 33 (Fall 1973): 3–42.

[33]William Haber and Merrill Murray, *Unemployment Insurance in the American Economy* (Homewood, Ill.: Irwin, 1966), pp. 26–35.

[34]Our discussion here draws heavily on Dale T. Mortensen, "Job Search, the Duration of Unemployment, and the Phillips Curve," *American Economic Review* 60 (December 1970): 847–62.

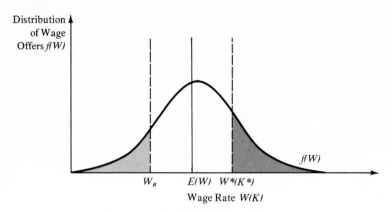

FIGURE 15.6 **Choice of Reservation Wage in a Model of Job Search**

model will make the key assumption that wages are associated with the characteristics of jobs, not with the specific individuals who fill them.[35]

Suppose that employers differ in the set of minimum hiring standards that they have. Hiring standards may include educational requirements, job training, work experience, performance on test scores, etc. For expositional convenience suppose this set of attributes can be summarized in a single variable, K, which will denote the minimum skill level a job requires. Associated with each job is a wage, $W(K)$—a wage that is a function of the required skill level and not of the particular characteristics of the people hired. We assume that the wage rate is an increasing function of the minimum required skill level and that two employers that have the same hiring standard will offer the same wage.

Because different employers have different hiring standards, there will be a distribution of wage offers associated with job vacancies in the labor market. This distribution of wage offers is denoted by $f(W)$ in Figure 15.6. As one moves to the right in the figure, the minimum required skill level and offered wage on a job increase. Since $f(W)$ represents a *probability distribution* of wage offers, the area under the curve sums to one (that is, the distribution contains 100 percent of all wage offers in the market). Each wage offer (on the horizontal axis) is shown in relation to that offer's share in the distribution (on the vertical axis).

Now suppose a given unemployed individual has skill level $K.^*$ Since no firm will hire a worker who does not meet its hiring standards, the maximum wage that this individual could hope to receive is $W^*(K^*)$. If he or she knew which firms had a hiring standard of K^*, he or she would apply to them and, since the individual meets their hiring standards, would be hired at a wage of W^*.

Suppose, instead, that job-market information is imperfect—in the sense that while the individual knows the shape of the distribution of wage offers, $f(W)$, he or she does *not* know what each individual firm's wage offer or hiring standard will be. One can conceptualize job search as a process in which the person ran-

---

[35]Such an assumption has been made in another context by Lester Thurow, *Generating Inequality* (New York: Basic Books, 1975).

domly knocks on the doors of personnel departments of firms. If the firm's hiring standard exceeds $K,*$ the person is rejected for the job. However, if the hiring standard is $K*$ or less, the person is offered the job. While the individual might find it advantageous to accumulate a number of jobs offers and then accept the best, job seekers—especially at the lower-skilled end of the skill ladder—are not always allowed such a luxury. Rather, they must make instantaneous decisions about whether or not to accept a job offer because otherwise the offer will be extended to a different applicant.

How does an unemployed worker know whether to accept any particular job offer? One strategy is to decide on a *minimum-acceptance* (or *reservation*) *wage* and then to accept (reject) any offer above (below) this level. The critical question then is, How is this reservation wage determined?

To answer this question, suppose W_R is the reservation wage that is chosen (in Figure 15.6) by a person who has skill level $K.*$ Now observe that this individual's job application will be rejected by any firm that offers a wage higher than $W* (K*)$; the person will not meet their minimum hiring standards. Similarly, the person will reject any job offers that call for a wage less than W_R. Hence, the probability that he or she will find an acceptable job in any period is simply the unshaded area under the curve between W_R and $W*$. The higher this probability the lower the expected duration of unemployment. Given that the person finds a job, his or her expected wage is simply the weighted average of the job offers in the W_R to $W*$ range. This average or expected wage is denoted by $E(W)$ in Figure 15.6.

If the individual were to choose a slightly higher reservation wage, his or her choice would have two effects. On the one hand, since the person would now reject more low-wage jobs, his or her expected or average wage (once employed) would increase. On the other hand, by rejecting more job offers he or she also decreases the probability of finding an acceptable job in any given period—thus increasing the expected duration of unemployment. Put another way, higher reservation wages lead to the costs of longer expected spells of unemployment but also to the benefits of higher expected wages once a job is found. Each unemployed individual will choose his or her reservation wage so that, at the margin, the expected costs of longer spells of unemployment just equal the expected benefits of higher postunemployment wages. That is, the reservation wage should be chosen so that the marginal benefit from a higher reservation wage just equals its marginal cost.

This simple model and associated decision rule lead to a number of implications. First, as long as the reservation wage is not set equal to the minimum wage offered in the market, the probability of finding a job will be less than one and hence some *search unemployment* will result. *Search unemployment* occurs when an individual does not necessarily accept the first job that is offered to him or her and is a rational strategy in a world of imperfect information.[36]

---

[36]Voluntary search unemployment is but one form of frictional unemployment and frictional unemployment is but one form of overall unemployment; thus, only a portion of unemployment is of the voluntary search nature. Indeed, the data suggest that many unemployed workers never reject any job offer; see, for example, U.S. Bureau of Labor Statistics, Bulletin 1886, *Job Seeking Methods Used by American Workers* (Washington, D.C.: U.S. Government Printing Office, 1975).

Second, since the reservation wage will always be chosen to be less than the wage commensurate with the individual's skill level, $W^*(K^*)$, virtually all individuals will be *underemployed* once they find a job (in the sense that their expected earnings will be less than W^*). This underemployment is a cost of imperfect information; better labor-market information would improve the job-matching process.

Third, due to random luck, otherwise identical individuals will wind up receiving different wages. Two identical individuals who have the same skill level should choose the same reservation wage and should have the same *expected* postunemployment wage. However, the wages they actually wind up with would depend upon pure luck—the wage offer between W_R and W^* they happened to find. In a world of imperfect information, then, no economic model can explain all of the variation in wages across individuals.

Fourth, anything that reduces the cost of an individual's being unemployed should lead the person to increase his or her reservation wage—and should thus lead to longer durations of unemployment and higher expected postunemployment wages. Since higher UI benefits reduce individuals' cost of unemployment, increasing such benefits should be associated with longer spells of unemployment and higher postunemployment wages.

In recent years, numerous studies have sought to estimate the effects of UI benefits on durations of unemployment and postunemployment wages.[37] In the main, these studies use data on individuals and exploit the fact that the replacement rate (the fraction of previous earnings that UI benefits replace) varies (*within* states) with individuals' previous earnings levels (see Figure 15.4) and also varies *across* states. Evidence from these studies suggests quite strongly that higher UI replacement rates are associated with longer durations of unemployment; raising the replacement rate from 0.4 to 0.5 of previous weekly earnings may increase the average spell of unemployment by one half to one week. In contrast, the evidence on the effects of postunemployment wages is much more mixed. For example, one study found that higher replacement rates were associated with higher postunemployment wage rates for adults but not for teenagers.[38]

Fifth, anything that increases individuals' discount rates—or their need for current income relative to future income—should lead to lower reservation wages and hence to shorter expected durations of unemployment and lower postunemployment wages. Thus, unemployed individuals from poor families may well set-

---

[37] See, for example, Ronald G. Ehrenberg and Ronald L. Oaxaca, "Unemployment Insurance, Duration of Unemployment and Subsequent Wage Gain," *American Economic Review* 66 (December 1976): 754–66. Many of the studies are summarized in Daniel S. Hamermesh, *Jobless Pay and the Economy* (Baltimore: Johns Hopkins University Press, 1977) and are critiqued in Finis Welch, "What Have We Learned From Empirical Studies of Unemployment Insurance," *Industrial and Labor Relations Review* 30 (July 1977): 451–61.

[38] Ehrenberg and Oaxaca, "Unemployment Insurance." The results for teens may imply that (a) unemployed teens do not search actively for work, (b) unemployed teens' job search is not productive, perhaps because of the narrow range of job opportunities they face, or (c) unemployed teens may search for jobs that offer greater training options and possible higher future wages, although not higher current wages. The available data do not permit one to determine which of these alternatives is correct.

Example 15.2
Unemployment-Insurance Benefits in Great Britain

Evidence that more generous unemployment-insurance benefits lead to higher levels of unemployment is not confined to the United States. For example, Daniel Benjamin and Levis Kochin have found three pieces of information that seem to confirm the relationship for Great Britain during the period between World Wars I and II:

1. Increases in the aggregate British unemployment rate, even after controlling for the level of aggregate demand, were associated with increases in the British UI replacement rate over the 1920–1938 period.
2. Teenagers—many of whom were either not eligible for UI benefits during this period or who received very low benefits relative to their wages—had unemployment rates that were only a fraction of the adult unemployment rate. Further, the unemployment rate jumped markedly at ages 18 and 21, when UI benefits increased.
3. In 1932, the year a change in the British UI regulations reduced the possibility that unemployed married women could receive UI benefits, the unemployment rate for married women dropped sharply relative to the rate for males.

SOURCE: See Daniel Benjamin and Levis Kochin, "Searching for an Explanation of Unemployment in Interwar Britain," *Journal of Political Economy* 87 (June 1979): 441–78.

tle for lower-paying jobs than equally skilled unemployed individuals from higher-income families.

Sixth, the shorter the length of time that an individual expects to be employed, the smaller will be the payoff to job search activities and hence the lower will be the reservation wage. This lower reservation wage will lead to shorter durations of unemployment and lower postunemployment wages for individuals with short expected job tenure.

Finally, increases in skill level—say, by means of participation in a government job-training programs—will have two effects on unemployed workers. On the one hand, their W^* will increase—which, other things equal, will increase the proportion of jobs they are qualified for, decrease their expected duration of unemployment, and increase their expected postunemployment wage. On the other hand, an increase in skill level will induce them to raise their reservation wage, which will increase the proportion of low-wage job offers they turn down and tend to increase both their expected duration of unemployment and their expected postunemployment wage. Thus, while unambiguously increasing expected postunemployment wages, an increase in skill levels has an ambiguous effect on the duration of unemployment. This final implication has direct bearing on how one should evaluate the effectiveness of government-sponsored training programs. One should *not* evaluate them on the basis of the initial post-program employment experience of program graduates; these individuals may rationally remain unemployed for a while, searching for jobs commensurate with their new skill levels. Rather, evaluations should be based on the longer run experiences of program graduates.[39]

NORMATIVE ISSUES IN UNEMPLOYMENT

Is unemployment a serious problem? Certainly some level of frictional unemployment is unavoidable in a dynamic world fraught with imperfect information. Moreover, as we have seen, the parameters of the UI system encourage both additional search unemployment and temporary layoff (cyclical and seasonal) unemployment. Nonetheless, when unemployment rises above its full-employment or natural level, resources are being wasted. More than 25 years ago Arthur Okun pointed out that every one-percentage-point decline in the aggregate unemployment rate was associated with a three-percentage-point increase in the output our society produces. That relationship appears to have held up through 1975, although since 1975 it is more in the range of a 2 percentage point increase in output. Even this latter number, however, suggests the great costs our society bears from excessively high rates of unemployment.[40] Thus, while it is unlikely that zero unemployment would be an optimal rate, policies to reduce cyclical unemployment (in a noninflationary manner) are clearly desirable. Improving the functioning of labor markets would also reduce frictional and structural unemployment; however, the benefits of reduced unemployment must be weighed against the costs generated by the policies designed to accomplish this objective in each case.

In addition to concern over the cost of unemployment, society should also be concerned about the distribution of unemployment across age/race/sex groups. As Table 15.3 indicated, the incidence of unemployment is higher among females than males, among nonwhites than whites, and among teens than nonteens. We have traced the labor-market flows that are associated with these differentials. White female adult unemployment rates are high because of proportionately large flows of women from employment to out-of-labor-force status, which suggests that some of their higher labor turnover (and unemployment) may be voluntary in nature. In contrast, the major cause of high nonwhite adult male unemployment rates is the high probability of members of that group leaving or losing their jobs to become unemployed; the fact that they remain attached to the labor force sug-

---

[39] An additional reason for doing this is that program effects may depreciate over time. For example, after completion of a training program, unemployed workers may be able to find a job. However, if they lose that job, the program may have no further positive effect on them. In this case, the short-run effects of a program might exceed its long-run effects. Knowledge of how long program effects last is clearly important.

[40] Arthur Okun, "Potential GNP: Its Measurement and Significance," reprinted in Arthur Okun, ed., *The Political Economy of Prosperity* (Washington, D.C.: Brookings Institute, 1970). Recent evidence suggests that the relationship is more in the range of 2.2 to 1. See Robert J. Gordon and Robert E. Hall, "Arthur M. Okun 1928–1980," *Brookings Papers on Economic Activity,* 1980–1, pp. 1–5.

gests that their unemployment problem is serious and that the case for government intervention is strong.

What about the high teenage unemployment rates, especially those of non-white teens? Is the high unemployment rate for teens a serious problem that poli-cymakers should address? Some doubt the seriousness of the problem, pointing out that unemployment rates decline rapidly as youths reach their early twenties (see Table 15.3). To these doubters, high teenage unemployment rates are symp-tomatic of the process of job turnover and search that occurs when new entrants to the labor force seek to acquire information about labor markets and their own productive ability. Moreover, proponents of this view could note that approxi-mately 50 percent of the unemployed 16 to 19 year olds and 90 percent of the unemployed 16 to 17 year olds are enrolled in school.[41] Of these in-school un-employed youths, 50 percent were searching only for temporary jobs in 1976 and only 10 percent had become unemployed by losing their previous job.[42] Finally, they could cite evidence that teenage unemployment is not always associated with low family incomes. For example, data from the *1976 Survey of Income and Education,* a large national survey conducted by the Census Bureau, indicate that less than 26 percent of unemployed youths age 16 to 24 came from families whose family income fell below the poverty line.[43]

Of course, these arguments neglect a number of important points. First, a substantial body of evidence indicates that youth unemployment is highly corre-lated with youth criminal activity; thus there are costs to society, as well as to the youths, of youth unemployment. Second, much youth unemployment is concen-trated among nonwhite youths—and the distributional implications of this fact may be unacceptable to society, especially given the higher correlation between youth unemployment and poverty that exists for nonwhites. Finally, it is possible that the effects of youth unemployment may be long lasting and that unemployed teenagers may face reduced long-run earnings and employment prospects, as com-pared to teenagers who do not suffer unemployment. Although unemployment rates do decline rapidly with age for younger adults, individuals who suffered unemployment as teenagers might be "scarred" in the sense of having relatively higher probabilities of adult unemployment or commanding relatively lower adult wage rates.

Somewhat surprisingly, until recently there was no evidence on the long-run effects of teenage unemployment. Indeed, as late as 1976 Richard Freeman as-serted that

---

[41]See Arvil Adams and Garth Mangum, *The Lingering Crisis of Youth Unemployment* (Kalamazoo, Mich.: W.E. Upjohn Institute, 1978), chap. 3.

[42]Adams and Mangum, *The Lingering Crisis of Youth Unemployment.*

[43]*U.S. Congressional Budget Office, Youth Unemployment: The Outlook and Some Policy Strategies* (Washington, D.C.: U.S. Government Printing Office, April 1978), Appendix Table A–5. It is worth noting, however, that this table also indicates that youth unemployment rates decline with family income and that more than 45 percent of unemployed *nonwhite* youths come from families with family incomes below the poverty line. Put another way, youth employment is much more highly correlated with poverty for nonwhites than it is for whites.

there is no evidence that having considerable unemployment and related poor work experience at a young age "scars" a person for life. Teenage unemployment *may* have deleterious effects on work attitudes, investment in job skills, and lifetime income, and related labor market experiences, but this has *not* been documented. Teenage unemployment may be purely a transitional problem without long-term consequences.[44]

Since 1976, however, four studies using data on younger males and standard statistical methods have addressed this issue.[45] These studies do *not* all 1. use data from a common time period, 2. use the same sample restrictions (out-of-school youths or all youths), 3. focus on the same outcome variable (earnings or unemployment), or 4. use the same research methodology (simple correlation or multiple-regression analysis). Nonetheless the evidence does appear to indicate that unemployment of *nonwhite* male teens is associated, on average, with long-run adverse labor-market effects. However, the evidence on persistence effects of white male teenage unemployment is less clear. Thus, these studies at first glance appear to support public concern, at least for nonwhites, about the long-run effects of teenage unemployment.

Unfortunately, these studies did *not* identify whether it is the experience of unemployment *per se* or some unobserved characteristics of the teenage unemployed that lead to subsequent adverse labor-market outcomes. If the experience of unemployment is responsible, then policies to reduce teenage unemployment may have long run positive effects. However, if unobservable characteristics are responsible—for example, if teens who become unemployed are less motivated or able, other things equal, than those who find employment—then it is less clear that policies to reduce teenage unemployment will have long-lasting effects. Other studies that have attempted to identify whether the experience of unemployment *per se* matters in the long run have yielded ambiguous results—such as the finding that an early employment experience has a positive effect on later employment for female teens but very little effect for male teens.[46] Thus, our knowledge about whether teenage unemployment has long-run scarring effects is still quite imprecise.

[44]Richard Freeman, "Teenage Unemployment: Can Reallocating Resources Help?" in U.S. Congressional Budget Office, *The Teenage Unemployment Problem: What Are the Options?* (Washington, D.C.: U.S. Government Printing Office, 1976).

[45]See Wayne Stevenson, "The Relationship Between Early Work Experience and Future Employability," in Adams and Mangum, *The Lingering Crisis of Youth Unemployment;* Paul Osterman, "Race Differentials in Male Youth Unemployment" in U.S. Department of Labor, *Conference Report on Youth Unemployment: Its Measurement and Meaning* (Washington, D.C.: U.S. Government Printing Office, 1978); Joseph Antos and Wesley Mellow, "The Youth Labor Market: A Dynamic Overview" (Washington, D.C.: Bureau of Labor Statistics, February 1978); and Brian Becker and Stephen Hills, "Teenage Unemployment: Some Evidence on the Long-Run Effects on Wages" *Journal of Human Resources* 15 (Summer 1980): 354–72.

[46]David Ellwood, "Teenage Unemployment: Permanent Scars or Temporary Blemishes"; Mary Corcoran, "The Employment, Wage, and Fertility Consequences of Teenage Women's Nonemployment"; and Robert Meyer and David Wise, "High School Preparation and Early Labor Force Experience"; all presented at the National Bureau of Economic Research (NBER) Conference on Youth Unemployment in May 1979.

REVIEW QUESTIONS

1. Labor economists offer many reasons for unemployment. In your judgment, what are the principal explanations for today's unemployment? Justify your answer.
2. A presidential hopeful is campaigning to raise unemployment-compensation benefits and lower the full-employment target from 4 percent to 3.5 percent. Comment on the compatibility of these goals.
3. Government officials find it useful to measure the nation's "economic health." The unemployment rate is currently used as a major indicator of the relative strength of labor supply and demand. Do you think the unemployment rate is becoming more or less useful as an indicator of labor-market tightness? What other measures might serve this purpose better?
4. The unemployment rate is a stock concept (something like the amount of water in a lake at a given time). The level of unemployment goes up or down as the *flows* into unemployment exceed or are slower than the flows out of unemployment. Is it important for policy purposes to accurately measure the *flows* into and out of unemployment, or is knowing the *level* of unemployment enough for most purposes? Justify your answer.
5. Is the following question true, false, or uncertain? "Increasing the level of unemployment-insurance benefits will prolong the average length of spells of unemployment. Hence a policy of raising UI benefit levels is not socially desirable." Explain your answer.

SELECTED READINGS

Bailey, Martin. "Wages and Employment Under Uncertain Demand." *Review of Economic Studies* 41 (January 1974): 37–50.

Clark, Kim B. and Lawrence Summers. "Labor Market Dynamics and Unemployment: A Reconsideration." *Brookings Papers on Economic Activity,* 1979–1, pp. 13–60.

Feldstein, Martin. "The Economics of the New Unemployment." *Public Interest* 33 (Fall 1973): 3–42.

Feldstein, Martin. "The Importance of Temporary Layoffs: An Empirical Analysis." *Brookings Papers on Economic Activity,* 1975–3, pp. 725–44.

Hamermesh, Daniel S. *Jobless Pay and the Economy.* Baltimore: Johns Hopkins University Press, 1977.

Marston, Steven. "Employment Instability and High Unemployment Rates." *Brookings Papers on Economic Activity,* 1976–1, pp. 169–203.

National Commission on Employment and Unemployment Statistics. *Counting the Labor Force.* Washington, D.C.: Government Printing Office, 1979.

The Relationship Between the Unemployment Rate and Labor-Market Flows

The objective of this appendix is to formally derive equation (15.2) on page 427, which relates a group's unemployment rate (**u**) to the proportions of its members that move between employment, unemployment, and not-in-the-labor-force status each month. As in equation (15.2), let P_{ij} denote the proportion of individuals in a group in labor-market state i that move to labor market state j during the period, where the different states are employed *(e)*, unemployed *(u)*, and not in the labor force *(n)*. The numbers of people in each of these states at the start of a period are denoted by E, U, and N, respectively.

Labor-market equilibrium is defined as a situation in which the number of employed individuals and the number of unemployed individuals both remain constant over time. In this case, the number of unemployed people at the start of a period who obtain jobs plus the number of people out of the labor force at the start of a period who obtain jobs is just equal to the number of people employed at the start of the period who become unemployed or drop out of the labor force during the period. That is,

$$P_{ue}U + P_{ne}N = (P_{eu} + P_{en})E \tag{15A.1}$$

$$\underset{\text{who become employed}}{\text{The number}} = \underset{\text{who leave employment}}{\text{the number}}$$

Similarly, in equilibrium the number of people who become unemployed during the period (because of losing or leaving their previous jobs or unsuccessfully entering the labor force) just equals the number who leave unemployment (either because they found a job or because they left the labor force).

'This appendix is based on Steven T. Marston, ''Employment Instability and High Unemployment Rates,'' *Brookings Papers on Economic Activity*, 1976–1, pp. 169–203.

$$P_{eu}E + P_{nu}N = (P_{ue} + P_{un})U \tag{15A.2}$$

$$\frac{\text{The number}}{\text{who become unemployed}} = \frac{\text{the number}}{\text{who leave unemployment}}$$

Multiplying (15A.1) by P_{nu} and (15A.2) by P_{ne} and then subtracting (15A.2) from (15A.1), one obtains:

$$P_{ue}P_{nu}U - P_{eu}P_{ne}E = (P_{eu} + P_{en})P_{nu}E - (P_{ue} + P_{un})P_{ne}U \tag{15A.3}$$

or

$$[P_{ue}P_{nu} + P_{ne}(P_{ue} + P_{un})]U = [P_{eu}P_{ne} + P_{nu}(P_{eu} + P_{en})]E \tag{15A.4}$$

Hence, in equilibrium the numbers of unemployed and employed individuals—solving from equation (15A.4)—are related by

$$E = U\frac{[P_{ue}P_{nu} + P_{ne}(P_{ue} + P_{un})]}{[P_{eu}P_{ne} + P_{nu}(P_{eu} + P_{en})]} \tag{15A.5}$$

$$= U\frac{[(P_{ne} + P_{nu})P_{ue} + P_{ne}P_{un}]}{[(P_{ne} + P_{nu})P_{eu} + P_{nu}P_{en}]}$$

The unemployment rate is now defined as the number of unemployed individuals divided by the sum of the unemployed and the employed:

$$\mathbf{u} = \frac{U}{(U + E)} \tag{15A.6}$$

Substituting (15A.5) into (15A.6) and simplifying yields:

$$\mathbf{u} = \frac{1}{1 + \left[\dfrac{(P_{ne} + P_{nu})P_{ue} + (P_{ne})(P_{un})}{(P_{ne} + P_{nu})P_{eu} + (P_{nu})(P_{en})}\right]}, \tag{15A.7}$$

which is, in fact, equation (15.2). Thus, a group's unemployment rate depends upon the flow of its members between all three labor-market states.

16

Inflation and Unemployment

INTRODUCTION

Throughout most of the 1970s the United States was faced with relatively high rates of wage and price *inflation* (that is, with relatively rapid and generally pervasive increases in wages and prices). Further, these increases were taking place in the context of rather high unemployment rates, so that the country seemed to suffer the consequences of both inflation *and* unemployment at the same time. Simultaneously high rates of inflation and unemployment challenged the long-held belief that inflation would diminish if unemployment rose—a belief that seemed to have held out hope that government fiscal or monetary policies could be skillfully used to manuever the economy to tolerable levels of both inflation and unemployment.

The causes and consequences of inflation—and the fiscal and monetary policies to remedy it—are beyond the scope of labor economics. Our intent in this chapter is to analyze the relationship between inflation and unemployment so that the connections between what happens in the labor market and what happens to prices in general are more clearly understood. Moreover, because our focus is on the labor market, we will emphasize the price of labor—the wage rate—when discussing the issue of inflation.

Measuring Wage Inflation

The overall rate of *wage inflation* in the economy is the annual percentage rate of increase in some composite measure of hourly earnings in the economy. The construction of such an index is a considerable task because *average* hourly earnings can change, even if the wage scales for every individual *job* remain constant. For example, if there is a shift in the distribution of employment towards high-wage industries (such as construction) and away from low-wage industries (such as retail trade), average hourly earnings will increase. Similarly, if there is a shift towards increased usage of highly paid skilled workers and away from lower paid

TABLE 16.1 Unemployment Rate and Percentage Change in Earnings and
Prices in the United States

Year	Percent Change in Adjusted Hourly Earnings of Nonsupervisory Workers in the Private Nonagricultural Sector	Unemployment Rate	Percent Change in the GNP Deflator
1960	3.4	5.5	1.7
1961	3.1	6.7	0.9
1962	3.3	5.5	1.9
1963	2.9	5.7	1.5
1964	2.7	5.2	1.6
1965	3.4	4.5	2.2
1966	4.5	3.8	3.3
1967	4.9	3.8	3.0
1968	6.2	3.6	4.5
1969	6.6	3.5	5.1
1970	6.6	4.9	5.3
1971	7.0	5.9	5.1
1972	6.4	5.6	4.1
1973	6.2	4.9	5.7
1974	7.9	5.6	9.3
1975	8.3	8.5	9.7
1976	7.3	7.7	5.1
1977	7.5	7.0	5.9
1978	8.2	6.0	7.3
1979	7.9	5.8	8.7

SOURCE: *1980 Economic Report of the President* (Washington, D.C.: U.S. Government Printing Office, 1980), Tables B3, B29, and B35.

unskilled workers, average hourly earnings will increase. To take another example, if the age distribution of the work force shifts towards relatively fewer lower-paid new entrants, average hourly earnings will increase. Finally, if more overtime hours for which premium pay is received are worked relative to straight time hours, average hourly earnings will again increase, other things equal.[1]

The problem involved in all of these examples is that average hourly earnings in the economy $(\overline{W})$ is a weighted average of the earnings of individuals in each industry/occupation/experience group (W_i). The weight assigned to each group's earnings (f_i) depends upon the fraction of all hours worked in the economy by individuals in the group and the fraction of hours worked by the group for which premium pay is received. Changes in average hourly earnings may therefore reflect changes in the weights as well as changes in the wage scales of each group.

---

[1] The regulated-industry example first discussed in Chapter 9 illustrated the importance of these factors. As part of the regulatory case, the rate of wage inflation had to be computed for a utility's employees over the August 1973 to August 1976 period. The cumulative percentage wage increase in union wage scales called for in the company's union contracts was 32.1 percent; however, the increase in average hourly earnings was 42.1 percent. The difference in this example was primarily due to the changing skill mix and age distributions of the utility's employees. For details, see Ronald Ehrenberg, *The Regulatory Process and Labor Earnings* (New York: Academic Press, 1979), chap. 2.

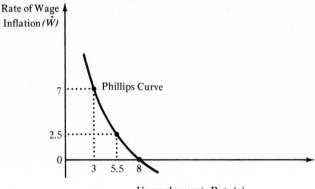

FIGURE 16.1   **"Phillips Curve" Showing the Trade-off Between Wage Inflation and Unemployment for 1960**

SOURCE: Adapted from Paul A. Samuelson and Robert M. Solow, "Our Menu of Policy Choices," *The Battle Against Inflation,* ed. Arthur M. Okun (New York: W. W. Norton, 1965), p. 74.

Focusing simply on the growth of average hourly earnings, then, may give one a misleading impression of what is happening to wage scales for particular jobs.[2]

To partially take the above problem into account, government statisticians have constructed an index of adjusted average hourly earnings for nonsupervisory workers in the private nonagricultural sector. This index, which controls for changes in the industrial composition of employment and changes in overtime hours in manufacturing, is one of the most comprehensive measures of wage changes that is available.[3] As Table 16.1 indicates, over the decades of the 1960s and 1970s, this index increased at annual percentage rates of roughly 3 to 8 percent, with the annual percentage increase apparently increasing over time.

---

[2]To see this point more clearly, suppose that there are n different industry/occupation/experience groups in the economy. Then average hourly earnings of all workers are given by

$$\dot{\overline{W}} = \sum_{i=1}^{n} W_i f_i$$

and the percentage change in average hourly earnings is *approximately* equal to

$$\dot{\overline{W}} \approx \sum_{i=1}^{n} \dot{W}_i f_i + \sum_{i=1}^{n} W_i \dot{f}_i + \sum_{i=1}^{n} \dot{W}_i \dot{f}_i,$$

where percentage change is indicated by a dot over a variable. Even if all wage rates were constant ($\dot{W}_i$ equal to zero for all i), average hourly earnings could still change if the weights changed, for in this case

$$\dot{\overline{W}} = \sum_{i=1}^{n} W_i \dot{f}_i.$$

[3]The index only partially controls for the problem of distinguishing between changes in wage scales and changes in the composition of employment because it makes no adjustment for changes in the *occupational* or *age* distributions of the work force.

The Inflation/Unemployment Trade-off

For many years economists believed that stable negative relationships, or *trade-off curves,* existed between the rates of wage (and price) inflation, on the one hand, and the overall unemployment rate in the economy, on the other. That is, higher levels of unemployment were thought to be associated with lower rates of wage and price inflation, and vice versa. The relationship between unemployment and wage inflation was dubbed the *Phillips Curve* after the noted economist who was an early observer of its existence.[4] The Phillips Curve was thought to provide a range of feasible options for policymakers—through the appropriate use of monetary or fiscal policy they could choose any unemployment/inflation combination along the curve. For example, a paper in 1959 by two well-known economists claimed that the country could choose among the following alternatives (illustrated in Figure 16.1): 8 percent unemployment and zero wage inflation, 5–6 percent unemployment and 2–3 percent wage inflation, and 3 percent unemployment and 7 percent wage inflation.[5]

Unfortunately, the well-defined, stable set of choices once thought to exist appears to have vanished. Table 16.1 contains data on both the unemployment rate and wage inflation during the 1960s and 1970s. These data indicate that during the 1960s a negative association did appear to exist between the unemployment rate and the rate of wage inflation. Indeed the steady tightening of labor markets and decreasing unemployment rates of the late 1960s were associated with increasing rates of wage inflation. However, during the 1970s the relationship appears, at first glance, to have broken down; one often observes a simultaneous increase in the rate of unemployment and the rate of wage inflation during that decade. The result is that while an unemployment rate of 5.5 percent was associated with a wage-inflation rate of 3.3 to 3.4 percent in the 1960s, an almost identical unemployment rate of 5.6 percent was associated with wage-inflation rates of 6.4 to 7.9 percent during the 1970s. These data tend to suggest that the belief in a stable negative trade-off between inflation and unemployment is unwarranted.

An alternative interpretation of these data, however, is that while a trade-off between the rates of inflation and unemployment exists at a *point in time,* the *position* of the trade-off curve is determined by a number of other factors that can change over time. The net effect of these other factors in recent years, it can be argued, has been to shift the trade-off curve shown in Figure 16.1 *upward and to the right.* Thus, the trade-off society faces in the early 1980s lies everywhere above the one that may have prevailed during the 1970s, which in turn was itself higher than the curve that prevailed during the 1960s (see Figure 16.2). Put another way, the argument underlying Figure 16.2 is that progressively higher rates of wage inflation ($\dot{W}_0$, $\dot{W}_1$, and $\dot{W}_2$) have become associated over time with any given level of unemployment ($\mathbf{u}_0$ in Figure 16.2). Conversely, progressively higher unemployment rates ($\mathbf{u}_0$, $\mathbf{u}_1$, $\mathbf{u}_2$) have become associated with any given

[4] See A. W. Phillips, "The Relation Between Unemployment and the Rates of Change of Money Wage Rates in the United Kingdom, 1862–1957," *Economica* 25 (November 1958): 283–99.

[5] Paul A. Samuelson and Robert M. Solow, "Our Menu of Policy Choices," in *The Battle Against Unemployment,* ed. Arthur M. Okun (New York: W. W. Norton, 1965), pp. 71–76.

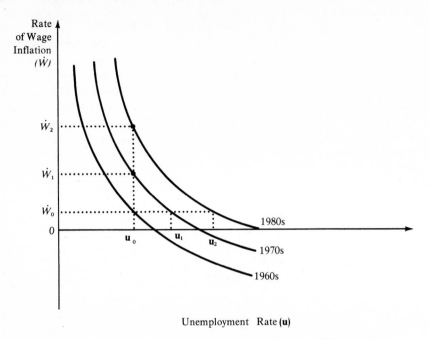

FIGURE 16.2   The Changing Trade-off Between the Rate of Wage Inflation
and the Level of the Unemployment Rate

level of wage inflation ($\dot{W}_0$). Indeed some economists suggest that between 1960 and 1980, the trade-off may have shifted to the right by as much as 3 percentage points.[6] It is also possible that the Phillips curve has become much flatter over recent years, so that the decrease in wage inflation accompanying a one-percentage-point increase in the unemployment rate is now smaller than it once was. This growing downward rigidity of wages has caused a loss of effectiveness in the traditional macroeconomic policies to combat inflation—and has increased the importance of alternative labor-market policies.

The next section presents a simple conceptual model that explains why the trade-off between wage inflation and unemployment may exist and discusses the forces that may have caused the trade-off to shift out over time. This model provides a framework that can be used to discuss the various labor-market policies that might enable policymakers to shift the trade-off curve in a more favorable direction.

This chapter will also discuss the relationship between wage and price behavior and consider the conditions under which a stable long-run trade-off between *price* inflation and unemployment will occur. Although *at a point in time* a trade-off may exist between the rate of *wage* inflation and the unemployment rate, it does not necessarily follow that *in the long run* a stable trade-off exists between the rate of *price* inflation and the unemployment rate. Indeed, one school of thought argues that this long-run trade-off curve is vertical and that attempts to

---

[6]See, for example, James Tobin, "Stabilization Policy Ten Years After," *Brookings Papers on Economic Activity*, 1980–1, 19–72.

keep the unemployment rate artificially low will lead to ever accelerating rates of inflation.[7]

The models discussed early in the chapter are models in which the direction of causation runs from the unemployment rate to the inflation rate. That is, changes in the unemployment rate are thought to cause changes in the rate of price or wage inflation. Later in the chapter, we will consider the possibility that it is the inflation rate that may influence the unemployment rate, not vice versa. We will return to the model of search unemployment presented in Chapter 15 and show that it is only *unexpected* or *unanticipated* inflation that influences the unemployment rate; fully anticipated inflation has no effect on unemployment. This model has obvious implications for whether government policies that increase inflation will have any payoff in terms of reduced unemployment.

This chapter will also consider the role of unions and the collective-bargaining process. It will explore why changing institutional arrangements—in particular the spread of *multiyear agreements* with *cost-of-living escalator clauses*—may have been partially responsible for the growing insensitivity of inflation to the unemployment rate.

The final section of the chapter returns to the central issue of how government policies might reduce the rate of inflation associated with any given level of unemployment. This section focuses on the various *incomes policies* that have been pursued in the United States since 1960—policies in which the government has tried directly to influence wages and prices by specifying "desired wage and price behavior," sometimes with enforcement mechanisms tied to the program (these include the wage-price guideposts of the Kennedy-Johnson years, the wage-price freeze and "Phase II" economic policies under the Nixon Administration, and the Carter voluntary anti-inflation guidelines). After discussing the available evidence on the effectiveness of these programs, we will analyze the proposals for new innovative types of *tax-based incomes policies* that were proposed during the 1970s.[8]

THE WAGE INFLATION/UNEMPLOYMENT TRADE-OFF

The Basic Model

Figure 16.3 represents a competitive labor market.[9] For simplicity we will *initially* take product prices as fixed so that the demand and supply curves can be drawn in terms of the money wage *(W)* rather than the real wage. In this labor market, the equilibrium wage is W_0, and the equilibrium employment level is E_0. We know from earlier chapters that whenever the wage is above W_0 it will fall, and that whenever it is below W_0 it will rise, to restore equilibrium.

---

[7]See for example, Milton Friedman, "The Role of Monetary Policy," *American Economic Review* 58 (March 1968): 1–17.

[8]See for example, Henry Wallich and Sidney Weintraub, "A Tax-Based Incomes Policy," *Journal of Economic Issues* 5 (June 1971):1–19 and Arthur Okun, "The Great Stagflation Swamp," *Challenge* 20 (November/December 1977): 6–13.

[9]This section initially draws heavily on Richard Lipsey, "The Relation Between Unemployment and the Rate of Change in Money Wage Rates in the United Kingdom, 1862–1957: A Further Analysis," *Economica* 27 (February 1960): 1–31.

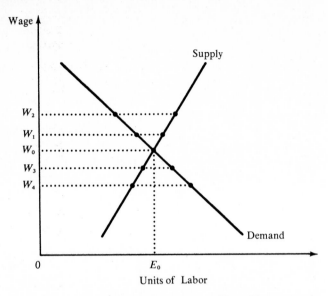

**FIGURE 16.3   The Relationship Between Wage Changes and
the Excess Demand for Labor:
Prices Held Constant**

How rapidly will the wage rate change when it is away from its equilibrium value? It seems reasonable to assume that the speed at which the wage rate changes is related to the extent to which the labor market is in disequilibrium, as measured by the excess demand for labor. Thus, although the wage rate will be increasing whenever the wage rate is below W_0 and a positive excess demand for labor exists, it is likely to be increasing more rapidly when it is at W_4 in Figure 16.3 than when it is at W_3. Similarly, while the wage rate will be falling whenever the wage rate is above W_0 and an excess supply (or negative excess demand) for labor exists, it is likely to be falling more rapidly when the wage rate is at W_2 than when it is at W_1.

The simplest possible way to formalize this idea is to assume that the percentage rate of change of wages $(\dot{W})$ is proportional to the excess demand for labor (X). Because a given *absolute* difference between demand and supply $(D - S = 1,000$, say) would indicate a greater degree of disequilibrium if 10,000 people were seeking work than if 100,000 were in the market, we will measure excess demand as $(D - S)/S$—so that:

$$\dot{W} = \alpha X = \alpha[(D - S)/S]. \tag{16.1}$$

This relationship is depicted in panel (a) of Figure 16.4; the larger α is the faster wages adjust to disequilibrium. Note that when supply exceeds demand, X—and hence $\dot{W}$—will be negative. (One could, of course, allow the responses to be nonsymmetric to excess demands and excess supplies. For example, if wages are *sticky* in a downward direction, α would be smaller—and the curve

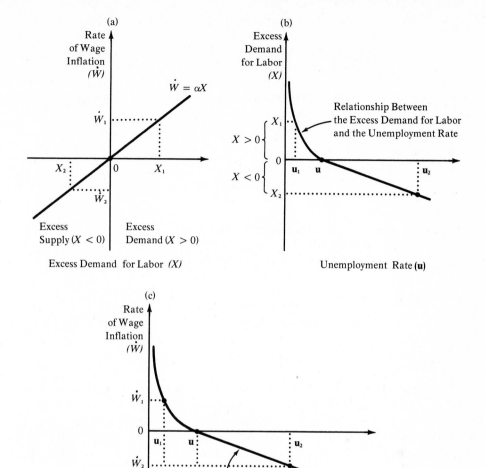

FIGURE 16.4 Derivation of the Trade-off Between the Rate of Wage Inflation and the Unemployment Rate

flatter—in the region of excess supply that lies to the left of the vertical axis. However, for expository convenience we will ignore this complication here.)

Unfortunately, because the excess demand for labor is usually not observable, it is necessary to replace it with an observable variable—such as the unemployment rate—when empirically analyzing wage changes. What is the relationship between the excess demand for labor and the unemployment rate $(\mathbf{u})$? We know from Chapter 15 that some unemployment exists even when labor markets are in balance with the overall demand for labor just equal to the overall supply $(X=0)$. This frictional unemployment occurs because normal job turnover and movements of people in and out of the labor market take place in circumstances where information is imperfect and job matching takes time. In panel (b) of Figure 16.4, **u** is the unemployment rate that exists when the excess demand for labor is zero; this is often referred to in the economics literature as the *natural* or *full-employment rate* of unemployment (see Chapter 15).

As the excess demand for labor increases and labor markets become tighter, the unemployment rate will fall. Although the time it takes to make job matches can be reduced, it will probably take some time to fill job vacancies. As a result, the unemployment rate is not likely to fall below some positive level, and as that level is approached, any increases in excess demand will call forth progressively smaller reductions in the unemployment rate. The result is a nonlinear relationship between the unemployment rate and the excess demand for labor, as drawn in the $X > 0$ region of panel (b). In contrast, in the region of excess supply (below the horizontal axis (where $X < 0$), increases in excess supply may well lead to proportional increases in the unemployment rate. Thus, the relationship between the unemployment rate and the excess demand for labor is perhaps linear in the region of excess supply, as illustrated in panel (b) of Figure 16.4.

The two relationships shown in panels (a) and (b)—the wage inflation/excess demand relationship and the unemployment rate/excess demand relationship, contain all the information that is required to derive the wage inflation/unemployment trade-off curve shown in panel (c). Refer in Figure 16.4 to the point where the excess demand for labor is zero. From panel (a), we know the rate of wage inflation is zero, and, from panel (b), we know that the unemployment rate is **u**. Thus, one point on our wage inflation/unemployment trade-off curve in panel (c) is $(0,\mathbf{u})$. When the excess demand for labor is X_1, wage inflation is $\dot{W}_1$, in (a), and the unemployment rate is $\mathbf{u}_1$, in (b). When the excess supply of labor is X_2, the wage inflation rate is $\dot{W}_2$, in (a), and the unemployment rate is $\mathbf{u}_2$, in (b). Thus, $(\dot{W}_1,\mathbf{u}_1)$ and $(\dot{W}_2,\mathbf{u}_2)$ are two additional points on the inflation/unemployment trade-off curve in panel (c). Repeating the argument for all possible values of the excess demand for labor leads one to trace out the entire trade-off curve in panel(c) of Figure 16.4.

In the context of this simple labor-market model, the trade-off between the rate of wage inflation and the unemployment rate arises from the postulated responsiveness of wages to the excess demand for labor. However, there are numerous forces that affect the *position* of the curve that traces out the aggregate relationship between the unemployment rate and the rate of wage inflation. Three of these forces are 1. the current and expected rates of price inflation, 2. the age/sex distribution of the labor force, and 3. the dispersion of unemployment rates across markets.

Forces Affecting the Wage Inflation/Unemployment Trade-Off

Price inflation.   So far we have assumed the price level to be fixed. However, current and expected future rates of price inflation clearly influence the rate of *money* wage inflation associated with any given level of excess demand for labor. Since both the demand and supply curves of labor are functions of the *real* wage rate, an increase in the *price* level requires a proportional increase in the *money* wage rate simply to keep the real wage and the excess demand for labor constant.

The relationship between wage changes and the excess demand for labor described in Figures 16.3 and 16.4 actually refers to changes in the real wage (prices were assumed fixed while wages changed). Hence, the effect of price inflation is to *increase* the rate of money-wage inflation associated with any given level of the excess demand for labor.

Our discussion so far has assumed that labor markets are competitive and that all real wages are renegotiated continuously as labor-market conditions change. Later in the chapter we will introduce several institutional features of the collective-bargaining process in the United States in our discussion. Here, we will consider how the introduction of one such feature—contracts that are negotiated only periodically—affects the analysis. From employees' perspectives, past price changes may influence wage demands during contract negotiations, because they signify that real wages are below the level employees expected *if* such price changes were not fully anticipated at the time of the previous contract negotiations. Expected future price changes may also matter, because they translate money-wage changes into expected real-wage changes. Similarly, from employers' perspectives, past and expected future price changes may affect their willingness to increase wages, as increases in output prices, *ceteris paribus,* reduce real wages and hence employers' costs of doing business.

Unambiguously then, higher expected price changes should lead to higher wage changes in a world where wages are adjusted only periodically. It is unclear, however, whether an extra 1 percent increase in expected price inflation will lead to an extra 1 percent increase in money wages; this depends, among other things, on the relative bargaining power of employees and employers. Let us assume that a 1 percent increase in the expected rate of price inflation $(\dot{P}^e)$ shifts the rate of money-wage inflation associated with a given excess demand for labor up by γ percent, where γ may be less than one.[10] That is,

$$\dot{W} = \alpha X + \gamma \dot{P}^e \qquad\qquad 0 \leq \gamma \leq 1. \qquad (16.2)$$

Equation (16.2) is illustrated by Figure 16.5. If the upward shift in the relationship between $\dot{W}$ and X in Figure 16.5 is translated back to panel (a) of Figure 16.4, and its implications for panel (c) are traced through panel (b), it should become clear that increases in the expected rate of price inflation cause the whole wage inflation/unemployment trade-off curve in panel (c) to shift up.[11]

Age/sex composition of the labor force.   Chapter 15 noted that females tend to have higher unemployment rates than males and that teenagers tend to have higher unemployment rates than adults. The aggregate unemployment rate associated with any given degree of labor-market *tightness*—or excess demand for labor—is simply the weighted average of the unemployment rates for the various age/sex groups, with the weights being the share of the group in the overall labor force.

---

[10] For simplicity, we have focused only on expected price inflation and ignored past price inflation per se here. We also have restricted γ to be no greater than one; this need not always be the case.

[11] Of course, since wages are a substantial fraction of production costs, increases in the rate of wage inflation should lead, other things equal, to increases in the rate of price inflation. This interdependency will be discussed later in the chapter.

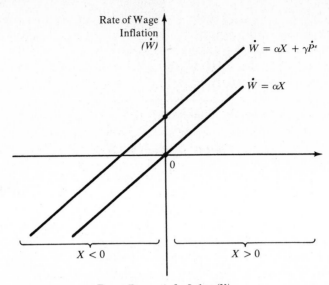

**FIGURE 16.5   Price Inflation Shifts Up the Wage-
Inflation/Excess-Demand-for-Labor Relationship**

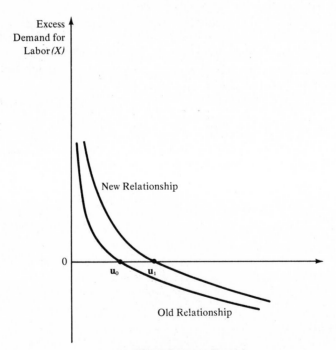

**FIGURE 16.6   Changing Age/Sex Composition of the Labor
Force Shifts Up the Excess-Demand-
for-Labor/Unemployment-Rate Relationship**

During the 1960s and 1970s the shares of teenagers and females in the labor force increased because of the growing share of teenagers in the population and increasing female labor-force-participation rates. Since these groups tend to have higher than average unemployment rates, the overall unemployment rate associated with any level of the excess demand for labor also increased, as illustrated in Figure 16.6.[12]

An increase in the level of unemployment associated with each level of the excess demand for labor implies, other things equal, that a higher unemployment rate will be associated with each rate of wage inflation. Put another way, the changing age/sex composition of the labor force has also caused the wage inflation/unemployment trade-off curve to shift up. At any level of the aggregate unemployment rate, the rate of wage inflation is higher than before. Furthermore, as indicated in Figure 16.6 (and in Chapter 15), the full-employment unemployment rate also has increased—from u_0 to u_1 in Figure 16.6.

The dispersion of unemployment rates. The model of the wage inflation/unemployment trade-off that we have presented applies to a *single* labor market.[13] To obtain the wage inflation/unemployment trade-off for the *economy,* one must aggregate all of the individual labor-market relationships. If the unemployment rate differs across labor markets, the aggregate rate of wage inflation associated with any given level of aggregate unemployment may be higher than it would be if the unemployment rate were the same in all markets.

To see why this is true, suppose there were only two labor markets in the whole economy, that they were identical in size, and that the same wage inflation/unemployment trade-off curve (represented by T_0 in Figure 16.7) existed in both. Given any overall level of unemployment, the aggregate rate of wage inflation is approximately equal to the average of the rates of wage inflation in the two markets.[14] If initially the unemployment rate were **u** in *each* market, the rate of wage inflation in each would be zero and the overall rate of wage inflation would also be zero.

Suppose now that the unemployment rate increases to **u** + ε in the first market and falls to **u** − ε in the second market, where ε is any positive number. Since the two markets are equal in size the overall unemployment rate will remain at **u.** However, wages will fall at the rate of $\dot{W}_H$ in the high-unemployment market and rise at the rate of $\dot{W}_L$ in the low-unemployment-rate market. As Figure 16.7 indicates, $\dot{W}_L$ is larger than $\dot{W}_H$ in absolute value, hence the average rate of wage inflation in the economy, $[(\dot{W}_H + \dot{W}_L)/2]$, is positive. The dispersion in unem-

---

[12]An early exposition of the importance of this factor is found in George Perry, "Changing Labor Markets and Inflation," *Brookings Papers on Economic Activity,* 1970–3, pp. 411–41.

[13]The role of geographic dispersion in unemployment rates was emphasized early by Lipsey and G. C. Archibald, "The Phillips Curve and the Distribution of Unemployment," *American Economic Review* 59 (May 1969): 124–34. The importance of dispersion of unemployment across age/sex groups was emphasized in George Perry, "Changing Labor Markets and Inflation," *Brookings Papers on Economic Activity,* 1970–3.

[14]We say "approximate" because once the unemployment rate differs between the two markets a slightly higher weight should be assigned to the low unemployment market that will have relatively more *employed* workers.

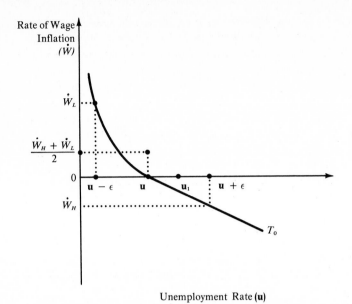

FIGURE 16.7   **Dispersion of Unemployment Rates Increase
the Rate of Wage Inflation Associated
with a Given Aggregate Unemployment Rate**

ployment rates has led to a higher overall rate of wage inflation. Indeed, increasing the dispersion in the unemployment rates (increasing ε) would lead to an even higher overall rate of wage inflation.

Why does this result occur? In our simple example it occurs because the relationship between the excess demand for labor and the unemployment rate is nonlinear to the left of the full-employment unemployment rate (as explained earlier in discussing Figure 16.4).[15] As a result, there is more upward pressure put on wages in the tight labor market by an ε-percentage-point *decline* in unemployment than there is downward pressure put on wages in the loose labor market by an ε-percentage-point *rise*. Thus, the average rate of wage inflation increases.

Figure 16.7 shows that an increase in the dispersion of unemployment rates will increase the aggregate rate of wage inflation (in this model) for any aggregate unemployment rate less than the full-employment rate (**u** in Figure 16.7). Since the unemployment/excess demand for labor relationship was assumed to be linear to the right of **u,** small increases in the dispersion of unemployment rates around an aggregate unemployment rate like **u₁** in Figure 16.7 will not necessarily lead to increases in the aggregate rate of wage inflation. However, if the dispersion is

---

[15]This nonlinearity is not necessary to derive the general result—nor is it necessary to have identical wage inflation/unemployment trade-off curves in the two markets. (On this see Archibald, ''The Phillips Curve and the Distribution of Unemployment.'') For example, if both curves are linear, as long as the wage inflation/excess demand for labor relationship is flatter in the market that has the higher unemployment rate, the same result will occur.

TABLE 16.2 **Female and Teenage
Shares of the Labor Force**

Year	Female Share	Teenage Share
1960	33.4	7.0
1965	35.2	7.9
1970	38.1	8.8
1975	39.9	9.5
1978	41.7	9.5

SOURCE: Based on *1979 Employment and Training Report
of the President* (Washington, D.C.: U.S. Government Printing Office, 1979), Table A3.

large enough that the nonlinear segment of T_0 is reached by the lower-unemployment market, then the aggregate rate of wage inflation will increase.

In sum, over a wide range of values of the unemployment rate, increases in the dispersion of unemployment rates across labor markets will increase the aggregate rate of wage inflation associated with the aggregate unemployment rate. Put another way, increases in the dispersion of unemployment rates can cause the aggregate wage inflation/unemployment trade-off curve to shift up. (While we have not yet defined precisely a *labor market* here, it is natural to think in terms of geographic markets. However, one could similarly analyze labor markets segmented by skill, age, sex, or race.)

Reasons for Shifts in the Trade-Off Curve Over Time

Have the three major factors discussed above been responsible for the upward shift of the short-run wage inflation/unemployment tradeoff throughout the 1960s and 1970s? First, as Table 16.1 indicates, the percentage rate of change in the gross national product (GNP) *implicit price deflator*—a broad measure of the prices of all goods produced in the economy—trended upwards over the period.[16] To the extent that past price changes affect expectations of *future* price changes, this trend should have shifted the trade-off curve out (as employees incorporated these expected price changes into their wage demands).

Second, as noted earlier in this chapter and in Chapter 15, during the 1960s and 1970s, there was an increase in the fraction of the labor force subject to higher than average unemployment rates. As Table 16.2 indicates, between 1960 and 1978 the share of teens in the labor force rose from 7.0 to 9.5 percent, and the share of females rose from 33.4 to 41.7 percent. Such demographic shifts alone have increased the overall rate of unemployment associated with any given level of wage inflation, perhaps by as much as 1 percentage point during the 1965-1980 period.[17]

---

[16]Another widely publicized price index is the Consumer Price Index (CPI), a measure of the cost of living for urban households that is published monthly by the Bureau of Labor Statistics. This index is in fact the one that is typically used to calculate cost-of-living increases due under union contracts with cost-of-living escalator clauses. Because the GNP deflator and CPI measure different things, year-to-year percentage changes in the two indices often differ. However, over longer periods of time they yield roughly the same picture about the upward trend in the inflation rate.

[17]James Tobin, "Stabilization Policy Ten Years After," *Brookings Papers on Economic Activity*, 1980-1, pp. 19-72.

Example 16.1
Wage Inflation and Unemployment
Around the World

The existence of a short-run trade-off between the rate of wage inflation and the unemployment rate is not unique to the United States. George
Perry sought to estimate the magnitude of this trade-off for nine industrialized nations during the early 1960s to mid 1970s period; some of his results are summarized in the table below. This table presents his estimates
of the percentage-point reduction in the rate of wage inflation that would
have occurred in each country in the first year after the country's unemployment rate was allowed to increase by 25 percent (*not* percentage
points). That is, if the unemployment rate in each country were increased
from its mean value during the period to a level that was 25 percent
higher, the table estimates how much lower the rate of wage inflation
would have been in the first year following the change.

While this table indicates that a short-run trade-off exists between the
rate of wage inflation and the level of the unemployment rate in all nine
countries, the marginal effects on wage inflation are strikingly different in
size. In the United States, the marginal effect of unemployment on wage
inflation—both in percentage-point terms and in relationship to the average level of wage inflation—is among the smallest listed. Determining why
this effect in the United States is so small relative to that in other countries
lies beyond the scope of this text, but these data reemphasize the fact
that aggregate demand policy alone will not be sufficient to reduce the
rate of wage inflation in the United States; alternative labor-market policies
will also be required.

Country	Percentage Point Change in the Rate of Wage Inflation in the First Year	Average Annual Rate of Wage Inflation 1961–1974 (percent)
Belgium	−1.7	11.9
Canada	−1.5	6.6
Germany	−1.0	10.6
Italy	−6.2	13.0
Japan	−0.6	16.6
Netherlands	−0.8	13.1
Sweden	−0.3	10.3
United Kingdom	−0.5	9.3
United States	−0.3	5.0

SOURCE: George L. Perry, "Determinants of Wage Inflation Around the World," *Brookings Papers on Economic Activity* 5 (1975–2), Tables 1 and 7.

SOURCE: George L. Perry, "Determinants of Wage Inflation Around the World," *Brookings Papers on Economic Activity* 5 (1975–2), pp. 403–35.

Finally, there is substantial evidence that the dispersion in the demographic distribution of unemployment rates has risen over the period. In particular, the unemployment rates of teenagers and white females have risen relative to the adult white male unemployment rate, and those for nonwhite teenagers have risen relative to those for white teenagers.[18] However, this increase in dispersion apparently has not had a substantial impact on the aggregate wage inflation/unemployment trade-off curve.[19]

Improving the Tradeoff

The analyses above suggest ways in which government policies can reduce the rate of wage inflation associated with any given unemployment rate:

1. They can attempt to reduce the rate of wage inflation associated with any level of excess demand for labor—or shift the curve in panel (a) of Figure 16.4 or in Figure 16.5 down.
2. They can attempt to reduce the unemployment rate associated with any given level of the excess demand for labor—or shift the curve in panel (b) of Figure 16.4 down.
3. Finally, they can attempt to reduce the geographic or demographic dispersion of unemployment rates.

A number of policy tools are potentially available to achieve each goal.

Turning to the wage-inflation/excess-demand-for-labor relationship first, one obvious objective here is to reduce the expected rate of growth of prices. Over long periods of time this goal is accomplished primarily by restrictive monetary or fiscal policy. In the short run, *incomes policies*—policies by which the government tries directly to control or influence wage and price levels by the specification of standards governing when prices or wages can be changed—may also have an effect. Examples here include wage-price guidelines, temporary wage-price freezes, and tax-based incomes policies. (The concluding section of this chapter will discuss incomes policies in some detail.)

The wage-inflation/excess-demand-for-labor relationship may also be shifted down through government policies that increase the competitiveness of labor markets and remove institutional barriers that reduce the downward flexibility of wages. Examples of such policies include eliminating or relaxing the Davis-Bacon Act (discussed in Chapter 12) and the deregulation of industries, such as airlines and trucking, that have been regulated in ways that tended to reduce competition. While such policies would undoubtedly reduce the rate of wage inflation, one must of course caution that these programs have other objectives, and the cost of giving up these objectives, if any, would have to be balanced against the gains from reduced wage inflation.

---

[18]Ronald Ehrenberg, ''The Demographic Structure of Unemployment Rates and Labor Market Transition Probabilities,'' *Research in Labor Economics* 3 (1980): 241–93.

[19]For econometric evidence on this point see Robert J. Gordon, ''Can the Inflation of the 1970s be Explained?'' *Brookings Papers on Economic Activity,* 1977–1, pp. 353–74.

With respect to reducing the rate of unemployment associated with any given level of excess demand for labor, the goal here would be to improve the efficiency of labor markets.[20] Many of the policies related to this goal were discussed in Chapter 15; they include improving job-market information, improving the "job matching services" offered by the U.S. Employment Service and private employment agencies, and increasing government-sponsored training programs to help reduce skill bottlenecks. One caution here, however, is that policies designed to reduce the unemployment rate may actually serve to increase it. For example, if potential job leavers—workers with some dissatisfaction with their jobs—knew that the government was actively pursuing a policy to reduce the length of time unemployed workers spent out of work, this knowledge might increase the probability that these workers would quit their jobs. One would have to balance the benefits from shorter durations of unemployment against the costs of a higher incidence of unemployment before deciding if such policies are worthwhile to implement.

The government can seek to reduce the geographic dispersion of unemployment rates by providing information about jobs in other areas to unemployed workers, by providing relocation allowances and subsidies for job search in different areas, and by administering public employment and training-program budgets in a way that increases allocations to areas with above-average unemployment rates.[21] The government can also seek to reduce the dispersion of unemployment rates across occupational or demographic groups by targeting employment and training programs, wage subsidies, tax credits, and relocation allowances on the groups with high unemployment rates.

Finally, independent of government policies, two demographic forces will be operating during the 1980s that will tend to reduce the unemployment rate associated with any level of excess demand for labor. First, the proportion of teenagers in the labor force will be declining. As a result of the decline in the birth rate in the 1960s and 1970s, less weight will be given to this relatively high unemployment rate group in computing the aggregate unemployment rate.

Second, while the proportion of females in the labor force will continue to increase, it is likely that the relative unemployment rate of females will decline. As discussed in Chapter 15, part of the reason for the relatively high unemployment rate of females is that many of them are fairly new entrants or reentrants to the labor force whose job turnover is high while they shop for desirable positions. However, as these women gain labor-market experience and as the perception increases that females' attachment to the labor force is as permanent as males', females' relative unemployment rates will likely fall. These two demographic trends, then, should serve to reduce the rate of wage inflation associated with any given level of overall unemployment during the 1980s.

---

[20] A long-time advocate of such policies is Charles Holt. See, for example, Charles Holt et al., "Manpower Proposals for Phase III," *Brookings Papers on Economic Activity,* 1971–3, pp. 703–22. For a more critical evaluation of these policies, see Robert Hall, "Prospects for Shifting the Phillips Curve Through Manpower Policy," *Brookings Papers on Economic Activity,* 1971–3, pp. 659–701.

[21] *Comprehensive Employment and Training Act (CETA)* program funds are administered in this way.

WAGE INFLATION, PRICE INFLATION, PRODUCTIVITY, AND THE LONG-RUN TRADE-OFF

To move from the relationship between *wage* inflation and unemployment to an understanding of the relationship between *price* inflation and unemployment requires a model of how producers determine their product prices. The simple model presented here highlights the role of labor productivity growth in the inflationary process and shows how increases in the growth of labor productivity can help to reduce price inflation.

Suppose that producers determine their product prices by using a *constant percentage markup* over unit labor cost rule. That is,

$$P = k \cdot ULC \tag{16.3}$$

where P represents product price, ULC represents unit labor cost—the labor cost of producing one unit of output—and k, which is a constant that is greater than one, represents the markup. Presumably k varies across firms as the share of labor cost in total costs of production varies (with smaller labor cost shares leading to larger values of k). It is also likely that k varies with the price elasticity of demand for the firms' products.[22] Although typically the size of markups do vary over the course of a business cycle, for expositional convenience we will ignore this fact here.[23]

Now unit labor costs are equal to the costs per labor hour divided by output per labor hour *(q)* or labor productivity. Suppose, for simplicity, that we ignore all labor costs other than straight-time wages. Then labor costs per labor hour are equal to the wage rate *(W)* and

$$ULC = W/q. \tag{16.4}$$

Substituting equation (16.4) into equation (16.3) and making use of the facts 1. that the percentage change in the *product* of two variables equals the sum of the percentage changes of the two variables and 2. that the percentage change in the *ratio* of two variables equals the percentage change in the numerator minus the percentage change in the denominator, one obtains

$$\dot{P} = \dot{k} + \dot{W} - m. \tag{16.5}$$

Here a dot over a variable represents a percentage change and m, equal to $\dot{q}$, is the rate of growth of output per labor hour (or the rate of labor productivity growth).

Over time the size of markups may change; for example, the drastic increase in the relative prices of energy since 1973 surely have led to increases in k. However, since this is a text in labor economics, not macroeconomics, we shall ignore

---

[22]Although we do not do so here, one can formally show that these statements are true for a profit-maximizing monopolist who faces a constant average-cost curve. In this case, the less elastic the price elasticity of demand for output, the greater k will be.

[23]For evidence on the cyclical variability of markups see Robert J. Gordon, "The Impact of Aggregate Demand on Prices," *Brookings Papers on Economic Activity*, 1975–3, pp. 613–63.

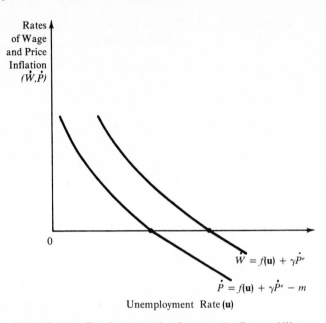

**FIGURE 16.8   The Relationships Between the Rates of Wage
and Price Inflation and (1) the Expected Rate
of Price Inflation and (2) the Rate
of Productivity Growth**

this complication and assume that k remains constant; the constancy of k implies that labor's share of output also remains constant). Under this assumption,

$$\dot{P} = \dot{W} - m. \tag{16.6}$$

Equation (16.6) asserts that the rate of price inflation equals the rate of wage inflation minus the rate of labor productivity growth. Thus, if wages increase at the rate of productivity growth *and* if markups do not change, prices will remain constant. Put another way, given any rate of wage inflation, an increase in the rate of growth of productivity will lead to a reduction in the rate of growth of prices, if markups are constant.

Moreover, if one characterizes the trade-off between wage inflation and unemployment as $\dot{W} = f(\mathbf{u}) + \gamma\dot{P}^e$, then one can substitute $f(\mathbf{u}) + \gamma\dot{P}^e$ for $\dot{W}$ in equation (16.6) to obtain

$$\dot{P} = f(\mathbf{u}) + \gamma\dot{P}^e - m. \tag{16.7}$$

That is, as Figure 16.8 indicates, as long as productivity growth is positive, the price-inflation/unemployment tradeoff that exists at any time lies everywhere below the wage-inflation/unemployment trade-off, with the vertical difference between the two curves being equal to the rate of labor productivity growth.

The Slowdown in Productivity Growth and Stagflation

During the late 1970s and early 1980s, one often read in the popular press that the slowdown in the rate of growth of labor productivity in the United States was at least partially responsible for high rates of price inflation that were associated

TABLE 16.3 Labor Productivity Growth in the United States (percent change per year)

Sector	1948–55	1955–65	1965–73	1973–78
Private business sector	2.5	2.4	1.6	0.8
Nonfarm	2.4	2.5	1.6	0.9
Manufacturing	3.2	2.8	2.4	1.5
Nonmanufacturing	2.1	2.2	1.2	0.5

SOURCE: *1980 Economic Report of the President* (Washington, D.C.: U.S. Government Printing Office, 1980), Table 16.

with high rates of unemployment—a phenomenon commonly referred to as *stagflation*. Table 16.3 presents data on labor productivity growth in the United States that support this claim. For the entire private business sector, productivity grew at about 2.5 percent per year over the 1948-1965 period. However, during 1965 to 1973 productivity growth fell to 1.6 percent a year, and during 1973-1978 it fell further to 0.8 percent a year. These shifts alone would cause the short-run aggregate price inflation/unemployment trade-off curve to be some 1.7 percentage points higher during the late 1970s than it was during the 1950s and early 1960s [see equation (16.7)]. This figure should, however, be contrasted to the 5 to 10 percent annual rates of increase in the GNP deflator that occurred during the late 1970s. Thus, while the slowdown in productivity growth contributed to the worsening inflation/unemployment trade-off, it was not the entire cause; the other factors we have mentioned clearly were important.[24]

The Long-Run Trade-off

Although *at a point in time* a tradeoff exists between the rate of price inflation and the unemployment rate, it does not necessarily follow that *in the long-run* a stable trade-off exists. Indeed, one school of thought argues that attempts to keep the unemployment rate artificially low—below the rate that is consistent with zero price inflation (when the expected rate of price inflation is zero)—will lead to ever-accelerating rates of inflation.[25] The reason for this acceleration is that attempts to reduce the unemployment rate through monetary or fiscal policy will lead to higher rates of wage and price inflation in the short run [see panel (c) of Figure 16.4 and Figure 16.8]. To the extent that expectations of inflation are conditioned by actual rates of inflation, such policies will increase the expected rate of price inflation, and the rates of wage and price inflation could continue to spiral upwards.

Whether this process will lead to ever-accelerating rates of wage and price inflation or ultimately to constant rates of wage and price inflation depends crucially on the responsiveness of money-wage increases to the expected rate of price inflation. In terms of our model, if all expected price increases are fully reflected

---

[24]A note of caution: one must be careful not to confuse cyclical changes in productivity growth (see Chapter 5) with changes in the underlying trend; the downward trend does tend to persist even after one controls for cyclical factors. Why this has occurred is not completely understood, although some explanations have been offered (see Chapter 4).

[25]See Friedman, ''The Role of Monetary Policy''; and Edmund Phelps, ''Phillips Curves, Expectations of Inflation, and Optimal Unemployment Over Time,'' *Economica* 34 (August 1967): 254–81, for early expositions of this view.

in higher wages [$\gamma = 1$ in equation (16.2)], no long-run trade-off exists; attempts to force unemployment below its natural rate will cause ever-accelerating rates of inflation. In contrast, if expected price increases are *not* fully reflected in higher wage increases ($\gamma < 1$), a stable long-run trade-off between price inflation and unemployment will exist (that is, a constant rate of inflation will eventually become associated with any level of unemployment).

The case of $\gamma < 1$.   Suppose, for the sake of simplicity, that the expected rate of price inflation in a period is equal to the actual rate of price inflation that occurred in the previous period. That is, suppose

$$\dot{P}^e = \dot{P}_{-1}. \tag{16.8}$$

Consider first the case when expected price increases are *not* fully reflected in wage increases, and—to take a specific example—suppose that γ is equal to $\frac{1}{2}$. In this case, the short-run price-inflation/unemployment tradeoff is given by

$$\dot{P} = f(\mathbf{u}) - m + \frac{1}{2}\dot{P}_{-1}. \tag{16.9}$$

If initially there were no price inflation in the economy, the trade-off curve would then be

$$\dot{P} = f(\mathbf{u}) - m. \tag{16.10}$$

Figure 16.9 provides a graphical representation of equation (16.10) (where T_0 is drawn as a straight line for expositional convenience). Note that if the unemployment rate were kept at $\mathbf{u}_0$, there would be no price inflation in the economy. (Note also that if labor productivity growth is positive, the price inflation/unemployment trade-off will lie below the wage inflation/unemployment trade-off, and, hence $\mathbf{u}_0$ will typically be *less than* the full-employment unemployment rate, $\mathbf{u}$. This statement ignores complications caused by the dispersion in unemployment rates.)

Now suppose that the government pursues a stimulative aggregate demand policy and reduces the unemployment rate to $\mathbf{u}_1$. As drawn in Figure 16.9, this policy would yield a 2 percent rate of price inflation—which, from equation (16.9), would shift the short-run trade-off in the next period up by 1 percentage point ($2 \times \frac{1}{2}$). This new curve is represented by T_1 in Figure 16.9, and, if the government sought to keep the unemployment rate at $\mathbf{u}_1$, the inflation rate would rise to 3 percent. However, this inflation rate would shift the trade-off in the next period up to T_2, which is $\frac{3}{2}$ ($3 \times \frac{1}{2}$) of a percentage point above the original trade-off, T_0. If the government again tried to keep the unemployment rate at $\mathbf{u}_1$, the rate of price inflation in the following period would rise to 3.5 percent.

This process of upward-shifting short-run trade-off curves would continue as long as the unemployment rate was kept at $\mathbf{u}_1$. Note, however, that because less than the expected price inflation rate is passed on in the form of higher wages ($\gamma < 1$), the magnitude of the shift becomes progressively smaller. Indeed, the inflation rate will eventually reach 4 percent, at which point the trade-off curve will have shifted to T_n, which is 2 percentage points above T_0. If the government then kept unemployment at $\mathbf{u}_1$, inflation in the next period would again be 4 percent and the upward spiral would stop. Hence, the inflation/unemployment combina-

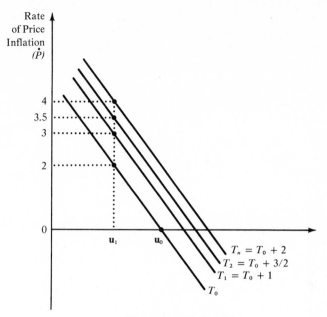

FIGURE 16.9   A Stable Long-Run Trade-off Between Price
Inflation and the Unemployment Rate:
$\dot{P} = f(\mathbf{u}) - m + \frac{1}{2} \dot{P}_{-1}$

tion $(4,\mathbf{u}_1)$ is a point on the long-run trade-off curve. One could repeat this line of reasoning for other unemployment rates and trace out the entire long-run trade-off curve.

More succinctly, the long-run trade-off will be the locus of inflation/unemployment combinations for which the *actual* rate of price inflation $(\dot{P})$ equals the *expected* rate of inflation $(\dot{P}^e)$. In terms of equation (16.7), one can replace the expected inflation rate by the actual rate to obtain

$$\dot{P} = f(\mathbf{u}) + \gamma \dot{P} - m. \tag{16.11}$$

Solving for the actual rate of inflation, one obtains:

$$\dot{P} = \frac{f(\mathbf{u})}{1 - \gamma} - \frac{m}{1 - \gamma}. \tag{16.12}$$

Equation (16.12) is the long-run price inflation/unemployment trade-off curve in our model. If wages respond at all to expected rates of price inflation (that is, if $\gamma > 0$), the long-run trade-off curve (T_L) will be steeper than the short-run trade-off curves, as indicated in Figure 16.10. Note in Figure 16.10 that the inflation/unemployment combinations of $(4,\mathbf{u}_1)$ and $(0,\mathbf{u}_0)$—each representing points where $\dot{P} = \dot{P}^e$—are both on T_L.

Put another way, increasing the unemployment rate by one percentage point will "buy" a larger reduction in inflation in the long run than it will in the short run if $\gamma > 0$. This difference in slope between the long-run and short-run trade-

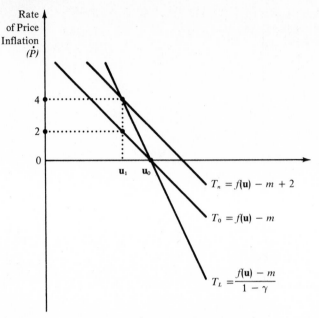

FIGURE 16.10   **The Relationship of the Short-Run
and Long-Run Trade-off Curves** $(\gamma = 1/2)$

offs increases as γ becomes larger. Furthermore, the larger is γ, the greater will be the effect of a change in the rate of productivity growth on the long-run inflation rate—with decreases in productivity growth causing the long-run trade-off curve to shift up by more than would be the case if γ were smaller. However, if $\gamma < 1$, a stable long-run relationship between $\dot{P}$ and $\mathbf{u}$ would exist.

The case of $\gamma = 1$.   If γ equals 1, however, there is no stable long-run trade-off between the rate of price inflation and the rate of unemployment. Attempts to reduce the unemployment rate below $\mathbf{u}_0$ will lead to ever-accelerating rates of price inflation. We will now assume that all of the expected increase in prices is transmitted into higher wages ($\gamma = 1$). As a result, the short-run trade-off curve is given by

$$\dot{P} = f(\mathbf{u}) - m + \dot{P}_{-1}. \tag{16.13}$$

The curve T_0 in Figure 16.11 represents the relationship in equation (16.13) when the economy is initially at $\mathbf{u}_0$ and the past inflation rate is zero. Suppose again that aggregate demand policy is pursued to reduce the unemployment rate to $\mathbf{u}_1$, and an inflation rate of 2 percent initially results. In this case, the short-run trade-off in the next period (T_1) shifts up by 2 percentage points, and if $\mathbf{u}_1$ is maintained, the inflation rate would be 4 percent in the next period.

It should be obvious that because of the one-for-one feedback from current price inflation to next period's wage inflation, the short-run trade-off curve will shift up vertically—*and* the actual rate of price inflation will *increase*—by 2 percentage points *every* period as long as the government keeps the unemployment

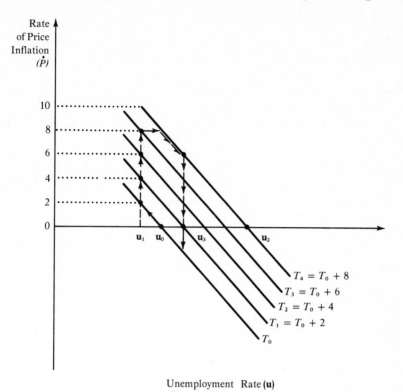

FIGURE 16.11   No Stable Long-Run Trade-off Between Price Inflation and the Unemployment Rate: $\dot{P} = f(\mathbf{u}) - m + \dot{P}_{-1}$

rate at $\mathbf{u}_1$. The attempt to keep the unemployment rate below $\mathbf{u}_0$ thus leads to ever-increasing rates of price inflation; no stable rate of inflation can be maintained. (In terms of equation (16.12), the long-run trade-off is infinite when $\gamma = 1$ because the denominator is zero.) For this reason $\mathbf{u}_0$ is often referred to in such models as the *nonaccelerating inflation rate of unemployment* or the *NAIRU*.

To get the process of accelerating inflation to stop in this model, the government must return the unemployment rate to the NAIRU. In Figure 16.11 if the unemployment rate is maintained at $\mathbf{u}_1$ for periods 0, 1, 2, and 3, the inflation rate will be 8 percent in period 3 and the trade-off curve will shift up to T_4 in period 4. *If* the government then allows the unemployment rate to rise to $\mathbf{u}_0$ in period 4, the inflation rate will remain at 8 percent. The trade-off curve in period 5 will be the same as the one in period 4, and, as long as the unemployment rate stays at $\mathbf{u}_0$, the inflation rate will remain at 8 percent. To reduce the inflation rate back to zero, the government could tolerate a massive increase in the unemployment rate (to $\mathbf{u}_2$) for one period, at which point $\dot{P} = 0$, and unemployment could be returned to $\mathbf{u}_0$. Alternatively, the government could let unemployment increase to $\mathbf{u}_3$ for 4 periods, after which the economy would be back on T_0 and unemployment could be returned to $\mathbf{u}_0$ (note the downward arrows in Figure 16.11).

If this model is correct, a short-run trade-off exists between the rate of price inflation and the level of the unemployment rate, but no such trade-off exists in the long run. Society can *temporarily* reduce the unemployment rate at the cost of *permanently* higher rates of price inflation. To bring these higher rates of inflation down requires a temporary increase in the unemployment rate.

Evidence on the long-run trade-off.   A key question for policymakers, then, is the extent to which expected increases in prices do lead to increases in wages. If the relationship is less than proportional ($\gamma < 1$), there *is* a stable long-run trade-off between price inflation and unemployment. If the relationship is one-for-one, however, no stable long-run trade-off exists.

Empirical evidence on this question is ambiguous, and some economists assert that it is nearly impossible to answer the question from statistical estimates of γ in equations such as (16.7).[26] The consensus appears to be, however, that the strict NAIRU hypothesis does not hold. That is, the consensus is that γ is less than one and that a stable long-run trade-off does exist. However, over time γ appears to have grown in size—leading to a less favorable short-run trade-off (in the sense that given any level of expected price inflation, the short-run trade-off curve is higher in the early 1980s than it was in the 1960s and early 1970s). The evidence also appears to indicate that the short-run curve is flatter; thus, the marginal effect of an increase in the unemployment rate on inflation appears to be smaller than it once was.[27]

EXPECTED VS. UNEXPECTED INFLATION

Our discussion of the inflation/unemployment trade-off has so far assumed that labor-market tightness and unemployment cause inflation, not vice versa. We also stressed the role of *expected* (or *anticipated*) inflation rates and ignored the role of *unexpected* (or *unanticipated*) inflation rates. This section will return to the simple model of job search presented in the last chapter to show how unexpected rates of wage and price inflation can cause a temporary decline in the unemployment rate but that fully expected inflation will have no causal effect on unemployment. Thus, when considering the inflation/unemployment trade-off, the direction of causation may run from *unanticipated* inflation to the unemployment rate.

As the actual rate of inflation trended upwards during the 1960s and 1970s (see Table 16.1), inflation also became much more variable. Table 16.4 presents data on the variance of the inflation rate over successive 5-year periods, and the variance clearly increased from the early 1960s to the 1970s—although the increase was larger for prices than wages. As such, individuals' ability to predict the actual inflation rate may well have declined, leading to an increased likelihood that *actual* wage or price level changes would differ from *expected* ones. As we

---

[26]See for example, Robert Lucas, "Econometric Testing of the Natural Rate Hypothesis" in *The Econometrics of Price Determination*, ed. Otto Eckstein (Washington, D.C.: Board of Governors of the Federal Reserve System, 1972).

[27]See, for example, Michael Wachter, "The Changing Cyclical Responsiveness of Wage Inflation," *Brookings Papers on Economic Activity*, 1976–1, pp. 115–59; and George Perry, "Inflation in Theory and Practice," *Brookings Papers on Economic Activity*, 1980–1, pp. 207–42.

**TABLE 16.4   Average Annual Rate of Increase in
Wages and the GNP Price Deflator—and Variance
in the Annual Rate of Increase of Each Over
Successive Five-Year Periods**

	Average Annual Increase		*Variance in the Annual Increases*[a]	
	Wages	*Prices*	*Wages*	*Prices*
1960–64	3.1	1.5	0.07	0.16
1965–69	5.1	3.6	1.35	1.09
1970–74	6.8	5.9	0.36	3.17
1975–79	7.8	7.3	0.15	2.90

[a]The *variance* is calculated by 1. computing the average (mean) annual increase for the five-year period, 2. calculating the difference between the increase for each year and the above average, 3. squaring the differences in step 2 and summing them over five years, and 4. dividing the sum in step 3 by 5. If yearly price increases start to vary much from each other, the calculated variance will rise.

SOURCE: Based on *1980 Economic Report of the President* (Washington, D.C.: U.S. Government Printing Office, 1980), Tables B3, B29, and B35.

will show, such a discrepancy tends to flatten the short-run inflation/unemployment trade-off curves.

Suppose that the initial distribution of money-wage offers facing a representative individual is given in panel (a) of Figure 16.12. Let the maximum wage commensurate with the individual's skill level be W^*, and suppose that the individual rationally chooses W_R^0 as his or her minimal *acceptance* (or *reservation*) *wage*. As noted in Chapter 15 (Figure 15.6), the area to the right of W^* under the wage distribution represents the proportion of jobs he or she is not qualified for and the area to the left of W_R^0 represents the proportion of jobs he or she will not accept. Together, then, the two areas tell us the probability that this representative individual will not find employment in any period and, thus, what the expected unemployment rate will be.

Suppose that there is a general increase in wages and prices that shifts the whole distribution of wage offers to the right but that the workers are initially *unaware* that this shift has occurred. If this inflation was truly unanticipated there would be no reason for workers to increase their acceptance wage. However, if they keep their acceptance wage at W_R^0, the probability that they will reject a job offer is reduced—the area to the left of W_R^0 after the shift in the distribution is reduced as can be seen in panel (b). Further, the proportion of jobs that these individuals are qualified for remains constant, which means that W^* shifts up by the same proportion as the rest of the wage distribution (to W_1^*). Thus, the probability of finding a job will increase and the unemployment rate will fall—and the greater the unexpected shift in the wage distribution the greater will be the fall in the unemployment rate. A short-run trade-off exists between unanticipated inflation and unemployment, with the direction of causation running from the former to the latter in this model.

Once the individual becomes aware of the overall wage inflation that has

(a) Initial Distribution of Wage Offers

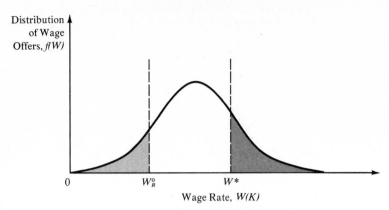

(b) Distribution of Wage Offers Shifts to the Right

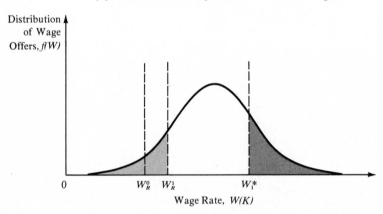

FIGURE 16.12   Effect of Anticipated and Unanticipated Wage
Inflation on Reservation Wages
and Unemployment

occurred, however, the trade-off ceases to exist. Individuals will revise their acceptance wage upward to W_R^1 in an effort to maintain their wage relative to others' and to obtain the benefits of the general increase in wage offers. As the reservation wage increases from W_R^0 to W_R^1, the area to the left of W_R^1 in panel (b) will be identical to the area to the left of W_R^0 in panel (a), and the unemployment rate will return to its full-employment level, **u.** Since unemployed individuals alter their acceptance-wage decisions in response to expected or anticipated inflation, changes in the expected rate of inflation will not lead to changes in the unemployment rate.

The trade-offs that are implied by this model are plotted in Figure 16.13. When inflation is unanticipated by job searchers, there is a negative trade-off, T^u, with the direction of causation running from the rate of unanticipated inflation to the unemployment rate. When inflation is fully anticipated or expected, no

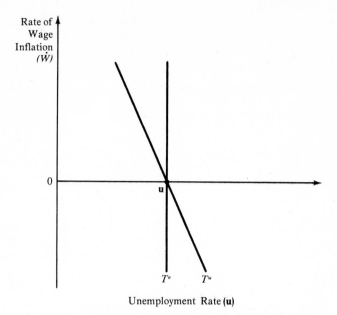

**FIGURE 16.13   Trade-off Between Inflation and Unemployment:
Expected vs. Unexpected Wage Inflation**

tradeoff exists and the level of anticipated inflation has no causal effect on the unemployment rate, as indicated by the curve T^e.

In summary, as the rates of wage and price inflation trended upward during the 1960s and 1970s they also became somewhat more variable (see Table 16.4); thus it became more difficult to anticipate the actual inflation rate. The model presented in this section would suggest, then, that over this period the curve showing the change in unemployment caused by wage inflation would begin to look more like T^u than T^e. Put another way, the fact that individuals became less able to fully anticipate the actual inflation rate may have contributed to the observed flattening of the trade-off curves between wage or price inflation and the unemployment rate.

UNIONS AND INFLATION

Less than 25 percent of the labor force are union members (see Chapter 12). In spite of this fact, unions and the collective-bargaining process in the United States are thought to exert a considerable influence on the position and shape of the wage inflation/unemployment trade-off curve for a number of reasons.

First, in several industries—such as steel, automobile, mining, trucking, and telephone—collective-bargaining negotiations are conducted at the national level and are well publicized in the media. The resulting settlements are often thought to set a pattern for wage settlements in other less heavily unionized industries and in the nonunion sector, either because of imitative behavior in the former or attempts to compete for labor and keep unions out in the latter.[28] Our model suggests that if the economic conditions facing firms and unions in only a few key industries heavily influence the rate of wage inflation in other sectors, the effect of the *aggregate* unemployment rate on inflation will be reduced.

Evidence to support this view is quite limited, however. For example, during the 1970s wages in the above highly unionized industries grew substantially relative to wages in the rest of the economy, suggesting that the settlements reached in these industries do not automatically spillover to other industries.[29] Moreover, attempts to formally test whether or not these key wage bargains, or union wage gains in general, set a pattern for the rest of the economy have not met with success.[30]

Second, union contracts have increasingly become multiyear in nature and call for wage increases not only at the time the contract is signed, but also in subsequent years. While these increases may well be sensitive to the unemployment rate at the time the contract is signed—or, more precisely, to unions' and employers' *expectations* of the unemployment rate over the term of the contract—the contractual increases are not directly affected by the *actual* unemployment rate during the duration of the contract.

Formal econometric analyses do in fact indicate that wage increases specified in the *first* year of multiyear union contracts appear to be about as sensitive to the unemployment rate as are wage increases in the nonunion sector. However, *deferred* wage increases specified in union contracts—those that occur in the second or third year of multiyear contracts—do not appear to be related to the actual unemployment rates during those years.[31] Hence, the increasing frequency of long-term union contracts in the economy *does* reduce the sensitivity of the overall rates of wage and price inflation to the unemployment rate, making the trade-off curves flatter.

Third, accompanying the growth of multiyear contracts has been the growth of *cost-of-living escalator clauses* in union contracts: clauses that call for wages to be automatically adjusted periodically as the price level changes. Approximately 20 percent of workers covered by major collective-bargaining agreements—that cover 1000 or more workers—had such provisions in their contracts in 1966. However, by 1976 this proportion had grown to 59 percent.[32]

---

[28] For an early exposition of this view, see Otto Eckstein and Thomas Wilson, "The Determination of Money Wages in American Industry," *Quarterly Journal of Economics* 76 (August 1962): 379–414.

[29] See Daniel Mitchell, *Unions, Wages, and Inflation* (Washington, D.C.: Brookings Institution, 1980); and Marvin Kosters, "Wage and Price Behavior: Prospects and Policies" in *Contemporary Economic Problems, 1977* ed. William Fellner (Washington, D.C.: American Enterprise Institute for Public Policy Research, 1977).

[30] See Daniel Mitchell, "Union Wage Determination: Policy Implications and Outlook," *Brookings Papers on Economic Activity, 1978–3,* pp. 537–82; and Robert Flanagan, "Wage Interdependence in Unionized Labor Markets," *Brookings Papers on Economic Activity, 1976–3,* pp. 635–73.

[31] Mitchell, "Union Wage Determination."

[32] Robert H. Ferguson, *Cost-of-Living Adjustments in Union-Management Agreements* (Ithaca, N.Y.: New York School of Industrial and Labor Relations, 1977).

Escalator clauses typically give workers less than 100 percent protection against price inflation. Such contracts usually call for wages to increase by less than one percent in response to each one percentage point increase in prices, and sometimes *caps*—or maximum allowable cost-of-living increases—are also specified. Nevertheless, their existence should increase the sensitivity of wage inflation to price inflation and the evidence bears this out; union wage changes, especially those in contracts that call for cost-of-living escalators, appear to be more sensitive to price changes than do nonunion wage changes.[33] As noted earlier, larger values of γ in equation (16.2) lead to a higher short-run price inflation/unemployment trade-off curve. Hence, the growing prevalence of cost-of-living escalator clauses in union contracts may well have contributed to the upward shift in the short-run trade-off curves.

A final reason why unions are thought to influence the position and shape of the trade-off curve is that union members are clearly concerned about maintaining their wage position relative to what they perceive are the wages of their *peer groups*. For example, at the national level automobile workers look at the wage gains won in the steel industry and vice versa. Whichever union settles first may set a pattern for the other union to follow in its negotiations, regardless of economic conditions in the latter industry. If this occurs, the responsiveness of wage and price inflation to unemployment would again be reduced.

Wage gains in several large national industries, such as automobile, steel, and rubber, clearly are highly correlated. However, it is difficult to disentangle the above *wage imitation* hypothesis from the hypothesis that wages in these industries are affected by a common set of variables. After all, steel is a major component of automobiles, as is rubber for the tires. It would, therefore, not be surprising to find that wage changes for workers in the three industries are highly correlated. Attempts to formally test whether wage imitation occurs among unions in these and other industries have not met with success.[34]

Our discussion suggests, then, that the collective-bargaining process *per se* may well have contributed to the flattening and shifting up of the short-run inflation/unemployment tradeoff curves during the 1970s. The increased prevalence of multiyear contracts is partially responsible for the flattening, and the increase in cost-of-living escalator clauses for the upward shift.[35] The effects of key settlements or other imitative behavior are uncertain.

---

[33]Mitchell, "Union Wage Determination."

[34]See for example, Robert Flanagan, "Wage Interdependencies in Unionized Labor Markets," *Brookings Papers on Economic Activity,* 1976–3: and Y. P. Mehra, "Spillovers in Wage Determination in U. S. Manufacturing Industries," *Review of Economics and Statistics* 58 (August 1976): 300–312.

[35]Another reason for the flattening of the trade-off curve in the nonunion sector relates to the growth of structured internal labor markets in which fluctuations in demand are met by temporary layoffs rather than money wage reductions, as discussed in Chapter 15. The "quantity adjustments" (layoffs) rather than "wage adjustments" at the individual firm level contribute to the growing insensitivity of wage changes to unemployment at the aggregate level. For an extensive discussion of this point, see Arthur Okun, "Inflation: Its Mechanics and Welfare Costs," *Brookings Papers on Economic Activity,* 1975–2, pp. 351–90; and Arthur Okun, *Prices and Quantities* (Washington, D. C.: Brookings Institution, 1981), pp. 351–90.

INCOMES POLICIES

The inflation/unemployment trade-offs—for both wages and prices—that we face in the early 1980s are distinctly unfavorable and appear to indicate that aggregate demand policy alone will not be an effective way of reducing inflation. One relatively optimistic observer has estimated that an extra percentage point of unemployment (which represents roughly 1 million jobs), if maintained for three years, would only lower the rate of price inflation by 0.7 percentage points by the end of the period.[36] How then can we hope to wind down the economy from the high inflation rates of the late 1970s and early 1980s?

Clearly, the answer is to resort to structural policies that will improve the inflation/unemployment trade-off *per se*. Many of these policies were discussed earlier in the chapter. In the remainder of the chapter we will focus in more detail on one of these—*incomes policies*. Incomes policies are policies in which the government tries to directly influence wage and price behavior by specifying *desired behavior*. Sometimes the policies are completely voluntary, and sometimes there are enforcement mechanisms built in to increase or guarantee compliance.

Incomes Policies in the United States

During the 1960-1980 period, a period over which the inflation/unemployment trade-off curve steadily shifted out, the United States tried several different types of incomes policies. In the early Kennedy-Johnson years (1962-1966), the Council of Economic Advisors tried to educate the public on the relationship between the rate of wage inflation, the rate of price inflation, and the rate of productivity growth—see equation (16.6). The council observed that if money-wage growth was held on average to the rate of labor productivity growth in the economy and if markups did not change, then prices would remain stable. The council suggested in 1964 that the trend rate of growth of productivity was roughly 3.2 percent per year (but compare this to the estimates in Table 16.3) and urged that employers and unions voluntarily limit their wage settlements to this level. This limitation would cause unit labor costs to rise in firms in which productivity growth was below average, leading to increases in prices there. However, unit labor costs would fall in firms with above-average rates of productivity growth, leading to price declines there (if profit margins remained constant). On average, then, prices would remain stable.

The guideposts worked reasonably well from 1962 to 1965 in the sense that the average rate of increase in wages was in fact below 3.2 percent during the period.[37] However, as labor markets tightened in the mid-1960s and as the price inflation rate rose above 2 percent, the guideposts broke down and by 1967 the program was abandoned.

The next experience with incomes policies occurred during the Nixon Administration in August of 1971. In response to increasing rates of price inflation (which averaged all of 5.3 percent in 1970), increasing unemployment, and a

---

[36]George Perry, "Slowing the Wage-Price Spiral: The Macroeconomic View," *Brookings Papers on Economic Activity,* 1978-2, pp. 259–91.

[37]This does not imply that the guideposts *caused* wage increases to average less than 3.2 percent. Evidence on their effect on the wage-inflation rate will be discussed below.

deteriorating trade balance, a comprehensive economic policy was announced. "Phase I," which lasted 90 days, called for a freeze on virtually all wages and prices. Phase I was followed in November of 1971 by Phase II, which set standards for wage increases of 5.5 percent a year. If productivity grew at 3 to 3.5 percent a year and if profit margins were maintained, prices would then grow at 2 to 2.5 percent a year—see equation (16.6). Compliance was required by law under the program. However, a sufficient number of exemptions were granted that average hourly earnings growth was well above 5.5 percent a year (see Table 16.1). The program was terminated in January of 1973 and replaced with a voluntary program of controls with no enforcement mechanism.

Finally, in October of 1978, the Carter Administration announced a voluntary system of wage standards to help reduce inflation. Average hourly earnings and fringes per company were to increase at a rate of no more than 7 percent a year; for contracts with cost-of-living escalator clauses compliance was evaluated at an assumed 6 percent price inflation rate over the life of the contract.[38] Several groups of workers were exempted from having to satisfy the standards, including low-wage workers.

Contract settlements under the Carter program were monitored by the Council on Wage and Price Stability. However, its enforcement power was limited to calling violations of the voluntary standards to public attention. Other arms of government—Congress and the President—contributed to enforcement of the standards, however, through implicit or explicit threats that firms violating the standards would lose government contracts. Threats of other government action were made to particular industries; these included relaxation of import quotas (steel), deregulation (trucking), and sale of government stockpiles (copper) if wage settlements in these industries were not in compliance. As inflation continued to accelerate in 1979, the levels of permissable wage increases were raised for 1980. After the defeat of President Carter in the 1980 election, the program was terminated.

Did U.S. Incomes Policies Work?

Numerous attempts have been made to appraise whether the Kennedy-Johnson wage/price guideposts and the Nixon Phase II economic program actually did succeed in reducing the rates of wage and price inflation below the levels that would have existed in the *absence* of the programs. It is worth emphasizing that the comparisons these studies make are *not* of actual levels of wage and price inflation during the periods that the incomes policies were in effect with levels of inflation during the *previous* periods. Since the forces that affect inflation, such as unemployment rates and expected rates of inflation, change over time, such comparisons would be meaningless. Put another way, such comparisons could not disentangle the change in inflation rates caused by the incomes policies from the change in inflation caused by changes in other variables.

Rather, the methodology used in these studies is to use historical data to estimate generalizations of the inflation/unemployment trade-off curves specified

---

[38]Actually the Carter Policy did *not* apply on a *company* basis but on an *employee-group* basis within each company. The three types of employee groups considered were supervisors, nonunion-non-supervisory employees, and workers covered by each collective-bargaining agreement.

earlier in this chapter and then to ask if these estimated relationships systematically changed during the periods that the incomes policies were in effect. That is,
the researchers tried to determine whether the rates of inflation that were *predicted*
using the historical relationship between unemployment and inflation (after controlling for the age/sex distribution of the labor force, the dispersion of unemployment rates, and expected inflation rates) really did exceed the *actual* inflation
rates that occurred. If *predicted* rates of inflation exceed *actual* rates, one could
argue that the incomes policies were effective in bringing down inflation.

The answers these studies yielded are somewhat ambiguous. For example,
George Perry found that the rate of wage inflation was some 0.6 to 1.2 points
lower during the Kennedy-Johnson guidepost period than his model would otherwise have predicted, but Robert J. Gordon found that the guideposts had no effect
on the rate of wage inflation.[39] In contrast, Gordon found that the rate of wage
inflation was held down during the Nixon Phase II incomes-policy period—a result other researchers have also found.[40]

In evaluating these studies, however, one must caution that the fact that the
rate of wage inflation appeared to be lower than a model predicts during the period
of time that the policy was in effect does not imply that the policy *caused* the
reduction in the rate of inflation. Factors not included in the model that reduce the
rate of wage inflation might have occurred at the same time. For example, the
period during which the Kennedy-Johnson wage/price guideposts were in effect
(1962-1966) was one of increased import competition for American steel manufacturers and one of rapid expansion of government-sponsored employee-training
programs to remove skill bottlenecks. Both of these forces should have served to
reduce the rate of wage inflation; the former by increasing the resistance of U. S.
steel manufacturers to union wage demands and the latter by reducing the excess
demand for labor. It is thus not an easy task to ascertain what the effects of
incomes policies really are.

Why are Incomes Policies Unpopular Among Economists?

Independent of the evidence on the effectiveness of incomes policies in moderating the rates of wage and price inflation, many economists are opposed to their
use because the policies create inequities and efficiency losses in the economy.[41]
The scope of this text does not permit our cataloging the case against incomes
policies, but a few arguments can be mentioned.

First, rigid guidelines or standards implicitly freeze the distribution of income

---

[39]Perry's initial study was George Perry, "Wages and the Guideposts," *American Economic Review*
57 (September 1967): 897–904. Additional results are found in George Perry, "Inflation in
Theory and Practice," *Brookings Papers on Economic Activity*, 1980-1, pp. 207–42. Gordon's
results are in his "Comment," *Brookings Papers on Economic Activity*, 1980–1, pp. 249–57.

[40]See Robert Gordon, "Wage Price Controls and the Shifting Phillips Curve," *Brookings Papers on
Economic Activity*, 1972–2, (pp. 385–421; and his "Comment", *Brookings Papers on Economic
Activity*, 1980–1, pp. 249–57. See also Bradley Askin and John Kraft, *Econometric Wage and
Price Models: Assessing the Impact of the Economic Stabilization Program* (Lexington, Mass.:
D.C. Heath, 1974).

[41]A now classic article that presents the case against incomes policies more completely is Milton
Friedman, "What Price Guideposts?" in *Guidelines, Informal Controls, and the Market Place*,
eds. George Shultz and Robert Alibers (Chicago: University of Chicago Press, 1966).

and create inequities. For example, individuals who recently have received large increases gain relative to those whose increases will be constrained by the policies. Unless most individuals are happy with their relative income positions at the time the policy is imposed and there is a social consensus for the need for the policy, the policy will invariably break down.

Second, such policies may create efficiency losses because rapidly expanding sectors of the economy that face personnel shortages are prevented from bidding up wages to attract labor. Once exceptions are systematically granted for the above reason, as was done in Phase II of the Nixon economic policy, the process of controlling wage increases becomes highly politicized—and the exceptions may be used to justify wage increases that exceed the standard in cases when waiving the standard is not justified by economic conditions. More generally, incomes policies tend to be unevenly applied to different groups; those with political power gain relative to those without.

Finally, the administrative costs of incomes policies that contain enforcement procedures may be enormous. Simply costing out tens of thousands of labor contracts to ascertain compliance is no trivial task, especially when numerous fringe benefits are involved—many of whose costs can only be actuarially estimated or guessed at, as is true with pensions. The resources devoted both by the government agencies monitoring the programs and by private employers to prove or assure that they are in compliance may represent a substantial cost to society.

Tax-Based Incomes Policies

Recently proposals have been set forth to establish a new form of incomes policy that would work through the federal personal and corporate income-tax systems.[42] These *tax-based incomes policy (TIP)* proposals are based upon the notion that the tax system can be used to provide incentives for employees or employers to moderate wage and price increases.

One form of TIP uses the "carrot" of lower personal income-tax rates, or tax credits. These would be granted to employees who work for firms whose average wage settlements do not exceed a specified critical value, if the rate of price inflation exceeds another specified value.[43] Panel (a) of Figure 16.14 shows the tax rate (t) on labor income for a representative individual whose wage settlement $(\dot{W})$ is less than the specified standard $(\dot{W}^c)$. If the actual rate of price increase exceeds V percent, the individual's normal tax rate (t_0) will be lowered by the fraction ϕ times the difference between the actual and critical value of the price inflation rate. That is,

$$
\begin{aligned}
t &= t_0 - \phi(\dot{P} - V) \quad &\text{if} \quad \dot{W} \le \dot{W}^c; \\
t &= t_0 \quad &\text{if} \quad \dot{W} > \dot{W}^c.
\end{aligned}
\tag{16.14}
$$

---

[42]See, for example, Henry Wallich and Sidney Weintraub, "A Tax-Based Incomes Policy," *Journal of Economic Issues* 5 (June 1971): 1–19; and Arthur Okun, "The Great Stagflation Swamp," *Challenge* 20 (November/December 1977): 6–13.

[43]See Okun, "The Great Stagflation Swamp." A variant of this emerged as the Carter Administration's "Real Wage Insurance" Proposal in January of 1979. For a discussion of this proposal, see Robert J. Flanagan, "Real Wage Insurance as a Compliance Incentive," *Eastern Economic Journal* 5 (October 1979): 367–78.

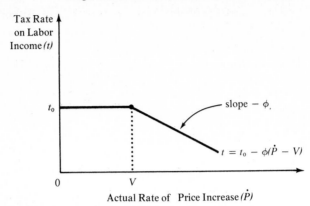

(a) Real Wage Insurance for Employees Whose Wage Increases Are Less Than the Guidelines

Tax Rate on Labor Income (t)

t_0

slope $-\phi$

$t = t_0 - \phi(\dot{P} - V)$

0 V

Actual Rate of Price Increase $(\dot{P})$

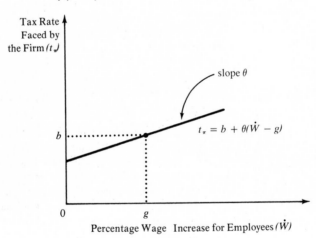

(b) Corporate Tax Rate Varies With Wage Increases

Tax Rate Faced by the Firm (t_π)

slope θ

b

$t_\pi = b + \theta(\dot{W} - g)$

0 g

Percentage Wage Increase for Employees $(\dot{W})$

FIGURE 16.14   Alternative Forms of Tax-Based Incomes Policies (TIPs)

By way of example, the Carter administration's Real Wage Insurance Proposal called for wage and price standards of 7 percent $(V = \dot{W}^C = 7)$ and called for each one-percentage-point increase in the price inflation rate to lead to a one percentage point decrease in the tax rate $(\phi = 1)$.[44]

The idea behind such a scheme is that if the actual rate of price inflation proves to be less than 7 percent, workers' real wages would not have declined if they had confined their wage settlements to 7 percent. If, however, prices wound

[44]This proposal was also subject to certain "caps" or limits on the tax rebates, one of which is discussed below. See Flanagan, "Real Wage Insurance as a Compliance Incentive," for details.

Example 16.2
Incomes Policies During the Roman Empire

The use of incomes policies to combat inflation is not a recent innovation—and neither is the inflexibility in resource allocation caused by policies that fix prices. In the year 301 AD, after years of severe inflation, the Emperor Diocletian issued an edict fixing maximum prices and wages for the whole Roman Empire. Maximum wages were specified for more than 130 different categories of labor, and severe punishment was promised to anyone who violated the standards.

One would expect that the establishment of a rigid occupational wage structure with a maximum wage specified for each occupation would have had two effects. First, workers would have sought to leave occupations where compensation levels were fixed at relatively low levels (considering the work involved) and would have sought employment where wages happened to be fixed at relatively higher levels. These occupational flows could not be accompanied by wage changes (because wages were fixed), so one would expect that permanent surpluses and shortages would have developed. Second, some workers might have decided that the prevailing maximum-wage scales did not offer sufficiently high rewards for their labor-force participation and would have chosen not to participate. Either effect would have led to a reduction in the overall level of output.

Diocletian was apparently well aware of these potential difficulties and tried to head them off by restricting both occupational mobility and labor-force-participation decisions. Each worker was effectively tied to his job, and it was required that his children be brought up to succeed him. Not surprisingly, however, the removal of individuals' freedom of choice coupled with the wage ceilings effectively killed any incentives workers had to work hard or exhibit initiative. According to R. H. Barrow, "Production fell, and with it the standard of living; the rigid uniformity of a lifeless and static mediocrity prevailed."

SOURCES: H. Michell, "The Edict of Diocletian: A Study of Price Fixing in the Roman Empire," *Canadian Journal of Economics and Political Science* 13 (February 1947): 1–12; R. H. Barrow, *The Romans* (Baltimore, Md.: Penguin Books, 1949), p. 177.

---

up increasing by more than 7 percent, workers would receive a tax credit or rebate to help protect their real earnings. However, the tax credit (and hence real earnings protection) would be granted *only* for the given year, and at the start of the next year their real after-tax earnings (assuming $\dot{W} = 7$) would have declined by $\dot{P} - 7$ percent. If $\dot{P}$ were substantially greater than 7 percent, the decline would be sizable. As such, it is not surprising that this form of TIP was opposed by organized labor and failed to win support in Congress.[45]

---

[45] The Carter proposal also "capped" the rebate, or decrease in the tax rate, at 3 percentage points—a move that was necessary to protect against an explosion in the size of the federal deficit. Not surprisingly this limit further reduced labor support for the proposal.

A TIP proposal that works through the corporate-profits tax rate and seeks to increase employers' incentives to bargain tough with their work forces seems to have more promise.[46] A representative scheme is plotted in panel (b) of Figure 16.14, where the tax rate on corporate profits faced by the firm, t_π, is assumed to vary directly with the actual average percentage wage increase *(W)* granted by the firm. Specifically,

$$t_\pi = b + \vartheta(\dot{W} - g), \tag{16.15}$$

where *b* is the normal corporate-profits tax rate, *g* is the specified wage standard, and ϑ is the marginal effect of a one percentage point increase in the wage settlement on the tax rate that the firm would pay.

If the actual wage settlement is equal to the standard $(\dot{W} = g)$, the corporate tax rate remains at its normal level. However, larger increases would lead to higher tax rates and smaller increases would lead to lower tax rates. This proposal thus combines both a "carrot" (lower taxes) and a "stick" (higher taxes) approach; unlike the employee tax-based proposal, it also provides an incentive for the firm to depress wage increases *below* the standard. Presumably, by tying the firms's share of after-tax profits to its wage settlement, the scheme gives employers an extra incentive to stiffen their resistance to union wage demands and to hold down wage increases. If price markups over costs remain unchanged, this policy would help reduce the rate of price inflation.

While such schemes hold out the promise of being able to shift inflation/unemployment trade-off curves down, they are not without potential drawbacks and weaknesses. First, they raise all sorts of administrative problems.[47] For example, how does one handle numerous small firms, firms with no corporate tax liabilities, private nonprofit firms, and government agencies?[48] Or how does one collect the data necessary to include nonwage forms of compensation in the calculations? In this respect, these policies suffer from the same type of problems that any incomes policy with an enforcement mechanism built in would face.

Second, these policies focus on wages rather than prices, even though public concern is ultimately with the latter. The focus on wages is due to the difficulties involved in monitoring and measuring prices for millions of different products that are heterogeneous and whose quality can be easily varied. Employees are not likely to be receptive, though, to government intervention in labor markets if no attention is explicitly paid to product prices. Furthermore, a firm might agree to a large wage increase, resulting in an increased corporate tax rate, and then seek

---

[46]See Wallich and Weintraub, "A Tax-Based Incomes Policy." A more recent advocate of a corporate-profit-based TIP is Laurence Seidman, "Tax-Based Incomes Policies," *Brookings Papers on Economic Activity,* 1978–2, pp. 301–48.

[47]For a discussion of these problems, see Larry L. Dildine and Emil M. Sunley, "Administrative Problems of Tax-Based Incomes Policies," *Brookings Papers on Economic Activity,* 1978–2, pp. 363–89.

[48]One could, of course, restrict the scheme to employees of large profitable private firms; however, this creates obvious equity problems.

to negate this effect by passing the increased wage *and* tax costs on to consumers in the form of higher prices. Even supporters of such a scheme are aware of this potential problem, although they discount its importance.[49]

Finally, union leaders and members are not likely to be sympathetic to the policy.[50] On the one hand, even if the policy works and union members' real wages do not fall, the government—not union leaders—will get "credit" for the improvement. Thus, union leaders are not likely to be enthusiastic about the policy (see Chapter 12 for a discussion of the difference between the goals of union members and leaders). On the other hand, union members and leaders are both likely to resent a policy that provides direct financial incentives to management to resist union wage demands (tax cuts) but provides nothing for them. Indeed, because of this, stiffened management resistance may well lead to increases in the frequency and duration of strike activity, especially immediately after the initial adoption of the policy.

In spite of these problems, the corporate profits variant of TIP does provide certain advantages over more traditional forms of incomes policies. Unlike direct controls or standards, it does not prohibit anything. Industries in which there is an excess demand for labor can agree to relatively high wage settlements, thereby avoiding shortages, as long as they are willing to pay the price of a higher corporate-profits tax rate. Furthermore, it provides a means by which policymakers can short-circuit the inflationary process generated in the late 1960s and 1970s in which inflationary shocks, like oil price increases, fed into wage increases—which were then passed on to price increases, leading to a further wage-price spiral even after the initial shock was long past. The hope is that a decrease in the rate of wage inflation induced by a TIP would cause a decrease in the rate of price inflation leading to further moderation in future wage and price increases and a winding down of inflation.

Of course, this line of reasoning suggests that any action the government takes that causes a one-time decline in the price level—or decreases the rate of growth of prices—will lead to lower wage increases, subsequent lower price increases, and thus also help to short-circuit the wage-price spiral. As a result, a number of such proposals have been advocated.[51] These proposals include reducing the federal payroll tax that finances social security (which enters into employers' costs and hence their product price decisions); eliminating federal excise taxes on alcohol and tobacco; and reducing minimum wage rates and substituting a wage subsidy program for low-income workers. Each of these proposals would directly reduce employers' costs or product prices. None would alone solve the inflation problem, but a combination of these and other proposals might cause a significant one-time reduction in the price level (compared to what it would oth-

[49]Seidman, "Tax-Based Incomes Policies."

[50]Albert Rees, "New Policies to Fight Inflation: Sources of Skepticism," *Brookings Papers on Economic Activity,* 1978–2, pp. 453–77.

[51]See for example, Robert W. Crandall, "Federal Government Initiatives to Reduce the Price," *Brookings Papers on Economic Activity,* 1978–2, pp. 401–40.

erwise be). To the extent that this would feed back into lower rates of wage and price inflation, such proposals would serve to improve the inflation/unemployment trade-offs that the United States faces.

A Regulated Industry TIP

We conclude by returning to the regulated-industry example that has been discussed throughout this book, which illustrates both the complexity of policy analysis and the variety of analytic tools that must often be applied to analyze a single policy issue. In the battle against inflation, what policies can state public utility commissions pursue to moderate the rate of wage increases of utility employees and hence utility price increases?

One possibility is for commissions to institute a variant of a tax-based incomes policy in the industries they regulate.[52] Under such a policy the fraction of negotiated increase in wage scales that a utility could pass on to consumers in the form of higher prices would be specified to be a function of the level of the increase, with greater increases corresponding to smaller fractional pass-throughs. Such a scheme would allow a utility to increase its revenues by *less* than its actual increase in wage costs if the increase in wages exceeded a specific amount, but by perhaps *more* than its actual increase if a smaller settlement were reached. In effect, this makes the utility's allowable rate of return a negative function of the size of the negotiated wage settlement, providing the utility with an extra incentive to resist union wage demands.

Examples of such schemes are shown in Figure 16.15, where the percent wage increase "allowed" for rate-setting purposes is plotted on the vertical axis (W_A) and the actual percent wage increase granted is plotted on the horizontal axis. The curve C in panel (a) of Figure 16.15 shows the percent wage increase that the commission will allow to be passed on to consumers in the form of higher prices for each level of the actual wage settlement. If the actual wage increase is h percent, the utility will be allowed to pass the entire settlement on to consumers. If it is more than h percent, the utility will recover less than the full increase; if it is less than h percent, it will recover more than the full increase. In the latter case, however, the increase faced by consumers will still be less than h percent (for example, if the actual settlement is h_1 the commission will act as if it is h_2), so consumers will have gained by the utility's holding its labor costs down below h percent.

If the commission is uncertain about what rate of increase in wages should be passed on to consumers fully, it can specify a range of full cost recovery.[53] For example, in panel (b) of Figure 16.15, the curve D now shows the rate of wage increase that the commission will allow to be passed on to consumers in the form of higher prices as a function of the actual settlement. Here, wage settlements in the range h_3 to h_4 can be fully passed on.

---

[52]The discussion that follows draws heavily on Ehrenberg, *The Regulatory Process and Labor Earnings,* pp. 167–173.

[53]See Ehrenberg, *The Regulatory Process and Labor Earnings,* for a discussion of how this level of full recovery might be specified.

(a)

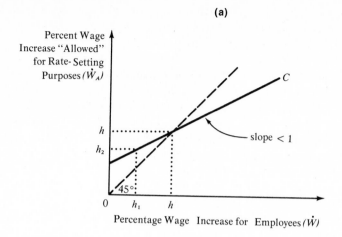

(b)

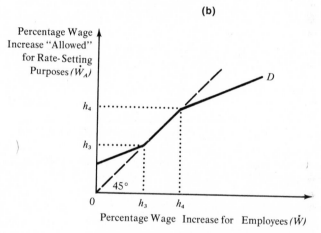

**FIGURE 16.15 Tax-Based Incomes Policies
for Regulated Industries**

Would such a scheme be an effective way of moderating inflation of utility prices? Many of the objections raised earlier to nationwide TIPs fail to hold here. Administrative problems would be minimal as commissions regularly set prices for a well-defined number of utilities (all who seek to earn profits), based upon detailed information about the utilities' costs. Since commissions set prices directly, one also does not have to worry about increased corporate-profits tax liabilities being passed on to consumers in the form of higher prices (as one would with a nationwide TIP that worked through the corporate-profits tax).

While these factors tend to increase the viability of the regulated-industry variant of a TIP, such a proposal would not win employee support. Indeed, workers in regulated industries might find an economy wide TIP easier to swallow, since under the regulated-industry TIP only *their* relative earnings would suffer. As such one might expect increases in the frequency and duration of strikes in regulated industries, especially during the first few years of operation of the schemes (before unions and management fully adjust to the change that has occurred in the bargaining environment).

Presumably such service disruptions could be minimized if the regulated-industry TIP focused on unit-labor-cost increases rather than wage-scale increases. This focus would allow unions in regulated industries to engage in explicit or implicit productivity bargaining; larger productivity gains permit larger wage increases without any price changes—see equation (16.6). Union support might also be increased if the focus were on all input costs, not just labor costs. Ultimately, however, society may have to decide if the potential reduction in inflation from having a nationwide or regulated-industry TIP more than offsets the costs of short-run increases in strike activity. If it does, a strong case for these policies can be made.

REVIEW QUESTIONS

1. Why are the size of wage increases and the unemployment rate thought to be negatively related? How (and why) is this negative relationship affected by price inflation and the rising labor-force participation of women? What can the government do to reduce the wage inflation associated with any level of unemployment?
2. Great Britain recently instituted three related policies. First, it increased unemployment-compensation benefits. Second, the government agreed to pay lump-sum benefits owed to anyone permanently fired by his or her employer. (Assume that previously the *employers* paid these benefits.) Third, the government placed a tax, to be paid by employers, on wages in *service* industries (wages in manufacturing were not taxed).
   a. Analyze the effects of these three policies on the labor market.
   b. Judging from the effects of these programs, what is (are) the *goal*(s) implicit in these policies?
3. Suppose the government were to adopt an incomes policy that allows workers to receive wage increases each January equal to the increase in the cost of living during the previous 12 months but *no* other increases. Would such a scheme help reduce the rate of inflation?
4. Some members of Congress have supported legislation requiring the federal government to undertake massive employment programs as long as the overall unemployment rate is above 4 percent. Evaluate such a program with respect to inflation.
5. How can unanticipated inflation lower the unemployment rate?
6. If you were President, what policies would you propose to reduce inflation? Why? What are the strengths and weaknesses of your policy proposals?
7. "Incomes policies that specify that workers should receive percentage wage increases equal to their rate of productivity growth are doomed to failure because they will cause managements' share of output to continually fall." Is this statement true, false, or uncertain? Explain your answer.

SELECTED READINGS

Flanagan, Robert. "Wage Interdependencies in Unionized Labor Markets." *Brookings Papers on Economic Activity*, 1976–3, pp. 635–73.

Friedman, Milton. "The Role of Monetary Policy." *American Economic Review* 58 (March 1968): 1–17.

Lipsey, Richard. "The Relation Between Unemployment and the Rate of Change in Money Wage Rates in the United Kingdom, 1862–1957: A Further Analysis." *Economica* 27 (February 1960): 1–31.

Mitchell, Daniel. *Unions, Wages and Inflation*. Washington, D.C.: Brookings Institution, 1980.

Okun, Arthur and George Perry, eds. "Innovative Policies to Slow Inflation." *Brookings Papers on Economic Activity*, 1978–2.

Perry, George. "Changing Labor Markets and Inflation." *Brookings Papers on Economic Activity*, 1970–3, pp. 411–41.

Tobin, James. "Stabilization Policy Ten Years After." *Brookings Papers on Economic Activity*, 1980–1, pp. 19–72.

Index